Early Virginia Immigrants

- 1623-1666 -

Southern Historical Press, Inc.
Book Publishers

By:
George Cabell Greer

This volume was reproduced from
An reprint edition located in the
Publisher's private library,
Greenville, South Carolina

Please direct all correspondence and orders to:

www.southernhistoricalpress.com
or
SOUTHERN HISTORICAL PRESS, Inc.
PO BOX 1267
375 West Broad Street
Greenville, SC   29601
southernhistoricalpress@gmail.com

Originally published: Richmond, VA 1912
ISBN #0-89308-814-5
All rights Reserved.
Printed in the United States of America

PREFACE.

Since the publication of "Hotten's Immigrants," no successful effort has been made to gather together, in one volume, a list of the thousands of persons who came into Virginia during the early period of her life.

The records of the Land Office in Richmond remain the only source from which these names can now be obtained. As the records stand, it is simply impossible, without the most extensive and expensive research, to obtain names of persons who came to Virginia, unless they themselves were patentees of land; and the great majority of immigrants to the colony do not appear as patentees.

A list of the immigrants to Virginia has always been a desideratum to the genealogist. To descendants of early Virginia immigrants this work will, in many cases, offer the only opportunity to trace their ancestry. It will often be the means of forming the "Missing Link," which is the genealogists' bane.

Nearly twenty-five thousand names have been collected from the original records and arranged in alphabetical order. The search has been systematic and thorough, and every name from 1623 (when the records begin) down to 1666 has been noted, with date of appearance.

It is believed that this work will be of interest to the general public and invaluable to the historian and antiquarian.

GEORGE CABELL GREER.

EARLY

VIRGINIA IMMIGRANTS

1623—1666

BY

GEORGE CABEL GREER

A

Aaron, Rich., 1643, by John Freeme, Charles Co.
Abathon, George, 1653, by Tho. Speake, ——— Co.
Abbcome, Isabell, 1638, by Thomas Sawyer, New Norfolk Co.
Abbeys, Wm., 1652, by Mrs. Jane Harmer, Northumberland Co.
Abbet, Su., 1653, by Corbet Piddel, Northumberland Co.
Abbeys, William, 1638, by Bennett Freeman, James City.
Abbins, James, 1638, by Thomas Burbage, Accomack Co.
Abbins, James, 1638, by Thomas Burbage, Accomack Co.
Abbins, James, 1638, by Thomas Burbage, Accomack Co.
Abbott, Bryan, 1642, by Tymothy Fenn, Isle of Wight Co.
Abbott, Samuell, 1643, by Richard Kemp, Esq., James City.
Abbott, Ann, 1652, by John Gresham, Northumberland Co.
Abbott, Jon., 1635, by Thos. by Crompe, James Co.
Abbott, Katherine, 1651, by Jonas Jackson, Northampton Co.
Abbott, Wm., 1653, by Toby Horton, Lancaster Co.
Abbott, Jane, 1656, by John Wood, ——— Co.
Abbott, James, 1636, by Wm. Fookes, ——— Co.
Abbott, Symon, 1636, by John Laydon, Warwick River Co.
Abbs, Tho., 1649, by Wm. Nesum, Tho. Sax, Miles Bathasby and John
    Pyne, Northampton Co.
Abby, Jon., 1653, by Robert Brasseur, Nansemond Co.
Abdale, John, 1652, by Mr. Geo. Foster, Northumberland Co.
Abdell, William, 1651, by Richard Vaughan, Northampton Co.
Abdey, Nicholas, 1637, by William Mills, James City.
Ablercrumme, John, 1639, by John Well, Charles City Co.
Abherlyn, Richard, 1636, by William Coleman, Charles River Co.
Abighlander, Hugh, 1653, by Geo. Cable, ——— Co.
Aboshew, James, 1643, by Mr. Phillipp Bennett, Upper Norfolk Co.
Abotham, George, 1654, by Nich. Merywether, Westmoreland Co.
Abbott, Christopher, 1635, by Jeremiah Clement, ——— Co.
Abraham, Geo., 1639, by Henry Perry, Charles City Co.
Abram, John, 1635, by George Minifie, James City Co.
Abrall, John, 1638, by Bennett Freeman, James City.

Note—The first-mentioned name in every instance is the immigrant and the name following the word "by" is the patentee or party bringing him over.

Abraham, John, 1636, by Mr. Georg Menifye, James City.
Abreshall, Tho., 1656, by Nicholas Merriwether and John Leach, James City Co.
Abry, John, 1650, by Capt. John Flood, Genl., and Jno. Flood, an ancient planter, James City Co.
Abshire, Lewis, 1637, by Theodore Moyser, James City.
Absolon, Dorman, 1655, by George Wall, Westmoreland Co.
Achman, Yosh., 1653, by Geo. Hack, Northampton Co.
Acken, John, 1653, by Colo. Wm. Clayborne, —— Co. (Sec. of State.)
Ackerman, Tho., 1653, by John Blackbourne, Surry Co.
Ackland, Mary, 1638, by John Wayne, Charles River Co.
Acone, Thos., 1642, by Wm. Ireland and Robt. Wallis, Yorke Co.
Acton, John, 1642, by Francis England, Isle of Wight Co.
Adams, Susan, 1653, by John Shepperd, Northumberland Co.
Adams, Thomas, 1649, by Joseph Croshawe, Yorke Co.
Adams, Tho., 1648, by Lewis Burwell, and Tho. Haws, York River Co.
Adams, Wm., 1652, by John Pouncey, —— Co.
Adams, Peter, 1653, by Jno. Hansford, Gloucester Co.
Adams, Geo., 1653, by Richard Carey, —— Co.
Adams, Geo., 1637, by Capt. Francis Eppes, Charles River Co.
Adams, John, 1642, by William Lawson, Isle of Wight Co.
Adams, Eede, 1638, by Richard Milton, Charles City.
Adams, Rich., 1654, by Capt. Nich. Marteaw, Westmoreland Co.
Adams, Wm., 1656, by Geo. Abbott, Nansemond Co.
Adams, John, 1645, by Roger Johns, Northampton Co.
Adams, Thos. 1637, Humphry Higgensin, Gent Co.
Adams, Andrew, 1637, by Francis Fowler, James River Co.
Adams, Rochell, 1636, by James Vanerit, Elizabeth City Co.
Adams, Eliz., 1638, by Capt. Wm. Pierse, —— Co.
Addams, Thos., 1636, by John Neale, Accomack.
Addams, Richard, 1643, by James Whiting, —— Co.
Adderby, Thos., 1637, by Argoll Yeardly, New Norfolk Co.
Addison, Thos., 1637, by Daniell Gookins, New Norfolk Co.
Addis, John, 1652, by John Bebey, —— Co.
Addison, Aug., by Saml. Ruthland, Lower Norfolk Co.
Addison, Eliz., 1653, by Wm. Morgan, —— Co.
Addington, Jonothan, 1639, by Edward Travis, James City.
Adea, Gabriel, 1637, by Henry Perry, Charles River Co.
Aden, Luke, 1637, by Capt. John Howe, Accomac Co.
Aden, Hugh, 1645, by John Shepard, York Co.
Adinson, Tho., 1645, by John Rode, Warwick Co.
Adkins, Richd., 1642, by John Boyles, —— Co.
Adkins, Robt., 1654, by Tho. Bell, Northampton Co.
Adkins, Elder, 1656, by James Price, Northampton Co.
Adkins, Henry, 1651, by Edward Deggs, Esq., Yorke Co.
Adkins, Alice, 1651, by Capt. John West, Esq., Yorke Co.
Adkins, Tho., 1643, by Henry Neale, James City Co.
Adkins, Robert, 1649, by John Merriman, —— Co.
Adkins, Robert, 1649, by John Merriman, —— Co.
Adkinson, Ja., 1649, by Nicholas Waddilow, Northampton Co.

Adkinson, Robert, 1651, by Mr. Robert Abrall, Yorke Co.
Adkinson, Alice, 1648, by Lewis Burwell, Gent., ———— Co.
Adrey, Hump., 1652, by Mrs. Jane Harmer, Northumberland Co.
Adridge, Rice, 1650, by Capt. Moore Fautleroy, ———— Co.
Adsden, Jno., 1652, by Tho. Boswell, ———— Co.
Adsdon, John, 1652, by Daniell Welch, Lancaster Co.
Adson, Richard, 1650, by Mrs. Frances Townshend (widow), North-
    umberland Co.
Adwell, Charles, 1642, by Adam Cooke, Charles Co.
Adwick, James, 1655, by John Dorman, Northampton Co.
Adwick, Grace, 1655, by John Dorman, Northampton Co.
Adye, John, 1639, by Edward Prince, Charles City.
Aekin, Jno., 1645, by John Rode, Warwick.
Aereland, Tho., 1648, by Mr. Phillip Bennet, Nansemond Co.
Aereoday, Mary, 1651, by Lieut. Col. Giles Brent, Northumberland Co.
Agajin, John, 1653, by Mr. Edmund Bowman, and Richard Starnell
    ———— Co.
Agar, Edward, 1635, by Edmund Scarborough, Accomack Co.
Agard, Edward, 1640, by Edmund Scarburgh, Accomack Co.
Age, Hugh, 1647, by Symon Symons, Nansemond Co.
Agger, John, 1656, by John Symons, Nansemond Co.
Aglett, John, 1653, by Mr. Edmund Bowman and Richard Starnell,
    ———— Co.
Agre, Hugh, 1649, by Mr. Wm. Hoccaday, ———— Co.
Ahoge, Richard, 1637, by Francis Osborne, ———— Co.
Airea, George, 1653, by Peter Knight and Baker Cutt, ———— Co.
Aires, John, 1654, by Wm. Lea, Charles City Co.
Akerhill, Ann, 1651, by Capt. Tho. Davis, Northumberland Co.
Akleson, Robert, 1654, by James Yates, ———— Co.
Alad, Samuel, 1652, by John Godfrey, Lower Norfolk Co.
Albett, Richd., 1651, by Humphrey Tabb, Northumberland Co.
Alchard, Edw., 1650, by Robert Blake and Samuell Elridge, Isle of
    Wight Co.
Alcock, Samuell, 1650, by George Taylor, ———— Co.
Alcock, Jos., 1653, by Ferdinando Austin, Charles City Co.
Alcock, Wm., 1650, by John Sevier, ———— Co.
Alcocke, James, 1650, by Tho. Blogg, Northumberland Co.
Alcott, A., 1636, by Henry Southell, ———— Co.
Alcutt, Eliza, 1637, by Lieut. Richard Popeley, New Norfolk Co.
Alden, Hugh, 1653, by John Shepperd, Northumberland Co.
Aldersey, Grace, 1646, by Col. Henry Bishopp, James City.
Aldis, John, 1652, by Ralph Paine, ———— Co.
Aldred, Robert, 1650, by John Perrott, Nansemond Co.
Aldride, Margorie, 1642, by Robert Lawrance, Isle of Wight Co.
Aldrige, Fr., 1637, by Bridges Freeman, James City.
Aldrige, Fr., 1636, by Bridges Freeman, ———— Co.
Aldridge, Wm., 1650, by John Sevier, ———— Co.
Aldridge, Tho., 1650, by Sr. Tho. Luntsford, Kt., and Baronette,
    ———— Co.
Aldrop, Michall, 1648, by Lewis Burwell, Gent., ———— Co.

Alesworth, Wm., 1654, by Alex. Madocks and James Jones, Northampton Co.

Alewood, John, 1652, by Henry Fleete, Lancaster Co.

Alexander, John, 1653, by Roger Walter, Northumberland Co.

Alexander, Robt., 1642, by Thomas Loving, James City Co.

Alexander, Patrick, 1638, by Georg Mynifie (merchant), ——— Co.

Alexander, Jon., 1653, by Roger Walker, Northumberland Co.

Alerdine, James, 1654, by John Wyre, John Gillet, Andrew Gilson and John Phillips, ——— Co.

Alexander, Jno., 1654, by Roger Walters, Northumberland Co.

Alher, John, 1655, by Arthur Upshott, Northampton Co.

Alherson, Ann, 1635, by Capt. Adam Thoroughgood, ——— Co.

Alice, Ellen, 1637, by William Spencer, ——— Co.

Alice, Ellen, 1635, by William Spencer, ——— Co.

Alice, Mary, 1650, by Capt. Richard Bond, Charles City Co.

Aliome, Xtop., 1651, by Capt. John West, Esq., Yorke Co.

Alkin, Sampson, 1653, by Capt. Nathaniel Hurd, Warrick Co.

Alkins, James, 1654, by Clement Thurush, Lancaster Co.

Allen, James, 1646, by Lancaster Levilt, ——— Co.

Allen, Charles, 1638, by Hugh Allen, Charles River Co.

Allen, Robt., 1638, by Mr. Thomas Wallis, James City.

Allen, Hugh, 1638, by Hugh Allen, Charles River Co.

Allen, John, 1638, by Wm. Rookins, James City Co.

Allen, Oliver, 1636, by Hannah Boyse, Henrico Co.

Allen, Geo., 1650, by Capt. Moore Fantleroy, ——— Co.

Allen, Valentine, 1650, by John Catlett and Ralph Rousey, ——— Co.

Allen, Judith, 1649, by Robert Mosely, Gent., ——— Co.

Allen, Richard, 1649, by Mr. Henry Woodhouse, Lower Norfolk Co.

Allen, Mary, 1648, by Job. Chanler, Lower Norfolk Co.

Allen, Tho., 1649, by Capt. Ralph Wormeley, ——— Co.

Allen, Nicho., 1653, by Peter Knight, Northumberland Co.

Allen, John, 1652, by Mr. Tho. Curtis, ——— Co.

Allen, Hezekiell, 1652, by Thomas Teakle, Northampton Co.

Allen, Wm., 1653, by Mr. Wm. Baldwin, York Co.

Allen, John, 1652, by Tho. Greenwood, Isle of Wight Co.

Allen, Wm., 1653, by Mr. Richard Barnhouse, Jr., Gloucester Co.

Allen, Rose, 1653, by John Levistone, Gloucester Co.

Allen, Patrick, 1653, by Jno. Hansford, Gloucester Co.

Allen, Richard, 1653, by Elias Hartru, Northampton Co.

Allen, John, 1639, by Edward Prince, Charles City.

Allen, Wm., 1640, by Robert Holt, James City.

Allen, Wm., 1638, by John Clarkson, Charles River Co.

Allen, Eliza, 1650, by John Landman, ——— Co.

Allen, Tho., 1651, by Joseph Hayes, Gent., Yorke Co.

Allen, Wm., 1650, by Mr. Robert Holt, James City Co.

Allen, Chr., 1651, by Edward Deggs, Esq., Yorke, Co.

Allen, Ant., 1653, by Francis Grey, Charles City Co.

Allen, Robt., 1653, by John Maddison, Gloucester Co.

Allen, Margaret, 1655, by Southy Littleberry, Northampton Co.

Allen, Geo., 1654, by Geo. Wyre, John Gillet, Andrew Gilson and John Phillips, ———Co.

Allen, James, 1653, by Toby Horton, Lancaster Co.
Allen, Fra., 1653, by Ferdinando Austin, Charles City Co.
Allen, Teague, 1653, by Ferdinando Austin, Charles City Co.
Allen, John, 1656, by Vincent Stanford, ——— Co.
Allen, Edward, 1656, by John Wood, ——— Co.
Allen, Wm., 1656, by Humphrey Tabb, Gent., Elizabeth City Co.
Allen, Rose, 1650, by Wingfield Webb and Richard Pate, ———Co.
Allen, Tho., 1656, by Nicholas Merriwether and John Leach, James
      City Co.
Allen, John, 1643, by Phillipp Taylor, Northampton, Co.
Allen, Chas. (son of Hugh Allen), 1638, by Hugh Allen, Charles River Co.
Allen, John, 1636, by William Rookens, James City Co.
Allen, Edward, 1635, by Mc William Stone, ——— Co.
Allen, Oliver, 1637, by Hannah Boyes, Henrico Co.
Allen, Mary, 1635, by Robert Hollom, Henrico.
Allen, John, 1651, by Geo. Trahett and Henry Edwards, Northampton
      Co.
Allen, Kath., 1650, by Daniell Luellin, Charles City Co.
Allen, Francis, 1643, by William Ewins, James City.
Allen, James, 1643, by Thomas Glascocke, ——— Co.
Allen, Grego., 1648, by George White, Lower Norfolk Co.
Allenby, Wm., 1648, by Tho. Lambert, Lower Norfolk Co.
Alleson, Wm., 1646, by Tho. Savedge, Northampton Co.
Allenteria, Peter, 1640, by William Crannage, Isle of Wight Co.
Alleston, Andrew, 1653, by Wm. Johnson, Lancaster Co.
Allin, James, 1651, by James Allen, Northumberland Co.
Allin, Thos., 1655, by Mrs. Margaret Brent, Lancaster Co.
Allin, Edward, 1644, by John Hill, Gent., Upper Norfolk Co.
Allin, Wm., 1638, by Robt. Holt and Richard Bell, James City Co.
Allington, Henry, 1652, by John Pouncey, ——— Co.
Allison, John, 1653, by Peter Knight, Northumberland Co.
Allison, Sarah, 1642, by Hugh Gwyn, Gent., ——— Co.
Allison, Sarah, 1656, by John Bromfeild, James City Co.
Allison, William, 1636, by Lewis Denwood, Accomack Co.
Alliston, Wm., 1654, by Francis Smith and Mr. John Smith, Westmore-
      land Co.
Allom, Jeremy, 1602, by Anthony Hoskins, Northampton Co.
Allott, Peter, 1655, by John Palmer, Northumberland Co.
Allumby, Diana, 1653, by Geo. Allumby (her husband), ——— Co.
Allumby, Wm., 1637, by Arthur Smith, Isle of Wight Co.
Allvit, Mary, 1656, by Mary Lewis, Northampton Co.
Allyson, Sarah, 1656, by John Bromfeild, James City Co.
Alsopp, Henry, 1648, by John Tiny, James City Co.
Alson, Thomas, 1637, by Francis Osborne, ——— Co.
Alsworth, Wm., 1652, by Mr. John Browne, Northampton Co.
Alpott, Jones, 1656, by Sir Henry Chichley, ——— Co.
Alpatt, Ann, 1636, by John Neale, Accomack Co.
Alporte, Jon., 1635, by Capt. Adam Thoroughgood, ——— Co.
Alter, Jno., 1642, by John Bayles, ——— Co.
Alwood, Hen., 1652, by Tho. Todd, ——— Co.
Aman, Wm., ———, by Tho. Binns, Surry Co.

Ambrose, Leonard, 1651, by Mr. John Walker, ———— Co.
Amber, Joseph, 1650, by Wingfield Webb and Richard Pate, ———— **Co.**
Amblieff, Spura, 1655, by Tho. Leatherberry, Northampton Co.
Ames, Wm., 1654, by Richard Johnson, negro, Northampton Co.
Ameyson, Dorrick, 1656, by Nicholas Waddilow, Northampton Co.
Amis, Thomas, 1638, by Thomas Symons, Upper Norfolk Co.
Amison, Grace, 1637, by Wm. Prior, Charles River Co.
Amolihan, Roger, 1655, by John Dorman, Northampton Co.
Amord, Hannert, 1645, by William Daynes, Lower Norfolk.
Anchile, Fra., 1653, by Capt. Giles Brent, Northumberland Co.
Ande, Sam., 1650, by Richard Tye and Charles Sparrowe, Charles City
    Co.
Anderson, Fran., 1647, by Elizabeth Barcroft, Isle of Wight Co.
Anderson, Wm., 1650, by George Taylor, ———— Co.
Anderson, John, 1648, by Richard Thompson, Northumberland Co.
Anderson, Alex., 1653, by Edward Dobson, ———— Co.
Anderson, Sarah, 1652, by Mr. Henry Soane, ———— Co.
Anderson, Roger, 1640, by William Wigg, James City Co.
Andrews, John, 1648, by Francis Ceely, ———— Co.
Andrews, Wm., 1639, by Edward Prince, Charles City.
Andrews, Tho., 1639, by Tho. Symons, James City Co.
Andrews, Richard, 1639, by Thomas Stamp, James City Co.
Andrews, Edward, 1639, by Georg Minifye, Esq., Charles River Co.
Andrews, John, 1639, by Richard Corke, Gent., Henrico Co.
Anderson, Roger, 1638, by Capt. Christopher Wormley, ———— Co.
Anderson, Roger, 1638, by Christopher Lawson, James City Co.
Anderson, John, 1639, by John Graves, Elizabeth City.
Anderson, Robert, 1653, by Geo. Watts, Northumberland Co.
Anderson, Thomas, 1651, by William Ginsey, Yorke Co.
Anderson, Jon., 1654, by Lt. Col. John Cheeseman and John **Adleoton,**
    ———— Co.
Anderson, Richard, 1654, by Robert Holt, James City Co.
Anderson, John, 1653, by Mrs. Mary Brent, ———— Co.
Anderson, Reynard, 1654, by Martin Coale, Northumberland Co.
Anderson, Tho., 1643, by Edward Murfey and John Vaughan, ——— **Co.**
Anderton, Jno., 1651, by Mr. Rowland Burnham, ———— Co.
Andrery, Wm., 1652, by Mrs. Mary Brent, Northumberland Co.
Andick, Daniell, 1637, by Jonathan Longworth, New Norfolk Co.
Andick, Daniell, 1637, by Jonathon Langworth, New Norfolk Co.
Andley, Teg., 1639, by Justinian Cooper, Isle of Wight Co.
Andrew, George, 1652, by Littleton Scarburg, ———— Co.
Andrew, Wm., 1655, by Richard Hamlet, James City Co.
Andrew, Rob., 1655, by Richard Hamlet, James City Co.
Andrew, John, 1654, by Tho. Harmanson, Northampton Co.
Andrew, Joan, and her son, 1654, by Tho. Harmanson, Northampton **Co.**
Andrew, Robert, 1643, by Mr. John Bishopp, James City Co.
Andrews, Richard, 1638, by Thomas Stampe, James City.
Andrews, Israell, 1642, by John Sweete, ———— Co.
Andrews, Richard, 1648, by John King and Laurence Ward, **Isle of**
    Wight Co.
Andrews, William, 1648, by Lewis Burwell, Gent., ———— Co.

Andrews, Mary, 1652, by Richard Dudley, ———— Co.
Andrews, Susan, 1652, by Mr. Tho. Purifye and Mrs. Temperence Reppitt, ———— Co.
Andrews, Margt., 1652, by Mr. Tho. Purifye and Mrs. Reppitt, ———— Co.
Andrews, George, 1652, by Tho. Johnson, Jr., Northampton, Co.
Andrews, Nicholas, 1638, by Georg Mynifie (merchant), ———— Co.
Andrews, Wm., 1652, by Mr. Tho. Purifye and Mrs. Temperence Reppitt, ———— Co.
Andrews, Tho., 1643, by Tho. Symonds, ———— Co.
Andrews, Mrs. Elizabeth, 1654, by Mrs. Fra. Harrison, widow, Westmoreland Co.
Andrews, Elizabeth, 1655, by Mr. Anthony Langston, New Kent Co.
Andrew, Richard, 1643, by Mr. Moore Fantleroy, Upper Norfolk Co.
Andrews, Wm., 1643, by Mr. John Bishopp, James City Co.
Andrews, Roger, 1643, by Sir Francis Wyatt, ———— Co.
Andrews, Wm., 1638, by Wm. Barker and associates, Charles City Co.
Andrews, Susan, 1638, by Henry Williams, Accomack.
Andrews, Eliza,1637, by Jno. Dennett, Charles River Co.
Andrews, Edward, 1637, by John Dennett, Charles River Co.
Andrews, Dorothy, 1637, by Georg Burcher, James City Co.
Andrews, Thomas, 1635, by George Minifie, James City Co.
Andrews, Susan, 1636, by Henry Williams, Accomack.
Andrews, Wm., 1635, by William Barber (a mariner), Charles City Co.
Andrews, Thos., 1636, by Mr. Georg Menifye, James City Co.
Andrews, Jon., 1636, by Richard Cocke, ———— Co.
Andrews, Susana, 1635, by Wm. Andrews (her husband), Accomac Co.
Andry, Ellin, 1642, by Thomas Symmons, ———— Co.
Aner, Thos., 1642, by Capt. Samuell Mathews, Esq., ———— Co.
Anənrie, Jon., 1638, by John Flood, James City Co.
Anesly, Sara, 1651, by Richard Kellum, Northampton Co.
Aney, Wm., 1642, by Georg Chowning, Upper Norfolk Co.
Angle, Elizabeth, 1652, by Mrs. Elinor Broras, Lancaster Co.
Angell, Wm., 1651, by Humphrey Tabb, Northumberland Co.
Anglin, Ruth, 1635, by Anthony Jones, ———— Co.
Angood, Wm., 1655, by Dr. Giles Mode, New Kent Co.
Anins, Robert, 1636, by Somme Edwards, James City Co.
Anley, Robt., 1643, by Tho. Symonds, ———— Co.
Annice, John, 1638, by John George, Charles City Co.
Annis, William, 1639, by William Burdett, Accomack Co.
Annis, Wm., 1639, by William Burdett, Accomack Co.
Annley, Robert, 1639, by Tho. Symons, James City Co.
Anthem, Mary, 1653, by Col. Wm. Clayborne (Sec. of State), ———— Co.
Antherson, Wm., 1635, by Wm. Carter, James City Co.
Anthony, Tho., 1652, by Edward Cannon and Tho. Allen, Lower Norfolk Co.
Anthony, Andrew, 1637, by Rich. Bellane and Christopher Lawson, James City Co.
Anssell, Freeman, 1650, by George Pate, Charles City Co.
Apleby, Walter, 1650, by John Olian, James City Co.
Apleton, Richard, 1636, by Mr. Georg Menifye, James City.
Apleton, Alice, 1643, by Rich. Hoe, Gent., ———— Co.

Apleton, George, 1653, by Henry Deadman, Lancaster Co.
Apliton, Gregory, 1653, by Abraham Moon, Lancaster Co.
Appes, Edw., 1650, by John Landman, ——— Co.
Appleby, John, 1652, by Nathaniel Bacon, Isle of Wight Co.
Appleton, Richard, 1635, by George Minifie, James City Co.
Appletree, Richard, 1652, by Nicholas George, ——— Co.
Apps, Edmond, 1650, by Thomas Mulford, Nansemond Co.
Aram, Jon., 1635, by Anthony Jones, ——— Co.
Arator, Eliza, 1650, by George Pate, Charles City Co.
Arbernean, Robt., 1635, by Thos. Crompe, James Co.
Arbson, Dorrick, 1656, by Nicholas Waddilow, Northampton Co.
Arch, John, 1654, by Francis Smith and Mr. John Smith, Westmoreland Co.
Archellen, Marg., 1636, by John Chandler, Elizabeth Citie Co.
Archer, Ann, 1653, by John Debar, ——— Co.
Archer, Alice, 1653, by Mr. Wm. Fry, James City Co.
Archer, John, 1645, by Lawrence Ward and John King, Isle of Wight Co.
Archer, Geo. 1642, by Justinian Cooper, Isle of Wight Co.
Archer, Geo., 1636, by Justinian Cooper, Warrasquinock Co.
Archerday, Tho., 1643, by Rich. Hoe, Gent., ——— Co.
Arden, Henry, 1638, by Thomas Plomer and Samuell Edmonds, James City Co.
Arden, Robt., 1638, by Epaphroditus Lawson, Upper Norfolk Co.
Ardington, Tho., 1656, by John Rosier Clarke, Westmoreland Co.
Arendeer, James, 1651, by Col. Guy Molsworth, ——— Co.
Arett, John, 1649, by James Miller, ——— Co.
Arey, Robt., 1646, by Col. Henry Bishopp, James City.
Arguse, Rich., 1637, by Capt. Thomas Osborne, Henrico Co.
Aris, John, 1651, by James Thelaball, Lower Norfolk Co.
Arkady, ———, 1652, by George Pace, Charles City Co.
Armes, Henry, 1649, by Richard Parrett, ——— Co.
Armes, Fra., 1651, by Capt. Tho. Davis, Northumberland Co.
Armetrading, Henry, 1635, by McWilliam Stone, ——— Co.
Armestrong, Geo., 1639, by John Pawley, James City.
Armeson, Robt., 1643, by Lt. Wm. Worleidge, ——— Co.
Armeson, Robt., 1650, by Lieut. Wm. Worleich, ——— Co.
Armestead, Ann, 1636, by Wm. Armestead (her husband), Elizabeth City.
Armhunt, Richard, 1653, by Charles Grymes, Lancaster Co.
Armie, Mary, 1635, by John Armie, Warrasquinoake Co.
Armie, John, 1635, by John Armie, Warrasquinoake Co.
Armie, William, 1635, by John Armie, Warrasquinoake Co.
Armiger, Wm., 1651, by James Thelaball, Lower Norfolk Co.
Armitage, Eliz., 1652, by John Meredith, Lancaster Co.
Armitage, Abra., 1652, by Mr. Geo. Foster, Northumberland Co.
Armitage, Joan, 1654, by John Watson and John Bognall, Westmoreland Co.
Armston, Abra., 1651, by Joseph Croshaw, Yorke Co.
Armstrong, Fra., 1652, by Nathaniel Bacon, Isle of Wight Co.
Armstronge, Robt., 1653, by John Ashley and John Hamper, ——— Co.

Armstrong, John, 1653, by Charles Grymes, Lancaster Co.
Armstrong, Richard, 1655, by Hugh Leo, Northampton Co.
Armstrong, Rich., 1654, by John Watson and John Bognall, Westmoreland Co.
Armstrong, Robt., 1654, by John Wyre, John Gillett, Andrew Gilson and John Phillips, ———— Co.
Armstrong, Geo., 1654, by Tho. Willoughby, Lower Norfolk Co.
Army, Tho., 1654, by Capt. David Mansell, Westmoreland Co.
Armye, Thomas, 1638, by David Mansell, James City Co.
Arnall, Robert, 1635, by William Spencer, ———— Co.
Arndall, Kath., 1639, by John Pawley, James City.
Arnee, Tho., 1650, by Hump. Lyster, ———— Co.
Arnis, Joyce, 1652, by Mr. James Warradine, ———— Co.
Arnold, Margarett, 1641, by Robert Burnett, Isle of Wight Co.
Arnold, Joyce, 1641, by Toby Smith, Warwick River Co.
Arnold, Henry, 1651, by Mr. Arthur Price, Yorke Co.
Arnold, Wm., 1647, by Thomas Johnson, Gent., Northampton Co.
Arnold, Willie, 1638, by John Fludd, James City Co.
Arnold, Robt., 1637, by William Spencer, ———— Co.
Arnoll, Mary, 1653, by Tho. Hawkins, Northumberland Co.
Arnoll, Robt., 1638, by Nicholas Jarnew, Charles River Co.
Arnoll, Wm., 1654, by Robert Hubard, Westmoreland Co.
Arnoll, Margaret, 1656, by Vincent Stanford, ———— Co.
Arnsell, Jon., 1637, by Capt. Thomas Panlett, Charles River Co.
Arnwood, Roger, 1638, by Rich. Hill and Roger Arnwood, James City Co.
Arnwood, Roger, 1635, by ThomasCrompe, James Co.
Arpe, Peter, 1638, by Georg Mynifie (merchant), ———— Co.
Arrge, Daniell, 1638, by Elizabeth Grayne, Charles City Co.
Arris, Jon., 1642, by Lieut. Francis Mason, ———— Co.
Arrens, Heilten, 1649, by John Merriman, ———— Co.
Arrundell, Mary, 1652, by Anthony Hoskins, Northampton Co.
Arteine, Roger, 1642, by John Bayles, ———— Co.
Arthur, Hugh, 1649, by Mr. Wm. Hoccaday, ———— Co.
Arthur, John, 1649, by Mr. Wm. Hoccaday, ———— Co.
Arthur, Eliz., 1654, by Tho. Harmanson, Northampton Co.
Arthur, James, 1642, by Thomas Bagwell, Charles City Co.
Arthur, Georg, 1637, by Justinian Cooper, Isle of Wight Co.
Arthurs, Christ., 1642, by John Valentine, Isle of Wight Co.
Arthurs, James, 1642, by John Valentine, Isle of Wight Co.
Arthurs, Alice, 1642, by John Valentine, Isle of Wight Co.
Arum, Richard, 1655, by Symon Symons, Charles City Co.
Arundell, James, 1637, by Thomas Holt, New Norfolk Co.
Arundell, Richard, 1650, by Mr. Stephen Hamelin, ———— Co.
Arundell, Richard, 1656, by Sir Henry Chichley, ———— Co.
Arundell, John, 1652, by Nicho. Seaborne, Lower Norfolk Co.
Arwin, Robert, 1650, by Tho. Tilsley, James City Co.
Asball, Geo., 1650, by Robert Bird, ———— Co.
Asbby, Thomas, 1635, by Jeremiah Clement, ———— Co.
Ascott, Patrick, 1653, by Wm. Hardidge, Northumberland Co.
Ascough, Richard, 1635, by Silvester Totnam, James Co.

Ash, John, 1651, by Wm. Hampton, ———Co.
Ashall, Georg, 1641, by Ambrose Bennett, Isle of Wight.
Ashbifoote, John, 1645, by Sir William Berkley, ——— Co.
Ashbournham, Edward, 1653, by Charles Grimes, Lancaster Co.
Ashbrooke, Tho., 1653, by Wm. Langly, Lower Norfolk Co.
Ashby, Robt., 1639, by Capt. Nicholas Martian, Charles River Co.
Ashby, Wm., 1651, by Joseph Croshaw, Yorke Co.
Ashby, Roger, 1651, by Col. Richard Lee, Esq., Glcucester Co.
Ashly, Robt., 1651, by Capt. Geo. Read, Lan:aster Co.
Ashcomb, Ann, 1650, by John Sevier, ——— Co.
Ashcomb, John, Jr., 1646, by John Ashcomb, Upper Norfolk Co.
Ashcomb, Winifred, 1646, by Jchn Ashcomb, Upper Norfolk.
Ashe, John, 1642, by Geo. Adkins and Wm. Foster, ——— Co.
Ashfield, James, 1636, by Wm. Rainshaw, Elizabeth City Co.
Ashley, David, 1652, by Mr. David Fox, Lancaster Co.
Ashton, Richard, 1653, by Charles Grymes, Lancaster Co.
Ashton, Warbow, 1638, by Mr. Walter Ashton, Charles City Co.
Ashton, Eliza, 1651, by Mrs. Anna Bernard, Northumberland Co.
Ashton, Isabell, 1652, by Mrs. Anna Barnett, Gloucester Co.
Ashton, Rachell, 1653, by Mrs. Mary Brent, ——— Co.
Ashton, Fra., 1655, by Major Wm. Hoccaday, New Kent Co.
Ashton, Thom., 1635, by Osbourne Jerkin, Charles City Co.
Ashwell, Anne, 1650, by Wm. Hodgson, Yorke Co.
Ashwell, Wm., 1653, by Wm. Delram, ——— Co.
Ashwell, Mary, 1652, by Mrs. Elinor Brocas, Lancaster Co.
Ashwell, Henry, 1639, by Georg Minifye, Esq., Charles River Co.
Ashworth, Wm., 1653, by Charles Scarburgh, Northampton. Co.
Aston, Richard, 1654, by Capt. Giles Brent, Westmoreland Co.
Asley, John, 1630, by John Russell, ——— Co.
Askue, Ann, ———, by Tho. Meares, Lower Norfolk Co.
Asse, Andrew, 1643, by Henry Neale, James City Co.
Asselbie, Elija, 1646, by Sir William Berkley, ——— Co.
Assell, Gilbert, 1653, by Gregory Rawlins, Surry Co.
Asenie, Alice, 1641, by Tho. Mathews, ——— Co.
Assey, Francis, 1639, by William Barker, Charles City Co.
Ashton, Joane, 1638, by Wm. Hatfield, Upper New Norfolk Co.
Aston, Thomas, 1647, by Thomas Wright, Lower Norfolk Co.
Aston, John, 1643, by Edward Tonstall, ——— Co.
Aston, Antho., 1650, by Capt. Moore Fantleroy, ——— Co.
Aston, James, 1650, by Tho. Hawkins, Charles River Co.
Aston, Charles, Isabell, his wife, Charles, his son, 1656, by Mr. Tho.
    Purifoy, ——— Co.
Aston, Walter, 1643, by Sir. Francis Wyatt, Kt., ——— Co.
Aston, Robt., 1637, by Theodore Moyser, James City.
Atcherson, Wm., 1638, by William Carter, James City Co.
Athanes, Thomas, 1650, by George Taylor, ——— Co.
Athaway, Wm., 1637, by Alice Edloe, Henrico Co.
Atherfold, Lanes, 1650, by Mrs. Francis Townshend (widow), **North-**
    umberland Co.
Athor, James, 1643, by Edward Dobson, ——— Co.
Atkins, Antho., 1648, by Tho. Broughton, ——— Co.

Atkins, Marmad, 1653, by Peter Knight, Northumberland Co.
Atkins, Eliz., 1653, by Maj. Wm. Lewis, —––— Co.
Atkins, Wm., 1640, by William Crannage, Isle of Wight Co.
Atkins, Silvester, 1637, by Capt. Francis Eppes, Charles City Co.
Atkins, Jon., 1653, by Leonard Chamberlaine, Gloucester Co.
Atkins, Tho., 1654, by Jno. Wyre, John Gillet, Andrew Gilson and John
    Phillipps, —––— Co.
Atkins, Robt., 1656, by John Williams, Northampton Co.
Atkins, George, 1654, by Edward Simpson, Gloucester Co.
Atkins, Anth., 1643, by Elizabeth Hull, —––— Co.
Atkins, Wm., 1642, by John Waltham, Jr., Accomac Co.
Atkins, William, 1635, by Capt. Adam Thoroughgood, —––— Co.
Atkins, Christopher, 1635, by Capt. Wm. Pierse, —––— Co.
Atkinson (Jr.), 1637, by Mathew Atkinson, New Norfolk Co.
Atkinson, Mathew (Sr.), 1637, by Mathew Atkinson, New Norfolk Co.
Atkinson, Marmaduke, 1642, by Christopher Boyce, —––— Co.
Atkinson, And., 1648, by Lewis Burwell, Gent., —––— Co.
Atkinson, Allis., 1648, by Lewis Burwell, Gent., —––— Co.
Atkinson, Henry, 1639, by John Lewin, Isle of Wight Co.
Atkinson, Thomas, 1642, by Peter Rigby, —––— Co.
Atkinson, Tho., 1652, by John Halton, —––— Co.
Atkinson, Mary, 1643, by John Batts, James City Co.
Atkinson, Matt, 1645, by John Rode, Warwick.
Atkinson, Tho., 1637, by Mathew Atkinson, New Norfolk Co.
Atmore, Thos., 1635, by Capt. Adam Thoroughgood, —––— Co.
Attaway, Ja., 1653, by John Merryman and Morgan Haynes, Lancaster
    Co.
Attera, Tho., 1637, by Wm. Prior, Charles River Co.
Attingsworth, Jno., 1646, by Sir William Berkley, —––— Co.
Attocke, Nagar, 1645, by Richard Jacob, Northampton Co.
Attore, Edward, 1650, by Mordecay Cooke, —––— Co.
Atwack, Jacob, 1648, by John Clarke, Lower Norfolk Co.
Atwell, Mary, 1649, by Wm. Hoccaday, —––— Co.
Atwell, Symon, 1648, by John Saynes, James City Co.
Atwell, Katherin, 1638, by Thomas Plomer and Samuell Edmonds,
    James City Co.
Atwell, Israell, 1635, by Vectoris Christmas, Elizabeth City Co.
Atwell, Nicholas, 1637, by William Spencer, —––— Co.
Atwell, Tho., and wife, 1650, by Edward Grimes, —––— Co.
Atwill, Nicholds, 1635, by William Spencer, —––— Co.
Atwood, Edw., 1653, by John Ware, —––— Co.
Atwood, Edmond, 1653, by Charles Grymes, Lancaster Co.
Atwood, An., 1635, by Richard Bennett, —––— Co.
Atwood, Ann, 1637, by Rich. Bennett, New Norfolk Co.
Axelby, John, 1652, by Capt. Tho. Hackett, Lancaster Co.
Axter, John, 1650, by John Sevier, —––— Co.
Axtill, John, 1653, by Col. Wm. Taylor, Esq., Gloucester Co.
Axton, John, 1648, by Lewis Burwell, Gent., —––— Co.
Austin, Samuell, 1643, by Obedience Robins, Gent., Northampton Co.
Audrey, Ellin, 1652, by Toby Smith, Gent., Lancaster Co.
Audreck, Wm., 1655, by Wm. Wright, Gent., Nansemond Co.

Auger, Jon., 1637, by Arthur Smith, Isle of Wight Co.
Aunoagan, Marine, 1653, by Tho. Speoke, ——— Co.
Aunt, Phillipp, 1635, by John Cheeseman, Charles River Co.
Austen, Tho., and wife, 1654, by Wm. Lea, Charles City Co.
Austin, Richard, 1638, by John Watkins, James Cittie Co.
Austin, James, 1650, by Mrs. Frances Townsland (widow), Northumberland Co.
Austin, Richard, 1654, by Wm. Lea, Charles City Co.
Austin, John, 1654, by Wm. Lea, Charles City Co.
Austin, Thos., wife and two children, 1642, Bertram Hobert, ———Co.
Austin, Geo., 1643, by Capt. Samuell Mathews, Esq., ——— Co.
Austin, Geo., 1643, by Capt. Samuell Mathews, Esq., ———Co.
Austin, Wm., 1637, by Francis Osborne, ——— Co.
Austine, Tho., 1652, by Mr. Tho. Gutheridge, Lower Norfolk Co.
Austine, James, 1652, by Robt. Bauldry, York Co.
Austine, Tho., 1650, by Mrs. Francis Townslend (widdow), Northumberland Co.
Auston, Jno., 1654, by John Drayton, Westmoreland Co.
Auston, Rich., 1648, by Wm. Ewen James City Co.
Aurllott, Ann, 1654, by Edw. Welch, ——— Co.
Autrobos, John, 1653, by Henry Lowne, Henrico Co.
Averry, Jon., 1642, by Hugh Gwyn, Gent., ——— Co.
Avery, Henry, and Ann, his wife, 1642, by Stephen Gill, Yorke River Co.
Avery, Tho., 1651, by Edward Deggs, Esq., Yorke Co.
Avery, Eliz., 1641, by Ambrose Bennett, Isle of Wight Co.
Avery, Marke, 1643, by Capt. Wm. Peirce, Esq., ——— Co.
Averitt, Christo., 1630, by Capt. John Chelsman, Charles River Co.
Avile, Eliza, 1649, by Wm. Hoccaday, ——— Co.
Avint, Phillip, 1636, by Capt. John Chelsman, Charles River Co.
Aykins, Jane, 1653, by Major John Westhrope, Charles City Co.
Ayres, Kath., 1651, by Mr. Wm. Armestead, ——— Co.
Ayres, Mr. Wm., 1652, by Mrs. Mary Brent, Northumberland Co.

B

Baats, Henry, 1639, by Robert Eley, Isle of Wight Co.
Babb, Edward, 1639, by Edward Panderson, ——— Co.
Babbington, Michaell, 1635, by Thos. Butler Clark and Pastor of Denbie, Warrasquinoake Co.
Babbinton, John, 1639, by John Jackson, Chalres River Co.
Babister, Richard, 1643, by Wm. Warder, ——— Co.
Bach, Thos., 1638, by Edw. Travis and John Johnson, James City Co.
Backcocke, Richard, 1652, by Henry Palin, and John Singleton, ———Co.
Backen, Eliza, 1649, by Henry Bishopp, Northampton Co.
Backham, Henry, 1650, by Samuell Smith, Northumberland Co.
Backwel, John, 1642, by Robert Lawrence, Isle of Wight Co.
Backsler, Wm., 1637, by Cheney Boyes, Charles City Co.
Backster, Jno., 1653, by John Levistone, Gloucester Co.
Backster, Roger, 1653, by Col. Wm. Clayborne, ——— Co. (Sec. of State.)
Bacon, Eliza, 1647, by John Little, Northampton Co.

Bacon, Eliza, 1657, by Mr. Wm. Armestead, —— Co.
Bacon, Tho., 1651, by Mr. Wm. Armestead, —— Co.
Bacon, Tho., 1653, by Jervais Dodson, Northumberland Co.
Bacon, Mary, 1652, James Forster, and Andry Bonnet, —— Co.
Bacon, Joseph, 1652, by Mrs. Anna Barnett, Gloucester Co.
Bacon, Jos., 1651, by Mrs. Anna Bernard, Northumberland Co.
Bacon, Eliza, 1650, by Stephen Carlton, Northampton Co.
Bade, Clem., 1641, by Thomas Morrey, Isle of Wight Co.
Badden, John, 1639, by William Davis, James City Co.
Badge, John, 1642, by Thomas Bagwell, Charles City Co.
Badger, Ann, 1648, by Richard Thompson, Northumberland Co.
Badger, Anne, 1653, by Mrs. Mary Brent, —— Co.
Badger, Ann, 1639, by William Parry, Elizabeth City Co.
Badham, Margarett, 1639, by Wm. Barker, Charles CityCo.
Badham, Jon., 1638, by Thomas Stout, —— Co.
Badham, John, 1639, by William Parry, Elizabeth City Co.
Badley, Thomas, 1642, by John Styles, Isle of Wight Co.
Badnall, John, 1642, by Thomas Wombwell, James City Co.
Badney, Richard, 1639, by Lieut. Richard Popeley, —— Co.
Badworth, James, 1639, by John Osborne, James Cittie Co.
Baerer, Ralph, 1655, by John Watson, Lancaster Co.
Bagly, Phillipp, 1639, by Robert Newman, Warwick River Co.
Bagby, Jon., 1636, by Mr. George Menifye, James City Co.
Bagley, Phill, 1650, by Epa. Lawson, —— Co.
Bagly, Richard, 1638, by William Banister, —— Co.
Bagly, Tho., 1641, by Wm. Storey, Upper Norfolk Co.
Bagby, Joan, 1636, by John Chandler, Elizabeth Citie Co.
Bagly, James, 1639, by Robert Rockwell, Upper New Norfolk Co.
Bagly, Jon., 1642, by Thomas Osborne, Henrico Co.
Bagly, Robert, 1653, by Robert Bayley, Northampton Co.
Bagly, Thomas, 1641, by Wm. Storey, Upper Norfolk Co.
Bagon, Mary, 1650, by David Peibles, Charles City Co.
Bagnall, Roger, 1637, by John Upton, Isle of Wight Co.
Bagnol, Roger, 1635, by Jno. Upton, Warrasquinoake Co.
Bagwell, Tho., 1653, by Colo. Wm. Clayborne, —— Co. (Sec. of State.)
Baldershell, Wm., 1650, by John Garwood, Nansemond Co.
Bading, Walter, 1654, by Walter Dickenson, Lancaster Co.
Baile, Mathew, 1656, by Wm. Justice, Charles City Co.
Bailey, Anthony, 1656, by Vincent Stanford, —— Co.
Baily, John, 1643, by Walter Aston, Gent., Charles City Co.
Baine, Elizabeth, 1656, by Richard Wheeler, Lower Norfolk Co.
Baines, Richard, ——, by Lt. Coll. John Cheesman, —— Co.
Baines, Geo., 1653, by Richard Carey, —— Co.
Bainer, Dorothy, 1652, by July Gardner, Northampton Co.
Bainsham, Tho., 1643, by James Bagnall, Lower Norfolk Co.
Baker, Francis, 1646, by Tho. Miles, Elizabeth City Co.
Baker, Walter, 1650, by Mrs. Frances Townshend (widdow), Northumberland Co.
Baker, Edward, 1650, by Daniell Luellin, Charles City Co.
Baker, Phillip, 1655, by Capt. Tho. Davis, Warwick Co.
Baker, Daniel, 1655, by Southy Littleberry, Northampton Co.

Baker, Maurice, 1651, by Thomas Thornbrough, Northampton Co.
Baker, Tho., 1653, by James Turner, ——— Co.
Baker, John, 1652, by John Gresham, Northumberland Co.
Baker, Ann, 1653, by Colo. Wm. Clayborne, ——— Co. (Sec. of State.)
Baker, Peter, 1651, by Richard Bayly, ——— Co.
Baker, Langay, 1654, by Edw. Cole, Northampton Co.
Baker, Susan, 1655, by Col. Hugh Gwyn, Lancaster Co.
Baker, Richard, 1653, by Edward Dobson, ——— Co.
Baker, Hangatt, 1649, by Richard Bayly, Northampton Co.
Baker, Mary, 1650, by Mr. James Williamson, ——— Co.
Baker, Wm., 1638, by Capt. Christopher Wormley, Charles River Co.
Baker, Martin, 1643, by Rowland Burnham, Yorke Co.
Baker, Lewis, 1638, by David Mansell, James City Co.
Baker, John, 1642, by Richard Morgan, Charles County.
Baker, Eliza, 1643, by Edward Tonstall, ——— Co.
Baker, John, 1645, by Mark Johnson, Elizabeth City Co.
Baker, Silvester, 1643, by Mr. Phillipp Bennett, Upper Norfolk Co.
Baker, Law., 1653, by John Maddison, Gloucester Co.
Baker, Richard, 1639, by Edward Oliver, James City Co.
Baker, Tho., 1653, by John Maddison, Gloucester Co.
Baker, Mary, 1653, by Tho. Hawkins, Northumberland Co.
Baker, Jon., 1638, by William Banister, ——— Co.
Baker, Daniel, 1635, by William Wilkinson (minister), ——— Co.
Baker, Wm., 1637, by Tho. Wheeler, Charles City Co.
Baker, Alice, 1642, by John Towlsen, Accomack Co.
Baker, John, 1635, by George Minifie, James City Co.
Baker, Wm., 1637, by Wm. Farrar, Henrico Co.
Baker, William, 1638, by Oliver Sprye, Upper New Norfolk Co.
Baker, Geo., 1637, by Henry Perry, Charles River Co.
Baker, Dorothy, 1637, by John Baker, Charles City Co.
Baker, Alice, 1637, by John Baker, Charles City Co.
Baker, John, 1637, by John Baker, Charles City Co.
Baker, Thigh., 1637, by John Baker, Charles City Co.
Baker, Richard, 1636, by Elizabeth Hawkins, Charles River Co.
Baker, Wm., 1637, by Theodore Moyser, James City Co.
Baker, Richard, 1639, by Edward Oliver, James City Co.
Baker, John, 1636, by Izabell Thresher, ——— Co.
Baker, John, 1636, by Mr. Georg Menefee, James City Co.
Baker, John, 1636, by Wm. Layton, ——— Co.
Baker, Daniel, 1637, by William Wilkinson, New Norfolk Co.
Baker, Ellis, 1635, by Bridges Freeman, James City Co.
Baker, Willliam, 1635, by John Vaster, Warrasquinoake Co.
Bakone, Elizabeth, 1656, by Richard Barnhouse, Gent., James City Co.
Balding, Francis, 1642, by John Moone, Isle of Wight Co.
Baldock, Dasey, 1638, by Nicholas Sabrell, James City Co.
Baldrige, Wm., 1651, by James Baldrige and Capt. Tho. Baldrige, Northumberland Co.
Baldrige, Mary, 1651, by James Baldrige and Capt. Tho. Baldrige, Northumberland Co.
Baldwin, Marles, 1647, by Richard Bland, ——— Co.
Baldwin, Jone, 1636, by John Baker, Henrico Co.

Baldwin, John, 1652, by Capt. John West, Esq., ——— Co.
Baldwin, Wm., 1650, by Robert Blake and Samuell Elridge, Isle of Wight Co.
Baldwin, Edward, 1650, by Hump. Lyster, ——— Co.
Baldwin, Wm., 1635, by Wm. Garry, Accomack Co.
Bales, Tho., 1636, by John Chandler, Elizabeth Citie Co.
Balewell, Robert, 1649, by Tho. Spake, Gent., Northumberland Co.
Baley, Wm., 1653, by John Medstard and John Edwards, Northumberland Co.
Balfe, Oliver, 1648, by Tho. Braughton, ——— Co.
Balfe, Oliver, 1643, by Elizabeth Hull, ——— Co.
Balistocke, Rich., 1642, by Thomas Bagwell, Charles City Co.
Ball, Tho., 1654, by Capt. John West, Esq., Gloucester Co.
Ball, James, 1654, by John Drayton, Westmoreland Co.
Ball, John, 1655, by Wm. Botham, Westmoreland Co.
Ball, Eliza, 1651, by Richard Smith, Northampton Co.
Ball, John, 1653, by Tho. Harmanson, Northampton Co.
Ball, Wm., 1653, by Robert Brasseur, Nansemond Co.
Ball, Wm., 1653, by Robert Brasseur, Nansemond Co.
Ball, Richard, 1651, by Mr. Richard Lawson, ——— Co.
Ball, Tho., 1650, by Edward Walker, Northumberland Co.
Ball, John, 1643, by Mr. Moore Fantleroy, Upper Norfolk Co.
Ball, John, 1652, by Mr. Peter Knight, Gloucester Co.
Ball, Michael, 1638, by John Jackson and Eliza Wingswill, James City Co.
Ball, Richard, 1638, by Humphry Tabb, Elizabeth City Co.
Ballance, Wm., 1656, by Wm. Justice, Charles City Co.
Ballister, Tho., 1656, by Wm. Crump and Mr. Humphry Vaulx, James City Co.
Ballard, An., 1653, by Corbet Piddee, Northumberland Co.
Ballard, Richard, 1656, by Tho. Busby, Surry Co.
Ballard, Judith, ———, by Tho. Binns, Surry Co.
Balleroe, James, 1650, by John Hallawes, Gent., Northumberland Co.
Balton, Wm., 1654, by Francis Gray, ——— Co.
Balver, Beves, 1642, by Thomas Bagwell, Isle of Wight Co.
Baly, Richard, 1636, by Robert Hollom, Henrico Co.
Bambas, Edward, 1653, by Geo. Cable, ——— Co.
Bambridge, Christopher, 1639, by Thomas Stoute, James City Co.
Bamforth, John, 1642, by Capt. Samuell Mathews, Esq., ——— Co.
Bancks, Jon., 1635, by Thomas Gray, James Co.
Bancks, John, 1638, by Thomas Gray, James City.
Bancks, Jon., 1637, by Capt. John Howe, Accomac Co.
Bancroft, Wm., 1640, by Randall Crew, Upper Norfolk Co.
Bandes, Wm., 1652, by John Smith, ——— Co.
Band, Wm., 1654, by Col. Argoll Yardley, Northampton Co.
Band, John, 1637, by Henry Catyler, New Norfolk Co.
Bandleson, Ja., 1650, by Wm. Clapham, ——— Co.
Bandon, Peter, 1654, by Tho. Willoughby, Lower Norfolk Co.
Bandwick, John, 1648, by Richard Wyatt, ——— Co.
Bandick, Richard, 1650, by Richard Hull, ——— Co.
Banister, Wm., 1650, by Robert Bird, ——— Co.
Banister, Henry, 1653, by Joseph Croshaw, York Co.

Banister, Thomas, 1639, by Dorothy Clarke, Henrico Co.
Banister, John, 1652, by Tho. Teakle, Northampton Co.
Banister, Wm., 1645, by Justinian Cooper, Gent., Isle of Wight Co.
Banister, Wm., 1638, by Wm. Banister, ——— Co.
Banister, John, 1636, by Arthur Washington, Warwick Co.
Bannister, William, 1637, by Justinian Cooper, Isle of Wight Co.
Bannister, Nicholas, 1642, by John Brooch, Charles River Co.
Bannister, Wm., 1636, by Justinian Cooper, Warrasquinoak Co.
Bankes, Eliza, 1650, by Richard Smith, Northampton Co.
Banks, John, 1652, by Nathaniel Bacon, Isle of Wight Co.
Banks, John, 1652, by Capt. Tho. Hackett, Lancaster Co.
Banks, Ja., 1650, by Mordecay Cooke, ——— Co.
Banks, Rich., 1637, by Capt. John Chelsman, Charles River Co.
Banks, Rich., 1636, by Wm. Armestead, Elizabeth City Co.
Banks, Ann, 1637, by William Reynolds, Charles River Co.
Banson, Peter, 1648, by Lewis Burwell and Tho. Haws, York River Co.
Banten, Thos., 1635, by John Parrott, ——— Co.
Banton, Carrington, 1642, by Victoris Christmas and Francis Finch,
    ——— Co.
Banton, Jane, 1653, by Mr. Tho. Breman, Gloucester Co.
Banton, Wm., 1650, by Jervace Dodson, Gent., Northumberland Co.
Banton, Wm., 1637, by Charles Barcroft, Isle of Wight.
Banen, Rich., 1635, by John Moone, Warrasquinoake Co.
Barricole, Phill., 1652, by Charles Scarburg, Northampton Co.
Baramus, Tho., 1643, by William Jacob, Lower Norfolk Co.
Barber, Fra., 1653, by Frances Emperor, Hugh Gale and Edward
    Morgan, Lower Norfolk Co.
Barbeard, Wm., 1647, by Wm. Whitington, Northampton Co.
Barber, Edw., 1650, by Capt. Moore Fautleroy, ——— Co.
Barber, John, 1636, by Wm. Neesam, James City Co.
Barber, Geog., 1638, by Edward Oliver, ——— Co.
Barber, Vic., 1654, by Thomas Binns, Surry Co.
Barber, John, 1656, by Wm. Justice, Charles City Co.
Barber, Hester, 1655, by Wm. Wright, Gent., Nansemond Co.
Barber, James, 1653, by Peter Knight and Baker Cutt, ——— Co.
Barber, Fra., 1647, by Tho. Wells, Lower Norfolk Co.
Barbor, John, 1651, by Toby Norton, Northampton Co.
Barby, Jane, 1656, by Vincent Stanford, ——— Co.
Barcost, Tho., 1636, by Richard Cocke, ——— Co.
Barcroft, Jane, wife of Jon. Barcroft, 1637, by Arthur Smith, Isle of
    Wight.
Barcroft, John, 1637, by Arthur Smith, Isle of Wight Co.
Barcroft, Charles, 1650, by Anthony Fulgain, ——— Co.
Barcroft, Charles, 1650, by John Mangor, ——— Co.
Barcroft, Char., 1647, by Elizabeth Barcroft, Isle of Wight Co.
Bard, Robt., 1635, by John Moone, Warrasquinoake Co.
Bard, John, 1651, by Ashwell Battin, Yorke Co.
Barden, Ann, 1653, by Joseph Croshaw, York Co.
Bardin, Geo., 1694, by Mr. Edmund Scarburg, Northampton Co.
Bare, Hen., 1654, by Randall Chamblett, ——— Co.
Baree, Anna, 1651, by Mr. Rowland Burnham, ——— Co.

Barefield, Jon., 1653, by Robert Brasseur, Nansemond Co.
Barefoot, Tho., 1650, by Mr. John Hallawes, Northumberland Co.
Bareman, Wm., 1651, by Wm. Hampton, ——— Co.
Bareman, Wm., 1651, by Wm. Hampton, ——— Co.
Barerofe, Charles, 1652, by Littleton Scarburg, ——— Co.
Barfeild, Tho., 1643, by Phillipp Taylor, Northampton Co.
Barfoote, Ann., 1636, by Richard Cocke, ——— Co.
Barham, Mary, 1654, by Sr. Henry Chickly, Kt., Lancaster Co.
Barkeley, Jane, daughter of Eliz. Martian, 1639, by Capt. Nicholas
    Martian, Charles River Co.
Barkeley, Mary, 1648, by George White, Lower Norfolk Co.
Barkeley, Ann, 1650, by Wm. Clapham, ——— Co.
Barker, Mary, 1650, by Hump. Lyster, ——— Co.
Barker, Tho., 1652, by Mr. Tho. Brice, Lancaster Co.
Barker, Henry, 1652, by Mr. James Warradine, ——— Co.
Barker, Nicholas, 1641, by Samuell Firmer, Upper New Norfolk Co.
Barker, Mary, 1650, by Tho. Wilkinson, ——— Co.
Barke, H., 1647, by Thomas Johnson, Gent., Northampton Co.
Barker, John, 1656, by Tho. Busby, Surry Co.
Barker, Eliz., 1650, by Capt. Moore Fantleroy, ——— Co.
Barker, Elizabeth, 1650, by John Sever, ——— Co.
Barker, Nathan, 1649, by Wm. Moore, ——— Co.
Barker, John, 1648, by Tho. Ludwell, Gent., James City Co.
Barker, Alice, wife Christo Barker, 1648, by John Watkins, James City.
Barker, Christo., 1648, by John Watkins, James City Co.
Barker, Wm., 1654, by John Drayton, Westmoreland Co.
Barker, Wm., 1656, by James Price, Northampton Co.
Barker, Georg, 1639, by Edward Oliver, James City Co.
Barker, Colte., 1643, by Capt. Thomas Pettus, ——— Co.
Barker, Jerimiah, 1638, by Edmund Scarborough, Accomac Co.
Barker, Sylvester, 1638, by Mr. Robert Bennett, Upper Norfolk Co.
Barker, Robt., 1638, by Bennett Freeman, James City Co.
Barker, James, 1637, by Edward Tunstall, Henrico Co.
Barker, Geo., 1637, by Henry Perry, Charles River Co.
Barker, Wm., 1637, by Arthur Bayly and Tho. Crosby, Henrico Co.
Barker, Jon., 1636, by Peter Johnson, Warrasquinoake Co.
Barker, Georg, 1636, by Richard Peirce, James City Co.
Barker, Jon., 1637, by Thomas Causey, Charles City Co.
Barker, Wm., 1639, by Samuell Almond, Henrico Co.
Barker, Geo. 1639, by Edward Oliver, James City Co.
Barker, James, 1636, by Edward Tonstall, ——— Co.
Barker, John, 1639, by William Dooi, James City.
Barker, Hugh, 1639, by Ambrose Cobbs, Henrico Co.
Barker, Christopher, 1640, by Christopher Kirke, Accomack Co.
Barker, Richard, 1639, Ambrose Cobbs, Henrico Co.
Barkwith, Robt., 1635, by Capt. Thos. Willowbye, ——— Co.
Barkworth, Jno., 1654, by Robert Hubard, Westmoreland Co.
Barkeworth, John, 1654, by Valentine Patten, Westmoreland Co.
Barlae, Francis, 1650, by Epa. Lawson, ——— Co.
Barleaw, Mrs. Jane, 1651, by Capt. Geo. Read, Lancaster Co.
Barlo, John, 1648, by Randall Crew, Nansemond Co.

Barlow, Wm., 1653, by Hump. Edey, ——— Co.
Barlow, Stafford, 1642, by Joseph Royall, ——— Co.
Barlow, John, 1652, by Wm. Up. Thomas, ——— Co.
Barlow, Tho., 1652, by Henry Barlow, ——— Co.
Barlow, Jon., 1642, by Christopher Boyce, ——— Co.
Barlow, Sus., 1654, by Capt. John West, Esq., Gloucester Co.
Barlowe, Tymothy, 1635, by Capt. Thos. Willowbye, ——— Co.
Barly, Roger, 1643, by Tho. Evans, ——— Co.
Barley, Antho., 1653, by John Barrow, Surry Co.
Barlye, Henry, 1650, by Robert Bird, ——— Co.
Barnaby, James, 1651, by Roger Johns, Northampton Co.
Barnaby, Sara, 1651, by Roger Johns, Northampton Co.
Barnaby, Sarah, 1640, by John Holloway, Accomack.
Barnaby, James, 1640, by John Holloway, Accomack.
Barnard, Wm., 1642, by John Benton, ——— Co.
Barnarde, Jon., 1635, by Capt. Adam Thoroughgood, ——— Co.
Barnbridge, Christopher, 1638, by Capt. Christopher Wormley, —— Co.
Barne, Eliz., 1654, by Col. Hump. Higgenson, Esq., and Abraham
   Moone, Westmoreland Co.
Barnes, Edw., 1651, by Humphry Tabb, Northumberland Co.
Barnes, Agnes, 1653, by Wm. Mellin, Northampton Co.
Barnes, Dorothy, 1653, by Charles scarburg, Northampton Co.
Barnes, Ann, 1646, by Thomas Bahe, Upper Norfolk Co.
Barnes, Edwd., 1654, by Tho. Deynes, ——— Co.
Barnes, Martin, 1642, by Augustine Warner, ——— Co.
Barnes, John, 1651, by Mr. Antho. Steevens, Northampton Co.
Barnes, Henry, 1651, by Edwards Diggs, Esq., Yorke Co.
Barnes, Edward, 1654, by Tho. Bell, Northampton Co.
Barnes, Fra., 1651, by Tho. Hales and Tho. Sheppard, Northumberland
   Co.
Barnes, Joan, 1653, by Hump. Edey, ——— Co.
Barnes, Chas., 1653, by James Magregory and Hugh Fauch, North-
   umberland Co.
Barnes, Henry, 1653, by Wm. Freeke, Northumberland Co.
Barnes, Henry, 1649, by Francis Brown, Northumberland Co.
Barnes, Geo., 1650, by Tho. Vaus, Gent., Northumberland Co.
Barnes, Wm., 1650, by John Baytes, Northumberland Co.
Barnes, Stephen, 1650, by John Major, Northampton Co.
Barnes, John, 1650, by John Mattrum, Northumberland Co.
Barnes, James, 1650, by Capt. Richard Bond, Charles City Co.
Barnes, Henry, 1653, by Abraham Moone, Lancaster Co.
Barnes, Wm., 1642, by Wm. Barnard, Esq., Isle of Wight Co.
Barnes, Wm., 1642, by Wm. Barnes, Esq., Isle of Wight Co.
Barnes, Wm., 1642, by Wm. Barnes, Esq., Isle of Wight Co.
Barnes, Wm., 1642, by Wm. Barnard, Esq., Isle of Wight Co.
Barnes, John, 1642, by Thomas Ray, ——— Co.
Barnes, Edward, 1639, by Edward Drew, Accomack Co.
Barnes, Henry, 1639, by Robert Eley, Isle of Wight Co.
Barnes, Barnaby, 1637, by Wm. Prior, Charles River Co.
Barnes, James, 1637, by Humphrey England, James City Co.

Barnes, James, 1640, by William Wigg, James City Co.
Barnett, Nich., 1638, by Thomas Swan, James Citie Co.
Barnett, Dorothy, 1638, by Edw. Travis and John Johnson, James City Co.
Barnett, Dorothy, 1637, by Edward Travis, James City Co.
Barnett, Robert, 1653, by Peter Knight, Northumberland Co.
Barnett, Richard, 1651, by Mrs. Anna Bernard, Northumberland Co.
Barnett, Eliza, 1651, by Mrs. Anna Bernard, Northumberland Co.
Barnett, Rich., 1635, by Wm. Swan, James Co.
Barnett, Stephen (his negro), 1636, by John Wilkins, Accomack Co.
Barnett, Nicho., 1638, by William Carter, James City Co.
Barnett, Stephen, 1637, by John Wilkins, New Norfolk Co.
Barnett, Jno., 1653, by Francis Emperor, Hugh Gale and Edward Morgan, Lower Norfolk Co.
Barnett, Corderoy, 1652, by Mrs. Anna Barnett, Gloucester Co.
Barnett, Eliza, 1652, by Mrs. Anna Barnett, Gloucester Co.
Barnett, Mrs. Richard, 1652, by Mrs. Anna Barnett, Gloucester Co.
Barnett, Richard, 1652, by Mrs. Anna Barnett, Gloucester Co.
Barnaed, Eliza., 1650, by Mr. Epaphroditus Lawson, ——— Co.
Barnett, Elizabeth, 1652, by John Robbins, Northampton Co.
Barnett, Joseph, 1642, by Stephen Gill, Yorke River Co.
Barney, Phon., 1650, by Lewis Burwell, Gent., Northumberland Co.
Barney, James, 1650, by Lewis Burwell, Gent., Northumberland Co.
Barnick, Wm., 1643, by William Ewins, James City Co.
Barogan, Richard, 1653, by Henry Corbell, Gloucester Co.
Boroughs, Wm., 1635, by Capt. Adam Thoroughgood, ——— Co.
Barr, Roger, 1656, by Wm. Millinge, Northampton Co.
Barrab, Abraham, 1655, by John Hampton, ——— Co.
Barres, Hugh, 1653, by Dennis Connier, Lancaster Co.
Barrfy, John, 1650, by John Maltrum, Northumberland Co.
Barrington, Wm., 1643, by Edward Murfey and John Vaughan, ——Co.
Barrington, Fra., 1648, by Lewis Burwell and Tho. Haws, York River Co.
Barrom, John, 1652, by Tho. Gloscock, Lancaster Co.
Bartlett, Christopher, 1639, by John Jackson, Charles River Co.
Bartlett, Richard, 1637, by John Judson, Charles River Co.
Bartlett, Michaell, 1638, by Wm. Cloys, Charles River Co.
Bartlett, Ann, 1653, by Fra. Gower, Lancaster Co.
Barrett, Avis., 1653, by John Dipdall, Charles City Co.
Barrett, Jane, 1653, by Charles Scarburg, Northampton Co.
Barrett, Henry, 1652, by Teague Floyne, Lancaster Co.
Barrett, Symon, 1650, by Mr. Epaphroditus Lawson, ——— Co.
Barrett, Richd., 1653, by John Merryman and Morgan Haynes, Lancaster Co.
Barrett, Sara, 1649, by Robert Mosely, Gent., ——— Co.
Barretts, Tho., 1652, by Capt. Augustine Warner, ——— Co.
Barrett, John, 1653, by Eppy Bonison, Lancaster Co.
Barrett, Tho., 1655, by John Woodward, Gloucester Co.
Barrow, John, 1642, by John Sweete, ——— Co.
Barrow, Henry, 1652, by Tho. Preston, ——— Co.
Barrow, Michaell, 1653, by Mr. Wm. Hoccoday, Yorke Co.

Barrow, John, 1654, by John Wyre, John Gillet, Andrew Gilson and John Phillipps, ——— Co.
Barrow, Tho., 1654, by Major Abraham Wood, Henrico Co.
Barrows, Mathew, 1656, by John Bromfeild, James City Co.
Barry, Garratt, 1651, by Lancaster Lovett, Lower Norfolk Co.
Barshall, John, 1652, by Mr. Edward, Overman, York Co.
Barshall, John, 1642, by Samuell Abbott, ——— Co.
Barston, Christ., 1638, by John Gater, Lower New Norfolk Co.
Bartlett, Alex., 1653, by Tho. Griffin, Lancaster Co.
Bartlett, Mary, 1656, by Major Wm. Lewis, ——— Co.
Bartlett, Jane, 1651, by Capt. Geo. Read, Lancaster Co.
Bartlett, Ann, 1654, by John Wyre, John Gillet, Andrew Gilson and John Phillipps, ——— Co.
Barthram, 1652, by Joane Yates, Lower Norfolk Co.
Bartin, Thos., 1637, by Capt. Thomas Osborne, Henrico Co.
Barter, James, 1655, by Jer. Dodson, Gent., Lancaster Co.
Bartler, Hen., 1650, by Mr. Robert Holt, James City Co.
Barton, Elias, 1642, by Richard Morgan, Charles Co.
Barton, William, 1639, by Walter Cooper, James City Co.
Barton, Nich., 1654, by John Watson and John Bognall, Westmoreland Co.
Barton, John, 1652, by Tho. Steevens, Warrick Co.
Barton, Wm., 1653, by Tho. Hawkins, Northumberland, Co.
Barton, Robt., 1637, by Nathaniel Floyd, Isle of Wight Co.
Barton, William, 1636, by Alice Edloe, Henrico Co.
Bartwright, Jon., 1653, by Henry Lee, York Co.
Barwood, Robert, 1639, by Henry Perry, Charles City Co.
Basaker, Edward, 1638, by John Gater, Lower New Norfolk Co.
Bashfeeld, Elizabeth, 1649, by Mr. Henry Lee, Yorke Co.
Bashfeild, Ann, 1650, by Laurence Peters, Nansemond Co.
Baskeville, Richard, 1639, by Walter Pakes, James City Co.
Baskerville, Robt., 1642, by John Robins, ——— Co.
Baskervill, Richard, 1639, by Walter Pakes, ——— Co.
Baskett, Wm., 1650, by Mr. Anthony Ellyot, ——— Co.
Baskett, Francis, 1643, by Rich. Hoe, Gent., ——— Co.
Basham, Ann, 1651, by Toby Norton, Northampton Co.
Basham, Andrew, 1639, by Henry Bogwell, Accomack.
Bashaw, And., 1654, by Hugh Lee, Northumberland Co.
Bashaw, Giles, 1648, by John Ellis, James Joones and John Taylor, Northampton Co.
Bashaw, Mary, 1654, by Hugh Lee, Northumberland Co.
Bashaw, Wm., 1654, by Hugh Lee, Northumberland Co.
Bashaw, Jane, 1654, by Hugh Lee, Northumberland Co.
Basoneth, Samuell, 1643, by James Basoneth (his brother), Yorke Co.
Bass, Gregory, 1642, by William Prior, Gent., ——— Co.
Bass, John, 1637, by Thos. Hampton Clarke, New Norfolk Co.
Bass, Tony, 1654, by Mr. Giles Brent, Westmoreland Co.
Bassett, Tho., 1654, by Mr. Giles Brent, Westmoreland Co.
Bassett, Ralph, 1655, by Wm. Wright, Gent., Nansemond Co.
Bassett, Mathew, 1638, by John Noone, ——— Co.
Bassett, Wm., 1638, by Thomas Dewe, Upper New Norfolk Co.

Bassett, Math., 1637, by John Moone, Isle of Wight Co.
Bassett, Georg., 1637, by Christopher Woodward, Charles City Co.
Bassett, Math., 1637, by John Moone, Isle of Wight Co.
Bassett, Isabell, 1639, by Samuel Trigg and Michael Joyner, James City Co.
Basnett, Jno., 1637, by Jno. Clarkson, Charles River Co.
Bassnett, Willi, 1637, by Lt. Richard Popeley, New Norfolk Co.
Bassye, Eliz, 1650, by Elias Edmonds, ——— Co.
Bastisks, Constant, 1653, by Major John Westhrope, Charles City Co.
Batchells, Mary, 1652, by Dr. George Hack, Northampton Co.
Batchelor, Mary, 1654, by John Whithers and Stephen Garey, Westmoreland Co.
Batcheler, Wm., 1648, by Richard Lee, Gent., ——— Co.
Batcheller, Mary, 1655, by Tho. Leatherberry, Northampton Co.
Bateman, Robt., 1643, by Richard Kemp, Esq., James City Co.
Bateman, Richard, 1653, by Benjamin Brasseur, ——— Co.
Bateman, Persiphall, 1647, by Thomas Johnson, Gent., Northampton Co.
Bateman, James, 1651, by Joseph Croshaw, Yorke Co.
Bateman, Robt., 1637, by William Mills, James City Co.
Batmason, Tho., 1653, by Wm. Hunt, ——— Co.
Bater, Charles, 1642, by Thomas Say, ——— Co.
Batiman, Tho., 1635, by Osbourne Jerkin, Charles City Co.
Bath, Thos., 1637, by Edward Travis, James City Co.
Bathelor, Mary, 1653, by Charles Scarburg, Northampton Co.
Bathers, Fra., 1648, by George Read, Gent., ——— Co.
Batho, John, 1642, by Peter Rigby, ——— Co.
Bartholmew, Hen., 1643, by John Carter, ——— Co.
Batman, Tho., 1637, by Francis Osborne, ——— Co.
Battle, Mathew, 1647, by Wm. Egberows, James City Co.
Battle, Tho., 1652, by Mr. James Warradine, ——— Co.
Battle, Elizabeth, 1654, by John Battell, ——— Co.
Battle, John, 1654, by John Battell, ——— Co.
Battock, Ralph, 1653, by John Levistone, Gloucester Co.
Batten, Wm., 1654, by John Wyre, John Gillett, Andrew Gilson and John Phillipps, ——— Co.
Batt, Mich., 1652, by Mrs. Jane Harmer, Northumberland Co.
Batts, Henry, 1643, by Tho. Symonds, ——— Co.
Batts, Wm., 1643, by Tho. Symonds, ——— Co.
Batts, Dorothy, 1643, by John Batts, James City Co.
Batts, Wm., 1650, by Robert Blake and Samuell Elridge, Isle of Wight Co.
Batts, Wm., 1648, by Wm. Barret, ——— Co.
Batts, Joseph, 1639, by Edward Travis, James City Co.
Batts, Mary, 1650, by Edward Walker, Northumberland Co.
Bates, Tho., 1650, by Mr. Epaphroditus Lawson, ——— Co.
Bates, Joseph, 1653, by Jno. Hansford, Gloucester Co.
Bates, Joane, 1651, by Giles Lawrence and John Turner, Nansemond Co.
Bates, Nicholas, 1637, by John Broche, Charles River Co.
Batts, Henry, 1639, by Thomas Symons, James City Co.

Batts, William, 1639, by Tho. Symons, James City Co.
Bates, Richard, 1654, by Nicholas Morris, Northumberland Co.
Bates, John, 1654, by John Skerrett, ——— Co.
Batty, Ashwell, 1653, by Mr. Henry Soanes, Gloucester Co.
Batley, Christo., 1652, by Wm. Moore, ——— Co.
Batrum, Lawrence, 1643, by Richard Kemp, Esq., James City Co.
Bauldwin, Tho., 1653, by Charles Grimes, Lancaster Co.
Bauldwin, Eliza, 1653, by Richard Braine, Charles Co.
Bauldwin, Wm., 1652, by Capt. Augustine Warner, ——— Co.
Baulke, Thomas, 1642, by Thomas Loving, James City Co.
Baulke, Wm., 1639, by Tho. Boulding, Elizabeth City Co.
Bauson, Eliz., 1650, by Capt. Moore Fantleroy, ——— Co.
Bausworth, Mary, 1653, by Henry Corbell, Gloucester Co.
Bavin, Mary, 1650, by John Blackborne, Surry Co.
Bawe, Joseph, 1652, by Savill Gaskins, Lower Norfolk Co.
Bawcocke, Tho., 1642, by Bertram Hobert, ——— Co.
Baxton, Jane, 1636, by William Rookins, James City Co.
Baxter, Wm., 1636, by Cheney Boyse, Charles City Co.
Baxter, Rich., 1638, by Thomas Clipwell, James City.
Baxter, Jane, 1638, by Wm. Rookins, James City Co.
Baxter, Wm., 1648, by John Manning, Lower Norfolk Co.
Baxter, John, 1651, by George Ludlow, Esq., ——— Co.
Baxter, Eleanor, 1642, by Wm. Durant, ——— Co.
Baxter, Tho., 1655, by George Wall, Westmoreland Co.
Bayant, John, 1635, by Capt. Wm. Pierse, ——— Co.
Bayard, Susan, 1648, by Lewis Burwell, Gent., ——— Co.
Bayse, Sarah, 1654, by Capt. John West, Esq., Gloucester Co.
Baycock, Wm., 1649, by Capt. Ralph Wormeley, ——— Co.
Bayer, Thomas, 1635, by Nathaniel Hoake, ——— Co.
Bayford, Hanna, 1639, by Georg Mallen, James City Co.
Bayles, Peter, 1642, by Thomas Symmons, ——— Co.
Bagley, Eliz., 1638, by Thomas Dew, Upper New Norfolk.
Bayley, Tho., 1652, by Wm. Up. Thomas, ——— Co.
Bayley, Jane, 1652, by Nicho. George, Tho. Taberer and Humphery
    Clarke, ——— Co.
Bayley, John, 1643, by Mr. Moore Fantleroy, Upper Norfolk Co.
Bayley, Tho., 1645, by William Storey, Upper Norfolk Co.
Bagley, James, 1639, by Wm. Barker, Charles City Co.
Bayley, Richd., 1653, by Joseph Croshaw, York Co.
Bayle, Mary, 1650, by Capt. Moore Fantleroy, ——— Co.
Bayle, Henry, 1637, by Patrick Kennedye, New Norfolk Co.
Baylie, Edward, 1652, by Christopher Robinson, and John Sturdevant,
    Henrico Co.
Bayly, Peter, 1637, by Rich. Bennett, New Norfolk Co.
Bayly, Henry, 1650, by Lewis Burwell, Gent., ——— Co.
Bayly, Richard, 1650, by Lewis Burwell, Gent., ——— Co.
Bayly, Jove, 1639, by Edward Drew, Accomack.
Bayly, Margarett, 1639, by Capt. Rich. Townsend, Charles River Co.
Bayly, Peter, 1635, by Richard Bennett, ——— Co.
Bayly, Hen., 1637, by James Harrison, James City Co.
Bayly, Rebena, 1637, by Phillipp Taylor, Accomack Co.

Bayly, Rich., 1643, by Capt. John Upton, Isle of Wight Co.
Bayly, Rebecca, 1643, by Phillipp Taylor, Northampton Co.
Bayly, Richard, 1638, by John Robins, James City Co.
Bayly, Rob., 1648, by Job. Chanter, Lower Norfolk Co.
Bayly, Tho., 1654, by Gregory Wells and Richard Williams, James City Co.
Bayly, Tho., 1655, by Mr. Robt. Bourne and Mr. Daniel Parke, York Co.
Bayly, John, 1654, by Mr. Tho. Fowke, Westmoreland Co.
Bayly, Robt., 1656, by Geo. Abbott, Nansemond Co.
Bayly, Tho., 1652, by George Pace, Charles City Co.
Baylye, Thomas, 1637, by Francis Osborne, ——— Co.
Baylye, Jon., 1638, by Abraham Wood, Charles City Co.
Baylye, Tho., 1650, by Andrew Gilson, ——— Co.
Bayne, Walter, 1637, by Leonard Yeo, Elizabeth City Co.
Baynebridge, Thomas, 1650, by Lawrence Peters, Nansemond Co.
Baywell, ———, 1635, by Thos. Baywell (her husband), ——— Co.
Bazgine, Symon, 1650, by Nathaniel Jones, Northumberland Co.
Bea, Christopher, 1639, by John Smith and Christo. Bea, Elizabeth City Co.
Beach, Ann, 1655, by George Kibble, Lancaster Co.
Beach, Stephen, 1639, by Georg Mallen, James City Co.
Beacham, Robt., 1653, by John Bebey, Lancaster Co.
Beachill, George, ———, by Mr. John Page, ——— Co.
Beachly, George, 1652, by Mr. Tho. Brice, Lancaster Co.
Beadell, John, 1636, by Richard Cocke, ——— Co.
Beadle, Jon., 1636, by Capt. Thomas Willoughby, ——— Co.
Beadle, Wm., 1650, by James Anorke, ——— Co.
Beadle, Phillip, 1653, by Wm. Thomas, Northumberland Co.
Beadle, Robt., 1656, by Wm. Pope, Nansemond Co.
Beadle, Phillip, 1653, by Abraham Moon, Lancaster Co.
Beadman, Eliz., 1650, by Henry Ashwell, ——— Co.
Beale, Eliza, 1650, by John Rosier, Northumberland, Co.
Beale, Susane, 1637, by Argoll Yeardly, New Norfolk.
Beale, Wm., 1653, by John Hillier, Northumberland Co.
Beamast, James, 1652, by Mr. Tho. Brice, Lancaster Co.
Beame, Dennock, 1655, by Capt. George Floyd, New Kent Co.
Beamond, Row., 1652, by Tho. Hoane, ——— Co.
Beamont, John, 1652, by Henry Fleete, Lancaster Co.
Beamont, Wm., 1655, by Mathew Huberd, Gent., York Co.
Beane, Robert, 1652, by Mr. Richard Cocke, Henrico Co.
Beane, Stephen, 1638, by Robt. Holt and Richard Bell, James City Co.
Beane, Stephen, 1640, by Robert Holt, James City Co.
Beane, Daniel, 1655, by John Woodward, Gloucester Co.
Beard, William, 1638, by Joseph Harmon, James City Co.
Beard, John, 1637, by Capt. Thomas Osborne, Henrico Co.
Beard, Christ., 1637, by Elizabeth Parker, Henrico Co.
Beard, Joane, 1638, by Joseph Harmon, James City Co.
Beard, Robert, 1650, by Sr. Tho. Luntsford, Kt., and Baronette, ——— Co.
Beard, Robt., 1650, by Walter Broodhurst, ——— Co.

Beard, John, 1654, by Tho. and Henry Preston, ——— Co.
Beard, Wm., 1647, by Richard Bland, ——— Co.
Beard, Mary, 1647, by Richard Bland, ——— Co.
Beard, Wm., 1654, by Capt. Nich. Marteaw, Westmoreland Co.
Bearde, Joane, 1635, by William Beard, James City Co.
Beardsley, Elizabeth, 1637, by Thos. Weekes, her husband, James City Co.
Bearkel, Jane, 1655, by Wm. Thomas, Northumberland Co.
Bearley, Job., 1655, by Saml. Eldridge, ——— Co.
Bearne, Jon., 1637, by Henry Perry, Charles River Co.
Bearne, Jon., 1637, by Henry Perry, Charles River Co.
Beare, Wm., 1643, by John Hoddin, ——— Co.
Beatall, Robert, 1637, by Elanor Day and Thom. Emmerson, Warwick River Co.
Beatall, Robt., 1637, by Eleanor Day and Thos. Emmerson, Warwick River Co.
Beatinge, John, 1653, by Tho. Sawyer, ——— Co.
Beaton, Tho., 1650, by George Pate, Charles City Co.
Beaumond, Peter, 1650, by John Sevier, ——— Co.
Beaushampe, Mary, 1652, by John Chambers, Northumberland Co.
Beaver, Mathew, 1638, by Wm. Morgan, ——— Co.
Beaw, Daniel, 1655, by John Smithey, ——— Co.
Beawmond, Rowland, 1654, by Francis Smith and Mr. John Smith, Westmoreland Co.
Bebee, John, 1638, by Epaphroditus Lawson, Upper New Norfolk Co.
Beccallitolby, Haneha, 1642, by Capt. Samuell Mathews, Esq., ——— Co.
Becham, Wm., 1639, by Richard, Preston, Upper New Norfolk Co.
Beck, James, 1651, by Mr. Wm. Armestead, ——— Co.
Beck, Edward, 1653, by John Dipdall, Charles City Co.
Beck, Richard, 1639, by Walter Pakes, James City Co.
Beckett, John, 1654, by Col. Argoll Yardley, Northampton Co.
Beckett, Tytus, 1652, by Anthony Doney and Enoch Hawker, Lancaster Co.
Beckett, Margarett, 1639, by Robt. Newman, Warwick River Co.
Beckland, Georg, 1638, by John Wagne, Charles River Co.
Beckweth, Jarret, 1636, by Hannibal Fletcher, James City Co.
Beddins, Edward, 1651, by Henry Hackney, ——— Co.
Beddus, Tho., 1650, by Mrs. Frances Townshend (widdow), Northumberland Co.
Bede, John, 1653, by Jno. Hansford, Gloucester Co.
Bedford, Jane, 1638, by Thomas Burbage, Accomack Co.
Bedham, Wm., 1652, by Mrs. Mary Brent, Northumberland Co.
Bedlem, Wm., 1650, by John Mattrum, Northumberland Co.
Bee, James, 1651, by James Foster, Nansemond Co.
Beebmer, Benis, 1638, by Thom. Bogwell, Charles City Co.
Beech, John, 1650, by Sr. Tho. Luntsford, Kt., and Baronett, ——— Co.
Beede, Tho., 1642, by Capt. Daniell Gookin, ——— Co.
Beedham, Rich., 1638, by John Robins, James City Co.
Beedman, Robt., 1650, by William Gooch, Gent., ——— Co.
Beedle, Edward, 1654, by Capt. Nich. Marteaw, Westmoreland Co.
Beedle, Alice, 1650, by George Taylor, ——— Co.

Beerfoote, Ann, 1639, by Richard Corke, Gent., Henrico Co.
Beeke, Thomas, 1638, by Wm. Cloys, Charles River Co.
Beel, Richard, 1638, by Robt. Holt and Richard Bell, James City Co.
Beely, James, 1635, by Capt. Adam Thoroughgood, —— Co.
Beeseley, Peter, 1636, by John Place, Elizabeth City Co.
Begg, Joshua, 1655, by Major Wm. Lewis, New Kent Co.
Beggon, Tho., 1655, by Philip Charles, —— Co.
Begnall, Fra., 1655, by Richard Foster, —— Co.
Beggs, Thomas, 1650, by David Peibles, Charles City Co.
Beife, John, 1650, by Wm. Yarrett and Fra. Wittington, —— Co.
Beih, Joseph, 1635, by Anthony Jones, —— Co.
Being, Elizabeth, 1652, by Mr. Tho. Curtis, —— Co.
Belcher, Wm., 1655, by Peter Ford, Gloucester Co.
Belcher, Walt., 1651, by Capt. Tho. Davis, Northumberland Co.
Belcher, Walt., 1645, by Thomas Davis, Warwick Co.
Belcher, Thomas, 1637, by John Seaward, Isle of Wight Co.
Beldam, Jon., 1637, by Capt. Thomas Panlett, Charles City Co.
Bell, John, 1657, by Ashwell Battin, Yorke Co.
Bell, Geo., 1650, by Wm. Yarrett and Fra. Wittington, —— Co.
Bell, John, 1648, by Lewis Burwell and Tho. Haws, York River Co.
Bell, Alex., 1654, by Tho. Willoughby, Lower Norfolk Co.
Bell, John, 1654, by Tho. Willoughby, Lower Norfolk Co.
Bell, John, 1655, by Tho. Willess, Lancaster Co.
Bell, John, 1642, by Georg Busse, —— Co.
Bell, Christian, 1650, by Andrew Munrow, Northumberland Co.
Bell, Richard, 1648, by Geo. Hardey, Tho. Wombwell and Peter Hall,
    Isle of Wight Co.
Bell, John, 1649, by Tho. Bourne, —— Co.
Bell, John, 1650, by Rice Jones, —— Co.
Bell, Wm., 1650, by Mr. Epaphroditus Lawson, —— Co.
Bell, Jarvis, 1643, by Mr. Moore Fautleroy, Upper Norfolk Co.
Bell, Picter, 1652, by Tho. Harris, Isle of Wight Co.
Bell, Tho., 1638, by Stephen Charlton, Accomack Co.
Bell, Geo., 1638, by John Fludd, James City Co.
Bell, Richard, 1651, by Mr. Robert Abrall, Yorke Co.
Bell, John, 1638, by William Carter, James City Co.
Bell, Wm., 1640, by Richard Williams, Charles City Co.
Bell, William, 1635, by Thomas Harwood, —— Co.
Bellan, Mary, 1638, by Alice Edloe, Henrico Co.
Bellings, Henry, 1651, by Humphrey Tabb, Northumberland Co.
Bellins, John, 1653, by Capt. Robt. Abrahal, Gloucester Co.
Belmon, Robt., 1651, by Abraham Moon and Thomas Griffen, Lan-
    caster Co.
Belsome, Ann, 1637, by Theodore Moyser, James City Co.
Belson, John, 1653, by Colo. Wm. Clayborne (Sec. of State), Co.
Belt, Richard, 1654, by Sarah Hancock, Lower Norfolk Co.
Belt, Thomp., 1636, by Wm. Clarke, Henrico Co.
Belvoir, Bevis, 1643, by Edward Dobson, —— Co.
Bemberry, John, 1646, by Geo. Ludlow, Esq., York Co.
Bembridge, Hen., 1642, by John Resbury, —— Co.
Bembridge, Thos., 1637, by Henry Perry, Charles River Co.

Bembridge, Wm., 1638, by Samuell Watkeyes, Charles River Co.
Bembridge, Tho., 1637, by Henry Perry, Charles River Co.
Bemrose, Tho., 1652, by Nicholas George, ———— Co.
Bemrose, Tho., 1651, by Anthony Johnson, Northampton Co.
Bemson, Ellis, 1656, by John Wood, ———— Co.
Benbow, Ann, 1652, by Ambrose Dixon and Stephen Horsely, North-
    ampton Co.
Bence, Wm., 1654, by Mrs. Mgt. Brent, Westmoreland Co.
Bence, John, 1653, by Geo. Thompson, ———— Co.
Bendall, Jeremiah, 1654, by John Wyre, John Gillet, Andrew Gilson
    and John Phillipps, ———— Co.
Benge, Will, 1653, by Geo. Hack, Northampton, Co.
Benering, John, 1651, by John Martin and Lancaster Lovett, Lower
    Norfolk Co.
Benhoios, Ann, 1656, by John Billiott, Northampton Co.
Benington, Jon., 1642, by Stephen Gill, ———— Co.
Benley, Wm., 1651, by Humphry Tabb, Northumberland Co.
Benleye, Tho., 1653, by John Blackbourne, Surry Co.
Benn, Stephen, 1637, by Wm. Prior, Charles River Co.
Bennet, Reb., 1653, by John Jaliffe, Isle of Wight Co.
Bennet, Math., 1655, by Southy Littleberry, Northampton Co.
Bennett, Christopher, 1653, by Peter Knight and Baker Cult, ———— Co.
Bennett, Eliz., 1653, by John Bennett, of Normany, Northumberland
    Co.
Bennett, Robt., 1653, by Richard Lake, Lancaster Co.
Bennett, Mary, 1654, by Tho. Willoughby, Lower Norfolk Co.
Bennett, Robert, 1654, by Edward Parker, Westmoreland Co.
Bennett, Eliz., 1650, by Bertram Obert, ———— Co.
Bennett, Sarah, 1642, by Stephen Hamblyn, York Co.
Bennett, John, 1654, by Sinkler Pagett, Nansemond Co.
Bennett, Edwd., 1654, by Edwin Conaway, Lancaster Co.
Bennett, John, 1653, by Colo. Wm. Clayborne, (Sec. of State), ————
    Co.
Bennett, Paule, 1651, by Edward Greenwood, James City Co.
Bennett, Ri., 1652, by Tho. Boswell, ———— Co.
Bennett, John, 1649, by Capt. Ralph Wormeley, ———— Co.
Bennett, Mary, 1649, by Capt. Ralph Wormeley, ———— Co.
Bennett, Henry, 1650, by Nathaniell Jones, Nortumberland Co.
Bennett, David, 1650, by Tho. Blogg, Northumberland Co.
Bennett, Rich., 1642, by Hugh Gwyn, Gent., ———— Co.
Bennett, Ri., 1650, by Mr. Epaphroditus Lawson, ———— Co.
Bennett, Morris, 1638, by Ambrose Bennett, Isle of Wight.
Bennett, Thomas, 1637, by Richard Bennett, New Norfolk Co.
Bennett, Eliza, 1652, by Daniell Welch, Lancaster Co.
Bennett, Robt., 1637, by Capt. Adam Thoroughgood, New Norfolk Co.
Bennett, Maselin, 1650, by Robert Bird, ———— Co.
Bennett, Jno., 1637, by David Mansell, James City Co.
Bennett, Jon., Thos. Crosby's servant, 1637, by Arthur Bayly and
    Tho. Crosby, Henrico Co.
Bennett, Eliz., 1637, by Jno. Broche, Charles River Co.
Bennett, Thos., 1636, by Richard Bennett, ———— Co.

Bennett, Gilbert, 1636, by John Neale, Accomack Co.
Bennett, John, 1639, by Samuell Almond, Henrico Co.
Bennett, Robt., 1635, by Capt. Adam Thoroughgood, ―――― Co.
Bennett, Richard, 1637, by Richard Bennett, New Norfolk Co.
Bennett, Ambrose, ――――, by Richard Bennett, New Norfolk Co.
Bennett, Eliz., 1635, by Charles Harwer, ―――― Co.
Bennett, Nich., 1635, by Wm. Clark, Eliz. City Co.
Bennett, Ambrose, 1635, by Richard Bennett, ―――― Co.
Bennett, Jon., 1635, by David Mansell, James Co.
Bennett, Mandlin, 1642, by Georg Chowning, Upper Norfolk Co.
Bennett, Robert, 1635, by John Slaughter, ―――― Co.
Benne, Richard, 1652, by Richard Hatton and Lambett Lambettson, Lancaster Co.
Bennes, Bennet, 1652, by Henry Fleete, Lancaster Co.
Bennes, Ann, 1654, by Major Miles Carey, Westmoreland Co.
Benny, Joseph, 1650, by John Baytes, Northumberland, Co.
Bennison, Eliza., 1648, by Lewis Burwell and Tho. Haws, York River Co.
Bentall, Robt., 1636, by Ellinor Dey, and Thos. Emmerson, Warwick River Co.
Bentley, Wm., 1639, by Richard Johnson, Henrico Co.
Bentley, Henry, 1650, by Capt. Ishiell Linch, ―――― Co.
Bentley, Elizabeth, 1655, by Martin Hamond, ―――― Co.
Bently, Hen., 1638, by Elizabeth Grayne, Charles City Co.
Benton, Cunningham, 1654, by Francis Gray, ―――― Co.
Benton, John, 1650, by Henry Lee and Wm. Clapham, ―――― Co.
Benton, John, 1642, by John Benton, ―――― Co.
Benton, Isabell, 1642, by John Benton, ―――― Co.
Benton, Abigail, 1642, by John Benton, ―――― Co.
Benton, Joane, wife of John Benton, 1642, by John Benton, ―――― Co.
Benton, Alice, 1642, by John Benton, ―――― Co.
Benton, Thos., 1635, by Richard Durrant, James Co.
Benton, John, 1635, by John Leonard, Warrasquinoake Co.
Bensbricke, Jove, 1639, by Tristram Nosworthy, Upper Norfolk.
Benson, John, 1650, by Capt. Charles Leech, Yorke Co.
Benson, Cuthbert, 1655, by Jno. Dodson, Gent., Lancaster Co.
Benson, Stephen, 1652, by Mrs. Mary Brent, Northumberland Co.
Benstead, Math., 1650, by George Gill, Yorke Co.
Beordwell, Tho., 1656, by Sir Henry Chichley, ―――― Co.
Beosly, Geo., 1652, by Edward Cannon and Tho. Allen, Lower Norfolk Co.
Bercher, John, 1652, by Henry Fleete, Lancaster Co.
Beadell, Mary, 1652, by John Sharpe, Lancaster Co.
Berker, Tho., 1652, by Richard Coleman, ―――― Co.
Bernard, Wm., 1651, by Mr. Rowland Burnham, ―――― Co.
Bernard, Mr. Richard, 1651, by Mrs. Anna Bernard, Northumberland Co.
Bernard, Thomas, 1638, by John George, Charles City Co.
Bernard, Stephen, 1635, by Capt. Adam Thoroughgood, ―――― Co.
Bernes, Richard, 1646, by Thomas Bahe, Upper Norfolk Co.
Berrick, Wm., 1651, by Phillip Charles, James City Co.

Berriman, Wm., 1648, by John Ellis, James Joones and John Taylor, Northampton Co.
Berrinan, John, 1654, by Major Miles Carey, Westmoreland Co.
Berry, Danll., 1653, by Wm. Johnson, Henrico Co.
Berry, Henry, 1655, by John Lawson, Lancaster Co.
Berry, Andrew, 1656, by John Wood, ——— Co.
Berry, Eppy, 1654, by John Wyre, John Gillett, Andrew Gilson and John Phillipps, ——— Co.
Berry, Lydia, 1648, by Richard Wyatt, ——— Co.
Berry, Mathew, 1650, by Laurence Peters, Nansemond Co.
Berry, Alice, 1650, by David Peibles, Charles City Co.
Berry, Henry, 1650, by Epa. Lawson, ——— Co.
Berry, John, 1642, by John Sweete, ——— Co.
Berry, Mich., 1636, by Wm. Rainshaw, Elizabeth City Co.
Berry, Francis, 1643, by Lt. Wm. Worleidge, ——— Co.
Berry, Robt., 1641, by Stephen Charleton, Accomack Co.
Berry, John, 1642, by Tho. Curtis, ——— Co.
Berry, Elizabeth, 1637, by James Berry, her husband, Accomack Co.
Berry, Wm., 1637, by Capt. Henry Browne, James River Co.
Berry, Wm., 1636, by William Julian, Elizabeth City Co.
Berry, Eliz., 1636, by James Berry, Accomack.
Bersey, John, 1642, by Capt. Samuell Mathews, Esq., ——— Co.
Bertram, Jno., 1650, by Mr. Anthony Ellyot, ——— Co.
Bartholemewe, Hen., 1647, by Laurence Peeters, "Nansimum" Co.
Berton, Wm., 1646, by Geo. Ludlow, Esq., York Co
Berwicke, Wm., 1648, by Wm. Ewen, James City Co.
Besairdier, Peter, 1640, by Robert Brasseur, Upper Norfolk Co.
Besairdier, Reeve, 1640, by Robert Brasseur, Upper Norfolk Co.
Besley, Walter, 1642, by Wm. Eyres, Upper New Norfolk Co.
Beson, Tho., 1638, by Robert Freeman, James City Co.
Besson, Thomas, 1640, by Thomas Stegg, Charles City Co.
Best, Christian, 1649, by Capt. Ralph Wormeley, ——— Co.
Best, Wm., 1643, by Henry Neale, James City Co.
Best, Tho., 1652, by James Forster and Audrey Bonny, ——— Co.
Best, Wm., 1650, by Mrs. Frances Townshend (widdow), Northumberland Co.
Best, Mary, wife of Thos. Best, 1640, by Toby Smith, Warwick River Co.
Best, John, and 2 children, 1640, by Toby Smith, Warwick River Co.
Best, Thomas, 1640, by Toby Smith, Warwick River Co.
Best, Georg, 1639, by Walter Pakes, James City Co.
Besse, Wm., 1652, by George Pace, Charles City Co.
Beston, Thomas, 1635, by William Wilkinson (minister), ——— Co.
Betbone, John, 1637, by Mathew Edloe, ——— Co.
Bethell, Wm., 1655, by Francis Clay, Gent., Northumberland Co.
Bethell, Wm., 1653, by Francis Clay, Northumberland Co.
Bett, Robt., 1653, by Capt. Robt. Abrahal, York Co.
Betts, Will., 1651, by Wm. Betts, Northumberland Co.
Betts, John, 1654, by Capt. Nich. Marteaw, Westmoreland Co.
Bevan, David, 1654, by Major Miles Carey, Westmoreland Co.
Beven, Nicho., 1650, by Geo. Ludlow, Esq., Northumberland Co.
Bevchamp, Mary, 1650, by James Metgrigar and Hugh Foutch, Northumberland Co.

Bevinton, Tho., 1650, by Lieut. Wm. Worleich, ——— Co.
Bevis, Elizabeth, 1654, by Tho. Deynes, ——— Co.
Beuford, Thomas, 1650, by Lewis Burwell, Gent., Northumberland Co.
Beufort, Richard, 1637, by John Moone, Isle of Wight Co.
Beuson, Eliz., 1650, by George Pate, Charles City Co.
Bew, Richard, 1655, by Richard Codsford, Westmoreland Co.
Bewly, Ambrose, 1642, by Stephen Hamblyn, York Co.
Bibby, Mary, 1636, by Wm. Bibby, Accomack.
Bicby, John, 1650, by Capt. John Flood, Gent., and Jno. Flood, an
    ancient mariner, James City Co.
Bick, Richard, 1636, by William Carter, Henrico Co.
Bick, Richard, 1638, by William Carter, James City Co.
Bick, Fr., 1636, by Wm. Carter, James City Co.
Bidd, Christopher, 1650, by Samull Smith, Northumberland Co.
Bigg, John, 1653, by Tho. White and Peter Sexton, Norfolk Co.
Bigg, Henry, 1649, by Wm. Nesum, Tho. Sax, Miles Bathasly and John
    Pyne, Northampton Co.
Bigg, Elinor, 1648, by Tho. Ludwell, Gent., James City Co.
Bigg, John, 1653, by Tho. Sawyer, ——— Co.
Biggs, Hen., 1654, by Lieut. Coll. Giles Brent, Westmoreland Co.
Biggs, Marg., 1655, by Richard Price, New Kent Co.
Biggs, Henry, 1651, by John Rookwood, Gent., Northumberland Co.
Biggs, Henry, 1651, by Lieut. Coll. Giles Brent, Northumberland Co.
Biggs, Richd., 1649, by Tho. Spake, Gent., Northumberland Co.
Biggs, Mellison, 1652, by Mr. Tho. Curtis, ——— Co.
Biggs, Francis, 1638, by John George, Charles City Co.
Biggens, Law., 1653, by Wm. Dittye, Charles City Co.
Bighill, Jno., 1647, by Elizabeth Barcroft, Isle of Wight Co.
Bigs, Tho., 1652, by George Pace, Charles City Co.
Biker, Ann, 1643, by Richard Richards, Charles River Co.
Bilbay, Jno., 1647, by Elizabeth Barcroft, Isle of Wight Co.
Bilbie, Margt., 1635, by Capt. Adam Thoroughgood, ——— Co.
Bilbrough, Wm., 1650, by Wm. Morgan, ——— Co.
Bill, Wenckfield, 1650, by Hump. Lyster, ——— Co.
Bill, Walter, 1637, by Henry Bradly, New Norfolk Co.
Billahea, Neale, 1638, by Epaphroditus Lawson, Upper Norfolk Co.
Billens, John, 1635, by Capt. Robt. Abrahall, Gloucester Co.
Billeings, Eliza., 1651, by Thomas Keeling, Lower Norfolk Co.
Billin, Michaell, 1642, by William Lawson, Isle of Wight Co.
Billins, John, 1640, by Thomas Causey, ——— Co.
Billing, Elizabeth, 1652, by Tho. Lucas, Gent., Lancaster Co.
Billings, Jon., 1636, by Izabell Thresher, ——— Co.
Billingsley, Wm., 1650, by Edward James, ——— Co.
Billingsley, Tho., 1650, by Edward James, ——— Co.
Billowes, Tho., 1635, by Wm. Pilkington, ——— Co.
Bilsbrough, Wm., 1653, by Wm. Morgan, ——— Co.
Bilsey, Francis, 1637, by James Knott, New Norfolk Co.
Bilson, Stafford, 1653, by Capt. Robt. Abrall, ——— Co.
Bind, Mary, ———, by Lt. Coll. John Cheesman, ——— Co.
Binds, Jon., 1654, by Lt. Colo. John Cheeseman and (John Addleston),
    ——— Co.

Bing, Jon., 1636, by Bridges Freeman, ——— Co.
Binge, Joan, 1654, by Tho. Felton, Charles City Co.
Binias, John, ———, by Mr. John Page, ——— Co.
Binion, Charles, 1651, by Robert Holt, James City Co.
Binion, John, 1656, by George Kibble, Lancaster Co.
Binion, Gabll., 1653, by Charles Grymes, Lancaster Co.
Binsteed, John, 1642, by Richard Bennett, ——— Co.
Birch, Geo., 1638, by Joseph Bourne, Charles City Co.
Bird, Ashwell, 1642, by Hugh Gwyn, Gent., ——— Co.
Bird, Richard, 1642, by Cornelius de Hull, ——— Co.
Bird, Wm., 1650, by Capt, Ishiell Linch, ——— Co.
Bird, Wm., 1650, by Sr. Tho. Luntsford, Kt., and Baronett, ——— Co.
Bird, Alice, 1652, by Tho. Glascock, Lancaster Co.
Bird, Wm., 1653, by John Dipdall, Charles City Co.
Bird, Wm., 1635, by James Merriman, Charles City Co.
Bird, Susan, 1642, by John Garrett, Upper New Norfolk Co.
Bird, Rich., 1637, by Richard Bennett, New Norfolk Co.
Bird, Richard, 1636, by Wm. Cox, Henrico Co.
Bird, Richard, 1635, by Richard Bennett, ——— Co.
Birkenhead, Wm., 1653, by Edward Kemp, Geo. Cortlough and **John** Meredith, Lancaster Co.
Birkett, Jno., 1650, by John Garwood, Nansemond Co.
Birth, Roger, 1655, by Ralph Green, New Kent Co.
Biscoe, Mathew, 1643, by Capt. Samuell Mathews, Esq., ——— Co.
Bishell, Fra., 1651, by George Eaton, ——— Co.
Bishopp, Ferdinando, 1643, by Sir Francis Wyatt, Kt., ——— Co.
Bishopp, Jno., 1651, by Mr. John Bishopp, ——— Co.
Bishopp, Eliza, 1651, by Mr. John Bishopp, ——— Co.
Bishopp, Mary, 1651, by Mr. John Bishopp, ——— Co.
Bishopp, Dorothy, 1649, by John Speltimber, James City Co.
Bishopp, Henry, 1652, by Nathaniel Bacon, Isle of Wight Co.
Bishopp, Walter, 1643, by Epaphroditus Lawson, Upper Norfolk **Co.**
Bishopp, John, 1643, by Mr. John Bishopp, James City Co.
Bishopp, ———, 1643, by Mr. John Bishopp (her husband), **James** City Co.
Bishopp, John, 1638, by Thomas Gray, James City Co.
Bishopp, Oliver, 1637, by Cheney Boyes, Charles City Co.
Bishopp, Oliver, 1636, by Cheney Boyse, Charles City Co.
Bishopp, Wm., 1641, by Thomas Morrey, Isle of Wight Co.
Bishopp, John, 1651, by Audrey Bennett, Nansemond Co.
Bisile, John, 1645, by Thomas Stephens, Elizabeth City Co.
Bisley, Wm., 1642, by Justinian Cooper, Isle of Wight Co.
Bisley, Franc., 1636, by James Knott, Elizabeth City Co.
Bittle, Fra., 1653, by Nathaniel Hickmon, Northumberland Co.
Bivins, Margarett, 1642, by Hugh Gwyn, Gent., ——— Co.
Blachard, John, 1650, by Richard Tye and Charles Sparrowe, **Charles** City Co.
Blancher, Tho., 1637, by Capt. Thomas Flint, Warwick River Co.
Blanchett, Eliza., 1650, by Nicholas Jernew, Gent., ——— Co.
Blackburne, John, 1642, by Wm. Eyres, Upper New Norfolk Co.
Black, Edw., 1637, by Capt. Adam Thoroughgood, New Norfolk **Co.**

Blacke, Francis, 1639, by Georg Minifye, Esq., Charles River Co.
Blacke, Robert, 1651, by Geo. Trahett and Henry Edwards, Northampton Co.
Blacke, John, 1649, by Richard Kemp, Esq. (Sec. of State), ——— Co.
Blackey, Wm., 1652, by Capt. John West, Esq., ——— Co.
Blackford, Mary, 1650, by Lieut. Wm. Worleich, ——— Co.
Blackford, Mary, 1649, by Francis Brown, Northumberland Co.
Blackhan, Alex., by Jervais Dodson, Northumberland Co.
Blackgrove, Geo., 1654, by Robert Tomlin, ——— Co.
Blackin, Wm., 1653, by John Shepperd, Northumberland Co.
Blackman, Phillis, 1639, by Thomas Sheppey, Henrico Co.
Blackman, Eliz., 1648, by Richard Pettibon, ——— Co.
Blackman, Hump., ———, by Mr. Wm. Presly, Northumberland Co.
Blackman, Wm., 1653, by Richard Thomas, Henrico Co.
Blackstone, Jon., 1635, by McWilliam Stone, ——— Co.
Blackston, Thomas, 1642, by Cornelius de Hull, ——— Co.
Blackwell, Roger, 1636, by Elizabeth Hawkins, Charles River Co.
Blackwell, Hanna, 1656, by Maj. Tho. Curtis, Westmoreland Co.
Blade, Timothy, 1654, by Walter Dickenson, Lancaster Co.
Blades, John, Jr., 1652, by Tho. Mairy, ——— Co.
Blades, Wm., Sr., 1652, by Tho. Mairy, ——— Co.
Blagg, David, 1654, by Wm. Mells, Lancaster Co.
Blake, Edw., 1635, by Capt. Adam Thoroughgood, ——— Co.
Blake, Walter, 1637, by James Knott, New Norfolk Co.
Blake, Wm. 1654, by John Black, ——— Co.
Blake, Mary, 1652, by Mr. George Clapham, ——— Co.
Blake, John, 1653, by Tho. Todd, ——— Co.
Blake, Walter, 1654, by Col. Argoll Yardley, Northampton Co.
Blake, James, 1655, by Major Wm. Hoccaday, New Kent Co.
Blake, Anne, 1653, by Joseph Hogkinson, Lower Norfolk Co.
Blakin, Ralph, 1640, by Robt. Holt, James City Co.
Blaiton, Joseph, 1651, by Mr. John Walker, ——— Co.
Blanch, Roger, 1637, by Daniell Gookins, New Norfolk Co.
Blanchernell, Chas., 1655, by Moses Lynton, Lower Norfolk Co.
Blancke, Tho., 1652, by Jno. Robinson, Lancaster Co.
Bland, Edward, 1636, by William Carter, Henrico.
Bland, Edward, 1638, by Wm. Carter, James City Co.
Bland, Fra., 1654, by Randall Chamblett, ——— Co.
Bland, Pewrigrin, 1642, by Richard Maior, Charles River.
Bland, Edw., 1647, by Richard Bland, ——— Co.
Bland, Eliza, 1647, by Richard Bland, ——— Co.
Bland, John, 1646, by Samuell Abbott, Nansemond Co.
Bland, Mary, 1653, by Richard Carey, ——— Co.
Blanks, Georg, 1639, by Dorothy Clarke, Henrico Co.
Blany, Francis, 1654, by James Yates, ——— Co.
Blany, James, 1654, by Nath. Pope, Westmoreland Co.
Blarks, Andrew, 1656, by Humphrey Tabb, Gent., Elizabeth City Co.
Beausteed, Mary, 1636, by Thomas Beausteed, James City Co.
Blay, Johne, 1654, by John Watson and John Bagnell, Westmoreland Co.
Blaye, Wm., 1636, by John Chandler, Elizabeth Citie Co.
Blear, Samll., 1643, by John Freeme, Charles Co.

Bleese, James, 1637, by Thomas Todd, New Norfolk Co.
Bletsoe, William, 1639, by Tho. Symons, James City Co.
Bletts, John, 1651, by Richard Turney, Northumberland Co.
Blettsoe, Wm., 1643, by Tho. Symonds, ——— Co.
Bletstoe, Mathew, 1641, by Richard Jackson, Isle of Wight Co.
Blew, Edward, 1642, by William Connhoe, ——— Co.
Blewett, Margery, 1654, by Capt. Nich. Marteaw, Westmoreland Co.
Bliba, Mary, 1651, by Mr. Wm. Armestead, ——— Co.
Blight, Jacob, 1637, by James Warradine, Charles City Co.
Blingston, Wm., 1652, by Nicholas Wadilow, Northampton Co.
Blittle, Tho., 1653, by Edward Hamond, Northampton, Co.
Blithe, ———, 1653, by Richard Starnell, ——— Co.
Blithe, James, 1638, by Stephen Charlton, Accomack Co.
Blockinsoys, Henry, 1653, by Charles Grymes, Lancaster Co.
Blocke, Elizabeth, 1649, by Roger Nicholls, James City Co.
Blocker, Eliza, 1638, by Joseph Harmon, James City.
Blocklock, Tho., his wife and child, 1655, by Southy Littleberry, Northampton Co.
Blockhaws, Sanders, 1642, by John George, Charles City Co.
Blockman, Humphrey, 1638, by Richard Wilcox, James City Co.
Blockwell, Andrew, 1638, by Richard Bennett, Isle of Wight Co.
Bloncks, Thos., 1637, by Elizabeth Parker, Henrico Co.
Blocock, Patrick, 1635, by Capt. Adam Thoroughgood, ——— Co.
Blodes, Wm., 1655, by Hugh Yeo, Northampton Co.
Blogg, John, 1650, by Nathaniell, Jones, Northumberland Co.
Blonch, Thomas, 1648, by Robert Pitt, Isle of Wight Co.
Bloodstone, Mary, 1653, by Richard Vardy, James City Co.
Blore, Eliza, 1653, by Capt. Francis Patt, Northampton Co.
Blow, John, 1650, by John Sevier, ——— Co.
Blowe, Georg, 1638, by Henry Catelyn, Upper Norfolk Co.
Blowe, Bartho., 1653, by Tho. Scroggin, Northumberland Co.
Blower, Geo., 1653, by Capt. Nathaniel Hurd, Warrick Co.
Bloyse, Thos., 1636, by John Chandler, Elizabeth City Co.
Blumfield, Kath., 1652, by July Gardner, Northampton Co.
Blunt, Wm., 1654, by Martin Coale, Northumberland Co.
Blunt, ———, 1652, by Gilbert Blunt (her father), ——— Co.
Blunt, ———, 1652, by Gilbert Blunt (her husband), ——— Co.
Blunt, Edw., 1653, by Colo. Wm. Clayborne,(Sec. of State), ——— Co.
Blunt, Jon., 1652, by George Kemp, Lower Norfolk Co.
Blunt, Tho., 1653, by Richard Budd, Northumberland Co.
Blunter, John, 1638, by Jonothan Langworth, Lower New Norfolk Co.
Bly, Mary, 1653, by Tho. Cowlinge, ——— Co.
Blyth, Jone, 1652, by Gilbert Blunt, ——— Co.
Blyth, Wm., 1652, by Gilbert Blunt, ——— Co.
Blyth, Mary, 1651, by Thomas Thornbrough, Northumberland Co.
Boare, Geo., 1652, by Tho. Todd, ——— Co.
Board, ———, wife Tho. Board, 1652, by Teague Floyne, Lancaster Co.
Board, George, 1639, by Thomas Mathews, Henrico, Co.
Boards, Tho., 1652, by Henry Fleete, Lancaster Co.
Boardman, Osgrand, 1645, by Mr. Bartholomew Hoskins, ——— Co.

Boarner, John, 1636, by Joseph Jolly, Charles River Co.
Boates, Geo., 1636, by James Place, Henrico Co.
Boatwright, John, 1654, by Humphry Dennis, Gloucester Co.
Boase, Tho., 1656, by Capt. Henry Fleete, ———— Co.
Bobonett, Patrick, 1641, by Thomas Morrey, Isle of Wight Co.
Bocker, Joane, 1651, by Richard Trigson, ———— Co.
Bocock, Thomas, 1646, by Geo. Ludlow, Esq., York Co.
Boddicutt, Robt., 1637, by Thomas Causey, Charles City Co.
Bodely, Arthur, 1642, by Thomas Loving, James City Co.
Bodman, Andrew, 1638, by Christopher Burrough, Lower Norfolk Co.
Bodney, Henry, 1642, by Thomas Plummer, ———— Co.
Bodin, Jno., 1635, by John Parrott, ———— Co.
Body, Robert, 1645, by Mr. Bartholomew Hoskins, ———— Co.
Body, Thomas, 1636, by Georg Sapheir, Elizabeth City Co.
Boein, John, 1650, by Anthony Fuljam, ———— Co.
Bogges, Mary, 1656, by Richard Wheeler, Lower Norfolk Co.
Bogges, John, 1656, by Richard Wheeler, Lower Norfolk Co.
Bogges, Robt., 1656, by Richard Wheeler, Lower Norfolk Co.
Boyle, Richard, 1638, by Lieut. John Upton, Isle of Wight Co.
Bogby, John, 1655, by Gilbert Deacon, Henrico Co.
Bognall, Sarah, 1654, by Richard Walker, ———— Co.
Bognall, Roger, 1637, by Lt. John Upton, Isle of Wight Co.
Bogwell, Jane, 1638, by Thom. Bogwell, Charles City Co.
Bogworth, John, 1637, by John Hampton Clarke, New Norfolk Co.
Boid, John, 1643, by Mr. Phillipp Bennett, Upper Norfolk Co.
Bolal, Leon., 1635, by Edward Osborne, Henrico Co.
Boles, Engo, 1637, by Theodore Moyser, James City Co.
Bolson, John, 1655, by Ralph Green, New Kent Co.
Bolton, Joane, 1636, by Capt. John Chelsman, Charles River Co.
Bolton, Jane, 1635, by John Cheeseman, Charles River Co.
Boman, Grace, 1651, by James Baldrige and Capt. Tho. Baldrige, Northumberland Co.
Boman, Sarah, 1651, by James Baldrige and Capt. Tho. Baldrige, Northumberland Co.
Bonas, John, 1654, by John Wyre, John Gillett, Andrew Gilson and John Phillipps, ———— Co.
Bonce, James, 1653, by Henry Deadman, Lancaster Co.
Bond, Sarah, 1642, by Stephen Gill, Yorke River Co.
Bond, Eliza, 1655, by Southy Littleberry, Northampton Co.
Bond, Tho., 1654, by George Kibble, Lancaster Co.
Bond, Henry, 1651, by Thomas Killing, Lower Norfolk Co.
Bond, John, 1638, by Henry Catelyn, Upper Norfolk Co.
Bond, Edw., 1636, by John Seaward, Isle of Wight Co.
Bond, Edward, and his wife, 1650, by Mordecay Cooke, ———— Co.
Bone, Wm., 1643, by Richard Kemp, Esq., James City Co.
Bone, Wm., 1649, by Edmund Scarburgh, Jr., Northampton Co.
Bone, Degery, 1638, by Christopher Lanson, ———— Co.
Boner, James, 1654, by Toby Smith, Lancaster Co.
Bones, Christopher, 1655, by Richard Hamlet, James City Co.
Boney, Henry, 1637, by Justinian Cooper, Isle of Wight Co.
Boniday, Wm., 1648, by George White, Lower Norfolk Co.

Bonnall, John, 1654, by Daniel Boucher, Isle of Wighte Co.
Bonne, Elia., 1635, by Robert Sheppard, ——— Co.
Bonner, And., 1650, by Capt. Moore Fantleroy, ——— Co.
Bonner, Tho., 1653, by Francis Emperor, Hugh Gale and Edward Morgan, Lower Norfolk Co.
Bonner, James, 1653, by Abraham Moon, Lancaster Co.
Bonner, Tho., 1647, by Tho. Wells, Lower Norfolk Co.
Bonner, Rich., 1643, by John Freeme, Charles Co.
Bonner, Tho., 1638, by Cornelius Loyd, ——— Co.
Bonner, John, 1638, by John Bishop, James City Co.
Bonney, Henry, 1636, by Justinian Cooper, Warrasquinoak Co.
Bonnor, James, 1653, by Eppy Bonison, Lancaster Co.
Bonton, Edward, 1637, by Theodore Moyser, James City.
Bony, Henry, 1642, by Justinian Cooper, Isle of Wight Co.
Bony, Susanna, 1637, by Thomas Davis, New Norfolk Co.
Boodes, John, 1637, by William Wilkinson, New Norfolk Co.
Boods, John, 1635, by William Wilkinson (minister), ——— Co.
Booker, Mrs. Margarett, and Mary, her daughter, 1654, by John Rosyer, clerk, ——— Co.
Booker, Mrs. Marg., and Mary, her daughter, 1653, by Jno. Rosyer, Northumberland Co.
Booker, Mary, 1653, by Capt. Francis Patt, Northampton Co.
Bookes, John, 1638, by Cornelius Loyd, ·——— Co.
Booker, Fra., 1653, by Christopher Boyce, Northumberland Co.
Booke, Tobie, 1635, by David Jones, Charles City Co.
Bookwood, John, 1653, by Capt. Giles Brent, Northumberland Co.
Boone, Mary, 1653, by Wm. Thomas, Northumberland Co.
Boone, Wm., 1642, by John Smith, James City Co.
Boone, Xtopher, 1653, by Wm. Debram, ——— Co.
Boone, Mar., 1652, by John Bayles, Lancaster Co.
Boost, Thos., 1636, by Thomas Beast, Elizabeth City Co.
Boost, Mary (wife of Thos. Boost), 1636, by Thomas Beast, Elizabeth City Co.
Boost, Rich. (son of Tho. Boost), 1635, by Thos. Beast, Elizabeth City Co.
Boord, Richard, 1643, by Jeremiah Clement, James City Co.
Boordman, Jon., 1653, by Wm. Haynes, ——— Co.
Boore, James, 1653, by Oliver Segar, Lancaster Co.
Boote, Joane, 1652, by Tho. Johnson, Jr., Northampton Co.
Booth, John, 1694, by Mr. Edmund Scarburg, Northampton Co.
Booth, Eliza, a maid, 1648, by Lewis Burwell and Tho. Haws, York River Co.
Booth, Wm., 1642, by Thomas Guyer, ——— Co.
Booth, Tho., 1654, by John Watson and John Bognall, Westmoreland Co.
Booth, John, 1649, by Edmund Scarburg, Jr., Northampton Co.
Booth, Mary, 1648, by Geo. Hardey, Tho. Wombwell and Peter Hall, Isle of Wight Co.
Booth, John, 1642, by Edmund Scarburgh, Accomack Co.
Booth, John, 1651, by Capt. Geo. Read, Lancaster Co.
Boothes, Abra., 1646, by Elizabeth and Ratchell Robins, Northampton Co.

Bootherton, Dennis, 1635, by Samuel Weaver, ——— Co.
Booton, Tho., 1638, by Edward Oliver, ——— Co.
Boice, Samuell, 1653, by Colo. Wm. Clayborne, (Sec. of State), ——— Co.
Boran, John, 1635, by William Dawson, ——— Co.
Bordman, John, 1637, by Margaret Rogers, James City Co.
Bordman, Jon., 1636, by Edward Rogers, Warrasquinoake Co.
Boreman, Eliza, 1639, by Richard Johnson, Henrico Co.
Boreing, John, 1656, by Geo. Abbott, Nansemond Co.
Borer, Georg, 1637, by Thomas Addison, New Norfolk Co.
Borer, Georg, 1637, by James Harrison, James City Co.
Borne, Barbary, 1636, by Francis Maulden, ——— Co.
Bord, Robt., 1654, by Wm. Robinson and Cornelius Johnson, Westmoreland Co.
Border, Robt., 1654, by John Wyre, John Gillet, Andrew Gilson and John Phillipps, ——— Co.
Border, Robt., 1653, by John Hillier, Northumberland Co.
Border, Rob., 1653, by Capt. Francis Morgan, Gloucester Co.
Borrowes, Mathew, 1654, by Mr. Mordecay Cooke, ——— Co.
Borwell, Anne, 1655, by Nich. Waddilow, Northampton Co.
Bosaker, Edward, 1636, by John Gates, Elizabeth City Co.
Boshae, John, 1649, by John King, Yorke Co.
Boshpoole, Gregory, 1652, by Capt. Francis Morgan and Ralph Green, Gloucester Co.
Bosman, William, 1649, by Mr. Ralph Barlowe, Northampton Co.
Bostock, Jonathan, 1654, by John Wyre, John Gillet, Andrew Gilson, and John Phillipps, ——— Co.
Bostocke, Eliza, 1653, by Gregory Rawlins, Surry Co.
Bostionke, Atwell, 1644, by Thomas Davis, Upper Norfolk Co.
Boston, Henry, 1643, by Mr. Obedience Robins, Northampton Co.
Boston, Elizabeth, 1656, by Major Tho. Curtis, ——— Co.
Boston, Henry, 1650, by Stephen Charlton, Northampton Co.
Boswell, Tho., 1655, by George Frizell and Tho. Moore, Northampton Co.
Boswell, Morch, 1655, by Wm. Wright, Gent., Nansemond Co.
Boswell, Ann, 1655, by Wm. Botham, Westmoreland Co.
Boswell, John, 1652, by Tho. Boswell, ——— Co.
Boswell, Samll., 1650, by Geo. Ludlow, Esq., Northumberland Co.
Boswell, Eliza., 1650, by Geo. Ludlow, Esq., Northumberland Co.
Botchane, Nicho., 1653, by Wm. Debram, ——— Co.
Bott, Jon., 1653, by Robert Brasseur, Nansemond Co.
Botton, Margar., 1652, by Mr. Wm. Waters, Northampton Co.
Bottom, Richd, 1653, by Frances Symons, Northumberland Co.
Bottomly, John, 1653, by Samuell Parry, Lancaster Co.
Bottomly, Do., 1651, by Lieut. Coll. Giles Brent, Northumberland Co.
Bottomly, Dorothy, 1651, by Lieut. Collo. Giles Brent, Northumberland Co.
Bouch, Rob., 1654, by Nath. Pope, Westmoreland Co.
Boucher, Andrew, 1650, by Lawrence Peters, Nansemond Co.
Boulding, Thomas, 1638, by John Jackson and Eliza Kingswill, James City Co.

Boule, Symon, 1650, by Richard Budd, Northumberland Co.
Boughton, Tho., 1639, by Edward Oliver, James City Co.
Boult, Geo., 1653, by John Dipdall, Charles City Co.
Boulton, Thos., 1635, by Capt. Adam Thoroughgood, ——— Co.
Bound, Elinor, 1637, by Georg Burcher, James City Co.
Bourham, Tho., 1649, by Richard Bayly, Northampton Co.
Bourne, Ben., 1652, by George Pace, Charles City Co.
Bourne, Benja., 1650, by George Pate, Charles City Co.
Bourne, Henry, 1649, by Thomas Curtis, ——— Co.
Bourne, Henry, 1649, by Edmund Scarburgh, Jr., Northampton Co.
Bourne, Thomas, 1638, by John Moone, ——— Co.
Bourne, Joseph, 1655, by Gilbert Deacon, Henrico Co.
Bourne, Jon., 1637, by Joseph Jolly, Charles River Co.
Bourne, James, 1654, by Wm. Mells, Lancaster Co.
Bourne, Tho., 1654, by Humphry Dennis, Gloucester Co.
Boves, Wm., 1653, by Wm. Debram, ——— Co.
Bow, Wm., 1637, by Capt. Henry Browne, James City Co.
Bowen, Saml., 1643, by Henry Neale, James City Co.
Bowen, Phillipp, 1643, by Henry Neale, James City Co.
Bowen, Moir.s, 1638, by Edward Hill, Charles City Co.
Bowers, Jonas, 1637, by Arthur Bayly, Henrico Co.
Bowden, Jane, 1653, by Richard Major, Gloucester Co.
Bowden, Phillipp, 1646, by Geo. Ludlow, Esq., York Co.
Bower, Henry, 1637, by Humphry Higginson, Gent., ——— Co.
Bowin, Elizabeth. 1649, by Wm. Peerce and Frances Symons, Northumberland Co.
Bowland, Jno., 1650, by Mr. Epaphroditus Lawson, ——— Co.
Bowles, Edw., 1654, by Francis Gray, ——— Co.
Bowles, Tho., 1655, by Jer. Dodson, Gent., Lancaster Co.
Bowles, Mr. Tho., 1655, by Dr. Giles Mode, New Kent Co.
Bowles, Ann, Jr., 1656, by Mr. Tho. Purifoy, ——— Co.
Bowles, Ann, Sr., 1656, by Mr. Tho. Purifoy, ——— Co.
Bowles, James, 1654, by Nich. Merywether, Westmoreland Co.
Bowles, James, 1653, by Nicho. Meriwether, Northumberland Co.
Bowles, John, 1651, by Phillips Charles, James City Co.
Bowles, Jonas, Arthur Bayly's servant, 1637, by Arthur Bayly and Tho. Crosby, Henrico Co.
Bowles, Geo., 1636, by John Neale, Accomack Co.
Bowles, Edward, 1639, by Capt. Nicholas Maritian, Charles River Co.
Bowles, William, 1639, by Thomas Mathews, Henrico Co.
Bowlton, Ann, 1635, by Capt. Adam Thoroughgood, ——— Co.
Bowman, Walter, 1643, by Capt. Samuell Mathews, Esq., ——— Co.
Bowman, Garthred, 1653, by Mr. Edmund Bowman and Richard Starnell, ——— Co.
Bowman, Sarah, 1653, by Mr. Edmund Bowman and Richard Starnell, ——— Co.
Bowman, Margt., 1653, by Mr. Edmund Bowman and Richard Starnell, ——— Co.
Bowman, Tho., 1652, by Robert West, Charles City Co.
Bowyer, Hen., 1653, by Capt. Francis Patt, Northampton Co.
Box, Thomas, Jr., 1638, by Mr. John Gookins, Upper New Norfolk Co.

Box, Mary, 1636, by Mary Boxe, Henrico Co.
Box, Thomas, 1636, by John Gookin, Gent., ——— Co.
Box, Benjamin, 1637, by Daniell Gookins, New Norfolk Co.
Box, John (ancient planter), 1636, by Mary Boxe, Henrico Co.
Box, Anth., 1637, by Capt. Francis Eppes, Charles River Co.
Box, Mary, 1637, by Mary Box, Henrico Co.
Box, Thomas, (Jr.,) 1636, by John Gookin, New Norfolk Co.
Box, John, 1637, by Mary Box, Henrico Co.
Box, Tho., 1654, by Abraham Moone, ——— Co.
Boxford, Tho., 1651, by John Martin and Lancaster Lovitt, Lower Nor-
    folk Co.
Boy, Thomas, 1635, by John Moore, Warrasquincake Co.
Boyce, Christo., 1642, by Christopher Boyce, ——— Co.
Boyce, Sarah, 1653, by Joseph Croshaw, York Co.
Boyd, James, 1650, by George Taylor, ——— Co.
Boyes, Francis, 1650, by Samuell Smith, Northumberland Co.
Boyes, Luke, 1637, by Hannah Boyes, Henrico Co.
Boyer, Stephen, 1652, by Capt. Francis Morgan and Ralph **Green,**
    Gloucester Co.
Boyer, Wm., 1636, by William Rainshaw, Elizabeth City Co.
Boyer, Andrew, 1635, by Capt. Adam Thoroughgood, ——— Co.
Boyle, Chr., 1645, by John Rode, Warwick Co.
Boyle, Luke, 1636, by Hannah Boyse, Henrico Co.
Boyss, George, 1651, by Humphry Tabb, Northumberland Co.
Brace, Walter, 1642, by Christopher Boyce, ——— Co.
Bracele, Wm., 1637, by Thomas Powell, New Norfolk Co.
Bracon, Wm., 1653, by Geo. Thompson, Gloucester Co.
Bradly, Eliza, 1637, by Henry Perry, Charles River Co.
Bradly, Eliza, 1637, by Henry Perry, Charles River Co.
Bradley, Henry, 1636, by John Layden, Warwick River Co.
Bradbury, John, 1650, by Sr. Tho. Luntsford, Kt., and Baronett, ———
    Co.
Bradberry, John, 1656, by Nicholas Merriwether and John **Leach,**
    James City Co.
Bradbury, John, 1636, by Walter Hacker, James River Co.
Bradchater, Jacob, 1637, by Hen. Woodhouse, New Norfolk Co.
Bradford, John, 1652, by Capt. Augustine Warner, ——— Co.
Bradford, Mathew, 1652, by Peter Knight, Gloucester Co.
Bradford, Rich., 1653, by Roger Walter, Northumberland Co.
Bradford, Susan, 1643, by Sir Francis Wyatt, Kt., ——— Co.
Bradford, Edy, 1650, by Mr. Epaphroditus Lawson, ——— Co.
Bradford, Nicho., 1647, by John Brooch, York River Co.
Bradford, Rich., 1653, by Roger Walker, Northumberland Co.
Bradford, Rich., 1654, by Roger Walters, Northumberland Co.
Bradford, Thos., 1640, by Robert Holt, James City Co.
Bradfield, Cornelius, 1639, by John Lewin, Isle of Wight Co.
Bradnadge, Tho., 1653, by Mr. Wm. Baldwen, York Co.
Bradin, Eliz., 1638, by Geo. Lobb, Tho. Perce, Tho. Warne, James **City**
    Co.
Bradiwell, Joan, 1655, by Richard Price, New Kent Co.
Bradly, John, 1653, by Mr. Henry Soanes, Gloucester Co.

Bradly, Dorothy, 1638, by John Fludd, James City Co.
Bradly, Frances, 1637, by Henry Bradly (her husband), New Norfolk Co.
Bradly, Margt., (wife) 1638, by John Fludd, James City Co.
Bradly, Mrs. Ann, 1650, by Sr. Tho. Luntsford, Kt., and Baronett, —— Co.
Bradly, Toby, 1653, by Robt. Sorrel, —— Co.
Bradly, Wm., 1654, by Peter Knight, Northumberland Co.
Bradley, Ann, 1653, by Tho. Mallard, Northumberland Co.
Bradley, Bartho., 1650, by John Hany, Northumberland Co.
Bradley, Wm., 1655, by Dr. Giles Mode, New Kent Co.
Bradley, John, 1642, by Hugh Gwyn, Gent., —— Co.
Bradley, Richard, 1643, by William Ewins, James City Co.
Bradshaw, Robt., 1640, by Thomas Harvey, James City Co.
Bradshaw, Hen., 1637, by Theodore Moyser, James City Co.
Bradshaw, John, 1654, by Edw. Welch, —— Co.
Bradshaw, John, ——, by Saml. Ruthland, Lower Norfolk Co.
Bradshaw, Rebecca, 1656, by John Bromfield, James City Co.
Bradshaw, Bernard, 1650, by John Watts, Gent., —— Co.
Bradshaw, Richard, 1643, by Capt. Samuell Mathews, Esq., —— Co.
Bradshaw, Wm., 1648, by Lewis Burgell and Tho. Haws, York River Co.
Bradwell, John, 1651, by Richard Whitehurst, Lower Norfolk Co.
Bradwell, Arthur, 1650, by John Sevier, —— Co.
Bradsten, Jon., 1635, by Capt. Adam Thoroughgood, —— Co.
Bragg, Wm., 1650, by Wingfield Webb and Richard Pate, —— Co.
Braene, Debora, 1647, by Wm. Blaskey, York Co.
Braine, Richard, 1653, by John Barrow, Surry Co.
Brake, Henry, 1648, by Lewis Burwell, Gent., —— Co.
Bramfeild, John, 1648, by Richard Thompson, Northumberland Co.
Bramley, Tho., 1650, by Thomas Powell, —— Co.
Bramley, Hugh, 1640, by William Hampton, Isle of Wight Co.
Bramley, Francis, 1635, Capt. by Adam Thoroughgood, —— Co.
Branch, Wm., 1652, by Littleton Scarburgh, —— Co.
Branch, Mary, Jr., 1656, by Richard Gible, Northumberland Co.
Branch, John, 1656, by Richard Gible, Northumberland Co.
Branch, Mary, 1656, by Richard Gible, Northumberland Co.
Branch, John, 1645, by William Daynes, Lower Norfolk Co.
Branch, Antho., 1643, by Tristram Nosworthy, Isle of Wight Co.
Branch, John, 1639, by Capt. Nicholas Martian, Charlcs River Co.
Branches, Christ., 1638, by William Morgan, James City Co.
Brand, Tho., 1652, by Anthony Hoskins, Northampton Co.
Brandon, Wm., 1653, by Collo. John Mottrom, Northumberland Co.
Brandly, Symon, 1655, by Wm. Johnson and Stephen Horsey, Northampton Co.
Braneston, Tho., 1638, by John Fludd, James City Co.
Branston, Thomas, 1636, by Wm. Cox, Henrico Co.
Brantly, Edward, 1638, by John Seaward, Isle of Wight Co.
Brasbridge, John, 1643, by John Wall, —— Co.
Brase, Wm., 1638, by Thomas Dew, Upper New Norfolk Co.
Brasey, Foulke, 1635, by Thomas Harwood, —— Co.

Brashall, Hen., 1643, by Walter Ashton, Gent., Charles City Co.
Brasherd, John, 1654, by Christopher Regault, Gloucester Co.
Bassett, Thos., 1646, by Sir. William Berkley, —— Co.
Brasseur, Kath., 1653, by Robert Brasseur, Nansemond Co.
Brasseur, Bennet, 1653, by Robt. Brasseur, Nansemond Co.
Brasseur, Persie, 1653, by Robert Brasseur, Nansemond Co.
Brasseur, Mary, 1653, by Robert Brasseur, Nansemond Co.
Brathard, Jno., 1654, by Randall Chamblett, —— Co.
Bratt, John, 1650, by Wm. Hodgson, Yorke Co.
Bratt, Isaac, 1650, by John Cooke, Northumberland Co.
Bratson, John, 1654, by Nath. Pope, Westmoreland Co.
Braughton, Wm., 1643, by Tho. Dew, Upper Norfolk Co.
Brawnes, Blanche, 1635, by Thos Harwood, —— Co.
Braxton, Robt., 1639, by Lieut. Richard Popeley, —— Co.
Bray, Mar., 1653, by Robert Sorrel, —— Co.
Bray, Nich., 1651, by Thomas Keeling, Lower Norfolk Co.
Bray, Henry, 1652, by Elias Edmond, Lancaster Co.
Brayden, Edw., 1642, by William Prior, Gent., —— Co.
Breaneer, Thomas, 1638, by Richard Maion, Charles River Co.
Breckler, Edward, 1653, by Colo. Wm. Clayborne (Sec. of State),
    —— Co.
Breed, Wm., 1650, by Rice Jones, —— Co.
Bregat, Wm., 1654, by Francis Smith and Mr. John Smith, Westmore-
    land Co.
Bregatmon, Henry, 1648, by Richard Wyatt, —— Co.
Breight, Robt., 1651, by Mr. Robert Abrall, Yorke Co.
Brem, Cleer., 1636, by Wm. Neesam, James City Co.
Breman, Wm., 1650, by Daniell Luellin, Charles City Co.
Brener, Jon., and Mary Brener, his wife, 1635, by Thos. Butler Clark
    and Pastor of Denbie, Warrasquinoake Co.
Brent, Hugh, 1642, by Francis England, Isle of Wight Co.
Brent, Richard, 1653, by Geo. Thompson, Gloucester Co.
Brent, Wm., 1651, by Geo. Colclough, Gent., Northumberland Co.
Brent, Capt., 1652, by Mrs. Mary Brent, Northumberland Co.
Brentwell, Robt., 1643, by Thomas Cassen, —— Co.
Bressey, Ann, 1637, by Robert Bennett, New Norfolk Co.
Brestow, Eliz., 1653, by Richard Burton, —— Co.
Bretherston, Dennis, 1637, by Thomas Weston, Charles River Co.
Brett, Emma, 1655, by Henry Huberd, —— Co.
Brett, Tho., 1650, by Nathaniel Jones, Northumberland Co.
Brett, Alex., 1638, by Roger Davis, Charles City Co.
Brett, Rich., 1637, by William Spencer, —— Co.
Brew, Sackfield, 1652, by Mrs. Jane Harmer, Northumberland Co.
Brewer, Tho., 1649, by Tho. Dale, —— Co.
Brewer, Elizabeth, 1651, by Thomas Thornbrugh, Northumberland Co.
Brewer, Paul, 1643, by Richard Kemp, Esq., James City Co.
Brewer, Tho., 1648, by John Landman, Nansimond Co.
Brewster, Anthony, 1652, by Mr. Wm. Waters, Northampton, Co.
Brewster, Jose., 1651, by Mr. Wm. Armestead, —— Co.
Brewster, Sackford, 1648, by George Read, Gent., —— Co.
Brewster, Stackforde, 1643, by Capt. John Upton, Isle of Wight Co.

Brewton, Jon., 1635, by Capt. Adam Thoroughgood, ——— Co.
Brice, James, 1652, by Andrew Munrow, Northumberland Co.
Brickbetten, Wm., 1639, by John Burland, Charles River Co.
Briste, Mathew, 1638, by Wm. Carter, James City Co.
Brice, Robt., 1648, by John Seward, Isle of Wight Co.
Brice, Wm., 1652, by Andrew Munrow, Northumberland Co.
Brice, James, 1653, by Abraham Moone, Lancaster Co.
Brice, John, 1653, by John Edwards, Lancaster Co.
Brice, James, 1653, by Abraham Moon, Lancaster Co.
Brice, Geo., 1650, by Capt. Moore Fautleroy, ——— Co.
Brice, Martha, 1652, by Mr. Tho. Brice, Lancaster Co.
Brice, Martha, 1648, by John Manning, Lower Norfolk Co.
Brice, John, 1650, by Nathaniell Jones, Northumberland Co.
Brice, Wm., 1650, by Tho. Blogg, Northumberland Co.
Brice, Wm., 1650, by Silvester Thatcher and Tho. Whittocke, ——— Co.
Brice, Francis, 1643, by Phillipp Taylor, Northampton Co.
Brice, Martha, 1653, by Tho. Hawkins, Northumberland Co.
Brick, Fr., 1638, by William Carter, James City Co.
Bridd, Tho., 1652, by Mr. George Clapham, ——— Co.
Bride, Richard, 1653, by Tho. Hawkins, Northumberland Co.
Bridgeman, Jacob, 1654, by John Phillips and John Batts, Lancaster Co.
Bridgman, Daniell, 1643, by William Ewins, James City Co.
Bridley, Robert, 1655, by Mr. Anthony Langston, New Kent Co.
Bridwell, Tho., 1642, by Wm. Eyres, Upper New Norfolk Co.
Bridge, John, 1654, by Nicholas Morris, Northumberland Co.
Bridge, John, 1652, by Nathaniel Bacon, Isle of Wight Co.
Bridge, John, 1652, by Capt. Tho. Hackett, Lancaster Co.
Bridge, John, 1637, by Bridges Freeman, James City Co.
Bridges, Thos., 1635, by Wm. Barber, Charles City Co.
Bridges, Nich., 1655, by Henry Huberd, ——— Co.
Bridges, Nich., 1642, by Samuell Abbott, ——— Co.
Bridges, Videm, 1651, by David Murray, Lower Norfolk Co.
Bridges, Margt., 1653, by Tho. Holmes, York Co.
Bridges, William, 1639, by John White, James Citie Co.
Bridges, Elizab., 1650, by John Cooke, Northumberland Co.
Bridges, Eliza, 1645, by Zachary Cripps, Warwick, Co.
Bridges, Ann, 1645, by Wm. Jacob, Upper Norfolk Co.
Bridges, Tho., 1643, by Sir Francis Wyatt, Kt., ——— Co.
Bridges, Jeremiah, 1638, by Lt. Robt. Bridges, James Co.
Bridges, Eliza, 1652, by Robt. Elam, Henrico Co.
Bridges, Nicho., 1652, by Mr. Edward Overman, York Co.
Bridges, Jon., 1637, by Thomas Causey, Charles City.
Bridges, Wm., 1639, by Thomas Stoute, James City Co.
Briggs, Wm., 1638, by Stephen Webb, James Citie Co.
Briggs, Seth, 1639, by Edward Prince, Charles City Co.
Brigson, Thomas, 1639, by John Graves, Elizabeth City Co.
Bright, Robt., 1656, by John Billiott, Northampton Co.
Bright, John, 1642, by Capt. Daniell Gookin, ——— Co.
Bright, Robt., 1653, by Capt. Robt. Abrall, ——— Co.
Bright, Robt., 1655, by Tho. Leatherberry, Northampton Co.

Bright, Dorothy, ——, by Sam'l. Ruthland, Lower Norfolk Co.
Bright, John, 1651, by Coll. Richard Lee, Esq., Gloucester Co.
Brightman, Henry, 1637, by Henry Woodhouse, New Norfolk Co.
Brignall, Richard, 1640, by Thomas Causey, —— Co.
Brignell, Henry, 1639, by Robt. Newman, Warwick River Co.
Brigton, Rachell, 1653, by Capt. Robt. Abrall, —— Co.
Brill, Puler, 1635, by Thos. Crompe, James City Co.
Brimstone, 1655, by Nich. Wadilow, Northampton Co.
Brinckley, Michaild, 1635, by Anthony Jones, —— Co.
Bringley, Symon, 1654, by Wm. Johnson, Northampton Co.
Briscot, Charles, 1655, by George Frizell and Tho. Moore, Northampton Co.
Bristoll, Jone, 1653, by Ferdinando Austin, Charles City Co.
Bristoe, John, 1637, by Robert Throckmorton, Charles River Co.
Bristoe, Fr., 1637, by Phillipp Taylor, Accomack Co.
Bristoe, Lan., 1637, by Capt. Henry Browne, James City Co.
Bristoe, John, 1637, by Robert Throckmorton, Charles River Co.
Bristow, Thomas, 1645, by Sir William Berkley, —— Co.
Brite, James, 1652, by Mr. David Fox, Lancaster Co.
Britcliffe, Richard, 1637, by Robert Throckmorton, Charles River Co.
Britcliffe, Richard, 1637, by Robert Throckmorton, Charles River.
Britten, Lyonell, 1655, by Mr. John Mottrow, Northumberland Co.
Britten, Rich., 1653, by Capt. Francis Patt, Northampton Co.
Britten, Richard, 1652, by Ambrose Dixon and Stephen Horsely, Jr., Northampton Co.
Brittin, Lyon, 1650, by Thomas Mulford, Nansemond Co.
Britts, Richard, 1653, by Tho. Hawkins, Northumberland Co.
Brittaine, John, 1638, by Cornelius Loyd, —— Co.
Brittaine, Robert, 1635, by Capt. Wm. Pierse, —— Co.
Brittenie, Tho., 1655, by John Biggs, Lower Norfolk Co.
Britton, Edward, 1650, by John Cox, —— Co.
Broad, Thos., 1636, by James Knott, Elizabeth City Co.
Broad, Thomas, 1637, by James Knott, New Norfolk Co.
Broadway, Tho., 1654, by Tho. Bell, Northampton Co.
Broane, Peter, 1656, by John Wood, —— Co.
Brocas, John, 1656, by Major Wm. Lewis, —— Co.
Brocas, John, 1651, by John Thomas, Gloucester Co.
Brocas, Mrs. Tabithe, 1653, by Dennis Connier, Lancaster Co.
Brocas, Georg, 1642, by John Robins, —— Co.
Broche, Barbary, 1637, by Jno. Broche, Charles River Co.
Brock, James, 1651, by Abraham Moone and Thomas Griffin Lancaster Co.
Brock, Wm., 1637, by Francis Osborne, —— Co.
Brockett, William, 1638, by Thomas Burbage, Accomack Co.
Brockham, Edmund, 1656, by John Billiott, Northampton Co.
Brownser, Tho., 1635, by Thos. Harwood, —— Co.
Browning, John, 1635, by Capt. Wm. Pierse, —— Co.
Broodhurst, Ra., 1652, by Toby Smith, Gent., Lancaster Co.
Broodman, Richard, 1650, by Walter Broodhurst, —— Co.
Brodway, Thos., 1656, by John Williams, Northampton Co.
Broodway, John, 1643, by John Norton, James City Co.

Brogg, Wm., 1649, by Capt. Randall Harle, Northampton Co.
Brooch, John, 1648, by George Read, Gent., ——— Co.
Brood, ——, 1654, by Robert Tomlin, ——— Co.
Broode, Humphrey, 1635, by William Hieres, Warrasquinoake Co.
Broodfeild, Ann, 1648, by John Clarke, Lower Norfolk Co.
Broodrihh, Joane, 1652, by Clement Thrush, ——— Co.
Brooke, Georg, 1639, by Capt. Nicholas Martian, Charles River Co.
Brooke, Georg, 1638, by Thomas Burbage, Accomack Co.
Brooke, ——, and two children, 1643, by William Brooke (her husband), Upper Norfolk Co.
Brooke, Wm., 1653, by Mr. Wm. Fry, James City Co.
Brooke, Tho., 1645, by Mark Johnson, Elizabeth City Co.
Brooke, John, 1647, by Tho. Wells, Lower Norfolk Co.
Brooke, Jno., 1653, by Frances Emperor, Hugh Gale and Edward Morgan, Lower Norfolk Co.
Brooke, Eliz., 1642, by Capt. Daniell Gookin, ——— Co.
Brooke, Lydia, 1650, by Henry Brooke, Northumberland Co.
Brooke, Eman., 1650, by Henry Brooke, Northumberland Co.
Brooke, Jane, 1650, by Henry Brooke, Northumberland Co.
Brooke, Tho., 1651, by Capt. Stephen Gill, Northumberland Co.
Brooke, Nicholas, Sr., 1650, by Capt. Charles Leech, Yorke Co.
Brooke, Nicholas, nephew to Sr., 1650, by Capt. Charles Leech, Yorke Co.
Brooke, Nicholas, Jr., 1650, by Capt. Charles Leech, Yorke Co.
Brooke, Charles, 1646, by William Hockaday, York Co.
Brookes, John, 1639, by Georg Minifye, Esq., Charles River Co.
Brooks, Thomas, 1637, by Thomas Shippey, Henrico Co.
Brookes, Jno., 1644, by John Hill, Gent., Upper Norfolk Co.
Brookes, Geo., 1648, by George Read, Gent., ———- Co.
Brookes, Jane, 1650, by Henry Brooke, Northumberland Co.
Brookes, Eliza., 1651, by John Martin and Lancaster Lovett, Lower Norfolk Co.
Brookes, Geo., 1651, by Capt. Geo. Read, Lancaster Co.
Brookes, Marg., 1651, by Phillip Hunley, ——— Co.
Brookes, Bestney, 1648, by Thomas Glascocke, Warwick River Co.
Brook, Wm., 1635, by Osborne Jerkin, Charles City Co.
Brooks, Thomas, 1635, by Capt. Adam Thoroughgood, ——— Co.
Brooks, John, 1640, by Richard Williams, Charles City Co.
Brooks, George, 1635, by William Barber (a mariner), Charles City Co.
Brooks, Peter, 1638, by Thomas Bush, Upper New Norfolk.
Brooks, Walter, 1638, by John Cookeney, Henrico Co.
Brooks, Georg, 1638, by Wm. Barker and associates, Charles City Co.
Brooks, Eliz., 1653, by John Bebey, Lancaster Co.
Brooks, Thos., 1643, by Benjamin Harryson, Gent., James City Co.
Brooks, Wm., 1643, by Obedience Robins, Gent., Northampton Co.
Brookwood, Wm., 1655, by Lt. Col. Anthony Ellyott, ——— Co.
Bromely, Danll., 1635, by Wm. Barber (a mariner), Charles City Co.
Bromfill, Tho., 1655, by Henry Barlow, ——— Co.
Bromfeild, Tho., 1655, by John Lynge, James City Co.
Broomfeild, Mary, 1654, by Alex. Madocks and James Jones, Northampton Co.
Bromfield, Mark, 1645, by James Bruss, Northampton Co.

Bromley, Alex., 1655, by John Hinman, Northampton Co.
Bromly, Hugh, 1651, by Wm. Hampton, —— Co.
Bromly, Daniell, 1638, by Wm. Baker and associates, Charles City Co.
Broper, Tho., 1643, by Edward Murfy and John Vaughan, —— Co.
Brorgin, Geo., 1653, by Maj. Wm. Lewis, —— Co.
Broshery, William, 1636, by John Gates, Elizabeth City Co.
Brotherston, Nester, 1636, by John Dansey, James City.
Brotherton, Henry, 1637, by Capt. Thomas Flint, Warwick River Co.
Brough, Thomas, 1637, by James Knott, New Norfolk Co.
Brough, Thos., 1636, by James Knott, Elizabeth City Co.
Brough, Edward, 1642, by Adam Cooke, Charles County Co.
Brough, Margery, 1647, by John Sidney, Lower Norfolk Co.
Broughoe, Nath., 1656, by Nicholas Waddilow, Northampton Co.
Broughton, Henry, 1643, by Randall Holt, —— Co.
Broughton, Tho., 1654, by Tho. Hobkins, Lancaster Co.
Broughton, Thomas, 1638, by Edward Oliver, James City Co.
Broughton, Jno., 1653, by Robt. Parfitt and Wm. Hatcher, Lancaster Co.
Broughton, Tho., 1650, by Lewis Burwell, Gent., Northumberland Co.
Broughton, 1638, by Thomas Dew, Upper New Norfolk Co.
Broughton, Edward, 1638, by Cobb Howell, Lower New Norfolk Co.
Brouse, Robt., 1639, by Robert Eley, Isle of Wight Co.
Broveck, Wm., 1655, by Edmund Scarbourgh, Jr., and Littleton Scar-
    bourgh, Northampton Co.
Brow, Weston, 1645, by William Jones, Northampton Co.
Broward, Robert, 1642, by Capt. Daniell Gookin, —— Co.
Brown, John, 1653, by George Collins, —— Co.
Brown, Jon., 1653, by Richard Carey, —— Co.
Brown, Wm., 1647, by William Blackey, York Co.
Brown, Eliza, wife Wm. Brown, 1647, by Wm. Blackey, York Co.
Brown, John, 1655, by Richard Hamlet, James City Co.
Brown, John, 1655, by Wm. Wright, Gent., Nansemond Co.
Brown, Tho., and Anne, his wife, 1656, by Edward Robinson and Tho.
    Hall, Lower Norfolk Co.
Brown, John, ——, by Henry Wesgate, Lower Norfolk Co.
Brown, Richard, 1655, by John Jenkins, Northampton Co.
Brown, Wm., 1651, by Mr. Antho. Steevens, Northampton Co.
Brown, Wm., 1653, by Ferdinando Austin, Charles City Co.
Brown, Ja., 1653, by Robt. Sorrel, —— Co.
Brown, John, 1653, by Robt. Sorrel, —— Co.
Brown, Kath., 1651, by Robt. Bradshaw, Charles River Co.
Brown, Nicho., and wife, 1651, by Robt. Bradshaw, Charles River Co.
Brown, John, 1651, by Tho. Wilsford, Gent., —— Co.
Brown, Francis, 1650, by Hump. Lyster, —— Co.
Brown, ——, 1650, by John Brown (her husband), Northampton Co.
Brown, Hester, 1650, by John Cox, —— Co.
Brown, Anne, 1653, by Tho. Davis, —— Co.
Brown, Robert, 1649, by Richard Kemp, Esq., (Sec. of State) ——
    Co.
Brown, Robt., 1648, by George Read, Gent., —— Co.
Brown, Patience, 1648, by Richard Thompson, Northumberland Co.
Brown, Francis, 1650, by Lieut. Wm. Worleich, —— Co.

Brown, Ursula, 1646, by John Brown, her husband, Northampton **Co.**
Brown, Joyce, 1643, by Mr. John Bishopp, James City Co.
Brown, Weston, 1652, by Mr. Tho. Gutheridge, Lower Norfolk **Co.**
Brown, Margaret, 1653, by Tho. Keene, Northumberland Co.
Brown, Wm., 1652, by Isaac Richson, Lancaster Co.
Brown, Wm., 1642, by Robert Eyres, Lower New Norfolk Co.
Brown, Richard, 1640, by Mr. Bridges Freeman, James City Co.
Brown, Jon., 1654, by Robert Holt, James City Co.
Brown, Nicho., 1648, by John Watkins, James City Co.
Brown, Richd., 1654, by Elward Revell, Northampton Co.
Browne, James, 1653, by Mr. Wm. Baldwin, York Co.
Browne, James, 1652, by Tho. Teakle, Northampton Co.
Browne, Robt., 1653, by Ralph Hacker, Lancaster Co.
Browne, Elize, 1635, by Wm. Garry, Accomacke Co.
Browne, Robt., 1638, by Thomas Gray, James City.
Browne, Thos., 1637, by Daniell Gookins, New Norfolk Co.
Browne, Christopher, 1642, by Thomas Mooreland, Yorke Co.
Browne, Giles, 1641, by Stephen Charleton, Accomack Co.
Browne, Chas., 1635, by Geo. Holmes, James Co.
Browne, Robt., 1635, by Thomas Gray, James Co.
Browne, Robt. (a servant), 1635, by Wm. Garry, Accomack Co.
Browne, John, 1636, by Georg Traveller, Accomack Co.
Browne, Robt., 1639, by Capt. Nicholas Martian, Charles River **Co.**
Browne, Jon., 1637, by Thos. Hampton Clarke, New Norfolk Co.
Browne, Randall, 1637, by Thomas Hampton, New Norfolk Co.
Browne, Tho., 1637, by Wm. Hatcher, ———— Co.
Browne, Willis, 1635, by Edw. Minter, James Co.
Browne, Natho, 1650, by Thomas Powell, ———— Co.
Browne, Robt., 1651, by Capt. Geo Read, Lancaster Co.
Browne, Tho., 1651, by Thomas Manning, Warwick Co.
Browne, Wm., 1642, by Capt. Samuell Mathews, Esq., ———— **Co.**
Browne, Hump., 1636, by Francis Maulden, ———— Co.
Browne, John, 1636, by Richard Cocke, ———— Co.
Browne, Nicholas, 1636, by Wm. Clarke, Henrico Co.
Browne, Robt., 1637, by Thomas Barnard, Warwick River Co.
Browne, Jeffry, 1637, by Thomas Shippey, Henrico Co.
Browne, Sarah, 1639, by William Davis, James City Co.
Browne, John, 1636, by John Dansey, James City Co.
Browne, ———, 1642, by John Browne (her husband), Accomac Co.
Browne, Mrs. Ann, 1637, by Capt. Henry Browne, James City Co.
Browne, Ellen, 1642, by John Lylley, ———— Co.
Browne, Wm., 1642, by Thomas Grey, James City Co.
Browne, Eliza, 1638, by John Fludd, James City Co.
Browne, Rebecca, 1652, by Henry Palin and John Singleton, ———— **Co.**
Browne, Tho., 1652, by Mr. Geo. Foster, Northumberland Co.
Browne, Tho., 1652, by Dr. George Hack, Northampton Co.
Browne, Tho., 1652, by Dr. George Hack, Northampton Co.
Browne, Tho., 1638, by John Jackson and Eliza Kingswill, James **City Co.**
Browne, Tho., 1638, by Wm. Hatfield, Upper New Norfolk Co.
Browne, Antho., 1635, by Wm. Barber, Charles City Co.
Browne, Tho., 1653, by Charles Scarburg, Northampton Co.

Browne, Henry, 1643, by Tho. Dew, Upper Norfolk Co.
Browne, Robert, 1643, by Wm. Tapinge, James City Co.
Browne, Wm., 1650, by John Baytes, Northumberland Co.
Browne, Wm., 1650, by John Essix, Northumberland Co.
Browne, Tho., 1641, by Thomas Pitt, Charles City Co.
Browne, Richard, 1648, by Thomas Woodhouse, James City Co.
Browne, Thos., 1636, by Georg Holmes, James City Co.
Browne, Stephen, 1637, by Capt. Henry Browne, James City Co.
Browne, Randall, 1637, by Thos. Hampton Clarke, New Norfolk Co.
Browne, Thomas, 1637, by Georg Holmes, James City Co.
Browne, Edward, 1637, by John Brodwell, James City Co.
Browne, Thomas, 1639, by William Burdett, Accomack Co.
Browne, Tho., 1652, by Tho. Steevens, Lancaster Co.
Browne, Wm., 1653, by Wm. Leech, Lancaster Co.
Browne, Tho., 1653, by Tho. Hawkins, ——— Co.
Browne, John, 1653, by Edward Dobson, ——— Co.
Browne, Marga., 1653, by Abraham Moon, Lancaster Co.
Browne, Rich., 1642, by Capt. Daniell Gookin, ——— Co.
Browne, Eliza., 1650, by Capt. John Flood, Gent., and Jno. Flood, an
    ancient mariner, James City Co.
Browne, Grace, 1651, by Lieut. Coll. Giles Brent, Northumberland Co.
Browne, Originall, 1653, by Colo. Wm. Clayborne, (Sec. of State) ———
    Co.
Browne, Grace, 1651, by John Rookwood, Gent., Northumberland Co.
Browne, Jacob, 1654, by Henry Walker, James City Co.
Browne, Eliz., 1652, by Tho. Dodford, ——— Co.
Browne, Wm., 1654, by Nath. Pope, Westmoreland Co.
Browne, Eliz., 1654, by Robert Hubard, Westmoreland Co.
Browne, Nich., and his wife, 1654, by Edw. Welch, ——— Co.
Browne, Ann, 1654, by Edw. Welch, ——— Co.
Browne, Sarah, 1654, by Edw. Welch, ——— Co.
Browne, Andrew, 1654, by Francis Smith and Mr. John Smith, West-
    moreland Co.
Browne, Cleare, 1654, by John Whithers and Stephen Garey, Westmore-
    land Co.
Browne, Nich., 1642, by Wm. Pudivatt, Isle of Wight Co.
Browne, Eliz., 1654, by Major Miles Carey, Westmoreland Co.
Browne, John, 1654, by Christopher Boon, Westmoreland Co.
Browne, Wm., 1654, by Abraham Moon, Gloucester Co.
Browne, Mary, 1654, by Abraham Moon, Gloucester Co.
Browne, David, 1654, by Walter Dickenson, Lancaster Co.
Browne, Grace, 1654, by Lieut. Coll. Giles Brent, Westmoreland Co.
Browne, John, 1654, by Sarah Hancock, Lower Norfolk Co.
Browne, Tho., 1650, by Mrs. Frances Townshend (widow), North-
    umberland Co.
Browne, Ellen, 1643, by Richard Kemp, Esq., James City Co.
Browne, Wm., 1643, by Richard Kemp, Esq., James City Co.
Browne, Tho., 1653, by Charles Scarburg, Northampton Co.
Browne, Richard, 1652, by Edward Revell, Northampton Co.
Browne, Darby, 1654, by Francis Land, Lower Norfolk Co.
Browne, Wm., 1652, by Mr. David Fox, Lancaster Co.

Brownes, Andrew, 1651, by James Allen, Northumberland Co.
Brower, Wm., 1638, by Wm. Rainshaw, Lower New Norfolk Co.
Brownelofe, John, 1638, by Capt. Christopher Wormley, Charles River Co.
Browning, Kath., 1655, by Robert Castle, James City Co.
Browning, Math., 1653, by Tho. Davis, ——— Co.
Browning, Wm., 1650, by John Hany, Northumberland Co.
Browning, Geo., 1635, by Hugh Cox, Charles City Co.
Browning, Jas., 1650, by Mrs. Francis Townshend, Northumberland Co.
Brownly, Luke, 1639, by Edward Travis, James City.
Brownson, Geo., 1643, by Capt. Samuell Mathews, Esq., ——— Co.
Brownridge, Math., 1637, by Wm. Farrar, Henrico Co.
Brron, Devorux, 1654, by John Watson and John Bagnall, Westmoreland Co.
Bruce, Richard, 1650, by Capt. John Flood, Gent., and Jno. Flood, an ancient planter, James City Co.
Brumfield, Kath., 1653, by Charles Scarburg, Northampton Co.
Bruham, Wm., 1653, by Tho. Read, Northumberland Co.
Brumly, David, 1649, by Christop. Lewis, James City Co.
Brumly, Fra., 1652, by Tho. Glascock, Lancaster Co.
Bruneall, Wm., 1650, by Henry Peaseley, ——— Co.
Bruse, James, 1645, by James Bruss, Northampton Co.
Bruse, Rich., 1638, by John Fludd, James City Co.
Brute, Walter, 1637, by Richard Preston, ——— Co.
Bruster, Anthony, 1647, by Thomas Johnson, Gent., Northampton Co.
Bryan, Kath., 1653, by Augustine Gillet, Upper Norfolk Co.
Bryan, Edward, 1652, by Mr. Wm. Waters, Northampton Co.
Bryan, Xtop., 1646, by Henry Sededen, Northampton Co.
Bryan, Wm., 1654, by Abraham Moone, ——— Co.
Bryan, Tho., 1655, by Patrick Miller, Lancaster Co.
Bryan, Richd., 1654, by Christopher Boon, Westmoreland Co.
Bryan, Garret, 1643, by John Batts, James City Co.
Bryan, Richard, 1654, by Toby Smith, Lancaster Co.
Bryan, Jon., 1653, by Robert Saven, ——— Co.
Bryan, Hen., 1650, by Capt. Moore Fantleroy, ——— Co.
Bryan, Tho., 1653, by John Holding, York Co.
Bryan, Teague, 1649, by Richard Kemp, Esq., (Sec. of State), ——— Co.
Bryan, Edw., 1647, by Thomas Johnson, Gent., Northampton Co.
Bryan, Tho., 1652, by Mr. Edward Travis, James City Co.
Bryan, Edward, 1638, by Thomas Stampe, James City Co.
Bryan, Richard, 1652, by Tho. Hackett, ——— Co.
Bryan, Robert, 1637, by James Knott, New Norfolk Co.
Bryan, Nick, 1637, by Tho. Edghill, Isle of Wight Co.
Bryan, Morgan, 1642, by John Beale, ——— Co.
Bryan, Henry, 1639, by Edward Panderson, ——— Co.
Bryan, Edward, 1639, by Thomas Stamp, James City Co.
Bryan, Tho., 1648, by Wm. Edwards and Rice Edwards, James City Co.
Bryant, John, 1656, by Capt. Henry Fleete, ——— Co.
Bryant, John, 1652, by John Spiltimber and John Brady, ——— Co.
Bryant, John, 1653, by Oliver Segar, Lancaster Co.

Bryant, Michaell, 1636, by John Wilkins, Accomac Co.
Bryant, Edmund, 1655, by George Parker, Northampton Co.
Bryce, Wm., 1654, by John Hallawes, Westmoreland Co.
Bryce, James, 1659, by Mrs. Mgt. Brent, Westmoreland Co.
Bryer, Robert, 1656, by Roger Wolmsly and Richard Ingram, James
   City Co.
Bryer, Wm., 1653, by Abraham Moon, Lancaster Co.
Bryer, Geo., 1650, by Wm. Underwood, Gent., ——— Co.
Bryun, Edmund, 1641, by Richard Jackson, Isle of Wight Co.
Bubith, Jonathan, 1654, by Daniel Boucher, Isle of Wight Co.
Buck, Old., 1650, by Sr. Tho. Luntsford, Kt., and Baronett, ——— Co.
Buck, John, 1642, by John Bayles, ——— Co.
Buck, Peter, 1637, by John Jackson, Charles River Co.
Buck, Thos., 1639, by William Canhooe, Charles River Co.
Buck, Thomas, 1640, by Thomas Harvey, James City Co.
Buck, Peter, 1635, by John Jackson, ——— Co.
Bucker, William, 1635, by McWilliam Stone, ——— Co.
Bucher, Richard, 1638, by Wm. Clays, Charles River Co.
Buckerin, John, 1649, by Richard Croshaw, Yorke Co.
Buckham, Richd., 1653, by Wm. Havett, ——— Co.
Buckham, Richard, 1649, by Ralph Harsly, Northumberland Co.
Buckham, Tho., 1649, by Wm. Peerce and Frances Symons, North-
   umberland Co.
Buckland, Richard, 1645, by James Bruss, Northampton Co.
Buckland, Jon., 1637, by Daniell Gookins, New Norfolk Co.
Buckley, Humphrey, 1639, by Capt. Rich. Townsend, Charles River Co.
Buckley, Rowland, 1637, by Lt. Rich. Popeley, New Norfolk Co.
Buckley, Richard, 1642, by James Pereene, Northampton Co.
Buckley, Arth., 1647, by Elizabeth Barcroft, Isle of Wight Co.
Buckly, Rowd., 1636, by Henry Southall, ——— Co.
Buckingham, Edwd., 1656, by Sir Henry Chichley, ——— Co.
Buckingham, Edward, 1650, by Mr. Stephen Hamelin, Charles City Co.
Buckmaster, Tho., 1655, by John Biggs, Lower Norfolk Co.
Buckmanreyne, Jno., 1650, by Mr. Epaphroditus Lawson, ——— Co.
Buckster, Elin., 1652, by Col. Geo. Ludlow, Esq., Gloucester Co.
Bucktrell, Rich., 1635, by Rich. Peirce, James City Co.
Buckworth, John, 1638, by John Fludd, James City Co.
Budd, Tho., 1643, by Capt. Samuell Mathews, Esq., ——— Co.
Budd, ———, 1650, by Richard Budd (her husband), Northumberland Co.
Budd, Giles, 1639, by William Burdett, Accomack Co.
Budder, Hugh, 1655, by Capt. Henry Fleet, ——— Co.
Buderhill, Edwd., 1648, by Thomas Woodhouse, James City Co.
Budford, James, 1652, by Nicholas George, ——— Co.
Budge, John, 1643, by Edward Dobson, ——— Co.
Budge, John, 1640, by Robert Holt, James City Co.
Budle, Alex., 1650, by Mr. Robt. Holt, James City Co.
Budway, John, 1650, by Mrs. Frances Townshend (widow, North-
   umberland Co.
Buffeild, Sarah, 1641, by Samuell Firment, Upper New Norfolk Co.
Buffeild, Tho., 1655, by Southy Littleberry, Northampton Co.
Buffin, John, 1635, by McWilliam Stone, ——— Co.

Buffkin, M. Henry, 1650, by Sr. Tho. Luntsford, Kt., and Baronett, ——— Co.
Bufort, Richard, 1637, by John Moon, Isle of Wight Co.
Bugg, Joan, 1654, by Christopher Regoult, ——— Co.
Bugg, Joan, 1655, by Ralph Green, New Kent Co.
Bugbly, Peter, 1651, by Anthony Johnson, Northampton Co.
Bugbye, John, 1635, by George Minifie, James City Co.
Buggs, Wm., 1639, by Stephen Webb, James City Co.
Bulcher, John, 1650, by Sr. Tho. Luntsford, Kt., and Baronett, ——— Co.
Bulker, Oneale, 1655, by Wm. Taylor, Northampton Co.
Bull, Tho., 1654, by Mrs. Fra. Harrison, widow, Westmoreland Co.
Bull, John, 1650, by Daniell Luellin, Charles City Co.
Bull, John, 1643, by Walter Aston, Gent., Charles City Co.
Bull, George, 1639, by Thomas Mathews, Henrico Co.
Bullard, Rich., 1654, by Col. Hump. Higgenson, Esq., and Abraham Moone, Westmoreland Co.
Bullard, Tho., 1654, by Col. Hump. Higgenson, Westmoreland Co.
Bullard, Thomas, 1637, by Humphry Higgenson, Gent., ——— Co.
Bullard, John, from Rendall, 1642, by Thomas Say, ——— Co.
Bullard, Henry, 1636, by Christopher Calthropp, Charles River Co.
Buller, Tho., 1642, by Stephen Hamblyn, York Co.
Buller, Tho., 1643, by Wm. Warder, ——— Co.
Bullifont, Rebecca, 1656, by Tho. Binns, Surry Co.
Bulliford, Ro., 1651, by Edward Deggs, Esq., Yorke Co.
Bulling, Tho., 1653, by Charles Grymes, Lancaster Co.
Bullock, George, 1654, by Edward Parker, Westmoreland Co.
Bullock, Wm., 1656, by Silvester Thatcher, ——— Co.
Bullock, Tho., 1654, by Richard Allen, Northampton Co.
Bullock, Richard, 1654, by Tho. Pensherman, York Co.
Bullock, Tho., 1652, by Tho. Johnson, Jr., Northampton Co.
Bullock, Joane, 1638, by William Clarke, Henrico Co.
Bullock, Wm., 1638, by Wm. Cloys, Charles River Co.
Bullock, Geo., 1637, by David Mansell, James City Co.
Bullock, Richard, 1641, by John Gookin, Lower Norfolk Co.
Bullock, Joane, 1636, by Wm. Clarke, Henrico Co.
Bullock, Geo., 1635, by David Mansell, James Co.
Bulmer, Benis, 1635, by Thos. Bagwell, ——— Co.
Bulmer, Tho., 1636, by Edward Rogers, Warrasquinoake Co.
Bulmur, Thos., 1637, by Margaret Rogers, New Norfolk Co.
Bulter, John, 1636, by John Gookin, Gent., ——— Co.
Bulter, Wm., 1635, by Christopher Branch, Henrico Co.
Bush, Tho., 1654, by Robert Holt, James City Co.
Bumpass, Richard, 1635, by Edw. Osborne, Henrico Co.
Bumpass, Richard, 1638, by Christopher Branch, Henrico Co.
Bumbridge, Christopher, 1639, by John White, James Citie Co.
Burbadge, Tho., 1653, by Wm. Walker, Northumberland Co.
Burber, John, 1652, by Tho. Preston, ——— Co.
Burbadge, Tho., 1654, by John Whithers and Stephen Garey, Westmoreland Co.
Burbanck, Mary, 1650, by Wm. Yarret and Fra. Wittington, ——— Co.
Burch, John, 1637, by Wm. Prior, Charles River Co.

Burchell, Ann, 1655, by Wm. Hall, New Kent Co.
Burcher, Joane, 1637, by Georg Burcher, James City.
Burcher, Humphry, 1639, by Richard Corke, Gent., Henrico Co.
Burcher, Abraham, 1638, by Oliver Sprye, Upper New Norfolk Co.
Burtcher, Jane, daughter of Geo., 1635, by George Burtcher, James City Co.
Burtcher, Ann, wife of Geo. B., 1635, by George Burtcher James City Co.
Burcher, Humphry, 1636, by Richard Cocke, ———— Co.
Burcher, Tho., 1638, by Joseph Harmon, James City Co.
Burcher, Ann, 1637, by Georg Burcher, her husband, James City Co.
Burcher, Geo., 1655, by Gilbert Deacon, Henrico Co.
Burd, John, 1649, by Tho. Bourne, ———— Co.
Burdett, Cris., 1648, by Lewis Burwell and Tho. Haws, York River Co.
Burdette, Mr. William, 1639, by William Burdett, Accomack Co.
Burden, John, 1637, by Bridges Freeman, James City Co.
Burden John, 1637, by John Gookin, New Norfolk Co.
Burden, John, 1637, by William Frye, James City Co.
Burden, John, 1637, by Daniell Gookins, New Norfolk Co.
Burden, Edw., 1637, by Daniell Gookins, New Norfolk Co.
Burden John, 1636, by John Gookin, Gent., ———— Co.
Burdyken, Mary, 1652, by Nicho. George, Tho. Taberer and Humphry Clarke, ———— Co.
Burden, John, 1638, by Mr. John Gookins, Upper New Norfolk Co.
Burdix, Jno., 1650, by Richard Axom and Tho. Godwin, ———— Co.
Burfe, James, 1635, by Henry Harte, James City Co.
Burfoote, Samll., 1637, by Capt. Henry Browne, James City Co.
Burford, Moddin, 1653, by Wm. Walker, Northumberland Co.
Burford, Wm., 1654, by Mr. Giles Brent, Westmoreland Co.
Burford, Emedlin, 1654, by John Whithers and Stephen Garey, Westmoreland Co.
Burford, Geo., Jr., 1643, by Thomas Hughes, Charles River Co.
Burford, Geo., Sr., 1643, by Thomas Hughes, Charles River Co.
Burford, Georg, 1643, by John Norton, James City Co.
Burford, Wm., 1637, by Thomas Osborne, Jr., Henrico Co.
Burfur, Wm., 1639, by William Davis, James City Co.
Burgeyny, Rich., 1642, by Stephen Gill, ———— Co.
Burger, Evan., 1643, by Mr. Moore Fantleroy, Upper Norfolk Co.
Burges, John, 1635, by Capt. Adam Thoroughgood, ———— Co.
Burges, John, 1639, by John Saines, ———— Co.
Burges, Wm., 1637, by William Mills, James City Co.
Burges, John, 1636, by Christopher Calthopher, Charles River Co.
Burges, John, 1637, by Capt. Adam Thoroughgood, New Norfolk Co.
Burges, Richard, 1638, by Robert Pitts, Isle of Wight Co.
Burges, Wm., 1650, by George Goldsmith, ———— Co.
Burges, Mary, 1643, by Benjamin Harryson, Gent., James City Co.
Burgess, Joseph, 1652, by Christopher Lewis, Isle of Wight Co.
Burgess, Robt., 1652, by Mr. James Warradine, ———— Co.
Burgis, John, 1639, by Georg Minifye, Esq., Charles River Co.
Burgis, Richard, 1640, by Robert Holt, James City Co.
Burgis, John, 1650, by Mr. Robert Holt, James City Co.

Burgis, Mary, 1650, by John Rosier, Northumberland Co.
Burgis, John, 1648, by John Sayner, James City Co.
Burgiss, Wm., 1651, by Richard Whitehurst, Lower Norfolk Co.
Burgesse, Ann, 1652, by Toby Smith, Gent., Lancaster Co.
Burher, Lewis, 1653, by Richard Carey, ———— Co.
Burk, Ann, 1647, by Richard Bland, ———— Co.
Burkett, ———, 1654, by Robert Tomlin, ———— Co.
Burkett, Ellins, 1636, by Wm. Clarke, Henrico Co.
Burbage, Wm., 1638, by Thomas Burbage, Accomack Co.
Burbage, Thomas, 1642, by Ellis Richerdson, Yorke Co.
Burleigh, Abell, 1652, by Mrs. Elnor Brocas, Lancaster Co.
Burlion, Jon., 1653, by Richard Carey, ———— Co.
Burner, Law., 1652, by John Johnson, Northampton Co.
Burnell, Robert, 1651, by George Eaton, ———— Co.
Burnell, Henry, 1656, by Major Wm. Lewis, ———— Co.
Burnell, Francis, 1656, by Major Wm. Lewis, ———— Co.
Burnett, Samuell, 1648, by William Mills, Isle of Wight Co.
Burnett, Hen., 1651, by Richard Bayly, ———— Co.
Burnett, James, 1639, by John Pawley, James City Co.
Burnett, Francis, 1637, by William Frye, James City Co.
Burnett, Nich., 1635, by William Carter, Henrico Co.
Burnham, John, 1643, by John Hoddin, ———— Co.
Burnham, Sus., 1651, by Mr. Rowland Burnham, ———— Co.
Burnham, Mrs. Alice, 1651, by Mr. Rowland Burnham, ———— Co.
Burnham, Tho., 1654, by Edw. Cole, Northampton Co.
Burnham, Katharine, 1649, by Rowland Burneham, Gent., ———— Co.
Burpott, Rich., 1635, by Christopher Wooddard, ———— Co.
Burr, Jeremiah, 1637, by Arthur Bayly and Tho. Crosby, Henrico Co.
Burr, Edward, 1637, by Lt. John Upton, Isle of Wight Co.
Burr, Edw., 1637, by John Upton, Isle of Wight Co.
Burr, Edwar d, 1635, by Jno. Upton, Warrasquinoake Co.
Burrell, Wm., 1644, by Edwyn Conaway, Northampton Co.
Burrell, Robt., his wife and three children, 1654, by Peter Knight, Northumberland Co.
Burrell, Tho., 1638, by Capt. Christopher, Wormley, ———— Co.
Burland, Dorothy, 1639, by John Burland, Charles River.
Burle, Eliza., 1653, by Christopher Boyce, Northumberland Co.
Burras, Mathew, 1642, by Thomas Say, ———— Co.
Burrick, Tho., 1652, by Francis England, Isle of Wight Co.
Burris, Kath., 1655, by Dr. Giles Mode, New Kent Co.
Burroge, Henry, 1652, by Capt. Augustine Warner, ———— Co.
Burrough, Rober, 1647, by Jonathan Gills, Northampton Co.
Burroughs, Ann, 1635, by Capt. Adam Thoroughgood, ———— Co.
Burroughs, Ann, 1636, by Christopher Burroughs, Elizabeth City Co.
Burroughs, Wm., 1636, by Christopher Burroughs, Elizabeth City Co.
Burrow, Mathew, 1639, by William Davis, James City Co.
Burrows, Mathews, 1635, by Thomas Harwood, ———— Co.
Burrowes, Eliz., 1653, by Samuell Bowman, Northumberland Co.
Burry, Garrie, ———, by Mr. Robt. Fontaine, Lower Norfolk Co.
Burt, Wm., 1654, by Mrs. Mgt. Brent, Westmoreland Co.
Burt, Edward, 1635, by McWilliam Stone, ———— Co.

Burtenwood,Wm., 1648, by Lewis Burwell and Tho. Haws,York River Co.
Burthen, Richard, 1635, by Capt. Wm. Pierce, ———— Co.
Burtlett, Thom., 1637, by Alice Edloe, Henrico Co.
Burton, Robt., 1651, by Joseph Croshaw, Yorke Co.
Burton, Issabell, 1652, by Tho. Teakle, Northampton, Co.
Burton, Ann, 1650, by Nicho. Jernew, Yorke Co.
Burton, Ann, 1650, by Nicholas Jernew, Gent., ———— Co.
Burton, Bryan, 1646, by Sir William Berkley, ———— Co.
Burton, Ralph, 1653, by Mr. Wm. Fry, James City Co.
Burton, Anne, 1652, by Wm. Ginsey, Gloucester Co.
Burton, John, 1643, by Henry Bradley, Upper Norfolk Co.
Burton, Wm., 1643, by Henry Bradley, Upper Norfolk Co.
Burly, Francis, 1638, by Robert Pitts, Isle of Wight Co.
Bushell, Nich., 1642, by Capt. Samuell Mathews, Esq., ———— Co.
Bussey, Georg, 1637, by Rich. Bennett, New Norfolk.
Burwelll Robt., 1654, by Tho. Hobkins, Lancaster Co.
Burwell,, Fra., 1648, by Lewis Burwell, Gent., ———— Co.
Burwell, Francis, 1648, by Lewis Burwell, Gent., ———— Co.
Burwell, Wm., 1648, by Tho. Braughton, ———— Co.
Burwell, Geo., 1648, by Tho. Braughton, ———— Co.
Burwell, Elizabeth, 1648, by Tho. Braughton, ———— Co.
Burwell, Lewis, 1648, by Tho. Braughton, ———— Co.
Burwell,, Wm., 1648, by Lewis Burwell and Tho. Haws, York River Co.
Burwell, Robt., 1652, by Mrs. Elnor Brocas, Lancaster Co.
Busby, Eliza, 1652, by Mrs. Mary Brent, Northumberland Co.
Busby, Ann, 1635, by Robert Bennett, ———— Co.
Busby, Tho., Arthur Bayly's servant, 1637, by Arthur Bayly and Tho.
    Crosby, Henrico Co.
Bush, Tho., 1637, by Oliver Sprye, New Norfolk Co.
Bush Nich., 1639, by Edward Panderson, ———— Co.
Bushe, Roger, 1654, by Col. Argoll Yardley, Northampton Co.
Bushell, Nich., 1635, by Jno. Upton, Warrasquinoake Co.
Bushell, Nicholas, 1637, by Lt. John Upton, Isle of Wight.
Bushell, Rich., 1637, by John Upton, Isle of Wight.
Busher, Mable, 1635, by Mr. Willis Heyly, ———— Co.
Bushoppe, Jon., 1635, by Thomas Gray, James Co.
Busby, Waller, 1651, by Capt. Tho. Davis, Northumberland Co.
Bussen, Jno., 1654, by Edward, Gilla, James City Co.
Bussie, Eliz., 1649, by Henry White, James City Co.
Bussy, Eliz., 1635, by Robert Bennett, ———— Co.
Bussey, George, 1635, by Richard Bennett, ———— Co.
Butler, Nicholas, 1652, by Mr. John Moltrom, Northumberland Co.
Butler, Wm., 1656, by Tho. Salsbury, Northumberland Co.
Butler, Tho., 1642, by Thomas Bagwell, Charles City Co.
Butler, John, 1642, by John Pratt, Henrico Co.
Butler, Francis, 1656, by Capt. Wm. Canfell, Surry Co.
Butler, John, 1653, by Colo. Wm. Clayborne, (Sec. of State), ————
    Co.
Butler, Elizabeth, 1653, by Nicholas Perry, Charles City Co.
Butler, Jon., 1638, by Richard Wilcox, James City Co.
Butler, Samuell, 1641, by Tho. Pitt, Charles City Co.

Butler, Tho., 1650, by John Hallawes, Gent., Northumberland Co.
Butler, Xtop., 1650, by John Hallawes, Gent., Northumberland Co.
Butler, John, 1650, by John Hallawes, Gent., Northumberland Co.
Butler, Natha., 1650, by John Hallawes, Gent., Northumberland Co.
Butler, Eliza, 1643, by Wm. Butler, James City Co.
Butler, Jon., 1643, by Wm. Butler, James City Co.
Butler, Mary, 1643, by Wm. Butler, James City Co.
Butler, John, 1643, by James Bagnall, Lower Norfolk Co.
Butler, John, 1638, by Mr. John Gookins, Upper New Norfolk Co.
Butler, Joane, 1638, by Georg White, clerk, Upper New Norfolk Co.
Bntler, Tho., 1638, by John Bough, Henrico Co.
Butler, Edward, 1638, by Robert Pitts, Isle of Wight Co.
Butler, Wm., 1650, by Capt. Richard Bond, Charles City Co.
Butler, Wm., 1651, by Phillip Charles, James City Co.
Butler, Wm., 1638, by Christopher Branch, Henrico Co.
Butler, Henry, 1637, by Charles Barcroft, Isle of Wight Co.
Butler, John, 1635, by John Gookin, New Norfolk Co.
Butler, Robt., 1635, by Capt. Edmund Scarborough, Accomack Co.
Butler, Joane, 1635, by Thos. Harwood, ———— Co.
Butler, Robt., 1640, by Edmund Scarburgh, Accomack Co.
Butler, Wm., 1649, by Richard Kemp., Esq., Sec., of State, ———— Co.
Butler, Henry, 1650, by Jervace Dodson, Gent., Northumberland Co.
Butler, Ann, 1654, by Col. Henry Higgenson, Esq., and Abraham
    Moone, Westmoreland Co.
Butross, Rich., 1637, by Capt. Thomas Flint, Warwick River Co.
Butt, James, 1650, by Wm. Clapham, ———— Co.
Butcher, Wm., 1642, by Thomas Bagwell, Charles City Co.
Butcher, Jon., 1654, by Wm. Bacon, Northumberland Co.
Butcher, Geo., 1655, by Southy Littleberry, Northampton Co.
Butcher, John, 1649, by Richard Bayly, Northampton Co.
Butcher, Amey, 1650, by Lawrence Peters, Nansemond Co.
Butcher, Tho., 1643, by Richard Richards, Charles River Co.
Butcher, Edward, 1643, by Richard Richards, Charles River Co.
Butcher, Mary, 1643, by Wm. Butcher, James City Co.
Butcher, Wm., 1643, by Wm. Warder, ———— Co.
Butcher, John, 1653, by Wm. Debram, ———— Co.
Butlerfield, Robt., 1650, by Benedick Barbar, Gent., ———— Co.
Butterum, John, 1637, by William Reynolds, Charles River Co.
Butterworth, Edw., 1639, by Peter Ridley, James City Co.
Buttey, Magt., 1655, by Geo. Coltclough, Northumberland Co.
Buttin, Eliz., 1642, by Capt. Samuell Mathews, Esq., ———— Co.
Butting, Tho., ————, by Tho. Lucas, ———— Co.
Buttinge, Thomas, 1636, by Elizabeth Hawkins, Charles River Co.
Buxton, Jon., 1637, by Mathew Edloe, ———— Co.
Buxton, Robert, 1646, by Sir William Berkley, ———— Co.
Byfeild, Antho., 1653, by John Merryman and Morgan Haynes, Lan-
    caster Co.
Byham, Ger., 1655, by John Coole, James City Co.
Byler, Wm., 1656, by Sir Henry Chichley, ———— Co.
Bynam, Robt., 1655, by Richard Foster, ———— Co.
Byrd, Wm., 1653, by Charles Grymes, Lancaster Co.

Byrd, Xtophur, 1651, by Henry Hackery, ——— Co.
Byrd, Ann, 1652, by James Sterling, Lower Norfolk Co.
Byrom, John, 1656, by Mr. Tho. Purifoy, ——— Co.
Bysant, Michaell, 1637, by John Wilkins, New Norfolk Co.

C

Cable, Tho., 1651, by Robert Holt, James City, Co.
Cable, John, 1650, by Capt. Moore Fautleroy, ——— Co.
Cabley, Barna, 1650, by Lewis Burwell, Gent., ——— Co.
Cade, Sarah, 1650, by Capt. Moore Fautleroy, ——— Co.
Cade, Peter, 1653, by Col. Hugh Gwyn, Lancaster Co.
Cade, Robert, 1652, by Capt. Augustine Warner, ——— Co.
Cade, Florence, 1655, by George Parker, Northampton Co.
Cade, James, 1654, by Toby Smith, Lancaster Co.
Cade, Peter, 1652, by Collo. Hugh Gwin, ——— Co.
Cade, William, 1640, by Toby Smith, Warwick River Co.
Cadin, Jno., 1650, by Mr. James Williamson, ——— Co.
Cadly, Tho., 1638, by William Banister, ——— Co.
Cadwell, Wm., 1650, by Lieut. Wm. Worleich, ——— Co.
Cadwellader, Humphry, 1641, by Samuell Firment, Upper New Nor-
     folk Co.
Caffeway, Nicho., 1652, by Tho. Green, ——— Co.
Cain, Charles, 1654, by Robert Holt, James City Co.
Cainhae, Richard, 1651, by Mr. Geo. Truhett, Northampton Co.
Cakebread, Tho., 1645, by Mr. Bartholomew Hoskins, ——— Co.
Caketread, John, 1643, by Phillipp Taylor, Northampton Co.
Calcott, Elizabeth, 1651, by Edward Greenwood, James City Co.
Calcup, Bridget, 1647, by Elizabeth Barcroft, Isle of Wight Co.
Caldhaus, Wm., 1653, by Ralph Green, Gloucester Co.
Calfe, Joseph, 1651, by Tho. Wilsford, Gent., ——— Co.
Calgey, Toby, 1655, by John Jenkins, Northampton Co.
Calkbrand, Tho., 1643, by Phillipp Taylor, Northampton Co.
Callahan, Chas., 1637, by Hugh Wynn, Isle of Wight Co.
Callaway, Edmund, 1639, by Wm. Barker, Charles City Co.
Callay, Peter, ———, by Mr. Wm. Presly, Northumberland Co.
Caldwell, Mr. Wm., 1650, by Sr. Tho. Luntsford, Kt. and Baronett,
     ——— Co.
Caldwell, Robt.,1646, by Geo. Ludlow, Esq., York Co.
Calfe, Wm., 1637, by Arthur Boyly and Tho. Crosby, Henrico Co.
Called, Samuel, 1652, by Edward Coles, Northumberland Co.
Callender, Wm., 1650, by Geo. Ludlow, Esq., Northumberland Co.
Callender, Wm., 1651, by George Ludlow, Esq., ——— Co.
Caller, Tho., 1653, by Charles Scarburg, Northampton Co.
Callowe, Steph., 1652, by Mr. Tho. Gutheridge, Lower Norfolk Co.
Callowet, Step., 1645, by William Jones, Northampton Co.
Calston, Francis, 1653, by Wm. Johnson, Lancaster Co.
Calton, Thomas, 1647, by James Warradine, ——— Co.
Calvery, John, 1652, by Mr. Edwin Connaway, ——— Co.
Calvert, Edwd., 1653, by John Debar, Lower Norfolk Co.
Calvin, Fra., 1654, by John Watson and John Bognall, Westmoreland Co.

Camber, Fr., 1638, by Edward Travis and John Johnson, James City Co.
Camblett, Robt., 1646, by Henry Sedenden, Northampton Co.
Camell, Alex., 1650, by Capt. Moore Fautleroy, —— Co.
Camell, Jno., 1653, by Tho. Youl, Northumberland Co.
Camell, Edmund, 1637, by Patrick Kennedye, New Norfolk Co.
Cameo, John, 1635, by Capt. Adam Thoroughgood, —— Co.
Camer, James, 1652, by Tho. Johnson, Jr., Northampton Co.
Cammell, Alex., 1650, by Mr. James Williams, —— Co.
Camnell Geo., 1653, by Wm. Memux and Demetre Murreen, —— Co.
Campeere, Grace (wife Robt. Campeere), 1637, by Richard Bennett, New Norfolk Co.
Campeere, Robt., 1637, by Rich. Bennett, New Norfolk Co.
Campton, Humphry, 1637, by James Harrison, James City Co.
Cannaday, Clement, 1642, by Thomas Loving, James City Co.
Cannaday, Jon., 1642, by Christopher Boyce, —— Co.
Canadia, Cornel., 1652, by Mr. Richard Cocke, Henrico Co.
Candeale, Robt., 1655, by Maltilda Scarbourgh, Northampton Co.
Candell, Anthony, 1656, by Sir Henry Chichley, —— Co.
Candell, Patrick, 1637, by Patrick Kennedye, New Norfolk Co.
Cane, John, 1638, by William Morgan, —— Co.
Canedy, Cornelius, 1650, by Tho. Gerrord, Gent., Northumberland Co.
Canes, Maudlin, 1638, by Edw. Sparshott, Charles City Co.
Canes, Edward, 1652, by Capt. Augustine Warner, —— Co.
Canida, Bryan, 1654, by Francis Smith and Mr. John Smith, Westmoreland Co.
Canlly, Robert, 1637, by Percival Champion, New Norfolk Co.
Cann, Tho., 1643, by Rich. Hoe, Gent., —— Co.
Cannana, Arthur, 1650, by John Smith, —— Co.
Canninge, John, 1652, by John Oliver, Isle of Wight Co.
Cannon, Edward, 1646, by Edward Hall, Lower Norfolk Co.
Cannon, Ann (wife Edw. Cannon), 1646, by Edward Hall, Lower Norfolk Co.
Cannon, Joane, 1652, by Mrs. Elinor Brocas, Lancaster Co.
Cannon, Joan, 1649, by Wm. Hoccaday, —— Co.
Canny, Richard, 1641, by Thomas Mathews, —— Co.
Cany, 1654, by Edward Cook, —— Co.
Cape, Robert,1638, by Cobb Howell, Lower New Norfolk Co.
Capell, John, 1656, by Mr. Jno. Paine, —— Co.
Caper, Wm., 1639, by William Burdett, Accomack Co.
Caper, Peter, 1652, by Mrs. Elinor Brocas, Lancaster Co.
Caps, Robt., 1645, by Wm. Jacob, Upper Norfolk Co.
Capsac, Walter, 1651, by James Allen, Northumberland Co.
Car, Wm., 1642, by John Harlow, Accomack Co.
Carr, Eliz., 1637, by James Warradine, Charles City Co.
Carby, Danny, 1656, by Wm. and Hancock Lee, Gloucester Co.
Carcott, Nich., 1650, by Stephen Charlton, Northampton Co.
Card, Mary, 1653, by John Madison, —— Co.
Carde, Robt., 1642, by Abraham Turner, —— Co.
Cardecur, Mary, 1654, by Major Miles Carey, Westmoreland Co.
Caree, Step., 1654, by Robert Yoe, Westmoreland Co.

Carilesse, Andrew, 1651, by Richard Coleman, ——— Co.
Carelesse, Joan, 1653, by Tho. Morgan, ——— Co.
Carelesse, Andrew, 1649, by Capt. Ralph Wormeley, ——— Co.
Cares, Tho., 1650, by George Pate, Charles City Co.
Caresy, Tho., 1654, by Capt. Nich. Marteaw, Westmoreland Co.
Caresy, Robt., 1654, by Capt. Nich. Marteaw, Westmoreland Co.
Caret, Micha., 1653, by Edward Hamond, Northampton Co.
Carew, Mannes, 1653, by Jno. Hansford, Gloucester Co.
Carge, Jon., 1638, by William Banister, ——— Co.
Carkawdy, Marga., 1651, by Lieut. Collo. Giles Brent, Northumberland
  Co.
Carleton, John, 1642, by John Harlowe, Northampton Co.
Carliere, John, ———, by Tho. Meares, Lower Norfolk Co.
Carlington, Joane, 1655, by Robt. Priddy, New Kent Co.
Carmake, Dan, 1654, by Coll. Jno. Matron, Westmoreland Co.
Carmen, Ludwick, 1651, by Abraham Moore and (Thomas Griffin),
  Lancaster Co.
Carnal, Angel, 1653, by Wm. Haynes, ——— Co.
Carnal, Rathal, 1653, by Wm. Haynes, ——— Co.
Carnall, Tho., 1653, by Wm. Haynes, ——— Co.
Carne, Abraham, 1638, by Hugh Allen, Charles River Co.
Carner, John, 1649, by Roger Nicholls, James City Co.
Carney, Wm., 1650, by Mr. Anthony Ellyot, ——— Co.
Carnock, Symon, 1642, by Tymothy Fenn, Isle of Wight Co.
Carnock, Mary, daughter of Symon Carnock, 1642, by Tymothy Fenn,
  Isle of Wight Co.
Carpenter, Arthur, 1652, by Mr. Peter Knight, Gloucester Co.
Carpenter, Anthony, 1655, by Nich. Wadilow, Northampton Co.
Carpenter, Alice, 1655, by Mr. Tho. Peck, Gloucester Co.
Carpenter, Mary, 1650, by Richard Axom and Tho. Godwin, ——— Co.
Carpenter, Fra., 1650, by Capt. Moore Fautleroy, ——— Co.
Carpenter, Anthony, 1652, by Nicholas Wadilow, Northampton Co.
Carpenter, Jon., 1637, by Henry Perry, Charles River Co.
Carpenter, Francis, 1642, by John Stocker, Isle of Wight Co.
Carpenter, Sy., 1654, by John Watson and John Bognall, Westmore-
  land Co.
Carpenter, Arthur, 1656, by Arthur Upshott, Northampton, Co.
Carpenter, Roger, 1643, by Sir Francis Wyatt, Kt., ——— Co.
Carpenter, Walter, 1638, by Mr. John Gookins, Upper New Norfolk Co.
Carpenter, Rich., 1637, by Capt. Thomas Panlett, Charles City Co.
Carpenter, Jon., 1637, by Henry Perry, Charles River Co.
Carpenter, John, 1636, by John Gookin, ——— Co.
Carpenter, Walter, 1637, by John Gookin, New Norfolk Co.
Caryslights, Pate, 1636, by Joane Bennett, Charles River Co.
Carr, Fra., 1652, by Tho. and Wm. Leithermore, ——— Co.
Carr, Fra., 1651, by Edmond Welch, ——— Co.
Carr, Auth., 1642, by Hugh Gwyn, Gent., ——— Co.
Carr, Antho., 1653, by Mr. Henry Soanes, Gloucester Co.
Carr, Francis, 1653, by Charles Kiggen, Yorke Co.
Carrar, Hester, 1650, by Robert Bird, ——— Co.
Carraway, Joane, 1639, by Richard Preston, Upper New Norfolk Co.

Carraway, Jon., 1642, by Christopher Boyce, ———— Co.
Carraway, John, 1644, by John Sydney, Gent., Lower Norfolk Co.
Carraway, Joane, 1644, by Toby Smith, Gent., Upper Norfolk Co.
Carre, John, 1642, by Francis Mandlin, Upper New Norfolk Co.
Carre, Wm., 1652, by Wm. Owen and Wm. Morgan, ———— Co.
Carrell, David, 1653, by Christopher Boyce, Northumberland Co.
Carrick, Richd., 1650, by Capt. Moore Fantleroy, ———— Co.
Carrill, Elizabeth, 1638, by Benjamin Carrill (her husband), James
    City Co.
Carrill, Henry, 1638, by Benjamin Carrill, James City Co.
Carrington, Michael, 1652, by James Forster and Audry Bonny, ——Co.
Carrington, Saml., 1652, by Col. Geo. Ludlow, Esq., Gloucester Co.
Carron, Hugh, 1639, by John Pawley, James City Co.
Carrow, Jon., 1643, by Capt. Samuell Mathews, Esq., ———— Co.
Cart, Wm., 1654, by Robert Hubard, Westmoreland Co.
Carter, Barb., 1649, by John Sibsey, Lower Norfolk Co.
Carter, Robt., 1649, by Stephen Gill, York Co.
Carter, Barbara, 1653, by Joseph Hogkinson, Lower Norfolk Co.
Carter, Jno., 1643, by Mr. Obedience Robins, Northampton Co.
Carter, Tho., 1654, by Mr. Mordecay Cooke, ———— Co.
Carter, Mary, 1655, by Wm. Wright, Gent., Nansemond Co.
Carter, Wm., 1655, by Mr. Tho. Peck, Gloucester Co.
Cartar, Wm., 1646, by William Hockaday, York Co.
Carter, Giles, 1653, by Mr. Wm. Fry, James City Co.
Carter, Mary, 1650, by Mr. Anthony Ellyot, ———— Co.
Carter, Richard, 1643, by Tho. Wheeler, Charles City Co.
Carter, Charles, 1643, by John Freeme, Charles Co.
Carter, Tho., 1650, by Andrew Gilson, ———— Co.
Cartar, Mandlin, 1650, by Capt. Moore Fautleroy, ———— Co.
Carter, Wm., 1648, by John Ellis, James Joones and John Taylor,
    Northampton Co.
Carter, Jon., 1653, by Wm. Johnson, Henrico Co.
Carter, Marg., 1652, by Tho. Sawyer, ———— Co.
Carter, Henry, 1639, by Lieut. Richard Popeley, ———— Co.
Carter, Wm., 1638, by Geo. Lobb, Tho. Perce and Tho. Warne, James
    City Co.
Carter, Hester, 1641, by Ambrose Bennett, Isle of Wight Co.
Carter, Henry, 1654, by Alexander Portus and Tho. Williams, Lancaster
    Co.
Carter, Thomas, 1638, by Edw. Sparshott, Charles City Co.
Carter, Rich., 1637, by Nathaniel Floyd, Isle of Wight Co.
Carter, Tho., 1638, by John Walton, Accomac Co.
Carter Richard, 1642, by John Meakes, ———— Co.
Carter, Fra., 1643, by John Neale, Gent., Northampton Co.
Carter, Wm., 1656, by Tho. Stephens, Surry Co.
Carter, John, 1644, by James Taylor and Lawrence Bake, James City
    Co.
Carter, Thos., 1637, by Arthur Smith, Isle of Wight Co.
Carter, Nath., 1638, by Robert Pitts, Isle of Wight Co.
Carter, Jon., 1635, by Reichard Peirce, James City Co.
Carter, Wm., 1636, by Edward Drew, Accomack Co.

Carter, Phillis, 1635, by Erasinees Carter, James City Co.
Carter, Michaell, 1635, by William Carter, James City Co.
Carty, Mahan, 1655, Lieut. Col. John Walker, —— Co.
Carse, Moses, 1643, by Capt. John Upton, Isle of Wight Co.
Carsino, Mich., 1638, by Edw. Travis and John Johnson, James City Co.
Cartar, Wm., 1649, by Joseph Croshawe, Yorke Co.
Carteanceaw, Jacob, Annie, his wife, John, Jacob, Wm., his sons, 1656, by Nathaniel Pope, Gent., Westmoreland Co.
Cartell, Tho., 1654, by Andrew Gibson, —— Co.
Cartigg, Richd., 1651, by Wm. Taylor, Northumberland Co.
Carts, David, 1654, by John Carr, —— Co.
Cartwright, Mr., 1650, by Sr. Tho. Luntsford, Kt. and Baronett, —— Co.
Cartwright, Tho., 1650, by Mr. James Williamson, —— Co.
Cartwright, John, 1642, by Stephen Gill, —— Co.
Cartwright, Tho., 1654, by Capt. Nich. Marteaw, Westmoreland Co.
Cartwright, Tho., 1639, by Capt. Nicholas Martran, Charles River Co.
Carey, Henry, 1656, by Tabitha and Matilda Scarburgh, Northampton Co.
Carey, Sampson, 1654, by Arthur Nash, New Kent Co.
Carey, Brid., 1654, by Mr. Tho. Fowke, Westmoreland Co.
Carey, Edw., 1654, by Mr. Tho. Fowke, Westmoreland Co.
Carey, Tho., 1653, by Richard Lee, Lancaster Co.
Carey, Wm., 1653, by Richard Carey, —— Co.
Carey, ——, 1653, by Charles Scarburg, Northampton Co.
Carey, John, 1653, by Charles Scarburgh, Northampton, Co.
Carvent, John, 1652, by Nicho. George, Tho. Taberer and Hmphrey Clarke, —— Co.
Carver, Lanc. and Eliza, his wife, 1643, by William Ewins, James City Co.
Cary, Richard, 1640, by William Hompton, Elizabeth City Co.
Cary, Richard, 1651, by Wm. Hampton, —— Co.
Cary, Meacom, 1649, by Robert Mosely, Gent., —— Co.
Cary, Hugh, 1650, by John Mangor, —— Co.
Carye, John, 1652, by Charles Scarburg, Northampton, Co.
Cascill, John, 1642, by Thomas Wombwell, James City Co.
Case, Richard, 1649, by Richard Parrett, —— Co.
Case, Elizabeth, 1653, by Jenkin Price, Northampton Co.
Case, Robt., 1654, by John Drayton, Westmoreland Co.
Case, Elizabeth, 1653, by Charles Scarburg, Northampton Co.
Casey, Rich., 1636, by Justinian Cooper, Warrasquinock Co.
Casley, Henry, 1637, by Daniell Gookins, New Norfolk Co.
Cason, John, 1653, by John Medstard and John Edwards, Northumberland Co.
Cason, Henry, 1643, by Capt. Samuell Mathews, Esq., —— Co.
Cass, John, 1639, by William Burdett, Accomack Co.
Casse, Richard, 1652, by Christopher Lewis, Isle of Wight Co.
Cassell, Humphrey, 1636, by Robert Hollom, Henrico Co.
Cassen, Ann, 1643, by John Sweete, Isle of Wight Co.
Cassens, John, 1652, by Nicholas George, —— Co.
Casey, Rich., 1637, by Justinian Cooper, Isle of Wight Co.

Caslife, Tho., 1642, by Samuell Abbott, —— Co.
Castell, Henry, 1639, by Thomas Mathews, Henrico Co.
Casteele, Wm., 1643, by Phillipp Taylor, Northampton Co.
Caster, Andrew, ——, by Mr. John Page, —— Co.
Castle, Humphrey, 1643, by Robert Haies, Lower Norfolk Co.
Castle, Robert, 1648, by Wm. Barret, —— Co.
Castle, Henry, 1653, by Richard Budd, Northumberland Co.
Castle, Tho., 1652, by Mr. Edward Overman, York Co.
Castle, Dorothy, 1639, by Tho. Symons, James City Co.
Castle, Dorothy, 1643, by Symonds, —— Co.
Castle, George, 1638, by Thomas Dewe, Upper New Norfolk Co.
Castle, Geo., 1637, by Tho. Powell, New Norfolk Co.
Castelford, Richard, 1648, by Christopher Burrows, —— Co.
Castleford Richd., 1651, by Christopher Burroughs, Lower Norfolk Co.
Castleton, Robt., 1651, by Wm. Betts, Northumberland Co.
Castleton, George, 1652, by Tho. Harwood, —— Co.
Castons, Mathew, 1651, by Audery Bennett, Nansemond Co.
Castons, Robert, 1637, by Alice Edloe, Henrico Co.
Catchman, Tho., 1650, by John Hany, Northumberland Co.
Catchman, Tho., 1635, by Mr. Geo. White, minister of the word of God,
      —— Co.
Catchmett, Tho., 1653, by Jervais Jones, Northumberiand Co.
Cater, Georg, 1642, by John Ewens, Jr., Charles City Co.
Caterer, Chas., 1648, by Lewis Burwell and Tho. Haws, York River Co.
Catesby, Robt., 1654, by Arthur Nash, New Kent Co.
Catesly, Jane, 1636, by John Chandler, Elizabeth Citie Co.
Cathrell, Mary, 1649, by Wm. Nesum, Tho. Fox, Miles Bathasly and
      John Pyne, Northampton Co.
Cathrell, Edw., 1636, by Capt. John Chelsman, Charles River Co.
Catlett, Nicho., 1650, by John Catlett and Ralph Rousey, —— Co.
Cattan, Nehemiah, 1654, by Obed. Williams, York Co.
Cattan, Sam., 1648, by Thomas Woodhouse, James City Co.
Cattle, Thomas, 1635, by John Parrott, —— Co.
Cattlett, John, 1653, by Charles Grymes, Lancaster Co.
Cansly, Thomas, 1636, by Rich. Peirce, James City Co.
Cansey, Tho., 1640, by Thomas Harvey, James City Co.
Cansey, John, 1635, by Wm. Berriman, Accomacke Co.
Causington, Walter, 1652, by Joane Yates, Lower Norfolk Co.
Causon, Nehemiah, 1643, by James Whiting, —— Co.
Cautrey, Wm., 1653, by Abraham Moon, Lancaster Co.
Cautrill, Phil., 1654, by Col. Argoll Yardley, Northampton Co.
Cave, Patrick, 1639, by Henry Perry, Charles City Co.
Cave, Marg., 1651, by Col. Guy Molsworth, —— Co.
Cavalier, Isaac, 1650, by Sr. Tho. Luntsford, Kt. and Barronett,
      —— Co.
Cavide, John, 1652, by Col. Geo. Ludlow, Esq., Gloucester Co.
Cawch, Lyon, 1652, by John Pouncey, —— Co.
Cawker, John, 1637, by Thom. Shippey, Henrico Co.
Cawling, Jos., 1650, by Capt. Moore Fautleroy, —— Co.
Ceely, Margery, 1640, by Toby Smith, Warwick River Co.
Ceely, Wm., 1652, by Wm. Moore, —— Co.

Cesar, Mary, 1653, by Francis Grey, Charles City Co.
Cess, John, 1655, by Francis Clay, Gent., Northumberland Co.
Chadwell, Dan., 1653, by Sampson Robins, Northampton Co.
Chadwell, Ann, 1651, by Palmer Hinton, ———— Co.
Chadworth, Tho., 1643, by Mr. Phillipp Bennett, Upper Norfolk Co.
Challice, James, 1653, by Tho. Hawkins, ———— Co.
Challenge, Sam., 1654, by Richard Hawkins, Westmoreland Co.
Challenge, Marjery, 1654, by Richard Hawkins, Westmoreland Co.
Challis, Edward, 1639, by Edward Panderson, ———— Co.
Chaloys, Sisly, 1655, by Henry Barlow, ———— Co.
Chaloys, Sisly, 1655, by John Lynge, James City Co.
Chamberlain, Leon, 1637, by William Frye, James City Co.
Chamberlin, Christ., 1643, by Capt. Samuell Mathews, Esq., ———— Co.
Chamberlin, Wm., 1652, by Peter Knight, Gloucester Co.
Chamberlane, Jon., 1643, by Richard Kemp, Esq., James City Co.
Chambers, Robt., 1655, by John Wyere, Lancaster Co.
Chambers, Nath., 1653, by Capt. Robt. Abrahal, Gloucester Co.
Chambers, Jon., 1654, by Robert Holt, James City Co.
Chambers, Marg., 1650, by David Peibles, Charles City Co.
Chambers, Francis, 1642, by Hugh Gwyn, Gent., ———— Co.
Chambers, Francis, 1656, by John Bromfeild, James City Co.
Chambers, Daniel, 1654, by John Grey, Northampton Co.
Chambers, John, 1642, by Stephen Gill, ———— Co.
Chambers, John, 1639, by Robert Rockwell, Upper New Norfolk Co.
Chambers, Jon., 1637, by Thomas Causey, Charles City Co.
Chambers, Francis, 1637, by Edward Travis, James City Co.
Chamber, Margery, 1652, by Mr. Peter Knight, Gloucester Co.
Chamber, Robert, 1639, by Georg Mallen, James City Co.
Chamby, Ann, 1651, by Robert Vans, Gent., Yorke Co.
Chamleich, Cha., 1652, by Mrs. Mary Brent, Northumberland Co.
Chamnes, John, 1652, by John Gresham, Northumberland Co.
Champion, John, 1643, by Richard Jackson, Isle of Wight Co.
Champion, Mary, 1637, by Arthur Smith, Isle of Wight Co.
Champion, Edward, 1638, by Thomas Swan, James Citie Co.
Champion, Mary, 1637, by Percival Champion (her husband), New
    Norfolk Co.
Champion, John, 1635, by Daniel Cugley, Accomac Co.
Champion, Pascal, 1652, by Mr. Tho. Gutheridge, Lower Norfolk Co.
Champin, Edw., 1635, by Wm. Swan, James Co.
Champins, Francis, 1637, Margaret Rogers, New Norfolk Co.
Chandler, Eliz., 1636, by John Chandler, Elizabeth City Co.
Chandler, Susan, 1642, by Peter Johnson, New Norfolk Co.
Chandler, Wm., 1641, by Tho. Mathews, ———— Co.
Chandler, Job., ————, by Mr. Robt. Fontaine, Lower Norfolk Co.
Chandler, Arthur, 1656, by Sir Henry Chichley, ———— Co.
Chandler, Joh., 1651, by John Martin and (Lancaster Lovett), Lower
    Norfolk Co.
Chandler, Richard, 1651, by Abraham Moone and (Thomas Griffin),
    Lancaster Co.
Chandler, Nicho., 1653, by Evan Davis and Henry Nicholls, Lancaster
    Co.

Chandler, John, 1652, by Richard King, Lower Norfolk Co.
Chandler, Daniel, 1652, by Tho. Hoane, ——— Co.
Chandler, Sarah, 1652, by Tho. Hoane, ——— Co.
Chandler, Anth., 1650, by Mr. Stephen Hamelin, Charles City Co.
Chandler, Ann, 1649, by Mr. Tho. Spake, Northumberland Co.
Chandler, Thos., 1635, by Capt. Adam Thoroughgood, ——— Co.
Chandly, Wm. (servant), 1638, by Thom. Plomer and Samuell Edmonds, James City Co.
Chaner, Phillipp, 1637, by Henry Hart, James Citie Co.
Chanke, John, 1635, by Mr. Willis Heyly, ——— Co.
Chant, Andrew, 1635, by Capt. Adam Thoroughgood, ——— Co.
Chant, Andrew, 1636, by Joane Bennett, Charles River Co.
Chantry, Richd., 1650, by Capt. Charles Leech, Yorke Co.
Chantry, Richard, 1656, by George Kibble, Lancaster Co.
Chapleman, Mary, 1650, by Mr. Epaphroditus Lawson, ——— Co.
Chaplin, Sarah, 1639, by William Parry, Elizabeth City Co.
Chaplin, John, 1651, by Phillip Cleades, James City Co.
Chaplyn, Robt., 1637, by Capt. Thomas Panlett, Charles City Co.
Chapman, Pascal, 1645, by William Jones, Northampton, Co.
Chapman, Richard, 1645, by William Jones, Northampton Co.
Chapman, Alex., 1638, by Stephen Charlton, Accomack Co.
Chapman, Barbary, 1638, by Joseph Moore, Elizabeth City Co.
Chapman, Adam, 1655, by Ralph Green, New Kent Co.
Chapman, Phill, 1637, by Daniell Gookins, New Norfolk Co.
Chapman, Tho., 1637, by Leonard Yeo, Elizabeth City Co.
Chapman, Barbary, 1636, by Joseph Moore, Elizabeth Citie Co.
Chapman, Jon., 1636, by Richard Cocke, ——— Co.
Chapman, John, 1639, by Geo. Minifye, Esq., Charles River Co.
Chapman, Barbary, 1642, by Thomas Symmons, ——— Co.
Chapman, Roger, 1639, by Richard Corke, Gent., Henrico Co.
Chapman, John, 1642, by John Beale, ——— Co.
Chapman, Humphry, 1640, by Thomas Stegg, Charles City Co.
Chapman, Mathew, 1642, by John Meakes, ——— Co.
Chapman, John, 1656, by Wm. Bird, ——— Co.
Chapman, Wm., 1656, by Richard Gible, Northumberland Co.
Chapman, John, 1651, by Richard Coleman, Yorke Co.
Chapman, Robert, 1651, by Capt. Stephen Gill, Northumberland Co.
Chapman, Tho., 1652, by Richard Coleman, ——— Co.
Chapman, Richard, 1652, by Mr. Tho. Gutheridge, Lower Norfolk Co.
Chapman, Mr. Wm., 1649, by Mr. Tho. Spake, Northumberland Co.
Chapman, Winter, 1649, by Tho. Spake, Gent., Northumberland Co.
Chapman, Tho., 1643, by Mr. Obedience Robins, Northampton Co.
Chapman, Nich., 1655, by Wm. Wright, Gent., Nansemond Co.
Chappell, Robt., 1639, by Richard Nance, Henrico Co.
Chappell, John, 1638, by Robert Freeman, James City Co.
Chappell, John, 1638, by Richard Wilcox, James City Co.
Chappell, Robt., 1642, by Capt. Samuell Mathews, Esq., ——— Co.
Chappell, Tho., 1650, by Richard Tye and Charles Sparrowe, Charles City Co.
Chappell, John, by Mr. Wm. Presly, Northumberland Co.

Chargwell, Samuell, 1638, by John Batts and John Davis, Charles River Co.
Charke, Richard, 1636, by Mr. Georg Menifye, James City Co.
Charles, Wm., 1638, by Robert Freeman, James City Co.
Charles, John, 1637, by Phillip Taylor, Accomack Co.
Charles, Wm., 1643, by Thomas Glascocke, ——— Co.
Charles, John, 1651, by Coll. Richard Lee, Gent., Gloucester Co.
Charles, Tho., 1652, by Nathaniel Bacon, Isle of Wight Co.
Charles, John, 1650, by Andrew Gilson, ——— Co.
Charles, Jo., ———, by Tho. Lucas, ——— Co.
Charlott, Hanafitts, 1653, by Oliver Segar and Fra. Brown, ——— Co.
Charnocke, John, 1643, by Tho. Williams, ——— Co.
Charnold, Tho., 1653, by Peter Knight and Baker Cutt, ——— Co.
Charter, John, 1638, by John Rolins, ——— Co.
Chaters, Fra., 1653, by Maj. Wm. Lewis, ——— Co.
Chase, Huedy, 1652, by Tho. Cartwright, Lower Norfolk Co.
Chase, Wm., 1652, by Mr. Tho. Purifye and Mrs. Temperence Reppitt, ——— Co.
Chatworth, Roger, 1654, by R. Lawson, ——— Co.
Chausler, John, 1649, by James Miller, ——— Co.
Cheaning, Robert, 1649, by Richard Kemp, Esq. (Sec. of State.) ——— Co.
Check, Hugh, 1648, by Wm. Ewen, James City Co.
Cheesome, Richard, 1643, by William Botts, ——— Co.
Cheesman, Edward, 1637, by Francis Morgan, Charles River Co.
Cheffeild, Anne, 1652, by Anthony Hoskins, Northampton Co.
Cheines, Margt., 1655, by Mr. Tho. Peck, Gloucester Co.
Cheins, Martin, 1654, by Major Miles Carey, Westmoreland Co.
Chelmedge, Wm., 1656, by Sir Henry Chichley, ——— Co.
Chenner, Nicho., 1653, by Robt. Sorrel, ——— Co.
Cherrick, Domine, 1652, by Tho. Boswell, ——— Co.
Cherry, Franc., 1643, by Georg Levitt, ——— Co.
Cherry, John, 1637, by Oliver Sprye, New Norfolk Co.
Cherry, Richard, 1655, by Mrs. Margaret Brent, Lancaster Co.
Chesee, Holliday, 1652, by Tho. Stevens, Lancaster Co.
Chesly, Hen., 1650, by Tho. Gerrord, Gent., Northumberland Co.
Chessheire, Robert, 1635, by McWilliam Stone, ——— Co.
Cheetood, John, 1651, by John Ward, Charles City Co.
Cheton, Marke, 1642, by Daniell Lewellyn, ——— Co.
Chetter, Phillip, 1656, by John Wood, ——— Co.
Chevell, Thomas, 1649, by Wm. Nessum, Tho. Sax, Miles Bathasby and John Pyne, Northampton Co.
Cheverell, Tho., 1651, by John Adleston, ——— Co.
Chew, John, 1623, by John Chew, Gent., Charles River Co.
Chew, John, 1622, by John Chew, Gent., Charles River Co.
Chewning, Geo., 1636, by John Chandler, Elizabeth Citie Co.
Cheynay, Robert, 1639, by Richard Corke, Gent., Henrico Co.
Cheyny, Robert, 1636, by Richard Cocke, ——— Co.
Chichester, Wm., 1652, by Wm. Up. Thomas, ——— Co.
Chigain, Wm., 1641, by Garrett Stephens, Warwick River Co.
Chilcott, Thomas, 1635, by McWilliam Stone, ——— Co.

Chilcurne, Wm., 1652, by Littleton Scarburg, ——— Co.
Child, Richard, 1635, by Stephen Webb, ——— Co.
Child, Tho., 1638, by John Jackson and Eliza Freeman, James City Co.
Child, John, 1652, by Henry Smith, Jr., ——— Co.
Child, Tho., 1652, by Mr. Geo. Foster, Northumberland Co.
Child, Thos., 1642, by Adam Cooke, Charles County.
Childe, Ann, 1654, by Valentine Patten, Westmoreland Co.
Child, Ann, 1654, by Robert Hubard, Westmoreland Co.
Childs, Richard, 1639, by Samuell Almond, Henrico Co.
Childs, Richd., 1637, by Arthur Bayly and Tho. Crosby, Henrico Co.
Childredge, Wm., 1650, by Mr. Stephen Hamelin, Charles City Co.
Childecock, John, 1656, by Wm. Crump and Mr. Humphry Vault, James City Co.
Chiles, Walter, Jr., 1638, by Walter Chiles, Charles Citie Co.
Chiles, Eliza, 1638, by Walter Chiles, Charles Citie Co.
Chiles, Wm., 1638, by Walter Chiles, Charles Citie Co.
Chiles, Walter, Sr., 1638, by Walter Chiles, Charles Citie Co.
Chiles, Geo., 1651, by Ashwell Battin, Yorke Co.
Chiles, Susan, 1653, by Wm. and George Worsman, Henrico Co.
Chiles, Sarah, 1653, by Wm. and George Worsman, Henrico Co.
Chiles, Law., 1650, by Capt. Moore Fautleroy, ——— Co.
Chilinan, Nicholas, 1646, by Col. Henry Bishopp, James City Co.
Chilton, Stephen, 1650, by Anthony Fuljam, ——— Co.
Chipnell, Joseph, 1650, by Geo. Ludlow, Esq., Northumberland Co.
Chisston, Paule, 1650, by Nicho. Jernew, Yorke Co.
Chiter, Anne, 1652, by Edward Hall, Lower Norfolk Co.
Chitwood, Wm., 1636, by Izabell Thresher, ——— Co.
Chiverfall, Hum., 1655, by Mr. Anthony Langston, New Kent Co.
Chovell, James, 1651, by Robert Cade, ——— Co.
Christian, Richard, 1643, by Capt. Samuell Mathews, Esq., ——— Co.
Christian, Wm., 1652, by Mrs. Jane Harmen, Northumberland Co.
Christo, Burston, 1636, by John Gater, Elizabeth City Co.
Chrisippe, Jno., 1645, by John Rode, Warwick, Co.
Christmas, Isabell, 1635, by Victoris Christmas, Elizabeth City Co.
Christmas, Rich., 1637, by Capt. Henry Browne, James City Co.
Christmas, Isabell, wife of Victoris Christmas, 1642, by Victoris Christmas and Francis Finch, ——— Co.
Chubb, Mary, 1651, by Robert Vans, Gent., Yorke Co.
Chudworth, Bridget, 1653, by Major John Westhrope, Charles City Co.
Chuebett, Eliz., 1651, by Christopher Burroughs, Lower Norfolk Co.
Chumer, Cuthbert, 1651, by Abraham Moone and (Thomas Griffin), Lancaster Co.
Church, Thomas, 1645, by James Bruss, Northampton Co.
Church, Samuel, 1636, by Wm. Clarke, Henrico Co.
Church, Martin, 1639, by Lieut. Richard Popeley, ——— Co.
Church, Elizabeth, 1655, by Moses Synton, Lower Norfolk Co.
Church, Nicho., 1650, by Sr. Tho. Luntsford, Kt. and Barronett, ——— Co.
Church, Henry, 1650, by Richard, Hull, ——— Co.
Church, Wm., 1653, by Abraham Moone, Lancaster Co.
Church, Wm., 1653, by Wm. Hardidge, Northumberland Co.

Churchwell, Samuell, 1651, by Henry Hackery, ——— Co.
Chycott, Phill., 1652, by Mr. Tho. Brice, Lancaster Co.
Cicann, Davis, 1642, by Abraham English, ——— Co.
Cicks, James, 1643, by Wm. Brooke, Upper Norfolk Co.
Cistner, Adam, 1637, by John Broche, Charles River Co.
Cittinge, Jno., 1653, by Capt. Francis Putt, Northampton Co.
Civill, Tho., 1652, by Mr. Geo. Foster, Northumberland Co.
Clanc, Tho. 1648, by Geo. Hardey, Tho. Wombwell and Peter Hall,
    Isle of Wight Co.
Clanly, Nicho., 1648, by Tho. Lambert, Lower Norfolk Co.
Clansey, James, 1638, by Epaphroditus Lawson, Upper New Norfolk
    Co.
Clannon, Geo., 1638, by John Bough, Henrico Co.
Clanterne, Edward, 1656, by Wm. Bird, ——— Co.
Clapp, Elija, 1648, by Lewis Burwell, Gent., ——— Co.
Clapps, Thom., 1651, by Mr. Wm. Armestead, ——— Co.
Clapham, Margery, 1655, by Lt. Col. Anthony Ellyott, ——— Co.
Clare, John, 1649, by Joseph Croshawe, Yorke Co.
Clare, John, 1651, by Joseph Croshaw, Yorke Co.
Clarford, Jno., 1650, by Bertram Obert, ——— Co.
Clark, John, 1654, by Major Miles Carey, Westmoreland Co.
Clarke, Nich., 1651, by Geo. Trahett and Henry Edwards, Northampton
    Co.
Clarke, Elizabeth, 1646, by Lucy Webster, Judith and Jane Webster,
    James City Co.
Clarke, John, 1644, by John Sydney, Gent., Lower Norfolk Co.
Clarke, John, 1638, by Joseph Boarne, Charles City Co.
Clarke, Mary, 1638, by Phillipp Clarke, James City Co.
Clarke, Elija, 1638, by Phillip Clarke, James City Co.
Clarke, Thomas, by Robt. Throckmorton, Charles River Co.
Clarke, Edward, 1637, by Henry Perry, Charles River Co.
Clarke, Eliz., 1637, by Capt. Thomas Panlett, Charles City Co.
Clarke, Wm., 1637, by Daniell Gookins, New Norfolk Co.
Clarke, Edward, 1638, by Randall Crew, Upper New Norfolk Co.
Clarke, Nicho., 1635, by Wm. Garry, Accomack Co.
Clarke, Douglass, 1637, by Hugh Wynn, Isle of Wight Co.
Clarke, Nathaniell, 1637, by Joseph Jolly, Charles River Co.
Clarke, Robt., 1636, by John Seaward, Isle of Wight Co.
Clarke, Richard, 1635, by George Minifie, James City Co.
Clarke, John, 1635, by Jno. Sparkes, ——— Co.
Clark, George, 1636, by James Vanerit, Elizabeth City Co.
Clarke, George, 1635, by John Parrott, ——— Co.
Clarke, John, 1637, by John Baker, Henrico Co.
Clarke, Uriah, 1636, by Robert Hollom, Henrico Co.
Clarke, Nathaniell, 1636, by Joseph Jolly, Charles River Co.
Clarke, Tho., 1639, by John Kempe, James City Co.
Clarke, Michaell, 1642, by Richard Gregson, Elizabeth City Co.
Clarke, Edward, 1638, by Cobb Howell, Lower New Norfolk Co.
Clarke, Charles, 1638, by Cobb Howell, Lower New Norfolk Co.
Clarke, David, 1638, by Lieut. John Upton, Isle of Wight Co.
Clarke, Thom., 1637, by Robert Throckmorton, Charles River Co.

Clarke, Edw., 1637, by Henry Perry, Charles River Co.
Clarke, Alex., 1638, by Georg Mynifie (merchant), ——— Co.
Clark, Pa., 1655, by John Lawson, Lancaster Co.
Clarke, Wm., 1655, by Southy Littleberry, Northampton Co.
Clarke, Annis, 1655, by Sampson Robins, Northampton Co.
Clarke, Fra., 1650, by Daniell Luellin, Charles City Co.
Clarke, John, 1646, by Edward Hall, Lower Norfolk Co.
Clarke, Rich., 1643, by Richard Kemp, Esq., James City Co.
Clarke, Edw., 1643, by Capt. Samuell Mathews, Esq., ——— Co.
Clarke, John, 1651, by Edward Deggs, Esq., Yorke Co.
Clarke, Daniell, 1650, by Mr. Robt. Holt, James City Co.
Clarke, James, 1651, by Ashwell Battin, Yorke Co.
Clarke, Henry, 1651, by Mr. John Walker, ——— Co.
Clarke, Mary, 1653, by Edward Hamond, Northampton Co.
Clarke, Wm., 1653, by Richard Slaughter, Nansemond Co.
Clarke, Edmond, 1653, by John Dipdall, Charles City Co.
Clarke, Tho., 1652, by Lawrence Dameron, Northumberland Co.
Clarke, Danl., 1652, by Richard Coleman, ——— Co.
Clarke, John, 1653, by Robert Bouth, Yorke Co.
Clarke, Tho., 1650, by Richard Jacob, Northampton Co.
Clarke, Dorothy, 1650, by Silvester Thatcher and Tho. Whitlocke, ——— Co.
Clarke, Richard, 1650, by William Gooch, Gent., ——— Co.
Clarke, John, 1650, by Geo. Ludlow, Esq., Northumberland Co.
Clarke, Patrick, 1650, by Epa. Lawson, ——— Co.
Clarke, Hum., 1650, by Robert Bird, ——— Co.
Clarke, Robert, 1650, by Robert Bird, ——— Co.
Clarke, Samuell, 1650, by Wm. Yarrett and Fra. Willington, ——— Co.
Clarke, Randall, 1642, by John Sweete, ——— Co.
Clarke, Edward, 1649, by Capt. Randall Harle, Northampton Co.
Clarke, James, 1649, by Tho. Bourne, ——— Co.
Clarke, Jo., 1649, by Rich. Croshaw, Yorke Co.
Clarke, Nicholas, 1649, by Richard Kemp, Esq. (Sec. of State), ——— Co.
Clarke, Dorothy, 1649, by George Burcher, Charles City Co.
Clarke, Ann, 1648, by Geo. Hardy, ——— Co.
Clarke, Robert, 1648, by Tho. Lambert, Lower Norfolk Co.
Clarke, James, 1652, by Mr. Peter Knight, Gloucester Co.
Clarke, Saml., 1652, by Mr. Peter Knight, Gloucester Co.
Clarke, Brian, 1652, by Littleton Scarburg, ——— Co.
Clarke, John, 1652, by Mr. John Cheesman, ——— Co.
Clarke, Fra., 1653, by Wm. Havett, ——— Co.
Clarke, Wm., 1653, by John Edwards, Lancaster Co.
Clarke, Hen., 1653, by John Debar, ——— Co.
Clarke, Mary, 1653, by John Edwards, Lancaster Co.
Clarke, Wm., 1653, by Abraham Moon, Lancaster Co.
Clarke, Wm., 1654, by John Wyre, John Gillett, Andrew Gilson and John Phillipps, ——— Co.
Clarkson, Jane, 1638, by John Clarkson, Charles River Co.
Clarkson, Ann, 1638, by John Clarkson, Charles River Co.
Clarkson, Ann (widow), 1638, by John Clarkson, Charles River Co.

Clarkson, John, 1649, by Wm., Peerce and Frances Symons, North-
umberland Co.
Clarister, Jon., 1636, by John Chandler, Elizabeth Citie Co.
Clartes, John, 1654, by Andrew Gibson, ——— Co.
Clary, Tho., 1642, by John King, Charles River Co.
Clarye, Tho., 1653, by John Day, Gloucester Co.
Clason, John, 1637, by John Baker, Charles City Co.
Claton, Peter, 1653, by Richard Budd, Northumberland Co.
Clay, John, 1654, by Coll. Jno. Matrom, Westmoreland Co.
Clay, Jon., 1642, by Thomas Guyer, ——— Co.
Clay, Jno., 1643, by Benjamin Harryson, Gent., James City Co.
Clay, Thomas, 1646, by Edward Hall, Lower Norfolk Co.
Clay, Mrs. Francis, 1652, by Edward Coles, Northumberland Co.
Clay, Edward, 1650, by John Hany, Northumberland Co.
Clayborne, Edw., 1636, by William Julian, Elizabeth City Co.
Claybourne, Wm., 1654, by Robert Yoe, Westmoreland Co.
Clayden, Ellean, 1638, by John George, Charles City Co.
Clayer, Jon., 1635, by John Moone, Warrasquinoake Co.
Clayre, Wm., 1653, by Peter Knight and Baker Cult, ——— Co.
Clayton, Rich., 1637, by Edward Tunstall, Henrico Co.
Clayton, Thos., 1637, by William Spencer, ——— Co.
Clayton, Thomas, 1635, by William Spencer, ——— Co.
Clayton, Rich., 1636, Edward Tonstall, ——— Co.
Clayton, William, 1651, by Tho. Tharnbrough, Northumberland Co.
Clave, Phillip, 1648, by Thomas Hart, James City Co.
Clavery, Andrew, 1650, by Richard Jacobs, Northampton, Co.
Cleake, Tho., 1650, by Richard Budd, Northumberland Co.
Cleaves, Jno., 1653, by Tho., Youel, Northumberland Co.
Cleaves, Tho., 1653, by Francis Clay, Northumberland Co.
Clemby, John, 1648, by Tho. Ludwell, Gent., James City Co.
Clement, Rich., 1640, by John Holloway, Accumack Co.
Clement, Margaritt, 1635, by Thos. Shippey, ——— Co.
Clement, John, 1635, by Jeremiah Clement, ——— Co.
Clement, Edey, 1635, by Jeremiah Clement (her husband), ——— Co.
Clement, Robert, 1638, by Thomas Boulding, Elizabeth City Co.
Clements, Margery, 1650, by Lieut. Wm. Worleich, ——— Co.
Clements, Richard, 1651, by Roger Johns, Northumberland Co.
Clements, Cornelius, 1643, by John Freeme, Charles Co.
Clements, Ezekiel, 1643, by Jeremiah Clement, James City Co.
Clements, Amey, 1643, by Jeremiah Clements, James City Co.
Clements, Rich., 1636, by Wm. Armistead, Elizabeth City Co.
Clements, Robert, 1639, by Tho. Boulding, Elizabeth City Co.
Clemens, John, 1650, by Robert Bleake and Samuell Elridge, Isle of
Wight Co.
Clemere Mark, 1638, by John Robins, James City Co.
Cleopman, Wm., 1637, by Arthur Smith, Isle of Wight Co.
Cleote, Thos., 1635, by Pierce Lemun, Charles City Co.
Clerck, Elizabeth, 1656, by Silvester Thatcher, ——— Co.
Clere, James, 1655, by Tho. Hale, Northumberland Co.
Clerk, Wm., 1655, by John Withers, Westmoreland Co.
Clerk, Robert, 1654, by Mrs. Fra. Harrison, widow, Westmoreland Co.

Clerk, John, 1654, by Rich. Bunduch, Northumberland Co.
Clerk, Tho., 1654, by Col. Henry Higgenson, Esq., and Abraham Moone, Westmoreland Co.
Clerk, Anthony, 1655, by Tho. Everidge, ――― Co.
Clerke, Richard, 1655, by Mr. Anthony Langston, New Kent Co.
Clerke, James, 1655, by Mrs. Margaret Brent, Lancaster Co.
Clerke, Richard, 1645, by William Daynes, Lower Norfolk Co.
Clerke, James, 1655, by John Watson, Lancaster Co.
Clerke, Wm., 1654, by Nich. Merywether, Westmoreland Co.
Clerke, John, 1653, by Roger Walter, Northumberland Co.
Clerke, James, 1654, by Richard Walker, ――― Co.
Clerke, John, 1653, by Eppy Bonison, Lancaster Co.
Clerke, Robt., 1653, by Maj. Wm. Lewis, ――― Co.
Clerke John, 1652, by Richard Coleman, ――― Co.
Clerke, Mary, 1653, by Mr. Anthony Langston, New Kent Co.
Clerke, Robt., 1653, by Roger Walker, Northumberland Co.
Clerke, Jon., 1653, by Tho. Holmes, York Co.
Clerke, Wm., 1653, by Nicho. Meriwether, Northumberland Co.
Clerke, Mary, 1652, by Tho. Hoane, ――― Co.
Clerke, Joseph, 1652, by Capt. Francis Morgan and Ralph Green Gloucester Co.
Clerke, Wm., 1652, by Mrs. Mary Brent, Northumberland Co.
Cleriton, Mary, 1636, by Justinian Cooper, Warrasquinook Co.
Clevedon, Wm., 1642, by Capt. Samuell Mathews, Esq., ――― Co.
Clever, Tho., 1655, by Francis Clay, Gent., Northumberland Co.
Clewley, Eliz., 1643, by Casar Puggett, Lower Norfolk Co.
Clewmore, Tymothy, 1650, by Tho. Vans, Gent., Northumberland Co.
Cley, John, 1639, by Henry Bogwell, Accomack Co.
Cliffe, Nich., 1638, by Elizabeth Grayne, Charles City Co.
Clifford, Oliver, 1640, by William Hampton, Isle of Wight Co.
Clifford, Martin, 1654, by Mr. Francis Hamond, York Co.
Clifton, Thomas, 1638, by William Berryman, Accomack Co.
Clifton, Paul, 1650, by Nicholas Jernew, Gent., ―――Co.
Clifton, Ye Lady, 1648, by Lewis Burwell and Tho. Haws, York River Co.
Clinn Cillina, 1656, by Tabitha and Matild Scarbough, Northampton Co.
Clint, John, 1654, by Mr. Francis Hamond, York Co.
Clinton, Mary, 1637, by Justinian Cooper, Isle of Wight Co.
Clinton, Cornelius, 1656, by Nicholas Waddilow, Northampton Co.
Clisse, Eliz., 1654, by John Watson and John Bognall, Westmoreland Co.
Clocke, Thomas, 1643, by Capt. Samuell Mathews, Esq., ――― Co.
Clockett, Leonard, 1638, by Wm. Morgan, ――― Co.
Clooke, Thomas, 1636, by John Laydon, Warwick River Co.
Closly, Eliz., 1650, by Lewis Burwell, Gent., Northumberland Co.
Closse, Patrick, 1641, by Thomas Bernard, Warwick River Co.
Clothier, Richard, 1653, by Geo. Cable, ――― Co.
Cloud, Robert, 1643, by Rich. Hoe, Gent., ――― Co.
Clurton, Stephen, 1650, by Tho. Wilkinson, ――― Co.
Clowdley, Wm., 1650, by John Lacker, ――― Co.

Clowman, Edmd., 1652, by Mrs. Jane Harmer, Northumberland Co.
Cloyd, Henry, 1648, by Richard Lee, Gent., ——— Co.
Coach, Fra., 1653, by Wm. Hunt, ——— Co.
Coale, Tho., 1653, by Robert Tomlin, ——— Co.
Coape, John, 1650, by Capt. Ishiell Linch, ——— Co.
Coard, Wm., 1655, by Christopher Calvert, Northampton Co.
Coate, Abraham, 1642, by John Benton, ——— Co.
Coates, John, 1650. by Henry Peaseley, ——— Co.
Coats, Jon., 1643, by William Ewins, James City Co.
Coax, Gabriell, 1652, by Wm. Ginsey, Gloucester Co.
Cob, John, 1637, by Cheney Boyes, Charles City Co.
Cobb, Eliza., 1637, by Joseph Cobb, Isle of Wight Co.
Cobb, Joseph (Jun.), 1637, by Joseph Cobb, Isle of Wight Co.
Cobb, Benjamin, 1637, Joseph Cobb, his father, Isle of Wight Co.
Cobb, Eliza., 1637, by Joseph Cobb, Isle of Wight Co.
Cobb, Mary, 1655, by Robert Castle, James City Co.
Cobb, Thomas, 1648, by Peter Knight, Isle of Wight Co.
Cobb, John, 1650, by John Major, Northampton Co.
Cobb, Andrew, 1649, by Stephen Gill, York Co.
Cobb, Tho., 1652, by Mr, Peter Knight, Gloucester Co.
Cobb, John, 1654, by John Phillips and John Batts, Lancaster Co.
Cobbre, John, 1650, by Wm. Holder, ——— Co.
Cobbs, Robert, 1639, by Ambrose Cobbs, his father, Henrico Co.
Cobbs, Margarett, 1639 by Ambrose Cobbs, her father, Henrico Co.
Cobbs, Ann, 1639, by Ambrose Cobbs, her husband, Henrico Co.
Cobe, Erasmas, 1649, by Capt, Ralph Wormeley, ——— Co.
Cobin, Christopher, 1655, by Wm. Wright, Gent., Nansemond Co.
Coblier, Daniell, 1637, by Cheney Boyes, Charles City Co.
Coblins, Daniell, 1636, by Cheney Boyse, Charles City Co.
Cock, Dale, James, 1649, by Mr. Robert Parker, Northampton Co.
Cock, Edward, 1648, by Tho. Browne, York Co.
Cock, Ann, 1642, John Bayles, ——— Co.
Cock, Lewis, 1638, by Francis Morgan, Charles River Co.
Cock, Richard, 1642, by Thomas Osborne, Henrico Co.
Cock, Robt., 1656, by Mr. Henry Soanes, New Kent Co.
Cocks, Edward, 1651, by Ashwell Battin, Yorke Co.
Cockcroft, Geo., 1641, by Richard Jackson, Isle of Wight Co.
Cocker, Wm., 1637, John Wilkins, New Norfolk Co.
Cocker, Lancet, 1652, by Anthony Doney and Enoch Hawker, Lancaster Co.
Cockery, John, 1652, by Wm. Moore, ——— Co.
Cockett, Robt., 1636, by Capt. John Chelsman, Charles River Co.
Cockett, Samuell, 1639, by John Pawley, James City Co.
Cockett, Henry, 1653, by Nicho. Meriwether, Northumberland Co.
Cocket, Henry, 1654, by Rich. Merywether, Westmoreland Co.
Cocket, Arthur, 1654, by Nich. Merywether, Westmoreland Co.
Cocket, James, 1654, by Nich. Merywether, Westmoreland Co.
Cockham, Geo., 1653, by John Gillett, Lancaster Co.
Cockman, Wm., 1653, by James Bonner, Lancaster Co.
Cockney, Stephen, 1649, by John Trussells, ——— Co.
Cockorum, Wm., 1639, by Robert Eley, Isle of Wight Co.

Cockrum, James, 1653, by Fredinando Austin, Charles City Co.
Cocksholt, Edward, 1635, by Capt. Wm. Pierse, ——— Co.
Cocwrick, Mary, 1650, by Mr. Epaphoditus Lawson, ——— Co.
Codd, Geo., 1643, by Capt. Thomas Pettus, ——— Co.
Code, Walter, and wife, 1648, by Wm. M. Thomas, Elizabeth City Co.
Codne, Mary, 1642, by Capt. Daniell Gookin, ——— Co.
Cody, Tho., 1651, by George Ludlow, Esq., ——— Co.
Coe, Susanna, 1655, by Lt. Col. Tho. Swan, Surry Co.
Coe, Sarah, 1655, by Lt. Col. Tho. Swan, Surry Co.
Coe, Timothy, 1652, by Mr. John Brown, Northampton Co.
Coe, Sarah, 1656, by Hester Obkham, James City Co.
Cofface, Abr., 1653, by Maj. Wm. Lewis, ——— Co.
Coffee, John, 1637, by Nicholas Hill, Eliz. City Co.
Coffin, Anne, 1650, by Silvester Thatcher and Tho. Whitlocke, ———
    Co.
Coffin, Francis, 1635, by Thomas Smith, James Co.
Coge, Peter, 1649, by Wm. Horcaday, ——— Co.
Coggin, Sarah, 1638, by William Clarke, Charles River Co.
Coggin, Tho., 1642, by Francis England, Isle of Wight Co.
Cogun, Fra., 1653, by Roger Walter, Northumberland Co.
Coheane, John, 1653, by Henry Corbele, Gloucester Co.
Coker, John, 1636, by Justinian Cooper, Warrasqunoah Co.
Colebourne, John, 1654, by Toby Smith, Lancaster Co.
Colby, Ann, 1655, by Major Wm. Horcaday, New Kent Co.
Colchester, Ann, 1643, by Thomas Wheeler, Charles City Co.
Colchester, Jane, 1637, by Tho. Wheeler, Charles City Co.
Coldron, Symon, 1641, by Wm. Burdett, Accomack Co.
Cole, Richard, 1635, by Jno. Sparkes, ——— Co.
Cole, Tho., 1635, by Erasmus Carter, James City Co.
Cole, Richard, 1655, by Tho. Jones, James City Co.
Cole, John, 1655, by George Parker, Northampton Co.
Cole, Millicent, 1643, by Wm. Berryman, Northampton Co.
Cole, Peter, 1652, by Littleton Scarburg, ——— Co.
Cole, Dennis, 1652, by Augustine Moore, ——— Co.
Cole, Dorothy, 1649, by Tho. Dale, ——— Co.
Cole, John, 1650, by Capt. John Flood, Gent., and Jno. Flood (an
    ancient mariner), James City Co.
Cole, Martha, 1650, by Robert Blake and Samuell Elridge, Isle of Wight
    Co.
Cole, Francis, 1650, by Nicholas Jernew, Gent., ——— Co.
Cole, James, 1652, by Mrs. Jane Harmer, Northumberland Co.
Coles, Edward, 1652, by Mr. Geo. Foster, Northumberland Co.
Cole, Fra., 1653, by Edward Kemp, Geo. Cartlough and John Mere-
    dith, Lancaster Co.
Cole, Richard, 1654, by Capt. John West, Esq., Gloucester Co.
Cole, Henry, 1650, by Capt. Richard Bond, Charles City Co.
Cole, Joane, 1656, by Mr. Henry Soanes, New Kent Co.
Cole, Antho., 1641, by Ambrose Bennett, Isle of Wight Co.
Cole, Tho., 1640, by Thomas Harvey, James City Co.
Cole, Edward, 1642, by Richard Gregson, Elizabeth City Co.
Cole, John, 1639, by John Kempe, James City Co.

Cole, John, 1636, by David Jones, Charles City Co.
Cole, With, 1635, by McWilliam Stone, ———— Co.
Cole, Jon., 1636, by Cheney Boyse, Charles City Co.
Cole, Robert, 1637, by Thomas Shippey, Henrico Co.
Cole, Thomas, 1635, by Charles Harwer, ———— Co.
Cole, John, 1637, by Leonard Geo., Elizabeth City Co.
Cole, Ann, 1642, by Joseph Royall, ———— Co.
Cole, Wm. (a servant), 1635, by Wm. Gary, Accomack Co.
Cole, Sarah, 1638, by Walter Chiles, Charles City Co.
Cole, Jon., 1638, by John Fludd, James City Co.
Cole, John, 1638, by Sarah Cloyden, Isle of Wight Co.
Cole, Wm., 1637, by Bennett Freeman, James city Co.
Cole, Anthony, 1638, by Ambrose Bennett, Isle of Wight Co.
Cole, Dorothy, 1638, by William Parker, Upper Norfolk Co.
Cole, Sarah, 1638, by Walter Chiles, Charles Citie Co.
Cole, Wm., 1643, by Casar Puggett, Lower Norfolk Co.
Cole, Tho., 1644, by Elizabeth Harmer, Northampton Co.
Cole, Dorothy, 1648, by John Landman, Nansemond Co.
Cole, John, 1646, by Sir. William Berkley, ———— Co.
Coles, Richard, 1637, by Francis Fowler, James River Co.
Colles, Richard, 1644, by James Taylor and Lawrence Baker, James City Co.
Coleman, Robert, 1638, by Thomas Symons, Upper Norfolk Co.
Coleman, Edw., 1637, by Capt. Adam Thoroughgood, Elizabeth City Co.
Coleman, Robert, 1637, by Wm. Farrar, Henrico Co.
Coleman, Katherine, 1636, by William Coleman, Elizabeth City Co.
Coleman, Robert, 1639, by Tho. Symons, James City Co.
Coleman, Morris, 1638, by Capt. Christopher Wormley, Charles River Co.
Coleman, John, 1654, by Lieut.-Col. Giles Brent, Westmoreland Co.
Coleman, Wm., 1656, by Wm. Justice, Charles City Co.
Coleman, Robt., 1643, by Tho. Symonds, ———— Co.
Coleman, Anne, 1652, by Tho. Dodford, Lower Norfolk Co.
Coleman, John, 1649, by Capt. Ralph Wormeley, ———— Co.
Coleman, John, 1653, by Mrs. Mary Brent, ———— Co.
Coleman, Jno., 1643, by Mr. Obedience Robins, Northampton Co.
Coleman, Rich., 1654, by Mrs. Mgt. Brent, Westmoreland Co.
Coleman, Samuel, 1654, by Edward Conaway, Lancaster Co.
Coleman, Sibil, 1655, by George Wall, Westmoreland Co.
Colert, Cleri., 1636, by Wm. Bibby, Accomac Co.
Collect, Geo., 1636, by Elizabeth Hawkins, Charles River Co.
Colledge, Geo., 1637, by Humphry Loyd, Charles River Co
Collect, Sam., 1653, by Robert Blake, Isle of Wight Co.
Collect, John, Jr., 1653, by Robt. Blake, Isle of Wight Co.
Collect, John, and Anne his wife, 1653, by Robt. Blake, Isle of Wight Co.
Collett, Richard, 1653, by Tho. Davis, ———— Co.
Collett, Richard, 1642, by Georg Busse, ———— Co.
Collett, James, 1654, by Valentine Patten, Westmoreland Co.
Collett, James, 1654, by Robert Hubard, Westmoreland Co.

Collett, Margarett, 1640, by William Jones, Accomack Co.
Collect, John, 1642, by Georg Smith, Accomack Co.
Collett, Eliz., 1637, by James Warradine, Charles City Co.
Collier, Mary, 1653, by Mr. Richard Barnhouse, Jr., Gloucester Co.
Collier, Henry, 1648, by Tho. Ludwell, Gent., James City Co.
Coleman, John, 1649, by Capt. Ralph Wormley, ——— Co.
Collinge, Eliz., 1654, by Randall Chamblett, ——— Co.
Collier, Tho., 1655, by John Hinman, Northampton Co.
Collington, Georg., 1636, by William Roper, Accomack Co.
Collison, Miles, 1639, by Richard Preston, Upper New Norfolk Co.
Collison, Eliza, 1650, by George Taylor, ——— Co.
Colmer, Thomas, 1643, by Capt. Wm. Peirce, Esq., ——— Co.
Collin, Stephen, 1652, by Peter Knight, Gloucester Co.
Collins, Richard, 1653, by Major Abra. Wood, Charles City Co.
Collins, John, 1655, by George Frizell and Tho. Moore, Northampton Co.
Collins, Elizabeth, 1654, by John Cox, Lancaster, Co.
Collins, Elios, 1638, by Edward Hill, Charles City Co.
Collins, William, 1640, by John Geary, Upper Norfolk Co.
Collins, William, 1639, by Oliver Sprye, Upper New Norfolk Co.
Collins, Tho., 1635, by Wm. Garry, Accomack Co.
Collins, Elizabeth, 1636, by Wm. Clarke, Henrico Co.
Collins, Giers, 1635, by Capt. Thos. Willowbye ——— Co.
Collins, Hen., by Hugh Cox, Charles City Co.
Collins, Walter, 1635, by Thos. Baywell, ——— Co.
Collins, Walter, 1638, by Thomas Bogwell, Charles City Co.
Collins, Jon., 1638, by Stephen Charlton, Accomack Co.
Collins, Richard, 1646, by Geo. Ludlow, Esq., York Co.
Collins, Arth., 1652, by Mrs. Jane Harner, Northumberland Co.
Collins, Eliza, 1652, by Tho. Cartwright, Lower Norfolk Co.
Collins, John, 1650, by Capt. Moore Fautleroy, ——— Co.
Collins, Chr., 1648, by John Manning, Lower Norfolk Co.
Collins, Eliza, 1649, by Roger Nicholls, James City Co.
Collins, Susan, 1653, by Wm. Walker, Northumberland Co.
Collins, Wm., 1654, by Edwin Conaway, Lancaster Co.
Collins, Susan, 1654, by John Whithers and Stephen Garey, Westmore-
    land Co.
Collins, Ann, 1655, by John Wyere, Lancaster Co.
Collis, John, 1651, by Audery Bennett, Nancemond Co.
Collor, Tho., 1652, by Dr. George Hack, Northampton Co.
Collybant, Sarah, 1635, by Wm. Barber (a mariner), Charles City Co.
Colly, Tho., 1636, by Wm. Fookes, ——— Co.
Collybancke, Sarah, 1638, by Wm. Baker and Associates, Charles City
    Co.
Colowell, Elies, 1647, by Elizabeth Barcroft, Isle of Wight Co.
Colran, Thomas, 1635, by Thomas Harwood, ——— Co.
Colson, Susan, 1635, by Capt. Adam Thoroughgood, ——— Co.
Colson, Jane, 1654, by John Watson and John Bognall, Westmore-
    land Co.
Colston, Jno., 1653, by Capt. Francis Patt, Northampton Co.
Coltrey, Phillip, 1650, by Richard Tye and Charles Sparrowe, Charles
    City Co.

Colt, Richard, 1656, by Vincent Stanford, —— Co.
Colt, Elinor, 1651, by Lieut. Coll. Giles Brent, Northumberland Co.
Colt, Geoorge, 1654, by Richard Codsford, Westmoreland Co.
Colton, Nicho., 1643, by Sir. Francis Wyatt, Kt., —— Co.
Colton, Anne, 1654, by Major Miles Carey, Westmoreland Co.
Combay Will, 1653, by Geo. Hack, Northampton Co.
Combes, Richard, 1635, by Vectoris Christmas, Elizabeth City Co.
Combey, Ann, 1635, by John Dennett, James Co.
Come, Debora, 1654, by Peter Knight, Northumberland Co.
Comes, Ann, 1650, by John Perrott, Nansemond Co.
Comelison, Comely, 1655, by Nich. Wadilow, Northampton Co.
Comell, Wm., 1654, by John Grey, Northampton Co.
Comellin, Edmond, 1638, by Benjamin Corrill, James City Co.
Comen, Tho., 1652, by July Gardner, Northampton Co.
Comesh, John, 1652, by Charles Scarburg, Northampton Co.
Comfrey, Robert, 1652, by Mrs. Mary Brent, Northumberland Co.
Comown, Arghil, 1651, by Richard Whitehurst, Lower Norfolk Co.
Compeere, Ralph, 1635, by Richard Bennett, —— Co.
Compton, John, 1643, by Tho. Williams, —— Co.
Compton, Francis, 1651, by Henry Hackery, —— Co.
Compton, Mary, 1649, by Tho. Harwood, —— Co.
Compton, Francis, 1648, by Georg Read, Gent., —— Co.
Conack, Phillip, 1652, by Mr. Geo. Foster, Northumberland Co.
Conady, John, 1652, by John Robinson, Jr., Northampton Co.
Condy, Jeffery, 1650, by Silvester Thatcher and Tho. Whitlocke, ——
    Co.
Cone, David, 1641, by Ambrose Bennett, Isle of Wight Co.
Congden, John, 1638, by Capt. Christopher Womley, Charles River Co.
Congdon, John, 1650, by Mr. Epaphroditus Lawson, —— Co.
Conington, Dan., 1656, by Tho. Harris, Lancaster Co.
Connagrane, Thomas, 1635, by McWilliams Stone, —— Co.
Connaway, John, 1638, by John Fludd, James City Co.
Connaway, Jarman, 1642, by Christopher Boyce, —— Co.
Connaway, Nicho., 1651, by Edward Deggs, Esq., Yorke Co.
Connaway, Freeman, 1652, by John Gresham, Northumberland Co.
Conaway, Henry, 1652, by Edward Hall, Lower Norfolk, Co.
Connaway, Martha, 1652, by Mr. Edwin Connaway (her husband),
    —— Co.
Connaway, John, 1650, by Capt. John Flood, Gent., and Jno. Flood,
    an ancient planter, James City Co.
Conway, Aron, 1642, by Capt. Samuell Mathews, Esq., —— Co.
Conner, Phillipp, 1638, Thomas Burbage, Accomack Co.
Connier, Dennes, 1652, by Capt. Francis Morgan and Ralph Green,
    Gloucester Co.
Conniers, Rich., 1654, by Mrs. Mgt. Brent, Westmoreland Co.
Coniers, Tho., 1654, by John Williams, Northumberland Co.
Conquest, Richd., 1649, by Henry White, James City Co.
Conquest, Lewis, 1649, by Capt. Ralph Wormeley, —— Co.
Constable, Sarah, 1656, by Major Wm. Lewis, —— Co.
Conle, Ralph, 1650, by Geo. Ludlow, Esq., Northumberland Co.
Courtier, Wm., 1637, by Henry Perry, Charles River Co.

Cousens, James, 1637, by Charles Barcroft, Isle of Wight Co.
Conway, Eliza, 1655, by Mr. Robt. Bourne and Mr. Daniel Parke, York Co.
Conusher, Stephen, 1635, by Jno. Sparkes, ——— Co.
Conyer, Tho., 1652, by Tho. Preston, Jr., ——— Co.
Coocs, Eliza, 1651, by Mr. Arillio Steevens, Northampton Co.
Cook, John, 1654, by Valentine Patten, Westmoreland Co.
Cook, Ann, 1635, by Williomi Prior, ——— Co.
Cook, Wm., 1653, by Coll. Wm. Taylor, Esq., Gloucester Co.
Cook, John, 1654, by Robert Hubard, Westmoreland Co.
Cook, Tobias, 1643, by Capt. Thomas Putters, ——— Co.
Cook, Wm., 1655, by Lt. Coll. Anthony Ellyot, ——— Co.
Cook, James, 1655, by Mr. Tho. Ballard, Gloucester Co.
Cooke, Tob., 1652, by Francis England, Isle of Wight Co.
Cooke, Joane, 1651, by Robt. Newman, Northumberland Co.
Cooke, Tho., 1650, by Richard Tye and Charles Sparrowe, Charles City Co.
Cooke, Kath., 1650, by Richard Tye and Charels Sparrowe, Charles City Co.
Cooke, Richard, 1650, by Richard Tye and Charles Sparrowe, Charles City Co.
Cooke, M., 1650, by Tho. Luntsford Kt., and Barronett, ——— Co.
Cooke, John and Elizabeth, his wife, 1652, by John Needles, ——— Co.
Cooke, John, Jr., 1652, by John Needles, ——— Co.
Cooke, Anne, 1653, by James Watson, Isle of Wight Co.
Cooke, Wm., 1653, by Charles Grymes, Lancaster Co.
Cooke, John, 1651, by Capt. Tho. Davis, Northumberland Co.
Cooke, Henry, 1651, by Abraham Moone and (Thomas Griffin), Lancaster Co.
Cooke, John, 1651, by John Adleston, ——— Co.
Cooke, James, 1648, by Lewis Burwell and Tho. Haws, York River Co.
Cooke, Wm., 1650, by John Landman, ——— Co.
Cooke, Wm., 1642, by Justiman Cooper, Isle of Wight Co.
Cooke, Edward, 1642, by Capt. Daniell Gookin, ——— Co.
Cooke, Mordecay, 1642, by Christopher Boyce, ——— Co.
Cooke, Alice, 1642, by John King, Charles River Co.
Cooke, Thomas, 1638, by Richard Kemp, Esq., ——— Co.
Cooke, John 1638, by John George, Charles City Co.
Cooke, Richard, 1639, by Richard Corke, Gent., Henrico Co.
Cooke, Wm., 1639, by Henry Peirey, Charles City Co.
Cooke, John, 1639, by Richard Cooke, Gent., Henrico Co.
Cooke, Mordecay, 1639, by Christopher Boyse, Charles River Co.
Cooke, Wm., 1640, by John Holloway, Accomack Co.
Cooke, Miles, 1639, by Samuell Almond, Hnerico Co.
Cooke, Edward, 1655, by Mrs. Margaret Brent, Lancaster Co.
Cooke, Wm., 1636, by Justinaina Cooper, Warrasquinock Co.
Cooke, John, 1635, by Alexander Stonar, ——— Co.
Cooke, Richard, 1636, by Richard Cocke, ——— Co.
Cooke, Jon., 1636, by Richard Cocke, ——— Co.
Cooke, Ann, 1637, by Willaim Prior, Charles River Co.
Cooke, Jon., 1637, by Theodore Moyser, James City Co.

Cooke, James, 1637, by Henry Poole, New Norfolk Co.
Cooke, Witti, 1636, by Elizabeth Packer, Henrico Co.
Cooke, Richard, 1638, by William Carter, James City Co.
Cooke, Wm., 1637, by Justinian Cooper, Isle of Wight Co.
Cooke, Barth., 1636, by Robert Hollom, Henrico Co.
Cooke, Ann, 1638, by Thomas Clipwell, James City Co.
Cooke, Richard, 1636, by William Carter, Henrico Co.
Cooke, Wm., 1637, by Elizabeth Parker, Henrico Co.
Cooke, Jon., 1638, by John Fludd, James City Co.
Cooke, Henry, 1638, by Cornelius Loyd, ——— Co.
Cooke, Gerrard, 1638, by William Clarke, Charles River Co.
Cooke, Christ., 1643, by Sir Francis Wyatt, Kt., ——— Co.
Cooke, Robt., 1638, by Tristrum Nosworthy, New Norfolk Co.
Cooke, John, 1643, by Sir Francis Wyatt, Kt., ——— Co.
Cooke, Richard, 1643, by Georg Levitt, ——— Co.
Cookeley, John, 1652, by Collo. Hugh Gwin, ——— Co.
Cookely, Ralph, 1655, by Patrick Miller, Lancaster Co.
Cooker, John, 1637, by Leonard Yeo, Elizabeth City Co.
Coole, Adam, 1639, by Georg. Minifye, Charles River Co.
Coole, Alexander, 1656, by Nicholas Waddilow, Northampton Co.
Coole, Fra., 1653, by Wm. Freeke, Northumberland Co.
Coomes, Cha., 1655, by Tho. Leatherberry, Northampton Co.
Cooner, Hen., 1654, by Tho. Harmanson, Northampton Co.
Coonwall, Pastrow, 1654, by Tho. Harmanson, Northampton Co.
Coop, Robert, 1653, by Colo. Wm. Clayborne, (Sec. of State), ———
    Co.
Coope, Eliza, 1651, by Capt. John West, Esq., Yorke Co.
Cooper, Anne, 1653, by Tho. Davis, ——— Co.
Cooper, Peeter, 1643, by Phillipp Taylor, Northampton Co.
Cooper, John, 1638, by Edward Minter, James City Co.
Cooper, Jon., 1638, by John Fludd, James City Co.
Cooper, Wm., 1637, by Capt. Thomas Panlett, Charles City Co.
Cooper, Jon., 1635, by Henry Harte, James City Co.
Cooper, Thomas, 1636, by Wm. Clarke, Henrico Co.
Cooper, Jon., 1636, by Edward Minter, ——— Co.
Cooper, Thos., 1638, by Willaim Clarke, Henrico Co.
Cooper, Hen., 1635, by Silvester Totnam, James Co.
Cooper, John, 1640, by Randall Crew, Upper Norfolk Co.
Cooper, Richard, 1642, by Roger Symmons, ——— Co.
Cooper, Richard, 1639, by Thomas Mathews, Henrico Co.
Cooper, Richard, 1641, by Robert Burnett, Isle of Wight Co.
Cooper, Edward, 1638, by Tho. Melton, Lower New Norfolk Co.
Cooper, Thomas, 1642, by Capt. Samuell Mathews, Esq., ——— Co.
Cooper, John, 1654, by Humphry Belt, Lower Norfolk Co.
Cooper, Daniel, 1655, by John Lawson, Lancaster Co.
Cooper, Tho., 1642, by Christopher Boyce, ——— Co.
Cooper, Justinian, and Ann, his wife, 1642, by Justinian Cooper, Isle
    of Wight Co.
Cooper, Wm., 1651, by Lieut. Collo. Giles Brent, Northumberland Co.
Cooper, Francis, 1653, by Tho. Davis, ——— Co.
Cooper, Symon, 1653, by Major Abra. Wood, Charles City Co.

Cooper, Walter, 1652, by Richard Nelmes, Northumberland Co.
Cooper, Edw. A., 1650, by John Hany, Northumberland Co.
Cooper, Eliza., 1652, by Tho. Todd, ——— Co.
Cooper, Lewis, 1643, by Wm. Butler, James City Co.
Cooper, Tho., 1650, by George Taylor, ——— Co.
Cooper, John, 1650, by Capt. John Flood, Gent., and Jno. Flood, an ancient planter, James City Co.
Cooper, Ann, 1650, by Capt. Moore Fautelroy, ——— Co.
Cooper, Bennet, 1650, by John Cox, ——— Co.
Cooper, Thomas, 1646, by Joseph Croshawe, Charles River Co.
Cooper, Richard, 1648, by Francis Ceely, ——— Co.
Cooper, John, 1645, by Mr. Robt. Eyres, ——— Co.
Cooper, Robert, 1652, by Anthony Dovey and Enoch Hawker, Lancaster Co.
Cooper, Anne, ——by, Mr. John Page, ——— Co.
Cooper, Wm., ———, by Tho. Lucas, ——— Co.
Cooper, Phild., ———, by Tho. Lucas, ——— Co.
Cooper, Mary, 1653, by John Jaliffe, Lower Norfolk Co.
Cooper, Walter, 1655, by Jenkin Price, Northampton Co.
Cooper, Wm., 1655, by Mrs. Margaret Brent, Lancaster Co.
Cooper, James, 1655, by Mr. Tho. Ballard, Gloucester Co.
Cooper, Geo., 1650, by Lewis Burwell, Gent., ——— Co.
Cooperson, Tho., 1650, by Mr. James Williamson, ——— Co.
Coosman, Wm., 1636, by John Wilkins, Accomack Co.
Coot, Jerem., 1563, by Richard Carey, ——— Co.
Coote, Wm., 1649, by Rich. Croshaw, Yorke Co.
Cootes, John, 1648, by Wm. Ewen, James City Co.
Cope, Guiles, 1654, by Major Wm. Andrews, Northampton Co.
Cope, Tho., 1655, by Hugh Yeo. Northampton Co,
Copeland, Hen., 1637, by Capt. Thomas Flint, Warwick River Co.
Copeland, Christopher, 1636, by Christopher Calthropp, Charles River Co.
Copeland, ———, 1638, by Humphry Tabb, Elizabeth City Co.
Copeland, John, 1651, by Mr. Rowland Lawson, ——— Co.
Copeland, Wm., 1653, by Gregory Rawlins, Surry Co.
Copeland, Wm., 1650, by Sr. Tho. Luntsford, Kt., and Barronett, ——— Co.
Coplestone, Annanias, 1635, by William Spencer, ——— Co.
Copleston, Armias, 1637, by William Spencer, ——— Co.
Coppell, Wm., 1642, by Stephen Gill, ——— Co.
Coram, Elizabeth, 1646, by John Ashamb, Upper Norfolk Co.
Corbett Robert, 1635, by John Cheesemen, Charles River Co.
Corbett, Ann, 1651, by Richard Kellum, Northampton Co.
Corbin, H., 1645, by Richard Jacob, Northampton Co.
Carbone, Babtisco, 1650, by Richard Tye and Charles Sparrowe, Charles City Co.
Corby, Ailie, 1650, by Richard Tye and Charles Sparrowe, Charles City Co.
Corde, John, 1642, by Wm. Durant, ——— Co.
Cordes, Kath., 1652, by Mrs. Mary Brent, Northumberland Co.
Cordell, James, 1654, by Arthur Nash, New Kent Co.

Corderoy, Ellinor, 1652, by Mrs. Anna Barnett, Gloucester Co.
Corderoy, Mrs. Elinor, 1651, by Mrs. Anna Bernard, Northumberland Co.
Corderoy, Wm., 1651, by Mrs. Anna Bernard, Northumberland Co.
Corderoy, Edward, 1651, by Mrs. Anna Bernard, Northumberland Co.
Cordey, Nathaniell, 1637, by Thomas Holt, New Norfolk Co.
Cordevar, Eliz., 1650, by Tho. Vans, Gent., Northumberland Co.
Cordroy, Edwd., 1652, by Mrs. Anna Barnett, Gloucester Co.
Cordon, Gregory, 1650, by Lewis, Burwell Gent., —— Co.
Cordwallet, Hump., 1650, by John Garwood, Nansemond Co.
Corewell, James, 1649, by Edmund Scarburgh, Jr., Northampton Co.
Corje, Jon., by John Jaliffe, Lower Norfolk Co.
Corhoor, Cor., 1645, by Justinian Cooper, Gent., Isle of Wight Co.
Corke, Jane, 1637, by Joseph Cobb, Isle of Wight Co.
Corke, Lewis, 1635, by Thomas Harwood, —— Co.
Corke, Jane, 1637, by Joseph Cobb, Isle of Wight Co.
Corkeley, Jno., 1650, by Mrs. Frances Townshend (widow), Northumberland Co.
Coringe, Elizabeth, 1652, by Lawrence Dameron, Northumberland Co.
Corkett, Henry, 1650, by Mordecay Cooke, —— Co.
Cormack Daniell, 1643, by John Freeme, Charles Co.
Cornish, Wm., 1650, by John Hany, Northumberland Co.
Corne, John, 1643, by Thomas Dew, Upper Norfolk Co.
Cornel, Cornel, 1652, by Nicholas Wadilow, Northampton Co.
Cornelia, Carona, 1655, by George Parker, Northampton Co.
Cornelies Mary, 1655, by John Dorman, Northampton Co.
Corners Gillion, 1656, by Capt. Wm. Canfill, Surry Co.
Cornewall, Pevice, 1652, by Mr. Tho. Brice, Lancaster Co.
Corney, Wm., 1637, by Daniell Gookins, New Norfolk Co.
Cornish, Robert, 1637, by William Spencer, —— Co.
Cornish, Mary, 1652, by Mrs. Elnor Brocas, Lancaster Co.
Cornish, John, 1649, by Capt. Ralph Wormeley, —— Co.
Cornishby, John, 1650, by Benedick Barbar, Gent., —— Co.
Cortes, Jno., 1637, by Tho. Symmons, Charles River Co.
Cosan, Step., 1655, by Southy Littleberry, Northampton Co.
Cosby, John, 1654, by Robert Yoe, Westmoreland Co.
Cosham, Henry, 1652, by Tho. Gloscock, Lancaster Co.
Cossin, James, 1650, by Jervace Dodson, Gent., Northumberland Co.
Cosmer, Richard, 1655, by Southy Littleberry, Northampton Co.
Cosones Nich., 1637, by Edward Travis, James City Co.
Costen, George, 1636, by Capt. John Chelsman, Charles River Co.
Costin, George, 1635, by John Cheeseman, Charles River Co.
Costen, Anne, 1652, by John Robbins, Northampton Co.
Costen, Stephen, 1652, by John Robbins, Northampton Co.
Costen, Eliz., 1653, by Tho. Willis, York Co.
Costerdine, Frank, 1635, by William Clark, Warrasquinoake Co.
Costh, Wm., 1651, by Richard Whitehurst, Lower Norfolk Co.
Cossens, Margarett, 1649, by Edmund Scarburgh, Jr., Northampton, Co.
Cotterell, Edward, 1635, by John Cheeseman, Charles River Co.
Cottin, Wm., 1650, by Richard Axom, and Tho. Godwin, —— Co.
Cotton, Cicely, 1637, by Arthur Smith, Isle of Wight Co.

Cotton, Wm., 1638, by William Banister, ——— Co.
Cotton, Rowland, 1637, by James Warradine, Charles City Co.
Cotton, Willi, 1637, by William Cotton, ——— Co.
Cotton, Margt., 1638, by Georg Mynifie (merchant), ——— Co.
Cotton, Housh, 1652, by Richard Longe, ——— Co.
Cottrell, Ambrose, 1649, by Robert Moseley, Gent., ——— Co.
Coude, Alexander, 1654, by Tho. Bell, Northampton Co.
Coughby, John, 1637, by Francis Osborne, ——— Co.
Coule, John, 1654, by Mr. Tho. Fowke, Westmoreland Co.
Coulston, Francis, 1656, by Wm. Johnson, ——— Co.
Coursie, Richard, 1642, by Justinian Cooper, Isle of Wight Co.
Court, Richard, 1637, by James Harrison, James City Co.
Court, Geo., 1653, by Capt. Francis Morgan, Gloucester Co.
Court, Geo., 1653, by Wm. Walker, Northumberland Co.
Court, Wm., 1654, by Robert Holt, James City Co.
Court, Grace, 1654, by John Wyre, John Gillet, Andrew Gibson, and
    John Phillipps, ——— Co.
Courtier, Wm., 1637, by Henry Perry, Charles River Co.
Courtman, Tho., 1655, by John Motley, Northumberland Co.
Courtney, James, 1635, by Charles Harwer, ——— Co.
Courser, Marg., 1652, by John Robbins, Northampton Co.
Cove, Margarett, 1643, by Tho. Wheeler, Charles City Co.
Covell, John, 1637, by Francis Morgan, Charles River Co.
Covell, Henry, 1652, by Henry Nicholls, Lancaster Co.
Covell, Nicho. 1648, by Lewis Burwell, Gent., ——— Co.
Covell, John, 1641, by John Gookin, Lower Norfolk Co.
Coventon, Nehemiah, 1647, by Stephen Harsey and Nich. Waddilow,
    Northampton Co.
Coventon, John, 1652, by Mrs. Mary Brent, Northumberland Co.
Coventon, Nehemiah, 1649, by Nicholas Waddilow, Northampton Co.
Cover, James, 1652, by Mr. David Fox, Lancaster Co.
Coward, Margarett, 1650, by Capt. Moore Fautleroy, ——— Co.
Cowden, Eman, 1650, by Lewis Burwell, Gent., ——— Co.
Cowdery, Wm., 1656, by John Rosier Clarke, Westmoreland Co.
Cowdwell, Henry, 1652, by John Howett, Northumberland Co.
Cowhead, Richard, 1654, by Nich. Merywether, Westmoreland Co.
Cowell, Elizabeth, 1645, by John Baugh, Gent., Henrico Co.
Cowken, Tho., 1653, by Richd. Haines, ——— Co.
Cowsland, Ann, 1653, by John Phillips, ——— Co.
Cowles, Sarah, 1654, by John Watson and John Bognall, Westmoreland
    Co.
Cowley, Sara, 1650, by Lewis Burwell, Gent., Northumberland Co.
Cowley, Wm., 1647, by Thomas Johnson, Gent., Northampton Co.
Cowley, Tobyas, 1650, by Lewis Burwell, Gent., Northumberland Co.
Cowen, Tho., 1653, by Charles Scarburgh, Northampton Co.
Cowen Edward, 1653, by Charles Scarburg, Northampton Co.
Cowins, Edward, 1652, by Dr. Geo. Hack, Northampton Co.
Cox, Thomas, 1637, by Capt. Thomas Panlett, Charles City Co.
Cox, Jon., 1637, by Daniell Gookins, New Norfolk Co.
Cox, Wm., 1637, by Mathew Edloe, ——— Co.
Cox, Joseph, 1639, by Lieut. Richard Popeley, ——— Co.

Cox, John, 1642, by John Benton, ——— Co.
Cox, Wm., 1637, by Nathaniel Floyd, Isle of Wight Co.
Cox, Jon., 1637, by Nathaniel Floyd, Isle of Wight Co.
Cox, John, 1654, by Capt. Nich. Marteaw, Westmoreland Co.
Cox, Christopher, 1656, by John Billiott, Northampton Co.
Cox, Jon., 1642, by John Davis, Henrico. Co.
Cox, Symon, 1648, by Robert Pitt, Isle of Wight Co.
Cox, Richard, 1651, by Mr. George Truhett, Northampton Co.
Cox, John, 1653, by John Poye, ——— Co.
Cox, Tho., 1652, by Edward Hall, Lower Norfolk Co.
Cox, John, 1652, by Ralph Paine, ——— Co.
Cox, Julyan, 1650, by Francis Hobbs, ——— Co.
Cox, John, 1650, by Francis Hobbs, ——— Co.
Cox, Henry, 1650, by Capt. Moore Fautleroy, ——— Co.
Cox, Mary, 1643, by Thomas Hughes, Charles River Co.
Cox, Wm., 1643, by Thomas Hughes, Charles River Co.
Cox, Eliza, 1650, by John Cox, ——— Co.
Cox, James, 1652, by Mr. David Fox, Lancaster Co.
Cox, Tho., 1654, by Edward Parker, Westmoreland Co.
Cox, Xper., 1655, by Nich. Wadilow, Northampton Co.
Coxa, Dennis, 1655, by Christopher Calvert, Northampton Co.
Coxe, Christop., 1652, by Nicholas Wadilow, Northampton Co.
Coxon, Bryan, 1655, by Wm. Graves, York Co.
Coxson, Thomas, 1637, by Arthur Smith, Isle of Wight Co.
Coyle, Willi, 1637, by Rich. Bellane and Christopher Lawson, James
    City Co.
Coyt, Wm., 1638, by Christopher Lawson, James City Co.
Cozier, Wm., 1636, by John Wilkins, Accomack Co.
Crabb, Jon., 1637, by Capt. Adam Thoroughgood, New Norfolk Co.
Crabb, Jon., 1635, by Capt. Adam Thoroughgood, ——— Co.
Crable Roger, 1638, by Richard Wilcox, James City Co.
Crable Robert, ———, by Mr. Wm. Presly, Northumberland Co.
Craford, Ann, 1637, by James Knott, New Norfolk Co.
Craft, Bridget, 1636, by John Wilkins, Accomack Co.
Craft, Jon., 1637, by Thomas Cansey, Charles City Co.
Craft, Bridget, 1637, by John Wilkins, New Norfolk Co.
Crafts, Oliver, 1643, by Fra. Mason, Lower Norfolk Co.
Craftin, Tho., 1635, by William Wilkinson (minister), ——— Co.
Crafford, Dorothy, 1642, by Capt. Samuell Mathews, Esq., ——— Co.
Craftin, Thos., 1637, by William Wilkinson, New Norfolk Co.
Crandell, Edward, 1653, by Patrick Margraffe, ——— Co.
Cradock, Robert, 1637, by Capt. Thomas Osborne, Henrico Co.
Crag, John, 1654, by John Wyre, John Gillet, Andrew Gibson, and
    John Phillipps, ——— Co.
Cragg, Thomas, 1637, by Theodore Moyser, James City Co.
Craggs, Mary, 1654, by Humphry Belt, Lower Norfolk Co.
Crane, Elizabeth, 1649, by Francis Brown, Northumberland Co.
Crand, Robert, 1650, by William Gooch, Gent., ——— Co.
Crane, Samll., 1653, by Richard Slaughter, Nansemond Co.
Crane, Wm., 1653, by Wm. Debram, ——— Co.
Crane, George, 1653, by Charles Grymes, Lancaster Co.

Craine, Fra., 1652, by Mrs. Elinor Brocas, Lancaster Co.
Cranage, Mary, 1637, by Wm. Cranage, New Norfolk Co.
Cranage, Edmund, 1637, by Wm. Craage, New Norfolk Co.
Cranage, Margarett, 1637, by Wm. Cranage, New Norfolk Co.
Cranage, Eliz., 1637, by Wm. Cranage (her husband), New Norfolk Co.
Cranage, Eliza, 1637, by William Cranage, New Norfolk Co.
Cranage, Margarett, 1639, by William Cranage, Isle, of Wight Co.
Cranell, Jon., 1637, by Francis Osborne, ——— Co.
Craner, Peter, 1650, by Capt. Moore Fautleroy, ——— Co.
Cranfield, Wm., 1638, by John Robins, ——— Co.
Cranfield, Peter, 1638, by Peter Monntegue, Upper Norfolk Co.
Cranfield, Ann, 1653, by Wm. Knott, Surry Co.
Cranford, John, 1653, by Ralph Green, Gloucester Co.
Crannage, Edmund, 1639, by William Crannage, Isle of Wight Co.
Crannage, Mary, 1639, by William Crannage, Isle of Wight Co.
Crannage, Ely, 1639, by William Crannage, Isle of Wight Co.
Crappage, Edw., 1648, by Lewis Burwell, Gent., ——— Co.
Crasford, Martin, 1647, by Elizabeth Barcroft, Isle of Wight Co.
Crashaw, Joseph, 1638, by Gloyd Bloys, Charles River Co.
Crave, Fra., 1649, by Wm. Hoccaday, ——— Co.
Craven, James, 1639, by Tho. Symons, James City Co.
Craven, Susan, 1655, by Lt. Col. Anthony Ellyott, ——— Co.
Craven, Tho., 1642, by John Benton, ——— Co.
Crawen, James, 1643, by Tho. Symonds, ——— Co.
Crawford, Ann, 1636, by James Knott, Elizabeth City Co.
Crawford, Wm., 1648, by Richard Lee, Gent., ——— Co.
Crawls, Henry, 1640, by William Wigg, James City Co.
Crawle, Wm., 1652, by Nathaniel Bacon, Isle of Wight Co.
Crawly, Michaell, 1641, by Stephen Charleton, Accomack Co.
Crew, John, 1642, by Edmund Scarburgh, Accomack Co.
Crew, Tho., 1652, by Mr. John Brown, Northampton Co.
Crew, Anne, 1652, by Anthony Doney and Enoch Hawkes, Lancaster Co.
Crew, John, 1694, by Mr. Edmund Scarburg, Northampton Co.
Crewe, Roger, 1638, by Joseph Boarne, Charles City Co.
Crewe, Rebecca, 1635, by Josepe Johnson, ——— Co.
Creaser, Thos., 1635, by Capt. Adam Thoroughgood, ——— Co.
Creaser, Eliza, 1635, by Capt. Adam Thoroughgood, ——— Co.
Creame, Samuell, 1642, by John Robins, ——— Co.
Creese, Marg., 1654, by Major Miles Carey, Westmoreland Co.
Creeton, Roger, 1655, by Mr. Anthony Langston, New Kent Co.
Creeye, Hugh, 1654, by John Curtis, Accomac Co.
Creppy, Math., 1651, by Robert Abrall, Yorke Co.
Cresmass, John, 1650, by Henry Peaseley, ——— Co.
Crespe, James, 1643, by Richard Kemp, Esq., James City Co.
Cressing, Eliz., 1650, by Epa. Lawson, ——— Co.
Crich, Richard, 1635, by William Carter, James City Co.
Cricklock, Jon., 1638, by Epaphroditus Lawson, Upper Norfolk Co.
Crippin, Kath., 1638, by Thomas Swan, James Citie Co.
Crippin, Kate, 1635, by Wm. Swan, James Co.
Cripps, Kate, 1635, by Wm. Swan, James Co.

Cripps, Kath., 1638, by Thomas Swan, James Citie Co.
Cripps, Antho., 1651, by Anthony Johnson, Northampton Co.
Cripps, La., 1652, by Joseph Gregory, ——— Co.
Cripps, Mary, 1650, by Capt. Moore Fautleroy, ——— Co.
Cripps, Mary, 1650, by Mr. James Williamson, ——— Co.
Cripps, Mathew, 1653, by Capt. Robt. Abrall, ——— Co.
Cripps, Wm., ———, by Tho. Lucas, ——— Co.
Crispe, John, 1639, by Christohper Boyse, Charles River Co.
Crispe, John, 1642, by Christopher Boyce, ——— Co.
Criste, Patrick, 1652, by Wm. Ginsey, Gloucester Co.
Crists, John, 1651, by Mr. Wm. Armestead, ——— Co.
Croadell, Eady, 1648, by Job. Chanter, Lower Norfolk Co.
Crocker, Tho., 1645, by Richard Jacob, Northampton Co.
Crocker, Pascall, 1635, by Daniel Augley, Accomac Co.
Crockell, Ja., 1649, by Joseph Croshawe, Yorke Co.
Croffa, Francis, 1656, by Geo. Abbott, Nansemond Co.
Croffield, Robt., 1638, by Georg Mynifie (merchand), ——— Co.
Crofford, Elizab., 1652, by George Smith, ——— Co.
Crofford, John, 1652, by Rice Hughes, ——— Co.
Crofford, Phill., 1652, by George Smith, ——— Co.
Crofford, John, 1652, by Mr. George Clapham, ——— Co.
Croft, Jon., 1638, by Wm. Baker and Associates, Charles City Co.
Croft, Hen., 1637, by Mathew Edloe, ——— Co.
Crofts, An, 1653, by John Ware, ——— Co.
Crofts, Ja., 1654, by John Wyre, John Gillett, Andrew Gibson and
    John Phillipps, ——— Co.
Crooke, Wm., 1636, by William Julian, Elizabeth City Co.
Crookneck, Nicho., 1646, by Henry Sedenden, Northampton Co.
Crollham, Peter, 1656, by Tho. Harris, Lancaster Co.
Cromey, Thom., 1638, by Abraham Wood, Charles City Co.
Cromp, William, 1648, by Lewis Burwell, Gent., ——— Co.
Crompton, Henry, 1650, by Mr. James Williamson, ——— Co.
Cronall, Tho., 1650, by Henry Ashwell, ——— Co.
Crooke, Alice, 1649, by Mr. Tho. Spake, Northumberland Co.
Crooke, Wm., 1649, by John Trussells, ——— Co.
Croply, Wm., 1652, by Tho. Johnson, Jr., Northampton Co.
Croply, John, 1652, by Tho. Johnson, Jr., Northampton Co.
Cropps, Tho., 1637, by Capt. Francis Eppes, Charles City Co.
Cropps, Henry, 1649, by Mr. Robert Parker, Northampton Co.
Crosben, Wm., 1637, by Capt. John Howe, Accomac Co.
Crosbow, Richard, 1650, by Wm. Hodgson, Yorke Co.
Crosby, Thom., 1637, by Mathew, Edloe, ——— Co.
Crosby, Hen., 1642, by Hugh Gwyn, Gent., ——— Co.
Crosby, Mary, 1654, by John Wyre, John Gillett, Andrew Gibson, and
    John Phillipps, ——— Co.
Crosbye, Hen., 1635, by Hugh Cox, Charles City Co.
Crose, Emanuel, 1654, by Tho. Harmonson, Northampton Co.
Croshaw, Richard, 1643, by Joseph Croshawe, ——— Co.
Crosia, Joseph, 1637, by William Parry, New Norfolk Co.
Cross, Kath., 1643, by Wm. Warder, ——— Co.
Crosse, Katherine, 1642, by Tho. Bagwell, Charels City Co.

Cross, Joane, 1649, by Robert Mosely, Gent., ——— Co.
Cross, Nich., 1643, by Robert Hails, Lower Norfolk Co.
Cross Jane, 1649, by Christop. Lewis, James City Co.
Cross, Jane, 1653, by Mr. James Tooke, Isle of Wight Co.
Cross, Jane, 1653, by Tho. Hampton, ——— Co.
Crosse, Eliza, 1650, by Richard Dunning, ——— Co.
Crossland, Geo., 1638, by John Fludd, James City Co.
Crossman, William, 1637, by John Wilkins, New Norfolk Co.
Crost, Jon., 1635, by William Barber (a mariner), Charles City Co.
Crostlewell, Debora, 1651, by Richard Whitehurst, Lower Norfolk Co.
Crostick, John, 1654, by Nich. Merywether, Westmoreland Co.
Crosticke, John, 1653, by Tho. Speoke, ——— Co.
Crosyer, Fra., 1655, by Mr. Tho. Ballard, Gloucester Co.
Croteto, Susan, 1656, by Girffith Deckinson, James City Co.
Crouch, Nicholas, 1637, by Leonard Yeo, Elizabeth City Co.
Crouch, Wm., 1635, by David Mansell, James Co.
Crouch, Robert, 1654, by John Drayton, Westmoreland Co.
Crouch, Eliza, 1653, by Robert Bouth, Yorke Co.
Crouch, Robert, 1650, by Mr. Stephen Hamelin, Charles City Co.
Crouch, Richard, 1655, by Mr. Anthony Langston, New Kent Co.
Crouch, Wm., 1637, by David Mansell, James City Co.
Crough, ———, 1643, by Edward Murfy and John Vaughan, ——— Co.
Croutch, Tho., 1639, by Edward Travis, James City Co.
Crow, Henry, 1636, by Walter Hacker, James River Co.
Crowder, Tho., 1654, by Nicho. Merywether, Westmoreland Co.
Crowell, Jane, 1653, by Nathaniel Hickmon, Northumberland Co.
Crowelden, John, 1636, by John Dansey, James City
Croxon, Alice, 1638, by William Carter, James City Co.
Croxon, Jno., 1651, by Joseph Croshaw, Yorke Co.
Crump Giles, 1637, by Wm. Farrar, Henrico Co.
Crump, Tho., 1655, by Mr. Tho. Ballard, Gloucester Co.
Crumpe, Tho., 1653, by Geo. Hack, Northampton Co.
Crumwell, Mary, 1655, by John Nicholls, Northampton Co.
Cruthen, Hen., 1650, by Richard Tye and Charles Sparrowe, Charles
　　City Co.
Cruxon, Alice, 1636, by William Carter, Henrico Co.
Cuck, Ann, 1650, by Elyas, Edmondes, ——— Co.
Cucknay, Henry, 1639, by Capt. Rich. Townsend, Charles River Co.
Cuddens, Sara, 1650, by Richard Tye and Charles Sparrowe, Charles
　　City Co.
Cuddington, Allin, 1653, by Mr. Henry Soanes, Gloucester Co.
Cuffin, Mary, 1656, by Major Wm. Lewis, ——— Co.
Cugley Patrick, 1650, by Stephen Charlton, Northampton Co.
Cugley, Jno., 1635, by Osbourne Jenkin, Charles City Co.
Cullaine, Kath., 1653, by Oliver Segar, Lancaster Co.
Cullam, John, 1650, by James Metgrigar and Hugh Foutch, North-
　　umberland Co.
Cullet, Jon., 1654, by Capt. John West, Esq., Gloucester Co.
Cullin, Joane, 1652, by Col. Geo. Ludlow, Esq., Gloucester Co.
Cullin, Joane, 1642, by Wm. Durant, ——— Co.
Cullins, Katherine, 1656, by Capt. Henry Fleete, ——— Co.

Cullumbine, Richard, 1635, by Richard Bennett, ——— Co.
Cullumbine, Rich., 1637, by Rich. Bennett, New Norfolk Co.
Culpeper, Jno., 1646, by Henry Sedenden, Northampton Co.
Culpeper, Hen., 1653, by Capt. Natha. Hurd, Warwick Co.
Cult, Francis, 1656, by Wm. Millinge, Northampton Co.
Cumig, Mary, 1654, by Lule Billington, Accomac Co.
Cunneck, Arthur, 1655, by Capt. George Floyd, New Kent Co.
Cunney, Henry, 1639, by Capt. Nicholas Martian, Charles River Co.
Cunney, James, 1652, by Mrs. Jane Harmer, Northumberland Co.
Cuningham, Wm., 1655, by Mr. Tho. Ballard, Gloucester Co.
Cunningham, Jon., 1637, by Capt. Thos. Panlett, Charles City Co.
Cuningham, Nehemiah, 1641, by Wm. Burdett, Accomack Co.
Cunningham, William, 1636, by Samuel Edwards, James City Co.
Cupperwharte, Thos., 1635, by Mr. Geo. Keth, Charles River Co.
Cure, Tho., 1653, by Wm. Debram, ——— Co.
Curle, Joane, 1652, by John Needles, ——— Co.
Curly, Alice, 1636, by Samuel Curly (her husband), James City Co.
Curnock, Alice, 1653, by Wm. Debram, ——— Co.
Curr, John, 1651, by Geo. Colclough, Gent., Northumberland Co.
Currant, Robert, 1636, by Wm. Clarke, Henrico Co.
Curant, Tho., 1654, by Capt. Nich. Marteaw, Westmoreland Co.
Currant, Robt., 1638, by William Clarke, Henrico Co.
Curret, Nich., 1645, by Roger Johns, Northampton Co.
Currey, John, 1652, by Dr. George Hack, Northampton Co.
Curtice, Alice, child, 1640, by William Hampton, Elizabeth City Co.
Curtis, Eliza, 1643, by Lt. Wm. Warleidge, ——— Co.
Curtis, Tho., 1637, by Daniell Gookins, New Norfolk Co.
Curtis, Jon., 1637, by Daniell Gookins, New Norfolk Co.
Curtis, John, 1637, by Justinian Cooper, Isle of Wight Co.
Curtis, Eliz., 1636, by Wm. Clarke, Henrico Co.
Curtis, Jon., 1636, by John Neale, Accomack Co.
Curtis, Eliza, 1638, by William Clarke, Henrico Co.
Curtis, John, 1636, by Justinian Cooper, Warrasquinoake Co.
Curtis, Alice, 1645, by Mr. Bartholomew Hoskins, ——— Co.
Curtis, John, 1654, by Richard Allen, Northampton Co.
Curtis, Elizabeth, 1650, by Lieut. Wm. Worelich, ——— Co.
Curtis, Joane, 1645, by Mr. Bartholomew Hoskins, ——— Co.
Curtis, John, 1652, by John Robinson, Jr., Northampton Co.
Curtis, Daniel, 1655, by Hugh Yeo, Northampton Co.
Curtisse, Eliza, 1635, by Capt. Adam Thoroughgood, ——— Co.
Cuane, Edmund, 1653, by Roger Walker, Northumberland Co.
Cuspe, Edmund, 1654, by Roger Walters, Northumberland Co.
Cuspe, Edw., 1653, by Roger Walter, Northumberland Co.
Curtis, Richard, 1653, by Robert Bayley, Northampton Co.
Cutchman, Thos., 1637, by Georg White, New Norfolk Co.
Cutler, Fra., 1653, by Mr. Edmund Bowman and Richard Starnell, ——— Co.
Cutler, Chr., 1637, by John Broche, Charles River Co.
Cutler, Tho., 1654, by Robert Hubard, Westmoreland Co.
Cynas, John, 1650, by Mrs Frances Townshend (widow), Northumberland Co.

D

Dabby, John, 1694, by Mr. Edmund Scarbough, Northampton Co.
Dabbs, James, 1652, by John Greenbough, Henrico Co.
Dabson, Elizab., 1652, by Mrs. Jane Harmer, Northumberland Co.
Daby, Anne, 1653, by Charles Scarburg, Northampton Co.
Dadberye, Eliz., 1653, by Edward Dabson, —— Co.
Daeby, Ann, 1652, by Charles Scarburg, Northampton Co.
Daerne, Tho., 1650, by Tho. Gerrard, Gent., Northumberland Co.
Daggett, Richard, 1651, by Mr. Antho. Stevens, Northampton Co.
Daigle, Christopher, 1652, by Wm. Up. Thomas, —— Co.
Daldye, Geo., 1653, by Robert Brasseur, Nansemond Co.
Dale, Judith, 1654, by John Watson and John Bognall, Westmoreland Co.
Dale, Edward, 1642, by Tymothy Fenn, Isle of Wight Co.
Dale, Humphry, ——, by Mr. Wm. Presly, Northumberland Co.
Dale, Tho., 1653, by Capt. Nallia Hurd, Warrick Co.
Dale, Judith, 1653, by John Earle, Northumberland Co.
Dale, John, 1653, by John Earle, Northumberland Co.
Dale, Robt., 1653, by Wm. Sidner, Lancaster Co.
Dale, Geo., 1652, by, Andrew Munrow, Northumberland Co.
Dale, George, 1652, by Edward Revell, Northampton Co.
Dale, John, 1638, by Eliabeth Grayne, Charles City Co.
Dale, Humphry, 1638, by Richard Wilcox, James City Co.
Dale, Walter, 1648, by Mr. Thomas Davis, Isle of Wight Co.
Dale, Nicholas, 1638, by Thomas Boulding, Elizabeth City Co.
Dallim, John, 1639, by William Burdett, Accomack Co.
Daller, George, 1653, by Christopher Boyce, Northumberland Co.
Daley, James, 1646, by Richard Moore and William Welton, Upper Norfolk Co.
Dalley, George, 1655, by Wm. Botham, Westmoreland Co.
Dallar, Mary, 1650, by John Rosier, Northumberland Co.
Daller, Dan., 1650, by Edward Grimes, —— Co.
Dally, Wm., 1655, by John Woodward, Gloucester Co.
Dallayhaye, Gringall, 1641, by Bryant Smith, Henrico Co.
Dalmes, John, 1653, by Richard Budd, Northumberland Co.
Daltie, Owen, 1638, by Thomas Burbage, Accomack Co.
Dalton, Jno., 1652, by Mr. Henry Pitt, —— Co.
Dalton, John, 1652, by Nicho. George, Tho. Taberer, Humphry Clarke, —— Co.
Dalton, John, 1654, by Humphry Haggett, Lancaster Co.
Dakins, Gilbert, 1638, by Joseph Boarne, Charles City Co.
Dam, Eliza, 1643, by Rich. Hoe, Gent., —— Co.
Dame, John, 1638, by Richard Hill and Roger Armwood, James City Co.
Dame, Jane, 1652, by July Gardner, Northampton Co.
Dampher, Alex., 1653, by Geo. Taylor, Lancaster Co.
Dams, George, 1653, by Geo. Hack, Northampton Co.
Dan, Geo., 1655, by Southy Littleberry, Northampton Co.
Danance, Richard, ..., by Thomas Meares, Lower Norfolk Co.
Danbury, Stephen, 1650, by Bertram Obert, —— Co.

Dane, Yorath, 1636, by Wm. Armstead, Elizabeth City Co.
Daniell, John, 1642, by John Harlowe, Northampton Co.
Daniell, Roger, Jr., 1654, by Major Miles Carey, Westmoreland Co.
Daniell, Roger, Sr., 1654, by Major Miles Carey, Westmoreland Co.
Daniell, Alex., 1655, by Ralph Green, New Kent Co.
Daniell, John, 1653, by Joseph Croshaw, York Co.
Daniell, John, 1649, by John King, Yorke Co.
Daniell, Thomas, 1649, by Mr. Ralph Barlowe, Northampton Co.
Daniell, John, 1648, by Tho. Ludwell, Gent., James City Co.
Daniell, John, 1648, by Richard Thompson, Northumberland Co.
Daniell, Tho. 1643, by John Neale, Gent., Northampton Co.
Daniel, Walter, 1653, by Capt. Francis Patt, Northampton Co.
Daniell, Thomas, 1653, by Wm. Thomas, Northumberland Co.
Daniell, Henry, 1652, by Mrs. Jane Harmer, Northumberland Co.
Daniell, Oliver, 1653, by Tho. Read, Northumberland Co.
Daniell, Wm., 1653, by Tho. Hawkins, Northumberland Co.
Daniell, Adam, 1653, by Peter Knight and Baber Cult, ——— Co.
Daniells, Danl., 1653, by Richard Lake, Lancaster Co.
Daniell, Edward, 1644, by Edwyn Conaway, Northampton Co.
Daniell, Hen., 1638, by John Jackson and Eliza Kingswill, James City
    Co.
Daniell, Edw., 1637, by Stephen Charlton, Accomack Co.
Daniell, Edw., 1636, by John Neale, Accomack Co.
Daniell, Peirce, 1637, by Capt. Thomas Flint, Warwick River Co.
Daniell, John, 1653, by Sampson Robins, Northampton Co.
Daniell, Eliza, 1635, by Henry, Daniell, James City Co.
Dane, Eustace, 1652, by John Robinson, Jr., Northampton Co.
Danebigg, Ralph, 1653, by Charles Grymes, clerk, Lancaster Co.
Dankes, Walter, 1637, by Henry Perry, Charles River Co.
Danielson, Marg, 1650, by David Peibles, Charles City Co.
Danister, James, 1650, by George Taylor, ——— Co.
Dany, Eliz., 1654, by John Watson and John Bognall, Westmoreland
    Co.
Dany, John, 1654, by Richard Jones, James City Co.
Darby, Henry, 1655, by Jenkins Price, Northampton Co.
Darby, Ann, 1650, by Mrs. Winefrid Morrison, ——— Co.
Darby, Thomas, 1635, by Samuel Weaver, ——— Co.
Darbye, Jon., 1637, by Thomas Weston, Charles River Co.
Darneby, William, 1635, by Thomas Harwood, ——— Co.
Darker, Tho., 1652, by Tobias Horton, Lancaster Co.
Darfield, Robt., 1654, by John Wyre, John Gillet, Andrew Gibson and
    John Phillipps, ——— Co.
Darfield, Robt., 1652, by Tho. Leechman and John Bennett, Gloucester
    Co.
Darling, Rich., 1648, by Wm. Ewen, James City Co.
Darling, Richard, 1641, by Henry Hawley, Isle of Wight Co.
Darling, Ruth, 1654, by Peter Knight, Northumberland Co.
Darling, Dorothy, 1647, by Elizabeth Barcroft, Isle of Wight Co.
Darrell, Wm., 1643, by Richard Richards, Charles River Co.
Darrell, Mary, 1654, by Mrs. Fra. Harrison, widow, Westmoreland
    Co.

Darrington, Wm., 1653, by John Goslin, —— Co.
Darrow, Anne, 1652, by Tho. Darrow (her husband), Northumberland Co.
Darson, Jonathan, 1638, by Benjamin Carrill, James City Co.
Dary, John, 1638, by Thomas Burbage, Accomack Co.
Dary, Lawrence, 1654, by Wm. Robinson and Cornelius Johnson, Westmoreland Co.
Daskins, Mary, 1653, by Carbet Piddle, Northumberland Co.
Dasvie, John, 1646, by Sir. William Berkley, —— Co.
Daughby, Edward, 1653, by John Knolt, —— Co.,
Dauks, Walter, 1655, by Jenkin Price, Northampton Co.
Daulding, Mary, 1650, by Thomas Panker, —— Co.
Daurnport, Hannah, 1650, by Wm. Hodson, Yorke Co.
Daune, Ann, 1650, by Mr. Robt. Holt, James City Co.
Dansey, Alice, 1636, by John Dansey, James City Co.
Dauson, Billcum, and Mary his wife, 1653, by John Goslin, —— Co.
Dauson, Richard, 1652, by Nicho. George, Tho. Taberer and Humphry Clarke, —— Co.
Dauter, Eliz., 1637, by Henry Perry, Charles River Co.
Dauter, Eliz., 1637, by Henry Perry, Charles River Co.
Dave, Tho., 1651, by Ashwell Battin, Yorke Co.
Davenport, Edwd., 1643, by Sir. Francis Wyatt, Kt., —— Co.
Davenport, Ann, 1637, by Thomas Hampton, New Norfolk Co.
Davicult, Robert, 1639, by Peter Ridley, James City Co.
Davins, Jon., 1636, by Georg Sapheir, Elizabeth City Co.
Davison, John, 1642, by William Lawson, Isle of Wight Co.
David, Wm., 1648, by Richard Lee, Gent., —— Co.
David, Evan, 1641, by Ambrose Bennett, Isle of Wight Co.
David, John, 1635, by Capt. Thos. Willowbye, Elizabeth City Co.
Davie, Richard, 1655, by David Boucher, Isle of Wight Co.
Davi, John, 1638, by Nicholas Jarnew, Charles River Co.
Davey, Richard, 1639, by Wm. Barker, Charles City Co.
Davie, John, 1639, by Richard Parsons, Lower New Norfolk Co.
Davis, Robert, 1639, by Tho. Boulding, Elizabeth City Co.
Davis, James, 1640, by Robert Holt, James City Co.
Davis, Nich., 1639, by Edward Sanderson, —— Co.
Davis, William, 1639, by William Davis, James City Co.
Davis, William, 1639, by Edward Travis, James City Co.
Davis, Jane, 1638, by John Robins, Elizabeth City Co.
Davis, Mary, 1642, by John Davis, her husband, Henrico Co.
Davis, Samuell, 1642, by Capt. Samuell Mathews, Esq., —— Co.
Davis, Mary, 1642, by Daniell Lewellyn, —— Co.
Davis, Margarett, 1642, by Capt. Daniell Gookin, —— Co.
Davis, Eliz., 1650, by Capt, Robert Sheppard, —— Co.
Davis, John, 1643, by Benjamin Harryson, Gent., James City Co.
Davis, John, 1642, by Justinian Cooper, Isle of Wight Co.
Davis, Edward, 1654, by Robert Bowers, —— Co.
Davis, James, 1654, by Edward Simpson, Gloucester Co.
Davis, Richard, 1643, by William Mills, Isle of Wight Co.
Davis, Lawrence, 1650, by Jervace Dodson, Gent., Northumberland Co.

Davis, Marg., 1650, by John Garwood, Nansemond Co.
Davis, Eliz., 1655, by Gilbert Deacon, Henrico Co.
Davis, John, 1642, by Samuell Abbott, ——— Co.
Davis, Grace, 1655, by Dr. Giles Mode, New Kent Co.
Davis, Devin, 1649, by Rowland Burneham, Gent., ——— Co.
Davis, Law., 1656, by Tho. Harris, Lancaster Co.
Davis, Francis, 1655, by Wm. Wright, Gent., Nansemond Co.
Davis, Robt., 1656, by Nathaniel Pope, Gent., Westmoreland Co.
Davis, Jane, 1656, by Capt. Wm. Confill, Surry Co.
Davis, Wm., 1655, by Mr. Anthony Langston, New Kent Co.
Davis, Wm., 1654, by Wm. Mells, Lancaster Co.
Davis, Runberon, 1655, by Mr. Anthony Langston, New Kent Co.
Davis, Richard, 1654, by John Williams, Northumberland Co.
Davis, Sarah, 1655, by Richard Foster, ——— Co.
Davis, Sabina, 1654, by John Williams, Northumberland Co.
Davis, Wm., 1655, by Robt. Priddy, New Kent Co.
Davis, Griffeth, 1647, by Richard Bland, ——— Co.
Davis, John, 1643, by Capt. Samuell Mathews, Esq., ——— Co.
Davis, Nico. 1650, by Mrs. Francis Townshend (widow), Northumberland Co.
Davis, John, 1650, by Thos. Blogg, Northumberland Co.
Davis, James, 1650, by Nathaniell Jones, Northumberland Co.
Davis, John, 1650, by John Armesbee, Northumberland Co.
Davis, Tho. 1650, by Sr. Tho. Luntsford, Kt., and Baronett, ——— Co.
Davis, Marg., 1650, by Mr. Epaphroditus Lawson, ——— Co.
Davis, Margarett, 1650, by George Taylor, ——— Co.
Davis, James, 1650, by Robert Bird, ——— Co.
Davis, Elizabeth, 1650, by Francis Hobbs, ——— Co.
Davis, Rich., 1637, by Wm. Prior, Gent., Charles River Co.
Davis, Wm., 1650, by Capt. Moore Fautleroy, ——— Co.
Davis, Richard, 1650, by Capt. Moore Fautleroy, ——— Co.
Davis, Robt., 1642, by Francis England, Isle of Wight Co.
Davis, Morgan, 1650, by Mr. James Williamson, ——— Co.
Davis, John, 1650, by Mr. James Williamson, ——— Co.
Davis, Mary, 1648, by Nicholas Dixson, Nansemond Co.
Davis, John, 1649, by Nicholas, Waddilowe, Northampton Co.
Davis, John, 1648, by Nichlas Dixson, Nansemond Co.
Davis, Justin, 1648, by Richard Thompson, Northumberland Co.
Davis, Richard, 1648, by Randall Crew, Nansemond Co.
Davis, James, 1651, by Geo. Colclough, Gent., Northumberland Co.
Davis, Jane, 1651, by Thomas Thornbraugh, Northumberland Co.
Davis, Wm., 1651, by Wm. Hampton, ——— Co.
Davis, John, 1651, by Capt. Stephen Gill, Northumberland Co.
Davis, Grace, 1651, by Capt. Stephen Gill, Northumberland Co.
Davis, Mary, 1651, by James Davis, Northumberland Co.
Davis, Wm., 1651, by Mr. Arthur Price, Yorke Co.
Davis, Jane, 1651, by Mr. W. Armestead, ——— Co.
Davis, Owen, 1651, by Mr. Rowland Burnham, ——— Co.
Davis, Jno., 1651, by Mr. Rowland Burnham, ——— Co.
Davis, John, 1651, by Thomas Keeling, Lower Norfolk Co.
Davis, Wm., 1653, by Robt. Sorrel, ——— Co.

Davis, Jon., 1653, by Tho. Mallard, Northumberland Co.
Davis, Mary, 1653, by Richard Jennings, ——— Co.
Davis, Wm., 1653, by Wm. Haynes, ——— Co.
Davis, Mary, 1653, by William Freeke, Northumberland Co.
Davis, Mary, 1653, by Henry Lee, Yorke Co.
Davis, Richard, by 1652, by John Gresham, Northumberland Co.
Davis, Hopkin, 1652, by Mr. John Moltrom, Northumberland Co.
Davis, Richard, 1652, by Capt. Augustine Warner, ——— Co.
Davis, Richard, 1652, by Tho. Preston, Jr., ——— Co.
Davis, Wm., 1652, by Mr. David Fox, Lancaster Co.
Davis, Wm., 1652, by Lt. Coll. John Cheesman, ——— Co.
Davis, Sabina, 1652, by Tho. Preston, Jr., ——— Co.
Davis, Tho., 1653, by Wm. Haynes, ——— Co.
Davis, Luce, 1652, by Mr. Richard Cocke, Henrico Co.
Davis, Morgan, 1652, by Richard Nelmes, Northumberland Co.
Davis, David, 1652, by Mrs. Jane Harmer, Northumberland Co.
Davis, Kath., 1653, by Mr. Henry Soanes, Gloucester Co.
Davis, Tho., 1653, by Abraham Moone, Northumberland Co.
Davis, Jane, 1653, by John King, Surry Co.
Davis, Mary, 1653, by Peter Knight and Baker Cult, ——— Co.
Davis, Wm., 1653, by Oliver Green, Gloucester Co.
Davis, Jane, 1653, by Charles Scarburg, Northampton Co.
Davis, Tho., 1652, by Henry Smith, Jr., ——— Co.
Davis, Robert, 1653, by Francis Symons, Northumberland Co.
Davis, Tho., 1653, by Corbet Piddle, Northumberland Co.
Davis, Jon., 1653, by Corbet Piddle, Northumberland Co.
Davis, Alex., 1652, by Mr. James Wairadine, ——— Co.
Davis, James, 1638, by Lieut. John Upton, Isle of Wight Co.
Davis, John, 1642, by John Benton, ——— Co.
Davis, Hugh, 1638, by John George, Charles City Co.
Davis, Elizabeth, wife of Samuell Davis, 1642, by John Benton, ———
    Co.
Davis, Samuell, Sr., 1642, by John Benton, ——— Co.
Davis, Robt. 1642, by John Robins, ——— Co.
Davis, Samuell, Jr., 1642, by John Benton, ——— Co.
Davis, Rich., 1639, by Capt. Robert Felgate, Charles River Co.
Davis, Henry, 1646, by Geo. Ludlow, Esq., York Co.
Davis, Thomas, 1648, by Mr. Thomas Davies, Isle of Wight Co.
Davis, Ann, 1643, by Wm. Brooke, Upper Norfolk Co.
Davis, Elizabeth, 1638, by Joseph Boarne, Charles City Co.
Davis, Robert, 1638, by Tristrum Nosworthy, New Norfolk Co.
Davis, Robt., 1643, by John Sweete, Isle of Wight Co.
Davis, Evan, 1643, by James Whiting, ——— Co.
Davis, John, 1638, by Thomas Boulding, Elizabeth City Co.
Davis, David, 1638, by John Jackson and Eliza Kingswell, James City
    Co.
Davis, Thomas, 1638, by Mr. Thomas Wallis, James Cith Co.
Davis, Wm., 1637, by Stephen Charlton, Accomack Co.
Davis, John, 1637, by Justinian Cooper, Isle of Wight Co.
Davis, Wm., 1637. by Lt. John Upton, Isle of Wight Co.
Davis, Eliz., 1642, by Wm. Barnard, Esq., Isle of Wight Co.

Davis, Rice, 1635, by Thos. Butler Clarke and Pastor of Denbie, Warrasquinoake Co.
Davis, Robt., 1636, by John Chandler, Elizabeth City Co.
Davis, Joane, 1637, by Margaret Rogers, New Norfolk Co.
Davis, Joane, 1636, by Edward Rogers, Warrasquinoake Co.
Davis, Wm., 1635, by Jno. Upton, Warrasquinoake Co.
Davis, Thomas, 1635, by Charles Harner, ——— Co.
Davis, Jon., 1636, by Justinian Cooper, Warrasquinoake Co.
Davis, William, 1635, by William Stone, ——— Co.
Davis, John, 1650, by John Lacker, ——— Co.
Davis, Dorothy, 1636, John Roberts, Elizabeth City Co.
Davye, Richard, 1639, by Dorothy Clarke, Henrico Co.
Dawbee, Huho., 1646, by Sir. William Berkley, ——— Co.
Dawber, Edward, 1651, by Abraham Moone and (Thomas Griffin), Lancaster Co.
Dawby, Eliz., 1643, by John Botts, James City Co.
Dawby, John, 1643, by John Batts, James City Co.
Dawby, Lawrence, 1653, by John Hillier, Northumberland Co.
Dawby, Lawrence, 1652, by Elias Edmond, Lancaster Co.
Dawen, Robt., 1648, by John Seward, Isle of Wight Co.
Dawes, Alice, 1650, by Elyas Edmonds, ——— Co.
Dawling, Cor., 1654, by Mr. Francis Hamond, York Co.
Dawkes, Henry, 1638, by Thomas Swann, James City Co.
Dawkins, Elizabeth, assignee of Richard Shootboult, 1654, by Humphry Gibbs, Warrick Co.
Dawn, John, 1648, by Lewis Burwell and Tho. Haws, York River Co.
Dawnes, Alex., 1649, by Stephen Gill, York Co.
Dawnes, Richd., 1653, by Francis Emperer, Hugh Gale and Edward Morgan, Lower Norfolk Co.
Dawnes, Mary, 1653, by Tho. Hampton, ——— Co.
Dawnes, Fr., 1638, by Elizabeth Grayne, Charles City Co.
Dawnes, J., 1655, by Richard Hamlet, James City Co.
Dawning, Richard, 1650, by Robert Bird, ——— Co.
Dawning, Anne, 1652, by Tho. Stevens, Lancaster Co.
Dawell, Elizabeth, 1654, by Obed. Williams, York Co.
Dawsey, Ann, 1639, by Christopher Dawsey, Elizabeth City Co.
Dawsey, Chi., 1636, by James Vanerit, Elizabeth City Co.
Dawson, John, 1650, by Henry Ashwell, ——— Co.
Dawson, John, 1654, by Capt. Nich. Marteaw, Westmoreland Co.
Dawson, John, 1643, by Stephen Gill, ——— Co.
Dawson, Edward, 1654, by Tho. Hobkins, Lancaster Co.
Dawson, Geo., 1643, by Capt. Samuell Mathews, Esq., ——— Co.
Dawson, Edw., 1650, by Lewis Burwell, Gent., Northumberland Co.
Dawson, Jane, 1650, by Hump. Lyster, ——— Co.
Dawson, Wm., 1652, by Mr. Henry Pitt, ——— Co.
Dawson, Thomas, 1638, by John Moone, ——— Co.
Dawson, John, 1637, by Oliver Sprye, New Norfolk Co.
Dawson, Jonathan, 1636, by Nathan Martin, Henrico Co.
Dawson, Gilbert, 1636, by Cheney Boyse, Charles City Co.
Dawson, Wm., 1637, by Wm. Farrar, Henrico Co.
Dawson, Thomas, 1635, by Capt. Wm. Pierce, ——— Co.

Dawson, Ann, 1636, by Capt. Thomas Willoughby, ——— Co.
Dawtres, John, 1636, by Jeremiah Clement, ——— Co.
Dawrigg, Susan, 1652, by Arthur Upshalt, Northampton Co.
Day, John, 1655, by Richard Price, New Kent Co.
Day, Rich., 1655, by John Biggs, Lower Norfolk Co.
Day, John, & Margery his wife, 1655, by George Wall, Westmoreland Co.
Day, Mary, 1654, by John Williams, Northumberland Co.
Day, Geo., 1650, by Capt. Moore Fautleroy, ——— Co.
Day, George, 1649, by Mr. Tho. Spake, Northumberland Co.
Day, Thomas, 1652, by Henry Tyler, Charles River Co.
Day, Henry, 1653, by Charles Grimes, Lancaster Co.
Day, Eliz., 1653, by John Ware, ——— Co.
Day, Richard, 1638, by Cornelius Loyd, ——— Co.
Day, Jon., 1636, by Peter Johnson, Warrasquinoake Co.
Day, Jno., 1635, by John Slaughter, ——— Co.
Dayes, John, 1642, by John Vallentine, Isle of Wight Co.
Dayes, John, 1639, by Tho. Boulding, Elizabeth City Co.
Daynes, John, 1652, by Mr. Edward Overman, York Co.
Daynes, Phillis, 1645, by William Daynes, her husband, Lower Norfolk Co.
Dayton, Mary, a maid, 1648, by Lewis Burwell and Tho. Haws, York River Co.
Dayson, Susan, 1655, by Mr. Tho. Peck, Gloucester Co.
Deacon, Mary, 1655, by John Motley, Northumberland Co.
Deacon, Triphany, 1655, by John Motley, Northumberland Co.
Deacon, Wm., 1655, by John Motley, Northumberland Co.
Deakes, William, 1638, by Richard Milton, Charles City Co.
Dean, Nich., 1654, by Edw, Welch, ——— Co.
Deane, Wm., 1637, by Mathew Edloe, ——— Co.
Deane, Richard, 1630, by John Russell, ——— Co.
Deane, John, 1636, by John Dansey, James City Co.
Deane, Nath., 1638, by Wm. Barker and Associates, Charles City Co.
Deane, Richard, 1639, by Thomas Grey, James City Co.
Deane, Richard, 1637, by Edward Moth, James River Co.
Deane, Mary, 1653, by Robert Bouth, Yorke Co.
Deane, Alice, 1652, by Nicholas Wadilow, Northampton Co.
Deane, Alice, 1655, by Nich. Wadilow, Northampton Co.
Deane, Wm., 1654, by Phillip Chesly and Dan. Wilde, Westmoreland Co.
Deane, Mary, 1654, by Richard Walker, ——— Co.
Deane, Richard, 1654, by Richard Walker, ——— Co.
Deane, Alice, 1656, by John Belliott, Northampton Co.
Deane, Wm., 1642, by Hugh Gwyn, Gent., ——— Co.
Deane, Elinor, 1643, by Tho. Symonds, ——— Co.
Deane, Elian., 1639, by Tho. Symons, James City Co.
Deanes, Tho., 1649, by Henry Bishopp, Northampton Co.
Deany, Ann, 1650, by Robert Bird, ——— Co.
Deare, Wm., 1653, by Charles Grymes, Lancaster Co.
Deare, Joseph, 1637, by William Spencer, ——— Co.
Dearing, Kath., 1653, by Capt. Nathaniel Hurd, Warrick Co.

Death, Eliz., 1641, by Ambrose Bennett, Isle of Wight Co.
Death, Richard, 1641, by Ambrose Bennett, Isle of Wight Co.
Death, Francis, 1651, by Abraham Moone and (Thomas Griffin), Lancaster Co.
Death, Susan, 1641, by Ambrose Bennett, Isle of Wight Co.
Deacon, Tho., 1636, by Wm. Fookes, ——— Co.
Deacon, Martha, 1637, by Wm. Wilkinson, New Norfolk Co.
Death Peter, 1637, by John Clarkson, Charles River Co.
Deaton, Wm., 1651, by Mr. George Truhett, Northampton Co.
Deball, Cornelius, 1636, by James Place, Henrico Co.
Deball, Vencent, 1636, by James Place, Henrico Co.
Debarr, Peeter, 1646, by David Jones, Charles City Co.
Deberton, Ann, 1653, by Robt. Sorrel, ——— Co.
Debnam, Wm., 1636, by Christopher Calthropp, Charles River Co.
Deby, Robert, 1648, by Lewis Burwell, Gent., ——— Co.
DeCarvalco, Saliman, 1649, by Capt. Ralph Wormeley, ——— Co.
DeCude, Allen, 1639, by Capt. Nicholas Martian, Charles River Co.
Dedervate, Richard, 1653, by Wm. Wyatt, Gloucester Co.
Dedgens, Bastian, 1653, by John King, Surry Co.
Deeber, Eliza, ——, by Samuel Heely and John Carter, Surry Co.
Deedham, Daniel, 1653, by Edward Hall, Lower Norfolk Co.
Deeren, John, 1652, by Anthony Hoskins, Northampton Co.
Deering, Edmond, 1653, by Col. Wm. Clayborne (Sec. of State), ——— Co.
Deering, Thomas, 1638, by Thomas, Beerbye, Upper New Norfolk Co.
Degaris, Elias, 1643, by Georg Levitt, ——— Co.
Delabeere, Richard, 1638, by Joseph Boarne, Charles City Co.
Delabere, Richard, 1655, by Gilbert Deacon, Henrico Co.
Delahay, Sarah, a servant, 1637, by Rich. Greete, ——— Co.
Delaware, Esay, 1637, by Daniel Gookins, New Norfolk Co.
Deler, Rey Jacques, 1636, by William Coleman, Elizabeth City Co.
Delf, Tho., 1655, by Major Wm. Hoccaday, New Kent Co.
Delois, Alice, 1641, by Stephen Charleton, Accomack Co.
Dellony, John, 1654, by Toby Smith, Lancaster Co.
Delton, Margaret, 1656, by Hester Obkham, James City Co.
Delton, Margaret, 1655, by Lt. Col. Tho. Swan, Surry Co.
Demacheto, Christian, 1643, by Tho. Williams, ——— Co.
Demaley, John, 1654, by Nicholas Morris, Northumberland Co.
Demecry, Ann, 1650, by Capt. Moore Fautleroy, ——— Co.
Demey, Geo., 1654, by Col. Argoll Yardley, Northampton Co.
Demkin, James, 1653, by Tho. Bourne, Lancaster Co.
Demond, Martin, 1638, by Wm. Cloys, Charles River Co.
Demson, Rowland, 1640, by Tho. Stegg, Charles City Co.
Demster, Wm., 1654, by John Wyre, John Gillet and Andrew Gilson & John Phillipps, ——— Co.
Densley, Wm., 1650, by John Landman, ——— Co.
Denchfeild, Jeffrey, 1643, by Mr. John Bishopp, James City Co.
Deney, Joan, 1654, by Col. Argoll Yardley, Northampton Co.
Denamere, ——, 1654, by John Watson and John Bagnall, Westmoreland Co.
Denham, Thomas, 1643, by Edward Murfey and JohnVaughan, ——— Co.

Denham, Walter, 1653, by Bartholomew Haskins, Lower Norfolk Co.
Denman, Ellice, 1656, by George Abbott, Nansemond Co.
Denmark, Fr., 1636, by James Vanerit, Elizabeth City Co.
Denn, Christ., 1637, by Nathaniel Floyd, Isle of Wight Co.
Dendy, John, 1653, by Colo. Wm. Clayborne (Sec. of State), ——— Co.
Dennes, John, 1639, by John Saines, ——— Co.
Denine, John, 1635, by Daniel Cugley, Accomac Co.
Denington, Oliver, 1636, by Wm. Clarke, Henrico Co.
Dennes, Humphry, 1639, by Georg Minifye, Esq., Charles River Co.
Denins, Wm., 1655, by George Frizell and Tho. Moore, Northampton Co.
Dennis, Shela, 1654, by Rich. Bunduch, Northampton Co.
Dennis, Ann, 1650, by Capt. Moore Fautleroy, ——— Co.
Dennis, Xpo., 1651, by Mr. Rowland Lawson, ——— Co.
Dennis, Ann, 1653, by Edward Hamond, Northampton Co.
Dennis, Joane, 1652, by Mrs. Mary Brent, Northumberland Co.
Denison, Hum., 1650, by Tho. Vaws, Gent., Northumberland Co.
Dennett, James, 1650, by John Cooke, Northumberland Co.
Dennett, John, 1635, by Thomas Harwood, ——— Co.
Dennitt, Richard, 1653, by John Hillier, Northumberland Co.
Dennington, Oliver, 1638, by William Clark, Henrico Co.
Denson, Wm., 1652, by Daniel Welch, Lancaster Co.
Denson, Wm., 1638, by Robert Pitts, Isle of Wight Co.
Dent, Eliza, 1643, by Sir. Francis Wyatt, Kt., ——— Co.
Denton, John, 1650, by Capt. Moore, Fautleroy, ——— Co.
Denwood, Den., 1655, by Sampson Robin, Northampton Co.
Deone, Martha, 1635, by William Wilkinson (minister), ——— Co.
Deones, Tho., 1650, by Stephen Charlton, Northampton Co.
Depona, Lewis, 1635, by Thos. Crompe, James City Co.
Derickson, Peter, 1653, by Anto. Hoskins, Northampton Co.
Derfield, Ro., 1653, by Capt. Francis Morgan, Gloucseter Co.
Dermon, of Collum, 1052, by Mr. Henry Soane, ——— Co.
Derott, Charles, 1642, by John Sweete, ——— Co.
Deroys, John, 1646, by Thomas Bahe, Upper Norfolk Co.
Derricke, Francis, 1639, by Mathew Gough, ——— Co.
Derry, Robt., 1635, by Mr. Geo. Keth, Charles River Co.
Derry, Orsell, 1656, by Tabitha and Matilda Scarbough, Northampton Co.
Deryell, Joseph, 1655, by George Parker, Northampton Co.
Dence, Tho., 1638, by Capt. Christopher Wormeley, ——— Co.
Devall, Jon., 1642, by Daniell Lewellyn, ——— Co.
Devall, John, 1642, by John Davis, Henrico Co.
Devell, George, 1655, by John Motley, Northumberland Co.
Devine, Mary, 1653, by Samuell Parry, Lancaster Co.
Devorax, Jon., 1654, by Alex., Maducks and James Jones, Northampton Co.
Dexton, Ellinor, 1653, by Richard Jennings, ——— Co.
Dewe, Edwd., 1654, by Tho. Deynes, ——— Co.
Dewee, David, 1640, by Richard Williams, Charles City Co.
Dewse, Mary, 1650, by Mr. Epaphroditus Lawson, ——— Co.
Dibbins, Richard, 1651, by Thomas Manning, Warwick Co.

Dibbins, Richard, 1652, by Tho. Steevens, Lancaster Co.
Dick, Jervis, 1637, by John Baker, Charles City Co.
Dicke, James, 1651, by Audery Bennett, Nansemond Co.
Dickenson, Giles, 1653, by Wm. Wyatt, Gloucester Co.
Dickenson, ——, 1653, by Mr. Wm. Debram, —— Co.
Dickenson, Elizabeth, 1656, by Griffith Dickinson, —— Co.
Dickes, Wm., 1637, by Christopher Stokes, Charles River Co.
Dickes, Edward, 1638, by Georg White, clerk, Upper New Norfolk Co.
Dickes, Eliza, 1637, by Christopher Stokes, Warwick River Co.
Dickers, Mary, 1651, by Gerge Ludlow, Esq., —— Co.
Dickeson, John, 1653, by Elias Hartru, Northampton Co.
Dickinson, Wm., 1645, by John Baker, Elizabeth City Co.
Dickinson, Anthony, 1640, by William Wigg, James City Co.
Dickinson, Andrew, 1648, by Mr. Thomas Davies, Isle of Wight Co.
Dickinson, Wm., 1635, by John Slaughter, —— Co.
Dickinson, John, 1650, by Mr. James Williamson, —— Co.
Dickinson, John, 1652, by Capt. John West, Esq., —— Co.
Dicks, Edw., 1648, by Richard Lee, Gent., —— Co.
Dickins, Wm., 1643, by Phillipp Taylor, Northampton Co.
Dickey, Danll., 1650, by Mr. Epaphoditus Lawson, —— Co.
Dickson, Richard, 1647, by Thomas Johnson, Gent., Northampton Co.
Dickson, Tho., 1638, by Thomas Symons, Upper Nrofolk Co.
Digg, Samll., 1650, by Lewis Burwell, Gent., —— Co.
Digg, Edward, 1650, by Lewis Burwell, Gent., —— Co.
Digby, Edward, 1650, by Lewis Burwell, Gent., Northumberland Co.
Diggs, Richard, 1645, by William Cock, Elizabeth City Co.
Dignell, Mich., 1642, by Capt. Samuell Mathews, Esq., —— Co.
Dillard, George, 1650, by Capt. Moore Fautleroy, —— Co.
Dillard, ——, 1652, by Elias Edmonds, Lancaster Co.
Dile, Dorothy, 1649, by Tho. Curtis, —— Co.
Dillse, Thomas, 1637, by William Prior, Gent., Charles River Co.
Dinglas, Wm., 1652, by Col. Geo. Ludlow, Esq., Gloucester Co.
Dingley, Wm., 1654, by John Dennes, —— Co.
Dingley, Wm., 1654, by John Wyre, John Gillet, Andrew Gibson and
    John Phillipps, —— Co.
Dinsdale, Tho., 1368, by Georg Mynifie (merchant), —— Co.
Dipple, Jon., 1636, by Epaphroditus Lawson, Warwick Co.
Dinty, John, 1650, by John Essix, Northumberland Co.
Dison, Tho., 1652, by Tho. Glascock, Lancaster Co.
Ditch, Andrew, 1645, by John Nuthall, Northampton Co.
Ditch, Eliza, 1650, by Epaphroditus Lawson, —— Co.
Dix, John, 1642, by William Lawson, Isle of Wight Co.
Dix, Henry, 1637, by Henry Perry, Charles River Co.
Dixon, Isabella, 1639, by Robert Glascock, Lower Norfolk Co.
Dixon, Ann, 1654, by Walter Dickenson, Lancaster Co.
Dixon, John, 1638, by Stephen Hamblyn, Charles City Co.
Dixon, Luke, 1656, by George Abbott, Nansemond Co.
Dixon, Eliz., 1656, by George Abbott, Nansemond Co.
Dixon, Ri., 1650, by Capt. Moore Fautleroy, —— Co.
Dixon, Geo., 1643, by John Freeme, Charles Co.

Dixon, Amb., 1649, by Richard Bayly, Northampton Co.
Dixon, Wm., 1653, by Jon. Slaughter, ——— Co.
Dixon, Tho., 1654, by Richard Jones, James City Co.
Dixon, Wm., 1642, by Thomas Osborne, Henrico Co.
Dixon, Richard ,1653, by Richard Larke, Lancaster Co.
Dixon, Mary, 1652, by Ambrose Dixon and Stephen Horsely, Jr., Northampton Co.
Dixon, Christian, 1647, by Thomas Johnson, Gent., Northampton Co.
Dixon, Math., 1638, by Robert Freeman, James City Co.
Dixon, Christopher, 1636, by John Forbrese, Accomack Co.
Dixon, Reich., 1636, by Robert Hollem, Henrico Co.
Dixon, Christopher, 1638, by Edmund Scarborough, Accomac Co.
Dixson, John, 1654, by Toby Smith, Lancaster Co.
Dixson, Nicholas, 1646, by Thomas Bohe, Upper Norfolk Co.
Doane, Tho., 1650, by John Rosier, Northumberland Co.
Doane, Nich., 1635, by William Barber (a mariner) Charles City Co.
Doan, Fra., 1649, by Tho. Spake, Gent., Northumberland Co.
Doar, John, 1654, by Toby Smith, Lancaster Co.
Dobbins, Richd., 1651, by Humphry Tabb, Northumberland Co.
Dobson, Richard, 1643, by Thomas Frye, James City Co.
Dobson, Fra., and wife, 1653, by Edward Dobson, ——— Co.
Dobson, John, 1652, by John Oliver, Isle of Wight Co.
Dobson, Edward, 1638, by Thomas Boulding, Elizabeth City Co.
Dodd, John, 1642, by Cornelius de Hull, ——— Co.
Dodd, Tho., 1642, by Hugh Gwyn, Gent., ——— Co.
Dodman, John, 1637, by William Spencer, ——— Co.
Dodman, Jon., 1635, by William Spencer, ——— Co.
Dodson, Benj., 1635, by Capt. Wm. Pierse, ——— Co.
Dodsley, Tho., 1643, by Wm. Butler, James City Co.
Dodson, Tho., 1643, by Richard Richards, Charles River Co.
Dodson, Anne, 1652, by Gilbert Blunt, ——— Co.
Doe, Jane, 1655, by John Westlock, Northampton Co.
Doe, Ral., 1652, by Nicholas Wadilow, Northampton Co.
Doe, John, 1635, by George Minifie, James City Co.
Doe Ralph, 1655, by Nich. Wadilow, Northampton Co.
Doe, John, 1635, by Richard Bennett, ——— Co.
Doe, Jon., 1637, by Rich. Bennett, New Norfolk Co.
Doe, John, 1636, by Mr. Georg Menifye, James City Co.
Doge, John, 1654, by William Howard, Gloucester Co.
Doge, David, 1650, by Rice Jones, ——— Co.
Doilby, Wm., 1650, by Anthony Fuljam, ——— Co.
Dolby, John, 1642, by Edmund Scarborough, Accomack Co.
Dolkin, John, 1640, by Christopher Kirke, Accomack Co.
Dollin, Wm., 1643, by Richard Kemp, Esq., James City Co.
Dolson, Andrew, 1649, by John Sibsey, Lower Norfolk Co.
Dolumaine, Alex., 1655, by George Wall, Westmoreland Co.
Donak, Christopher, 1655, by Southy Littleberry, Northampton Co.
Donart, David, 1653, by Geo. Thompson, Gloucester Co.
Donaway, Step., 1654, by John Wyre, John Gillet, Andrew Gilson and John Phillipps, ——— Co.
Donell, Walter, 1654, by Mrs. Mgt. Brent, Westmoreland Co.

Donell, Moragha, 1655, by Edmund Scarborough, Jr., and Littleton Scarborough, Northampton Co.
Donellin, Mary, 1655, by Wm. Johnson, and Stephen Horsey, Northampton Co.
Donet, Clement, 1639, by William Burdett, Accomack Co.
Donnellin, Tho., 1655, by Wm. Johnson and Stephen Horsey, Northampton Co.
Donflin, Martin, 1637, by Joseph Cobb, Isle of Wight Co.
Donibell, Margery, 1653, by Capt. Robt. Alrahal, Gloucester Co.
Donn, Clem., 1639, by William Burdett, Accomack Co.
Donn, Arthur, 1643, by Elizabeth Hull, ———— Co.
Donne, John, 1653, by Colo. Wm. Clayborne (Sec. of State), ———— Co.
Donne, Richard, 1639, by Tho. Symons, James City Co.
Donnell, James, 1654, by Mrs. Mgt. Brent, Westmoreland Co.
Donnell, James, 1653, by Peler Knight, Northumberland Co.
Donned, Arth., 1648, by Tho. Broughton, ———— Co.
Donniell, Tho., 1653, by Abraham Moon, Lancaster Co.
Donouge, Roger, 1655, by John Woodward, Gloucester Co.
Dookes, Jon., 1638, by Elizabeth Grayne, Charles City Co.
Doone, Daniel, 1653, by Edward Hall, Lower Norfolk Co.
Dorcas, Foster, Jr., 1653, by Richard Foster, Lower Norfolk Co.
Dordon, Step., 1651, by Robert Brassem, Nansemond Co.
Dorfeild, Rob., 1654, by Richard Codsford, Westmoreland Co.
Dorman, Richard, 1656, by Tho. Harris, Lancaster Co.
Dorman, Sarah, 1655, by John Dorman, Northampton Co.
Dorman, John, 1648, by Tho. Broughton, ———— Co.
Dorman, Peter, 1652, by Richard Coleman, ———— Co.
Dorothy, Behethland, 1638, by Randall Crew (her husband), Upper New Norfolk Co.
Dorsett, Jon., 1643, by John Sweete, Isle of Wight Co.
Dorsey, Edward, 1646, by Thomas Brown, Lower Norfolk Co.
Dorsey, Edward, 1652, by Francis Fleetwood, Lower Norfolk Co.
Dorwin, Tho., 1647, by Richard Bland, ———— Co.
Dowde, Thos., 1656, by Geo. Abbott, Nansemond Co.
Dowland, Edmund, 1654, by Tho. Willoughby, Lower Norfolk Co.
Dowland, Peter, 1650, by Mr. Anthony Ellyot, ———— Co.
Dowling, Fr., 1643, by Capt. Samuell Mathews, Esq., ———— Co.
Downer, Henry, 1654, by Mrs. Fra. Harrison, widow, Westmoreland Co.
Downes, Walter, 1643, by Benjamin Harryson, Gent., James City Co.
Downes, Joyce, 1655, by Symon Symons, Charles City Co.
Downes, John, 1650, by James Metgrigar and Hugh Foutch, Northumberland Co.
Downes, Walter, 1642, by John Boyles, ———— Co.
Downes, Wm., 1637, by John Brodwell, James City Co.
Downes, Eustace, 1637, by Wm. Fairar, Henrico Co.
Downes, Walter, 1637, by Wm. Prior, Charles River Co.
Downinge, Geo., 1652, by Mr. Edward Overman, York Co.
Downing, Anne, 1652, by Capt. Augustine Warner, ———— Co.
Downing, Richd., 1653, by Robt. Sorrel, ———— Co.

Downing, Enoch, 1651, by Mr. Rowland Burnham, —— Co.
Downings, Wm., 1651, by Wm. Vincent, Northumberland Co.
Downing, Wm., 1647, by Elizabeth Barcroft, Isle of Wight Co.
Downman, Cressell, 1654, by Col. Argoll Yardley, Northampton Co.
Downman, Zach., 1654, by Col. Argoll Yardley, Northampton Co.
Downton, John, 1655, by Lt. Col. Anthony Ellyott, —— Co.
Downing, Susan, 1655, by Nich. Wadilow, Northampton Co.
Dowridge, Susan, 1656, by John Billiott, Northampton Co.
Dowringe, Susan, 1652, by Nicholas Wadilow, Northampton Co.
Dowry, John, 1654, by Tho. Harmanson, Northampton Co.
Dowse, Charles, 1643, by Richard Kemp, Esq., James City Co.
Dowse, Katharine, 1637, by Edward Travis, Isle of Wight Co.
Dowse, Kath., 1638, by Edw. Travis and John Johnson, James City Co.
Dowser, Ann, 1654, by Robert Younge, Lancaster Co.
Dowson, Gilbert, 1637, by Cheney Boyes, Charles City Co.
Doubly, Mary, 1637, by Arthur Boyly and Tho. Crosby, Henrico Co.
Doubt, Sampson, 1636, by Samuel Curby, James City Co.
Doughert, David, 1655, by Richard Codsford, Westmoreland Co.
Douglas, John, 1655, by Lt. Col. Tho. Swan, Surry Co.
Douglas, Lee, Wm., 1655, by Major Wm. Lewis, New Kent Co.
Douglass, Archiball, 1652, by Col. Geo. Ludlow, Esq., Gloucester Co.
Douglass, Dan., 1653, by Mr. Edmund Vowman, —— Co.
Douse, Barbara, 1645, by Mr. Bartholomew Hoskins, —— Co.
Dove, William, 1643, by Randall Holt, —— Co.
Dove, John, 1650, by William, Gooch Gent., —— Co.
Dove, John, 1638, by Geo. Dobb, Tho. Perce, Tho. Warne, James City Co.
Dover, Timo., 1651, by Mr. Rowland Burnham, —— Co.
Doza, John, 1655, by Christopher Calvert, Northampton Co.
Draiton, John, 1654, by John Drayton, Westmoreland Co.
Drake, Ann, 1638, by Richard Maion, Charles River Co.
Drake, James, 1639, by Robert Eley, Isle of Wight Co.
Drake, Elizabeth, Filia, 1636, by Robert Drake, Accomack Co.
Drake, Robt., (Senr.), 1636, by Robert Drake, Accomack Co.
Drake, Joan, 1636, by Robert Drake, Accomack Co.
Drake, John, 1637, by Thomas Holt, New Norfolk Co.
Drap, Richard, 1654, by Tho. Willoughby, Lower Norfolk Co.
Drap, John, 1653, by Peter Knight and Baber Cult, —— Co.
Drap, Robt., 1652, by John Phillips, Lancaster Co.
Draper, Jane, 1655, by George Kibble, Lancaster Co.
Draper, Mary, 1654, by Robert Yoe, Westmoreland Co.
Draper, Jon., 1535, by Capt. Thos. Willowbye, —— Co.
Draper, Hen., 1650., by Robert Bird, —— Co.
Draper, James, 1652, by Mrs. Elinor Brocas, Lancaster Co.
Drapp, James, 1649, by Wm. Hoccaday, —— Co.
Dratt, Antho., 1643, by Richard Kemp, Esq., James City Co.
Drawater, Ann, 1637, by Rich. Bellam and Christopher Lawson, James City Co.
Drawten, Ann, 1635, by Capt. Wm. Pierse, —— Co.
Draywood, Tho., 1637, by Capt. Thomas Osborne, Henrico Co.
Dreaton, John, 1642, by John Benton, —— Co.

Dregg, Robt., 1635, by Jno. Sparkei, —— Co.
Drew, John, 1642, by Adam Cooke, Charles Co.
Drew, Symon, 1638, by John Robins, James City Co.
Drew, Edward, 1647, by Wm. Whitington, Northampton Co.
Drew, Capt. Thomas, 1650, by Lawrence Peters, Nansemond Co.
Drew, Tho., 1649, by Bertram Obert, —— Co.
Drew, Tho., 1649, by Wm. Hoccaday, —— Co.
Drew, Hugh, 1653, by Augustine Gillet, Upper Norfolk Co.
Drew, Richd., 1654, by Capt. John West, Esq., Gloucester Co.
Drew, Henry, 1635, by Henry Harte, James City Co.
Drew, Wm., 1636, by Georg Travellor, Accomack Co.
Drewer, Joseph, 1638, by John Batts and John Davis, Charles River Co.
Drewery, Abigail, 1639, by William Davis, James City Co.
Drewry, Robert, 1638, by Robert Freeman, James City Co.
Drewrye, Alice, by John Baker, Charles City Co.
Drewett, John, 1643, by Capt. Samuell Mathews, Esq., —— Co.
Drinkedater, John, 1653, by Wm. Cox, —— Co.
Drinckwater, David, 1650, by William Gooch, Gent., —— Co.
Drinkwater, Jon., 1637, by Arthur Bayly, Henrico Co.
Dimock, Martin, 1637, by Wm. Farrar, Henrico Co.
Driver, Jane, 1649, by Frances Land, Norfolk Co.
Drocatt, Wm., 1642, by Tymothy Fenn, Isle of Wight Co.
Droner, Jean, 1655, by George Frizell and Tho. Moore, Northampton Co.
Droner, Robt., 1655, by George Frizell and Tho. Moore, Northampton Co.
Droner, Richard, 1655, by George Frizell and Tho. Moore, Northampton Co.
Droner, Fra., 1655, by George Frizell and Tho. Moore, Northampton Co.
Dronycold, Peter, 1652, by Robert Elam, Henrico Co.
Drooyt, Elizabeth, 1655, by Tho. Jones, James City Co.
Drop, Wm., 1653, by Abraham Moon, Lancaster Co.
Drout, Tho., 1653, by Capt. Robt. Abrall, —— Co.
Drove, Tho., 1651, by Mr. Robert Abrall, Yorke Co.
Dru, Wm., 1654, by Mr. Francis Hamond, York Co.
Dru, Edward, 1653, by Capt. Wm. Whitington, Northampton Co.
Druct, Wm., 1648, by Tho. Ludwell, Gent., James City Co.
Drud, Thomozim, 1652, by Mrs. Elinor Brocas, Lancaster Co.
Drue, Rich., 1643, by Tho. Symmonds, —— Co.
Druell, Mary, 1653, by John Dipdall, Charles City Co.
Druery, Mary, 1652, by John Pounsey, —— Co.
Drurey, Charles, 1653, by Benjamin Brasseur, —— Co.
Drury, Eliz., 1653, by Tho. Kibby, Northumberland Co.
Drummen, John, 1652, by Jenkin Price, Northampton Co.
Drummer, John, 1655, by Jenkin Price, Northampton Co.
Drumond, Wm., 1639, by Stephen Webb, James City Co.
Drye, Wm., 1654, by Tho. Harmonson, Northampton Co.
Dryner, Giles, 1656, by Tho. Harris, Lancaster Co.
Dubes Anne, 1652, by Mrs. Elnor Brocas, Lancaster Co.
Duch, Jon., 1637, by Arthur Bayly and Tho Crosby, Henrico Co.

Ducket, John, 1646, by Tho. Miles, Elizabeth City Co.

Ducke, William, 1639, by Justinian Cooper, Isle of Wight Co.

Dudifer, John, son Mary Dudifer, 1650, by Wm. Garett and Fra. Wittington, —— Co.

Dudifer, Ann, 1650, by Mr. Wm. Garrett and Fra. Wittington, —— Co.

Dugdale, Benj., 1638, by Georg Mynifie (merchant), —— Co.

Dudley, Ben., 1651, by William Ginsey, Yorke Co.

Dudley, Edw., 1637, by Thos. Hampton Clarke, New Norfolk Co.

Duglass, Tho., 1650, by Richard Tye and Charles Sparrowe, Charles City Co.

Duglass, Geo., 1650, by Richard Tye and Charles Sparrowe, Charles City Co.

Duglass, Jam., 1650, by Richard Tye and Charles Sparrowe, Charles City Co.

Duell, Tho., 1654, by Nich. Merywether, Westmoreland Co.

Duffell, James, 1650, by Lawrence Peters, Nansemond Co.

Dugert, Sarah, 1652, by Nicho. George, Tho. Taberer and Humphry Clarke, —— Co.

Duke, Geo., 1648, by John Seward, Isle of Wight Co.

Dukes, Samll., 1650, by Jervace Dobson, Gent., Northumberland Co.

Dulkly, Lucy, 1639, by Capt. Richard Townsend, Charles River Co.

Dunaton, Cicily, 1639, by John Dunston, James City Co.

Dunbar, Wm., 1650, by Mr. Epaphroditus Lawson, —— Co.

Dunbarr, Alexander, 1654, by Fra. Spright, Nansemond Co.

Duncley, Edw., 1638, by Thom. Plower, and Samuell Edmonds, James City Co.

Duncombe, Tho., 1653, by Major John Westhrope, Charles City Co.

Duncombe, John, 1637, by Lt. Richard Popeley, New Norfolk Co.

Duncome, Jon., 1636, by Henry Southell, —— Co.

Duneridge, John, 1656, by Richard Gible, Northumberland Co.

Dunery, John, 1648, by Richard Pettibon, —— Co.

Durham, Elizabeth, 1653, by Mr. Edmond Bowman, and Richard Slarnell,—— Co.

Dunham, Robert, 1650, by George Pate, Charles City Co.

Dunham, Tho., 1650, by John Baytes, Northumberland Co.

Dunherheath, Elias, 1635, by Thos. Harwood, —— Co.

Dunington, Nich., 1651, by Mr. Antho. Steevens, Northampton Co.

Dunn, Robt., 1650, by Mr. James Williamson, —— Co.

Dunne, Tho., 1650, by Mrs. Frances Townshend (widow), Northumberland Co.

Duning, Rich., 1635, by John Cheeseman, Charles River Co.

Duning, Rich., 1636, by Capt. John Chalsmen, Charles River Co.

Dunning, Sarah, 1650, by Richard Dunning (her husband), —— Co.

Dunings, Georg, 1642, by Stephen Webb, James City Co.

Dunings, Teo., 1642, by Samuell Abbott, —— Co.

Dunkan, Peter, 1650, by Stephen Charlton, Northampton Co.

Dunningham, Richard, 1635, by Nathaniel Hooke, —— Co.

Dunrich, John, 1650, by Epa. Lawson, —— Co.

Dunridge, Ellis, 1637, by Epaphroditus Lawson, Isle of Wight Co.

Dunrich, John, 1650, by Epa. Lawson, —— Co.

Dunrich, Ellis, 1650, by Epa. Lawson, ——— Co.
Dunston, Cicely, 1636, by John Dunston (her husband), James City Co.
Dunston, Andrew, 1653, by John Hellier, Northumberland Co.
Dunston, Wm., 1654, by James Yates, ——— Co.
Dunton, Tho., 1653, by Tho. Renalls, ——— Co.
Dunton, Thomas, 1647, by John Sidney, Lower Norfolk Co.
Dupen, James, 1642, by Cornelius de Hull, ——— Co.
Durand, William, 1635, by Richard Bennett, ——— Co.
Durand, Wm., 1639, by Walter Pakes, James City Co.
Duran, John, 1654, by Mrs. Fra. Harrison, widow, Westmoreland Co.
Durant, Tho., 1654, by Capt. Nich. Marteaw, Westmoreland Co.
Durant, Tho., 1654, by Wm. Beach, Westmoreland Co.
Durand, William, 1637, by Richard Bennett New Norfolk Co.
Durant, Ja., 1650, by Richard Tye and Charles Sparrowe, Charles City Co.
Durecing, Hono., 1653, by Jervais Dodson, Northumberland Co.
Durish, Francis, 1638, by Geo. Lobb, Tho. Perce, Tho. Warne, James City Co.
Durrant, ———, 1635, by Richard Durrant (her husband), James Co.
Durrington, Richard, 1643, by John Wall, ——— Co.
Durwell, Fra., 1653, by Tho. Speoke, ——— Co.
Durwell, Fra., 1654, by Nich. Merywether, Westmoreland Co.
Dutch, Robt., 1645, by John Baker, Elizabeth City Co.
Dutchfield, Eliz., 1654, by John Phillips and John Batts, Lancaster Co.
Dutton, Debora, 1652, by Tho. Johnson, Jr., Northampton Co.
Dutton, Dorothy, 1654, by John Drayton, Westmoreland Co.
Duvitt, Jacob, 1637, by Elizabeth Parker, Henrico Co.
Dyamond, Eliz., 1650, by Wm. Clapham, ——— Co.
Dyar, Tho., 1653, by Richard Thomas, Henrico Co.
Dycott, Robt., 1654, by Mr. Tho. Fowke, Westmoreland Co.
Dye, Robert, 1653, by Wm. Morgan, ——— Co.
Dye, John, 1655, by John Hinman, Northampton Co.
Dye, Robert, 1650, by Wm. Morgan, ——— Co.
Dyer, Ann, 1643, by Henry Neale, James City Co.
Dyer, Tho., 1651, by Phillip Hunley, ——— Co.
Dyer, David, 1653, by John King, Surry Co.
Dryver, John, 1654, by Mr. Tho. Fowke, Westmoreland Co.
Dyer, Tho., 1638, by Capt. Christopher Wormley, ——— Co.
Dyer, John, 1647, by Thomas Johnson, Gent., Northampton Co.
Dyer, John, 1635, by Capt. Adam Thoroughgood, ——— Co.
Dyer, Richard, 1655, by Christopher Calvert, Northampton Co.
Dyers, John, 1655, by Christopher Calvert, Northampton Co.
Dyers, Mary, 1654, by Christopher Calvert, Northampton Co.
Dyes, John, 1642, by Thomas Curtis, ——— Co.
Dyner, Thomas, 1635, by Daniel Cugley, Accomac Co.
Dyon, William, 1649, by Joseph Croshawe, Yorke Co.
Dyos, Thomas, 1642, by Wm. Ireland and Robt. Wallis, Yorke Co.

E

Eadly, Ambrose, 1637, by John Brodwell, James City Co.

Eager, Alex, 1650, by Richard Tye and Charles Sparrowe, Charles City Co.

Eagle, George, 1635, by Capt. Wm. Pierse, —— Co.

Ealerye, Emerie, 1637, by Tho. Symmons, Charles River Co.

Earle, Mary, Sr., 1652, by John Earle, Northumberland Co.

Earle, John and wife, 1653, by Tho. Keene, Northumberland Co.

Earle, Mary, Jr., 1652, by John Earle, Northumberland Co.

Earles, Wm., 1654, by Robert Tomlin, —— Co.

Eartes, Joane, 1642, by William Prier, Gent., —— Co.

East, Henry, 1653, by Colo. Wm. Clayborne (Sec. of State), —— Co.

East, Wm., 1653, by Francis Jordan, Surry Co.

East, Wm., 1638, by John Fludd, James City Co.

East, Edwd., 1654, by Capt. John West, Esq., Gloucester Co.

East, Wm., 1643, by Wm. Lawrance, James City Co.

Easterfeild, Lyd., 1654, by John Watson and John Bognall, Westmoreland Co.

Easterfield, Lydia, 1656, by John Evans, Northampton Co.

Easterfield, Lydia, 1656, by Robt. Bayly, Northampton Co.

Eastern, Dor., 1653, by Capt. Nathaniel Hurd, Warrick Co.

Easthrop, Brid., 1654, by John Watson and John Bognall, Westmoreland Co.

Easton, John, 1652, by Mrs. Elnor Brocas, Lancaster Co.

Eaterne, John, 1649, by John Trussells, —— Co.

Eaton, John, 1651, by George Eaton, —— Co.

Eaton, John, 1643, by Wm. Lawrance, James City Co.

Eaton, Peter, 1641, by John Seaword, Isle of Wight Co.

Eaton, Nathaniel, 1635, by Jeremiah Clement, —— Co.

Eaton, Nathanl., 1652, by John Phillips, Lancaster Co.

Eaton, Wm., 1652, by John Howett, Northumberland Co.

Eaton, Winifred, 1653, by John Coale, James City Co.

Eaton, Fra., 1654, by John Watson and John Bognall, Westmoreland Co.

Eaton, Wm., 1654, by John Watson and John Bognall, Westmoreland Co.

Eaton, Elizabeth, 1656, by James Price, Northampton Co.

Eaton, Peter, 1637, by Margaret Rogers, New Norfolk Co.

Eaton, Sam., 1635, by Henry Harte, James City Co.

Eaton, Henry, 1638, by Ambrose, Bennett Isle of Wight Co.

Eaton, Geo., 1654, by Tho. Hobkins, Lancaster Co.

Eaton, John, 1654, by Tho. Hobkins, Lancaster Co.

Eastwood, Richard, 1642, by John Garrett, Upper New Norfolk Co.

Eastindian, Antho., 1636, by Mr. Georg Menifye, James City Co.

Eastindian, Tony, 1635, by George Minifie, James City Co.

Easill, Christ., 1637, by Cheney Boyes, Charles City Co.

Eason, Edward, 1637, by John Neall, Aaccomck Co.

Eaworth, Mary, 1635, by Thos. Harwood, —— Co.

Ebbell, Eliz., 1648, by James Mason, James City Co.

Eberoney, Garturagut, 1648, by Wm. Edwards and Rice Edwards, James City Co.

Ebernathell, Robt., 1652, by Robert West, Charles City Co.
Ebnes, Wm., 1651, by Joseph Croshaw, Yorke Co.
Ebourne, Wm., 1652, by Mr. John Brown, Northampton Co.
Ebsworth, Anthony, 1637, by Daniell Gookin, New Norfolk Co.
Ebsworth, Ann, 1637, by Daniell Gookins, New Norfolk Co.
Edaw Mary, 1653, by Charles Scarburg, Northampton Co.
Edea, Gabriel, 1637, by Henry Perry, Charles River Co.
Edden, John, 1642, by Thomas Symmons, ——— Co.
Eddow, Mary, 1652, by Charles Scarburg, Northampton Co.
Edens, Alice, 1635, by Wm. Swan, James Co.
Edes, Eliz., 1638, by William Hatfield, Upper New Norfolk Co.
Edis, Jereney, 1651, by Wm. Hampton, ——— Co.
Edes, Tho., 1655, by John Coole, James City Co.
Edes, John, 1654, by Wm. Wright, Gent., Nansemond Co.
Edey, ———, 1653, by Hump. Edey (her husband), ——— Co.
Edgar, Mary, 1652, by Dr. George Hack, Northampton Co.
Edgar, Charles, 1642, by Daneill Lewellyn, ——— Co.
Edgcourt, John, 1648, by Mr. Thomas Davies, Isle of Wight Co.
Edge, Tho., 1637, by John Graves, Elizabeth City Co.
Edge, Tho., 1653, by Richard Carey, ——— Co.
Edge, Tho., 1651, by Wm. Parry, Northumberland Co.
Edger, Mary, 1653, by Charles Scarburg, Northampton Co.
Ediford, Wm., 1643, by Tho. Williams, ——— Co.
Edlin, John, 1638, by Rich. Hill and Roger Arnwood, James City Co.
Ednall, Edw., 1638, by Stephen Charlton, Accomack Co.
Edmonds, Wm., 1650, by Robert Bird, ——— Co.
Edmonds, Charles, 1654, by Mr. Francis Hamond, York Co.
Edmonds, Ann, 1638, by Edward Oliver, ——— Co.
Edmond, Tho., 1654, by Francis Smith and Mr. John Smith, Westmoreland Co.
Edmund, Scarborough, 1635, by Capt. Edmond Scarborough, Accomack Co.
Edmonds, Ann, 1639, by Edward Oliver, James City Co.
Edmunds, Job, 1655, by John Dormain, Northampton Co.
Edward, William, 1635, by Capt. Wm. Pierse, ——— Co.
Edwards, Humphrys, 1635, by Thos. Shipper, ——— Co.
Edwards, Jno., 1635, by Thos. Harris, Henrico Co.
Edwards, Wm., 1636, by Humphrey Scowne, Warrasquinoack Co.
Edwards, Wm., 1635, by Capt. Adam Thoroughgood, ——— Co.
Edwards, Rich., 1637, by Theodore Moyser, James City Co.
Edwards, Rich., 1637, by Capt. Henry Browne, James City Co.
Edwards, Tho., 1637, by Phillipp Taylor, Accomack Co.
Edwards, Ellen, 1638, by Thomas Watts, Lower New Norfolk Co.
Edwards, Edmond, 1638, by Abraham Wood, Charles City Co.
Edwards, John, 1638, by Capt. Tho. Harris, Henrico Co.
Edwards, Robt., 1643, by Sir Francis Waytt, Kt., ——— Co.
Edwards, Thos., 1639, by Edward Oliver, James City Co.
Edwards, Jon., 1653, by Wm. Haynes, ——— Co.
Edwards, Hen., 1653, by Wm. Haynes, ——— Co.
Edwards, Mary, 1653, by Wm. Haynes, ——— Co.
Edwards, Mary, 1653, by Gregory Rawlins, Surry Co.

Edwards, Henry, 1643, by Mr. Obedience Robins, Northampton Co.
Edwards, Henry, 1651, by Phillip Hunley, ——— Co.
Edwards, Dorothy, 1648, by Wm. Edwards (her husband) and Rice
    Edwards, James City Co.
Edward, Walter, 1648, by Francis Ceely, ——— Co.
Edwards, Andrew, 1649, by Bartholomew Hoskins, ——— Co.
Edwards, Hump., 1650, by Lieut. Wm. Worleich, ——— Co.
Edwards, Mary, 1646, by John Broach, York Co.
Edwards, Wm., 1643, by Richard Kemp, Esq., James City Co.
Edwards, Alice, 1648, by John Seward, Isle of Wight Co.
Edwards, Tho., 1652, by Christopher Robinson and John Sturdwant,
    Henrico Co.
Edwards, Mary, 1652, by Edward Cole, Northumberland Co.
Edwards, W—., Sr., 1652, by Col. Geo. Ludlow, Esq., Gloucester Go.
Edwards, W., Jr., 1652, by Col. Geo. Ludlow, Esq., Gloucester Co.
Edwards, Tho., 1652, by Richard Hill, Northampton Co.
Edwards, John, 1652, by John Johnson, Northampton Co.
Edwards, Hugh, 1653, by Benjamin Brasseur, ——— Co.
Edwards, Elizabeth, 1640, by Thomas Harvey, James City Co.
Edwards, John, 1653, by James Watson, Isle of Wight Co.
Edwards, Wm., 1653, by Robert Wild and Phillip Chesley, York Co.
Edwards, Wm., 1653, by John Dipdall, Charles City Co.
Edwards, Jenkin, 1653, by John Medstard and John Edwards, North-
    umberland Co.
Edwards, Wm., 1653, by Colo. Wm. Clayborne (Sec. of State), —— Co.
Edwards, John, 1654, by John Williams, Northampton Co.
Edwards, Mary, 1654, by John Williams, Northampton Co.
Edwards, Margt., 1654, by John Williams, Northampton Co.
Edwards, James, 1654, by Richard Allen, Northampton Co.
Edwards, Sam., 1642, by Capt. Samuell Mathews, Esq., ——— Co.
Edwards, Wm., 1642, by Capt. Samuell Mathews, Esq., ——— Co.
Edwards, Robt., 1638, by Georg Mynifie (merchant), ——— Co.
Edwards, Rebecca, 1638, by Georg Mynifie (merchant), ——— Co.
Edwards, Thos., 1639, by John Pawley, James City Co.
Edwards, Thomas, 1639, by Edward Oliver, James City Co.
Edwards, Andrew, 1639, by Tristram Nosworthy, Upper Norfolk Co.
Edwards, Francis, 1638, by Edward Oliver, ——— Co.
Edwards, Tho., 1652, by Littleton Scarburg, ——— Co.
Edwards, John, 1652, by Dr. George Hack, Northampton Co.
Edwards, Amy, 1655, by Dr. Giles Mode, New Kent Co.
Edwards, Mary, 1655, by Francis Clay, Gent., Northumberland Co.
Edwards, Near., 1654, by Major. Wm. Andrews, Northampton Co.
Edwin, Tho., 1642, by Peter Johnson, New Norfolk Co.
Edwin, James, 1642, by Peter Johnson, New Norfolk Co.
Eggleston, Arthur, 1635, by Capt. Adam Thoroughgood, ——— Co.
Egglestone, Jon., 1653, by Capt. Robt. Abrahal, Goucester Co.
Egleston, Rich., 1637, by Thomas Hampton Clarke, New Norfolk Co.
Eecles, Richard, 1653, by Charles Grymes, Lancaster Co.
Eeds, Alice, 1638, by Thomas Swan, James Citie Co.
Elay, Lancelott, 1638, by John Moone, ——— Co.
Eeven, Jane, 1648, by Nicholas Dixson, Nansemond Co.

Eeven, John, 1648, by Nicholas Dixson, Nansemond Co.
Elam, Robert, 1638, by Christopher Branch, Henrico Co.
Elcher, Henry, 1653, by Ralph Green, Gloucester Co.
Elcock, John, 1653, by Charles Grymes, clerk, Lancaster Co.
Elcock, John, 1651, by Tho. Hales and Tho. Sheppard, Northumberland Co.
Elcocke, Joane, 1653, by Tho. Hawkins, Northumberland Co.
Eldredge, Samuell, 1637, by Justinian Cooper, Isle of Wight Co.
Eldrege, Samuell, 1642, by Justinian Cooper, Isle of Wight Co.
Eldrige, Saml., 1636, by Justinian Cooper, Warrasquinoak Co.
Eldrige, Hugh, 1652, by Richard Coleman, ——— Co.
Eldrige, Debo., 1653, by Major Abra. Wood, Charles City Co.
Elderwell, Elizabeth, 1651, by Richard Ripley, ——— Co.
Elam, Ann, 1652, by Robert Elam, Henrico Co.
Elinge, John, 1651, by Geo. Trakett and Henry Edwards, Northampton Co.
Eliock, Aron, 1649, by Rowland Burneham, Gent., ——— Co.
Elis, Wm., 1653, by Robert Tomlin, ——— Co.
Elkeson, Andrew, 1654, by James Yates, ——— Co.
Elkton, Wm., 1637, by Bridges Freeman, James City Co.
Ellerge, Charity, 1638, by John Wayne, Charles River Co.
Elles, Robt., 1655, by Wm. Steevens, Northampton Co.
Elliot, Lewis, 1648, by Wm. Ewen, James City Co.
Elliot, John, 1650, by John Bone, ——— Co.
Elliot, Wm., 1643, by John Freeme, Charles Co.
Eley, Christop., 1651, by Abraham Moone and Thomas Griffen, Lancaster Co.
Elitherby, Mary, 1649, by Henry Brakes, Lower Norfolk Co.
Ellice, Elianor, 1639, by Wm. Denham, Isle of Wight Co.
Ellis, Samuell, 1636, by Wm. Layton, ——— Co.
Ellis, John, 1636, by Mr. Georg Menifye, James City Co.
Ellis, John, 1635, by George Minifie, James City Co.
Ellis, Samuel, 1635, by Mr. Robt. Cane, ——— Co.
Ellis, John, 1642, by Thomas Emerson, ——— Co.
Ellis, Edward, 1636, by Nathan Martin, Henrico Co.
Ellis, Wm., 1637, by Daniell Gookins, New Norfolk Co.
Ellis, John, 1642, by Thomas Emerson, ——— Co.
Ellis, Michaell, 1642, by Wm. Warren, ——— Co.
Ellis, Edward, 1638, by Benjamin Carrill, James City Co.
Ellis, Ra., 1653, by Robert Brasseur, Nansemond Co.
Ellis, Jno., 1643, by Mr. Obedience Robins, Northampton Co.
Ellis, Edward, 1643, by John Neale, Gent., Northampton Co.
Ellis, David, 1650, by Francis Hobbs, ——— Co.
Ellis, Sarah, 1643, by Richard Kemp, Esq., James City Co.
Ellis, Samuel, 1652, by Mr. George Clapham, ——— Co.
Ellis, Israel, 1652, by Mr. George Clapham, ——— Co.
Ellis, Alice, 1652, by Mr. Edwin Connaway, ——— Co.
Ellis, Alice, 1654, by Edwin Conaway, Lancaster Co.
Ellis, Rowland, 1654, by Walter Pritchard, ——— Co.
Ellis, Willi, 1641, by Ambrose Bennett, Isle of Wight Co.
Ellis, Isaac, 1640, by John George, Charles City Co.

Ellis, David, 1642, by John Benton, ——— Co.
Elliot, Wm., 1650, by Mr. Tho. Purifoy, ——— Co.
Ellis, Elinor, 1652, by Capt. Tho. Hackett, Lancaster Co.
Ellin, William, 1635, by Capt. Wm. Pierse, ——— Co.
Ellin, Wm., 1638, by Georg Mynifie (merchant), ——— Co.
Ellin, Mary, 1655, by Wm. Hall, New Kent Co.
Ellins, Bridgett, 1645, by Mr. Robert Eyres, ——— Co.
Ellix, Richard, 1643, by Mr. Moore Fautleroy, Upper Norfolk Co.
Ellom, Robt., 1635, by Edward Osborne, Henrico Co.
Ellmore, Tho., 1654, by Capt. Nich. Marteaw, Westmoreland Co.
Elmore, Henry, 1653, by Henry Corbell, Gloucester Co.
Elnor, Tho., 1654, by Wm. Beach, Westmoreland Co.
Ells, Henry, 1652, by Capt. Augustine Warner, ——— Co.
Ells, John, 1656, by Roger Wolmsly and Richard Ingram, James City Co.
Ellyott, Robert, 1650, by Edward Grimes, ——— Co.
Ellyott, Fra., 1653, by Tho. Sawyer, ——— Co.
Ellyott, Robt., 1555, by John Palmer, Northumberland Co.
Ellyott, Ann, 1654, by John Whithers and Stephen Garey, Westmore-
    land Co.
Ellyott, Phillip, 1654, by John Whithers and Stephen Garey, Westmore-
    land Co.
Ellyott, Edward, 1654, by John Whithers and Stephen Garey, West-
    moreland Co.
Ellyotts, Kath., 1655, by Robt. Priddey, New Kent Co.
Ellyott, Hen., 1654, by Capt. Nich Marteaw, Westmoreland Co.
Ellyns, Wm., 1653, by Colo. Wm. Clayborne (Sec. of State), ——— Co.
Ellyson, Robt., 1653, by Hen. Soanes, Gent., Gloucester Co.
Ellyson, Robert, 1656, by Mr. Henry Soanes, New Kent Co.
Elsly, Augustine, 1653, by Major Abra. Wood, Charles City Co.
Elsey, John, 1652, by Mr. Tho. Purifye and Mrs. Reppitt, ——— Co.
Elsey, John, 1654, by John Watson and John Bognall, Westmoreland Co.
Elson, John, 1652, by Tho. Johnson, Jr., Gloucester Co.
Elsmore, Eliz., 1653, by John Coale, James City Co.
Elton, Ed., 1653, by Wm. Johnson, Henrico Co.
Elwood, Jno. 1645, by John Rode, Warwick Co.
Ely, Joane, 1636, by Richard Cocke, ——— Co.
Elly, John, 1649, by Rich. Croshaw, Yorke Co.
Elly, John, 1652, by Israell Johnson and Mrs. Rich. Mayfield,—— Co.
Ely, Joane, 1639, by Richard Corke, Gent., Henrico Co.
Embrock, Richd., 1650, by Elias Edmondes, ——— Co.
Embrooke, Richard, 1649, by Henry White, James City Co.
Emerby, Isaac, 1651, by Richard Kellum, Northampton Co.
Emery, Andrew, 1638, by Geo. Lobb, Tho. Perce, Tho. Warne, James
    City Co.
Emery, Hen., 1653, by Margarett Upton, Lancaster Co.
Emerye, Isa., 1653, by Capt. Natha. Hurd, Warrick Co.
Emeroy, Lydia, 1647, by Richard Bland, ——— Co.
Emerson, Nich., 1653, by Margarett Upton, Lancaster Co.
Emerson, Nicholas, 1642, by Thomas Emerson, ——— Co.
Emeson, Wm., 1656, by Mr. Jno. Paine, ——— Co.
Emmerton, Ann, 1636, by Edward Minter, ——— Co.

Emmerton, Alice, 1636, by Wm. Hatcher, Henrico Co.
Emmerton, Alice, 1637, by Wm. Hatcher, ——— Co.
Emmerton, Ann, 1638, by Edward Minter, James City Co.
Emmerson, Ed., 1651, by John Adlston, ——— Co.
Emmerson, Arthur, 1643, by Wm. Berryman, Northampton Co.
Emonds, Ann, 1638, by Edward Oliver, James City Co.
Emson, Wm., 1650, by Walter Broodhurst, ——— Co.
Engard, Charles, 1646, by William Hockaday, York Co.
England, John, 1637, by Humphrey England, James City Co.
England, John (brother of Humphrey England, Sr.), 1636, by Humphrey England, James City Co.
England, Humphrey, (Jun.), son of Humphrey England, Sr., 1636, by Humpry England, Sr., James City Co.
England, Humphry, (Sr.), 1636, by Humphrey England, James City Co.
England, Mary (wife of Humphrey, Sr.), 1636, by Humphrey England, James City Co.
England, Ralph, 1650, by Mr. James Williamson, ——— Co.
England, Sarah, 1642, by Frances England, Isle of Wight Co.
England, Israell, 1650, by John Mattrum, Northumberland Co.
England, Jon., 1638, by Stephen Charlton, Accomack Co.
Engler, James, 1652, by Wm. Ginsey, Gloucester Co.
English, Jon., 1637, by Thomas Barnard, James City Co.
English, William, 1638, by George Higgins, Charles River Co.
English, John, 1653, by Colo. Wm. Clayborne (Sec. of State), ——— Co.
English, Wm., 1649, by Capt. Ralph Wormeley, ———Co.
English, Jane, 1654, by Mr. Francis Hamond, York Co.
English, Wm., 1638, by Capt. Christopher Wormley, Charles River Co.
English, Joane, 1642, by William English, ——— Co.
English, Kath., 1655, by John Lawson, Lancaster Co.
English, Walter, 1655, by Lieut. Coll. John Walker, ——— Co.
Emhamby, Geo., 1650, by Tho. Vaus, Gent., Northumberland Co.
Enies, John, 1635, by Capt., Adam Thoroughgood, ——— Co.
Ennis, James, 1650, by Francis Hobbs, ——— Co.
Enngood, Rich., 1642, by Edmund Scarburgh, Accomack Co.
Ensell, Christopher, 1635, by Cheney Boyse, Charles City Co.
Ensworth, Jno., 1653, by Nathaniel Hickmon, Northumberland Co.
Enysson, With, 1635, by William Heires, Warrasquinoake Co.
Epherby, Geo., 1650, by Lewis Burwell, Gent., Northumberland Co.
Erefined, Mary, 1649, by John Cabbedge, Lower Norfolk Co.
Errence, Joseph, 1656, by Wm. Justice, Charles City Co.
Errington, Richard, 1642, by William Prior, Gent., ——— Co.
Erwin, Georg, 1640, by Richard Hynes, New Norfolk Co.
Ewin, Wm., 1636, by Epaphroditus Lawson, Warwick Co.
Escholl, Joyse, 1652, by Tho. Mairy, ——— Co.
Essex, John, 1636, by Georg Travellor, Accomack Co.
Essex, John, and his wife, 1653, by Martin Cole, Northumberland Co.
Essington, Thomas, 1637, by James Harrison, James City Co.
Esson, Edward, 1637, by Wm. Cotton, ——— Co.
Esquire, John, 1638, by Mr. Walter Ashton, Charles City Co.
Etes, John, 1637, by Theodore Moyser, James City Co.
Etes, Wm., 1653, by John Gillett, Lancaster Co.

Ethell, Tho., 1646, by Sir William Berkley, ——— Co.
Etherton, Samuell, 1643, by Richard Kemp, Esq., James City Co.
Etheridge, Hen., 1654, by Wm. Johnson, Northampton Co.
Eubanke, Henry, 1653, by Colo. Wm. Clayborne (Sec. of State), ———Co.
Eules, Richard, 1652, by Tho. Steevens, Lancaster Co.
Eusam, Nich., 1654, by Nich. Merywether, Westmoreland Co.
Euson, Nicho., 1653, by Tho. Speake, ——— Co.
Eustis, James, 1635, by Capt. Wm. Pierse, ——— Co.
Evan, Joan, 1650, by Geo. Ludlow, Esq., Northumberland Co.
Evan, Hump., 1653, by Benjamin Brasseur, ——— Co.
Evan, Thompson, 1638, by Thomas Burbage, Accomack Co.
Evan, Robt., 1655, by Wm. Wright, Gent., Nansemond Co.
Evand, Wm. 1645, by John Rode, Warwick Co.
Evand, Tho., 1652, by Anthony Hoskins, Northampton Co.
Evans, John, 1636, by Wm. Ravenett, Warwick River Co.
Evans, Ann, 1636, by Randall Holt, James City Co.
Evans, Curi, 1636, by John Chew, Gent., Charles River Co.
Evans, Morgan, 1637, by John Upton, Isle of Wight Co.
Evans, James, 1637, by Arthur Bayly, Henrico Co.
Evans, Henry, 1642, by John Waltham, Jr., Accomac Co.
Evans, John, 1642, by John Towlson, Accomack Co.
Evans, Jon., 1635, by Wm. Garry, Accomack Co.
Evans, Richard, 1637, by Oliver Sprye, New Norfolk Co.
Evans, Morgan, 1637, by Lt. John Upton, Isle of Wight Co.
Evans, Edward, 1637, by Arthur Bayly and Tho. Crosby, Henrico Co.
Evans, Jonas, 1637, by David Mansell, James City Co.
Evans, John, 1638, by Nicholas Georg. and John Grynisditch, Isle of
  Wight Co.
Evans, Tho., 1645, by William Jones, Northampton Co.
Evans, Kath., 1653, by Jon. Slaughter, ——— Co.
Evans, Joan, 1653, by Corbet Piddle, Northumberland Co.
Evans, Rowland, 1651, by Richard Vaughan, Northampton Co.
Evans, Richard, 1651, by Wm. Rennoles, Northumberland Co.
Evans, Wm., 1651, by Hugh Fauch and James Magregory, Northum-
  berland Co.
Evans, Cleri, 1637, by John Chew, Charles River Co.
Evans, Jonas, 1635, by David Mansell, James Co.
Evans, Richard, 1635, by Wm. Andrews, Accomac Co.
Evans, Clem., 1636, by Justinian Cooper, Warrasquinoak Co.
Evans, ——, 1636, by Richard Cocke, ——— Co.
Evans, Jno., 1635, by John Spackmon, Warrasquinoake Co.
Evans, James, 1647, by Tho., Gibson, York Co.
Evans, Mary, 1649, by John Sibsey, Lower Norfolk Co.
Evans, Marg., 1650, by John Mattrum, Northumberland Co.
Evans, Jane, 1643, by Richard Richards, Charles River Co.
Evans, Mary, 1650, by Thomas Milford, Nansemond Co.
Evans, Christ., 1643, by Capt. Samuell Mathews, Esq., ——— Co.
Evans, Tho., Jr., 1643, by Capt. Samuell Mathews, Esq., ——— Co.
Evans, Geo., 1643, by Capt. Samuell Mathews, Esq., ——— Co.
Evans, Lucy, 1647, by Richard Bland, ——— Co.
Evans, Mary, 1653, by Joseph Hogkinson, Lower Norfolk Co.

Evans, John, 1653, by Coll. Wm. Taylor, Esq., Gloucester Co.
Evans, Tho., 1652, by Mr. Tho. Gutheridge, Lower Norfolk Co.
Evans, Geo., 1652, by Capt. Francis Morgan and Ralph Green, Gloucester Co.
Evans, Dan., 1652, by Robt. West, Charles City Co.
Evans, Row., 1652, by Dr. George Hack, Northampton Co.
Evans, Edward, 1652, by Dr. George Hack, Northampton Co.
Evans, Law, 1652, by Peter Knight, Gloucester Co.
Evans, Wm., 1652, by Peter Knight, Gloucester Co.
Evans, Abigail, 1653, by John Earle, Northumberland Co.
Evans, John, 1653, by John Earle, Northumberland Co.
Evans, Abigail, 1653, by John Earle, Northumberland Co.
Evans, Anne, 1653, by John Evans, Northumberland Co.
Evans, Francis, 1654, by Benjamin Mathews, Northampton Co.
Evans, Susan, 1654, by Richard Walker, ——— Co.
Evans, Thos., Sr., 1642, by Capt. Samuell Mathews, Esq., ——— Co.
Evans, Lawrence, 1638, by Thomas Burbage, Accomack Co.
Evans, John, 1639, by Abraham Wood, Henrico Co.
Evans, Richard, 1639, by Richard Parsons, Lower New Norfolk Co.
Evans, Humphry, 1639, by Edward Panderson, ——— Co.
Evans, Thos., 1639, by Henry Bognell, Accomack Co.
Evans, Edw., 1639, by Samuell Almond, Henrico Co.
Evans, Ann, 1639, by Randall Holt, James City Co.
Evans, Jeffery, 1638, by John George, Charles City Co.
Evans, Morgan, 1638, by Lieut, John Upton, Isle of Wight Co.
Evans, Thomas, 1638, by Jonathan Langworth, Lower New Norfolk Co.
Evans, Daniell, 1639, by Richard Corke, Gent., Henrico Co.
Evans, Rowland, 1653, by Charles Scarburg, Northampton Co.
Evans, Edward, 1653, by Charles Scarburg, Northampton Co.
Evans, John, 1653, by Geo. Hack, Northampton Co.
Evans, Edward, 1650, by Capt. Charles Leech, Yorke Co.
Evans, John, 1642, by Thomas Loving, James City Co.
Evans, Rachell, 1642, by John Ewens, Jr., Charles City Co.
Evans, John, 1642, by Georg Busse, ——— Co.
Evans, Ann, 1654, by Nicholas Morris, Northumberland Co.
Evans, Henry, 1655, by Francis Clay, Gent., Northumberland Co.
Evans, Lesley, 1654, by Major Abraham Wood, Henrico Co.
Evans, Joan, 1654, by Major Abraham Wood, Henrico Co.
Evans, Elizabeth, 1654, by Major Abraham Wood, Henrico Co.
Evelin, Mary, 1648, by John Seward, Isle of Wight Co.
Everat, Wm., and Ann, his wife, 1655, by Symons Symons, Charles City Co.
Everard, Thomas, 1648, by John King and Lawrence Ward, Isle of Wight Co.
Evere, John, 1645, by John Nuthall, Northampton Co.
Everett, Christopher, 1635, by John Cheeseman, Charles River Co.
Everette, Joane, 1651, by Robert Abrall, Yorke Co.
Everedge, Wm., 1638, by William Clarke, Henrico Co.
Everedge, Wm., 1636, by Wm. Clarke, Henrico Co.
Everfleet, Wm., 1650, by Capt. Moore Fautleroy, ———Co.
Everns, John, 1650, by Liet. Wm. Worleich, ——— Co.

Everson, Mathew, 1653, by John Madison, ——— Co.
Every, Nicho., 1643, by Mr. Obedience Robins, Northampton Co.
Everye, Edward, 1652, by Lt. Coll. John Cheesman, ——— Co.
Everye, Richard,———, by Lt. Coll. John Cheesman, ——— Co.
Eves, Jon., 1636, by Henry Southall, ——— Co.
Eves, John, 1637, by Lt. Rich. Popeley, New Norfolk Co.
Ewens, John, Sr., 1642, by John Ewens, Jr., Charles City Co.
Ewens, Ann, wife John Ewens, Sr., 1642, by John Ewens, Jr., Charles City Co.
Ewen, Nicholas, 1638, by Richard Ewen, Upper New Norfolk Co.
Ewens, Clement, 1642, by Justinian Cooper, Isle of Wight Co.
Exxell, Anne, 1654, by William Howard, Gloucester Co.
Exton, Geo., 1643, by John Foster, Northtmpton Co.
Exton, Nich., 1630, by John Russell, ——— Co.
Eyer, William, 1649, by Joseph Croshawe, Yorke Co.
Eyres, Jon., 1642, by Bertram Hobert, ——— Co.
Eyses, Wm., 1649, by Arthur Allen, James City Co.

F

Fabbett, Henry, 1652, by Mrs. Anna Barnett, Gloucester Co.
Fabett, Henry, 1651, by Mrs. Anna Bernard, Northumberland Co.
Fabian, Gilbert, 1648, by Mr. Thomas Davies, Isle of Wight Co.
Fabin, Tho., 1652, by Col. Geo. Ludlow, Esq., Gloucester Co.
Fabin, Tho., 1651, by George Ludlow, Esq., ——— Co.
Fae, Peter, 1654, by Richard Walker, ——— Co.
Failes, Abraham, 1656, by Margaret Miles, Westmoreland Co.
Fairing, Elin., 1650, by Tho. Tiisley, James City Co.
Fairebrother, Nath., 1638, by Lietu. John Upton, Isle of Wight Co.
Fairbank, John, 1653, by Peter Knight and Baker Cult, ——— Co.
Faire, Richard, 1643, by John Wright, Upper Norfolk Co.
Faire, Mathew, 1643, by John Wright, Upper Norfolk Co.
Fakin, Gilbert, 1651, by Ashwell Battin, Yorke Co.
Faker, John, 1636, by Thomas Markham, Henrico Co.
Falconer, Richard, 1638, by Elizabeth Grayner, Charles City Co.
Fallards, ———, 1653, by Henry Corbell, Gloucester Co.
Fallup, Wm., 1653, by Colo. Wm. Clayborne (Sec. of State, ——— Co.
Falston, Eliz., 1642, by Capt. Samuell Mathews, Esq., ——— Co.
Fannell, Wm., 1640, by Thomas Stegg, Charles City Co.
Fanner, James, 1656, by Mr. Martin Baker, New Kent Co.
Fanner, Mary, 1655, by Wm. Botham, Westmoreland Co.
Farborne, Lawrence, 1636, by Wm. Clarke, Henrico Co.
Farbuth, Danll, 1652, by John Cooke, ——— Co.
Farburne, Lawrence, 1637, by Thos. Causey, Charles City Co.
Farly, Ann, 1643, by John Sweet, Isle of Wight Co.
Farly, John, 1655, by Edward Pettaway, Surry Co.
Farly, Fra., 1655, by Edward Pettaway, Surry Co.
Farly, Joyce, 1655, by Edward Pettaway, Surry Co.
Farge, Ann, 1638, by Joseph Farge, Charles City Co.
Fargason, Thomas, 1639, by Wm. Barker, Charles City Co.
Farley, Wm., 1652, by Mrs. Jane Harner, Northumberland Co.

Farly, Joseph, 1655, by Edward Pettaway, Surry Co.
Farlin, Peter, 1652, by Tho. Preston, ——— Co.
Farlo, Joice, 1648, by Wm. Barret, ——— Co.
Farloe, Grace, 1655, by Mr, Tho. Ballard, Gloucester Co.
Farlow, Alex., 1654, by Arthur Nash, New Kent Co.
Farmar, Humph., 1650, by Walter Broodhurst, ——— Co.
Farmar, John, 1655, by John Hinman, Northampton Co.
Farmer, John, 1639, by Thomas Smith, Accomac Co.
Farmer, Jno., 1654, by John Watson, and John Bognall, Westmore-
　　land Co.
Farmer, John, 1652, by Peter Knight, Gloucester Co.
Farmer, Mary, 1653, by Robt. Parfitt and Wm. Hatcher, Lancaster Co.
Farmer, Richd., 1650, by Andrew Munrow, Northumberland Co.
Farnell, Mary, 1655, by Mr. Tho. Peck, Gloucester Co.
Farr, Mary, 1650, by Lewis Burwell, Gent., Northumberland Co.
Farr, Jno. (servant), 1635, by William Stafford, ——— Co.
Farrow, Jon, 1635, by Capt. Thos. Willowbye, ——— Co.
Farrington, Charles, 1635, by McWilliam Stone, ——— Co.
Farrell, Patrick, 1638, by John Robins, James City Co.
Farrell, Garrett, 1637, by Geo. Hull, Charles River Co.
Farrell, Alexander, 1656, by John Wood, ——— Co.
Farrell, Garrett, 1638, by Georg Mynifie (merchant), ——— Co.
Farrahoe, John, 1645, by John Godfrey, Lower Norfolk Co.
Farror, John, 1648, by Richard Lee, Gent., ——— Co.
Farrar, Anna, 1647, by Richard Bland, ——— Co.
Farra, Wm., 1650, by Wm. Garrett and Fra. Wittington, ——— Co.
Farthing, Barth., 1638, by William Clarke, Henrico Co.
Farthing, Berr, 1636, by William Clarke, Henrico Co.
Farthing, Robert, 1637, by Richard Bennett, New Norfolk Co.
Farthin, Robt., 1636, by Richard Bennett, ——— Co.
Farwell, Tho., 1652, by Tho. Preston, ——— Co.
Faslowe, Elias, 1653, by Robt. Blake, Isle of Wight Co.
Fatherell, Jno., 1654, by Major Miles Carey, Westmoreland Co.
Fathergall, Wm., 1654, by Francis Smith, and Mr. John Smith, West-
　　moreland Co.
Faulkner, Margaret, 1639, by Thomas Faulkner, her husband, —— Co.
Faulsham, Jon., 1653, by Roger Walker, Northumberland Co.
Faun, William, 1635, by Henry Coleman, Elizabeth City Co.
Fauster, Wm., 1650, by Mrs. Frances Townshend (widow), Northum-
　　berland Co.
Fautleroy, Geo., 1643, by Mr. Moore Fautleroy, Upper Norfolk Co.
Fautres, Fardinn, 1648, by Christopher Burrows, ——— Co.
Fauch, Tho., 1653, by Capt. Natha. Hurd, Warrick Co.
Fautres, Ferd, 1651, by Christopher Burroughs, Lower Norfolk Co.
Faulkner, Tho., 1653, by Charles Grymes, Clerk, Lancaster Co.
Favesham, John, 1653, by Roger Walter, Northumberland Co.
Fawcett, Adam, 1654, by John Williams, Northumberland Co.
Fawne, Mary, 1656, by John Billiott, Northampton Co.
Fawne, Wm., 1635, by Capt. Adam Thoroughgood, ——— Co.
Fawne, Tho., 1654, by Martin Coale, Northumberland Co.
Fay, Tho., 1655, by John Coole, James City Co.

Fay, Williams, 1652, by Capt. Henry Fleet, Lancaster Co.
Fayden, Jonathan, 1637, by Arthur Smith, Isle of Wight Co.
Faylor, James, 1643, by John Hoddin, ——— Co.
Fearbrace, Roger (a servant), 1635, by Wm. Garry, Accomack Co.
Feason, Nicho., 1648, by Wm. Ewen, James City Co.
Feasly, Robt., 1642, by Justinian Cooper, Isle of Wight Co.
Feathergill, Christo., 1648, by Richard Lee, Gent., ——— Co.
February, John, —, by Mr. Wm. Presly, Northumberland Co.
February, John, 1638, by Richard Wilcox, James City Co.
Feild, Jon., 1635, by Wm. Barber, Charles City Co.
Feild, Edw., 1650, by Richard Dunning, ——— Co.
Feild, Chas., 1642, by Richard Maior, Charles River Co.
Feild, James, 1642, by Wm. Durant, ——— Co.
Feild, John, 1655, by Wm. Hall, New Kent Co.
Feild, Wm., 1655, by Mr. Anthony Langston, New Kent Co.
Feild, Richard, 1655, by Richard Codsford, Westmoreland Co.
Feild, Christ., 1639, by Thomas Stamp, James City Co.
Feild, Richard, 1638, by Wm. Cloys, Charles River Co.
Feild, Mary, 1651, by Wm. Taylor, Northumberland Co.
Feild, Tho., 1652, by Mrs. Anna Barnett, Gloucester Co.
Feild, James, 1652, by Col. Geo. Ludlow, Esq., Gloucester Co.
Feild, Tho., 1653, by Major Abra. Wood, Charles City Co.
Feild, Chr., 1653, by Capt. Francis Patt, Northampton Co.
Feild, Ann, 1643, by John Freeme, Charles Co.
Feild, Tho., 1643, by John Freeme, Charles Co.
Felgate, Capt. Robt., his son Erasmus, and his wife Sebbella, 1651, by
     John Perines, Yorke Co.
Felgate, Erasmus, 1639, by Capt. Robt. Felgate, his father, Charles
     River Co.
Felgate, Margarett, 1639, by Capt. Robt. Felgate, her husband, Charles
     River Co.
Felgate, Judith, 1639, by Capt. Robt. Felgate, her father, Charles
     River Co.
Felgate, Capt. Robert, and Erasmus his son, and wife Sibella, 1654, by
     Mr. Giles Brent, Westmoreland Co.
Felix, Jno., 1653, by Wm. Sidner, Lancaster Co.
Fell, Wm., 1654, by Tho. Willoughby, Lower Norfolk Co.
Fells, John, 1642, by Christopher Boyce, ——— Co.
Fellkin, Robt., 1656, by Daniel Jaines and Jon. Jenings, ——— Co.
Fells, John, 1645, by John Rode, Warwick Co.
Fells, John, 1638, by Thomas Todd, Lower New Norfolk Co.
Felter, Timo., 1653, by David Phillips, Northumberland Co.
Felton, John, 1648, by George Read, Gent., ——— Co.
Felton, Andrew, 1651, by Humphry Tabb, Northumberland Co.
Felton, John, 1642, by Henry Bradly, Upper Norfolk Co.
Felton, John, 1640, by Henry Bradly, New Norfolk Co.
Felton, John, 1639, by Capt. Nicholas Martian, Charles River Co.
Felton, Jon., 1637, by Henry Bradly, New Norfolk Co.
Feltham, Tho., 1649, by Robert Mosely, Gent., ——— Co.
Fence, John, 1637, by Thomas Osborne, Jr., Henrico Co.
Fenn, Wm., 1642, by William Eyres, Upper New Norfolk Co.

Fenn, Samuell, 1637, by John Davis, James City Co.
Fenner, Edward, 1654, by Mr. Giles Brent, Westmoreland Co.
Fennell, John, 1650, by Mr. James Williamson, ——— Co.
Fenton, Jane, 1652, by Tho. Steevens, Lancaster Co.
Fenton, Henry, 1638, by Richard Kemp, Esq., ——— Co.
Fentrice, Robt., 1642, by Christopher Boyce, ——— Co.
Fentrice, Ro., 1645, by John Rode, Warwick Co.
Feo, Neale, 1638, by Epaphroditus Lawsen, Upper Norfolk Co.
Ferewether, Fra., 1649, by Capt. Ralph Wormeley, ——— Co.
Ferepoint, Jon., 1637, by Theodore Moyser, James City Co.
Ferke, Tho., 1643, by Sir Francis Wyatt, Kt., ——— Co.
Fermer, Samll., and wife, 1650, by John Cox, ——— Co.
Fernice, Wm., 1652, by Edward Revell, Northampton Co.
Ferr, Mary, 1653, by Tho. Cowlinge, ——— Co.
Ferrell, Kath., 1649, by Mr. Tho. Spake, Northumberland Co.
Ferrant, Phillip, 1654, by Francis Smith and Mr. John Smith, West-
moreland Co.
Ferrest, Joseph, 1650, by Mrs. Frances Townshend (widow), North-
umberland Co.
Ferreby, Thos., 1637, by James Knott, New Norfolk Co.
Ferreby, Thos., 1636, by James Knott, Elizabeth City Co.
Ferris, Richard, 1636, by Robert Hollom, Henrico Co.
Ferynes, Wm., 1643, by Rich. Hoe, Gent., ——— Co.
Fescott, Symon, 1642, by John Towlson, Accomack Co.
Fetherstone, Ch., 1653, by Major Abra. Wood, Charles City Co.
Fetherston, Ellen, 1642, by Wm. Warren, ——— Co.
Fewman, Nutro, 1648, by Tho. Broughton, ——— Co.
Fibaults, Robt., 1643, by Georg Levitt, ——— Co.
Fickling, John, 1643, by Capt. Thomas Pettus, ——— Co.
Fidings, Richard, 1650, by George Taylor, ——— Co.
Field, Daniell, 1637, by Thomas Causey, Charles City Co.
Field, Danll., 1648, by Mr. Phillip Bennet, Nansemond Co.
Field, John, 1650, by Capt. Richard Bond, Charles City Co.
Field, Thos., 1637, by Daniell Gookins, New Norfolk Co.
Field, Ann, 1653, by John Day, Gloucester Co.
Field, Christopher, 1638, by Thomas Stampe, James City Co.
Figg, Jon., 1643, by Capt. Samuell Mathews, Esq., ——— Co.
Figg, John, 1636, by Walter Hacker, James River Co.
Figgison, Peter, 1636, by Edward Drew, Accomack Co.
Figgs, Arthur, 1653, by Colo. Wm. Clayborne (Sec. of State), ——— Co.
Filby, Joane, 1640, by John Maior, Accomack Co.
Filch, Joseph, 1653, by Capt. Francis Patt, Northampton Co.
Filch, Mary, 1651, by Joseph Croshaw, Yorke Co.
Filkin, Robert, 1655, by George Kibble, ——— Co.
Filline, James, 1656, by Capt. Wm. Canfill, Surry Co.
Filton, John, 1651, by Capt. Geo. Read, Lancaster Co.
Finch, Mary, 1649, by Richd. Croshaw, Yorke Co.
Finch, William, 1649, by Richard Croshaw, Yorke Co.
Finch, John, 1649, by Richard Croshaw, Yorke Co.
Finch, Elizabeth, 1649, by Richard Croshaw, Yorke Co.
Finch, Richard, 1649, by Richard Croshaw, Yorke Co.

Finch, Anne, 1653, by Robert Woody, Lower Norfolk Co.
Finch, Wm., 1653, by Wm. Walker, Northumberland Co.
Finch, Wm., 1654, by John Whithers and Stephen Garey, Westmoreland Co.
Finch, Frances (daughter of Margt.), 1638, by John Fludd, James City Co.
Finch, Fra., 1650, by Capt. John Flood, Gent., and Jno. Flood, an ancient planter, James City Co.
Finny, Richard, 1639, by Thomas Stoute, James City Co.
Firby, Eliza, 1650, by George Taylor, ——— Co.
Freeman, Jane, 1637, by Henry Perry, Charles River Co.
Firmant, Samuell, 1638, by Wm. Hatfield, Upper New Norfolk Co.
Fish, Wm., 1651, by Robert Abrall, Yorke Co.
Fisher, Masld., 1645, by Mr. Bartholomew Hoskins, ——— Co.
Fisher, John, 1653, by Capt. Richard Barnhouse, James City Co.
Fisher, John, 1651, by Humphry Tabb, Northumberland Co.
Fisher, Edward, 1642, by Stephen Gill, ——— Co.
Fisher, Eliz., 1640, by Toby Smith, Warwick River Co.
Fisher, John, 1654, by John Watson and John Bognall, Westmoreland Co.
Fisher, John, 1654, by John Wyre, John Gillet, Andrew Gilson, and John Phillipps, ——— Co.
Fisher, Grace, 1655, by Mr. Tho. Ballard, Gloucester Co.
Fisher, Robert, 1655, by Mr. Tho. Ballard, Gloucester Co.
Fisher, Mary, 1656, by George Abbott, Nansemond Co.
Fisher, Edw., 1650, by Richard Axom, and Tho. Godwin, ——— Co.
Fisher, Will, 1655, by Southy Littleberry, Northampton Co.
Fisher, Geo., 1656, by Mr. Martin Baker, New Kent Co.
Fisher, Richard, 1639, by Robert Eley, Isle of Wight Co.
Fisher, Sarah, 1645, by Justinian Cooper, Gent., Isle of Wight Co.
Fisher, John, 1643, by Thomas Brice, Upper Norfolk Co.
Fisher, Tho., 1638, by William Hatfield, Upper New Norfolk Co.
Fisher, Bridget, 1636, by Wm. Neesam, James City Co.
Fisher, Jon., 1636, by John Chandler, Elizabeth Citie Co.
Fisher, Sarah, 1636, by Wm. Neesam, James City Co.
Fistull, John, 1655, by Major Miles Cary, Warwick Co.
Fitch, Mary, 1646, by Geo. Ludlow, Esq., York Co.
Fitch, Samuell, 1638, by Christopher Branch, Henrico Co.
Fitcher, Edward, 1654, by Tho. Willoughby, Lower Norfolk Co.
Fitchett, John, 1638, by Lieut. John Upton, Isle of Wight Co.
Fitchett, Jon., 1637, by Lt. John Upton, Isle of Wight Co.
Fitchett, Jno., 1635, by Jno. Upton, Warrasquinoake Co.
Fits, John Robt., 1650, by John Lacker, ——— Co.
Fiveash, Francis, 1639, by Thomas Grey, James City Co.
Five, Lewis, 1654, by John Watson and John Bognall, Westmoreland Co.
Fixer, James, 1651, by Mr. Rowland Lawson, ——— Co.
Fixmus, Richard, 1644, by Edwyn Conaway, Northampton Co.
Fixton, John, 1641, by Stephen Charleton, Accomack Co.
Fitzgarret, Redman, 1635, by Thos. Butler Clark and Pastor of Denbie, Warrasquinoake Co.
Flabarty, James, —, by Mr. Robert Fontaine, Lower Norfolk Co.

Flake, Giles, 1653, by James Mason, James City Co.
Flake, Robt., 1640, by Thomas Harvey, James City Co.
Flaharty, Jam., 1651, by Lancaster Lovett, Lower Norfolk Co.
Flaminge, Alexander, 1655, by Wm. Wright, ———— Co.
Flanny, Teague, 1655, by John Smithey, ———— Co.
Flathy, Elizabeth, 1655, by Jer. Dodson, Gent., Lancaster Co.
Flaxton, John, 1648, by Wm. Ewen, James City Co.
Fleece, Robt., 1643, by Fra. Mason, Henrico Co.
Fleet, John, 1652, by Mrs. Mary Brent, Northumberland Co.
Fleetwood, David, 1650, by George Ludlow, Esq., Northumberland Co.
Flenman, Nich., 1643, by Elizabeth Hull, ———— Co.
Flemin, Chas., 1653, by Francis Emperor, Hagle Gale, and Edward
    Morgan, Lower Norfolk Co.
Flemin, Patrick, 1652, by Anthony Hoskins, Northampton Co.
Fleming, Eliza, 1650, by John Olian, James City Co.
Fleming, Christopher, 1653, by Colo. Wm. Clayborne (Sec. of State),
    ———— Co.
Fleming, Richard, 1643, by Robert Haies, Lower Norfolk Co.
Fleming, Robert, 1643, by Tho. Dew, Upper Norfolk Co.
Fleming, John, 1653, by Joseph Croshaw, York Co.
Fleming, Teague, 1655, by Coll. Richard Lee, Gloucester Co.
Fletcher, Peter, 1643, by Capt. Samuell Mathews, Esq., ———— Co.
Fletcher, Wm., 1650, by Sr. Tho. Luntsford, Kt., and Barronett,
    ———— Co.
Fletcher, Jno., 1646, by Joseph Croshawe, Charles River Co.
Fletcher, Ann, 1649, by Tho. Dale, ———— Co.
Fletcher, Ryon, 1649, by Richard Kemp, Esq. (Sec. of State), ———— Co.
Fletcher, Nathan, 1653, by John Shepperd, Northumberland Co.
Fletcher, Robt., 1652, by Tho. and Wm. Leithermore, ———— Co.
Fletcher, Isaac, 1651, by Joseph Croshaw, Yorke Co.
Fletcher, John, 1639, by John Howell, Henrico Co.
Fletcher, Valentine, 1639, by Richard Corke, Gent., Henrico Co.
Fletcher, Elizabeth, 1656, by Wm. Crump and Mr. Humphry Vaulx,
    James City Co.
Fletcher, Isabell, 1655, by Mr. Robert Bourne, and Mr. Daniel Parke,
    York Co.
Fletcher, Michaell, 1642, by Thomas Loving, James City Co.
Fletcher, Silvester, 1638, by Rich. Bennett, Isle of Wight Co.
Fletcher, Tho., 1643, by John Hoddin, ———— Co.
Fletcher, Anthony, 1643, by William Storey, Accomack Co.
Fletcher, Valent., 1636, by Richard Cocke, ———— Co.
Fletcher, James, 1635, by McWilliam Stone, ———— Co.
Fletcher, Wm., 1635, by Capt. Adam Thoroughgood, ———— Co.
Fletcher, Elizabeth, 1634, by Hanibal Fletcher (her husband), ————
    Co. (In ship Primrose of London.)
Flewellin, Ann, 1643, by Henry Neale, James City Co.
Flewellin, Tho., 1643, by Henry Neale, James City Co.
Flexneye, Thomas, 1637, by Francis Fowler, James River Co.
Fling, John, 1638, by John Batts and John Davis, Charles River Co.
Flint, Mary, 1652, by by Wm. Ratton and Richard Flint, Lancaster Co.
Flint Richard, 1645, by Wm. Jacob Upper Norfolk Co.

Flint, Jno., 1646, by Geo. Ludlow, E.q., York Co.
Flinton, Eliza, 1650, by Elias Edmonds, ——— Co.
Flinton, Eliza, 1638, by Jeremiah Dickenson, James City Co.
Flitt, Robert, 1652, by Mr. Tho. Sawyer, Lower Norfolk Co.
Floid, James, 1654, by Nath. Pope, Westmoreland Co.
Flood, David, 1637, by Capt. Thomas Panlett, Charles City Co.
Flood, Thos., 1656, by Vincent Stanford, ——— Co.
Flood, Richard, 1639, by Henry Perry, Charles City Co.
Flood, Joane, 1652, by Clement Thrush, ——— Co.
Flood, John, 1652, by Clement Thrush, ——— Co.
Flood, Rich., 1635, by Wm. Swan, James Co.
Flood, Mary, 1650, by Capt. John Flood, Gent., and Jno. Flood, an
    ancient planter, James City Co.
Flood, Abra., 1650, by William Gooch, Gent., ——— Co.
Flood, Robt., 1637, by Bridges Freeman, James City Co.
Flood, Samll., 1637, by Capt. Henry Browne, James City Co.
Flood, Jon., 1635, by Wm. Swann, James Co.
Floreday, Morgan, 1642, by William Connhoe, ——— Co.
Flovian, Wm., 1653, by Richard Lee, Lancaster Co.
Flower, Nicho., 1649, by Tho. Harwood, ——— Co.
Flower, Ann, 1655, by Mathew Huberd, Gent., York Co.
Flowerday, Eliza, 1644, by John Sydney, Gent., Lower Norfolk Co.
Flower, Xtop, 1649, by Robert Mosely, Gent., ——— Co.
Flowerdon, Eliz., 1642, by Christopher Boyce, ——— Co.
Floyd, Arth., 1647, by Elizabeth Barcroft, Isle of Wight Co.
Floyd, Rich., 1639, by John Pawley, James City Co.
Floyd, Richard, 1650, by John Essix, Northumberland Co.
Floyd, Richard, 1652, by Capt. Augustine Warner, ——— Co.
Floyd, Richard, 1653, by Tho. Hampton, ——— Co.
Floyd, Tho., 1639, by William Davis, James City Co.
Floyd, Flug, 1637, by Nathaniel Floyd, Isle of Wight Co.
Floyd, Nich., 1654, by Abraham Moone, ——— Co.
Floyd, David, 1654, by Abraham Moon, Gloucester Co.
Floyd, Melchisedick, 1638, by Mr. Thomas Wallis, James City Co.
Floyd, Newell, 1637, by Humphry Higginson, Gent., ——— Co.
Fludd, John, 1648, by Thomas Woodhouse, James City Co.
Fludd, Martha, 1638, by Elizabeth Grayne, Charles City Co.
Fludd, John, 1638, by Thomas Swan, James Citie Co.
Fludd, Richard, 1638, by Thomas Swan, James Citie Co.
Fludd, John Junr., 1638, by John Fludd, James City Co.
Fluellin, Wm., 1653, by Peter Knight, Northumberland Co.
Flute, Robert, 1638, by Elizabeth Grayne, Charles City Co.
Flye, John, 1637, by Thomas Barnard, James City Co.
Foard, John, 1643, by Thomas Cassen, ——— Co.
Foard, Richard, 1653, by Charles Grimes, Lancaster Co.
Foard, Wm., 1653, by Geo. Thompson, ——— Co.
Foard, Chalice, 1652, by Henry Fleete, Lancaster Co.
Foard, Adrian, 1643, by Mr. John Bishopp, James City Co.
Foard, Dennis, 1654, by R. Lawson, ——— Co.
Foard, Jon., 1636, by Ellinor Day and Thos. Emmerson, Warwick
    River Co.

Foard, Hester, 1650, by Mr. James Williamson, ———— Co.
Fogg, Whitting, 1653, by Collo. John Mottrom, Northumberland Co.
Foker, John, 1637, by Thomas Markham, Henrico Co.
Folder, Katherin, 1637, by Nathaniel Floyd, Isle of Wight Co.
Folly Xprion, 1651, by Jonas Jackson, Northampton Co.
Fookes, John, 1652, by Mrs. Elnor Brocas, Lancaster Co.
Fookes, John, 1651, by George Eaton, ———— Co.
Fookes, Ann, 1638, by Charles River, Charles River Co.
Fookes, John, 1654, by John Sharpe, Lancaster Co.
Foolee, Prissell, 1652, by Mr. John Brown, Northampton Co.
Foot, John, 1654, by Robert Hubard, Westmoreland Co.
Foote, Wm., 1653, by Colo. Wm. Clayborne (Sec. of State), ———— Co.
Foote, Thomas, 1650, by Edward Walker, Northumberland Co.
Forbush, Jon., 1638, by William Banister, ———— Co.
Forbush, John, 1650, by Geo. Ludlow, Esq., Northumberland Co.
Forby, Ben., 1652, by Toby Smith, Gent., Lancaster Co.
Ford, Peter, 1648, by Georg Read, Gent., ———— Co.
Ford, Richard, 1652, by Mrs. Jane Harmer, Northumberland Co.
Ford, Richard, 1651, by Richard Grigson, ———— Co.
Ford, Richard, 1638, by Georg Mynifie (merchant), ———— Co.
Ford, John, 1637, by Eleanor Day and Thom. Emmerson, Warwick
    River Co.
Ford, William, 1637, by Richard Bennett, New Norfolk Co.
Ford, John, 1637, by Robert Bennett, New Norfolk Co.
Ford, John, 1637, by Eleanor Day, and Thos. Emmerson, Warwick
    River Co.
Ford, Wm., 1636, by Reichard Bennett, ———— Co.
Ford, Ch., 1636, by Edward Minter, ———— Co.
Ford, Jon., 1635, by Robert Bennett, ———— Co.
Forden, Mathew, 1637, by William Frye, James City Co.
Forecroft, Tho., 1652, by Tho. Hoane, ———— Co.
Foreman, Wm., 1653, by Charles Grymes, Lancaster Co.
Forester, Toby, 1655, by Mr. Tho. Ballard, Gloucester Co.
Forgeson, Patrick, 1652, by Mr. Tho. Curtis, ———— Co.
Forke, John, 1635, by Thomas Warren, Charles City Co.
Forrest, Tho., 1652, by Mr. Henry Pitt, ———— Co.
Forscue, Martin, 1639, by Robert Rockwell, Upper New Norfolk Co.
Forsetch, John, 1649, by Edmund Scarburgh, Jr., Northampton Co.
Forshew, Hugh, 1639, by Henry Perry, Charles City Co.
Forst, Robert, 1653, by John Maddison, Gloucester Co.
Forest, Danll., 1651, by Phillip Hunley, ———— Co.
Forest, James, 1654, by Nich. Merywether, Westmoreland Co.
Fortescue, Nich., 1635, by Capt. Thos. Willowbye, ———— Co.
Forth, Jennett, 1651, by Edward Greenwood, James City Co.
Forville, Tho., 1650, by Hump. Lyster, ———— Co.
Fosehead, John, 1653, by Wm. Knott, Surry Co.
Foskett, Elizabeth, 1653, by Agnes Barnes, Northampton Co.
Foskett, Symon, 1653, by Agnes Barnes, Northampton Co.
Foskutt, Eliz., 1653, by James Barnaby, Northampton Co.
Foskutt, Simon, 1654, by James Barnaby, Northampton Co.
Fossett, Wm., 1653, by John Hillier, Northumberland Co.

Fossett, Robert, 1642, by John Boyles, ——— Co.
Fossett, Robt., 1637, by Wm. Prior, Charles River Co.
Foster, Giles, 1643, by Tho. Williams, ——— Co.
Foster, Henry, 1646, by Samuell Abbott, Nansemond Co.
Foster, James, 1643, by Peter Knight, Isle of Wight Co.
Foster, Phillip, 1650, by Tho. Vans, Gent., Northumberland Co.
Foster, Mary, 1650, by Ralph Green, ——— Co.
Foster, Mr., 1650, by Sr. Tho. Luntsford, Kt., and Barronett, ——— Co.
Foster, James, 1650, by Lieut. Wm. Worleich, ——— Co.
Foster, Edward, 1648, by Lewis Burwell, Gent., ——— Co.
Foster, Pernett, 1645, by Mr. Robt. Eyres, ——— Co.
Foster, Richard, 1648, by Bartholomew Hoskins, ——— Co.
Foster, Hen., 1652, by Toby Smith, Gent., Lancaster Co.
Foster, Susanna, 1653, by Tho. Watkins, ——— Co.
Foster, Dorcar, Sr., 1653, by Richard Foster, Lower Norfolk Co.
Foster, James, 1652, by Peter Knight, Gloucester Co.
Foster, Susan, 1652, by Mr. Tho. Teagle, Northampton Co.
Foster, Tho., 1652, by Mrs. Mary Brent, Northunberland Co.
Foster, Francis and Mary, 1653, by Robt. Bouth, Yorke Co.
Foster, Susan, 1653, by Charles Scarburg, Northampton Co.
Foster, Henry, 1638, by Richard Milton, Charles City Co.
Foster, Jane, 1639, by Dorothy Clarke, Henrico Co.
Foster, Mary, 1655, by Richard Foster, ——— Co.
Foster, Robert, 1654, by Edward Simpson, Gloucester Co.
Foster, John, 1654, by Peter Knight, Northumberland Co.
Foster, Ellen, 1655, by Richard Foster, ——— Co.
Foster, Ann, 1655, by John Motley, Northumberland Co.
Foster, James, 1642, by Daniell Lewellyn, ——— Co.
Foster, Mary, 1642, by Stephen Gill, Yorke River Co.
Foster, Bridgett, 1643, by John Foster, her husband, Northampton Co.
Foster, James, 1646, by Lancaster Levilt, ——— Co.
Foster, Rich., 1638, by Mr. Thomas Wallis, James City Co.
Foster, Margarett, 1637, by Bennett Freeman, James City Co.
Foster, Zachariah, 1635, by Vectoris Christmas, Elizabeth City Co.
Foster, Nicholas, 1635, by Wm. Swan, James Co.
Foster, Eliza, 1637, by Wm. Farrar, Henrico Co.
Foster, Wm., 1637, by Theodore Moyser, James City Co.
Foster, Armstrong, 1635, by McWilliam Stone, ——— Co.
Foster Phillipp, 1636, by Richard Cocke, ——— Co.
Foster, Nicholas, 1638, by Thomas Swan, James Citie Co.
Foster, Mark, 1635, by Thos. Shippey, ——— Co.
Foster, John, 1641, by Henry Hawley, Isle of Wight Co.
Foulsham, Jno., 1654, by Roger Walters, Northumberland Co.
Fowke, Gerard, 1654, by Mr. Tho. Fowke, Westmoreland Co.
Fowke, Wm., 1646, by Sir William Berkley, ——— Co.
Fowkes, Wm., 1654, by Nath. Pope, Westmoreland Co.
Fowler, Tho., 1650, by Silvester Thatcher and Tho. Whitlocke, ——— Co.
Fowler, Tho., by Mr. Wm. Presly, Northumberland Co.
Fowler, John, 1653, by Charles Grimes, Lancaster Co.
Fowler, Tho., 1638, by Richard Wilcox, James City Co.
Fowler, Susan, 1653, by Capt. Wm. Whittington, Northampton Co.

Fowler, Hanna, 1654, by John Whethers and Stephen Garey, Westmoreland Co.
Fowler, John, 1655, by John Coole, James City Co.
Fowler, Tho., 1655, by Southy Littleberry, Northampton Co.
Fowler, James, 1635, by Hugh Cox, Charles City Co.
Fowler, William, 1635, by Richard Bennett, ———Co.
Fowler, Willi, 1637, by Rich. Bennett, New Norfolk Co.
Fowles, John, 1650, by William Gooch, Gent., ——— Co.
Fox, Jane, 1650, by Francis Hobbs, ——— Co.
Fox, Edward, 1649, by Joseph Croshaw, Yorke Co.
Foxmond, Edm., 1648, by Wm. Barret, ——— Co.
Fox, Edw., and a maid servant, 1639, by Saml. Watkeyes, Charles River Co.
Fox, Mary, 1654, by Toby Smith, Lancaster Co.
Fox, Hugh, 1637, by Henry Perry, Charles River Co.
Fox, Francis, 1639, by Edward Panderson, ——— Co.
Fox, Hugh, 1637, by Henry Perry, Charles River Co.
Foxly, Mary, 1646, by Henry Sedenden, Northampton Co.
Fraford, V., 1635, by Capt. Adam Thoroughgood, ——— Co.
Fralley, Timothy, 1656, by Wm. Millinge, Northampton Co.
Frame, Rebecca, 1656, by Wm. Justice, Charles City Co.
Frame, Jon., 1637, by Wm. Farrar, Henrico Co.
France, John, 1651, by Mr. Arthur Price, Yorke Co.
France, Wm., 1654, by Toby Smith, Lancaster Co.
Francis, Wm., 1653, by James Mason, James City Co.
Francis, Mary, 1648, by Job. Chanter, Lower Norfolk Co.
Francis, Rebecca, 1642, by John Smith, James City Co.
Francis, Ann, Alice, children, 1641, by Henry Hawley, Isle of Wight Co.
Francis, James, 1640, by William Hampton, Isle of Wight Co.
Francis, Wm., 1655, by Peter Ford, Gloucester Co.
Francis, John, 1655, by George Frizell and Tho. Moore, Northampton Co.
Francis, Bedford, 1642, by Stephen Gill, Yorke River Co.
Francis, Thomas, 1638 ,by Christopher Burrough, Lower Norfolk Co.
Francis, John, 1637, by Richard Bennett, New Norfolk Co.
Francis, John, 1635, by Richard Bennett, ——— Co.
Franciss, Tho., 1648, by John King and Lawrence Ward, Isle of Wight Co.
Francklin, Geo., 1637, by Christopher Woodward, Charles City Co.
Franklin, Isaac, 1656, by Major Wm. Lewis, ——— Co.
Franke, Hen., 1653, by Richard Slaughter, Nansemond Co.
Franke, Robt., 1642, by Humphry Tabb, Elizabeth City
Franklaind, Ann, 1643, by Edward Murfey, and John Vaughan, ——— Co.
Franklin, Wm., 1655, by Robert Castle, James City Co.
Franklin, Henry, 1635, by Capt. Adam Thoroughgood, ——— Co.
Francklin, Francis, 1634, by Hanibel Fletcher, ——— Co. (In ship Revenge.)
Franklin, John, 1651, by John Stratton, Lower Norfolk Co.
Franklin, Marg., 1653, by Major John Westhrope, Charles City Co.
Franklin, Henry, 1652, by Wm. Tautlett, ——— Co.

Franklin, Mary, 1653, by Wm. Johnson, Henrico Co.
Franklind, Ann, 1643, by Edward Murfey, and John Vaughan, ——— Co.
Frarie, Rebecca, 1649, by John Merriman, ——— Co.
Frasey, Tho., 1651, by Mr. Wm. Armestead, ——— Co.
Frasey, Wm., 1651, by Mr. Wm. Armestead, ——— Co.
Frasey, Barbore, 1651, by Mr. Wm. Armestead, ——— Co.
Frayle, Togo, 1642, by Daniell Lewellyn, ——— Co.
Freake, Wm., 1650, by John Hallawes, Gent., Northumberland Co.
Freddar, John, 1655, by Wm. Johnson and Stephen Horsey Northampton Co.
Frederick, Xpian, 1649, by Capt. Ralph Wormeley, ——— Co.
Fredericke, Jno., 1651, by John Rookwood, Gent., Northumberland Co.
Frederick, Jno., 1651, by Lieut. Coll. Gile Brent, Northumberland Co.
Frederick, John, 1655, by Robt. Priddy, New Kent Co.
Frederick, John, 1638, by Edward Hill, Charles City Co.
Freederick, John, 1654, by Lieut. Coll. Giles Brent, Westmoreland Co.
Freeke, Wm., 1654, by Tho. Hobkins, Lancaster Co.
Freeland, Wm., 1643, by Mr. Moore Fautleroy, Upper Norfolk Co.
Freehorne, Jno., 1643, by Wm. Berryman, Northampton Co.
Freeman, Wm., 1650, by Mr. James Williamson, ——— Co.
Freeman, Wm., 1647, by Wm. Whitington, Northampton Co.
Freeman, Wm., 1653, by Colo. Wm. Clayborne (Sec. of State), ——— Co.
Freeman, Fra., —, by Tho. Lucas, ——— Co.
Freeman, Tho., 1652, by John Pouncey, ——— Co.
Freeman, Tho., 1651, by Robert Cade, ——— Co.
Freeman, Henry, 1651, by Robert Cade, ——— Co.
Freeman, Mill, 1635, by Christopher Stoakes, Elizabeth Co.
Freeman, Jane, 1637, by Henry Perry, Charles River Co.
Freeman, John, 1637, by Wm. Crouch, New Norfolk Co.
Freeman, Ann, 1642, by Capt. Humphry Higgenson, ——— Co.
Freeman, Wm., 1653, by Capt. Wm. Whittington, Northampton Co.
Freeman, Wm., 1654, by Mr. Francis Hamond, York Co.
Freeman, Tho., 1654, by Mr. Francis Hamond, York Co.
Freeman, Ann, 1656, by Mr. Tho. Purifoy, ——— Co.
Freeman, Edwd., 1656, by Sir Henry Chichley, ——— Co.
Freeman, Wm., 1637, by Christopher Stoakes, Charles River Co.
Freeman, Richard, 1636, by John Place, Elizabeth City Co.
Freeman, Bridgett, 1635, by Bridges Freeman, James City Co.
Freeman, Bennett, 1635, by Bridges Freeman, James City Co.
Freeme, Ann, 1643, by John Freeme (her husband), Charles Co.
Freez, Arnace, 1636, by John Chew, Gent., Charles River Co.
Freestone, Henry, 1652, by Clemment Thrush, ——— Co.
Freeze, Rachell, 1636, by Wm. Julian, Elizabeth City Co.
Freeze, Arnall, 1637, by John Chew, Charles River Co.
Freind, Peter, 1643, by Epaphroditus Lawson, Upper Norfolk Co
Freith, Robert, 1654, by John Drayton, Westmoreland Co.
French, Richd., 1649, by Wm. Nesum, Tho. Sax, Miles Bathasby and John Pyne, Northampton Co.

French, Docto., 1649, by Richard Kemp, Esq. (Sec. of State), ——— Co.
French, Henry, 1653, by Charles Grimes, Lancaster Co.
French, Wm., 1654, by Capt. Nich. Marteaw, Westmoreland Co.
French, Peter and wife, 1655, by Mr. Robert Bourne and Mr. Daniel Parke, Yorke Co.
Frere, Robert, 1641, by Thomas Bernard, Warwick River Co.
Fresby, Ann, 1637, by Henry Perry, Charles River Co.
Fresh, Jno., 1651, by Wm. Vincent, Northumberland Co.
Fresh, Mary, 1656, by John Symons, Nansemond Co.
Freiston, Robt., 1638, by John Batts and John Davis, Charles River Co.
Freshwater, Geo., 1655, by Southy Littleberry, Northampton Co.
Fresser, Mary, 1648, by Lewis Burwell, Gent., ——— Co.
Fretthorne, John, 1638, by Wm. Parker, Warrasquinoake Co.
Frey, Humphrey, 1639, by Edward Travis, James City Co.
Frice, Ann, 1653, by Richard Stornell, ——— Co.
Frick, Francis, 1638, by Lieut. John Upton, Isle of Wight Co.
Fricker, John, 1638, by Robert Freeman, James City Co.
Friner, Andrew, 1651, by Lieut. Coll. Anthony Elliott, ——— Co.
Fringworth, Naul, 1651, by Abraham Moone and (Thomas Griffen), Lancaster Co.
Frisby, Ann, 1637, by Henry Perry, Charles River Co.
Frisell, George, 1649, by Edmund Scarburgh, Jr., Northampton Co.
Frisselle, Dan., Sr., 1654, by Capt. Augustine Warner and Mr. John Robins, ——— Co.
Frissell, Dan., Jr., 1654, by Capt. Augustine Warner, and Mr. John Robins, ——— Co.
Frith, Henry, 1647, by Leonard Pettock, Accomac Co.
Frizger, John, 1655, by Richard Coole and David Anderson, Westmoreland Co.
Frost, Wm., 1649, by Stephen Gill, York Co.
Frost, Geo., 1653, by Robert Saven, ——— Co.
Frost, Wm., 1654, by Christopher Regault, Gloucester Co.
Frouk, Robert, 1651, by Humphry Tabb, Northumberland Co.
Frowne, Eliz., 1642, by Wm. Barnard, Esq., Isle of Wight Co.
Frowell, Edward, 1650, by John Cooke, Northumberland Co.
Fry, Henry, 1650, by Capt. Moore Faulteroy, ——— Co.
Fry, Tho., 1650, by John Mangor, ——— Co.
Fry, Tho., 1652, by Henry Palin and John Singleton, ——— Co.
Fry, Mary, 1654, by Randall Chamblett, ——— Co.
Fry, Alice, 1650, by Lewis Burwell, Gent., ——— Co.
Fryar, Edward, 1654, by Tho. Hobkins, Lancaster Co.
Frye, Wm., 1638, by John Seaward, Isle of Wight Co.
Frye, Wm., 1637, by Francis Fowler, James River Co.
Frye, Wm., 1635, by Francis Fowler, James City Co.
Frye, Jeffry, 1637, by Georg Holmes, James City Co.
Fryer, Edwd., 1650, by John Hallawes, Gent., Northumberland Co.
Fryse, Wm., 1651, by Mr. Arthur Price, Yorke Co.
Fryth, Robert, 1650, by Mr. Stephen Hamelin, Charles City Co.
Fryth, Dyana, 1650, by Lewis Burwell, Gent., Northumberland Co.

Fuer, Sam., 1652, by John Greenbough, Henrico Co.
Fulcher, John, 1652, by Peter Knight, Gloucester Co.
Fulcher, John, 1653, by John Holding, York Co.
Fuller, Alice, 1637, by Theodore, Moyser, James City Co.
Fuller, John, 1653, by Peter Knight and Baker Cutt, ——— Co.
Fuller, John, 1652, by Mrs. Anna Barnett, Gloucester Co.
Fuller, Jno., 1651, by Mrs. Anna Bernard, Northumberland Co.
Fuller, Alex., 1643, by Francis Rice, ——— Co.
Fulton, Henry, 1638, by Walter Chiles, Charles City Co.
Furboyes, Fra., 1649, by Joseph Croshawe, Yorke Co.
Furbush, Fra., 1636, by John Dunston, James City Co.
Furbush, David, 1655, by Jer. Dodson, Gent., Lancaster Co.
Furbush, Fr., 1639, by John Dunston, James City Co.
Furbusher, Wm., 1654, by Col. Hump. Higgenson, Esq., and Abraham
    Moone, Westmoreland Co.
Furr, Wm., 1655, by John Jenkins, Northampton Co.
Fuston, Richard, 1652, by Henry Fleete, Lancaster Co.
Fybill, Jacob, 1643, by Casar Puggett, Lower Norfolk Co.

G

Gabriel, Jone, 1653, by David Phillips, Northumberland Co.
Gaely, Joane, 1639, by Lieut. Richard Popeley, ——— Co.
Gaffe, Jon., 1653, by Henry Lee, Yorke Co.
Gage, Wm., 1638, by Jeremiah Dickinson, James City Co.
Gage, Elizabeth, 1652, by Richard Halton and Lambett, Lambettson,
    Lancaster Co.
Gage, Wm ., 1638, by John Fludd, James City Co.
Gage, Wm., 1654, by Valentine Patten, Westmoreland Co.
Gage, Fra., 1654, by Roger Walters, Northumberland Co.
Gaines, Eliz., 1654, by R. Lawson, ——— Co.
Gaines, Geo., 1656, by Vincent Stanford, ——— Co.
Gaines, Bernard, 1654, by R. Lawson, ——— Co.
Gainine, Robert, 1635, by Capt. Adam Thoroughgood, ——— Co.
Galbourne, Edwd., 1654, by Wm. Lea, Charles City Co.
Galdhorne, Edward, 1642, by Bertram Hobert, ——— Co.
Gale, John, 1640, by John Radford, Lower Norfolk Co.
Gale, Daniell, 1649, by Richard Kemp, Esq. (Sec. of State), ——— Co.
Galepin, Wm., 1648, by George Read, Gent., ——— Co.
Gallant, Glode, 1649, by Capt. Ralph Wormeley, ——— Co.
Gallard, Wm., 1643, by Richard Kemp, Esq., James City Co.
Galler, John, 1654, by Nicholas Morris, Northumberland Co.
Gallett, Wm., 1637, by Jon Judson, Charles River Co.
Galliott, John, 1639, by Cpat. Nicholas Martian, Charles River Co.
Gallingson, Chris., 1650, by Wingfield, Webb, and Richard Pate, ———
    Co.
Gallop, Allen, 1652, by Savill Gaskins, Lower Norfolk Co.
Gallopin, Wm., 1635, by Jno. Sparkes, ——— Co.
Galloway, Richard, 1646, by John Ashcomb, Upper Norfolk Co.
Galloway, Mary, 1646, by John Ashcomb, Upper Norfolk Co.
Gally, Richard, 1637, by Francis Osborne, ——— Co.

Gallypin, Wm., 1651, by Capt. Geo. Read, Lancaster Co.
Garland, Francis, 1652, by Littleton Scarburg, ——— Co.
Galey, John, 1650, by Mrs. Frances Townshend (widow), Northumberland Co.
Gamberson, Con., 1654, by Tho. Hobkins, Lancaster Co.
Gambling, Josias, 1636, by Thomas Gaskins, Accomack Co.
Gammock, Robt. and 5 negroes, 1639, by Thom. Mathews, Henrico Co.
Gancer, Tymothy, 1649, by Edmund Scarburgh, Jr., Northampton Co.
Ganes, Richard, 1636, by John Wilkins, Accomack Co.
Ganey, Richard, 1639, by Thomas Smith, Accomac Co.
Gang, Alice, 1642, by Lieut. Francis Mason, ——— Co.
Gangrine, Nicho., 1648, by George Read, Gent., ——— Co.
Gannt, Jeffrey, 1642, by John Towlson, Accomack Co.
Gannt, Rich., 1638, by Robert Pitts, Isle of Wight Co.
Gapin, Wm., 1653, by Capt. Francis Patt, Northampton Co.
Gapper, John, 1650, by Richard Tye and Charles Sparrowe, Charles City Co.
Gaprelle, Edward, 1649, by Capt. Ralph Wormeley, ——— Co.
Gardener, Bryan, 1639, by John Well, Charles City Co.
Gardener, Rich., 1638, by Christopher Burrough, Lower Norfolk Co.
Gardiner, Thomas, 1642, by John Sytles, Isle of Wight Co.
Gardner, Archibald, 1655, by Lt. Col. Anthony Ellyott, ———Co.
Gardner, Philip, 1655, by Southy Littleberry, Northampton Co.
Gardner, Kath., 1656, by John Evans, Northampton Co.
Gardner, Rich., 1655, by John Hinman, Northampton Co.
Gardner, Step., 1654, by Mrs. Fra. Harrison, widow, Westmoreland Co.
Gardner, Richard, 1653, by Mr. Edmund Bowman, and Richard Starnell, ——— Co.
Gardner, Mary, 1650, by Ralph Green, ——— Co.
Gardner, John, 1650, by Hump. Lyster, ——— Co.
Gardner, Fra., 1649, by Edmund Scarburgh, Jr., Northampton Co.
Garden, George, 1649, by Edmund Scarburgh, Jr., Northampton Co.
Gardner, Mary, 1649, by Mr. Wm. Hoccaday, ——— Co.
Gardner, Don., 1651, by Lieut. Coll. Giles Brent, Northumberland Co.
Gardner, James, 1652, by Edward Revell, Northampton Co.
Gardner, Dan., 1654, by Lieut. Coll. Giles Brent, Westmoreland Co.
Gardner, Joseph, 1651, by Capt. John West, Esq., Yorke Co.
Gardner, Daniell, 1651, by John Rookwood, Gent., Northumberland Co.
Gardner, Tho., 1650, by Mrs. Frances Townshend, Northumberland Co.
Gordon, Dan., 1651, by John Martin and Lancaster Lovett, Lower Norfolk Co.
Gare, Robert, 1648, by Richard Thompson, Northumberland Co.
Gare, Israell, 1653, by Mr. Wm. Debram, ——— Co.
Gargame, Eliz., 1636, by Richard Cocke, ——— Co.
Gargame, Ellis, 1639, by Richard Corke, Gent., Henrico Co.
Gargen, Fra., 1653, by Roger Walker, Northumberland Co.
Gargrave, Isam, 1635, by Mr. Geo. Keth, Charles River Co.
Garingae, Samll., 1652, by Robert West, Charles City Co.
Garland, Peter, 1655, by George Kibble, ——— Co.
Garland, Robt., 1655, by Wm. Hall, New Kent Co.

Garland, Peter, 1656,.by Daniel Jaines and Jno. Jenings, —— Co.
Garland Peter, 1650, by Capt. Charles Leech, Yorke Co.
Garlick, Robt., 1650, by Capt. Moore Fautleroy, —— Co.
Garlington, Xtop., 1649, by Francis Brown, Northumberland Co.
Garner, Jon., 1637, by Daniell Gookins, New Norfolk Co.
Garnan, Richard, 1640, by William Crannage, Isle of Wight Co.
Garner, John, 1654, by Tho. Hobkins, Lancaster Co.
Garner, Wm., 1641, by Thomas Mathews, —— Co.
Garner, Daniel, 1638, by Edward Hill, Charles City Co.
Garner, Ellen, 1641, by Samuell Firment, Upper New Norfolk Co.
Garner, John, 1650, by Lewis Burwell, Gent., Northumberland Co.
Garner, Ann, 1648, by Geo. Hardey, Tho. Wombwell and Peter Hall,
     Isle of Wight Co.
Garner, Mary, 1652, by Mr. Edwin Connaway, —— Co.
Garner, Mary, 1638, by John Robins, —— Co.
Garner, Richard, 1637, by Wm. Cranage, New Norfolk Co.
Garner, Nicholas, 1637, by Humphry Loyd, Charles River Co.
Garner, John, 1637, by Wm. Farrar, Henrico Co.
Garner, Rich., 1637, by Wm. Farrar, Henrico Co.
Garner, Alex., 1637, by Rich. Bennett, New Norfolk Co.
Garner, Alex, 1635, by Richard Bennett, —— Co.
Garner, Phillip, 1650, by Mordecay Cooke, —— Co.
Garney, Jane, 1656, by Capt. Wm. Canfill, Surry Co.
Garnett, Jane, 1650, by Capt. Ishiell Linch, —— Co.
Garnett, Wm., 1650, by Edward Walker, Northumberland Co.
Garrett, Eliz., 1642, by Stephen Gill, Yorke River Co.
Garrett, John, 1650, by John Garwood, Nansemond Co.
Garrett, Mathew, 1654, by Benjamin Mathews, Northampton Co.
Garrett, Francis, 1639, by Georg Minifye, Esq., Charles River Co.
Garrett, Jon., 1639, by John Dunston, James City Co.
Garrett, Thomas, 1640, by Randall Crew, Upper Norfolk Co.
Garrett, John, 1639, by Henry Perry, Charles City Co.
Garrett, Eliza, 1647, by John Brooch, York River Co.
Garrett, Tho., 1647, by Thomas Godby, Lower Norfolk Co.
Garrett, John, 1648, by Tho. Lambert, Lower Norfolk Co.
Garrett, Wm., 1648, by Wm. Ewen, James City Co.
Garaway, Evans, 1637, by Jonathan Longworth, New Norfolk Co.
Garraway, Jon., 1654, by Capt. John West, Esq., Gloucester Co.
Garret, Jon., 1653, by Richard Major, Gloucester Co.
Garrett, Henry, 1653, by Robert Bayley, Northampton Co.
Garrett, Miller, 1653, by John King, Surry Co.
Garrett, Geo., 1653, by Abraham Moone, Northumberland Co.
Garrett, Marius, —, by Mr. John Page, —— Co.
Garrett, Wm., 1640, by Richard Hynes, New Norfolk Co.
Garrett, Eliz., 1636, by John Chandler, Elizabeth Citie Co.
Garrett, Rowland, 1637, by Leonard Yeo, —— Co.
Garrett, Jon., 1637, by William Mills, James City Co.
Garrett, Adry, 1637, by Theodore Moyser, James City Co.
Garrett, John, 1636, by John Dunston, James City Co.
Garrince, John, 1638, by George Mynifie (merchant), —— Co.
Garry, Henry, 1635, by Wm. Garry, his brother, Accomack Co.

Garry, Ann, 1635, by Wm. Garry, her husband, Accomack Co.
Garry, Wm., 1635, by Wm. Garry, his father, Accomack Co.
Garryson, Amos, 1654, by Richard Jacob, Northampton Co.
Gaskins, Eliz., 1636, by Thomas Gaskins, Accomack Co.
Garsuch, Richard, 1652, by Tho. Hoane, Gent., Lancaster Co.
Garsuch, Robt., 1652, by Tho. Hoane, Gent., Lancaster Co.
Garsuch, Anne, 1652, by Tho. Hoane, Gent., Lancaster Co.
Garwes, James, 1654, by Andrew Gibson, ——— Co.
Gary, Walter, 1640, by John Geary, Upper Norfolk Co.
Gaskin, Cebell, 1638, by Wm. Rainshaw, Lower New Norfolk Co.
Gaskins, Josias, 1635, by Thomas Gaskins, Accomack Co.
Gaskins, Alice, 1635, by Thomas Gaskins, Accomack Co.
Gaskins, Mary, 1635, by Thomas Gaskins, Accomack Co.
Gasmore, Eliz., 1635, by Capt. Adam Thoroughgood, ——— Co.
Gass, John, 1635, by Thomas Smith, James Co.
Gassent, John, 1654, by Mr. Mordecay Cooke, ——— Co.
Gasser, Marke, 1653, by Charles Grymes, clerk, Lancaster Co.
Gassett, Judith, 1654, by Luke Bellington, Accomac Co.
Gastcock, Wm., 1635, by Capt. A. Thoroughgood, ——— Co.
Gastrey, Thomas, 1648, by George White, Lower Norfolk Co.
Gatehouse, John, 1652, by Mr. Henry Pitt, ——— Co.
Gately, John, 1636, by Wm. Parker, Warrasquinoake Co.
Gater, James, 1638, by John Gates, Lower New Norfolk Co.
Gater, Joane, 1636, by John Gater, Elizabeth City Co.
Gaterson, James, 1637, by Capt. Thos. Osborne, Henrico Co.
Gates, Jon., 1643, by Sir Francis Wyatt, Kt., ——— Co.
Gates, Mathew, 1639, by Tho. Boulding, Elizabeth City Co.
Gaton, Georg, 1638, by Richard Maion, Charles River Co.
Gatricke, Ann, 1654, by Francis Land, Lower Norfolk Co.
Gandye, Eman., 1653, by John King, Surry Co.
Gaunt, Robt., 1637, by Theodore Moyser, James City Co.
Gautlett, ———, 1652, by Wn. Gautlett (his son), ——— Co.
Gawin, Wm., 1653, by Mr. Wm. Hoccoday, Yorke Co.
Gawing, Jon., 1635, by Thos. Crompe, James Co.
Gaying, Bernard, 1643, by Capt. Samuell Mathews, Esq., ——— Co.
Gayler, John, 1652, by Tho. Greenwood, Isle of Wight Co.
Gaylor, Peter, 1638, by Epaphroditus Lawson, Upper Norfolk Co.
Gayne, Tho., 1652, by Nicho. George, Tho. Taberer, and Humphry
   Clarke, ———Co.
Gaynes, Edw., 1650, by Edward Walker, Northumberland Co.
Gaynes, Jane, 1650, by Andrew Gibson, ——— Co.
Gayney, Richd., 1655, by John Ninman, Northampton Co.
Gayny, Robt., 1654, by Col. Argoll Yardely, Northampton Co.
Geadston, Jno., 1643, by John Batts, James City Co.
Geaf, Wm., 1637, by Henry Perry, Charles River Co.
Geat, Wm., 1637, by Henry Perry, Charles River Co.
Gebbons, Oliver, 1642, by Wm. Warren, ——— Co.
Giby, Prudence, 1650, by George Pate, Charles City Co.
Gedley, Richard, 1637, by Leonard Yeo. Elizabeth City Co.
Gedon, Anne, 1636, by Wm. Bibby, Accomack Co.
Gee, Tho., 1654, by Tho. Willoughby, Lower Norfolk Co.

Gee, William, 1639, by Randall Holt, James City Co.
Gee, Edward, 1643, by Mr. Moore Fautleroy, Upper Norfolk Co.
Gee, Jon., 1637, by Hen. Thompson, James River Co.
Geere, Fr., 1638, by Randall Crew, Upper New Norfolk Co.
Geers, John, 1640, by Christopher Kirk, Accomack Co.
Geey, Wm., 1650, by Mordecay Cooke, ——— Co.
Geiles, Henry, 1636, by John Gater, Elizabeth City Co.
Gelding, Wm., 1639, by William Burdett, Accomack Co.
Gelding, Elizabeth, 1648, by John Clarke, Lower Norfolk Co.
Gemple, Mary, 1654, by Elizabeth Hutton, Surry Co.
Gent., Tho., 1638, by Roger Davis, Charles City Co.
Geobe, John, 1640, by John George, Charles City Co.
Geogn, Hugh, 1649, by Richard Kemp, Esq. (Sec. of State), ——— Co.
Georg, Robert, 1642, by Roger Symmons, ——— Co.
Georg, Griffith, 1643, by William Ewins, James City Co.
Georg, Thomas, 1638, by Wm. Hatfield, Upper New Norfolk Co.
George, John, 1638, by Lieut. John Upton, Isle of Wight Co.
George, Silvester, 1650, by Lewis Burwell, Gent., ——— Co.
George, Wm., 1654, by Robert Hubard, Westmoreland Co.
George, Griffith, 1648, by Wm. Ewen, James City Co.
George, Anne, 1653, by Jervais, Dodson, Northumberland Co.
George, Nich., 1653, by Capt. Francis Patt, Northampton Co.
George, Jno., 1653, by Capt. Francis Patt, Northampton Co.
George, Richd., 1654, by Capt. John West, Esq., Gloucester Co.
George Hall, 1652, by John Pounsey, ——— Co.
George, Marg., 1652, by Nicholas George, ——— Co.
George, Richard, 1650, by Richard Dunning, ——— Co.
George, Jane, 1638, by John George (her husband), Charles City Co.
Geoynn, Abigail, 1653, by Geo. Wadding, Lancaster Co.
Gepperson, Hewett, 1652, by Tho. Todd, ——— Co.
Gerdon, Daniel, —, by Mr. Robt. Fontaine, Lower Norfolk Co.
Gerey, John, 1642, by John Benton, ——— Co.
Gerford, John, 1646, by Geo. Ludlow, Esq., York Co.
Gerrard, Peter, 1653, by Ferdinando Austin, Charles City Co.
Gerrard, Gilbert, 1643, by Richard Kemp, Esq., James City Co.
Gerrard, Jon., 1635, by Mr. Geo. Keth, Charles River Co.
Gerrish, John, 1641, by Thomas Bernard, Warwick River Co.
Gerris, Stephen, 1642, by Walter Chiles, Charles Co.
Gerrard, Susana, 1650, by Tho. Gerrord, Gent., Northumberland Co.
Gerrard, Susa, 1650, by Tho. Gerrord, Gent. (her father), Northumberland Co.
Gerrard, Temp., 1650, by Tho. Gerrord, Gent., Northumberland Co.
Gerrard, John, 1650, by Tho. Gerrord, Gent., Northumberland Co.
Gerrard, Fra., 1650, by Tho. Gerrord, Gent., Northumberland Co.
Gerrard, Justinian, 1650, by Tho. Gerrard, Northumberland Co.
Gerry, John, 1638, by Walter Chiles, Charles Citie Co.
Gerry, John, 1638, by Walter Chiles, Charles City Co.
Gesorroro, Jno., 1651, by Anthony Johnson, Northampton Co.
Gestee, Henry, 1651, by Mr. Rowland Burnham, ——— Co.
Gey, Wm., 1653, by Mr. Wm. Baldwen, York Co.
Gibbs, Wm., 1654, by Tho. Harmanson, Northampton Co.

Gibbs, Edward, 1654, by Francis Smith and Mr. John Smith, Westmoreland Co.
Gibbs, Robt., 1655, by Peter Ford, Gloucester Co.
Gibbs, Humphry, 1639, by John Hayward, James City Co.
Gibbs, Joell, 1650, by Tho. Gerrord, Gent., Northumberland Co.
Gibbs, John, 1649, by Mr. Nesum and others, Northumberland Co.
Gibbs, Natha., 1652, by George Kemp, Lower Norfolk Co.
Gibbs, Edward, 1652, by Tho. Steevens, Lancaster Co.
Gibbs, Edward, 1653, by Charles Grymes, Lancaster Co.
Gibbs, Joell, 1652, by Tho. Hallinard, ——— Co.
Gibbs, Edward, 1638, by Percivall Champion, Upper New Norfolk Co.
Gibbins, Olmer, 1640, by John Radford, Lower Norfolk Co.
Gibbons, John 1641, by Wm. Burdett, Accomack Co.
Gibett, Hen., 1654, by Robert Young, Lancaster Co.
Giblin, John, 1650, by Richard Axom, and Tho. Godwin, ——— Co.
Gibson, John, 1655, by Wm. Thomas, Northumberland Co.
Gibson, Nich., 1642, by Hugh Gwyn, Gent., ——— Co.
Gibson, Tho., 1639, by John Howell, Henrico Co.
Gibson, Jon., 1643, by John Freeme, Charles Co.
Gibson, Walter, 1639, by John Osborne, James Citie Co.
Gibson, Tho., 1647, by John Brooch, York River Co.
Gibson, Robt., 1652, by Nicholas Wadilow, Northampton Co.
Gibson, Edward, 1652, by Mr. James Warradine, ——— Co.
Gibson, Nicholas, 1638, by John Caugden, Charles River Co.
Gibson, John, 1638, by Christopher Branch, Henrico Co.
Gibson, Robt., 1655, by Nich. Waddilow, Northampton Co.
Gibson, Edw., 1637, by Humphry Higginson, Gent., ——— Co.
Gibson, Jon., 1637, by Wm. Farrar, Henrico Co.
Gibson, John, 1635, by Christopher Branch, Henrico Co.
Gibson, Geoman, 1637, by Thomas Holt, New Norfolk Co.
Giffry, Richard, 1642, by John Sweete, ——— Co.
Gidney, John, 1639, by John Pawley, James City Co.
Gilbert, Penelope, —, by Saml. Ruthland, Lower Norfolk Co.
Gilbert, Robt., 1643, by Robert Haies, Lower Norfolk Co.
Gilbert, Rog., Jr., 1645, by Mr. Bartholomew Hoskins, ——— Co.
Gilbert, Rog., Sr., 1645, by Mr. Bartholomew Hoskins, ——— Co.
Gilbert, Sam., 1645, by Richard Jacob, Northampton Co.
Gilbert, Thomas, 1645, by James Jackson, Northampton Co.
Gilbert, Jane, 1643, by Thomas Cassen, ——— Co.
Gilbert, Elizabeth, 1637, by Robert Bennett, New Norfolk Co.
Gilbert, Rich., 1637, by Thomas Barnard, James City Co.
Gilbert Eliz., 1635, by Robert Bennett, ——— Co.
Gilbert, George, 1635, by Joseph Johnson, ——— Co.
Gilbert, Reynolds, 1636, by Joseph Moore, Elizabeth City Co.
Gilcock, Wm., 1642, by William Durant, ——— Co.
Gildinge, John, 1652, by Mrs. Jane Harner, Northumberland Co.
Giles, John, 1654, by Francis Smith and Mr. John Smith, Westmoreland Co.
Giles, James, 1639, by Capt. Robt. Felgate, Charles River Co.
Giles, John, 1639, by George Giles, Upper Norfolk Co.
Giles, Wm., 1654, by Alex. Madocks and James Jones, Northampton Co.

Giles, George, 1652, by Christopher Lewis, Isle of Wight Co.

Giles, Robt., 1652, and Hanna his wife, and Hannah his daughter, by Nicho. George, Tho. Taberer and Humphry Clarke, ———— Co.

Giles, John, 1642, by Wm. Barnard, Esq., Isle of Wight Co.

Giles, Henry, 1635, by Joseph Johnson, ———— Co.

Giles, John, 1635, by Jeremiah Clement, ———— Co.

Gilgraffe, Tho., 1652, by Capt. John West, Esq., ———— Co.

Gilford, Peter, 1653, by John King, Surry Co.

Gilford, Robt., 1651, by Richard Grigson, ———— Co.

Gill, John, 1654, by Col. Argoll Yardley, Northampton Co.

Gill, Ellnor, 1655, by John Ayres, ———— Co.

Gill, Stephen, 1642, by Stephen Gill, Yorke River Co.

Gill, Jon., 1637, by Henry Perry, Charles River Co.

Gill, Jon., 1653, by Margarett Upton, Lancaster Co.

Gill, Richard, 1643, by Lt. Wm. Worleidge, ———— Co.

Gill, Wm., 1638, by Thomas Bogwell, Charles City Co.

Gill, John, 1637, by Edward Tunstall, Henrico Co.

Gill, Jon., 1637, by Henry Perry, Charles River Co.

Gill, Wm., 1635, by Thomas Bagwell, ———— Co.

Gill, Edward, 1636, by John Neale, Accomack Co.

Gill, John, 1636, by Edward Tonstall, ———— Co.

Gillam, Wm., 1650, by Mordecay Cooke, ———— Co.

Gillar, Susan, 1654, by Edward Gilla, James City Co.

Gillcy, Robert, 1650, by Silvester Thatcher and Tho. Whitlocke, ———— Co.

Gilleailow, Coner, 1655, by Edmund Scarbourgh, Northampton Co.

Giller, John, 1650, by Francis Hobbs, ———— Co.

Gillgate, John, 1638, by Lieut. John Upton, Isle of Wight Co.

Gillin, George, 1638, by Liut. John Upton, Isle of Wight Co.

Gillingham, Henry, 1642, by John Robins, ———— Co.

Gillins, Daniell, 1650, by Nathaniell Jones, Northumberland Co.

Gillis, Elin, 1649, by John Merriman, ———— Co.

Gillmon, Richard, 1653, by Mr. Wm. Hoccoday, Yorke Co.

Gilnett, Tho., 1654, by John Drayton, Westmoreland Co.

Gillet, John, 1655, by Wm. Steevens, Northampton Co.

Gillett, Jon., 1637, by Nathaniel Floyd, Isle of Wight Co.

Gillett, John, 1652, by Richard Hatton, Lancaster Co.

Gillett, Elizabeth, 1652, by Richard Allen, Elizabeth City Co.

Gilpin, Jane, 1652, by Mrs. Mary Brent, Northumberland Co.

Giltered, John, 1652, by Col. Geo. Ludlow, Esq., Gloucester Co.

Gimblet, Dan., 1655, by Wm. Wright, Gent., Nansemond Co.

Gina, Mark, 1643, by Casar Puggett, Lower Norfolk Co.

Gingey, Wm., 1638, by Capt. Christopher Wormley, Charles River Co.

Ginkin, Wm., 1649, by Capt. Ralph Wormeley, ———— Co.

Ginings, Wm., 1654, by Valentine Patten, Westmoreland Co.

Ginings, Wm., 1654, by Robert Hubard, Westmoreland Co.

Ginsly, Sarah, 1654, by Capt. Nich. Marteaw, Westmoreland Co.

Ginsey, Wm., 1649, by Capt. Ralph Wormeley, ———— Co.

Gintham, John, 1642, by Joseph Royall, ———— Co.

Gittens, Jane, 1656, by Tho. Best and Christopher Ashly, Nansemond Co.

Giving, Grace, 1650, by John Mattrum, Northumberland Co.
Glade, Wm., 1652, by Mr. Henry Soane, ——— Co.
Gladen, Mary, 1655, by Tho. Leatherberry, Northampton Co.
Gladenie, Howel, 1655, by Tho. Leatherberry, Northampton Co.
Gladeing, Haell, 1653, by Charles Scarburg, Northampton Co.
Glading, Howell, 1652, by Wm. Colborne, Northampton Co.
Glamfield, Jno., 1654, by John Curtis, Accomac Co.
Glan, John, 1655, by Dr. Giles Mode, New Kent Co.
Glan, Robert, 1652, by Nathaniel Bacon, Isle of Wight Co.
Glantum, John, 1653, by Colo. Wm. Clayborne (Sec. of State), ———
    Co.
Glascock, Rich., 1637, by Rich. Bennett, New Norfolk Co.
Glascock, Richard, 1635, by Richard Bennett, Warrasquinoak Co.
Glascocke, Jane, 1643, by Thomas Glascocke, her husband, ——— Co.
Glascock, Richard, 1635, by Richard Bennett, ——— Co.
Glass, Duncan, 1652, by James Sterling, Lower Norfolk Co.
Glass, Mary, 1651, by John Senior, ——— Co.
Glasse, Duning, 1652, by Nathaniel Bacon, Isle of Wight Co.
Glayne, George, Jr., 1655, by Tho. Everidge, ——— Co.
Glayne, George, and Mary his wife, 1655, by Tho. Everidge, ——— Co.
Gleames, Kat., 1650, by Elias Edmonds, ——— Co.
Gleare, Peter, 1637, by John Moone, Isle of Wight Co.
Gleed, Thos., 1638, by Lieut. John Upton, Isle of Wight Co.
Glem, Jane, 1654, by Wm. Lea, Charles City Co.
Glendener, Wm., 1653, by Richard Braine, Charles Co.
Glenister, Robt., 1636, by Wm. Armestead, Elizabeth City Co.
Glissen, Eliza, 1655, by Wm. Thomas, Northumberland Co.
Glisson, Fra., 1654, by John Watson and John Bognell, Westmoreland
    Co.
Glight, Thomas, 1642, by Stephen Webb, James City Co.
Gloaer, Morgan, 1643, by William Ewins, James City Co.
Glonfeild, Joane, 1642, by Victoris Christmas and Francis Finch, ———
    Co.
Gloss, John, 1653, by Ralph Green, Gloucester Co.
Glouce, Ann, 1653, by Richard Burton, ——— Co.
Glovise, Lew., 1635, by Stephen Webb, ——— Co.
Glover, Tho., 1651, by Audery Bennett, Nansemond Co.
Glover, John, 1651, by James Thelaball, Lower Norfolk Co.
Glover, Dorothy, 1637, by Tho. Symmons, Charles River Co.
Glover, Sarah, 1637, by Alice Edloe, Henrico Co.
Glover, Edward, 1638, by Lieut. John Upton, Isle of Wight Co.
Glover, Elin., 1655, by Southy Littleberry, Northampton Co.
Glover, John, 1655, by Martin Hamond, ——— Co.
Glover, James, 1655, by Mr. Tho. Ballard, Gloucester Co.
Glover, Margaret, 1639, by Wm. Barker, Charles City Co.
Gloves, Wm., 1638, by John Walton, Accomac Co.
Glower, Tho., 1655, by Mr. John Mottrow, Northumberland Co.
Glowers, Edward, 1651, by Audery Bennett, Nansemond Co.
Glyn, Morris, 1653, by Wm. Haynes, ——— Co.
Goardon, Tho., 1650, by Robert Bird, ——— Co.
Godbeare, Hector, 1637, by William Spencer, ——— Co.

Godbeard, Nestor, 1635, by William Spencer, ——— Co.
Godby, Tho., 1653, by Frances Emperor, Hugh Gale and Edward Morgan, Lower Norfolk Co.
Godbery, Joane, 1636, by Samuel Edwards, James City Co.
Godbye, Thomas, 1637, by Arthur Smith, Isle of Wight Co.
Goddin, Wm., 1650, by Robert Bird, ——— Co.
Goddin, Jon., 1653, by Symon Thorogood, Elizabeth City Co.
Godfrey, Wm., 1640, by William Crannage, Isle of Wight Co.
Godfrey, Richard, 1652, by Mr. Tho. Brice, Lancaster Co.
Godfrey, Sarah, 1652, by Tho. Dodford, Lower Norfolk Co.
Godfrye, John, 1638, by Capt. Thomas Harris, Henrico Co.
Godfry, Wm., 1637, by William Mills, James City Co.
Godfrye, Jno., 1635, by Thos. Harris, Henrico Co.
Godle, Nathan, 1637, by Eleanor Day and Thom. Emmerson, Warwick River Co.
Godle, Nathan, 1637, by Eleanor Day and Thos. Emmerson, Warwick River Co.
Godsmen, John, 1653, by Joseph Croshaw, York Co.
Godson, Christopher, 1650, by Sr. Tho. Luntsford, Kt., and Barronett, Co.
Godson, Tho., 1652, by Mr. James Warradine, ——— Co.
Godson, Richd., 1650, by Mr. Robt. Holt, James City Co.
Godwen, John, 1650, by Anthony Fulgam, ——— Co.
Godwin, Jo., 1653, by Capt. Wm. Whittington, Northampton Co.
Godwin, Eliz., 1653, by Capt. Wm. Whittington, Northampton Co.
Godwin, Devorux, 1653, by Capt. Wm. Whittington, Northampton Co
Godwin, Mat., 1654, by Henry Walker, James City Co.
Godwin, John, 1656, by Wm. Pope, Nansemond Co.
Godwin, Jno., 1647, by Elizabeth Barcroft, Isle of Wight Co.
Godwin, Daniel, 1635, by William Barber (a minister), Charles City Co.
Godyal, Edwd., 1653, by Margarett Upton, Lancaster Co.
Goeman, Tho., 1637, by Capt. John Howe, Accomac Co.
Goffe, Walton, 1637, by John Judson, Charles River Co.
Gogs, Jeane, 1656, by Wm. Crump and Mr. Humphry Vaulx, James City Co.
Golby, Ann, 1647, by Richard Morgan, Lower Norfolk Co.
Gold, Richard, 1651, by Mr. Wm. Armestead, ——— Co.
Goldcock, Tho., 1653, by Samuell Parry, Lancaster Co.
Golden, Geo., 1652, by Tho. Holliwell, ——— Co.
Golding, John, 1638, by John Jackson, and Eliza Kingswill, James City Co.
Golding, Tho., 1638, by Edward Oliver, ——— Co.
Golding, Dorothy, 1638, by Edward Oliver, ——— Co.
Golding, Dorothy, 1639. by Edward Oliver, James City Co.
Golding, Thomas, 1639, by Edward Oliver, James City Co.
Golding, Gabriell, 1650, by Mr. Epaphroditus Lawson, ——— Co.
Golding, Tho., 1650, by Capt. Moore Fautleroy, ——— Co.
Golding, John, 1651, by Richard Ripley, ——— Co.
Golding, Tho., 1639, by Edward Oliver, James City Co.
Golding, Wm., 1637, by Thomas Weston, Charles River Co.
Golding, Wm., 1636, by Wm. Parker, Warrasquinoake Co.

Goldsmith, Richard, 1648, by John Seward, Isle of Wight Co.
Goldsmith, Nicho., 1639, by William Davis, James City Co.
Goldsmith, John, 1650, by Tho. Gerrord, Gent., Northumberland Co.
Goldsmith, ——, and three children, 1650, by Geo. Goldsmith (her husband), —— Co.
Goldsmith, John, 1652, by Anthony Hoskins, Northampton Co.
Goldsmith, Mary, 1652, by Richard Starnell, —— Co.
Goldsmith, Wm., 1638, by John Gater, Lower New Norfolk Co.
Goldston, Richard, 1653, by Mr. Edmund Bowman, and Richard Starnell, —— Co.
Gole, Edward, 1650, by William Gooch, Gent., —— Co.
Gondaine, Marg., 1650, by Jervace Dodson, Gent., Northumberland Co.
Gonlson, Danll., 1648, by John King and Lawrence Ward, Isle of Wight Co.
Gonnion, James, 1650, by John Cox, —— Co.
Gonnion, Robt., 1650, by John Cox, —— Co.
Gonth, Christ., 1638, by Edward Hill, Charles City Co.
Good, Richard, 1655, by Mrs. Margaret Brent, Lancaster Co.
Goodall, Rich., 1636, by Nathan Martin, Henrico Co.
Gooday, Richard, 1640, by John Geary, Upper Norfolk Co.
Goodcrost, James, 1646, by John Ashcomb, Upper Norfolk Co.
Goode, Richard, 1651, by Joseph Hayes, Gent., Yorke Co.
Goodgaine, Henry, 1642, by William Prior, Gent., —— Co.
Gookins, Samuell, 1642, by Capt. Daniell Gookin, —— Co.
Gookins, Mrs. Mary, 1642, by Capt. Daniell Gookin, —— Co.
Goordlord, Tho., 1643, by Sir Francis Wyatt, Kt., —— Co.
Goodman, Marg., 1655, by Capt. Tho. Davis, Warwick Co.
Goodman, Richard, 1638, by Thomas Beerboye, Upper New Norfolk Co.
Goodman, John, 1638, by Thomas Burbage, Accomack Co.
Goodman, Geo., 1653, by Tho. White and Peter Sexton, Norfolk Co.
Goodman, Richard, 1652, by Henry Fleete, Lancaster Co.
Goodman, Wm., 1651, by Richard Coleman, Yorke Co.
Goodman, Kath., 1653, by Richard Major, Gloucester Co.
Goodman, Francis, 1638, by Thomas Dewe, Upper New Norfolk Co.
Goodman, Francis, 1637, by Tho. Powell, New Norfolk Co.
Goodnought, Luke, 1642, by Jerimiah Grey, James City Co.
Goodrich, Anne, 1653, by Peter Sexton, —— Co.
Goodrich, Tho., 1653, by Peter Sxeton, —— Co.
Goodridge, Ann, 1637, by Francis Fowler, James River Co.
Goodriffe, Grace, 1648, by Richard Thompson, Northumberland Co.
Goodron, Henry, 1636, by Christopher Calthropp, Charles River Co.
Goods, Wm., 1643, by Richard Kemp, Esq., James City Co.
Goodson, John, 1638, by Thomas Swan, James Citie Co.
Goodson, Jon., 1635, by Wm. Swan, James Co.
Goodwin, Sam., 1656, by Sir Henry Chichley, —— Co.
Goodwin, Samll., 1650, by Mr. Stephen Hamelin, Charles City Co.
Goodwin, Sarah, 1643, by Rich. Hoe, Gent., —— Co.
Goodwin, Step., 1638, by Wm. Baker and Associates, Charles City Co.
Goodwin, Daniell, 1638, by Wm. Baker and Associates, Charles City Co.
Goodwin, John, 1635, by William Wilkinson (minister), —— Co.

Goodwin, Stephen, 1635, by William Barber (a mariner), Charles City Co.
Goodwin, Geo., 1637, by John Chew, Charles River Co.
Goodwin, John, 1637, by William Wilkinson, New Norfolk Co.
Goone, John, 1650, by Walter Broodhurst, ——— Co.
Goman, Anne, 1653, by Capt. Nathaniel Hurd, Warrick Co.
Gordon, Henry, 1652, by Henry Snaile, Lower Norfolk Co.
Gordale, Tho., 1653, by Tho. Scoggin, Northumberland Co.
Gordon, Nich., 1635, by Wm. Garry, Accomacke Co.
Gordione, Thomas, 1651, by Robert Absall, Yorke Co.
Gordon, Gerog, 1636, by John Chew, Gent., Charles River Co.
George, Jon., 1637, by Patrick Kennedye, New Norfolk Co.
Gore, John, 1654, by Tho. Willoughby, Lower Norfolk Co.
Gorrell, Tho., 1642, by Christopher Boyce, ——— Co.
Gorsuch, Elizabeth, 1652, by Tho. Hoane, ——— Co.
Gorsuch, Lovelace, 1652, by Tho. Hoane, ——— Co.
Gorsuch, Charles, 1652, by Tho. Hoane, ——— Co.
Gorsuch, Kath., 1652, by Tho. Hoane, ——— Co.
Goverson, Cor., 1651, by George Eaton, ——— Co.
Gosall, Jon., 1638, by James Warradin, Charles City Co.
Gosse, Christopher, 1637, by Alice Edloe, Henrico Co.
Gosling, John, 1643, by Wm. Lawrance, James City Co.
Gosnell, Eliz., 1653, by Richd. Haines, ——— Co.
Gosnell, Marg., 1653, by Richd. Haines, ——— Co.
Goste, Rich., 1644, by Thomas Davis, Upper Norfolk Co.
Gouch, Mathew, 1636, by George Sapheir, Elizabeth City Co.
Gouch, Oplier, 1651, by Lieut. Coll. Giles Brent, Northumberland Co.
Gouch, Xtop, 1651, by John Rookwood, Gent., Northumberland Co.
Gourdon, Georg., 1654, by Edward Cook, ——— Co.
Gouge, John, 1650, by Capt. Moore Fautleroy, ——— Co.
Goulding, Jane, 1650, by Richard Tye and Charles Sparrowe, Charles City Co.
Goulding William 1635 by Samuel Weaver, ——— Co.
Gourd, Andrew, 1652, by George Pace, Charles City Co.
Gourd, John, 1655, by Edward Moore, Northampton Co.
Gouth, Xpher, 1654, by Lieut. Coll. Giles Brent, Westmoreland Co.
Goward, Wm., 1655, by Mr. Wm. Nutt, Northumberland Co.
Gower, Edward, 1655, by Mr. John Mottrow, Northumberland Co.
Gower, John, 1653, by John Edwards, Lancaster Co.
Gower, Nich., 1638, by Stephen Charlton, Accomack Co.
Gower, Rich., 1637, by Percival Champion, New Norfolk Co.
Gowlate, Richd., 1653, by Capt. Natha. Hurd, Warrick Co.
Gowin, John, 1650, by John Armesbee, Northumberland Co.
Gowsey, Wm., 1656, by Tabitha and Matilda Scarburgh, Northampton Co.
Gover, Tho., 1653, by Francis Emperor, Hugh Gale and Edward Morgan, Lower Norfolk Co.
Goverby, Ellis, 1654, by Richard Jacob, Northampton Co.
Goverson, Corn., 1652, by Mrs. Elnor Brocas, Lancaster Co.
Grace, George, 1639, by Thomas Mathews, Henrico Co.
Grace, Isabell, 1653, by Mr. Wm. Hoccoday, Yorke Co.

Grace, Robt., 1635, by Francis Fowler, James City Co.
Grace, Roger, 1637, by Francis Fowler, James River Co.
Grainger, Hen., 1639, by Randall Holt, James City Co.
Gracewood, Benedict, 1653, by Wm. Debram, ——— Co.
Graddon, Nich., 1654, by Col. Argoll Yardley, Northampton Co.
Gradin, Edw., 1637, by Charles Barcroft, Isle of Wight Co.
Gragg, Mary, 1653, by Augustus Warner, ——— Co.
Graham, Ant., 1651, by Capt. Tho. Davis, Northumberland Co.
Graham, Mary, 1653, by Mr. Wm. Hoccoday, Yorke Co.
Grand, John, 1650, by Richard Tye and Charles Sparrowe, Charles City Co.
Grand, Mary, 1639, by Lieut. Richard Popeley, ——— Co.
Grande, Tho., 1651, by Joseph Croshaw, Yorke Co.
Grands, Chr., 1647, by Leonard Pettock, Accomac Co.
Branfeild, Xtop., 1650, by Mr. James Williamson, ——— Co.
Granger, Richard, 1654, by Mr. Tho. Fowke, Westmoreland Co.
Granger, Elizabeth, 1653, by Samuell Parry, Lancaster Co.
Granger, Tho., 1653, by Wm. Sidner, Lancaster Co.
Granger, Tho., 1653, by John Gillett, Lancaster Co.
Granger, Wm., 1637, by Daniell Gookins, New Norfolk Co.
Granger, Wm., 1641, by John Gookin, Lower Norfolk Co.
Grangrave, Brin., 1655, by Edmund Scarbourgh, Jr., and Littleton Scarbourgh, Northampton Co.
Granely, Jone, 1638, by John Fludd, James City Co.
Grames, William, 1639, by Edward Oliver, James City Co.
Grannt, Joane, 1638, by Samuell Trigg and Michael Joyner, James City Co.
Grant, Joane, 1640, by Henry Porter and Raphaell Joyner, James City Co.
Grant, Wm., 1656, by Tho. Best and Christopher Ashly, Nansemond Co.
Grant, Elizabeth, 1650, by Wm. Holder, ——— Co.
Grant, Duncom, 1650, by Elyes Edmonds, ——— Co.
Grant, Antho., 1652, by Col. Geo. Ludlow, Esq., Gloucester Co.
Grant, Bened, 1652, by Col. Geo. Ludlow, Esq., Gloucester Co.
Grant, John, 1638, by Geo. Lobb, Tho. Perce, Tho. Warne, James City Co.
Grant, Christ., 1637, by Argoll Yeardly, New Norfolk Co.
Grave, Joane, 1639, by John Burland, Charles River Co.
Grave, John, 1639, by Dorothy Clarke, Henrico Co.
Graves, William, 1639, by Edward Oliver, James City Co.
Graves, Robt., 1643, by Capt. Samuell Mathews, Esq., ——— Co.
Graves, Edw., 1647, by Elizabeth Barcroft, Isle of Wight Co.
Graves, Robins, 1650, by Francis Hobbs, ——— Co.
Graves, Alexander, 1653, by Evan Davis and Henry Nicholls, Lancaster Co.
Graves, Richard, 1653, by Wm. Thomas, Northumberland Co.
Graves, Tho., and Katherine his wife, 1651, by William Parry, Northumberland Co.
Graves, Ann, 1653, by Edward Hall, Lower Norfolk Co.
Graves, John, 1651, by Wm. Parry, Northumberland Co.

Graves, Tho., Jr., 1651, by Wm. Parry, Northumberland Co.
Graves, Tho., 1651, by Capt. Stephen Gill, Northumberland Co.
Graves, Rich., 1637, by Robert Pitts, Isle of Wight Co.
Graves, George, 1642, by Thomas Grey, James City Co.
Graves, Richard, 1637, by John Redman and John Neale, Accomac Co.
Graves, Jon., of Pattentee, 1637, by John Graves, Elizabeth City Co.
Graves, Thom., Sr., 1637, by John Graves, Elizabeth City Co.
Graves, Reichard, 1636, by John Neale, Accomack Co.
Graves, Ann, 1637, by Wm. Cotton, ——— Co.
Graves, Kath., 1637, by John Graves, Elizabeth City Co.
Graves, Tho., Jr., 1637, by John Graves, Elizabeth City Co.
Graves, Richard, 1637, by John Wilkins, New Norfolk Co.
Gravelin, Joan, 1650, by Capt. John Flood, Gent., and Jno. Flood, an
    ancient mariner, James City Co.
Gray, Josua, 1656, by Tho. Salsbury, Northumberland Co.
Gray, Ann, 1656, by Tho. Salsbury, Northumberland Co.
Gray, Geo., 1654, by Humphry Belt, Lower Norfolk Co.
Gray, Mary, 1656, by Tho. Salsbury, Northumberland Co.
Gray, Francis, and Alice his wife, 1656, by Tho. Salsbury, Northum-
    berland Co.
Gray, Miles, 1655, by John Hinman, Northampton Co.
Gray, Wm., 1656, by Tho. Busby, Surry Co.
Gray, Wm., 1654, by Benjamin Mathews, Northampton Co.
Gray, Alice, 1650, by John Hallawes, Gent., Northumberland Co.
Gray, Mary, 1650, by John Hallawes, Gent., Northumberland Co.
Gray, Wm., 1650, by Silvester Thathcher and Tho. Whitlocke, ———
    Co.
Gray, John, 1651, by Coll. Richard Lee, Esq., Gloucester Co.
Gray, Henry, 1651, by Tho. Hales and Tho. Sheppard, Northumber-
    land Co.
Gray, Thomas, 1652, by Capt. Augustine Warner, ——— Co.
Gray, Wm., 1652, by Tho. Teakle, Northampton Co.
Gray, Elizabeth, 1653, by Richard Budd, Northumberland Co.
Gray, Rebecca, 1638, by Thomas Gray, James City Co.
Gray, Wm., 1638, by Thomas Gray, James City Co.
Gray, Avis, 1638, by Thomas Gray, James City Co.
Gray, Rebecca, 1635, by Thomas Gray, she being his second wi fe
    James Co.
Gray, Annis, 1635, by Thos. Gray, her husband, James Co.
Gray, Fran., 1635, by Joseph Johnson, ——— Co.
Gray, Henry, 1650, by Lewis Burwell, Gent., ——— Co.
Grayes, Thomas, 1638, by Samuell Watkeyes, Charles River Co.
Grange, John, 1637, by William Mills, James City Co.
Grayne, Jonathan, 1638, by Edward Sparshott, Charles City Co.
Grayne, Rowland, 1638, by Elizabeth Grayne, Charles City Co.
Grayne, Jonathan, 1638, by Edward Sparshott, Charles City Co.
Grayne, James, 1638, by Elizabeth Grayne, Charles City Co.
Grear, Tho., 1649, by Christop. Lewis, James City Co.
Greed, And., 1654, by Col. Argoll Yardley, Northampton Co.
Greeke, Rich, 1637, by Wm. Farrar, Henrico Co.
Greeman, Wm., 1654, by Mr. Francis Hamond, York Co.

Gremisdelch, Tho., 1649, by Mr. Nesum and others, Northumberland Co.
Gremston, Anthony, 1637, by Wm. Prior, Charles River Co.
Green, Tho., 1653, by Margarett Upton, Lancaster Co.
Green, Pres., 1651, by Edward Deggs, Yorke Co.
Green, Marjary, 1653, by Peter Knight, Northumberland Co.
Green, Richard, 1652, by Tho. Lewis, Gent., Lancaster Co.
Green, Ann, 1650, by Capt. Richard Bond, Charles City Co.
Green, John, 1653, by Joseph Hogkinson, Lower Norfolk Co.
Green, Dorcas, 1654, by Alex. Madocks, and James Jones, Northampton Co.
Green, Richd., 1653, by Richd. Haines, ——— Co.
Green, James, 1653, by Tho. Kidd, Lancaster Co.
Green, Mary, 1653, by Leonard Chamberlaine, Gloucester Co.
Green, Millisent, 1652, by Mr. John Brown, Northampton Co.
Green, John, 1647, by Tho. Gibson, York Co.
Green, Peeter, 1649, by Mr. Wm. Hoccaday, ——— Co.
Green, John, 1650, by Silvester Thatcher and Tho. Whitlocke, ——— Co.
Green, Tho., 1650, by Richard Jacob, Northampton Co.
Green, Ann, 1655, by Tho. Jones, James City Co.
Green, Edmond, 1647, by Elizabeth Barcroft, Isle of Wight Co.
Green, Tho., 1653, by Ferdinando Austin, Charles City Co.
Green, Tho., 1654, by Robert Hubard, Westmoreland Co.
Green, Armogall, 1656, by Francis Hutchins, Nansemond Co.
Green, Tho., 1654, by Nich. Merywether, Westmoreland Co.
Green, John, 1654, by James Yates, ——— Co.
Green, Ann, 1655, by John Palmer, Northumberland Co.
Green, Mary, 1655, by John Palmer, Northumberland Co.
Green, Tho., 1654, by Valentine Patten, Westmoreland Co.
Green, Sarah, 1656, by John Billiott, Northampton Co.
Green, Tho., 1654, by Richard Hawkins, Westmoreland Co.
Green, John, 1654, by John Wyre, John Gillet, Andrew Gilson and John Phillipps, ——— Co.
Green, Kath., 1655, by John Green, ——— Co.
Green, Mary, 1643, by Joseph Croshawe, ——— Co.
Green, Richard, 1655, by John Green, ——— Co.
Green, Alexander, and Joane his wife, 1650, by Mordecay Cooke, ——— Co.
Greene, Edward, 1650, by Mordecay Cooke, ——— Co.
Greene, John, 1635, by Thomas Harwood, ——— Co.
Greene, Robert, 1637, by Patrick Kennedye, New Norfolk Co.
Greene, Elin, 1636, by Cheney Boyse, Charles City Co.
Greene, Eliz., 1637, by Cheney Boyes, Charles City Co.
Greene, Wm., Arthur Bayly's servant, 1637, by Atrhur Bayly and Tho. Crosby, Henrico Co.
Green, Judith, 1635, by Wm. Swan, James Co.
Greene, Charles, 1637, by Henry Perry, Charles River Co.
Greene, Judith, 1638, by Thomas Swan, James Citie, Co.
Greene, John, 1643, by Capt. John Upton, Isle of Wight Co.
Greene, Henry, 1653, by Wm. Cox, ——— Co.

Greene, Cha., 1653, by Capt. Francis Patt, Northampton Co.
Greene, Margarett, 1652, by Nicho Searborne, Lower Norfolk Co.
Greene, Tho., 1652, by Mr. John Browne, Northampton Co.
Greene, Tho., 1648, by Geo. Hardey, Tho. Wombwell and Peter Hall, Isle of Wight Co.
Greene, David, 1648, by Geo. Hardey, Tho. Wombley, and Peter Hall, Isle of Wight Co.
Greene, John, 1648, by Wm. Barret, ——— Co.
Greene, Judith, 1648, by Thomas Hart, James City Co.
Greene, Mary, 1650, by Wm. Hodgson, Yorke Co.
Greene, Charles, 1637, by Henry Perry, Charles River Co.
Greene, Peter, 1642, by William Lawson, Isle of Wight Co.
Greene, Richard, 1642, by John Ewens, Jr., Charles City Co.
Green, Eliz., 1654, by John Wyre, John Gillet, Andrew Gilson and John Phillipps. ——— Co.
Greene, Tho., 1639, by Georg Minifye, Esq., Charles River Co.
Greene, George, 1639, by Thomas Mathews, Henrico Co.
Greene, William, 1638, by Thomas Croutch, James City Co.
Greene, Jones, 1642, by William Lawson, Isle of Wight Co.
Greene, John, 1639, by Abraham Wood, Henrico Co.
Greene, John, 1650, by John Cox, ——— Co.
Greene, John, 1649, by Wm. Moore, ——— Co.
Greene, Edw., 1650, by Geo. Ludlow, Esq., Northumberland Co.
Greene, John, 1650, by Henry Lee and Wm. Clapham, ——— Co.
Greene, Richard, 1650, by Sr. Tho. Luntsford, Kt., and Barronett, ——— Co.
Greensfeild, Robt., 1635, by Tho. Phillipps, James City Co.
Grundy, Jno., 1635, by Jno. Sparkes, ——— Co.
Greenfield, John, 1638, by Joel Vinon, James City Co.
Greenfield, John, 1638, by Christopher Thomas, Accomac Co.
Greenfeild, Jno., 1650, by Edward Walker, Northumberland Co.
Greenhoe, Tho., 1652, by Richard Coleman, ——— Co.
Greenland, Oliver, 1653, by Wm. and George Worsman, Henrico Co.
Greenleaf, Robt., 1633, by Thomas Markham, Henrico Co..
Greenleaf, Robt., 1635, by Thomas Warren, Charles City Co.
Greenleaf, Susan, 1635, by Thomas Warren, Charles City Co.
Greenleaf, Robt., 1637, by Thomas Markham, Henrico Co.
Greening, John, 1655, by Nich. Wadilow, Northampton Co.
Greening, John, 1652, by Nicholas Wadilow, Northampton Co.
Greenshan, John, 1653, by Mr. Richard Barnhouse, Jr., Gloucester Co.
Grested, Wm., 1650, by John Mattrum, Northumberland Co.
Grenvate, Henry, 1655, by Wm. Wright, Nansemond Co.
Grenwell, Richd., 1650, by Capt. Moore Fautleroy, ——— Co.
Grenwill, Rob., 1653, by Robert Bouth, Yorke Co.
Greenwood, Judith, 1651, by Ashwell Battin, Yorke Co.
Grenwood, Rich., 1736, by Capt. Thomas Osborne, Henrico Co.
Greenwood, Eliza, 1637, by William Parry, New Norfolk Co.
Greet, Elian, 1637, by Richard Greet (her husband), ——— Co.
Greet, Alice, 1637, by Richard Greet (her husband), ——— Co.
Greete, Richard, 1636, by James Place, Henrico Co.
Greete, Geo., 1653, by John Robinson, Jr., Northampton Co.

Greeves, John, 1650, by George Taylor, —— Co.
Greggs, Tho., 1648, by Richard Thompson, Northumberland Co.
Gregman, ——, 1653, by Robert Capps, and Robert Springs, —— Co.
Gregory, Benjamine, 1637, by Wm. Hatcher, —— Co.
Gregory, Charles, 1654, by Mr. Tho. Fowke, Westmoreland Co.
Gregory, Francis, 1656, by John Wood, —— Co.
Gregory, Ja., 1653, by Ferdinando Austin, Charles City Co.
Gregory, Tho., 1653, by Ferdinando Austin, Charles City Co.
Gregory, Tho., 1638, by John Stratton, Lower New Norfolk Co.
Gregory, Ben., 1653, by John Dipdall, Charles City Co.
Gregory, Charles, 1652, by Mrs. Jane Harner, Northumberland Co.
Gregory, Joseph, 1651, by Mr. Robert Abrall, Yorke Co.
Gregory, Alex., 1653, by Richard Jackson, —— Co.
Gregory, Georg, 1638, by William Barker and associates, Charles City Co.
Gregory, Thomas, 1637, by Capt. Thomas Panlett, Charles City Co.
Gregory, George, 1635, by William Barber (a mariner), Charles City Co.
Grenwill, Jas., 1642, by Christopher Boyce, —— Co.
Grenalefield, Thos., 1635, by Thos. Crompe, James Co.
Grensly, Francis, 1655, by Mrs. Margaret Brent, Lancaster Co.
Greocheare, Donell, 1655, by Edmund Scarbourgh, Jr., and Littleton Scarbourgh, Northampton Co.
Gresham, Ed., 1650, by Bertram Obert, —— Co.
Greveman, Jno., 1651, by Capt. Tho. Davis, Northumberland Co.
Grey, Tho., 1654, by John Wyre, John Gillet, Andrew Gilson and John Phillips ——Co.
Grey, Ann, 1654, by Robert Yoe, Westmoreland Co.
Grey, Miles, 1654, by John Watson and John Bognall, Westmoreland Co.
Grey, Daniel, 1654, by Valentine Patten, Westmoreland Co.
Grey, Dunton, 1654, by Col. Hump. Higgenson, Esq., and Abraham Moone, Westmoreland Co.
Grey, Tho., 1654, by Mr. Tho. Fowke, Westmoreland Co.
Grey, Miles, 1656, by John Evans, Northampton Co.
Grey, John, 1656, by John Williams, Lower Norfolk Co.
Grey, Robert, 1650, by Wm. Morgan, —— Co.
Grey, San., 1654, by Robt. Hubard, Westmoreland Co.
Grey, Richard, 1642, by John Benton, —— Co.
Grey, Alex., 1648, by Lewis Burwell, Gent., —— Co.
Grey, John, 1652, by John Sharpe, Lancaster Co.
Grey, Christopher, 1652, by John Fleet, Yorke Co.
Grey, Robt., 1653, by Wm. Morgan, —— Co.
Grey, John, 1653, by Tho. Morgan, —— Co.
Gridwell, Henry, 1643, by Tho. Cassen, Lower Norfolk Co.
Griffin, Bridges, 1654, by Walter Pritchard, —— Co.
Griffin, Wm., 1654, by Tho. Willoughby, Lower Norfolk Co.
Griffen, Joan, 1654, by John Skerrett, —— Co.
Griffen, Willm, 1654, by Tho. Willoughby, Lower Norfolk Co.
Griffen, Mary, 1643, by Edward Murfy, and John Vaughan, —— Co.
Griffen, John, 1653, by Ralph Green, Gloucester Co.

Griffen, John, 1653, by Ferdinando Austin, Charles City Co.
Griffen, Dorothy, 1654, by Nicholas Morris, Northumberland Co.
Griffen, Ann, 1648, by Richard Wyatt, ——— Co.
Griffen, Wm., 1635, by Wm. Barber (a mariner), Charles City Co.
Griffin, David, 1656, by Richard Gible, Northumberland Co.
Griffin, Wm., 1655, by Dr. Giles Mode, New Kent Co.
Griffin, Wm., 1638, by Capt. Christopher Wormley, ——— Co.
Griffin, Edward, 1637, by Jonathan Longworth, New Norfolk Co.
Griffin, Tho., 1642, by Ellis Richardson, Yorke Co.
Griffin, Georg., 1638, by Christopher Lawson, James City Co.
Griffin, Hopkin, 1643, by Capt. Samuell Mathews, Esq., ——— Co.
Griffin, Thomas, 1642, by Abraham Wood, Henrico Co.
Griffin, John, 1650, by Tho. Hawkins, Charles River Co.
Griffin, Hugh, 1649, by Mr. Nesum and others, Northumberland Co.
Griffin, Tho., 1649, by Mr. Nesum and orthers, Northumberland Co.
Griffin, Richard, 1653, by John Maddison, Gloucester Co.
Griffin, Hugh, 1652, by Rice Hughes, ——— Co.
Griffen, Edw., 1638, by Joseph Harmon, James City Co.
Griffin, Mathew, 1643, by Sir. Francis Wyatt, Kt., ——— Co.
Griffin, Wm., 1638, by Wm. Barker and associates, Charles City Co.
Griffin, Ann, 1638, by Wm. Hatfield, Upper New Norfolk Co.
Griffin, Symon, 1638, by Wm. Hatfield, Upper New Norfolk Co.
Griffin, Geo., 1638, by Lt. Robt. Sheppard, James City Co.
Griffin, Edw., 1637, by Jonathan Longworth, New Norfolk Co.
Griffin, Elias, 1637, by Daniell Gookins, New Norfolk Co.
Griffin, John, 1641, by Wm. Storey, Upper Norfolk Co.
Griffin, Tho., 1642, by John Brooch, Charles River Co.
Griffin, Wm., 1636, by John Seaward, Isle of Wight Co.
Griffin, Willi, 1737, by Theodore Moyser, James City Co.
Griffin, Ann, 1637, by Thomas Davis, New Norfolk Co.
Griffett, Herbert, 1639, by Edward Prince, Charles City Co.
Griffeth, Tho., 1654, by Capt. Nich. Marteaw, Westmoreland Co.
Griffith, Jane, 1656, by John Wood, ——— Co.
Griffeth, Tho., 1646, by Thomas Holmes, York River Co.
Griffeth, Ralph, 1641, by Thomas Morrey, Isle of Wight Co.
Griffeth, Wm., 1650, by Sr. Tho. Luntsford, Kt., and Barronett, ———
    Co.
Griffeth, Antho., 1650, by Sr. Tho. Luntsford, Kt. and Baronett, ———
    Co.
Griffeth, Silvanus, 1649, by Robert Moseley, Gent., ——— Co.
Griffeth, Lt. Collo., and Anne, his wife, 1652, by Richard Longe,
    ——— Co.
Griffeth, Mary, 1652, by Mr. John Browne, Northampton Co.
Griffeth, Mary, 1653, by Charles Scarburgh, Northampton Co.
Griffeth, Tho., 1651, by Richard Turney, Northumberland Co.
Griffeth, Margarett, 1651, by Robert Cade, ——— Co.
Griffeth, Jon., 1653, by Samuell Bonam, Northumberland Co.
Griffeth, Edward, 1653, by Colo. Wm. Clayborne (Sec. of State),
    ——— Co.
Griffeth, Tho., 1646, by Sir William Berkeley, ——— Co.
Griffih, Tho., 1643, by Richard Kemp, Esq., James City Co.

Grigg, Blanche, 1650, by Capt. Ishiell Linch, ——— Co.
Griggs, Robt., 1653, by Wm. Debrane, ——— Co.
Griggs, Tho., 1637, by John Graves, Elizabeth City Co.
Griggs, Xtop., 1650, by Jervace Dodson, Gent., Northumberland Co.
Grigs, John, 1639, by Samuell Jackson, Isle of Wight Co.
Grimes, John, 1655, by Richard Hamlet, James City Co.
Grimes, John, 1650, by Jervace Dodson, Gent., Northumbreland Co.
Grimes, Elizabeth, 1654, by John Newman, Lancaster Co.
Grimes, Edw., 1643, by Thomas Frye, James City Co.
Grimes, John, 1650, by Jervace Dodson, Northumberland Co.
Grimes, Hen., 1650, by Capt. Moore Fautleroy, ——— Co.
Grimes, Edw., 1653, by Capt. Francis Patt, Northampton Co.
Grimes, Arthur, 1638, by Francis Morgan, Charles River Co.
Grimes, Walter, 1635, by Richard Durrant, James City Co.
Grimes, John, 1635, by George Minifie, James City Co.
Grimes, John, 1636, by Georg. Menifye, James City Co.
Grimstone, Tho., 1654, by John Watson and John Bognall, Westmore-
    land Co.
Grindall, Tho., 1638, by Edward Oliver, ——— Co.
Grindall, Thos., 1639, by Edward Oliver, James City Co.
Grindall, Thomas, 1639, by Edward Oliver, James City Co.
Grinder, Alice, 1651, by Wm. Parry, Northumberland Co.
Grindon, Thos., by 1637, Thomas Paule, James City Co.
Grinett, Alice, 1635, by John Grinett, her husband, ——— Co.
Grinett, Elizabeth, 1635, by John Grinett, her now husband, ———Co.
Grinfield, Robt., 1639, by Nicholas Comings, Charles River Co.
Grinfield, John, 1651, by Richard Grigson, ——— Co.
Gringer, Robert, 1643, by Wm. Butler, James City Co.
Grimshaw, Wm., 1651, by Joseph Croshaw, Yorke Co.
Gringwood, Dorothy, 1641, by Thos. Grinwood, Isle of Wight Co.
Grinwood, Mary, 1641, by Thos. Grinwood, her husband, Isle of Wight Co.
Grissell, Wm., 1654, by Richard Marshfeild, ——— Co.
Grizell, Humphrey, 1636, by Robt. Hollom, Henrico Co.
Groce, Roger, 1637, by Francis Fowler, James River Co.
Grodson, Jno., 1637, by James Warradine, Charles City Co.
Grogan, Alex., 1652, by Tho. Dodford, ——— Co.
Groomer, Jos., 1650, by Capt. Moore Fautleroy, ——— Co.
Gromwell, Gersen, 1637, by John Seaward, Isle of Wight Co.
Gross, Thompson, 1637, by Arthur Smith, Isle of Wight Co.
Grott, A. Jonas, 1650, by Mr. Stephen Hamelin, Charles City Co.
Grotte, Antoinade, 1639, by Thomas Faulkner, ——— Co.
Groves, Wm., 1654, by Capt. Nich, Marteaw, Westmoreland Co.
Groves, John, 1652. by Tho. Preston, ——— Co.
Groves, Richard, 1653, by Abraham Moone, Lancaster Co.
Grubb, John, 1650, by John Rosier, Northumberland Co.
Grunn, Eliz., 1653, by Capt. Francis Pott, Northampton Co.
Grunsditch, John, 1642, by Stephen,Gill, ——— Co.
Gruting, Wm., 1652, by Tobias Horton, Lancaster Co.
Gryer, Wm., 1650, by George Pate, Charles City Co.
Grymes, Wm., 1638, by Geo. Lobb, Tho. Perce, Tho. Warne, James
    City Co.

Grymes, John, 1652, by Nathaniel Bacon, Isle of Wight Co.
Grymes, Tho., 1653, by Charles Grymes, clerk, Lansaster Co.
Grymes, Elizabeth, 1653, by Tho. Griffin, Lancaster Co.
Grymes, Ann, 1642, by Wm. Warren, ——— Co.
Guavis, Tho., 1637, by Arthur Smith, Isle of Wight Co.
Gudle, Nathan, 1636, by Ellinor Dey and Thos. Emmerson, Warwick
    River Co.
Guest, Geo., 1647, by Richard Stearnell, Lower Norfolk Co.
Gug, Margt., 1653, by James Johnson, Nansemond Co.
Gugleston, Edward, 1636, by John Dunston, James City Co.
Gugson, Tho., 1653, by Mrs. Mary Brent, ——— Co.
Guige, Tho., 1651, by Phillip Hunley, ——— Co.
Guilham, Thomas, 1642, by Joseph Royall, ——— Co.
Guilloe, Chargaree, 1656, by Vincent Stanford, ——— Co.
Guilt, Nicho., 1650, by Lieut. Wm. Worleich, ——— Co.
Guinsey, Wm., 1651, by William Ginsey, Yorke Co.
Gullam, John, 1655, by Capt. Tho. Davis, Warwick Co.
Gullis, John, 1646, by William Berkeley, ——— Co.
Gulton, John, 1640, by Thomas Stegg, Charles City Co.
Gum, Jon., Sr., 1653, by Robt. Chewninge, Lancaster Co.
Gum, Jon., Jr., 1653, by Robt., Chewninge, Lancaster Co.
Gum, Christian, and his wife, 1643, by John Hoddin, ——— Co.
Gummey, Richard, 1656, by Tho. Rolfe, Gent., James City Co.
Gumsby, Jno, 1654, by John Drayton, Westmoreland Co.
Gun, Margery, 1642, by Lieut. Francis Mason, ——— Co
Gun, William, 1635, by Vectoris Christmas, Elizabeth City Co.
Gundry, Eliza., 1650, by John Gundry, ——— Co.
Gundry, John, Jr., 1650, by John Gundry, ——— Co.
Gundry, John, 1650, by John Gundry (his brother), ——— Co.
Gunn, John, 1654, by John Skerrett, ——— Co.
Gunnell, Wm., 1650, by Mr. Epaphroditus Lawson, ——— Co.
Gunner, Geo., 1642, by John Benton, ——— Co.
Gunner, Thos., 1642, by William Prior, Gent., ——— Co.
Gunney, Sarah, 1653, by John Gillett, Lancaster Co.
Gunny, Rich., 1637, by Theodore Moyser, James City Co.
Guntler, Richard, 1650, by Lewis Burwell, Gent., ——— Co.
Gunter, Edwd., 1654, by Tho. Salsbury, Lancaster Co.
Gunter, Edward, 1652, by Ambrose Dixon, and Stephen Horseley, Jr.,
    Northampton Co.
Gunter, Jacob, 1651, by Abraham Moon and (Thomas Griffen), Lan-
    caster Co.
Gunston, Antho., 1642, by John Bayles, ——— Co.
Gurnett, John, 1650, by Capt. Ishiell Linch, ——— Co.
Gurrington, John, 1653, by Wm. Debram, ——— Co.
Gutt, Henry, 1645, by William Jones, Northampton Co.
Gutt, Hen., 1562, by Mr. Tho. Gutheridge, Lower Norfolk Co.
Guttridge, Peeter, 1648, by John Seward, Isle of Wight Co.
Guttridge, Henry, 1653, by Tho. Griffin, Lancaster Co.
Guy, John, 1651, by Humphry Tabb, Northumberland Co.
Guy, Henry, 1637, by John Broche, Charles River Co.
Guy, Gilbert, 1636, by Wm. Armestead, Elizabeth City Co.

Guy, John, 1647, by John Brooch, York River Co.
Gwaepmey, Tho., 1650, by Wm. Yarret and Fra. Willington, —— Co.
Gwany, Henry, 1654, by Francis Smith and Mr. John Smith, West-
    moreland Co.
Gwin, John, 1652, by Littleton Scarburg, ——— Co.
Gwin, Griffin, 1652, by Edward Cannon, and Tho. Allen, Lower Nor-
    folk Co.
Gwillin, Georg, 1650, by George Taylor, ——— Co.
Gwyn, Mrs. Ann, 1642, by Hugh Gwyn, Gent., ——— Co.
Gwyn, Hugh, 1642, by Hugh Gwyn, Gent., ——— Co.
Gwyne, Anne, 1650, by Robert Bird, ——— Co.
Gye, Gilbert, 1635, by Capt. A. Thoroughgood, ——— Co.
Gyllom, Hen., 1637, by Wm. Farrar, Henrico Co.
Gylyard, Richard, 1637, by Thomas Sawyer, New Norfolk Co.
Gymes, Geo., 1653, by Joseph Croshaw, York Co.

H

Habeane, Richd., 1653, by Colo. Wm. Clayborne (Sec. of State), ———
    Co.
Habitiel, Geo., 1637, by Tho. Symmons, Charles River Co.
Hacke, Richard, 1652, by Jno. Robinson, Lancaster Co.
Hackett, Jane, 1653, by Geo. Wadding, Lancaster Co.
Hackett, Tho., 1653, by Mr. Henry Soanes, Gloucester Co.
Hackett, Tho., 1650, by George Gill, Yorke Co.
Hackett, Tho., 1642, by Richard Lee, ——— Co.
Hacker, Margery, 1637, by Geo. Sanghier, Elizabeth City Co.
Hackes, Elell, 1638, by Thomas Stout, ——— Co.
Hackerly, Elias, 1654, by Col. Argoll Yardley, Northampton Co.
Hackery, Tho., 1649, by Stephen Gill, York Co.
Hackerstone, Tho., 1650, by John Major, Northampton Co.
Hackley, Jane, 1653, by John Shepperd, Northumberland Co.
Hackley, Richard, 1653, by Abraham Moone, Lancaster Co.
Hackley, Jon., 1638, by Wm. Rainshaw, Lower New Norfolk Co.
Hackney, Wm., 1638, by John Clarkson, Charles River Co.
Hacock, John, 1637, by Theodore Moyser, James City Co.
Hacro, Wm., 1653, by Major John Westhrope, Charles City Co.
Haddy, John, 1639, by John Burland, Charles River Co.
Hadway, Wm., 1650, by John Mangor, ———Co.
Hadwell, Wm., 1643, by Casar Puggett, Lower Norfolk Co.
Haeding, Nath., 1652, by Capt. Augustine Warner, ——— Co.
Haggist, Humphry, 1654, by Tho. Deynes, ——— Co.
Hagleton, Symon, 1655, by Richard Hamlet, James City Co.
Haies, Nath., 1643, by Robert Haies, Lower Norfolk Co.
Haies, John, 1651, by Tho. Hales and Tho. Sheppard, Northumber-
    land Co.
Haies, Eliza, 1653, by Capt. Robt. Abrall, ——— Co.
Haies, Alex., 1643, by Robert Haies, Lower Norfolk Co.
Haies, Isabell, 1643, by Thomas Frye, James City Co.
Haies, Elizabeth, 1655, by John Dorman, Northampton Co.
Haies, Ann, 1655, by John Dorman, Northampton Co.

Haies, Richard, 1637, by Robert Bennett, New Norfolk Co.
Haines, Richard, 1653, by John Shepperd, Northumberland Co.
Haines, Susanna, 1652, by Richard Allen, Elizabeth City Co.
Haines, Henry, 1638, by Georg Mynifie (merchant), ——— Co.
Haines, George, 1645, by John Shepard, York Co.
Haines, Robt., 1646, by Sir William Berkley, ——— Co.
Haines, Richd., 1645, by John Separd, York Co.
Haines, Rich., and Ann his wife, 1643, by John Sweete, Isle of Wight
    Co.
Haines, Rich., 1643, by John Sweete, Isle of Wight Co.
Haire, James, 1642, by Hugh Gwyn, Gent., ——— Co.
Hainard, Mary, 1654, by John Watson and John Bognall, Westmore-
    land Co.
Halbar, John, 1654, by Mr. Tho. Fowke, Westmoreland Co.
Halbar, Rich., 1654, by Mr. Tho. Fowke, Westmoreland Co.
Halden, Arch., 1655, by Wm. Wright, Gent., Nansemond Co.
Hales, Barbara, 1651, by Lieut. Coll. Giles Brent, Northumberland
    Co.
Hale, Edw., 1653, by Colo. Wm. Clayborne (Sec. of State), ——— Co.
Hale, James, 1651, by Capt. Stephen Gill, Northumberland Co.
Hale, Tho., 1652, by Richard Longe, ——— Co.
Hale, Nicholas, 1653, by John Maddison, Gloucester Co.
Hale, Tho., 1652, by Richard Hill, Northampton Co.
Hale, Ann, 1641, by Thomas Morrey, Isle of Wight Co.
Hale, Nath., 1653, by James Turner, ——— Co.
Hale, Lew, 1636, by John Gater, Elizabeth Co.
Hale, Susan, 1637, by Capt. Thomas Panlett, Charles City Co.
Hale, Tho., 1638, by John Gater, Lower New Norfolk Co.
Haling, Jno., 1654, by Randall Chamblett, ——— Co.
Hall, Susan, 1646, by Joseph Croshawe, Charles River Co.
Hall, John, 1652, by Mr. Edward Travis, James City Co.
Hall, Patience, 1650, by John Garwood, Nansemond Co.
Hall, Elizabeth, 1652, by Capt. Augustine Warner, ——— Co.
Hall, Mary, 1651, by Phillip Hunley, ——— Co.
Hall, Richd., 1653, by Corbet Piddle, Northumberland Co.
Hall, James, 1653, by Capt. Francis Patt, Northampton Co.
Hall, John, 1653, by John Holding, York Co.
Hall, Hum., 1646, by Edward Hall, Lower Norfolk Co.
Hall, Fra., 1651, by John Hull, Northumberland Co.
Hall, Mathew, 1652, by Richard Coleman, ——— Co.
Halls, Tho., 1652, by Wm. Gautlett, ——— Co.
Hall, Joseph, 1652, by Dr. Richard Hall, ——— Co.
Hall, Samuel, 1652, by Dr. Richard Hall, ——— Co.
Hall, Kath., 1652, by Dr. Richard Hall, ——— Co.
Hall, Richard, Sr., 1652, by Dr. Richard Hall, ——— Co.
Hall, Math., 1652, by Mr. Tho. Gutheridge, ——— Co.
Hall, Richard, Jr., 1652, by Dr. Richard Hall, ——— Co.
Hall, Robert, 1652, by Nathaniel Bacon, Isle of Wight Co.
Hall, Henry, 1653, by Capt. Robt. Abrall, ——— Co.
Hall, Wm., 1653, by Tho. Renalls, ——— Co.
Hall, Step., 1650, by Capt. Moore Fautleroy, ——— Co.

Hall, Richard, 1650, by Capt. Moore Fautleroy, ——— Co.
Hall, George, 1649, by Nicholas Waddilow, Northampton Co.
Hall, George, 1648, by John Baldwin, Northampton Co.
Hall, David, son, Geo. Hall, 1648, by Tho. Broughton, ——— Co.
Hall, Edmund, son, Geo. Hall, 1648, by Tho. Broughton, ——— Co.
Hall, George, 1648, by Tho. Broughton, ——— Co.
Hall, Eliza., wife, Geo. Hall, 1648, by Tho. Broughton, ——— Co.
Hall, Fra., 1648, by Wm. Edwards and Rice Edwards, James City Co.
Hall, Robert, 1642, by Lieut. Francis Mason, ——— Co.
Hale, Richard, 1638, by John Clarkson, Charles River Co.
Hall, Jon., 1643, by Richard Kemp, Esq., James City Co.
Hall, James, 1650, by Silvester Thatcher and Tho. Whitlockes, ———
   Co.
Hall, Saml., 1643, by Henry Neale, James City Co.
Hall, Alexander, 1654, by John Curtis, Accomac Co.
Hall, John, 1654, by Robert Hubard, Westmoreland Co.
Hall, Tho., 1654, by Mr. Giles Brent, Westmoreland Co.
Hall, Dorothy, 1655, by Wm. Wright, ——— Co.
Hall, Mary, 1656, by Capt. Wm. Canfill, Surry Co.
Hall, Edward, 1635, by Thomas Harwood, ——— Co.
Hall, Georg, 1636, by Edward Drew, Accomack Co.
Hall, John, 1637, by James Warradine, Charles City Co.
Hallaway, Wm., 1650, by John Garwood, Nansemond Co.
Hallaway, Rich., 1653, by Robt. Capps and Robert Spring, ——— Co.
Halley, Merciful, 1635, by Capt. Adam Thoroughgood, ——— Co.
Halley, Joseph, 1637, by James Berry, Accomack Co.
Halley, John, 1656, by Major Wm. Lewis, ——— Co.
Halliard, Fra., 1652, by Richard Dudley, ——— Co.
Hallinard, Alice, 1652, by Tho. Hallinard (her husband), ——— Co.
Hallingham, Wm., 1652, by Richard Coleman, ——— Co.
Hallis, Wm., 1653, by Charles Scarburg, Northampton Co.
Hallome, Frances, 1642, by Daniell Lewellyn, ——— Co.
Hallome, Robt., 1642, by Daniell Lewellyn, ——— Co.
Hallond, Edward, 1636, by Hannah Boyse, Henrico Co.
Hallow, Robt., 1655, by George Parker, Northampton Co.
Halloway, John, 1636, by Nathan Martin, Henrico Co.
Hallows, John, 1654, by Tho. Hobkins, Lancaster Co.
Hallowes, Restitute, Jr., 1650, by John Hallowes, Gent., Northumber-
   land Co.
Hallowes, Res., Jr., 1650, by John Hallowes, Gent., Northumberland
   Co.
Hallum, Robert, 1637, by Hannah Boyes, Henrico Co.
Hallum, Robt., 1636, by Hannah Boyse, Henrico Co.
Hally, Jos., 1636, by James Berry, Accomack Co.
Hallyson, Wm., 1654, by John Wyre, John Gillet, Andrew Gibson and
   John Phillipps, ——— Co.
Halsey, Robt., 1653, by Colo. Wm. Clayborne (Sec. of State), ———
   Co.
Halsey, Ann, 1650, by Epa. Lawson, ——— Co.
Halsey, Robt., 1639, by Lieut. Richard Popeley, ——— Co.
Halston, Susan, 1653, by Capt. Francis Patt, Northampton Co.

Halsworth, Rob., 1650, by John Mattrum, Northumberland Co.
Halt, Geo., 1652, by Wm. Gautlett, ——— Co.
Halt, Henry, 1650, by Lieut. Wm. Worlick, Worlich Co.
Halt, Edwd., 1648, by Geo. Hardey, Tho. Wombwell and Peter Hall, Isle of Wight Co.
Haner, Pee, 1653, by John Dipdall, Charles City Co.
Hardy, John, 1647, by Elizabeth Barcroft, Isle of Wight Co.
Harris, Thomas, 1643, by Peter Knight, Isle of Wight Co.
Harris, Israell, 1647, by Lawrence Peeters, Nansemond Co.
Harson, Walter, 1648, by George White, Lower Norfolk Co.
Hatton, John, 1653, by John Dipdall, Charles City Co.
Haly, James, Anne his wife, Fra., Ann and Alice his children, 1654, by Peter Knight, Northumberland Co.
Ham, Kath., 1654, by Toby Smith, Lancaster Co.
Hama, Nich., 1654, by Francis Gray, ——— Co.
Haman, Mark, 1638, by Georg Mynifie (merchant), ——— Co.
Hambleton, Geo., 1654, by Alex. Madock and James Jones, Northampton Co.
Hamer, Percy, 1651, by Richard Turney, Northumberland Co.
Hamelton, John, 1656, by Mr. Henry Soanes, New Kent Co.
Hamilton, Amos., 1650, by Richard Axom and Tho. Godwin, ——— Co.
Hamelton, Danll., 1652, by Col. Geo. Ludlow, Esq., Gloucester Co.
Hamilton, Ma., 1648, by Lewis Burwell, Gent., ——— Co.
Hamilton, James, 1655, by Mrs. Margaret Brent, Lancaster Co.
Hamilton, James, 1655, by Nich. Bush, James City Co.
Hamilton, David, 1655, by Mr. Tho. Peck, Gloucester Co.
Hamlin, Phillip, 1653, by Colo. Wm. Clayborne (Sec. of State), ——— Co.
Hamlin, Margaret, 1653, by John Gillett, Lancaster Co.
Hammack, Wm., 1656, by James Price, Northampton Co.
Hammond, Wm., 1652, by Richard Coleman, ——— Co.
Hammond, Hen., 1653, by Wm. Morgan, ——— Co.
Hammond, John, 1638, by Richard Milton, Charles City Co.
Hamon, Peircy, 1653, by Wm. Walker, Northumberland Co.
Hannon, Richard, 1655, by Wm. Wright, Gent., Nansemond Co.
Hamon, Christ., 1637, by Thomas Sawyer, New Norfolk Co.
Hamond, Tho., 1653, by Tho. Speake, ——— Co.
Hamond, Martin, 1639, by John Dunstin, James City Co.
Hamond, Fra., 1654, by Mr. Francis Hamond, York Co.
Hamond, Edward, 1650, by Capt. Moore Fautleroy, ——— Co.
Hamond, Mana., 1654, by Mr. Francis Hamond, York Co.
Hamond, Mark, 1655, by Edward Moore, Northampton Co.
Hamond, Mary, 1655, by Ralph Green, New Kent Co.
Hamond, Tho., 1654, by by Nich. Merywether, Westmoreland Co.
Hamond, Perty, 1654, by John Withers and Stephen Garey, Westmoreland Co.
Hamond, John, 1654, by John Withers and Stephen Garey, Gloucester Co.
Hamond, Christopher, 1638, by Thom. Sawyer, New Norfolk Co.
Hampron, Bridgett, 1651, by Thomas Keeling, Lower Norfolk Co.
Hampton, Ed., 1653, by Richard Lee, Lancaster Co.

Hampton, Philad., 1651, by Wm. Hampton, —— Co.
Hampton, John, 1649, by Capt. Ralph Wormeley, —— Co.
Hampton, Willi, child., 1640, by William Hampton, Elizabeth City Co.
Hampton, Eliza, 1640, by William Hampton, Isle of Wight Co.
Hampton, Grace, 1640, by William Hampton, Isle of Wight Co.
Hampton, Joane, 1640, by Wm. Hampton, her husband, Isle of Wight Co.
Hampton, John, 1638, by Capt. Christopher Wormley, Charles River Co.
Hampton, Richard, 1654, by Capt. Giles Brent, Westmoreland Co.
Hampton, Thos., 1637, by Thomas Hampton Clarke, New Norfolk Co.
Hampton, Peter, 1637, by Humphry Higginson, Gent., —— Co.
Hamssisgonnett, Jno., 1644, by Thomas Davis, Upper Norfolk Co.
Hamwood, John, 1653, by Wm. Debram, —— Co.
Hanand, Edward, 1636, by Mary Boxe, Henrico Co.
Hanbury, Peter, 1639, by William Canhooe, Charles River Co.
Hance, Wm., 1639, by Henry Perry, Charles City Co.
Hanch, John, 1650, by John Hallowes, Gent., Northumberland Co.
Hancklae, Henry, 1650, by Geo. Ludlow, Esq., Northumberland Co.
Hancock, Mat., 1654, by Tho. Willoughby, Lower Norfolk Co.
Hancock, Edwd., 1651, by Ashwell Baltin, Yorke Co.
Hancock, Richard, 1650, by Capt. Richard Bond, Charles City Co.
Hancocke, Mary, 1652, by Mr. Tho. Brice, Lancaster Co.
Hancocke, James, by John Taylor, Lancaster Co.
Hancocke, Audrey, 1649, by Capt. Ralph Wormeley, —— Co.
Hancocke, John, 1639, by Thomas Grey, James City Co.
Hancorne, Gerrard, 1648, by Lewis Burwell, Gent., —— Co.
Hand, Samuell, 1651, by Abraham Moone and (Thomas Griffen), Lancaster Co.
Hand, Robert, 1646, by John Broach, York Co.
Hande, Robert, 1656, by Sir Henry Chichley, —— Co.
Handly, Nicho., 1652, by Tho. Lucas, Gent., Lancaster Co.
Handley, Wm., 1648, by Wm. Edwards and Rice Edwards, James City Co.
Hane, Thomas, 1637, by Richard Bennett, New Norfolk Co.
Hanerly, Do., 1654, by Col. Hump. Higgenson, Esq., and Abraham Moone, Westmoreland Co.
Hanes, Mathew, 1652, by Tho. Cartwright, Lower Norfolk Co.
Hanes, Jno., 1650, by John Hany, Northumberland Co.
Hanes, John, 1655, by John Nicholls, Northampton Co.
Hanes, Edward, 1635, by Capt. Wm. Pierse, —— Co.
Hanes, Wm., 1635, by Capt. Adam Thoroughgood, —— Co.
Hanly, Rich., 1642, by Stephen Gill, Yorke River Co.
Hanly, Sarah, 1642, by Stephen Gill, Yorke River Co.
Hankes, Tho., 1654, by Mr. Tho. Fowke, Westmoreland Co.
Hankin, Georg, 1640, by William Hampton, Isle of Wight Co.
Hankins, Richd., 1652, by Richard Coleman, —— Co.
Haninge, Jno., 1651, by Capt. John West, Esq., Yorke Co.
Hannig, Wm., 1642, by John George, Charles City Co.
Hanning, Ann, 1655, by Nich. Bush, James City Co.
Hannah, Neal, 1654, by James Yates, —— Co.

Hanscome, Robert, 1643, by Mr. John Bishopp, James City Co.
Hansen, Tho., 1655, by George Kibble, ——— Co.
Hansford, John, 1651, by Richard Hansford, Charles River Co.
Hansford, Eliza., 1653, by Jno. Hansford, Gloucester Co.
Hanson, Tho., 1650, by Capt. Charles Leech, Yorke Co.
Hanson, Tho., 1656, by George Abbott, Nansemond Co.
Hansworth, Fra., 1654, by Mr. Giles Brent, Westmoreland Co.
Hansworth, Thomas, 1651, by Richard Coleman, Yorke Co.
Happ, Row., 1652, by Nathaniel Bacon, Isle of Wight Co.
Hapton, Wm., 1642, by John Bayles, ——— Co.
Harback, Henry, 1639, by William Wigg, ——— Co.
Harbard, Ann, 1642, by John Towlson, Accomack Co.
Harbattle, John, 1652, by Christopher Lewis, Isle of Wight Co.
Harber, Fra., 1647, by Leonard Pettock, Accomac Co.
Harbolt, Richard, 1643, by Richard Richards, Charles River Co.
Harbrough, Edw., 1653, by Richard Burton, ——— Co.
Harby, Mathew, 1655, by David Boucher, Isle of Wight Co.
Harcock, John 1639, by John Dunstin, James City Co.
Harcocke, Jon., 1636, by John Dunston, James City Co.
Hard, Xtop., 1651, by Robt. Newman, Northumberland Co.
Harden, Ja., 1646, by Henry Sedenden, Northampton Co.
Hardy, Thomas, 1642, by Georg Harding, ——— Co.
Hardy, Mary, 1653, by Jervais Dodson, Northumberland Co.
Hardy, Tho., 1650, by Lewis Burwell, Gent., Northumberland Co.
Hardy, Wm., 1654, by John Carr, ——— Co.
Hardy, Samuell, 1655, by Edward Pettaway, Surry Co.
Hardin, Ann, 1656, by Mr. Henry Soanes, New Kent Co.
Harding, Sarah, 1643, by Benjamin Harryson, Gent., James City Co.
Harding, Ja., 1651, by Mr. Rowland Burnham, ———– Co.
Harding, Ann, 1651, by Henry Nicholls, Lower Norfolk Co.
Hardinge, Tho., 1652, by Henry Nicholls, Lancaster Co.
Harding, Joane, 1642, by Jeremiah Grey, James City Co.
Harding, Mary, 1653, by Anto. Hoskins, Northampton Co.
Harding, Mary, 1637, by Richard Bennett, New Norfolk Co.
Harding, Tho., 1650, by Capt. Moore Fautleroy, ——— Co.
Harding, Mary, 1635, by Richard Bennett, ——— Co.
Hardway, James, 1654, by John Drayton, Westmoreland Co.
Hardwell, John, 1653, by Charles Scarburgh, Northampton Co.
Hardway, Jno., 1650, by Richard Tye and Charles Sparrowe, Charles
    City Co.
Hardwell, John, 1652, by Mr. John Browne, Northampton Co.
Hardwin, Grace, 1643, by Casar Puggett, Lower Norfolk Co.
Hare, Andrew, 1653, by Jervais Dodson, Northumberland Co.
Hare, James, 1652, by Richard Coelman, ——— Co.
Hare, James, 1653, by Mr. Henry Soanes, Gloucester Co.
Hare, James, 1654, by Richard Hawkins, Westmoreland Co.
Hare, James, 1654, by Nich. Merywether, Westmoreland Co.
Hares, Jon., 1637, by Wm. Farrar, Henrico Co.
Hare, Nicho., 1649, by Tho. Harwood, ——— Co.
Hare, Susan, 1638, by William Morgan, ——— Co.
Harecourt, Tho., 1650, by Capt. Robert Sheppard, ——— Co.

Harebridge, Tho., 1653, by Wm. Sidner, Lancaster Co.
Harewood, John, 1638, by Tristrum Nosworthy, New Norfolk Co.
Hargrave, Alice, 1646, by Tho. Savedge, Northampton Co.
Hargrave, Christopher, 1639, by Wm. Barker, Charles City Co.
Harford, Mary, 1636, by Wm. Parker, Warrasquinoake Co.
Hargas, Geo., 1642, by John Benton, ——— Co.
Hargrave, Barbara, 1650, by William Gooch, Gent., ——— Co.
Hargrave, Peter, 1654, by Col. Hump. Higgenson, Esq., and Abraham
 Moone, Westmoreland Co.
Hargrave, Christopher, 1637, by James Harrison, James City Co.
Harker, Alice, 1636, by Walter Hacker, Charles River Co.
Harkwood, Benj., 1643, by Richard Kemp, Esq., James City Co.
Harky, Rich., 1641, by Tho. Mathews, ——— Co.
Harland, Georg, 1642, by Christopher Boyce, ——— Co.
Harleston, Geo., 1643, by Capt. Samuell Mathews, Esq., ——— Co.
Harlewood, John, 1654, by John Williams, Northampton Co.
Harloe, John, and his wife Ann, 1651, by Toby Norton, Northampton
 Co.
Harloe, Mary, 1651, by Toby Norton, Northampton Co.
Harloe, Step., 1651, by Toby Norton, Northampton Co.
Harlow, Ann, 1642, by John Harlow, Accomack Co.
Harlow, Stephen, 1642, by John Harlow, Accomack Co.
Harlow, John, 1652, by Mr. James Warradine, ——— Co.
Harlowe, Agnes, 1635, by John Harlow, her brother, Accomack Co.
Harlowe, Ann, 1636, by John Harlowe (her husband), Accomack Co.
Harlowe, Stephen, 1636, by John Harlowe (his father), Accomack Co.
Harltand, Tho., 1649, by Joseph Croshawe, Yorke Co.
Harman, Mary, 1653, by Jervais Dodson, Northumberland Co.
Harman, Joane, 1636, by John Wilkin, Accomack Co.
Harman, Elias, 1636, by John Neale, Accomack Co.
Harmar, John, 1652, by Mr. Tho. Curtis, ——— Co.
Harmon, Jon., 1653, by Wm. Walker, Northumberland Co.
Harmon, Andrew, 1650, by Thomas Powell, ——— Co.
Harmons, Wm., 1651, by George Eaton, ——— Co.
Harmon, John, 1639, by John Kempe, James City Co.
Harmon, Eliz., 1654, by John Watson and John Bognall, Westmore-
 land Co.
Harmon, Ellin, 1655, by Dr. Giles Mode, New Kent Co.
Harmon, John, 1637, by Elizabeth Parker, Henrico Co.
Harner, Roger, 1650, by Capt. John Fludd, Gent., and Jno. Flood, an
 ancient planter, James City Co.
Harnett, John, 1643, by Tho. Williams, ——— Co.
Harnings, Robert, 1650, by John Garwood, Nansemond Co.
Harmota, Abraham, 1642, by John Robins, ——— Co.
Harper, Patrick, 1653, by Leonard Chamberlaine, Gloucester Co.
Harper, John, 1642, by Peter Rigby, ——— Co.
Harper, Wm., 1638, by Epaphroditus Lawson, Upper Norfolk Co.
Harper, Wm., 1650, by Nathaniel Jones, Northumberland Co.
Harper, Wm., 1650, by Richard Budd, Northumberland Co.
Harper, Joseph, 1654, by Martin Coale, Northumberland Co.
Harper, Francis, 1654, by Robt. Bowers, ——— Co.

Harper, Symon, and his wife, 1654, by Robert Bowers, ——— Co.
Harper, John, 1654, by Toby Smith, Lancaster Co.
Harper, Richard, 1655, by Walter Dickenson, Lancaster Co.
Harper, Rob., 1655, by Christopher Calvert, Northampton Co.
Harper, Richard, 1655, by Capt. George Floyd, New Kent Co.
Harper, Francis, 1635, by Hugh Cox, Charles City Co.
Harrald, John, 1655, by John Jenkins, Northampton Co.
Harrard, Gerrard, 1655, by Symon Symons, ——— Co.
Harren, James, 1654, by Abraham Moone, ——— Co.
Harringham, Phillipp, 1638, by Lieut. Robt. Sheppard, James City Co.
Harrington, Wm., 1653, by Capt. Wm. Whittington, Northampton Co.
Harrington, Edw., 1643, by Capt. Samuell Mathews, Esq., ——— Co.
Harrington, Susan, 1653, by John Barrow, Surry Co.
Harrington, Ralph, 1639, by Henry Perry, Charles City Co.
Harris Abraham, 1656, by Mr. Henry Soanes, New Kent Co.
Harris, John, 1656, by Richard Wheeler, Lower Norfolk Co.
Harris, Eliza, 1642, by Wm. Durant, ——— Co.
Harris, Tho., 1643, by Samuell Abbott, James City Co.
Harris, Giles, 1651, by Roger Johns, Northampton Co.
Harris, Eliza., 1651, by Roger Johns, Northampton Co.
Harris, Edw., 1651, by Capt. Tho. Davis, Northumberland Co.
Harris, Kath., 1653, by Richard Smith, Northampton Co.
Harris, Ann, 1653, by Robert Tomlin, ——— Co.
Harris, Jane, 1653, by Richd., Haines, ——— Co.
Harris, Anne, 1653, by John Earle, Northumberland Co.
Harris, Jonathan, 1653, by Tho. Morgan, ——— Co.
Harris, John, 1653, by Nicholas Perry, Charles City Co.
Harris, Wm., 1648, by John Seward, Isle of Wight Co.
Harris, John, 1653, by Benjamin Brasseur, ——— Co.
Harris, John, 1652, by John Taylor, Lancaster Co.
Harris, John, 1652, by John Halton, ——— Co.
Harris, Charles, 1652, by John Phillips, Lancaster Co.
Harris, Tho., 1653, by Oliver Segar, Lancaster Co.
Harris, James, 1653, by Jenkin Price, Northampton Co.
Harris, Anne, 1653, by John Gillett, Lancaster Co.
Harris, James, 1653, by Charles Scarburg, Northampton Co.
Harris, Grace, 1652, by John Bryan, ——— Co.
Harris, Eliza., 1652, by Col. Geo. Ludlow, Esq., Gloucester Co.
Harris, Daniell, 1650, by George Taylor, ——— Co.
Harris, Bavill, 1650, by Capt. Moore Fautleroy, ——— Co.
Harris, John, —, by Tho. Meares, Lower Norfolk Co.
Harris, Thomas, 1648, by Randall Crew, Nansemond Co.
Harris, Wm., 1639, by Richard Corke, Gent., Henrico Co.
Harris, Anthony, 1640, by Phillip Clarke, James City Co.
Harris, Owen, 1639, by William Burdett, Accomack Co.
Harris, John, 1642, by Capt. Samuell Mathews, ——— Co.
Harris, Elias, 1642, by Lieut. Francis Mason, ——— Co.
Harris, Owen, 1639, by William Burdett, Accomack Co.
Harris, John, 1639, by Tho. Boudling, Elizabeth City Co.
Harris, Richard, 1642, by Jerimiah Grey, James City Co
Harris, Jane, 1639, by John White, James Citie Co.

Harris, Adry, 1638, by Tho. Harris, Capt. (her husband), Henrico Co.
Harris, John, 1639, by Randall Holt, James City Co.
Harris, Wm., 1637, by John Moon, Isle of Wight Co.
Harris, Jon., 1637, by Henry Perry, Charles River Co.
Harris, Jane, 1642, by John Robins, ——— Co.
Harris, Tho., 1650, by Mr. Stephen Hamelin, Charles City Co.
Harris, Roger, 1643, by Tho. Evans, ——— Co.
Harris, Penellope, 1650, by Sr. Tho. Luntsford, Kt., and Barronett,
    ——— Co.
Harris, John, 1650, by Richard Tye and Charles Sparrowe, Charles
    City Co.
Harris, Mary, 1654, by John Wyre, John Gillet, Andrew Gilson and
    John Phillipps, ——— Co.
Harris, Wm., 1655, by Jenkin Price, Northampton Co.
Harris, Edward, 1655, by Mathew Huberd, Gent., York Co.
Harris, John, 1655, by Wm. Steevens, Northampton Co.
Harris, Tho., 1656, by Sir Henry Chichley, ——— Co.
Harris, Tho., 1656, by Capt. Henry Fleete, ——— Co.
Harris, Richard, 1637, by Thomas Hampton, New Norfolk Co.
Harris, Eliza., 1637, by Thomas Hampton, New Norfolk Co.
Harris, Henry, 1635, by McWilliams Stone, ——— Co.
Harris Richard, 1637, by John Redman and John Neale, Accomac Co.
Harris, Wm., 1636, by Richard Cocke, ——— Co.
Harris, John, 1635, by Capt. Adam Thoroughgood, ——— Co.
Harris, Henry, 1635, by Samuel Weaver, ——— Co.
Harris, Thomas, 1637, by Cheney Boyes, Charles City Co.
Harris, William, 1636, by Wm. Fookes, ——— Co.
Harris, John, 1636, by Randall Holt, James City Co.
Harris, Richard, 1636, by John Neale, Accomack Co.
Harris, Tho., 1636, by Cheney Boyse, Charles City Co.
Harris, Wm., 1637, by John Moone, Isle of Wight Co.
Harris, Henry, 1637, by Thomas Weston, Charles River Co.
Harris, Wm., 1637, by Arthur Bayly and Tho. Crosby, Henrico Co.
Harris, Jon., 1637, by Henry Perry, Charles River Co.
Harris, Richard, 1642, by Wm. Barnard, Esq., Isle of Wight Co.
Harris, Wm., 1643, by Mr. Phillipp Bennett, Upper Norfolk Co.
Harris, Israell, 1643, by John Carter, ——— Co.
Harris, Eliz., 1638, by William Cotton, Accomack Co.
Harris, Elin., 1656, by Tho. Harris, Lancaster Co.
Harreson, Roger, 1654, by James Yates, ——— Co.
Harrison, William, 1638, by Richard Bennett, Isle of Wight Co.
Harrison, Fra., 1644, by Edwyn Conaway, Northampton Co.
Harpery, Wm., 1650, by Sr. Tho. Luntsford, Kt., and Barronett, ———
    Co.
Harratt, Jon., 1637, by Capt. Thomas Flint, Warwick River Co.
Harrimon, Martin, 1636, by John Dunston, James City Co.
Harrison, Katharine, 1638, by Mr. Thomas Wallis, James City Co.
Harrison, James, 1638, by Wm. Banister, ——— Co.
Harrison, Henry, 1635, by Capt. Wm. Pierse, ——— Co.
Harrison, Thomas, 1636, by Lewin Denwood, Accomack Co.
Harrison, Eras., 1636, by Richarde Cocke, ——— Co.

Harrison, James, 1635, by Capt. William Pierse, ——— Co.
Harrison, John, and negroe woman, 1635, by David Jones, Charles City Co.
Harrison, Georg., 1636, by Richard Cocke, ——— Co.
Harrison, Geo., 1655, by Wm. Johnson and Stephen Horsey, Northampton Co.
Harrison, Wm., 1656, by George Abbott, Nansemond Co.
Harrison, John, 1655, by Henry Huberd, ——— Co.
Harrison, Dr. Jeremy, 1654, by Mrs. Fra. Harrison (widow), Westmoreland Co.
Harrison, Richard, 1654, by Rich. Bunduch, Northampton Co.
Harrison, Barth., 1654, by John Wyre, John Gillet, Andrew Gilson and John Phillipps, ——— Co.
Harrison, Edward, 1654, by Edward Gilla, James City Co.
Harrison, John, 1639, by Georg Mallen, James City Co.
Harrison, Georg., 1638, by Richard Kemp, Esq., ——— Co.
Harrison, Wm., 1638, by Georg Mynifie (merchant), ——— Co.
Harrison, Erasmus, 1639, by Richard Corke, Esq., Henrico Co.
Harrison, Georg, 1639, by Richard Corke, Gent., Henrico Co.
Harrison, John, 1641, by Tho. Mathews, ——— Co.
Harrison, Fra., and wife, 1648, by Lewis Burwell and Tho. Haws, York River Co.
Harrison, Wm., 1650, by Mr. James Williamson, ——— Co.
Harrison, Robert, 1649, by Edmund Scarburgh, Jr., Northampton Co.
Harrison, Wm., 1649, by John Merriman, ——— Co.
Harrison, John, 1652, by Mr. Edward Overman, York Co.
Harrison, Richard, 1652, by Tho. Holme, Yorke Co.
Harrison, Robt., 1651, by Wm. Rennoles, Northumberland Co.
Harrison, Robert, 1647, by Edmond Scarborough, Northampton Co.
Harrison, Tho., 1653, by John Merryman and Morgan Haynes, Lancaster Co.
Harrison, Francis, 1653, by Dennis Conniers, Lancaster Co.
Harrison, Richd., 1653, by Tho. Holmes, York Co.
Harrison, Anth., 1653, by Samuell Bonam, Northumberland Co.
Harrison, Joseph, 1653, by Richard Smith, Northampton Co.
Harrison, Isaac, 1651, by Tho. Wilsford, Gent., ——— Co.
Harrison, Fra., 1643, by Edward Murfey and John Vaughan, ——— Co.
Harrison, Jon., 1642, by Samuell Abbott, ——— Co.
Harrison, Jon., 1642, by Stephen Hamblyn, York Co.
Harrison, Eliza., 1650, by Mrs. Frances Townshend (widow), Northumberland Co.
Harrison, Wm., 1650, by Wingfield Webb and Richard Pate, ——— Co.
Harrow, Richard, 1650, by Richard Axom, and Tho. Godwin, ——— Co.
Harroge, Eliza., 1652, by Tho. Boswell, ——— Co.
Harry, James, 1651, by Wm. Rennales, Northumberland Co.
Harry, Joseph, 1654, by John Watson and John Bognall, Westmoreland Co,
Harryson, Edward, 1653, by Capt. Francis Patt, Northampton Co.
Harswell, Rebecca, 1653, by Robt. Warren, Northampton Co.

Hart, Eliza, 1637, by Bridges Freeman, James City Co.
Hart, Hen., 1637, by Capt. Henry Browne, James River Co.
Hart, Elizabeth, 1637, by Henry Hart, her husband, James Citie Co.
Hart, Eliza., 1636, by Bridges Freeman, ——— Co.
Hart, Wm., 1656, by Sir Henry Chichley, ——— Co.
Hart, Tho., 1654, by Nich. Merywether, Westmoreland Co.
Hart, Elizabeth, 1654, by Nich. Merywether, Westmoreland Co.
Hart, James, 1655, by Patrick Miller, Lancaster Co.
Hart, Teague, 1655, by Matilda Scarbourgh, Northampton Co.
Hart, Robt., 1654, by John Williams, Northampton Co.
Hart, James, 1654, by Nath. Pope, Westmoreland Co.
Hart, Eliz., 1654, by Richard Hawkins, Westmoreland Co.
Hart, David, 1654, by Wm. Mills, Lancaster Co.
Hart, Daniell, 1640, by Toby Smith, Warwick River Co.
Hart, Thomas, 1638, by Georg Mynifie (merchant), ——— Co.
Hart, John, 1649, by Stephen Gill, York Co.
Hart, Methusalem, 1650, by Mr. James Williamson, ——— Co.
Hart, Nicholas, 1652, by Capt. Augustine Warner, ——— Co.
Hart, Walter, 1650, by John Boone, ——— Co.
Hart, James, 1653, by Abraham Moone, Northumberland Co.
Hart, Tho., 1652, by Richard Coleman, ——— Co.
Hart, Aug., 1652, by Tho. and Wm. Leithermore, ——— Co.
Hart, Tho., 1651, by Capt. Stephen Gill, Northumberland Co.
Hart, Ja., 1653, by Corbet Piddle, Northumberland Co.
Hart, Wm., 1653, by Wm. Reynolds, Northumberland Co.
Hart, Lyddy, 1653, by Tho. Philpot, Northumberland Co.
Hart, Mandlin, 1653, by Fra. Symons, Northumberland Co.
Hart, Tho., 1653, by Fra. Symons, Northumberland Co.
Hart, Aug., 1651, by Edmond Welch, ——— Co.
Harte, Thomas, 1642, by Abraham Turner, ——— Co.
Harte, Rebecca, 1635, by Henry Harte (her husband), James City Co.
Hartford, Edwd., 1653, by Capt. Francis Patt, Northampton Co.
Hartley, Eliza., 1655, by Wm. Wright, Gent., Nansemond Co.
Hartley, Thomas, 1642, by Hugh Gwyn, Gent., ——— Co.
Hartop, Edw., 1637, by Humphry Higginson, Gent., ——— Co.
Hartopp, John, 1654, by John Grey, Northampton Co.
Hartswood, Tho., 1656, by Wm. Justice, Charles City Co.
Hartwell, Jane, 1655, by Wm. Botham, Westmoreland Co.
Harvey, Joan, 1650, by John Rosier, Northumberland Co.
Harvey, Jane, 1653, by John Barbur, ——— Co.
Harvey, Tho., 1653, by John Barlow, ——— Co.
Harvey, Jon., 1653, by John Barbur, ——— Co.
Harvey, John, 1653, by Wm. Debram, ——— Co.
Harvey, Eliza, 1652, by Daniell Welch, Lancaster Co.
Harvey, Edwd., 1649, by Stephen Gill, York Co.
Harvey, Geo., and wife, 1648, by Geo. Hardey, Tho. Wombwell and
    Peter Hall, Isle of Wight Co.
Harvey, John, 1640, by Thomas Harvey, his father, James City Co.
Harvey, Henry, 1640, by Toby Smith, Warwick River Co.
Harvey, Mary, 1640, by Thos. Harvey, her husband, James City Co.

Harvey, Valentine, 1650, by Sr. Tho. Luntsford, Kt., and Barronett, ―― Co.
Harvis, Tho., 1652, by Capt. Francis Morgan and Ralph Green, Gloucester Co.
Harwell, John, 1636, by Capt. John Chelsman, Charles River Co.
Harwell, John, 1635, by John Cheeseman, Charles River Co.
Hartwell, Edw., 1638, by Robert Pitts, Isle of Wight Co.
Harway, Richard, 1648, by Bartholomew Hoskins, ―― Co.
Harwer, Ann, 1635, by Charles Harwer (her husband), ―― Co.
Harwood, Giles, 1637, by Georg Burcher, James City Co.
Harwood, Ralph, 1637, by John Upton, Isle of Wight Co.
Harwood, Ralph, 1635, by Jno. Upton, Warrasquinoake Co.
Harwood, Humphry, 1642, by Thomas Plummer, ―― Co.
Harwood, Wm., 1650, by Lawrence Peters, Nansemond Co.
Harwood, Peter, 1641, by Ambrose Bennett, Isle of Wight Co.
Harwood, Robert, 1645, by Bartholomew Hoskins, ―― Co.
Harwood, Wm., 1652, by Nathaniel Bacon, Isle of Wight Co.
Harwood, Charles, 1653, by Nicho. Meriwether, Northumberland Co.
Harwood, Eliz., 1653, by James Bonner, Lancaster Co.
Harwood, Eliz., 1653, by Hump. Edey, ―― Co.
Harwood, Jon., 1654, by Edward Revell, Northampton Co.
Harwood, Ralph, 1637, by Lt. John Upton, Isle of Wight Co.
Harwood, Tho., 1643, by Mr. Phillipp Bennett, Upper Norfolk Co.
Harrwood, Georg, 1643, by Tho. Cassen, Lower Norfolk Co.
Haskins, John, 1653, by Richard Budd, Northumberland Co.
Haskins, John, ――, by Tho. Meares, Lower Norfolk Co.
Hasledine, Marg., 1651, by Richard Griegson, ―― Co.
Hasleton, Priscilla, 1643, by James Bagnall, Lower Norfolk Co.
Hasleton, Symon, 1643, by Mr. John Bishopp, James City Co.
Haslewood, Jane., 1653, by Edward Dodson, ―― Co.
Haslewood, Rich., 1640, by Thomas Stegg, Charles City Co.
Hasleworth, Henry, 1652, by John Howett, Northumberland Co.
Hassall, Wm., 1653, by Tho. Salisbury, Northumberland Co.
Hassall, Jon., 1653, by Tho. Salisbury, Northumberland Co.
Hasson, Edw., 1653, by Elias Hartru, Northampton Co.
Hastewood, Edward, 1639, by Edward Panderson, ―― Co.
Hastewood, Walter, 1636, by John Chew, Gent., Charles River Co.
Hasting, Jno., 1648, by Lewis Burwell, and Tho. Haws, York River Co.
Hastings, Wm., 1639, by Richard Corke, Gent., Henrico Co.
Hastings, Wm., 1636, by Richard Cocke, ―― Co.
Hatcher, Ja., 1653, by John Edwards, Lancaster Co.
Hatcher, John, 1636, by Thomas Curtis, Charles River Co.
Hatcher, Sarah, 1636, by John Chandler, Elizabeth Citie Co.
Hatcher, Tho., 1645, by John Baker, Elizabeth City Co.
Hatcherly Scippia, 1654, by Col. Argoll Yardley, Northampton Co.
Hatchett, Elizabeth, 1642, by Thomas Plummer, ―― Co.
Hatchway, Thomas, 1643, by Henry Hawley, Elizabeth City Co.
Hatcock, Thomas, 1635, by McWilliam Stone, ―― Co.
Haten, John, 1654, by Mr. Tho. Fowke, Westmoreland Co.
Hatfeild, Tho., 1653, by Jno. Hansford, Gloucester Co.
Hatfeild, Grace, 1655, by Richard Price, New Kent Co.

Hattfield, Thomas, 1637, by Samuel Jones, Charles River Co.
Hathaway, Fra., 1652, by Capt. Augustine Warner, ———— Co.
Hathaway, Thom., 1638, by Edmund Scarborough, Accomac Co.
Hatburn, Hen., 1654, by Mr. Tho. Fowke, Westmoreland Co.
Hatherne, John, 1638, by Lt. Robt. Sheppard, James City Co.
Hathrone, John, 1656, by Mr. Henry Soanes, New Kent Co.
Hatley, John, 1656, by Wm. Justice, Charles City Co.
Hatly, Elizabeth, 1656, by John Symons, Nansemond Co.
Hatred, Mary, 1637, by Jonathan Longworth, New Norfolk Co.
Hatt, John, 1652, by Tho. Hallinard, ———— Co.
Hatton, Thomas, 1638, by Georg Mynifie (merchant), ———— Co.
Hatton, Wm., 1654, by Nath. Pope, Westmoreland Co.
Hatton, William, 1635, by Capt. Adam Thoroughgood, ———— Co.
Hatton, Jeffery, 1635, by George Minifie, James City Co.
Hatton, John, 1643, by Casar Puggett, Lower Norfolk Co.
Hatton, John, 1638, by William Parker, Upper Norfolk Co.
Hauton, Mary, 1637, by James Harrison, James City Co.
Haughton, Robt., 1635, by William Wilkinson (minister), ———— Co.
Hauton, Mathew, 1637, by James Harrison, James City Co.
Havant, Eliz., 1650, by Capt. Moore Fautleroy, ———— Co.
Havert, Wm., 1639, by John Kempe, James City Co.
Haverell, George, 1636, by Walter Hacker, James City Co.
Haw, Hamlett, 1642, by Capt. Samuell Mathews, Esq., ———— Co.
Haward, Richard, 1648, by George Read, Gent., ———— Co.
Haward, Alice, 1641, by Thomas Bernard, Warwick River Co.
Hawell, Andrew, 1636, by Joseph Jolly, Charles River Co.
Hawes, Walter, 1652, by John Robbins, Northampton Co.
Hawes, Richard, 1639, by Richard Parsons, Lower New Norfolk Co.
Hawes, Ann, 1654, by Rich. Bunduch, Northampton Co.
Hawkins, Hen., 1643, by Samuell Abbott, James City Co.
Hawkins, Jno., 1653, by Richard Well, Northumberland Co.
Hawkins, John, and Elizabeth his wife, 1653, by Robt. Blake, Isle of
    Wight Co.
Hawkins, Jon., 1654, by Robert Holt, James City Co.
Hawkins, Tho., —, by Tho. Lucas, ———— Co.
Hawkins, John, —, by Tho. Lucas, ———— Co.
Hawkins, Robt., 1653, by Charles Grymes, Lancaster Co.
Hawkins, Tho., Jr., 1653, by Tho. Hawkins, ———— Co.
Hawkins, ————, 1653, by Tho. Hawkins, Sr. (her husband), ———— Co.
Hawkins, Nicholas, 1650, by John Mangor, ———— Co.
Hawkins, James, 1639, by Georg Minifye, Esq., Charles River Co.
Hawkins, Phillipp, 1643, by Wm. Gapinge, James City Co.
Hawkins, Robt., 1654, by John Watson and John Bognall, Westmore-
    land Co.
Hawkins, Mich., 1654, by Col. Argoll Yardley, Northampton Co.
Hawkins, Henry, 1654, by Toby Smith, Lancaster Co.
Hawkins, Wm., 1637, by Theodore Moyser, James City Co.
Hawkins, Hen., 1648, by Randall Crew, Nansemond Co.
Hawkins, Mary, 1655, by Lt. Col. Tho. Swan, Surry Co.
Hawkins, Robt., 1638, by Owen Lancaster, Lower Norfolk Co.
Hawkins, John, 1651, by Thomas Axby, Northumberland Co.

Hawkes, Mary, 1643, by Henry Neale, James City Co.
Hawkes, Ellin, 1643, by Henry Neale, James City Co.
Hawkes, Edward, 1650, by Sr. Tho. Luntsford, Kt., and Barronett, ——— Co.
Hawkes, Hen., 1635, by Wm. Swan, James Co.
Hawkes, Mary, 1635, by Wm. Swan, James Co.
Hawkes, Mary, 1638, by Thomas Swan, James Citie Co.
Hawley, Ann, 1641, by Henry Hawley, her husband, Isle of Wight Co.
Hawly, Leonard, 1643, by Richard Kemp, Esq., James City Co.
Hawkwood, Fra., 1650, by Richard Tye and Charles Sparrowe, Charles City Co.
Hawis Richard, 1651, by James Davis, Northampton Co.
Hawten, Richard, 1643, by Thomas Cassen, ——— Co.
Harwood, Humphry, 1638, by Thomas Plomer and Samuell Edmonds, James City Co.
Hawravly, Darby, 1653, by Oliver Segar and Fra. Brown, ——— Co.
Haxter, Hen., 1654, by Henry Walker, James City Co.
Hay, Eliz., 1654, by John Watson and John Bognall, Westmoreland Co.
Hayall, John, 1655, by Robert Castle, James City Co.
Hayar, Rich., 1653, by Edward Dobson, ——— Co.
Hayden, Richd., 1650, by John Hany, Northumberland Co.
Haye, John, 1652, by John Taylor, Lancaster Co.
Hayes, Antho., 1643, by Tho. Symonds, ——— Co.
Hayes, Robt., 1642, by Cornelius de Hull, ——— Co.
Hayes, Fra., 1653, by Richard Carey, ——— Co.
Hayes, Alex., 1654, by Thomas Binus, Surry Co.
Hayes, Edward, 1653, by Major Abra. Wood, Charles City Co.
Hayes, Eliza, 1651, by Robert Abrall, Yorke Co.
Hayes, Ann (wife), 1643, by Robert Haies, Lower Norfolk Co.
Hayes, Mary, 1654, by Mr. Giles Brent, Westmoreland Co.
Hayes, Cha., 1637, by Patrick Kennedye, New Norfolk Co.
Hayes, Peter, 1637, by John Upton, Isle of Wight Co.
Hayes, Richard, 1635, by Robert Bennett, ——— Co.
Hayes, David, 1638, by John Fludd, James City Co.
Hayes, Mary, 1637, by Robt. Rockwell, New Norfolk Co.
Hayes, William, 1638, by Thomas Beerboye, Upper New Norfolk Co.
Hayes, Peter, 1637, by Lt. John Upton, Isle of Wight Co.
Hayes, Henry, 1638, by Jeremiah Dickinson, James City Co.
Hayfieild, Ben., 1650, by Capt. Moore Fautleroy, ——— Co.
Hayler, Henry, 1651, by George Eaton, ——— Co.
Hayle, Nicho., 1645, by Mark Johnson, Elizabeth City Co.
Hayles, Barbara, 1651, by John Rookwood, Gent., Northumberland Co.
Hayles, Barbara, 1654, by Lieut. Coll. Giles Brent, Westmoreland Co.
Hayles, Jer., 1638, by Edward Sparshott, Charles City Co.
Hayly, Georg, 1638, by John Poteet, Charles River Co.
Hayicke, John, 1652, by Lt. Coll. John Cheesman, ——— Co.
Haymon, Jon., 1653, by Robt. Blake, Isle of Wight Co.
Hayne, Wm., 1655, by Wm. Botham, Westmoreland Co.
Haynes, Richard, 1642, by Samuell Abbott, ——— Co.
Haynes, Antho., 1654, by William Haward, Gloucester Co.

Haynes, Susan, 1652, by Richard Nelmes, Northumberland Co.
Haynes, Jam., 1652, by Mr. Henry Pitt, ——— Co.
Haynes, Leeke, 1650, by Mrs. Frances Townshend (widow), Northumberland Co.
Haynes, Henry, 1649, by Henry Bishopp, Northampton Co.
Haynes, Geo., 1650, by Mr. Stephen Hamlin, Charles City Co.
Haynes, George, 1656, by Sir Henry Chichley, ——— Co.
Haynes, Mary, 1637, by Wm. Farrar, Henrico Co.
Haynes, Henry, 1650, by Stephen Charlton, Northampton Co.
Hayres, John, 1654, by Major Miles Carey, Westmoreland Co.
Hayward, Wm., and Elian his wife, 1652, by Christopher Robinson and John Sturdwant, Henrico Co.
Hayward, Francis, 1639, by John Hayward, James City Co.
Hayward, Tho., 1655, by Mr. Robert Bourne and Mr. Daniel Parke, York Co.
Hayward, Ellen, 1638, by Wm. Hayward, Charles City Co.
Hayward, Susan, 1638, by William Wigg, James City Co.
Hayward, Hugh, 1638, by William Wigg, James City Co.
Haywood, Wm., 1643, by Sir Francis Wyatt, Kt., ——— Co.
Hayword, Howell, 1635, by Capt. Thos. Willowbye, Elizabeth City Co.
Hazard, Sarah, 1654, by Capt. John West, Esq., Gloucester Co.
Hazlewad, Walter, 1637, by John Chew, Charles River Co.
Head, Tho., 1638, by John George, Charles City Co.
Head, James, 1638, by William Burdett, Accomack Co.
Head, Grace, 1654, by Mr. Giles Brent, Westmoreland Co.
Head, James, 1636, by John Neale, Accomack Co.
Header, Richard, 1638, by Capt. Christopher Wormley, Charles River Co.
Headry, John, 1637, by John Redman and John Neale, Accomac Co.
Heady, Richard, 1654, by Humphry Haggett, Lancaster Co.
Heakley, Henry, 1646, by Henry Sedenden, Northampton Co.
Heakley, Henry, wife Henry Heakley, 1646, by Henry Sedenden, Northampton Co.
Heald, Nicho., 1652, by Capt. Francis Morgan, and Ralph Green, Gloucester Co.
Healter, Ellynor, 1655, by Wm. Johnson and Stephen Horsey, Northampton Co.
Heard, Walter, 1650, by Robert Bird, ——— Co.
Hearne, Robert, 1652, by Mr. John Brown, Northampton Co.
Hearne, Tho., 1639, by Georg Minifye, Esq., Charles River Co.
Hearne, Tho., 1650, by Bertram Obert, ——— Co.
Hearne, John, 1639, by Richard Corke, Esq., Henrico Co.
Hearne, Jon., 1636, by Richard Cocke, ——— Co.
Heasell, Robt., 1635, by Capt. Adam Thoroughgood, ——— Co.
Heashaw, Tho., 1653, by Dennis Conniers, Lancaster Co.
Heath, Ferdinand, 1642, by Capt. Daniell Gookin, ——— Co.
Heath, Nicho., 1653, by Thomas Kidd, Lancaster Co.
Heath, John, 1653, by Raleigh Travers, ——— Co.
Heath, Mary, 1646, by Thomas Holmes, York River Co.
Heath, Margaret, 1651, by John Stratton, Lower Norfolk Co.
Heath, Wm., 1653, by Tho. Sawyer, ——— Co.

Heath, Jno., 1653, by Alexander Addison, ――――― Co.
Heath, Amey, 1653, by Alexander Addison, ――――― Co.
Heath, Abm., 1653, by Alexander Addison, ――――― Co.
Heath, Jane, 1650, by Epa. Lawson, ――――― Co.
Heath, Wm., 1650, by John Brown, Northampton Co.
Heath, Amery, wife of Wm. Heath, 1650, by John Brown, Northampton Co.
Heath, John, 1650, by John Brown, Northampton Co.
Heath, Wm., 1650, by John Browne, Northampton Co.
Heath, Amy, wife of Wm. Heath, 1650, by John Browne, Northampton Co.
Heath, John, and his wife, 1650, by John Browne, Northampton Co.
Heath, Isabell, 1654, by John Watson and John Bognall, Westmoreland Co.
Hearth, Eliza, 1656, by Wm. Justice, Charles City Co.
Heath, Thomas, 1636, by Henry Southell, ――――― Co.
Heath, John, 1635, by Capt. Wm. Pierse, ――――― Co.
Heath, Thos., 1637, by Lt. Richard Popeley, New Norfolk Co.
Heath, Jane, 1643, by Capt. John Upton, Isle of Wight Co.
Heather, Rich., 1647, by John Brooch, York River Co.
Heaves, Phillipp, 1642, by Andrew Terry, ――――― Co.
Hebden, John, 1651, by Richard Whitehurst, Lower Norfolk Co.
Hedlin, Jon., 1635, by Wm. Garry, Accomack Co.
Hedyes, Tho., 1653, by Wm. Debram, ――――― Co.
Heede, Francis, 1650, by Mr. John Hallawes, Northumberland Co.
Heeding, Robt., 1654, by Edward Parker, Westmoreland Co.
Heggins, Hump., 1652, by Collo. Hugh Gwin, ――――― Co.
Hegnove, Anto., 1653, by Charles Grymes, clerk, Lancaster Co.
Heifer, John, 1654, by Sinkler Pagett, Nansemond Co.
Heighman, Geo., 1651, by Thomas Thornbrough, Northumberland Co.
Heily, Erwin, 1643, by John Freeme, Charles Co.
Heines, Elizabeth, 1656, by Nicholas Merriwether and John Leach, James City Co.
Heiward, Charles, 1654, by Nich. Merywether, Westmoreland Co.
Helleny, Dyan, 1642, by John Robins, ――――― Co.
Heleme, Sara, 1650, by Wm. Clapham, ――――― Co.
Heler, Richard, 1654, by Abraham Moone, ――――― Co.
Helgate, Erasmus, 1637, by Capt. Robt. Helgate, Charles River Co.
Hellier, Jon., 1637, by Daniell Gookins, New Norfolk Co.
Helin, Mary, 1653, by Capt. Nathaniel Hurd, Warrick Co.
Helter, Kath., 1655, by Hugh Yeo, Northampton Co.
Helton, Margaret, 1656, by John Bromfeild, James City Co.
Hely, John, 1643, by Benjamin Harryson, Gent., James City Co.
Hely, Jon., 1637, by Wm. Farrar, Henrico Co.
Hely, Robt., 1635, by Mr. Willis Heyly, ――――― Co.
Hely, Willi, 1637, by David Mansell, James City Co.
Hemenig, Hugh, 1655, by Philip Charles, ――――― Co.
Hemlocke, Jane, 1650, by Capt. Robert Sheppard, ――――― Co.
Henman, Jno., 1648, by Lewis Burwell and Tho. Haws, York River Co.
Hemstead, Richard, 1652, by John Johnson, Northampton Co.

Hemsley, Wm., 1654, by John Watson and John Bognall, Westmoreland Co.
Henboone, Kath., 1637, by John Baker, Charles City Co.
Henchley, Sarah, 1638, by Jeremiah Dickenson, James City Co.
Hencill, Wm., 1652, by George Pace, Charles City Co.
Hencing, Jon., 1636, by Georg Sapheir, Elizabeth City Co.
Hencock, Richard, 1655, by Capt. George Floyd, New Kent Co.
Henderson, Gilbert, 1652, by Tho. Johnson, Jr., Northampton Co.
Henderson, Alex., 1650, by John Landman, ——— Co.
Henderson, Mathew, —, by Henry Wesgate, Lower Norfolk Co.
Hendly, Robt., 1652, by Mr. Nicholas Jernew, Gloucester Co.
Hendrickson, Hona Maria, 1652, by Wm. Capps, Lower Norfolk Co.
Hendrige, John, 1636, by John Neale, Accomack Co.
Hendwarth, Eliza., 1651, by Joseph Croshawe, Yorke Co.
Hengan, Roger, 1649, by Mr. Ralph Barlowe, Northampton Co.
Henry, Andrew, 1651, by Richard Vaughan, Northampton Co.
Henry, David, 1654, by Capt. Giles Brent, Westmoreland Co.
Henry, Richard, 1655, by Saml. Eldridge, ——— Co.
Henry, John, —, by Samuel Heely and John Carter, Surry Co.
Henscott, Ruth, 1635, by David Mansell, James Co.
Henly, John, 1650, by John Essix, Northumberland Co.
Hensett, Tho., 1650, by Mr. Anthony Ellyot, ——— Co.
Hensly, Robt., 1654, by John Sharpe, Lancaster Co.
Hentlands, Jon., 1637, by Capt. Thomas Flint, Warwick River Co.
Henton, John, 1652, by Mr. Peter Knight, Gloucester Co.
Henton, Tho., 1655, by Geo. Coltclough, Northumberland Co.
Henton, Tho., 1656, by Daniel James and Jno. Jenings, ——— Co.
Henvitt, Alice, 1652, by Joseph Gregory, ——— Co.
Henwalk, Rich., 1649, by Joseph Croshawe, Yorke Co.
Henys, Robt., 1651, by Coll. Richard Lee, Esq., Gloucester Co.
Herbert, Tho., 1651, by Mr. Antho. Steevens, Northampton Co.
Herbert, John, 1639, by Thomas Sheppey, Henrico Co.
Herecastle, Math., 1650, by Elias Edmonds, ——— Co.
Heresa, Finla, 1654, by John Phillips and John Batts, Lancaster Co.
Herricksein, Tho., 1636, by John Chandler, Elizabeth Citie Co.
Herrick, Thos. (Jun.), 1636, by John Chandler, Elizabeth Citie Co.
Herricke, John, 1643, by Zachariah Cripps, ——— Co.
Herring, John, 1642, by Robert Eyres, Lower New Norfolk Co.
Herring, Jon., 1642, by Stephen Gill, ——— Co.
Herry, Lawrance, 1643, by Richard Kemp, Esq., James City Co.
Herris, Joan, 1655, by Sampson Robins, Northampton Co.
Herst, John, 1640, by John Geary, Upper Norfolk Co.
Herton, Kath., 1655, by Wm. Wright, Gent., Nansemond Co.
Hesten, Eliza, 1639, by Robert Eley, Isle of Wight Co.
Hetchcock, Magdalin, 1653, by Geo. Mallard, Northmuberland Co.
Heth, William, 1637, by Georg Vuwin, New Norfolk Co.
Hether, Jon., 1635, by Wm. Garry, Accomack Co.
Hetherson, Jos., 1651, by Joseph Croshaw, Yorke Co.
Hetts, Carry, 1648, by Francis Ceely, ——— Co.
Heves, William, and his wife, 1642, by John Sweete, ——— Co.
Hewe, Wm., 1645, by John Rode, Warwick Co.

Hewet, Gyles, 1643, by John Foster, Northampton Co.
Hewett, Wm., 1652, by Mr. David Fox, Lancaster Co.
Hewett, Fra., 1652, by Mrs. Jane Harmer, Northumberland Co.
Hewett, Fra., 1653, by Abraham Moone, Lancaster Co.
Hewett, Kath., 1650, by Mr. Epaphroditus Lawson, ——— Co.
Hewett, Randall, 1654, by Humphry Belt, Lower Norfolk Co.
Hewett, John, 1636, by Richard Cocke, ——— Co.
Hewett, Antho., 1636, by William Julian, Elizabeth City Co.
Hewes, Richard, 1642, by Cornelius de Hull, ——— Co.
Hewes, Jon., 1654, by Tho. Morecock, James City Co.
Hewes, Wm., 1646, by Samuell Abbott, Nansemond Co.
Hewes, Tho., 1652, by Tho. Steevens, Lancsater Co.
Hewes, James, 1652, by Christopher Robinson and John Sturdwant,
    Henrico Co.
Hewes, Elizabeth, 1652, by Savill Gaskins, Lower Norfolk Co.
Hewes, Richard, 1653, by Francis Jordan, Surry Co.
Hewes, Richard, 1653, by John Knott, ——— Co.
Hewes, Richard, 1653, by Alexander Addison, ——— Co.
Hewes, Henry, 1649, by Richard Kemp, Esq. (Sec. of State), ——— Co.
Hewes, Garrett, 1639, by John Dunston, James City Co.
Hewes, Richard, 1636, by Wm. Cox, Henrico Co.
Hewes, Ralph, 1635, by Richard Bennett, ——— Co.
Hewes, Francis, 1637, by Francis Poythers, Charles City Co.
Hewes, Rich., 1638, by John Fludd, James City Co.
Hewes, James, 1638, by Wm. Hayward, Charles City Co.
Hewes, Tho., 1638, by William Banister, ——— Co.
Hews, Tho., 1652, by Mr. Tho. Teagle, Northampton Co.
Hews, Richard, 1650, by Tho. Hawkins, Charles River Co.
Hewitt, Rich., 1648, by Lewis Burwell and Tho. Haws, York River Co.
Hewitt, James, 1651, by Wm. Vincent, Northumberland Co.
Hewitt, Rich., 1637, by Capt. John Howe, Accomac Co.
Hewson, Tho., 1638, by Edw. Travis and John Johnson, James City Co.
Heyden, Jane, 1650, by David Peibles, Charles City Co.
Heydon, Humphry, 1648, by Francis Ceely, ——— Co.
Heyes, Peter, 1635, by Jno. Upton, Warrasquinoake Co.
Heyes, Hugh, 1635, by McWilliam Stone, ——— Co.
Heylens, Hester, 1649, by Francis Brown, Northumberland Co.
Heyly, Eleanor, 1635, by Mr. Willis Heyly, ——— Co.
Heyly, Wm., 1635, by David Mansell, James Co.
Heynes, Fra., 1653, by Wm. Wyatt, Gloucester Co.
Heynes, Ro., 1654, by Major Miles Carey, Westmoreland Co.
Heynes, Tho., 1654, by Major Miles Carey, Westmoreland Co.
Heyward, Ann, 1639, by John Pawley, James City Co.
Heyward, Wm., 1643, by Rowland Burnham, Yorke Co.
Heyward, Rand., 1637, by Mathew Edloe, ——— Co.
Heyward, Humphrey, 1635, by Capt. Adam Thoroughgood, ——— Co.
Heyward, John, 1635, by Thomas Harwood, ——— Co.
Heywood, Richard, 1652, by Robert Elam, Henrico Co.
Heywood, Robert, 1638, by Robert Freeman, James City Co.
Heywood, John, 1650, by George Pate, Charles City Co.
Hibs, Nohal, 1655, by John Wise, Northampton Co.

Hickes, Richard, 1653, by Jno. Hansford, Gloucester Co.
Hickes, Richard, 1650, by John Cox, ——— Co.
Hickes, John, 1642, by John Brooch, Charles River Co.
Hickhocke, Tho., 1650, by Geo. Hack, Northampton Co.
Hickins, Francis, 1642, by Wm. Barnard, Esq., Isle of Wight Co.
Hickman, Tho., 1652, by Tho. Bell, Gloucester Co.
Hickman, Hen., 1635, by Christo. Stoakes, Elizabeth Co.
Hickman, Tho., 1653, by James Turner, ——— Co.
Hickman, Wm., 1655, by John Dorman, Northampton Co.
Hickman, Sarah, 1641, by Wm. Burdett, Accomack Co.
Hickman, Henry, 1637, by Christopher Stoakes, Charles River Co.
Hickmon, ———, 1653, by Nathaniel Hickmon (her husband), Northumberland Co.
Hicks, Jeremy, 1654, by Randall Chamblett, ——— Co.
Hicks, Samuel, 1637, by Peter Roy and William Jacob, Isle of Wight Co.
Hicks, James, 1637, by Oliver Sprye, New Norfolk Co.
Hide, Edward, 1651, by John Thomas, Gloucester Co.
Hide, Samll., 1643, by John Freeme, Charles Co.
Hiderick, Robert, 1645, by John Rode, Warwick Co.
Higate, John, 1653, by James Watson, Isle of Wight Co.
Higbie, Edw., 1646, by Sir William Berkley, ——— Co.
Higby, Jonathan, 1653, by Jno. Hansford, Gloucester Co.
Higgeson, Joane, 1637, by Edward Tunstall, Henrico Co.
Higgens, Hum., 1653, by Col. Hugh Gwyn, Lancaster Co.
Higgins, John, 1639, by Edward Travis, James City Co.
Higgins, Dan., 1654, by James Yates, ——— Co.
Higgins, Jone, 1638, by Abraham Wood, Charles City Co.
Higgins, John, 1639, by Edward Prince, Charles City Co.
Higgins, Fra., 1651, by George Ludlow, Esq., ——— Co.
Higgenson, Robt., 1653, by Alexander Addison, ——— Co.
Higgenson, Wm., 1638, by William Carter, James City Co.
Higgenson, Mrs., 1654, by Col. Hump. Higgenson, Esq., and Abraham Moone, Westmoreland Co.
Higgenson, Ellinor, 1655, by John Dorman, Northampton Co.
Higginson, Christo., 1642, by Hugh Gwyn, Gent., ——— Co.
Higginson, Eliza, 1642, by Hugh Gwyn, Gent., ——— Co.
Higginson, Peter, 1648, by John Ellis, James Joones and John Taylor, Northampton Co.
Higginson, Hugh, 1649, by Capt. Ralph Wormeley, ——— Co.
Higginson, Peter, 1642, by John Towlson, Accomack Co.
Higginson, Eliz., 1637, by Humphrey Higginson, Gent., ——— Co.
Higson, Ralph, 1638, by Joseph Royall, Charles Citie Co.
Hiles, Eliz., 1654, by John Wyre, John Gillet, Andrew Gilson and John Phillips, ——— Co.
Hill, Eliza, 1650, by Richard Dunning, ——— Co.
Hill, Nicho., 1650, by George Pate, Charles City Co.
Hill, Rich., 1638, by William Morgan, James City Co.
Hill, Peter, 1638, by Edw. Travis, and John Johnson, James City Co.
Hill, Abraham, 1638, by John Hacker, James City Co.
Hill, Peter, 1638, by William Croutch, Lower Norfolk Co.
Hill, Mr. Wm., 1644, by John Hill, Gent., Upper Norfolk Co.

Hill, Charles, 1645, by John Shepard, York Co.
Hill, John, 1637, by John Jackson, Charles River Co.
Hill, Wm., 1636, by Wm. Julian, Elizabeth City Co.
Hill, Jon., 1635, by Capt. Adam Thoroughgood, ——— Co.
Hill, Mary, 1635, by Capt. Adam Thoroughgood, ——— Co.
Hill, Rich., 1637, by John Neale, Accomack Co.
Hill, Anthony, 1637, by William Spencer, ——— Co.
Hill, Rose, 1636, by John Dunston, James City Co.
Hill, Abraham, 1636, by John Harker, ——— Co.
Hill, Henry, 1635, by Capt. Adam Thoroughgood, ——— Co.
Hill, Richard, 1636, by Richard Cocke, ——— Co.
Hill, Richard, 1637, by Wm. Cotton, ——— Co.
Hill, Mary, 1635, by Capt. Adam Thoroughgood, ——— Co.
Hill, John, 1655, by Sampson Robins, Northampton Co.
Hill, John, 1655, by Wm. Steevens, Northampton Co.
Hilll, Charles, 1655, by George Kibble, Lancaster Co.
Hill, James, 1655, by Edward Pettaway, Surry Co.
Hill, George, 1654, by Tho. Willoughby, Lower Norfolk Co.
Hill, James, 1654, by Peter Knight, Northumberland Co.
Hill, Wm., 1654, by Tho. Harmanson, Northampton Co.
Hill, Antho., 1654, by Richard Walker, ——— Co.
Hill, John, 1654, by John Watson and John Bognall, Westmoreland Co.
Hill, Tho., 1650, by Richard Tye and Charles Sparrowe, Charles City Co.
Hill, William, 1650, by Samuell Smith, Northumberland Co.
Hill, Jacob, 1650, by Mrs. Frances Townshend (widow), Northumberland Co.
Hill, William, 1639, by Thomas Mathews, Henrico Co.
Hill, Katharine, wife Rich Hill, 1638, by Rich Hill and Roger Arnwood, James City Co.
Hill, John, 1639, by Edward Panderson, ——— Co.
Hill, John, 1639, by John Jackson, Charles River Co.
Hill, Thomas, 1639, by Edward Travis, James City Co.
Hill, Thomas, 1639, by Walter Pakes, ——— Co.
Hill, Rose, 1639, by John Dunston, James City Co.
Hill, Rose, 1638, by William Carter, James City Co.
Hill, Richard, 1639, by Richard Corke, Gent., Henrico Co.
Hill, Wm., 1639, by Georg Minifye, Esq., Charles River Co.
Hill, Tho., 1639, by Walter Pakes, James City Co.
Hill, Barbery, 1648, by Wm. Edwards and Rice Edwards, James City Co.
Hill, Ann, 1648, by Wm. Edwards and Rice Edwards, James City Co.
Hill, John, 1647, by Richard Stearnell, Lower Norfolk Co.
Hill, Robert, 1649, by Wm. Hoccaday, ——— Co.
Hill, Richard, 1649, by Joseph Croshawe, Yorke Co.
Hill, Mary, wife of Robt. Hill, 1642, by Francis England, Isle of Wight Co.
Hill, Tho., 1650, by Capt. Moore Fautleroy, ——— Co.
Hill, Fra., 1650, by Capt. Moore Fautleroy, ——— Co.
Hill, Mary, 1650, by Capt. Moore Fautleroy, ——— Co.
Hill, John, 1652, by Lt. Coll. John Cheeseman, ——— Co.

Hill, Mary, Sr., 1652, by Richard Hill, Northampton Co.
Hill, Mary, Jr., 1652, by Richard Hill, Northampton Co.
Hill, John, 1652, by Mr. John Mattrom, Northumberland Co.
Hill, Susan, 1652, by John Godfrey, Lower Norfolk Co.
Hill, John, 1652, by Henry Smith, Jr., ——— Co.
Hill, Anne, —, by Mr. John Page, ——— Co.
Hill, Tower, 1653, by Tho. Read, Northumberland Co.
Hill, John, 1653, by Robert Bouth, Yorke Co.
Hill, Richard, 1652, by Mr. George Clapham, ——— Co.
Hill, James, 1652, by Mr. John Browne, Northampton Co.
Hill, James, 1652, by Richard Coleman, ——— Co.
Hill, Charles, 1653, by John Sheppard, Northumberland Co.
Hill, Georg, 1648, by John Ellis, James Joones and John Taylor, Northampton Co.
Hill, George, 1653, by Major Abra. Wood, Charles City Co.
Hill, Martha, 1653, by Tho. Davis, ——— Co.
Hill, Joseph, 1653, by Capt. Francis Patt, Northampton Co.
Hill, Eliza, 1653, by Capt. Francis Patt, Northampton Co.
Hill, Robert, 1653, by Elianor Brocas, Lancaster Co.
Hill, Richd., 1653, by Colo. Wm. Clayborne (Sec. of State), ——— Co.
Hill, Benja., 1651, by Giles Lawrence and John Turner, Nansemond Co.
Hill, Robert, 1642, by Francis England, Isle of Wight Co.
Hill, Wm., 1650, by Henry Ashwell, ——— Co.
Hill, Tho., 1650, by Mrs. Frances Townshend (widow), Northumberland Co.
Hill, Peter, 1637, by Robert Taylor, New Norfolk Co.
Hills, Wm., 1638, by Benjamin Carrell, James City Co.
Hills, Henry, 1648, by John Troy, James City Co.
Hills, Henry, 1652, by Tho. Green, ——— Co.
Hillary, Susan, 1652, by Collo. Hugh Gwin, ——— Co.
Hillary, Susana, 1655, by Patrick Miller, Lancaster Co.
Hillard, Wm., 1654, by Mr. Giles Brent, Westmoreland Co.
Hillery, Susan, 1653, by Col. Hugh Gwyn, Lancaster Co.
Hilliar, Geo., 1654, by Robert Hubard, Westmoreland Co.
Hilliard, John, 1651, by Henry Singleton, ——— Co.
Hilliard, Geo., 1638, by John Fludd, James City Co.
Hillier, ———, 1653, by John Hillier (her husband), Northumberland Co.
Hillyer, Lawrence, 1655, by John Wise, Northampton Co.
Hilton, Ann, 1648, by Georg Read, Gent., ——— Co.
Hilton, Wm., 1654, by Francis Smith and Mr. John Smith, Westmoreland Co.
Hilton, Henry, 1643, by Tho. Taylor, Warwick Co.
Hinakly Thomas, 1635, by Thomas Harwood, ——— Co.
Hinam, Wm., 1650, by Edward Walker, Northumberland Co.
Hincastle, Jiles, 1650, by Geo. Ludlow, Esq., Northumberland Co.
Hinderson, Mathew, 1651, by James Allen, Northumberland Co.
Hind, Alexander, 1654, by Nich. Merywether, Westmoreland Co.
Hinde, James, 1652, by Mr. Nicholas Jernew, Gloucester Co.
Hinde, Eliz., 1653, by Wm. Haynes, ——— Co.
Hinde, Wm., his three wives and three children, 1647, by Tho. Gibson, York Co.

Hinde, Alex., 1654, by Richard Hawkins, Westmoreland Co.
Hinde, Wm., 1642, by Wm. Warren, ——— Co.
Hinde, Rich., 1638, by John Fludd, James City Co.
Hinds, Tho., 1656, by Capt. Henry Fleete, ——— Co.
Hine, Anthony, 1653, by Samuell Parry, Lancaster Co.
Hine, Tho., 1653, by Oliver Segar, Lancaster Co.
Hinshaw, Ann, 1653, by Richard Major, Gloucester Co.
Hinshaw, Mary, 1653, by Richard Major, Gloucester Co.
Hint, James, 1654, by Wm. Beach, Westmoreland Co.
Hinton, Tho., 1653, by Samuell Parry, Lancaster Co.
Hinton, Tho., 1651, by Palmer Hinton, ——— Co.
Hinton, Jone, wife Farrar Hinton, 1650, by Elias Hinton, ——— Co.
Hinton,, Farrar, 1650, by Elias Edmonds, ——— Co.
Hinton John, 1642, by John Harlowe, Northampton Co.
Hinton, Wm., 1636, by Richard Cocke, ——— Co.
Hinton, Mr. Tho., 1637, by Capt. Henry Browne, James River Co.
Hitchcock, Richd., 1653, by Francis Emperor, Hugh Gale and Edward
    Morgan, Lower Norfolk Co.
Hitchcox, Hen., 1642, by Daniell Lewellyn, ——— Co.
Hitchcox, John, 1639, by Tho. Boulding, Elizabeth City Co.
Hitchcox, Rich., 1636, by Edward Osborne, Henrico Co.
Hitchcox, Richard, 1636, by Robert Hollom, Henrico Co.
Hitchcox, 1635, by Wm. Barber, Charles City Co.
Hitchcox, Richard, 1637, by Capt. Thomas Osborne, Henrico Co.
Hix, William, 1638, by Richard Wilcox, James City Co.
Hixams, Robt., 1648, by Francis Fludd, York Co.
Hixon, Ralph, 1642, by Joseph Royall, ——— Co.
Hixon, Joan, 1653, by Jon. Slaughter, ——— Co.
Hoard, Elias, 1654, by Capt. John West, Esq., Gloucester Co.
Hobert, Sarah, wife of Bertram Hobert, 1642, by Bertram Hobert,
    ——— Co.
Hobert, Bertram, 1642, by Bertram Hobert, ——— Co.
Hobbs, Isaac, 1651, by Coll. Guy Molsworth, ——— Co.
Hobbs, Geo., 1650, by James Hurd, ——— Co.
Hobbs, John, 1650, by John Mangor, ——— Co.
Hobbs, Thomas, 1642, by Andrew Terry, ——— Co.
Hobbs, John, 1638, by Mr. Walter Ashton, Charles City Co.
Hobbs, Jone, 1643, by Georg Levitt, ——— Co.
Hobson, Elizabeth, 1656, by John Williams, Northampton Co.
Hobson, John, 1653, by Col. Wm. Clayborne (Sec. of State), ——— Co.
Hobson, Richard, 1653, by Wm. Debram, ——— Co.
Hobson, Roger, 1652, by Mrs. Jane Harmer, Northumberland Co.
Hobson, Tho., 1650, by Elias Edmonds, ——— Co.
Hobson, John, 1648, by George White, Lower Norfolk Co.
Hobson, Eliz., 1654, by Tho. Bell, Northampton Co.
Hobson, Robert, 1647, by Thomas Johnson, Gent., Northampton Co.
Hoccadie, Wm., 1653, by Mr. Wm. Fry, James City Co.
Hock, Isaac, 1643, by Capt. Samuell Mathews, Esq., ——— Co.
Hockett, Elizabeth, 1653, by John Day, Gloucester Co.
Hockett, Mary, 1653, by John Day, Gloucester Co.
Hockett, Henry, 1651, by Capt. Stephen Gill, Northumberland Co.

Hockerton, Ralph, 1654, by Richard Allen, Northampton Co.
Hockins, Georg, 1637, by Thomas Codd, New Norfolk Co.
Hockly, Rowld., 1653, by Wm. Haynes, ——— Co.
Hockson, Robt., 1653, by Abraham Moone, Lancaster Co.
Hockwell, Kath., 1656, by Tho. Rolfe, Gent., James City Co.
Hockwell, Katharine, 1637, by Theodore Moyser, James City Co.
Hoddin, John, 1643, by John Hoddin, ——— Co.
Hoddon, Michaell, 1649, by Robert Moseley, Gent., ——— Co.
Hoddy, John, 1642, by William Connhoe, ——— Co.
Hodge, Edward, 1653, by Mr. Wm. Hoccodoy, Yorke Co.
Hodge, Ellen, 1652, by John Dier, Lower Norfolk Co.
Hodge, William, 1639, by John Dunston, James City Co.
Hodge, Wm., 1636, by John Dunston, James City Co.
Hodgee, Joane, 1655, by John Hinman, Northampton Co.
Hodges, Margaret, 1652, by James Sterling, Lower Norfolk Co.
Hodges, Roger, 1650, by Mr. Epaphroditus Lawson, ——— Co.
Hodges, Joane, 1641, by Ambrose Bennett, Isle of Wight Co.
Hodges, Tho., 1650, by Silvester Thatcher and Tho. Whitlocke, ———
    Co.
Hodges, Jane, 1654, by Mr. Francis Hamond, York Co.
Hodges, Charles, 1655, by Richard Jones, ——— Co.
Hodges, Robt., 1636, by John Gookin, Gent., ——— Co.
Hodges, Eliza, 1637, by Bridges Freeman, James City Co.
Hodges, John, 1637, by Thomas Causey, Charles City Co.
Hodges, Robert, 1637, by John Gookin, New Norfolk Co.
Hodges, Jon., 1638, by Tristrum Nosworthy, ——— Co.
Hodges, John, 1643, by Mr. Phillipp Bennett, Upper Norfolk Co.
Hodges, Robert, 1638, by Mr. John Gookins, Upper New Norfolk Co.
Hodges, John, 1638, by Mr. Robert Bennett, Upper Norfolk Co.
Hodgines, John, 1650, by Jervace Dodson, Gent., Northumberland Co.
Hodgkenson, Wm., 1649, by Capt. Ralph Wormeley, ——— Co.
Hodgkins, Mary, 1638, by John George, Charles City Co.
Hodin, John, 1652, by Andrew, Munrow, Northumberland Co.
Hodson, John, 1637, by John Hucks, James Citie Co.
Hoe, Car., 1655, by Sampson Robins, Northampton Co.
Hoeding, Jon., 1635, by William Spencer, ——— Co.
Hoell, Charles, 1653, by Tho. Speoke, ——— Co.
Hoer, Andrew, 1637, by Thomas Paule, James City Co.
Hoes, Owen, 1637, by Leonard Yeo, Elizabeth City Co.
Hoffeild Henry, 1655, by Capt. George Floyd, New Kent Co.
Hogg, Andrew, 1653, by John Ashby and Jh. Hamper, ——— Co.
Hogg, Will, 1650, by John Armesbee, Northumberland Co.
Hogg, Tho., 1655, by Southy Littleberry, Northampton Co.
Hogard Peter, 1654, by Francis Smith and Mr. John Smith, Westmore-
    land Co.
Hogate, Janus, 1639, by Edward Panderson, ——— Co.
Hogges, Mary, 1650, by John Cooke, Northumberland Co.
Hogson, Wm., 1655, by John Browne, Gent., Northampton Co.
Holburton, Walter, 1642, by Capt. Samuell Mathews, Esq., ——— Co
Hold, Christopher, 1638, by John Hacker, James City Co.

Holden, Joane, 1652, by Ambrose Dixon and Stephen Horsely, North-
    ampton Co.
Holden, John, 1637, by William Spencer, ——— Co.
Holder, John, 1638, by John Robins, Elizabeth City Co.
Holder, Eliz. (wife John Holder), 1638, by John Robins, Elizabeth City
    Co.
Holdick, Richard, 1650, by Sr. Tho. Luntsford, Kt., and Barronett,
    ——— Co.
Holding, Geo., 1653, by Abraham Moon, Lancaster Co.
Holdinge, George, 1653, by John Edwards, Lancaster Co.
Holding, James, 1638, by Richard Maior, Charles River Co.
Holding, Robt., 1653, by Maj. Wm. Lewis, ——— Co.
Holding, Ja., 1653, by John Merryman and Morgan Haynes, Lancaster
    Co.
Holding, Rich., 1650, by Edward Walker, Northumberland Co.
Holding, Grace, wife Rich. Holding, 1650, by Edward Walker, North-
    umberland Co.
Holding, John, 1654, by Wm. Johnson, Northampton Co.
Holding, Isaac, 1655, by Capt. Henry Fleet, ——— Co.
Hole, Barbary, 1638, by Edward Hill, Charles City Co.
Holder, Mary, 1652, by John Earle, Northumberland Co.
Holeman, Xtop, 1650, by John Cox., ——— Co.
Holland, John, 1650, by Stephen Charlton, Northampton Co.
Holland, Wm., 1636, by Cheney Boyse, Charles Citie Co.
Holland, Fra., 1651, by Mr. Antho. Steevens, Northumberland Co.
Holland, Tho., 1651, by Mr. Arthur Price, Yorke Co.
Holland, John, 1649, by Henry Bishopp, Northampton Co.
Holland, Francis, 1643, by Francis Rice, ——— Co.
Holland, Mary, —, by Samuel Heely and John Carter, Surry Co.
Holland, Henry, 1635, by McWilliam Stone, ——— Co.
Holland, Edw., 1635, by Robt. Hollom, Henrico Co.
Holland, Wm., 1637, by Cheney Boyes, Charles City Co.
Holland, Edward, 1637, by Hannah Boyes, Henrico Co.
Holland, Wm., 1638, by John Batts and John Davis, Charles River Co.
Hollaway, Jno., 1655, by Mr. Wm. Nutt, Northumberland Co.
Holley, Lyonell, 1642, by John Robins, ——— Co.
Holliway, Oliver, 1648, by Mr. Bartholomew Haskins, Lower Norfolk
    Co.
Holloway, Peter, 1535, by Hugh Cox, Charles City Co.
Holleffe, John, 1642, by Capt. Samuell Mathews, ——— Co.
Holliday, Tho., 1656, by Major Wm. Lewis, ——— Co.
Holliday, John, 1638, by Capt. Christopher Wormley, ——— Co.
Holliday, Geo., 1638, by John Robins, ——— Co.
Holliday, Eliza, 1655, by John Dorman, Northampton Co.
Holliday, Wm., 1637, by William Mills, James City Co.
Holliday, Tho., 1650, by John Lacker, ——— Co.
Holliday, Geo., 1650, by George Pate, Charles City Co.
Holliman, ———, 1653, by John Sheerlock, Lancaster Co.
Holliman, Judith, 1653, by John Sheerlock, Lancaster Co.
Hollimen, Wm., 1656, by Tho. Rolfe, Gent., James City Co.
Hollingham, Thos., 1639, by William Canhooe, Charles River Co.

Hollingsworth, Sarah, wife of John Hollingsworth, —, by Mr. Thomas Wallis, James City Co.
Hollingsworth, John, 1638, by Mr. Thomas Wallis, James City Co.
Holliock, Roger, 1635, by Mr. Willis Heyly, ——— Co.
Hollis, Thomas, 1648, by Tho. Lambert, Lower Norfolk Co.
Hollis, John, 1642, by Capt. Samuell Mathews, Esq., ——— Co.
Hollis, Restitute, Jr., 1654, by Tho. Hobkins, Lancaster Co.
Hollis, Restitute, Sr., 1654, by Tho. Hobkins, Lancaster Co.
Hollman, Christop., 1653, by John Sheerlock, Lancaster Co.
Hollock, Andrew, 1643, by Capt. Samuell Mathews, Esq., ——— Co.
Hollman, Judith, 1653, by John Cox, Lancaster Co.
Holloman, Judith, 1650, by Tho. Wilkinson, ——— Co.
Hollowell, Edward, 1650, by John Watts, Gent., ——— Co.
Hollowell, Tho., 1649, by Stephen Gill, York Co.
Hollowes, Restitute, Sr., 1650, by John Hollowes, Gent., Northumberland Co.
Hollowes, Robt., 1650, by Sr. Tho. Luntsford, Kt. and Barronett, ——— Co.
Holly, John, 1650, by Capt. Moore Fautleroy, ——— Co.
Holly, Tyomll., 1652, by Mr. Geo. Foster, Northumberland Co.
Holman, Robert, 1638, by Elizabeth Grayne, Charles City Co.
Holman, Wm., 1638, by John Batts and John Davis, Charles River Co.
Holmer, Morris, 1643, by Sir Francis Wyatt, Kt., ——— Co.
Holmes, Tho., 1652, by Nicho. George, Tho. Taberer and Humphry Clarke, ——— Co.
Holmes, Jane, 1653, by Christopher Boyce, Northumberland Co.
Holmes, George, 1653, by Christopher Boyce, Northumberland Co.
Holmes, And., 1650, by Capt. Moore Fautleroy, ——— Co.
Holmes, Rich., 1648, by Bartholomew Hoskins, ——— Co.
Holmes, Fran., 1648, by Richard Pettibon, ——— Co.
Holmes, Marg., 1648, by John Baldwin, Northampton Co.
Holmes, David, 1648, by Tho. Braughton, ——— Co.
Holmes, Eliza., 1648, by Geo. Hardey, Tho. Wombwell and Peter Hall, Isle of Wight Co.
Holmes, Thomas, 1639, by George Minifye, Esq., Charles River Co.
Holmes, John, 1655, by John Westlock, Northampton Co.
Holmes, John, 1636, by James Vanerit, Elizabeth City Co.
Holmes, Rebecca, 1637, by Georg Holmes, her husband, James City Co.
Holmes, Rebecca, 1636, by Geo. Holmes (her husband), James City Co.
Holmes, Rebecca, 1635, by Geo. Holmes, her hsuband, James Co.
Holmes, David, 1643, by Elizabeth Hull, ——— Co.
Holmes, Mathew, 1638, by Chrisotpher Lawson, ——— Co.
Holnell, Tho., 1653, by Margarett Upton, Lancaster Co.
Holse, Wm., 1648, by John Baldwin, Northampton Co.
Holsteed, Henry, 1651, by Christopher Burroughs, Lower Norfolk Co.
Holt, Wm., 1652, by Dr. George Hack, Northampton Co.
Holt, Randall, 1653, by Capt. Francis Patt, Northampton Co.
Holt, Edward, 1651, by Wm. Taylor, Northumberland Co.
Holt, Alice, 1651, by Robert Holt, James City Co.
Holt, Edward, 1653, by Edward Harrington, Northampton Co.
Holt, Edward, 1653, by Charles Scarburg, Northampton Co.

Holt, Francis, 1639, by Randall Holt, James City Co.
Holt, Math., 1645, by William Jones, Northampton Co.
Holton, Jno., 1635, by Capt. Adam Thoroughgood, ——— Co.
Hombleton, John, 1650, by Mr. Robt. Holt, James City Co.
Home, Hen., 1651, by James Davis, Northampton Co.
Home, Wm., 1653, by Tho. Davis, Gent., Nansemond Co.
Home, Jno., 1653, by Tho. Mallard, Northumberland Co.
Home, Wm., 1651, by Mr. Robert Abrall, Yorke Co.
Homes, Peter, 1637, by Mathew Edloe, ——— Co.
Homert, Adam, 1653, by John Earle, Northumberland Co.
Homigwood, Robt., 1638, by Edw. Sparshott, Charles City Co.
Hommond, Henry, 1650, by Wm. Morgan, ——— Co.
Hond, Dorcas, 1655, by Jenkin Price, Northampton Co.
Hone, John, 1642, by Wm. Barnard, Esq., Isle of Wight Co.
Honine, Jane, 1638, by Roger Davis, Charles City Co.
Honnett, Rich., 1654, by Tho. Harmanson, Northampton Co.
Honnywood, Robt., 1638, by Edward Sparshott, Charles City Co.
Honyborne, Robt., 1649, by John Trussells, ——— Co.
Hooker, Tho., 1643, by Sir Francis Wyatt, Kt., ——— Co.
Hooker, Robt., 1653, by Tho. Cowlinge, ——— Co.
Hooke, Richd., 1650, by Capt. Moore Fautleroy, ——— Co.
Hooke, Joseph, 1655, by Lt. Col. Anthony Ellyott, ——— Co.
Hooke, Edwd., 1637, by Wm. Farrar, Henrico Co.
Hookes, Wm., 1637, by Daniell Gookins, New Norfolk Co.
Hooks, Wm., 1643, by Wm. Butler, James City Co.
Hooks, John, 1654, by Tho. Hobkins, Lancaster Co.
Hooper, Arthur, 1653, by Tho. Cowlinge, ——— Co.
Hooper, John, 1643, by Thomas Wheeler, Charles City Co.
Hooper, Peter, 1635, by John Grinett, ——— Co.
Hooper, Thos., 1635, by Wm. Barker, Charles City Co.
Hooper, Richard, 1643, by Tristram Nosworthy, Isle of Wight Co.
Hoopes, Henry, 1654, by John Drayton, Westmoreland Co.
Hoord, Aalan, 1650, by Capt. Moore Fautleroy, ——— Co.
Hoote, Joan, 1654, by Valentine Patten, Westmoreland Co.
Hooton, Christopher, 1643, by William Botts, ——— Co.
Hooton, Mich., 1654, by John Watson and John Bognall, Westmore-
    land Co.
Hoover, Margaret, 1656, by Tho. Merredith, New Kent Co.
Hope, Fra., 1646, by Joseph Croshawe, Charles River Co.
Hopkin, Wm., 1649, by Mr. Ralph Barlowe, Northampton Co.
Hopkins, Mathew, 1652, by Richard Coleman, ——— Co.
Hopkins, John, 1656, by Mr. Henry Soanes, New Kent Co.
Hopkins, Richard, 1647, by Wm. Blackey, York Co.
Hopkins, Wm., 1652, by Mrs. Jane Harmer, Northumberland Co.
Hopkins, Peter, 1652, by Capt. Augustine Warner, ——— Co.
Hopkins, Eliza, 1650, by George Taylor, ——— Co.
Hopkins, William, 1641, by Thomas Bernard, Warwick River Co.
Hopkins, Robert, 1642, by Peter Rigby, ——— Co.
Hopkins, David, 1637, by Nathaniel Floyd, Isle of Wight Co.
Hopkins, Richd., 1650, by Edward Walker, Northumberland Co.
Hopkins, Robt., 1635, by Jno. Sparkes, ——— Co.

Hopkinson, Daniell, 1637, by Daniell Gookins, New Norfolk Co.
Hoppards, Mayses, 1650, by Mrs. Frances Townshend (widow), North-
umberland Co.
Hopps, Robt., 1642, by Daniell Lewellyn, ——— Co.
Hopswood, Jno., 1652, by Henry Woodhouse, Lower Norfolk Co.
Horim, Hugh, 1653, by Jno. Hansford, Gloucester Co.
Horlaw, Tho., 1650, by Richard Axom and Tho. Godwin, ——— Co.
Horner, James, 1636, by Robt. Hollom, Henrico Co.
Horne, Wm., 1653, by Capt. Robt. Abrall, ——— Co.
Horne, Adam, 1652, by Tho. Hallinard, ——— Co.
Horne, Jon., 1637, by Margaret Rogers, New Norfolk Co.
Horne, Jon., 1636, by James Knott, Elizabeth City Co.
Horne, John, 1636, by Edward Rogers, Warrasquinoake Co.
Horne, John, 1637, by James Knott, New Norfolk Co.
Horner, Thomas, 1642, by John Robins, ——— Co.
Horner, Roger, 1638, by John Fludd, James City Co.
Horse, Step., 1643, by Mr. Obedience Robins, Northampton Co.
Horsley, Jane, 1652, by Ralph Horsely, Northumberland Co.
Horsley, Joseph, 1652, by Ralph Horsley, Northumberland Co.
Hort, John, 1656, by Wm. Crump and Mr. Humphry Vaulx, James
City Co.
Horton, Walter, 1653, by Capt. Francis Patt, Northampton Co.
Horton, Robert, 1648, by Robert Pitt, Isle of Wight Co.
Horton, Barth., 1650, by Capt. John Flood, Gent., and Jno. Flood, an
ancient planter, James City Co.
Horton, Wm., 1649, by Mr. Nesum and others, Northumberland Co.
Horton, Isaac, 1639, by Richard Corke, Gent., Henrico Co.
Horton, Eliza, 1650, by Mr. James Williamson, ——— Co.
Horton, Rich., 1654, by Mr. Tho. Fowke, Westmoreland Co.
Horton, Isaac, 1636, by Richard Cocke, ——— Co.
Horton, Barth., 1638, by John Fludd, James City Co.
Horton, Tobias, 1638, by Wm. Hatcher, ——— Co.
Hoskins, Alice, 1652, by Anthony Hoskins, Northampton Co.
Hoskins, Mandlin, 1656, by Nathaniel Pope, Gent., Westmoreland
Co.
Hoskins, Susan, 1656, by Nathaniel Pope, Gent., Westmoreland Co.
Hoskins, Richard, 1545, by Mr. Bartholomew Hoskins, ——— Co.
Hosnard, Dorothy, 1649, by Edmund Scarburgh, Jr.. Northampton Co
Hoster, Francis, ———, by Samuel Heely and John Carter, Surry Co.
Hotes, John, 1642, by Richard Bennett, ——— Co.
Houghton, Christop., 1652, by John Gresham, Northumberland Co.
Hould, Christopher, 1636, by John Harke, ——— Co.
Hound, Dorcas, 1637, by Georg Vuwin, New Norfolk Co.
Hound, Darias, 1635, by Thos. Butler Clark and Pastor of Denbie,
Warrasquinoake Co.
House, Wm., 1652, by John Howett, Northumberland Co.
House, Jane, 1652, by Mr. Henry Pitt, ——— Co.
House, Edw., 1650, by Capt. Moore Fautleroy, ——— Co.
Houshorne, Henry, 1647, by Leonard Pettock, Accomac Co.
Houston, Tho., 1655, by Richard Hamlet, James City Co.
Houseward, Fra., 1652, by John Meredith, Lancaster Co.

Houtirupp, Francis, 1653, by Colo. Wm. Clayborne (Sec. of State), ——— Co.
Hoveller, Jeremiah, 1637, by Thomas Osborne, Jr., Henrico Co.
Hovist, Wm., 1637, by Capt. Thomas Panlett, Charles City Co.
How, John, 1653, by Nicho. Meriwether, Northumberland Co.
How, Jane, 1648, by John Seward, Isle of Wight Co.
How, John, 1638, by Richard Kemp, Esq., ——— Co.
How, Richard, 1640, by Thomas Stegg, Charles City Co.
How, John, 1654, by John Drayton, Westmoreland Co.
How, John, 1654, by Nich. Merywether, Westmoreland Co.
How, Abigael, 1655, by Wm. Botham, Westmoreland Co.
How, Andrew, 1637, by Capt. Thomas Panlett, Charles City Co.
Howals, John, 1650, by John Hallowes, Gent., Northumberland Co
Howard, John, 1642, by Adam Cooke, Charles Co.
Howard, Edward, 1651, by Coll. Richard Lee, Esq., Gloucester Co.
Howard, John, 1653, by Augustus Warner, ——— Co.
Howard, Richard, 1648, by Lewis Burwell, Gent., ——— Co.
Howard, Grace, 1650, by James Arrorke, ——— Co.
Howard, Ben., 1646, by William Hockaday, York Co.
Howard, Robert, 1650, by Rici Jones, ——— Co.
Howard, Tho., 1654, by Richard Walker, ——— Co.
Howard, John, 1654, by Robert Yoe, Westmoreland Co.
Howard, James, 1656, by Sir Henry Chickley, ——— Co.
Howard, John, 1636, by James Vanerit, Elizabeth City Co.
Howard, Edward, 1637, by Mary Box, Henrico Co.
Howard, William, 1641, by Wm. Storey, Upper Norfolk Co.
Howard, Frances, 1648, by Mr. Thomas Davies, Isle of Wight Co.
Howard, Thomas, 1638, by Mr. Robert Bennett, Upper Norfolk Co.
Howden, Rob., 1653, by Symon Thorogood, Elizabeth City Co.
Howe, Wm., 1635, by Edward Osborne, Henrico Co.
Howe, John, 1637, by Capt. John Howe, Accomac Co.
Howe, John, 1635, by William Ravenett, Denbeigh Co.
Hower, Henry, 1650, by Mrs. Frances Townshend (widow), Northumberland Co.
Howes, Ralph, 1637, by Rich. Bennett, New Norfolk Co.
Howes, Garrett, 1636, by John Dunston, James City Co.
Howell, Owen, 1635, by Jno. Upton, Warrasquinoake Co.
Howell, Richard, 1653, by Capt. Nathaniel Hurd, Warrick Co.
Howell, Jone, 1653, by John Earle, Northumberland Co.
Howell, Mary, 1653, by Wm. Hardidge, Northumberland Co.
Howell, Alice, 1653, by Peter Knight, Northumberland Co.
Howell, Tho., 1649, by Henry Bishopp, Northampton Co.
Howell, Walkin, 1641, by Ambrose Bennett, Isle of Wight Co.
Howell, Andrew, 1639, by William Davis, James City Co.
Howell, Tho., 1650, by Mr. Stephen Hamelin, Charles City Co.
Howell, Richard, 1654, by Mr. Francis Hamond, York Co.
Howell, Charles, 1654, by Nich. Merywether, Westmoreland Co.
Howell, Tho., 1656, by Sir Henry Chichley, ——— Co.
Howell, Chas., 1637, by Wm. Hatcher, ——— Co.
Howell, Walter, 1635, by Capt. Tho. Willowbye, ——— Co.
Howell, Andrew, 1637, by Joseph Jolly, Charles River Co.

Howell, Owen, 1637, by John Upton, Isle of Wight Co.
Howell, Cob., 1635, by Capt. Adam Thoroughgood, ⸺ Co.
Howell, Henry, 1637, by Wm. Farrar, Henrico Co.
Howell, John, 1637, by Richard Greete, Henrico Co.
Howell, Owen, 1637, by Lt. John Upton, Isle of Wight Co.
Howell, John, 1650, by Stepehen Charlton, Northampton Co.
Howet, Jno., and wife, 1652, by Tho. Boswell, ⸺ Co.
Howgate, Tho., 1641, by Thomas Bernard, Warwick River Co.
Howgate, John, 1636, by John Lathropp, James City Co.
Howler, Tho., 1639, by Georg Minifye, Esq., Charles River Co.
Howlet, Tho., 1655, by Wm. Steevens, Northampton Co.
Howman, Elizabeth, 1656, by Wm. Johnson, James City Co.
Howman, Jon., 1637, by Wm. Farrar, Henrico Co.
Hownson, Wm., 1650, by Capt. Moore Fautleroy, ⸺ Co.
Howranley, Darby, 1656, by Capt. Henry Fleete, ⸺ Co.
Howse, Robert, 1638, by Lt. Robt. Sheppard, James City Co.
Howse, Wm., 1654, by Edw. Cole, Northampton Co.
Howson, Edw., 1637, by Wm. Farrar, Henrico Co.
Howtree, Mary, 1642, by Cornelius de Hull, ⸺ Co.
Hoyes, James, 1638, by Jeremiah Dickenson, James City Co.
Hoyles, Jeremiah, 1638, by Edw. Sparshott, Charles City Co.
Huby, Samuell, 1643, by William Ewins, James City Co.
Hubbard, Benjamin, 1639, by Nicholas Comings, Charles River Co.
Hubbard, Rich., 1642, by Capt. Samuell Mathews, Esq., ⸺ Co.
Hubberd, Henry, 1648, by Lewis Burwell, Gent., ⸺ Co.
Huckel, Andrew, 1643, by John Sweete, Isle of Wight Co.
Huckley, John, 1644, by James Taylor and Lawrence Baker, James
    City Co.
Huckins, Jno., 1651, by Mr. Rowland Burnham, ⸺ Co.
Hudsdale, Henry, 1653, by Charles Grymes, Lancaster Co.
Hudsey, Peter, 1637, by Elizabeth Parker, Henrico Co.
Hudson, John, 1650, by Mrs. Frances Townshend (widow), Northum-
    berland Co.
Hudson, John, 1653, by Henry Corbell, Gloucester Co.
Hudson, Elizabeth, 1652, by Capt. John West, Esq., ⸺ Co.
Hudson, Tho., 1649, by Francis Brown, Northumberland Co.
Hudson, Henry, 1649, by Mr. Robert Parker, Northampton Co.
Hudson, Mary, 1650, by Mr. James Williamson, ⸺ Co.
Hudson, Geo., 1645, by Mr. Robt. Eyres, ⸺ Co.
Hudson, Tho., 1651, by Mr. Wm. Armestead, ⸺ Co.
Hudson, Wm., 1654, by Robert Holt, James City Co.
Hudson, Mathew, 1648, by Wm. Edwards and Rice Edwards, James
    City Co.
Hudson, John, 1638, by Capt. Christopher Wormley, ⸺ Co.
Hudson, Robert, 1639, by Wm. Barker, Charles City Co.
Hudson, Robt., 1650, by George Gill, Yorke Co.
Hudson, Eliza, 1635, by Henry Daniell, James City Co.
Hudson, Robert, 1635, by Thomas Harwood, ⸺ Co.
Hudson, Edw., 1637, by Capt. Thomas Flint, Warwick River Co.
Hudson, Samuell, 1638, by Mr. Thomas Wallis, James City Co.
Huebunt, Anthony, 1656, by Tho. Busby, Surry Co.

Hues, Fra., 1650, by John Rosier, Northumberland Co.
Hues, Elizabeth, 1653, by Jno. Royser, Northumberland Co.
Hues, Jno., 1653, by Francis Emperor, Hugh Gale and Edward Morgan, Lower Norfolk Co.
Hues, Frances, 1649, by Tho. Dale, ——— Co.
Hues, John, 1647, by Richard Stearnell, Lower Norfolk Co.
Hues, Thomas, 1650, by Thomas Mulford, Nansemond Co.
Hues, Richard, 1650, by Nicholas Perkins, Henrico Co.
Hues, Elizabeth, 1654, by John Rosyer, Clerk, ——— Co.
Hues, David, 1654, by Francis Smith, and Mr. John Smith Westmoreland Co.
Hues, Richard, 1642, by John Pratt, Henrico Co.
Hues, Richard, 1637, by Oliver Sprege, New Norfolk Co.
Hues, John, 1638, by Edmund Scarburgh, Accomac Co.
Huett, Robert, 1649, by Richard Kemp, Esq., Sec. of State, ——— Co.
Huett, John, 1639, by Richard Corke, Gent., Henrico Co.
Huett, Robert, 1638, by David Mansell, James City Co.
Huett, Francis, 1642, by John Robins, ——— Co.
Huett, Morgan, 1635, by Mr. Robert Cane, ——— Co.
Huey, Mich., 1650, by Richard Tye and Charles Sparrowe, Charles City Co.
Huffe, Mary, 1636, by Richard Cocke, ——— Co.
Huffe, Abr., 1653, by Corbet Piddle, Northumberland Co.
Huffer, John, 1639, by Wm. Barker, Charles City Co.
Huges, Mangeby, 1651, by Wm. Taylor, Northumberland Co.
Hughe, Richard, 1638, by John Robins, James City Co.
Hughes, Villemille, 1653, by Joseph Croshawe, York Co.
Hughes, Elizabeth, 1651, by Mr. Arthur Price, Yorke Co.
Hughes, Xtop., 1652, by Wm. Gautlett, ——— Co.
Hughes, Tho., 1652, by Tho. Todd, ——— Co.
Hughes, Tho., 1654, by Humphry Haggett, Lancaster Co.
Hughes, John, 1650, by Mr. John Hallawes, Northumberland Co.
Hughes, Arthur, 1639, by John Pawley, James City Co.
Hughes, Richard, 1639, by Thomas Symons, James City Co.
Hughes, Allen, 1642, by John Garrett, Upper New Norfolk Co.
Hughes, Tho., 1642, by John Benton, ——— Co.
Hughes, Xtop., 1650, by Mr. Anthony Ellyot, ——— Co.
Hughes, Tho., 1643, by Richard Richards, Charles River Co.
Hughes, Wm., 1654, by John Wyre, John Gillet, Andrew Gibson and John Phillipps, ——— Co.
Hughes, Jeffery, 1655, by John Jenkins, Northampton Co.
Hughes, Tho., 1642, by Bartholomew Knipe, ——— Co.
Hughes, Geo., 1646, by Sir William Berkley, ——— Co.
Hughes, Richard, 1637, by Arthur Smith, Isle of Wight Co.
Hughes, Rich., 1643, by Tho. Symonds, ——— Co.
Hughs, Eliz., 1653, by James Johnson, Nansemond Co.
Hughs, John, 1653, by Richard Well, Northumberland Co.
Hughs, Wm., 1651, by Mr. Rowland Burnham, ——— Co.
Huggeson, Jones, 1635, by Mr. Geo. Keth, Charles River Co.
Hugon, Vereto, 1655, by David Boucher, Isle of Wight Co.
Huitt, Catherine, 1653, by John Holding, York Co.

Hull, Mary, 1656, by Hester Obkham, James City Co.
Hull, Sarah, 1650, by John Hull (her husband), Northumberland Co.
Hull, Tho., 1654, by Capt. Nich. Marteaw, Westmoreland Co.
Hull, John, 1655, by Symon Symons, Charles City Co.
Hull, Geo., and Sons David and Edward, 1643, by Elizabeth Hull, ——— Co.
Hull, Eliza., wife David Hull, 1643, by Elizabeth Hull, ——— Co.
Hulett, Lawrence, 1652, by Teague Floyne, Lancaster Co.
Humble, Roger, 1637, by Capt. Thomas Osborne, Henrico Co.
Hume, James, 1648, by Lewis Burwell, Gent., ——— Co.
Humpheryes, Wm., 1651, by James Baldrige and Capt. Tho. Baldrige, Northumberland Co.
Humphereys, Wm., 1650, by Lieut. Wm. Worleich, ——— Co.
Humphreys, John, ——, by Tho. Lucas, ——— Co.
Humphrey, Amey, 1637, by Capt. Henry Browne, James City Co.
Humphrey, Wm., 1643, by Lt. Wm. Worleidge, ——— Co.
Humphrey, John, 1638, by William Clark, Henrico Co.
Humphrys, Jno., 1648, by George Read, Gent., ——— Co.
Humphry, James, 1653, by Wm. Johnson, Henrico Co.
Humphry, Wm., 1652, by Evan Griffeth, Lancaster Co.
Humphry, Jone, 1652, by Tho. Harwood, ——— Co.
Humphry, Tho., 1654, by John Cox, Lancaster Co.
Humphry, John, 1636, by Wm. Clarke, Henrico Co.
Humphry, Gunn, 1643, by John Hoddin, ——— Co.
Humpries, Jno., 1644, by James Taylor and Lawrence Baker, James City Co.
Huncer, Robt., 1649, by Edmund Scarburgh, Jr., Northampton Co.
Hunckle, Tho., 1650, by James Hurd, ——— Co.
Hundley, Hen., 1642, by Stephen Gill, ——— Co.
Hungerford, Sarah, 1650, by Andrew Munrow, Northumberland Co.
Hungerford, Joane, 1650, by Mr. John Hallowes, Northumberland Co.
Hungerton, John, 1651, by Christopher Burroughs, Lower Norfolk Co.
Hungerton, John, 1648, by Christopher Burrows, ——— Co.
Huningford, Jno., 1651, by Phillip Hunley, ——— Co.
Hunly, Robert, 1651, by Mr. Wm. Armestead, ——— Co.
Hunly, Elizabeth, 1651, by Mr. Wm. Armestead, ——— Co.
Hunstan, Wm., 1649, by Richard Parrett, ——— Co.
Hunt, Mary, 1651, by Abraham Moone and (Thomas Griffen), Lancaster Co.
Hunt, Symon, 1653, by Robert Tomlin, ——— Co.
Hunt, Henry, 1653, by Colo. Wm. Clayborne (Sec. of State), ——— Co.
Hunt, John, 1650, by John Landman, ——— Co.
Hunt, Wm., 1651, by Geo. Colclough, Gent., Northumberland Co.
Hunt, John, 1652, by Clement Thrush, Lancaster Co.
Hunt, Winified, 1652, by John Bayworth, ——— Co.
Hunt, Antho., 1650, by Richard Axom and Tho. Godwin, ——— Co.
Hunt, John, 1650, by Mr. John Hallowes, Northumberland Co.
Hunt, Wm., 1649, by Joseph Crowshawe, Yorke Co.
Hunt, Wm., 1649, by Christop. Lewis, James City Co.
Hunt, John, 1648, by Richard Lee, Gent., ——— Co.
Hunt, James, 1649, by Stephen Gill, York Co.

Hunt, Wm., 1638, by Cobb Howell, Lower New Norfolk Co.
Hunt, Edw., 1639, by John Dunston, James City Co.
Hunt, James, 1638, by Christopher Branch, Henrico Co.
Hunt, John, 1650, by John Essix, Northumberland Co.
Hunt, Richard, 1650, by William Gooch, Gent., ———— Co.
Hunt, Ja., 1654, by Christopher Boon, Westmoreland Co.
Hunt, Martha, 1655, by John Motley, Northumberland Co.
Hunt, Henry, 1655, by Hugh Yeo, Northampton Co.
Hunt, Jno., 1635, by Thos. Shippey, ———— Co.
Hunt, Christopher, 1636, by Wm. Rainshaw, Elizabeth City Co.
Hunt, James, 1636, by Christopher Branch,, Henrico Co.
Hunt, Edward, 1636, by John Dunston, James City Co.
Hunt, Ralph, 1636, by John Chandler, Elizabeth Citie Co.
Hunt, Thomas, 1636, by Thomas Hunt, Accomack Co.
Hunt, Thos. 1637, by Capt. Thomas Osborne, Henrico Co.
Hunt, Tho., 1643, by Edward Dobson, ———— Co.
Hunt, Joseph, 1650, by John Sevier, ———— Co.
Hunter, Richard, 1646, by Thomas Brown, Lower Norfolk Co.
Hunter, James, 1653, by John Joliffe, Lower Norfolk Co.
Hunter, James, 1653, by Wm. Johnson, Lancaster Co.
Hunter, Wm., 1651, by Edward Degg, Esq., Yorke Co.
Hunter, Richard, 1652, by Gregory Parrett, Lower Norfolk Co.
Hunter, James, 1652, by Nathaniel Bacon, Isle of Wight Co.
Hunter, Jon., 1642, by Stephen Gill, ———— Co.
Hunter, Mary, 1646, by David Jones, Charles City Co.
Hunter, Archibald, —, by Mr. Robt. Fontaine, Lower Norfolk Co.
Huntington, Lydia, 1642, by Andrew Terry, ———— Co.
Huntington, Andrew, 1642, by Andrew Terry, ———— Co.
Huntless, Edward, 1651, by John Rookwood, Gent., Northumberland
    Co.
Huntley, Edw., 1651, by Lieut. Coll. Giles Brent, Northumberland Co.
Huntley, Robt., 1652, by Littleton Scarburg, ———— Co.
Huntley, John, 1655, by George Truett, Northampton Co.
Huntly, Hannah, 1654, by Capt. David Mansell, Westmoreland Co.
Huntly, Edw., 1654, by Lieut. Coll. Giles Brent, Westmoreland Co.
Hurd, Ann, 1650, by James Hurd (her husband), ———— Co.
Hurd, Chris., 1652, by Tho. and Wm. Leithermore, ———— Co.
Hurd, Fra., 1652, by Capt. Augustine Warner, ———— Co.
Hurdis, Wm., 1635, by Jno. Sparkes, ———— Co.
Hurim, Nowell, 1642, by Joseph Royall, ———— Co.
Hurisatt, Natha., 1653, by Tho. Davis, ———— Co.
Hursh, Gilbert, 1649, by Robert Mosely, Gent., ———— Co.
Hurrs, Eliza., 1651, by Coll. Richard Lee, Esq., Gloucester Co.
Hurt, Tho., 1653, by Nicho. Meriwether, Northumberland Co.
Hurt, Edward, 1650, by Mr. James Williamson, ———— Co.
Hurt, Wm., 1650, by Mr. Stephen Hamelin, Charles City Co.
Husband, Tho., 1649, by Wm. Moore, ———— Co.
Huse, Kath., 1652, by Mr. Peter Knight, Gloucester Co.
Huse, Abigael, 1650, by Mr. James Williamson, ———— Co.
Huse, John, 1648, by Mr. Phillip Bennet, Nansemond Co.
Huses, Mary, 1651, by William Barber, Yorke Co.

Husey, David, 1648, by Wm. Edwards, and Rice Edwards James City Co.
Husley, Eliza., 1637, by Richard Bennett, New Norfolk Co.
Husly, James, 1654, by Francis Smith and Mr. John Smith, Westmoreland Co.
Husman, Tho., 1654, by Walter Pritchard, ——— Co.
Huson, John, 1639, by Georg Mallen, James City Co.
Huson, Elizabeth, 1638, by John Clarkson, Charles River Co.
Huson, Tho., 1637, by Edward Travis, James City Co.
Huss, Edward, 1652, by John Pouncey, ——— Co.
Hussey, Milkey, 1652, by Tho. Green, ——— Co.
Hussey, David, 1648, by Wm. Edwards and Rice Edwards, James River Co.
Hust, James, 1653, by Wm. Debram, ——— Co.
Huston, Robt., 1652, by Edward Revell, Northampton Co.
Huston, John, 1656, by Tho. Rolfe, Gent., James City Co.
Hutchin, Eliz., 1642, by Wm. Warren, ——— Co.
Hutcheson, Wm., 1652, by Capt. Augustine Warner, ——— Co.
Hutcheson, Jane, 1653, by Mr. Henry Soanes, Gloucester Co.
Hutcheson, William, 1637, by John Wilkins, New Norfolk Co.
Hutcheson, John, 1655, by Mrs. Margaret Brent, Lancaster Co.
Hutchins, Lewis, 1650, by Capt. Moore Fautleroy, ——— Co.
Hutchins, Fra., 1654, by Capt. David, Mansell, Westmoreland Co.
Hutchins, Sarah, 1654, by Francis Smith and Mr. John Smith, Westmoreland Co.
Hutchins, Isaac, 1637, by Capt. Thomas Osborne, Henrico Co.
Hutchinson, John, 1651, by Lieut. Collo. Giles Brent, Northumberland Co.
Hutchinson, Hector, 1652, by Nathaniel Bacon, Isle of Wight Co.
Hutchinson, Andre, 1652, by Nathaniel Bacon, Isle of Wight Co.
Hutchinson, Edward, 1639, by Stephen Webb, James City Co.
Hutchinson, Nich., 1638, by Thomas Burbage, Accomack Co.
Hutchinson, John, 1654, by John Wyre, John Gillet, Andrew Gibson and John Phillipps, ——— Co.
Hutchinson, Eliz., 1650, by Richard Tye and Charles Sparrowe, Charles City Co.
Hutchinson, Wm., 1654, by Nicho. Merywether, Westmoreland Co.
Hutchinson, Enoch, 1655, by Wm. Wright, Gent., Nansemond Co.
Hutchinson, Francis, 1636, by Fransic Maulden, ——— Co.
Hutchinson, James, 1637, by John Redman and John Neale, Accomack Co.
Hutchinson, Wm., 1636, by John Wilkins, Accomack Co.
Hutchinson, James, 1636, by John Neale, Accomack Co.
Hutchinson, Edward, 1638, by Joseph Farge, Charles City Co.
Hutchinson, Eliz., 1638, by Thomas Dew, Upper New Norfolk Co.
Hutson, Robert, 1651, by James Baldrige and Capt. Tho. Baldrige, Northumberland Co.
Hutt, Tho., 1652, by Mr. James Warradine, ——— Co.
Hutt, Joseph, 1653, by Tho. Sawyer, ——— Co.
Hutt, Wm., 1650, by Mr. James Williamson, ——— Co.
Hutt, Thom., 1637, by Capt. Henry Browne, James City Co.

Hutter, James, 1650, by Lawrence Peters, Nansemond Co.
Huttey, John, 1650, by Jervace Dodson, Gent., Northumberland Co.
Huttibell, Eliza, 1653, by Edward Hall, Lower Norfolk Co.
Hutton, James, 1653, by Wm. Wyatt, Gloucester Co.
Hutton, Fra., 1650, by Tho. Gerrord, Gent., Northumberland Co.
Hutton, Antho., 1650, by John Olian, James City Co.
Hutton, Eliz., 1654, by Col. Hump. Higgenson, Esq., and Abraham
    Moone, Westmoreland Co.
Hutton, Daniel, 1635, by Capt. Adam Thoroughgood, ——— Co.
Hutton, Joane, 1651, by Edward Deggs, Esq., Yorke Co.
Huttons, Wm., 1649, by Richard Vaughan, Northampton Co.
Hux, Alex., 1648, by Geo. Hardye, Tho. Wombwell and Peter Hall,
    Isle of Wight Co.
Hyde, Richard, 1638, by Edward Minter, James City Co.
Hyett, Tho., 1652, by Nathaniel Bacon, Isle of Wight Co.
Hygate, Christian, 1655, by Saml. Eddridge, ——— Co.
Hynde, Wm., 1653, by Wm, Haynes. ——— Co.
Hynde, Tho., 1642, by Stephen Hamblyn, York Co.
Hynes, Marimus, 1640, by Richard Hynes, New Norfolk Co.
Hynes, Sarah, 1640, by Richard Hynes, New Norfolk Co.
Hynes, Thos., 1637, by John Moone, Isle of Wight Co.
Hynes, Thomas, 1637, by John Moone, Isle of Wight Co.
Hyre, John, 1638, by Thomas Burbage, Accomack Co.
Hyves, Henry, 1638, by Capt. Christopher Wormley, Charles River Co.
Hyupp, Tho., 1654, by Nich. Merywether, Westmoreland Co.

I

Idam, Robt., 1637, by Capt. Thos. Flint, Warwick River Co.
Iden, Hen., 1643, by Sir Francis Wyatt, Kt., ——— Co.
Iker, John, 1635, by Wm. Clark, Eliz City Co.
Injam, Peter, 1654, by Capt. Nich. Marteaw, Westmoreland Co.
Inges, Michael, 1653, by Abraham Moon, Lancaster Co.
Inghram, Sara., 1652, by Henry Weeker, ——— Co.
Inghton, Ann, 1651, by Mr. John Bishopp, ——— Co.
Ingland, Jasse, 1652, by Francis England, Isle of Wight Co.
Inman, Hugh, 1650, by Wm. Holder, ——— Co.
Innervald, Tho., 1652, by Mrs. Elinor Brocas, Lancaster Co.
Ingram, Rich., 1642, by Hugh Gwyn, Gent., ——— Co.
Ingram, John, 1656, by Herbert Smith, Gent., Westmoreland Co.
Ingram, Toby, 1653, by Peter Knight and Baber Cutt, ——— Co.
Ingram, Richard, 1653, by Mr. Henry Soanes, Gloucester Co.
Ingram, John, 1652, by Tho. Gloscock, Lancaster Co.
Ingram, Joseph, 1652, by Mr. John Brown, Northampton Co.
Iran, Symon, 1653, by Robert Brasseur, Nansemond Co.
Ireland, Jno., 1640, by Thomas Harvey, James City Co.
Ireland, John, 1638, by Mathew Ireland Charles River Co.
Ireland, Martha, wife of John Ireland, 1638, by Mathew Ireland, Charles
    River Co.
Ireland, John, Junr., 1638, by Mathew Ireland, Charles River Co.
Ireland, Mathew, 1638, by Mathew Ireland, Charles River Co.

Ireland, Martha, 1638, by Mathew Ireland, Charles River Co.
Ireland, Jon., 1643, by Wm. Butler, James City Co.
Irish, Jone, 1653, by Ferdinando Austin, Charles City Co.
Irishman, Daniel, 1655, by Southy Littleberry, Northampton Co.
Ironmonger, Fra., 1651, by Mrs. Anna Bernard, Northumberland Co.
Ironmonger, Wm., 1651, by Mrs. Anna Bernard, Northumberland Co.
Ironmonger, Eliza, 1652, by Mrs. Anna Barnett, Gloucester Co.
Ironmonger, Fra., 1652, by Mrs. Anna Barnett, Gloucester Co.
Ironmonger, Wm., 1652, by Mrs. Anna Barnett, Gloucester Co.
Irwin, Wm., 1642, by Capt. Samuell Mathews, Esq., —— Co.
Isaac Christ., 1643, by Lt. Wm. Worleidge, —— Co.
Isac, ——, 1639, by William Davis, James City Co.
Isham, Dan., 1652, by Thomas Teakle, Northampton Co.
Isham, Roger, 1649, by Edmund, Scarburgh, Jr., Northampton Co.
Ishaleman, Dorman, 1655, by John Browne, Gent., Northampton Co.
Islea, Henry, 1652, by Henry Fleete, Lancaster Co.
Isom, Margaret, 1656, by Major Wm. Lewis, —— Co.
Isum, Math., 1643, by Richard Richards, Charles River Co.
Ison, Edward, 1642, by Robert Lawrence, Isle of Wight Co.
Issall, Timothy, 1656, by Capt. Wm. Canfell, Surry Co.
Issabell, Sandie, 1655, by Lt. Col. Anthony Ellyott, —— Co.
Ivell, John, 1637, by Stephen Charlton, Accomack Co.
Ives, Robt., 1643, by Capt. Samuell Mathews, Esq., —— Co.
Iveson, Abr., 1636, by James Vanerit, Elizabeth City Co.
Ivory, Geo., and Florence his wife, 1653, by Robert Brasseur, Nansemond Co.

J

Jack, Wm., 1652, by Thomas Teakle, Northampton Co.
Jackgive, John, 1639, by Capt. Robt. Felgate, Charles River Co.
Jackleston, Hum., 1654, by Col. Argoll Yardley, Northampton Co.
Jacksall, Richard, 1655, by Lt. Col. Tho. Swan, Surry Co.
Jackson, Sam., 1654, by John Watson and John Bognall, Westmoreland Co.
Jackson, Wm., 1635, by Wm. Barber (a mariner), Charles City Co.
Jackson, Thos., 1635, by Mr. Geo. Keth, Charles River Co.
Jackson, Robert, 1635, by John Jackson, —— Co.
Jackson, Rich., 1635, by Capt. Thos. Willowbye, Elizabeth City Co.
Jackson, L., 1636, by Wm. Clarke, Henrico Co.
Jackson, Robert, 1636, by John Lathropp, James City Co.
Jackson, Hen., 1636, by John Lathropp, James City Co.
Jackson, Randall, 1637, by Margaret Rogers, New Norfolk Co.
Jackson, Robt., 1637, by Capt. Adam Thoroughgood, Elizabeth City Co.
Jackson, Rich., 1637, by John Upton, Isle of Wight Co.
Jackson, Rich., 1637, by Lt. John, Upton Isle of Wight Co.
Jackson, Lanc., 1638, by Benjamin Carrill, James City Co.
Jackson, Wm., 1638, by Wm. Baker, and Associates, Charles City Co.
Jackson, Rich., 1643, by Casar Puggett, Lower Norfolk Co.
Jackson, Wm., 1646, by Sir William Berkley, —— Co.
Jackson, Jane, 1643, by Wm. Berryman, Northampton Co.

Jackson, Robt., 1643, by Wm. Berryman, Northampton Co.
Jackson, Jonah, 1643, by Wm. Berryman, Northampton Co.
Jackson, Wm., 1642, by Christopher Boyce, ——— Co.
Jackson, Eliza, 1642, by Daniell Lewellyn, ——— Co.
Jackson, Wm., 1642, by Stephen Gill, Yorke River Co.
Jackson, Tho., 1656, by Mr. Martin Baker, New Kent Co.
Jackson, Wm., 1656, by Wm. Pulliam, New Kent Co.
Jackson, John, 1655, by Southy Littleberry, Northampton Co.
Jackson, Eliz., 1654, by Nich. Merywether, Westmoreland Co.
Jackson, Antho., 1653, by James Turner, ——— Co.
Jackson, Cuthbert, 1655, by Mr. Tho. Ballard, Gloucester Co.
Jackson, Ursula, 1655, by Mr. Tho. Peck, Gloucester Co.
Jackson, Mary, 1654, by Tho. Deynes, ——— Co.
Jackson, John, 1654, by Fra. Spright, Nansemond Co.
Jackson, Hen., 1642, by Lieut. Francis Mason, ——— Co.
Jackson, Mary, 1639, by Edward Travis, James City Co.
Jackson, Mary, 1639, by Tristram Nosworthy, Upper Norfolk Co.
Jackson, Patrick, 1640, by Richard Williams, Charles City Co.
Jackson, Robt., 1653, by Wm. Hardidge, Northumberland Co.
Jackson, Jon., 1653, by Robert Capps and Robert Spring, ——— Co.
Jackson, Anne, 1653, by Wm. Hunt., ——— Co.
Jackson, Richd., 1653, by Tho. Holmes, York Co.
Jackson, Phillip, 1651, by Jonos Jackson, Northampton Co.
Jackson, Ann, 1653, by Xpher Rivers, ——— Co.
Jackson, James, 1651, by Mr. Rowland Lawson, ——— Co.
Jackson, Wm., 1652, by Mrs. Jane Harmer, Northumberland Co.
Jackson, Ralph, 1652, by John Paunsey, ——— Co.
Jackson, John, 1652, by Lt. Coll. John Cheesman, ——— Co.
Jackson, Don., 1652, by John Robinson, Jr., Northampton Co.
Jackson, Jane, 1652, by Mr. Wm. Waters, Northampton Co.
Jackson, John, 1649, by Capt. Ralph Wormeley, ——— Co.
Jackson, Tho., 1649, by Capt. Ralph Wormeley, ——— Co.
Jackson, John, 1650, by Mr. James Williamson, ——— Co.
Jackson, Wm., 1650, by Mr. James Williamson, ——— Co.
Jackson, Charles, 1649, by Richard Parrett, ——— Co.
Jackson, Tho., 1650, by Mrs. Winefrid Morrison, ——— Co.
Jackson, John, 1643, by John Norton, James City Co.
Jackson, John, 1650, by Lewis Burwell, Gent., Northumberland Co.
Jackson, Antho., 1650, by William Gooch, Gent., ——— Co.
Jackson, Walter, 1643, by Capt. Samuell Mathews, Esq., ——— Co.
Jackson, Wm., 1648, by John Seward, Isle of Wight Co.
Jackson, Ann, 1647, by Stephen Harsey and Nicho. Waddilow, North-
    ampton Co.
Jacob, Wm., 1652, by Clement Thrush, Lancaster Co.
Jacob, Fra., 1653, by John Day, Gloucester Co.
Jacob, Richard, 1653, by Capt. Wm. Whittington, Northampton Co.
Jacob, Susan, 1654, by John Thomas, Nansemond Co.
Jacob, Andrew, 1638, by Thomas Swan, James Citie Co.
Jacob, Andrew, 1635, by Wm. Swan, James Co.
Jacob, Martha, 1642, by Joseph Royall, ——— Co.
Jacob, William, 1636, by Wm. Reoper, Accomack Co.

Jacob, Willi, 1637, by Peter Roy and William Jacob, Isle of Wight Co.
Jacob, Richard, 1647, by Wm. Whitington, Northampton Co.
Jacobson, Jacob, 1650, by John Sevier, ———— Co.
Jaine, Tho., 1650, by Robert Bird, ———— Co.
Jakes, John, 1652, by Capt. Augustine Warner, ———— Co.
James, Robt., 1636, by Edward Osborne, Henrico Co.
James, Wm., 1636, by James Vanerit, Elizabeth City Co.
James, Wm., 1637, by William Parry, New Norfolk Co.
James, Mary, 1637, by Wm. Spencer, ———— Co.
James, Wm., 1642, by William Prior, Gent., ———— Co.
James, Jon., 1637, by Capt. Adam Thoroughgood, New Norfolk Co.
James, Robert, 1637, by Capt. Thomas Osborne, Henrico Co.
James, Samll., 1643, by Lt. Wm. Worleidge, ———— Co.
James, Jon., 1643, by Georg Levitt, ———— Co.
James, Michael, 1644, by Thomas Davis, Upper Norfolk Co.
James, Alice, 1650, by Wingfield Webb and Richard Pate, ———— Co.
James, Wm., 1655, by Patrick Miller, Lancaster Co.
James, Anne, 1655, by Peter Ford, Gloucester Co.
James, Wm., 1654, by Toby Smith, Lancaster Co.
James, Renold, 1654, by Walter Dickenson, Lancaster Co.
James, Wm., 1654, by Walter Dickenson, Lancaster Co.
James, Richard, 1654, by Abraham Moon, Gloucester Co.
James, John, 1654, by Wm. Beach, Westmoreland Co.
James, Wm., 1654, by Wm. Beach, Westmoreland Co.
James, Rich., 1654, by Nath. Pope, Westmoreland Co.
James, Eliz., 1654, by Nath. Pope, Westmoreland Co.
James, Wm., 1654, by Nath. Pope, Westmoreland Co.
James, Richard, 1640, by Thomas Stegg, Charles City Co.
James, Thomas, 1639, by Thomas Sheppey, Henrico Co.
James, John, 1639, by Lieut. Richard Popeley, ———— Co.
James, Vernitt, 1652, by John Robbins, Northampton Co.
James, Fra., 1653, by Abraham Moon, Lancaster Co.
James, Wm., 1653, by Fra. Gower, Lancaster Co.
James, Richd., 1653, by John Merryman and Morgan Haynes, Lancaster
    Co
James, Walter, 1653, by Oliver Green, Gloucester Co.
James, George, 1652, by Mrs. Jane Harmer, Northumberland Co.
James, John, 1652, by Mrs. Jane Harmer, Northumberland Co.
James, David, 1653, by Coll. Wm. Taylor, Esq., Gloucester Co.
James, John, 1652, by Isaac Richeson, Lancaster Co.
Janes, Mary, 1652, by Richard Longe, ———— Co.
James, Edward, 1652, by Wm. Moore, ———— Co.
James, Richd., 1652, by Capt. Francis Morgan and Ralph Greene,
    Gloucester Co.
James, Wm., 1652, by Andrew Munrow, Northumberland Co.
James, Bryan, 1652, by Henry Weeker, ———— Co.
James, Patr., 1653, by Tho. Hallinard, Lancaster Co.
James, Watkin, 1652, by Richard Coleman, ———— Co.
James, Francis, 1649, by Stephen Gill, York Co.
James, Hen., 1649, by Mr. Wm. Hoccaday, ———— Co.
James, Richard, 1650, by Wm. Holder, ———— Co.

James, Wm., 1650, by Robert Bird, ——— Co.
James, Lucretia, 1650, by George Goldsmith, ——— Co.
James, Ann, 1650, by Richard Axom and Tho. Godwin, ——— Co.
James, Wm., 1650, by Silvester Thatcher and Tho. Whitlocke, ———
    Co.
James, Edw., 1650, by John Baytes, Northumberland Co.
James, John, 1650, by Tho. Blogg, Northumberland Co.
James, John, 1650, by John Essix, Northumberland Co.
James, John, 1650, by Nathaniell Jones, Northumberland Co.
James, Andrew, 1650, by Nathaniell Jones, Northumberland Co.
James, Antho., 1646, by Elizabeth and Ratchell Robins, Northampton
    Co.
James, Richard, 1643, by Obedience Robins, Gent., Northampton Co.
Jankin, Thomas, 1638, by Capt. Christopher Wormley, Charles River
    Co.
Jankins, Alice, 1642, by Lieut. Francis Mason, ——— Co.
Jankinson, Rich., 1637, by Humphrey Tabb, Eliz. City Co.
Jannaway, Susanah, 1639, by William Wigg, ——— Co.
Jarret, Ralph, 1649, by Stephen Gill, York Co.
Jarrie, Richard, 1654, by Thomas Binus, Surry Co.
Jarre, John, 1642, by Tho. Curtis, ——— Co.
Jarrell, Fitz., 1636, by Wm. Bibby, Accomack Co.
Jarvis, Tho., 1650, by Mr. Anthony Ellyot, ——— Co.
Jasper, John, 1641, by Thomas Mathews, ——— Co.
Jawes, Jon., 1635, by Capt. Adam Thoroughgood, ——— Co.
Jax., Eliz., 1637, by Mathew Edloe, ——— Co.
Jealy, Avis, 1653, by Coll. Fran. Epps, Esq., Charles City Co.
Jede, John, 1649, by Joseph Croshawe, Yorke Co.
Jeeves, John, 1654, by John Wyre, John Gillett, Andrew Gilson and
    John Phillipps, ——— Co.
Jefferson, Wm., 1650, by Mr. James Williamson, ——— Co.
Jefferson, Alice, 1648, by Tho. Ludwell, Gent., James City Co.
Jefferson, Mary, 1653, by Richard Carey, ——— Co.
Jefferson, John, 1635, by George Burtcher (his wife's son), James City
    Co.
Jefferson, John, 1637, by John Burcher, James City Co.
Jefferson, Robert, 1639, by Justinian Cooper, Isle of Wight Co.
Jefferson, James, 1638, by Mr. Walter Ashton, Charles City Co.
Jeffries, Thomas, 1637, by Richard Bennett, New Norfolk Co.
Jeffries, Jabe, 1637, by Robert Newman, New Norfolk Co.
Jeffries, Thomas, 1636, by Richard Bennett, ——— Co.
Jeffers, Thos., 1642, by John Beale, ——— Co.
Jeffers, John, 1640, by Randall Crew, Upper Norfolk Co.
Jeffery, Wm., 1652, by John Bayles, Lancaster Co.
Jeffery, Samuell, 1643, by Tho. Dew, Upper Norfolk Co.
Jefferyes, Mary, 1650, by Capt. Richard Bond, Charles City Co.
Jefferyes, Thomas, 1638, by Hugh Allen, Charles River Co.
Jefferys, Francis, 1651, by Mr. George Truhett, Northampton Co.
Jefferys, Wm., 1653, by Abraham Moon, Lancaster Co.
Jefferys, John, 1653, by Tho. Hawkins, Northumberland Co.
Jefferys, Hugh, 1655, by John Coole, James City Co.

Jefferys, John, 1639, by Lieut. Richard Popeley, ——— Co.
Jefferys, Job., 1639, by Robt. Newman, Warwick River Co.
Jefferys, Hen., 1636, by James Vanerit, Elizabeth City Co.
Jeffreys, Arthur, 1653, by Capt. Francis Patt, Northampton Co.
Jeffrys, John, 1654, by Capt. Nich. Marteaw, Westmoreland Co.
Jeffrys, Ann, 1655, by George Kibble, Lancaster Co.
Jego, Richard, 1635, by Capt. Adam Thoroughgood, ——— Co.
Jego, Nicho., 1646, by Geo. Ludlow, Esq., York Co.
Jelfe, Edwd., 1654, by Edw. Welch, ——— Co.
Jelly, Tho., 1656, by Mr. Jno. Paine, ——— Co.
Jemens, Peter, 1650, by Henry Peaseley, ——— Co.
Jeneric Rich., 1635, by Capt. Adam Thoroughgood, ——— Co.
Jenings, Thomas, 1636, by Walter Daniell, James City Co.
Jenings, Richard, 1636, by Wm. Clarke, Henrico Co.
Jenings, Symon, 1643, by Rich. Hoe, Gent., ———Co.
Jenings, Nath., 1643, by Wm. Lawrence, James City Co.
Jenison, Anthony, 1654, by John Wyre, John Gillet, Andrew Gilson
    and John Phillipps, ——— Co.
Jenison, Wm., 1654, by Clement Thurush, Lancaster Co.
Jenkins, Jon., 1637, by Francis Fowler, James River Co.
Jenkins, Thos., 1638, by Bennett Freeman, James City Co.
Jenkins, Katherine, 1643, by Wm. Morgan, ——— Co.
Jenkins, Sabina, 1643, by Elizabeth Hull, ——— Co.
Jenkins, Daniell, 1643, by William Mills, Isle of Wight Co.
Jenkins, Wm., 1642, by Stephen Gill, Yorke River Co.
Jenkins, Tho., 1656, by Richard Barnhouse, Gent., James City Co.
Jenkins, Charity, 1656, by John Billiott, Northampton Co.
Jenkins, Wm., 1655, by Patrick Miller, Lancaster Co.
Jenkens, Tho., 1654, by Nath. Pope, Westmoreland Co.
Jenkins, Edward, 1638, by Capt. Chrisopther Wormley, ——— Co.
Jenkins, John, 1653, by Edward Hall, Lower Norfolk Co.
Jenkins, Tho., 1642, by John Robins, ——— Co.
Jenkins, Fra., 1653, by John Hillier, Northumberland Co.
Jenkins, Wm., 1653, by Peter Knight, Northumberland Co.
Jenkins, David, 1653, by Mr. Henry Soanes, Gloucester Co.
Jenkins, John, 1654, by John Black, ——— Co.
Jenkins, Ja., 1652, by John Hatton, ——— Co.
Jenkins, Robert, 1652, by Mr. Geo. Foster, Northumberland Co.
Jenkins, Sibella, 1648, by Tho. Braughton, ——— Co.
Jenkins, David, 1642, by Hugh Gwyn, Gent., ——— Co.
Jenkins, John, 1648, by John Ellis, James Joones and John Taylor,
    Northampton Co.
Jenkinson, Richard, 1651, by Mr. Rowland Lawson, ——— Co.
Jenkinson, Fred., 1654, by Richd. Jones, James City Co.
Jenkinson, Fra., 1654, by John Wyre, John Gillet, Andrew Gilson and
    John Phillipps, ——— Co.
Jenning, Wm., 1635, by Thos. Shippey, ——— Co.
Jennings, Richard, 1636, by Elizabeth Hawkins, Charles River Co.
Jennings, Jon., 1635, by Francis Fowler, James City Co.
Jennings, John, 1637, by Francis Fowler, James River Co.
Jenings, Thomas, 1639, by Walter Daniell, James City Co.

Jennings, Tho., 1638, by Roger Davis, Charles City Co.
Jennings, Jon., 1638, by Edw. Travis and John Johnson, James City Co.
Jennings, Rich., 1638, by William Clarke, Henrico Co.
Jennings, Jon., 1637, by Edward Travis, James City Co.
Jennings, John, 1643, by Georg Fowler, ——— Co.
Jennings, John, 1656, by Wm. Pulliam, New Kent Co.
Jenings, Mathew, 1642, by Capt. Samuell Mathews, Esq., ——— Co.
Jennings, Richd., 1653, by Mathew Tomlin, Northumberland Co.
Jennings, Richard, 1651, by George Eaton, ——— Co.
Jennings, Edward, 1643, by John Wall, ——— Co.
Jenney, Richard, 1639, by John White, James Citie Co.
Jerman, David, 1648, by Mr. Thomas Davies, Isle of Wight Co.
Jernew, Francis, 1650, by Nicholas Jernew, Gent., ——— Co.
Jernew, Francis, 1650, by Nicho. Jernew, Yorke Co.
Jerrell, John, 1654, by Peter Knight, Northumberland Co.
Jervis, Thomas, 1642, by William Prior, Gent., ——— Co.
Jervis, Tho., 1652, by Peter Knight, Gloucester Co.
Jessett, Eliza., 1639, by John Osborne, James Citie Co.
Jewell, Robt., 1637, by Daniel Gookins, New Norfolk Co.
Jewerles, Jno., 1648, by George Read, Gent., ——— Co.
Jills, Jeffry, 1650, by Stephen Charlton, Northampton Co.
Jnoson, Derrick, 1653, by Anto. Hoskins, Northampton Co.
Jnoson, Robt., 1654, by John Watson and John Bognall, Westmoreland Co.
Jnoson, Mary, 1654, by John Watson and John Bognall, Westmoreland Co.
Jnoson, Ann, 1654, by Mark Foster, ——— Co.
Jnoson, James, 1654, by Abra. Moone, Lancaster Co.
Joanes, Eliza, 1637, by Margaret Rogers, New Norfolk Co.
Joanes, John, 1653, by Edward Harrington, Northampton Co.
Joanes, John, 1653, by Abraham Moone, Lancaster Co.
Joanes, Magd., 1653, by Abraham Moone, Lancaster Co.
Joanes, John, 1652, by Tho. Hackett, ——— Co.
Joames, John, 1653, by Major Abra. Wood, Charles City Co.
Joanes, Tho., 1652, by Col. Geo. Ludlow, Esq., Gloucester Co.
Joanes, Morgan, 1649, by John King, Yorke Co.
Jobb, Joane, 1637, by Thomas Davis, New Norfolk Co.
Jock, Wm., 1654, by Luke Billington, Accomac Co.
Joggins, Antho., 1635, by Francis Fowler, James City Co.
Jochett, Snalter, 1638, by Wm. Clays, Charles River Co.
Jockman, Wm., 1652, by Gilbert Blunt, ——— Co.
Johannes, Augustine, 1656, by Mr. Tho. Purifoy, ——— Co.
John, David, 1656, by Tabitha and Matilda Scarburgh, Northampton Co.
John, Thomas, 1651, by Richard Coleman, Yorke Co.
John, Hills, 1648, by Francis Ceely, ——— Co.
John, Parris, 1653, by Roger Walker, Northumberland Co.
Johns, Mary, 1652, by Nicho. George, Tho. Taberer and Humphry Clarke, ——— Co.
Johns, Richard, 1655, by Southy Littleberry, Northampton Co.
Johns, Richard, 1645, by Roger Johns, Northampton Co.

Johns, Jacob, 1645, by Roger Johns, Northampton Co.
Johnson, Jno., 1643, by Samuell Abbott, James City Co.
Johnson, Georg, 1636, by Ellinor Dey and Thos. Emmerson, Warwick River Co.
Johnson, Thomas, 1635, by Capt. Wm. Pierse, ——— Co.
Johnson, Robert, 1635, by Wm. Andrews, Accomac Co.
Johnson, Eliza, 1635, by Joseph Johnson, ——— Co.
Johnson, John, 1636, by Richard Cocke, ——— Co.
Johnson, Alice, 1635, by Wm. Carter, James City Co.
Johnson, Eliza, 1635, by William Carter, Henrico Co.
Johnson, John, 1637, by William Wilkinson, New Norfolk Co.
Johnson, Henry, 1635, by McWilliam Stone, ——— Co.
Johnson, Henry, 1637, by Richard Bennett, New Norfolk Co.
Johnson, Wm., 1636, by Wm. Johnson, Warwick Co.
Johnson, Mary, 1635, by Jno. Upton, Warrasquinoake Co.
Johnson, Rich., 1637, by Wm. Farrar, Henrico Co.
Johnson, Choyce, 1635, by Capt. Adam Thoroughgood, ——— Co.
Johnson, Israell, 1636, by Cheney Boyse, Charles City Co.
Johnson, Thos., 1635, by Capt. Adam Thoroughgood, ——— Co.
Johnson, Richard, 1635, by Capt. Adam Thoroughgood, ——— Co.
Johnson, Henry, 1635, by Richard Bennett, Grace (his wife), ——— Co.
Johnson, Rich., 1635, by Butler Clark and Pastor of Denbie, Warrasquinoake Co.
Johnson, Israell, 1637, by Cheney Boyes, Charles City Co.
Johnson, Mary, 1637, by John Upton, Isle of Wight Co.
Johnson, Jon., 1635, by William Wilkinson (minister), ——— Co.
Johnson, Mary, 1637, by Lt. John Upton, Isle of Wight Co.
Johnson, Wm., 1642, by William Prior, Gent., ——— Co.
Johnson, Wm., 1638, by John Gater, Lower New Norfolk Co.
Johnson, Georg, 1637, by Eleanor Day and Thos. Emmerson, Warwick River Co.
Johnson, Choyse, 1637, by Capt. Adam Thoroughgood, New Norfolk Co.
Johnson, Thomas, 1638, by Lt. Robt. Sheppard, James City Co.
Johnson, James, 1638, by Henry Catelyn, Upper Norfolk Co.
Johnson, Wm., 1643, by Sir Francis Wyatt, ——— Co.
Johnson, John, wife and three children, 1638, by Edward Travis and John Johnson, James City Co.
Johnson, Walter, 1638, by Edw. Travis and John Johnson, James City Co.
Johnson, Jon., 1637, by Edward Travis, James City Co.
Johnson, ——, wife and 2 children of Jon. Johnson, 1637, by Edw. Travis, James City Co.
Johnson, Walter, 1637, by Edward Travis, James City Co.
Johnson, Stephen, 1646, by Sir William Berkley, ——— Co.
Johnson, Wm., 1643, by Samuell Abbott, James City Co.
Johnson, Abra., 1648, by George White, Lower Norfolk Co.
Johnson, John, 1650, by John Garwood, Nansemond Co.
Johnson, Geo., 1656, by Nicholas Waddilow, Northampton Co.
Johnson, Eliza, 1656, by John Evans, Northampton Co.

Johnson, Gabriell,—, by Mr. Robt. Fontaine, Lower Norfolk Co.
Johnson, John, 1655, by Southy Littleberry, Northampton Co.
Johnson, Robt., 1655, by Wm. Wright, Gent., Nansemond Co.
Johnson, Richard, 1655, by John Nicholls, Northampton Co.
Johnson, Eliz., 1655, by John Hinman, Northampton Co.
Johnson, James, 1654, by Nich. Merywether, Westmoreland Co.
Johnson, Daniel, 1655, by Symon Symons, ——— Co.
Johnson, Richard, 1653, by Ralph Green, Gloucester Co.
Johnson, Xan., 1653, by James Turner, ——— Co.
Johnson, Benjamin, 1654, by Obed. Williams, York Co.
Johnson, Richard, 1655, by Mr. Anthony Langston, New Kent Co.
Johnson, John, 1655, by Tho. Willess, Lancaster Co.
Johnson, Stephen, 1655, by John Motley, Northumberland Co.
Johnson, Wm., 1655, by Mr. Tho. Ballard, Gloucester Co.
Johnson, Elizabeth, 1655, by Martin Hamond, ——— Co.
Johnson, George, 1654, by Toby Smith, Lancaster Co.
Johnson, Eliz., 1654, by Richard Marshfield, ——— Co.
Johnson, Antho., 1654, by Coll. Jno. Matrom, Westmoreland Co.
Johnson, Ann, 1654, by Richard Allen, Northampton Co.
Johnson, Walter, 1654, by Major Miles Carey, Westmoreland Co.
Johnson, James, 1654, by Math. Pope, Westmoreland Co.
Johnson, Dennis, 1654, by John Wyre, John Gillet, Andrew Gilson and
    John Phillipps, ——— Co.
Johnson, Derrick, 1654, by John Wyre, John Gillett, John Phillipps
    and Andrew Gilson, ——— Co.
Johnson, Derick, 1653, by Eppy Bonison, Lancaster Co.
Johnson, Eliz., 1654, by John Watson and John Bognall, Westmoreland
    Co.
Johnson, John, 1642, by Lieut. Francis Mason, ——— Co.
Johnson, Mary, 1642, by John Stocker, Isle of Wight Co.
Johnson, Hen., 1642, by John Stocker, Isle of Wight Co.
Johnson, John, 1638, by Georg Mynifie (merchant), ——— Co.
Johnson, Walter, 1641, by Thomas Pitt, Charles City Co.
Johnson, Edward, 1639, by Edward Travis, James City Co.
Johnson, Elizabeth, 1639, by Richard Johnson, Henrico Co.
Johnson, Francis, 1639, by Richard Johnson, Henrico Co.
Johnson, Tymothy, 1639, by Justinian Cooper, Isle of Wight Co.
Johnson, John, 1639, by Christopher Boyse, Charles River Co.
Johnson, Wm., 1639, by WilliamBurdett, Accomack Co.
Johnson, John, 1639, by William Burdett, Accomack Co.
Johnson, Alice, 1641, by Robert Burnett, Isle of Wight Co.
Johnson, Georg, 1637, by Eleanor Day and Thom. Emmerson, Warwick
    River Co.
Johnson, John, 1638, by Thomas Todd, Lower New Norfolk Co.
Johnson, Alice, 1638, by William Carter, James City Co.
Johnson, Eliz., 1638, by William Carter, James City Co.
Johnson, Gilbert, 1653, by Tho. Hampton, ——— Co.
Johnson, James, 1653, by Tho. Hawkins, Northumberland Co.
Johnson, John, 1653, by Capt. Robt. Abrall, ——— Co.
Johnson, Jane, 1653, by Mr. Wm. Hoccoday, Yorke Co.

Johnson, James, 1653, by Edward Kemp, Geo. Cartlough and John Meredith, Lancaster Co.

Johnson, James, 1653, by Geo. Wadding, Lancaster Co.

Johnson, Henry, 1653, by Geo. Watts, Northumberland Co.

Johnson, Wm., 1653, by John Merryman and Morgan Haynes, Lancaster Co.

Johnson, Eliz., 1653, by Richard Haines, ——— Co.

Johnson, Peter, 1653, by Corbet Piddle, Northumberland Co.

Johsnon, Samuell, 1643, by John Neale, Gent., Northampton Co.

Johnson, Fra., 1653, by John Edwards, Lancaster Co.

Johnson, Richard, 1651, by Anthony Johnson, Northampton Co.

Johnson, John, 1651, by Mr. Robert Abrall, Yorke Co.

Johnson, Wm., 1653, by Coll. Fran. Epps, Esq., Charles City Co.

Johnson, James, 1652, by Wm. Ginsey, Gloucester Co.

Johnson, Eliza., 1652, by Isreall Johnson and Mrs. Richard Mayfield, ——— Co.

Johnson, Mary, 1652, by John Johnson, Northampton Co.

Johnson, John, 1648, by Randall Crew, Nansemond Co.

Johnson, Wm., 1648, by Randall Crew, Nansemond Co.

Johnson, Angle, 1649, by John Merriman, ——— Co.

Johnson, Thomas, 1649, by Mr. Henry Lee, York Co.

Johnson, John, 1649, by Tho. Bourne, ——— Co.

Johnson, John, 1649, by Frances Land, Norfolk Co.

Johnson, David, 1650, by Capt. Moore Fautleroy, ——— Co.

Johnson, Antho., 1650, by Capt. Moore Fautleroy, ——— Co.

Johnson, Jno., 1650, by Mr. Epaphroditus Lawson, ——— Co.

Johnson, Edward, 1643, by Wm. Butler, James City Co.

Johnson, Xpian, 1650, by William Gooch, Gent., ——— Co.

Johnson, James, 1650, by John Cooke, Northumberland Co.

Johnson, John, 1646, by Richard Moore and William Walton, Upper Norfolk Co.

Johnson, Jon., 1642, by Christopher Boyce, ——— Co.

Johnson, Tho., 1646, by Samuell Abbott, Nansemond Co.

Johnson, William, 1646, by Richard Moore and William Walton, Upper Norfolk Co.

Johnsons, Mary, 1638, by Thomas Clipwell, James City Co.

Joice, John, 1637, by Georg White, New Norfolk Co.

Joice, Peter, 1652, by George Kemp, Lower Norfolk Co.

Joiner, Edmund, 1656, by Wm. Justice, Charles City Co.

Joiner, Mary, 1652, by Arthur Robbins, Northampton Co.

Jolly, Margery, 1636, by Joseph Jolly (her husband), Charles River Co.

Jolly, Jon., 1636, by Richard Bennett, ——— Co.

Jolly, Margery, 1637, by Joseph Jolly, her husband, Charles River Co.

Jolly, Joseph, 1637, by Henry Perry, Charles River Co.

Jolly, John, 1637, by Richard Bennett, New Norfolk Co.

Jolly, John, 1642, by John Pratt, Henrico Co.

Jolly, Wm., 1656, by Mr. Henry Soanes, New Kent Co.

Jolly Joseph, 1637, by Henry Perry, Charles River Co.

Jolly, Jon., 1653, by John Bebey, Lancaster Co.

Jolley, John, 1648, by Richard Pettibon, ——— Co.

Jolly, Licha., 1648, by Richard Pettibon, ——— Co.

Jolly, Fra., 1648, by Richard Pettibon, ——— Co.
Jolly, Joseph, 1643, by Capt. Samuell Mathews, Esq., ——— Co.
Jones, Elias, 1635, by Mr. Geo. Keth, Charles River Co.
Jones, Thomas, 1636, by Walter Hacker, James River Co.
Jones, Sarah, 1636, by Joseph Jolly, Charles River Co.
Jones, David, 1636, by Bridges Freeman, ——— Co.
Jones, Thomas, 1635, by Richard Bennett, ——— Co.
Jones, Thomas, 1635, by David Jones, Charles City Co.
Jones, Thomas, 1635, by Henry Coleman, Elizabeth City Co.
Jones, Wm., 1635, by Thos. Harris, Henrico Co.
Jones, Jon., 1636, by Richard Cocke, ——— Co.
Jones, Thomas, 1637, by Rich. Bennett, New Norfolk Co.
Jones, Wm., 1637, by Thomas Weekes, James City Co.
Jones, Chri., 1637, by Mathew Edloe, ——— Co.
Jones, Rich., 1635, by Jno. Upton, Warrasquinoake, Co.
Jones, Thom., 1635, by Osbourne Jenkin, Charles City Co.
Jones, Humphrey, 1636, by Cheney Boyce, Charles City Co.
Jones, Morgan, 1650, by Capt. Moore Fautleroy, ——— Co.
Jones, Hugh, 1637, by William Parry, New Norfolk Co.
John, James, 1636, by John Dansey, James City Co.
Jones, Alice, 1636, by Georg. Travellor, Accomack Co.
Jones, Hugh, 1637, by William Wilkinson, New Norfolk Co.
Jones, Morris, 1637, by Wm. Reynolds, Charles River Co.
Jones, David, 1637, by Bridges Freeman, James City Co.
Jones, Robt., 1637, by Capt. Henry Browne, James City Co.
Jones, Evan, 1635, by Charles Harwer, ——— Co.
Jones, Edward, 1635, by Capt. Adam Thoroughgood, ——— Co.
Jones, Jon., 1536, by William Barber (a mariner), Charles City Co.
Jones, Edward, 1636, by Elizabeth Packer, Henrico Co.
Jones, Lewis, 1635, by Elizabeth Packer, Henrico Co.
Jones, Thomas, 1637, by Georg Burcher, James City Co.
Jones, Humphrey, 1637, by Cheney Boyes, Charles City Co.
Jones, Charles, 1636, by John Seaward, Isle of Wight Co.
Jones, Sarah, 1637, by Joseph Jolly, Charles River Co.
Jones, Rich., 1637, by John Upton, Isle of Wight Co.
Jones, Tho., 1642, by John Waltham, Jr., Accomac Co.
Jones, Rich., 1635, by Francis Fowler, James City Co.
Jones, Thos., 1635, by Christopher Woodard, ——— Co.
Jones, Rich., 1635, by William Swan, James Co.
Jones, Hugh, 1635, by Willaim Wilkinson (minister), ——— Co.
Jones, Richard, 1637, by Lt. John Upton, Isle of Wight Co.
Jones, Richard, 1637, by Francis Fowler, James River Co.
Jones, James, 1641, by Stephen Charlton, Accomack Co.
Jones, Hugh, 1637, by Daniell Gookins, New Norfolk Co.
Jones, Hugh, 1637, by Daniell Gookins, New Norfolk Co.
Jones, Wm., 1637, by Capt. Thomas Osborne, Henrico Co.
Jones, Rich., 1637, by Argoll Yeardly, New Norfolk Co.
Jones, Edward, 1637, by Elizabeth Parker, Henrico Co.
Jones, Lewis, 1637, by Elizabeth Parker, Henrico Co.
Jones, Mandlin, 1637, by James Knott, New Norfolk Co.

Jones, Rich., 1638, by Ambrose Bennett, Isle of Wight Co.
Jones, John, 1638, by Percivall Champion, Upper New Norfolk Co.
Jones, John, 1638, by Randall Crew, Upper New Norfolk Co.
Jones, Wm., 1638, by Capt. Tho. Harris, Henrico Co.
Jones, Jon., 1638, by Wm. Baker and Associates, Charles City Co.
Jones, Hannah, 1638, by Thomas Stampe, James City Co.
Jones, Richard, 1638, by Thomas Swan, James Citie Co.
Jones, Wm., 1637, by Arthur Smith, Isle of Wight Co.
Jones, Richard, 1648, by John Landmand, Nansimond Co.
Jones, Hester, 1644, by James Taylor, and Lawrence Baker, James City Co.
Jones, Robt., 1646, by Sir William Berkley, ———— Co.
Jones, Wm., 1650, by Mrs. Frances Townshend, Northumberland Co.
Jones, Thos., 1642, by Adam Cooke, Charles Co.
Jones, Walter, 1642, by Cornelius de Hull, ———— Co.
Jones, Isaac, 1643, by Edward Murfey and John Vaughan, ———— Co.
Jones, Foulke, 1642, by Stephen Webb, James City Co.
Jones, Evan, 1642, by John Moone, Isle of Wight Co.
Jones, Nicholas, 1642, by Hugh Gwyn, Gent., ———— Co.
Jones, John, 1656, by Geo. Abbott, Nansemond Co.
Jones, Wm., 1656, by Griffith Deckinson, ———— Co.
Jones, Tho., 1655, by Mr. John Mottrom, Northumberland Co.
Jones, Morgan, —, by Henry Wesgate, Lower Norfolk Co.
Jones, Tho., 1655, by George Truett, Northampton Co.
Jones, Ann, 1655, by Mary Lewis, Northampton Co.
Jones, Murell, 1656, by Tabitha and Matilda Scarburgh, Northampton Co.
Jones, Kath., 1655, by Wm. Bothane, Westmoreland Co.
Jones, Wm., 1655, by John Dorman, Northampton Co.
Jones, Margarett, 1654, by Francis Smith and Mr. John Smith, Westmoreland Co.
Jones, Henry, 1656, by Tho. Harris, Lancaster Co.
Jones, Tho., 1655, by Christopher Calvert, Northampton Co.
Jones, Elizabeth, 1654, by James Yates, ———— Co.
Jones, David, 1654, by Nich. Merywether, Westmoreland Co.
Jones, Mandlin, 1655, by Tho. Jones, James City Co.
Jones, Richard, 1654, by Wm. Mills, Lancaster Co.
Jones, Henry, 1655, by Mrs. Margaret Brent, Lancaster Co.
Jones, Roger, 1655, by Mr. Anthony Langston, New Kent Co.
Jones, John, 1655, by John Withers, Westmoreland Co.
Jones, Farn, Jr., 1655, by George Parker, Northampton Co.
Jones, Sarah, 1655, by George Parker, Northampton Co.
Jones, Farmer, Sr., 1655, by George Parker, Northampton Co.
Jones, Wm., 1655, by Robt. Priddy, New Kent Co.
Jones, Wm., 1655, by Francis Clay, Gent., Northumberland Co.
Jones, Amy, 1655, by Henry Barlow, ———— Co.
Jones, Tho., 1654, by Toby Smith, Lancaster Co.
Jones, Mary, 1654, by Nich. Wadilow, Northampton Co.
Jones, Ann, 1655, by John Lynge, James City Co.
Jones, Jno., 1655, by Nich. Bush, James City Co.
Jones, Wm., 1654, by Abraham Moone, ———— Co.

Jones, Tho., 1654, by R. Lawson, ——— Co.
Jones, James, 1654, by Peter Knight, Northumberland Co.
Jones, Robert, 1653, by Mathew Williams, James City Co.
Jones, John, 1654, by John Grey, Northmapton Co.
Jones, Ann, 1654, by Capt. David Mansell, Westmoreland Co.
Jones, John, 1654, by Nath. Pope, Westmoreland Co.
Jones, Rich., 1654, by Nath. Pope, Westmoreland Co.
Jones, Davy, 1654, by Abra. Moone, Lancaster Co.
Jones, Richard, 1653, by Eppy Bonison, Lancaster Co.
Jones, Edward, 1654, by by Edward Gilla, James City Co.
Jones, Ben, 1654, by John Watson and John Bognall, Westmoreland Co.
Jones, Mabill, 1654, by John Watson and John Bognall, Westmoreland Co.
Jones, Jon., 1642, by Capt. Samuell Mathews, Esq., ——— Co.
Jones, Hen., 1642, by Capt. Samuell Mathews, Esq., ——— Co.
Jones, Howell, 1642, by Capt. Samuell Mathews, Esq., ——— Co.
Jones, Thomas, 1642, by Capt. Samuell Mathews, Esq., ——— Co.
James, Owen, 1638, by Georg Mynifie (merchant), ——— Co.
Jones, Phillipps, 1641, by Samuell Firment, Upper New Norfolk Co.
Jones, Eliza, 1641, by Thomas Babb, Upper New Norfolk Co.
Jones, Walter, 1639, by Richard Preston, Upper New Norfolk Co.
Jones, Alice, 1639, by Rich. Hoe, James City Co.
Jones, Hamon, 1639, by Thomas Stamp, James City Co.
Jones, Morgan, 1639, by Samuell Watkeyes, Charles River Co.
Jones, Edward, 1639, by Edward Drew, Accomack Co.
Jones, John, 1639, by Robert Eley, Isle of Wight Co.
Jones, Katherine, 1639, by Thomas Smith, Accomac Co.
Jones, William, 1639, by Thomas Marsh, Upper Norfolk Co.
Jones, Elizabeth, 1640, by William Jones, her husband, Accomack Co.
Jones, John, 1639, by John Bell, Charles River Co.
Jones, Samuell, 1638, by Capt. Christopher Wormley, Charles River Co.
Jones, Reynold, 1642, by William Connhoe, ——— Co.
Jones, Wm., 1642, by John Robins, ——— Co.
Jones, Wm., 1638, by Mr. Walter Ashton, Charles City Co.
Jones, Tho., 1638, by John George, Charles City Co.
Jones, Henry, 1638, by Wm. Rainshaw, Lower New Norfolk Co.
Jones, Wm., 1639, by Georg Minifye, Esq., Charles River Co.
Jones, John, 1653, by Charles Scarburg, Northampton Co.
Jones, Mary, 1652, by Arthur Upshall, Northampton Co.
Jones, Wilncott, 1653, by Peter Knight and Baber Cutt, ——— Co.
Jones, Richard, 1653, by Mr. Wm. Hoccoday, Yorke Co.
Jones, Wm., 1653, by Wm. Leech, Lancaster Co.
Jones, Susan, 1653, by Jervais Dodson, Northumberland Co.
Jones, Wm., 1653, by Edward Kemp, Geo. Cortlough and John Mere-
    dith, Lancaster Co.
Jorvis, Sarah, 1653, by Tho. Griffin, Lancaster Co.
Jones, Wm., 1653, by George Wadding, Lancaster Co.
Jones, Wm., 1653, by Francis Clay, Northumberland Co.
Jones, Hugh, 1653, by James Bonner, Lancaster Co.
Jones, Rowland, 1653, by Wm. Debram, ——— Co.
Jones, John, 1653, by Wm. Hardidge, Northumberland Co.

Jones, Edmond, 1653, by John Earle, Northumberland Co.
Jones, Vincent, 1653, by Tho. Bourne, Lancaster Co.
Jones, Reg., 1653, by John Edwards, Lancaster Co.
Jones, Silvester, 1653, by Peter Knight, Northumberland Co.
Jones, Jon., 1652, by Wm. Colborne, Northampton Co.
Jones, Wm., 1653, by Capt. Nathaniel Hurd, Warwick Co.
Jones, Richd., 1653, by James Johnson, Nansemond Co.
Jones, Hugh, 1653, by John Phillips, ——— Co.
Jones, Jon., 1653, by Corbet Piddle, Northumberland Co.
Jones, Fra., 1654, by Edward Revel, Northampton Co.
Jones, Wm., 1651, by Tho. Hales and Tho. Sheppard, Northumberland
    Co.
Jones, Hen., 1651, by Mr. Rowland Burnham, ——— Co.
Jones, Thomas, 1651, by Richard Turney, Northumberland Co.
Jones, Henry, 1651, by Lieut. Collo. Giles Brent, Northumberland Co.
Jones, Tho., 1651, by Phillip Hunley, ——— Co.
Jones, Flor., 1651, by Mr. Wm. Armestead, ——— Co.
Jones, William, 1651, by Mr. Arthur Price, Yorke Co.
Jones, Isaac, 1651, by Edward Deggs, Esq., Yorke Co.
Jones, Wm., 1651, by Wm. Rennoles, Northumberland Co.
Jones, Wm., 1651, by Wm. Vincent, Northumberland Co.
Jones, Wm., 1651, by Hugh Fauch and James Magregory, Northum-
    berland Co.
Jones, Evan, 1652, by Evan Griffith, Lancaster Co.
Jones, Wm., 1652, by Anthony Doney and Enoch Hawker, Lancaster
    Co.
Jones, Wm., 1652, by Mrs. Jane Harmer, Northumberland Co.
Jones, Christopher, 1652, by Mr. Tho. Brice, Lancaster Co.
Jones, Wm., 1652, by Capt. Francis Morgan and Ralph Green, Glou-
    cester Co.
Jones, Chr., 1652, by Mr. Henry Pitt, ——— Co.
Jones, Tho., 1652, by Mr. Henry Pitt, ——— Co.
Jones, Richard, 1652, by Tho. Holliwell, ——— Co.
Jones, Mary, 1652, by Richard Coleman, ——— Co.
Jones, Saml., 1652, by Richard Coleman, ——— Co.
Jones, Richard, 1653, by Mrs. Mary Brent, Northumberland Co.
Jones, Wm., 1652, by John Bayworth, ——— Co.
Jones, Morgan, 1652, by Edward Coles, Northumberland Co.
Jones, Mary, 1652, by Nicholas Waddilow, Northampton Co.
Jones, Wm., 1648, by John Saynes, James City Co.
Jones, Isaac, 1648, by Francis Fludd, York Co.
Jones, Wm., 1647, by Symon Symons, Nansemond Co.
Jones, Ann, 1648, by Thomas Lambert, Lower Norfolk Co.
Jones, John, 1648, by Tho. Lambert, Lower Norfolk Co.
Jones, Sam., 1649, by Capt. Ralph Wormeley, ——— Co.
Jones, Wm., Jr., 1649, by Mr. Wm. Hoccaday, ——— Co.
Jones, Tho., 1648, by Richard Pettibon, ——— Co.
Jones, Hugh., Jun., 1649, by Mr. Wm. Hoccaday, ——— Co.
Jones, Tho., 1649, by John Waltham, Northampton Co.
Jones, Wm., 1650, by Mr. James Williamson, ——— Co.
Jones, Leon, 1650, by Mr. James Williamson, ——— Co.

Jones, Richard, 1649, by Wm. Nesum and others, Northumberland Co.
Jones, Richard, 1649, by Tho. Dale, ——— Co.
Jones, Wm., 1649, by Richard Vaughan,, Northampton Co.
Jones, Tho., 1649, by Edmund Scarburgh, Jr., Northampton Co.
Jones, Kath., 1650, by George Goldsmith, ——— Co.
Jones, Rice, 1650, by Wm. Yarrett and Fra. Wittington, ——— Co.
Jones, Ri., 1650, by Capt. Moore Fautleroy, ——— Co.
Jones, Tho., 1650, by Capt. Moore Fautleroy, ——— Co.
Jones, Richard, 1650, by Wm. Holder, ——— Co.
Jones, Sarah, 1650, by Mr. Epaphroditus Lawson, ——— Co.
Jones, Joane, 1650, by Lieut. Wm. Worleich, ——— Co.
Jones, Elinor, 1650, by John Mattram, Northumberland Co.
Jones, Wm., 1650, by Sr. Tho. Luntsford, Kt., and Barronett, ———
    Co.
Jones, Yarmer, 1650, by Sr. Tho. Luntsford, Kt., and Barronett, ———
    Co.
Jones, Wm., 1643, by Henry Neale, James City Co.
Jones, Marg., 1650, by Lawrence Peters, Nansemond Co.
Jones, Mary, 1650, by Thomas Mulford, Nansemond Co.
Jones, Honour, 1650, by Thomas Mulford, Nansemond Co.
Jones, Marg., 1650, by Rice Jones, ——— Co.
Jones, Stephen, 1650, by Henry Peaseley, ——— Co.
Jones, Tho., 1650, by Richard Hawkins, Northumberland Co.
Jones, Wm., 1650, by John Essix, Northumberland Co.
Jones, Marian, 1646, by William Hockaday, York Co.
Jones, Winifred, 1646, by John Ashcomb, Upper Norfolk Co.
Jones, Henry, 1646, by John Ashcomb, Upper Norfolk Co.
Jones, James, 1643, by Capt. Samuell Mathews, Esq., ——— Co.
Jones, John, 1648, by John Seward, Isle of Wight Co.
Jordan, Georg., 1637, by Capt. Henry Browne, James City Co.
Jordan, Jon., 1635, by Thos. Butler Clark and Pastor of Denbie, War-
    rasquinoake Co.
Jordan, Anth., 1635, by John Moone, Warrasquinoake Co.
Jordan, Ann, 1655, by John Jenkins, Northampton Co.
Jordan, Patrick, 1655, by Matilda Scarbourgh, Northampton Co.
Jordan Dorothy, 1654, by Wm. Thorne, Northampton Co.
Jordan, Wm., 1654, by Wm. Thorne, Northampton Co.
Jordan, Georg., 1642, by Capt. Samuell Mathews, Esq., ——— Co.
Jordan, Tho., 1653, by John Ware, ——— Co.
Jordan, Edward, 1654, by Robert Holt, James City Co.
Jorden, Abbigall, 1648, by John Troy, James City Co.
Jorden, Ann., 1654, by James Barnaby, Northampton Co.
Jordin, Anne, 1653, by Agnes Barnes, Northampton, Co.
Jordain, Eliza, 1651, by Richard Smith, Northampton Co.
Jordaine, Jacob, 1649, by Mr. Moore, ——— Co.
Jordaines, Eliza, 1650, by Richard Smith, Northampton Co.
Joseph, Evan, 1639, by John Well, Charles City Co.
Joules, Thomas, 1652, by John Meredith, Lancaster Co.
Joy, Thomas, 1652, by Capt. Henry Fleete, Lancaster Co.
Joy, Asher, 1635, by Hugh Cox, Charles City Co.
Joy, Richard, 1656, by Wm. and Hancock Lee, Gloucester Co.

Joyce, Robert, 1637, by Nathaniel Floyd, Isle of Wight Co.
Joyce, Jno., 1635, by Mr. Geo. White, minister of the Word of God, ───── Co.
Joyce, John, 1637, by Thomas Weston, Charles River Co.
Joyce, Giles, 1654, by Toby Smith, Lancaster Co.
Joyce, Crowder, 1639, by Lieut. Richard Popeley, ───── Co.
Joyce, John, 1650, by Richard Tye and Charles Sparrowe, Charles City Co.
Joyce, Mart., 1650, by Lawrence Peters, Nansemond, Co.
Joyce, Mary, 1652, by Collo. Hugh Gwin, ───── Co.
Joyhe, John, 1635, by Samuel Weaver, ───── Co.
Joyner, Ambrose, 1637, by Edward Travis, James City Co.
Joyner, James, 1656, by John Wood, ───── Co.
Joyner, Mary, 1655, by Capt. George Floyd, New Kent Co.
Joyner, Mary, 1655, by Nich. Waddilow, Northampton Co.
Joyner, Mary, 1654, by Mr. Tho. Fowke, Westmoreland Co.
Joyner, Mary, 1652, by Nicholas Wadilow, Northampton Co.
Joyner, Thomas, 1646, by Elizabeth and Ratchell Robins, Northampton Co.
Juce, John, 1652, by Mrs. Elnor Brocas, Lancaster Co.
Juche, Oliver, 1638, by Stephen Hamblyn, Charles City Co.
Judd, Christ., 1642, by Adam Cooke, Charles Co.
Judd, Herbert, 1654, by Robert Holt, James City Co.
Judd, Herbert, 1651, by Edward Deggs, Gent., Yorke Co.
Judd, Eliza, 1642, by Adam Cooke, Charles Co.
Jue, Elias, 1638, by Jeremiah Dickinson, James City Co.
Jues, Timothy and Margaret his wife, —, by John Marshall, Lower Norfolk Co.
Juett, Francis, 1653, by Wm. Hardidge, Northumberland Co.
Jugan, Thos., and Elizabeth his wife, 1656, by Geo. Abbott, Nansemond Co.
Juges, Michael, 1653, by Wm. Thomas, Northumberland Co.
Jugleton, Edward, 1639, by John Dunston, James City Co.
Jugleton, Jacob, 1647, by Thomas Johnson, Gent., Northampton Co.
Junge, Jane, 1650, by Edward James, ───── Co.
Junkin, Robert, 1656, by Mr. Henry Soanes, New Kent Co.
Jurne, James, 1654, by Capt. Nich. Marteaw, Westmoreland Co.
Jury, Eliz., 1654, by Col. Hump. Higgenson, Esq., and Abraham Moone, Westmoreland Co.
Jury, Wm., 1650, by Mr. James Williamson, ───── —Co.
Just, Robt., 1654, by Arthur Nash, New Kent Co.
Justman, An., 1635, by McWilliam Stone, ───── Co.
Jyillings, Geo., 1653, by Mr. Wm. Debram, ───── Co.

K

Kaas, Robert, 1653, by James Turner, ───── Co.
Kable, Mary, 1637, by James Berry, Accomack Co.
Kaddle, Richard, 1653, by Ralph Hacker, Lancaster Co.
Kahan, Phillip, 1655, by Edmund Scarbourgh, Jr., and Littleton Scarbourgh, Northampton Co.

Kaiton, James, 1652, by Tho. Boswell, ——— Co.
Kallaway, Katherine, 1642, by John King, Charles River Co.
Kalman, John, 1650, by Richard Axomi and Tho. Godwin, ——— Co.
Kalmo of Cameno, 1637, by Hen. Woodhouse, New Norfolk Co.
Kan, Dorothy, ———, by Samuel Heely and John Carter, Surry Co.
Kann, Hanly, 1656, by Tabitha and Matilda Scarburgh, Northampton Co.
Karmon, Wm., 1648, by Lewis Burwell and Tho. Haws, York River Co.
Kate, James, 1643, by Capt. Samuell Mathews, Esq., ——— Co.
Kath, a French maid, 1650, by John Hany, Northumberland Co.
Kathorne, Lee, 1653, by Col. Wm. Taylor, Esq., Gloucester Co.
Katson, Edward, 1650, by John Garewood, Nansemond Co.
Katon, James, 1652, by Daniell Welch, Lancaster Co.
Kasey, Hester, 1638, by Wm. Rabnett, Warwick River.
Kayne, Wm., 1654, by Tho. Harmonson, Northampton Co.
Kayupp, Kath., 1643, by Sir. Francis Wyatt, Kt., ——— Co.
Keach, Christ., 1643, by Lt. Wm. Worleidge, ——— Co.
Keator, Tho., 1650, by Richard Axom, and Tho. Godwin, ——— Co.
Kedale, John, 1650, by Wingfield Webb and Richard Pate, ——— Co.
Kedbey, Thomas, 1639, by Thomas Marsh, Upper Norfolk Co.
Kedd, Wm., 1654, by Tobey Smith, Lancaster Co.
Keeding, Ann, 1639, by William Davis, James City Co.
Keelin, Sarah, 1638, by Elizabeth Grayne, Charles City Co.
Keely, Henry, 1654, by Nich. Merywether, Westmoreland Co.
Keely, Mundiff, 1656, by Margaret Miles, Westmoreland Co.
Keely, Elias 1637, by Daniell Gookins, New Norfolk Co.
Keene, Mary, 1653, by Tho. Keene, Northumberland Co.
Keene, Wm., 1653, by Tho. Kcene, Northumberland Co.
Keene, Tho., 1653, by Colo. Wm. Clayborne (Sec. of State), ———
     Co.
Keene, Susan, 1653, by Jervais Dodson, Northumberland Co.
Keene, Abraham, 1637, by Wm. Prior, Charles River Co.
Keffin, David, 1636, by John Wilkins, Accomack Co.
Kegs, Sarah, 1654, by James Yates, ——— Co.
Kelle, Xpher, 1655, by George Kibble, Lancaster Co.
Kelleston, Dungue, 1650, by John Landman, ——— Co.
Kelly, Alice, 1651, by John King, Gloucester Co.
Kellin, David, 1654, by Mrs. Mgt. Brent, Westmoreland Co.
Kelly, Alice, 1654, by Capt. John West, Esq., Gloucester Co.
Kelly, Elizabeth, 1653, by Samuell Parry, Lancaster Co.
Kelly, Thomas, 1652, by Richard King, Lower Norfolk Co.
Kelly, Abraham, 1643, by Wm. Berryman, Northampton Co.
Kelly, Bryan, 1638, by William Berryman, Accomack Co.
Kelly, Bryan, 1636, by John Neale, Accomack Co.
Kellum, Richard, 1649, by Nicholas Waddilowe, Northampton Co.
Kelman, Geo., 1650, by Richard Axom and Tho. Godwin, ——— Co.
Kelway, Tho., 1653, by Ferdinando Austin, Charles City Co.
Kembell, Thomas, 1642, by Stephen Gill, ——— Co.
Kemerley, Dor., 1652, by Tho. Hallinard, ——— Co.

Kemp, Tho., 1638, by Capt. Tho. Harris, Henrico Co.
Kemp, James, 1649, by Mr. Ralph Barlowe, Northampton Co.
Kemp, Tho., 1653, by John Jaliffe, Isle of Wight Co.
Kemp, Edmond, 1653, by Edward Kemp, Geo. Cortlough and John
    Meredith, Lancaster Co.
Kemp, Wm., 1652, by Tho. Steevens, Warrick Co.
Kemp, Tho., 1642, by Christopher Boyce, ——— Co.
Kemp, Evans, 1637, by Mathew Edloe, ——— Co.
Kemp, Tho., 1635, by Tho. Harris, Henrico Co.
Kempe, Kath., 1653, by Christopher Boyce, Northumberland Co.
Kempe, George, and Mary his wife, 1653, by Wm. Langly, Lower
    Norfolk Co.
Kempe, William, 1635, by Capt. Adam Thoroughgood, ——— Co.
Kempton, Wm., 1653, by Wm. Debram, ——— Co.
Keneller, Tho., 1649, by John Cabbedge, Lower Norfolk Co.
Kendal, Mary, 1653, by James Magregory and Hugh Fauch, Northum-
    berland Co.
Kendal, Wm., 1653, by James Magregory and Hugh Fauch, Northum-
    berland Co.
Kendall, Wm., 1652, by Tho. Hackett, ——— Co.
Kendall, Cha., 1653, by James Magregory and Hugh Fauch Northum-
    berland Co.
Kendall, Tho., 1653, by Colo. Wm. Clayborne (Sec. of State), ———
    Co.
Kendall, John, 1650, by Elyas Edmondes, ——— Co.
Kendall, John, 1638, by Wm. Hayward, Charles City Co.
Kendall, Wm., 1655, by John Nicholls, Northampton Co.
Kendall, Robt., 1636, by Wm. Armestead, Elizabeth City Co.
Ken, Henry, 1654, by Capt. John West, Esq., Gloucester Co.
Ken, Edwd., 1654, by Capt. John West, Esq., Gloucester Co.
Ken, Rich., 1654, by Capt. John West, Esq., Gloucester Co.
Keneis, Wm., 1654, by James Yates, ——— Co.
Keniston, Rich., 1655, by John Watson, Lancaster Co.
Kennell Hores, 1656, by Tabitha and Matilda Scarburgh, Northamp-
    ton Co.
Kennerly, Plule, 1637, by John Upton, Isle of Wight Co.
Kennett, Martin, 1638, by Geo. Mynifie (Merchant), ——— Co.
Kennett, Peter, 1655, by John Browne, Gent., Northampton Co.
Kennicke, Hugh, 1656, by Capt. Wm. Canfill, Surry Co.
Kennon, Geo., 1639, by Georg Minifie, Esq., Charles River Co.
Kenney, James, 1642, by John Robins, ——— Co.
Kenney Roger, 1638, by Abraham Wood, Charles City Co.
Kenseck, Edward, 1653, by James Watson, Isle of Wight Co.
Kennersly, Phillipp, 1635, by Jno. Upton, Warrasquinoake Co.
Kennersley, Phillip, 1637, by Lt. John Upton, Isle of Wight Co.
Kennso, Derrich, 1653, by Richard Carey, ——— Co.
Kenny, Rich., 1637, by Jonathon Langworth, New Norfolk Co.
Kenny, Richard, 1637, by Jonathon Longworth, New Norfolk Co.
Kenny, Edward, 1655, by Lt. Col. Anthony Ellyott, ——— Co.
Kenny Edmund, 1655, by John Woodward, Gloucester Co.

Kent, Nicho., 1653, by Francis Emperor, Hugh Gale and Edward Morgan, Lower Norfolk Co.
Kent, Robert, 1639, by Justinian Cooper, Isle of Wight Co.
Kent, Elizabeth, 1655, by Mr. Anthony Langston, New Kent Co.
Kent, Joseph, 1656, by John Wood, ——— Co.
Kerley, Richard, 1642, by Hugh Gwyn, Gent., ——— Co.
Kerby, Richard, 1651, by Mr. Arthur Price, Yorke Co.
Kerke, Thomas, 1637, by Thomas Sawyer, New Norfolk Co.
Kerle, Joan, 1662, by Mr. John Mottrom, Northumberland Co.
Kerney, David, 1654, by John Black, ——— Co.
Kerton, John, 1653, by Wm. Cox, ——— Co.
Kersh, John, 1650, by Elyas Edmondes, ——— Co.
Keth, Mary, 1650, by David Peibles, Charles City Co.
Keth, Barbara, 1656, by David Peibles, Charles City Co.
Keth, George, 1652, by Wm. Gautlett, ——— Co.
Keth, Barbary, 1653, by Nicholas Perry, Charles City Co.
Keth, Mrs. Martha, 1635, by Mr. Geo. Keth, Charles River Co.
Keth, Jon., 1635, by Mr. Geo. Keth, Charles River Co.
Ketle, Thos., 1635, by Thos. Butler Clerk and Pastor of Denbie, Warrasquinoake Co.
Ketchin, Nicholas, 1650, by Tho. Blogg, Northumberland Co.
Key, Robt., 1650, by William Gooch, Gent., ——— Co.
Key, Wm., 1650, by John Mattrum, Northumberland Co.
Key, Sarah, 1649, by Tho, Dale, ——— Co.
Key, Katharine, 1648, by Lewis Burwell, Gent., ——— Co.
Key, Tho., 1649, by Nicholas Waddilow, Northampton Co.
Key, Tho., 1648, by John Baldwin, Northampton Co.
Key, Peter, 1653, by Coll. Wm. Taylor, Esq., Gloucester Co.
Key, Adam, 1639, by Georg Minifye, Esq., Charles River Co.
Keye, John, 1654, by Tho. Harmanson, Northampton Co.
Keye, Tho., 1642, by John Towlson, Accomack Co.
Keyes Walter, 1650, by John Mangor, ——— Co.
Keyes, Thomas, 1640, by Robert Holt, James City Co.
Keyes, Daniell, 1638, by Joseph Boarne, Charles City Co.
Keyes, Tho., 1638, by Robt. Holt and Richard Bell, James City Co.
Keys, Tho., 1654, by Robert Holt, James City Co.
Keynan, John, 1655, by Edmund Scarbough, Jr., and Littleton Scarbourgh, Northampton, Co.
Keytin, Nicholas, 1639, by Lieut. Richard Popeley, ——— Co.
Kevin, Robt., 1642, by Justinian Cooper, Isle of Wight Co.
Kible, Joane, 1653, by John Edwards, Lancaster Co.
Kicke, Wm., 1643, by John Freeme, Charles Co.
Kickett, Christ, 1642, by William Connhoe, ——— Co.
Kidd, Tho., 1648, by Richard Lee, Gent., ——— Co.
Kiffe, Morris, 1656, by Tabitha and Matilda Scarburgh, Northampton Co.
Kigon, Karbury, 1643, by Wm. Storey, Upper Norfolk Co.
Kiggan, Cha., 1651, by Edmond Welch, ——— Co.
Kilbye, Henry, 1637, by Thomas Osborne, Jr., Henrico Co.
Killicke James, 1648, by Wm. W. Thomas, Elizabeth City Co.
Kilridge, Wm., 1636, by Capt. Thomas Willoughby, ———Co.

Kimberlin, Jon., 1642, by Walter Chiles, Charles Co.
Kineott, Rich., 1637, by David Mansell, James City Co.
Kindall, John, 1652, by Christopher Robinson and John Sturdwant, Henrico Co.
Kindall, Mary, 1652, by Mrs. Mary Brent, Northumberland Co.
Kinerose, Alex., 1654, by William Haward, Gloucester Co.
King, Alice, 1635, by Capt. Wm. Pierse, ——— Co.
King, Charles, 1650, by Mordecay Cooke, ——— Co.
King, Richard, 1650, by Capt. Moore Fantleroy, ——— Co.
King, Henry, 1635, by John Leonard, Warrasquinoake, Co.
King, Eliz., 1637, by John Upton, Isle of Wight Co.
King Mathias, 1642, by Geo. Addins, and Wm. Foster, ——— Co.
King, Eliz., 1642, by Wm. Barnard, Esq., Isle of Wight Co.
King, Eliza, 1637, by Lt. John Upton, Isle of Wight Co.
King, Jon., 1637, by Captain Thomas Panlett, Charles City Co.
King, John, 1643, by John Hoddin, ——— Co.
King, John, 1643, by Mr. Moore Fantleroy, Upper Norfolk Co.
King James, 1645, by Michael Masters, Henrico Co.
King, Ann, 1642, by John King (her husband), Charles River Co.
King, Katherine, 1642, by Thomas Guyer, ——— Co.
King, Wm., 1656, by Vincent Stanford, ——— Co.
King, John, 1655, by Capt. George Floyd, New Kent Co.
King, Henry, 1655, by Lt. Col. Anthony Ellyott, ——— Co.
King, John, 1654, by Nich. Wadilow, Northampton Co.
King Jno., 1654, by Mr. Francis Hamond, York Co.
King, Henry, 1654, by Mr. Francis Hamond, York Co.
King, Alex., 1654, by Mr. Francis Hamond, York Co.
King, Wm., 1642, by Capt. Samuell Mathews, Esq., ——— Co.
King, Alice, 1640, by Toby Smith, Warwick River Co.
King, Robt., 1653, by Charles Scarburg, Northampton Co.
King, Robert, 1653, by Edward Harrington, Northampton Co.
King, John, 1652, by Nicholas Wadilow, Northampton Co.
King, Richard, 1653, by John Hillier, Northumberland Co.
King, Kath., 1653, by Wm. Reynolds, Northumberland Co.
King, Mary, 1651, by Richard Kellum, Northampton Co.
King, Henry, 1646, by James Bruss, Northampton Co.
King, Jno., 1648, by Wm. Barret, ——— Co.
King, Robt., 1649, by Edmund Scarburgh, Northampton Co.
King, Edw., 1649, by Mr. Tho. Spake, Northumberland Co.
King, Ann, 1650, by Mr, Tho. Spake, Northumberland Co.
King, John, 1648, by John King and Laurence Ward, Isle of Wight Co.
King, Walter, 1650, by John Mangor, ——— Co.
King, Ri., 1650, by Mr. Epaphroditus Lawson, ——— Co.
King, John, 1650, by Henry Lee and Wm. Clapham, ——— Co.
King, Mathew, 1643, by James Whiting, ——— Co.
King, Mary, 1650, by John Hallawes, Gent., Northumberland Co.
King, Sarah, 1647, by John Sidiney, Lower Norfolk Co.
King, Jon., 1643, by Capt. Samuell Mathews, Esq., ——— Co.
King, Elizabeth, wife of John King, 1648, by John King and Laurence Ward, Isle of Wight Co.

King, Eliz., 1635, by Jno. Upton, Warrasquinoake Co.
Kingde, Pable, 1653, by Robt Capps and Robert Spring, ——— Co.
Kinge, Fra., 1653, by Capt. Giles Brent, Northumberland Co.
Kinge, Robt., 1652, by Christopher Robinson and John Sturdwant, Henrico Co.
Kinge, Anne, 1653, by Edward Dobson, ——— Co.
Kingman, Hen., 1653, by John Phillips, ——— Co.
Kingman, Lee, 1650, by John Hany, Northumberland Co.
Kingswell, Tho., 1642, by William Prior, Gent. ——— Co.
Kingsbury, John, 1642, by Lieut. Francis Mason, ——— Co.
Kingsbury, Robert, 1642, by William Prior, Gent., ——— Co.
Kingford, Nicholas, 1641, by Richard Jackson, Isle of Wight Co.
Kingsland, Nathan, 1648, by John Clarke, Lower Norfolk Co.
Kingsley, Wm., 1642, by Capt. Samuel Mathews, Esq., ——— Co.
Kingston, Jno., 1637, by Henry Perry, Charles River Co.
Kingswell, Edwd., 1648, by Lewis Burwell and Thomas Haws, York River Co.
Kingswell, Anthony, 1648, by Lewis Burwell and Tho. Haws, York River Co.
Knighton, John, 1643, by Capt, Samuell Mathews, Esq., ——— Co.
Kinkee, Kath., 1653, by Coll. Wm. Taylor, Esq., Gloucester Co.
Kinse, Edward, Sr., 1639, by Froncis Martin, Accomack Co.
Kinse, Edward Jr., 1639, by Froncis Martin, Accomack Co.
Kinse, Abigail, 1639, by Froncis Martin, Accomack Co.
Kinse, Elion, 1639, by Froncis Martin, Accomack Co.
Kinse, Eliza, 1639, by Froncis Martin, Accomack Co.
Kinsey, Edward, 1637 by Angoll Yeardly, New Norfolk Co.
Kinsey Paul, 1655, by Mr. Hugh Kinsey, Lancaster Co.
Kirby, Wm., 1650, by Richard Tye and Charles Sparrowe, Charles City Co.
Kirby, James, 1651, by Tho. Foote and John Barham, Northumberland Co.
Kirby, Ann, 1655, by Lt. Col. Anthony Ellyott, ——— Co.
Kirby, Hump., and Alice his wife, 1651, by Tho. Foote and John Barham,——— Co.
Kirbye, Thos. 1839, by Lieut. Richard Popeley, ——— Co.
Kirke, Mary, 1653, by Tho. Davis,
Kirke, John, 1651, by Lancaster Lovett, Lower Norfolk Co.
Kirke, Richard, 1651, by John Addeston, ——— Co.
Kirke, Tho., 1638, by Thomas Sawyer, New Norfolk Co.
Kirke, Tho., 1643, by Capt. John Upton, Isle of Wight Co.
Kirke, Bridgett, 1650, by Jewace Dodson, Gent. Northumberland Co.
Kirke, James, 1656, by John Wood, ——— Co.
Kirke, John, by Mr. Robt. Fontaine, Lower Norfolk, Co.
Kirshaw, Tho., 1646, by Joseph Croshawe, Charles River Co.
Kirtam, James, 1651, by Audery Bennett, Nansemond Co.
Kisfin, David, 1637, by John Wilkins, New Norfolk Co.
Kitchin, Elizabeth, 1652, by Tho. Hoane, ——— Co.
Kitchin, Jon., 1637, by Jonathan Langworth, New Norfolk Co.
Kitchin, Jon., 1638, by Joseph Harmon, James City Co.
Kitchen, Jon., 1637, by Jonathan Longworth, New Norfolk Co.

Kite, John, 1656, by William Bird, —— Co.
Kithley, Thomas, 1642, by Wm. Ireland and Robt. Wallis, Yorke Co.
Kittemue, James, 1651, by Mr. Wm. Armestead, —— Co
Kitson, Marmaduke, 1639, by John Dunston, James City Co.
Kitson, Merma., 1636, by John Dunston, James City Co.
Kleg, Edis, 1652, by Edward Revell, Northampton Co.
Kleg, Edis, 1632, by Andrew Munrow, Northumberland Co.
Knap, Tho., 1653, by John Holding, York Co.
Knapton, Jane, 1652, by Mr. Tho. Curtis, —— Co.
Knatchpoole, Jno., 1654, by Mr. Francis Hamond, York Co.
Knight, Edmund, 1642, by Thomas Emerson, —— Co.
Knight, Robert, 1638, by John Watkins, James Cittie.
Knight, Tho., 1644, by Edwyn Conaway, Northampton Co.
Knight, Mary, 1644, by Edwyn Conaway, Northampton Co.
Knight, John, 1656, by John Evans, Northampton Co.
Knight, John, 1655, by John Hinman, Northampton Co.
Knight, John, 1654, by John Watson and John Bognall, Westmoreland Co.
Knight, Rich., 1654, by Wm. Thorne, Northampton Co.
Knight Edm., 1638, by Epaphroditus Lawson, Upper New Norfolk Co.
Knight, Christollel, 1639, by John Pawley, James City Co.
Knight, Wm., 1642, by Henry Coleman, Elizabeth City Co.
Knight, John, 1652, by Christopher Lewis, Isle of Wight Co.
Knight, Fra., 1653, by Charles Scarburgh, Northampton Co.
Knight, Francis, 1652, by Littleton Scarburg, —— Co.
Knight, Wm., 1652, by Tho. Hackett, —— Co.
Knight, Fra., 1652, by Mr. Tho. Teagle, Northampton, Co.
Knight, Mary, 1653, by John Earle, Northumberland Co.
Knight, John, 1653, by John Earle, Northumberland Co.
Knight, Jon., 1653, by Mr. Henry Soanes, —— Co.
Knight, Mary, 1653, by Mr. Henry Soanes, —— Co.
Knight, Tho., 1653, by Mr. Henry Soanes, —— Co.
Knight, Wm., 1648, by Wm. Ewen, James City Co.
Knight, Robert, 1648, by Thomas Hart, James City Co.
Knight, John, 1642, by Hugh Gwyn, Gent., —— Co.
Knott, John, 1650, by John Hallawes, Gent., Northumberland Co.
Knott, James, 1560, by Richard Hawkins, Northumberland Co.
Knott, John, 1650, by John Hallowes, Gent., Northumberland Co.
Knighthill, John, 1652, by Peter Knight, Gloucester Co.
Knighton, Jno., 1650, by Richard Tye and Charles Sparrowe, Charles City Co.
Knocks, Wm., 1655, by Lt. Col. Anthony Ellyott, —— Co.
Knott, Eleanor, 1636, by James Knott, Elizabeth City Co.
Knopp, Wm., 1641, by Wm. Burdett, Accomack Co.
Knott, Elian, 1637, by James Knott, New Norfolk Co.
Knott, Susan, 1656, by Mr. Henry Soanes, New Kent Co.
Knott, John, 1654, by Tho. Hobkins, Lancaster Co.
Knott, Robert, 1653, by Peter Knight and Baber Cult, —— Co.
Knotts, Wm., 1652, by Mr. Tho. Curtis, —— Co.

Knott, Richard, 1651, by Thomas Thornbrough, Northumberland Co.
Knott, Richard, 1642, by Thomas Loving, James City Co.
Knight, Wm., 1651, by Thomas Thornbrough, Northumberland Co.
Knight, Towasin, 1643, by Rowland Burnham, Yorke Co.
Knight, Richard, 1646, by Edward Hall, Lower Norfolk Co.
Knowells, Henry, 1648, by John Seward, Isle of Wight Co.
Knowles, Peter, ..., by Tho. Binns, Surry Co.
Knowles, Tho., 1656, by Vincent Stanford, ——— Co.
Knowles, Robert, 1655, by Wm. Steevens, Northampton Co.
Knowles, Mich., 1642, by Lt. Francis Mason, ——— Co.
Knowles, Sands, 1652, by Capt. Augustine Warner, ——— Co.
Knowles, Wm., 1645, by Mr. Bartholomew Hoskins, ——— Co.
Knowles, Ann, 1656, by Walter Broodhurst, ——— Co.
Kogan, Harbor, 1645, by William, Storey, Upper Norfolk Co.
Koggan, Robert, 1650, by Richard Axom and Tho. Godwin, ——— Co.
Korne, Jon., 1635, by Pierce Lemon, Charles City Co.
Krogg, Benj., 1642, by Thomas Bagwell, Charles City Co.
Krimy, Edw., 1654, by Col. Argoll Yardley, Northampton Co.
Kurlin, Jenkin, 1652, by July Gardner, Northumberland Co.
Kuogard, Richard, 1655, by Edmund Scarbourgh, Jr., and Littleton Scarbrough, Northampton Co.
Kunnagh, Mor., 1655, by Edmund Scarbourgh, Jr., and Littleton Scarbourgh, Northampton Co.

L

Labbins, Peter, 1648, by Lewis Burwell, Gent., ——— Co.
Labor, Wm., 1652, by Col. Geo. Ludlow, Esq., Gloucester Co.
Lacey, Eliz, 1654, by Wm., Bacon, Northumberland Co.
Lacke, Wm., 1654, by John Hallawes, Westmoreland Co.
Lacke, John, 1651, by Geo. Colclough, Gent., Northumberland Co.
Lackhill, Andrew, 1650, by Wingfield Webb and Richard Pate, ——— Co.
Lacy, Rich., 1637, by Thomas Weston, Charles River Co.
Lacy, Eliza, 1649, by Richard Bayly, Northampton Co.
Lacy, James, 1653, by Geo. Thompson, Gloucester Co.
Lacye, Wm., 1652, by Capt. John West, Esq., ——— Co.
Ladd, Jon., 1653, by Wm. Diltye, Charles City Co.
Lady, Zackary, 1650, by John Mangor, ——— Co.
Lae, Wm., 1650, by Mr. Anthony Ellyot, ——— Co.
Laflyn, Jasper, 1637, by Oliver Sprye, New Norfolk Co.
Laflyn, Jasper, 1639, by Richard Parsons, Lower New Norfolk Co.
Lahay, Arthur, 1649, by Capt. Ralph Wormeley, ——— Co.
Laine, Henry, 1653, by Hopkins Howell, Nansemond Co.
Laishfoiler, Elizabeth, 1656, by John Phips, James City Co.
Lake, Tho., 1653, by John Day, Gloucester Co.
Lake, Robt., 1653, by Colo. Wm. Clayborne (Sec. of State),—— Co.
Lake, Gilbert, 1646, by John Ashcomb, Upper Norfolk Co.
Lake, Wm., 1655, by John Watson, Lancaster Co.
Lam, Rachael, 1635, by Capt. Adam Thoroughgood, ——— Co.
Lamb, Robert, 1642, by Wm. Barnard, Esq., Isle of Wight Co.

Lamb, Wm., 1650, by Wingfield Webb, and Richard Pate, ——— Co.
Lamb, Robt., 1653, by James Mason, James City Co.
Lamb, Robt., 1654, by Edward Simpson, Gloucester Co.
Lamb, Wm., 1646, by Sir. William Berkley, ——— Co.
Lambdin, Wm., 1638, by John Senior and Henry Carmon, James City Co.
Lambdin, Robert, 1638, by John Senior and Henry Carmon, James City Co.
Lambe, Abra., 1653, by Tho. Holmes, York Co.
Lambert, Henry, 1656, by Sir Henry Chichley, ——— Co.
Lambert, Hum., 1650, by Jervace Dodson, Gent., Northumberland Co.
Lambert, Richard, 1653, by John Jobinson, Lancaster Co.
Lambert, Fra., 1653, by Abraham Moone, Northumberland Co.
Lambert, Anne, 1653, by Wm. Moseley, Lower Norfolk Co.
Lambert, Henry, 1653, by Coll. Wm. Taylor, Esq., Gloucester Co.
Lambert, Henry, 1652, by Richard Starnell, ——— Co.
Lambkin, Martha, 1638, by John Senior and Henry Carman, James City Co.
Lambstone, James, 1652, by Henry Weekes, ——— Co.
Lampkin, David, 1654, by Capt. Giles Brent, Westmoreland Co.
Lance, Gowin, 1638, by Thom. Melton, Lower New Norfolk Co.
Lanceford, Phild., 1654, by Wm. Bacon, Northumberland Co.
Lancelott, Nicho., 1649, by John Trussells, ——— Co.
Lancelott, John, 1651, by Mr, Wm. Armestead, ——— Co.
Lancton, Thomas, 1639, by William Burdett, Accomack Co.
Land, Symond, 1650, by George Ludlow, Esq., Northumberland Co.
Land Phillip, 1648, by Mr. Bartholomew, Haskins, Lower Norfolk Co.
Land, Ja., 1551, by Mr. Rowland Burnham, ——— Co.
Land, Wm., 1653, by John Levistone, Gloucester Co.
Land, Tho., 1654, by Randall Chamblett, ——— Co.
Land, Rob., 1654, by Mr. Tho. Fowke, Westmoreland Co.
Land, Mary, 1655, by Samuel Sollace, Northampton Co.
Land, Edmund, 1653, by Tho. Read, Northumberland Co.
Land, James, 1652, by Tho. Preston, ——— Co.
Landford, Phill., 1649, by Richard Bayly, Northampton Co.
Landson, Robert, 1653, by Tho. Hawkins, Northumberland Co.
Landwood, John, 1644, by Edwyn Conaway, Northampton Co.
Landye, Francis, 1653, by Anthony Lenton, Northumberland Co.
Lane, Thomas, 1637, by Capt. Adam Thoroughgood, Elizabeth City Co.
Lane, John, 1635, by Richard Bennett, ——— Co.
Lane, Tho., 1636, by Richard Cocke, —— Co.
Lane, Daniell, 1635, by Thomas Harwood, —— Co.
Lane, John, 1643, by William Ewins, James City Co.
Lane, John, 1650, by Robert Bird, —— Co.
Lane, Walter, 1649, by Edmund, Scarburgh, Jr., Northampton Co.
Lane, Thomas, 1648, by Lewis Burwell, Gent., ——— Co.
Lane, Robt., 1654, by John Wyre, John Gillet, Andrew Gibson and John Phillipps, ——— Co.
Lane, Wm., 1654, by Col. Argoll Yardley, Northampton Co.

Lane, Edward, 1654, by John Drayton, Westmoreland Co.
Lane, Walter, 1652, by Littleton Scarburgh, ——— Co.
Lane, Anne, 1653, by Abraham Moore, Northumberland Co.
Lane, Rob., 1654, by Richard Codsford, Westmoreland Co.
Lane, Rob., 1653, by Capt. Francis Morgan, Gloucester Co.
Lane, Robt., 1652, by Tho. Leechman and John Bennett, Gloucester Co.
Lane, Wm., 1653, by Colo. Wm. Clayborne (Sec. of State), ——— Co.
Lane, Robt., 1653, by John Merryman and Morgan Haynes, Lancaster Co.
Lane, Tho., 1653, by Wm. Debrane, ——— Co.
Laner, Temperence, 1653, by John Shepperd, Northumberland Co.
Lanere, Mark, 1652, by Edward Cole, Northumberland Co.
Lanett, Wm., 1652, by John Taylor, Lancaster Co.
Langfield, Phillipp, 1636, by John Neale, Accomack Co.
Langford, Walter, 1643, by Capt. Samuell Mathews, Esq., ——— Co.
Langford, John, 1651, by Wm. Hampton, ——— Co.
Langford, Eliza., 1653, by John Earle, Northumberland Co.
Langford, Edward, 1638, by Wm. Morgan, ——— Co.
Langford, Meredith, 1652, by Mr. Richard Cocke, Henrico Co.
Langford, 1652, by Richard Coleman, ——— Co.
Lanford, Tho., 1651, by James Baldrige and Capt. Tho. Baldridge, Northumberland Co.
Langley, Henry, 1650, by Capt. Moore Fautleroy, ——— Co.
Langhson, Edward, 1638, by William Parker, Upper Norfolk Co.
Langley, Richard, 1637, by James Warradine, Charles City Co.
Langley, John, 1642, by Wm. Warren, ——— Co.
Langston, Jon., 1635, Tho. Butler Clark and Pastor of Denbie, Warrosquinoake Co.
Lanmore, Marsey, 1642, by Capt, Daniell Gookin, ——— Co.
Lamom, Richard, 1655, by Gilbert Deacon, Henrico Co.
Lanory, Mary, 1656, by Vincent Stanford, ——— Co.
Lans, Elady, 1641, by Stephen Charleton, Accomack Co.
Lansey, Joseph, 1656, by Mr. Tho. Purifoy, ——— Co.
Lant, Wm., 1653, by Robt. Sorrel, ——— Co.
Lapham, Richd., 1650, by Richard Axom and Tho. Godwin, ——— Co.
Lapworth, Michaell, 1643, by Sir, Francis Wyatt, Kt., ——— Co.
Large, Robert, 1643, by Lt. Wm. Worleidge, ——— Co.
Large, Wm., 1643, by Joseph Coshawe, ——— Co.
Large, Wm., 1636, by Mr. George Menifye, James City Co.
Large William,, 1635, by George Minife, James City, Co.
Large, Wm., 1651, by Wm. Vincent, Northumberland Co.
Larkin, Wm., 1650, by John Smith, ——— Co.
Larkin, Edwd., 1654, by Richard Hawkins, Westmoreland Co.
Larkin, Eliz., 1654, by Phillip Chesly and Dan. Wilde, York Co.
Larkin, Eliz, 1637, by Lt. John Upton, Isle of Wight Co.
Larkin Eliz, 1637, by John Upton, Isle of Wight Co.
Larking, Eliz., 1635, by Jno. Upton, Warrasquinoake Co.
Larock, Step., 1648, by Richard Pettibon, ——— Co.
Larramore, Henry, 1640, by John Maior, Accomack Co.
Laramore, Tho, 1649, by Rich. Croshaw, Yorke Co.

Larrett, Wm., 1653, by John Merryman and Morgan Haynes, Lancaster Co.
Lary, Richard, 1635, by Samuel Weaver, ——— Co.
Lash, Stephen, 1638, by Capt, Christopher Wormley, Charles River Co.
Lasher, Wm., 1646, by John Ashcomb, Upper Norfolk Co.
Lasey, Joane, 1653, by Wm. Hardedge, Northumberland Co.
Lasley, ———, 1643, by Capt. John Upton, Isle of Wight Co.
Lasling, Wm., 1639, by Thomas Iles, Charles River Co.
Lasse, William, 1648, by Lewis Burwell, Gent., ——— Co.
Laste, Hugh, 1655, by Edmund Scarborough, Jr., and Littleton Scarborough, Northampton Co.
Lastly, John, 1652, by Peter Knight, Gloucester Co.
Lasting, Jossy, 1643, by Capt. Samuell Mathews, Esq., ———Co.
Latchett, Robt., 1637, by William Spencer, ——— Co.
Latham Wm., 1653, by Richard Burton, ——— Co.
Latham, Jane, 1651, by Thomas Keeling, Lower Norfolk Co.
Lathberry, Richard, 1652, by Mr. Peter Knight, Gloucester Co.
Lathburg, Richd., 1653, by Mr. Henry Soanes, ——— Co.
Lather, Peter, 1638, by Arthur, Smith Isle of Wight Co.
Lathrop, John, 1654, by John Drayton, Westmoreland Co.
Lathropp, Wm., 1638, by Wm. Rabnett, Warwick River Co.
Lathropp, Bridget, 1636, by John Lathropp, James City Co.
Latner, Francis, 1637, by Theodore Moyser, James City Co.
Laton, Judith, 1653, by John Day, Gloucester Co.
Lattard, Hen., 1652, by John Spiltimber and John Brady, ——— Co.
Lattimore, Clement, 1642, by John Moone, Isle of Wight Co.
Lattimore, Hugh, 1652, by John Chambers, Northumberland Co.
Laughlin, Tho., 1654, by Toby Smith, Lancaster Co.
Laughly, Mathew, 1638, by Geo. Lobb, Tho. Perce, Tho. Warne, James City Co.
Laughton, Leon., 1636, by Elizabeth Packer, Henrico Co.
Laughton, Robt., 1637, by William Wilkinson, New Norfolk Co.
Laur, Wm., 1647, by Elizabeth Barcroft, Isle of Wight Co.
Laurel, Penelope, 1641, by Tho. Pitt, Charles City Co.
Laurwell, John, 1637, by Percival Champion, New Norfolk Co.
Law, Wm., 1635, by Wm. Barber, Charles City Co.
Law, Mary, 1643, by Elizabeth Hull, ——— Co.
Lawden, James, 1635, by Richard Tisdale, ——— Co.
Lawdere, Henry, 1637, by John Brodwell, James City Co.
Lawford, Mary, 1649, by Joseph Croshawe, Yorke Co.
Lawley, Tho., 1638, by William Clarke, Henrico Co.
Lawley, Thomas, 1636, by William Clarke, Henrico Co.
Lawmer, John, 1650, by George Pate, Charles City Co.
Lawrance, Joane, 1643, by Wm. Lawrance (her husband), James City Co.
Lawrance, Wm., 1643, by Richard Kemp, Esq., James City Co.
Lawrance, Jon., 1638, by John Fludd, James City Co.
Lawrance, John, 1642, by Wm. Barnard, Esq., Isle of Wight Co.
Lawrance, Eliza., 1642, by Robert Lawrance, Isle of Wight Co.
Lawrance, Benj., 1642, by Capt. Humphrey Higgenson, ——— Co.

Lawrance, Geo., 1641, by Tho. Mathews, ———— Co.
Lawrance, John, 1638, by John Robins, James City Co.
Lawrence, Mary, 1656, by Wm. Justice, Charles City Co.
Lawerence, James, 1652, by Richd. Coleman, ———— Co.
Lawerence, Robt., 1653, by Francis Grey, Charles City Co.
Lawrence, John, 1652, by James Forster and Audry Bonny, ———— Co.
Lawrence, Eliza., 1653, by Peter Knight and Baker Cult, ———— Co.
———— Co.
Lawrence, James, 1654, by John Hallawes, Westmoreland Co.
Lawrence, Robt., 1654, by Mrs. Mgt. Brent, Westmoreland Co.
Lawrence, Robert, 1655, by Richard Codsford, Westmoreland Co.
Lawrence, Alex., 1656, by Tho. Harris, Lancaster Co.
Lawrence, Sarah, 1656, by Wm. Justice, Charles City Co.
Lawrence, Ann, 1656, by Wm. Justice, Charles City Co.
Lawrence, Wm., 1656, by Wm. Justice, Charles City Co.
Lawrence, John, 1656, by John Rosier Clarke, Westmoreland Co.
Lawrence, Jon., 1654, by Richard Kellam, Northampton Co.
Lawrence, John, 1650, by John Bone, ———— Co.
Lawrence, John, 1650, by Capt. John Flood, Gent., and Jno. Flood,
    an ancient planter, James City Co.
Lawrence, Melchesider, 1638, by Wm. Morgan, ———— Co.
Lawrenson, Fra., Sr., 1654, by Mr. Francis Hamond, York Co.
Lawrenson, Fra., Jr., 1654, by Mr. Francis Hamond, York Co.
Lawren John, 1654, by Francis Gray, ———— Co.
Lawrey, Tho., 1650, by Richard Axom and Tho. Godwin, ———— Co.
Lawson, Eliza., 1637, by Capt. Adam Thoroughgood, New Norfolk Co.
Lawson, Robert, 1636, by Lewis Denwood, Accomack Co.
Lawson, Eliza., 1635, by Capt. Adam Thoroughgood, ———— Co.
Lawson, Hugh, 1636, by James Vanerit, Elizabeth City Co.
Lawson, Alice, 1635, by Capt. Wm. Pierse, ———— Co.
Lawson, Susan, 1653, by Tho. Kibby, Northumberland Co.
Lawson, Ann, 1653, by Corbet Piddle, Northumberland Co.
Lawson, George, 1655, by Jer. Dodson, Gent., Lancaster Co.
Lawson, Wm., 1654, by Christopher Boon, Westmoreland Co.
Lawson, William, 1639, by Thomas Mathews, Henrico Co.
Lawson, Rowland, 1638, by Epaphroditus Lawson, Upper Norfolk Co.
Lawson, William, 1638, by Epaphroditus Lawson, Upper Norfolk Co.
Lawson, Lettice, 1638, by Epaphroditus Lawson, Upper Norfolk Co.
Lawton, Tho., 1651, by Christopher Burroughs, Lower Norfolk Co.
Lawyer, Jos., 1648, by John Saynes, James City Co.
Laydon, Virginia, 1636, by John Laydon, Warwick River Co.
Laydon, ————, 1636, by John Laydon (her husband), Warwick River
    Co.
Layne, Robert, 1643, by Elizabeth Hull, ———— Co.
Layne, Robert, 1648, by Tho. Braughton, ———— Co.
Layton, Eliza., 1636, by William Layton, ———— Co.
Layton, Wm., 1637, by Lt. Richard Popeley, New Norfolk Co.
Layton, Wm., 1636, by Henry Southell, ———— Co.
Leach, Rebecca, 1639, by Edward Travis, James City Co.
Leach, Wm., 1656, by George Kibble, Lancaster Co.
Leach, Peter, 1655, by George Kibble, ———— Co.

Leach Charles, 1655, by George Kibble, —— Co.
Leach, Wm., 1650, by Capt. Charles Leech, Yorke Co.
Leaderd, Robert, 1637, by Nathaniel Floyd, Isle of Wight Co.
Leading, James, 1635, by Capt. Adam Thoroughgood, —— Co.
Leager, Thos., 1636, by John Yates, Elizabeth City Co.
Leathott, Marga., 1652, by Wm. Ratton and Richard Flint, Lancaster Co.
Leak, John, 1635, by Capt. Adam Thoroughgood, —— Co.
Leake, Andrew, 1642, by Capt. Humphry Higgenson, ——Co.
Leake, Richard, 1639, by Robert Newman, Warwick River Co.
Leake, John, 1635, by Capt. Adam Thoroughgood, —— Co.
Leake, John, 1642, by John Lylley, —— Co.
Leake, Richard, 1636, by John Wilkins, Accomack Co.
Leake, Rich., 1637, by John Wilkins, New Norfolk Co.
Leake, Richard, 1643, by James Bagnall, Lower Norfolk Co.
Leake, Christopher, 1650, by Lieut. Wm. Worleich, —— Co.
Leake, Richard, 1650, by James Metgrigar and Hugh Foutch, Northumberland Co.
Leake, Mary, 1654, by Alex. Madocks and James Jones, Northampton Co.
Leake, Fra., 1653, by Peter Knight, Northumberland Co.
Leamin, Roger, 1648, by George Read, Gent., —— Co.
Lear, Mort., 1649, by Rich. Croshaw, Yorke Co.
Leather, Richard, 1655, by Dr. Giles Mode, New Kent Co.
Leatherberry, Ellu., 1655, by Tho. Leatherberry, Northampton Co.
Ledrick, John, 1654, by Major Miles Carey, Westmoreland Co.
Ledmond, Ed., 1648, by Thomas Woodhouse, James City Co.
Lee, Wm., 1637, by Henry Perry, Charles River Co.
Lee, Anthony, 1637, by John Baker, Charles River Co.
Lee, John, 1654, by Col. Argoll Yardley, Northampton Co.
Lee, Richard, 1656, by Wm. Justice, Charles City Co.
Lee, Bridges, 1656, by Capt. Henry Fleete, —— Co.
Lee, Richard, 1643, by Mr. Moore Fautleroy, Upper Norfolk Co.
Lee, Richard, 1643, by Tho. Cassen, Lower Norfolk Co.
Lee, Henry, 1638, by Joseph Harmon, James City Co.
Lee, Anthony, 1638, by Nicholas Georg and John Grymoditch, —— Co.
Lee, Jon., 1637, by Robert Bennett, New Norfolk Co.
Lee, Wm., 1637, by Henry Perry, Charles River Co.
Lee, Grace, 1637, by Thomas Barnard, James City Co.
Lee, Henry, 1637, by James Berry, Accomack Co.
Lee, Gilbert, 1635, by Richard Bennett, —— Co.
Lee, John, 1635, by Robert Bennett, —— Co.
Lee, George, 1636, by John Wilkins, Accomack Co.
Lee, Willi, 1636, by Randall Holt, James City Co.
Lee, Henry, 1636, by James Berry, Accomack Co.
Lee, Georg, 1637, by John Wilkins, New Norfolk Co.
Lee, Gilbert, 1637, by Rich. Bennett, New Norfolk Co.
Lee, Nick., 1635, by Anthony Jones, —— Co.
Lee, Richard, 1636, by Anthony Jones, Warwick Co.
Lee, Tho., 1648, by Lewis Burwell and Tho. Haws, York River Co.

Lee, John, 1649, by Mr. Henry Lee, Yorke Co.
Lee, Mathew, 1648, by Richard Lee, Gent., ——— Co.
Lee, John, 1651, by Robt. Newman, Northumberland Co.
Lee, Matt., 1651, by Mr. Wm. Armestead, ——— Co.
Lee, Francis, 1651, by Thomas Clifton, Northampton Co.
Lee, Phild., and Girull, his wife, 1653, by Tho. Salisbury, Northumberland Co.
Lee, William, 1653, by John Bell, Lancaster Co.
Lee, Kath., 1653, by Jervais Dodson, Northumberland Co.
Lee, John, 1652, by John Gresham, Northumberland Co.
Lee, Humphry, 1652, by Mr. Tho. Purifye and Mrs. Temperence Reppitt, ——— Co.
Lee, Tho., 1652, by John Meredith, Lancaster Co.
Lee, John, 1652, by Mr. Tho. Purifye and Mrs. Temperence Reppitt, ——— Co.
Lee, David, 1652, by Mr. David Fox, Lancaster Co.
Lee, Tho., 1652, by Henry Palin and John Singleton, ——— Co.
Lee, Richard, 1652, by Edward Cannon and Tho. Allen, Lower Norfolk Co.
Lee, Eliza., 1652, by Anthony Dorey and Enock Hawker, Lancaster Co.
Lee, John, 1654, by Francis Gray, ——— Co.
Leech, Mark, 1639, by Capt. Nicholas Martian, Charles River Co.
Leech, Peter, 1650, by Capt. Charles Leech, Yorke Co.
Leech, John, 1636, by Wm. Bibby, Accomack Co.
Leech, Jno., 1653, by Geo. Thompson, Gloucester Co.
Leech, Jenkin, 1653, by Major Abra. Wood, Charles City Co.
Leech, Thomas, 1652, by Teague Floyne, Lancaster Co.
Leechman, Tho., 1650, by Bertram Obert, ——— Co.
Leeke, Marg., 1651, by Wm. Taylor, Northumberland Co.
Leely, Edward, 1637, by Henry Catalyn, New Norfolk Co.
Leeling, Thomas, 1635, by Capt. Adam Thoroughgood, ——— Co.
Leeman, Sarah, 1651, by Joseph Hayes, Gent., Yorke Co.
Leeth, Peter, 1656, by Daniel Jaines and Jno. Jennings, ——— Co.
Leeth, Chas., 1656, by Daniel Jaines and Jno. Jnenings, ——— Co.
Leeth, Jane, 1656, by Margaret Miles, Westmoreland Co.
Leevis, Eliz., 1637, by David Mansell, James City Co.
Lefford, Mary, 1656, by John Billiott, Northampton Co.
Legg, Marg., 1653, by Ferdinando Austin, Charles City Co.
Legg, Edy, 1653, by Richard Budd, Northumberland Co.
Legg, Grace, 1652, by Tho. Steevens, Lancaster Co.
Leidge, John, 1652, by Francis Fleetwood, Lower Norfolk Co.
Leigh, Thomas, 1639, by John Hayward, James City Co.
Leigh, Georg, 1637, by Wm. Prior, Gent., Charles River Co.
Leigh, John, 1647, by Thomas Wright, Lower Norfolk Co.
Leigh, Jon., 1643, by Wm. Butler, James City Co.
Leigh, Wm., 1649, by Capt. Ralph Wormeley, ——— Co.
Leigh, James, 1653, by Geo. Thompson, Gloucester Co.
Leigh, Wm., 1653, by Corbet Piddle, Northumberland Co.
Leigh, Tho., 1647, by Richard Bland, ——— Co.
Leine, Sarah, 1636, by Samuel Edwards, James City Co.

Lemon, Sar., 1655, by Mrs. Margaret Brent, Lancaster Co.
Lemans, Tho., 1649, by John King, Yorke Co.
Lemmare, Mercy, 1640, by John George, Charles City Co.
Lemon, John, 1654, by Tho. Harmanson, Northampton Co.
Lemon, Wm., 1655, by John Jenkins, Northampton Co.
Lemon, Edmund, 1643, by Pierce Lemon, Charles City Co.
Lemon, Rebecca, 1643, by Pierce Lemon (her husband), Charles City Co.
Lemon, Rebecca, 1635, by Pierce Lemon, Charles City Co.
Lemon, Wm., 1648, by George White, Lower Norfolk Co.
Lemon, Wm., 1648, by John Smith, Lower Norfolk Co.
Lemon, Will., 1652, by Gregory Parrett, Lower Norfolk Co.
Lemond, Gho., 1654, by Tho. Harmanson, Northampton Co.
Lemond, Mary, 1654, by Tho. Harmanson, Northampton Co.
Lendall, Richd., 1650, by William Gooch, Gent., ———— Co.
Lendall, Wm., 1653, by Abraham Moon, Lancaster Co.
Lenereman, Luke, 1651, by John Martin and (Lancaster Lovett) Lower Norfolk Co.
Lenn, Math., 1653, by Frances Emperor, Hugh Gale and Edward Morgan, Lower Norfolk Co.
Lentall, Geo., 1637, by Lt. Rich. Popeley, New Norfolk Co.
Lentall, Tho., 1654, by Alex Madocks and James Jones, Northampton Co.
Lentill, Barb., 1650, by Mordecay Cooke, ———— Co.
Lento, Geo., 1636, by Henry Southall, ———— Co.
Lenton, Wm., 1654, by John Sharpe, Lancaster Co.
Leonard, James, 1637, by Robert Bennett, New Norfolk Co.
Leonard, Katharine, 1637, by Bridges Freeman, James City Co.
Leonard, James, 1635, by Robert Bennett, ———— Co.
Leonard, Katharine, 1636, by Bridges Freeman, ———— Co.
Leonarde, Leonard, 1635, by Daniel Cugley, Accomac Co.
Lepard, John, 1654, by Toby Smith, Lancaster Co.
Lerch, Stephen, 1639, by George Minifye, Esq., Charles River Co.
Lercush, Inlian, N., 1656, by Mr. Henry Soanes, New Kent Co.
Lesley, Nico., 1650, by Mrs. Frances Townshend (widow), Northumberland Co.
Leshley, Alex., 1650, by Capt. Moore Fautleroy, ———— Co.
Lest, Walter, 1636, by Stephen Webb, James City Co.
Lester, Ralph, 1643, by Mr. John Bishopp, James City Co.
Lester, James, 1637, by Tho. Symmons, Charles River Co.
Lester, Robert, 1649, by John King, York Co.
Lester, Tho., 1653, by Colo. Wm. Clayborne (Sec. of State), ———— Co.
Lesting, Angell, 1643, by Epaphroditus Lawson, Upper Norfolk Co.
Lestis, Wm., 1647, by Thomas Johnson, Gent., Northampton Co.
Lether, John, 1639, by Thomas Curtis, ———— Co.
Lethermore, Tho., and Elinore, his wife, 1645, by John Baker, Elizabeth City. Co.
Lethermore, Wm., 1638, by Wm. Banister, ———— Co.
Lethrington, Tho., 1652, by Richard Nelmes, Northumberland Co.
Lett, Eliza., 1648, by Lewis Burwell and Tho. Haws, York River Co.
Lett, Leonard, 1651, by Mrs. Anna Bernard, Northumberland Co.

Lett, Tho., 1652, by Mrs. Anna Barnett, Gloucester Co.
Lett, John, 1651, by Joseph Croshaw, Yorke Co.
Letts, Mary, 1651, by Joseph Croshaw, Yorke Co.
Leullin, Robert, 1649, by Robert Moseley, Gent., ——— Co.
Leverich, Sarah, 1636, by William Julian, Elizabeth City Co.
Levin, Tho., 1654, by Valentine Patten, Westmoreland Co.
Lewis, Richard, 1638, by Capt. Chrisotpher Wormeley, Charles River
    Co.
Levin, Tho., 1654, by Robert Hubard, Westmoreland Co.
Levitt, Robert, 1654, by John Drayton, Westmoreland Co.
Levitt, Alice, 1643, by Georg Levitt (her husband), ——— Co.
Leviston, Jno., 1650, by Wingfield Webb and Richard Pate, ——— Co.
Lewd, Rich., 1637, by Wm. Farrar, Henrico Co.
Lewellen, Margt., 1654, by James Yates, ——— Co.
Lewellin, Daniell, 1637, by Henry Perry, Charles River Co.
Lewellin, John, 1655, by Mr. Tho. Peck, Gloucester Co.
Lewellin, Jon., 1637, by Capt. Thomas Paulett, Charles City Co.
Lewellin, Daniell, 1637, by Henry Perry, Charles River Co.
Lewellin, Wm., 1650, by Capt. Moore Fautleroy, ——— Co.
Lewen, Jon., 1636, by William Coleman, Charles River Co.
Lewes, Tho., 1638, by Georg Mynifie (merchant), ——— Co.
Lewes, Grace, 1656, by Wm. Millinge, Northampton Co.
Lewins, Wm., 1656, by Mr. Henry Soanes, New Kent Co.
Lewis, Christ., 1638, by Lieut. John Upton, Isle of Wight Co.
Lewis, Jonathan, 1640, by Edmund Scarburgh, Accomack Co.
Lewis, Wm.. 1639, by Rich. Hoe, James City Co.
Lewis, John, 1642, by Capt. Samuell Mathews, Esq., ——— Co.
Lewis, Tho., 1654, by Robert Yoe, Westmoreland Co.
Lewis, Evan, 1654, by Major Miles Carey, Westmoreland Co.
Lewis, James, 1654, by Arthur Nash, New Kent Co.
Lewis, Dorothy, 1654, by Lieut. Coll. Giles Brent, Westmoreland Co.
Lewis, Wm., 1655, by Sam. Sollace and Robert Trolliver, Gloucester
    Co.
Lewis, Tho., 1655, by Edward Pettaway, Surry Co.
Lewis, James, 1655, by John Withers, Westmoreland Co.
Lewis, Wm., 1654, by James Yates, ——— Co.
Lewis, John, 1655, by Lt. Col. Tho. Swan, Surry Co.
Lewis, Kath., 1642, by Christopher Boyce, ——— Co.
Lewis, Wm., 1650, by Mrs. Frances Townshend (widow), Northum-
    berland Co.
Lewis, Katherine, 1645, by John Rode, Warwick Co.
Lewis, Thomas, 1646, by Geo. Ludlow, Esq., York Co.
Lewis, David, 1638, by Thomas Symons, Upper Norfolk Co.
Lewis, Katherine, 1638, by Nicholas Sabrell, James City Co.
Lewis, Godfrey, 1637, by Capt. Thomas Osborne, Henrico Co.
Lewis, John, 1638, by Joseph Farge, Charles City Co.
Lewis, Christ., 1637, by Lt. John Upton, Isle of Wight Co.
Lewis, John, 1636, by John Forbuse, Accomack Co.
Lewis, Thomas, 1637, by Francis Osborne, ———Co.
Lewis, Tho., 1636, by Hannah Boyse, Henrico Co.
Lewis, Christopher, 1635, by Jno. Upton, Warrasquinoake Co.

Lewis, Roger, 1636, by Izabell Thresher, ———— Co.
Lewis, John, 1635, by William Spencer, ———— Co.
Lewis, Thomas, 1637, by Hannah Boyes, Henrico Co.
Lewis, Robert, 1636, by Richard Cocke, ———— Co.
Lewis, Thomas, 1635, by Thomas Harwood, ———— Co.
Lewis, Eliz., 1635, by David Mansell, James Co.
Lewis, Jon, 1643, by Richard Kemp, Esq., James City Co.
Lewis, John, 1647, by Elizabeth Barcroft, Isle of Wight Co.
Lewis, John, Jr., 1643, by Capt. Samuell Mathews, Esq., ———— Co.
Lewis, Wm., 1650, by Tho. Blogg, Northumberalnd Co.
Lewis, John, 1650, by Mr. Epaphroditus Lawson, ———— Co.
Lewis, Robert, 1650, by John Cox, ———— Co.
Lewis, Richard, 1649, by Richard Kemp, Esq. (Sec. of State), ————
    Co.
Lewis, Rich., 1649, by Capt. Ralph Wormeley, ———— Co.
Lewis, Bartho., 1651, by James Baldrige and Capt. Tho. Baldrige,
    Northumberland Co.
Lewis, Jane, 1650, by Seymon Thoroughgood, Eliz. City Co.
Lewis, Dorothy, 1651, by John Rookwood, Gent., Northumberland Co.
Lewis, Dorothy, 1651, by Lieut. Coll. Giles Brent, Northumberland Co.
Lewis, Edwd., 1653, by Mr. John Lewis, Gloucester Co.
Lewis, Wm., 1653, by Mr. Jchn Lewis, Gloucester Co.
Lewis, John, Jr., 1653, by Mr. John Lewis, Gloucester Co.
Lewis, Lidia, 1653, by Mr. John Lewis, Gloucester Co.
Lewis, Margt., 1653, by Leonard Chamberlain, Gloucester Co.
Lewis, Ar., 1653, by John Joliffe, Lower Norfolk Co.
Lewis, Mary, 1653, by Geo. Thompson, ———— Co.
Lewis, Wm., 1653, by Robt. Parfitt and Wm. Hatcher, Lancaster Co.
Lewis, Jane, 1653, by John Robinson, Lancaster Co.
Lewis, Richard, 1652, by Wm. Owen and Wm. Morgan, ———— Co.
Lewis, Daniel, 1652, by Tobias Horton, Lancaster Co.
Ley, John, 1635, by John Dennett, James Co.
Leye, John, 1652, by John Meredith, Lancaster Co.
Leyes, Peter, 1650, by Jervace Dodson, Gent., Northumberland Co.
Leyes, Amy, 1650, by Jervace Dodson, Gent., Northumberland Co.
Leyes, Hector, 1650, by Jervace Dodson, Gent., Northumberland Co.
Leynes, Ann, 1650, by Jervace Dodson, Gent., Northumberland Co.
Licermore, John, 1653, by Charles Grymes, Lancaster Co.
Licheston, John, 1637, by Mathew Edloe, ———— Co.
Liddel, Jon., 1653, by Gregory Rawlins, Surry Co.
Liddle, Thomas, 1650, by David Peibles, Charles City Co.
Lide, Richard, 1642, by Abraham Wood, Henrico Co.
Lidwith, Garrett, 1655, by Lt. Col. Anthony Ellyott, ———— Co.
Liege, Wm., 1653, by Edward Kemp, Geo. Cortleigh and John Mere-
    dith, Lancaster Co.
Light, Geo., 1652, by John Fleet, Lancaster Co.
Light, Mary, 1653, by Wm. Thomas, Northumberland Co.
Light, Mary, 1653, by Abraham Moon, Lancaster Co.
Light, George, 1648, by Richard Lee, Gent., ———— Co.
Light, Elias, 1637, by Lt. Richard Popeley, New Norfolk Co.
Light, Rich., 1637, by Lt. Richard Popeley, New Norfolk Co.

Light, Elias, 1636, by Henry Southell, —— Co.
Light, Richard, 1636, by Henry Southall, —— Co.
Lightall, Tho., 1654, by Fra. Spright, Nansemond Co.
Lightfoot, John, 1650, by George Pate, Charles City Co.
Lightfoot, Ann, 1635, by McWilliam Stone, —— Co.
Lighthollier, Wm., 1637, by Francis Osborne, —— Co.
Lile, Daniel, 1639, by Edward Panderson, —— Co.
Lile, John, 1656, by Mr. Martin Baker, New Kent Co.
Lilley, Henry, 1642, by James Pereene, Northampton Co.
Lilly, Henry, 1653, by Tho. Speoke, —— Co.
Lilly, Robert, 1654, by Obed. Williams, York Co.
Limbson, Nich., 1654, by Col. Hump. Higgenson, Esq., and Abraham
    Moone, Westmoreland Co.
Limicar, John, 1649, by Mr. Wm. Hoccaday, —— Co.
Lincey, Occory, 1656, by Capt. Wm. Confill, Surry Co.
Lincey, James, 1651, by Thomas Keeling, Lower Norfolk Co.
Lincle, John, 1646, by Tho. Savedge, Northampton Co.
Linch, Jere, 1649, by Capt. Ralph Wormeley, —— Co.
Lincolne, Edward, 1639, by Lieut. Edward Popeley, —— Co.
Line, Hen., 1642, by Stephen Gill, Yorke River Co.
Line, Dary, 1653, by Mr. Edmund Bowman and Richard Starnell,——
    Co.
Lineer, Marke, 1642, by Lieut. Francis Mason, —— Co.
Linfield, Richd., 1652, by John Meredith, Lancaster Co.
Linfield, Nicho., 1652, by John Meredith, Lancaster Co.
Linford, Ann, 1650, by Thomas Powell, —— Co.
Linge, John, 1652, by Mr. David Fox, Lancaster Co.
Lingford, Nich., 1642, by Capt. Samuell Mathews, Esq., —— Co.
Linn, John, 1653, by Geo. Wadding, Lancaster Co.
Linsey, Alexander, 1655, by Symon Symons, —— Co.
Linth, Geo., 1642, by Georg Harding, —— Co.
Linuce, Tho., 1653, by Major Abra. Wood, Charles City Co.
Lippett, John, 1638, by John Seaward, Isle of Wight Co.
Lippett, John, 1642, by Francis England, Isle of Wight Co.
Liplad, Jon., 1642, by Christopher Boyce, —— Co.
Lipson, John, 1656, by Mr. Henry Soanes, New Kent Co.
Lisbourne, Henry, 1655, by Capt. Henry Fleet, —— Co.
Liscatt, Jon., 1636, by Cheney Boyse, Charles City Co.
Lish, Thomas, 1639, by Henry Perry, Charles City Co.
Lisman, Mary, 1651, by Audeay, Bennett, Nansemond Co.
Litefoot, Joane, 1653, by Tho. Hancks, Gloucester Co.
Lithcain, Barnaby, 1652, by Lawen Lancaster, Charles River Co.
List, Henry, 1639, by Capt. Nicholas Martian, Charles River Co.
Litler, Richard, 1647, by Richard Bland, —— Co.
Little, Alice, 1652, by John Cooke, —— Co.
Little, Margery, 1653, by Capt. Francis Patt, Northampton Co.
Little, Lach., 1650, by Capt. Richard Bond, Charles City Co.
Little, Anthe., 1650, by Capt. Richard Bond, Charles City Co.
Little, Fra., 1650, by John Cox, —— Co.
Little, Antho., 1650, by Wm. Yarrett and Fra., Wittington —— Co.
Little, John James, 1635, by Wm. Andrews, Accomac Co.

Little, Jane, 1640, by Thomas Harvey, James City Co.
Littleboy, Lawrance, 1639, by Tho. Stamp, James City Co.
Littleboy, Charles, 1638, by Thomas Stampe, James City Co.
Littlefield, ———, 1653, by Henry Corbell, Gloucester Co.
Littleton, Geo., 1649, by John King, York Co.
Littlegage, Tho., 1653, by Geo. Wadding, Lancaster Co.
Littleton, George, 1653, by Wm. Wyatt, Gloucester Co.
Littleton, Anne, 1652, by Edward Cannon and Tho. Allen, Lower Norfolk Co.
Littlewood, Mrs. Eliza., 1642, by Richard Kemp, Esq., James City Co.
Littlewood, Mr. Wm., 1649, by Richard Kemp, Esq. (Sec. of State), ——— Co.
Litton, Nicho., 1650, by William Gooch, Gent., ——— Co.
Liver, Silvester, 1653, by Eppy Bonison, Lancaster Co.
Lleye, Donell, 1655, by Edmund Scarborough, Jr., and Littleton Scarborugh, Northampton Co.
Lloyd, Richd., 1653, by Major Abra Wood., Charles City Co.
Lloyd, John, 1650, by Thomas Mulford, Nansemond Co.
Lloyd, John, 1643, by Mr. Moore Fautleroy, Upper Norfolk Co.
Lloyd, James, 1654, by Peter Knight, Northumberland Co.
Lloyd, Robert, 1637, by Thomas Powell, New Norfolk Co.
Loare, Henry, 1655, by Samuel Smith, James City Co.
Lock, Tho., 1653, by Wm. Johnson, Henrico Co.
Lock, Tho., 1653, by Francis Emperor, Lower Norfolk Co.
Lock, Wm., 1642, by William Connhoe, ——— Co.
Lock, Georg, 1637, by Rich. Bennett, New Norfolk Co.
Lock, Thomas, 1635, by William Beard, James City Co.
Lock, Geo., 1651, by Ashwell Battin, Yorke Co.
Lock, Andrew, 1654, by Tho. Harmanson, Northampton Co.
Lock, Wm., 1639, by John Burland, Charles River Co.
Locke, Geo., 1651, by John Thomas, Gloucester Co.
Locker, Eliza., 1653, by Tho. Boswell, ——— Co.
Locker, George, 1635, by Richard Bennett, ——— Co.
Lockington, Elmor, 1654, by Francis Smith and Mr. John Smith, Westmoreland Co.
Lockley, Charles, 1639, by Thomas Stamp, James City Co.
Lockley, Charles, 1638, by John Batts and John Davis, Charles River Co.
Lockley, Thomas, 1638, by John Batts, and John Davis, Charles River Co.
Lodkley, Charles, 1638, by Thomas Stompe, James City Co.
Lockley, Ann, 1648, by Georg Read, Gent. ——— Co
Lockly, Josias, 1651, by Richard Ripley, ——— Co.
Loctins, Giles, 1650, by Mr. Moore Fautleroy, ——— Co.
Locu, James, 1651, by Geo. Colclough, Gent., Northumberland Co.
Locus, George, 1653, by Tho. Griffin, Lancaster Co.
Lodey, Wm., 1649, by Joseph Croshawe, Yorke Co.
Lodge, Thomas, 1637, by John Davis, James City Co.
Lodge, Georg, 1638, by Randall Crew, Upper New Norfolk Co.
Lodwell, James, 1653, by Oliver Segar, Lancaster Co.
Loftis, Willi, 1642, by John Robins, ——— Co.

Loes, Edward, 1649, by Joseph Croshawe, Yorke Co.
Loganell, John, 1653, by Mr. Wm. Baldwen, York Co.
Logat, Jon., 1635, by Capt. William Pierse, ——— Co.
Loid, James, 1653, by Tho. Hawkins, Northumberland Co.
London, Humphry, 1639, by Georg Minifye, Esq., Charles River Co.
London, John, 1637, by John Burnette, New Norfolk Co.
London, John, 1636, by John Gookin, Gent., ——— Co.
Londry, G., 1648, by Lewis Burwell, Gent., ——— Co.
Lone, John, 1637, by Georg Burcher, James City Co.
Lone, John, 1630, by Capt. Wm. Pierse, ——— Co.
Lonell, Robt., 1635, by Francis Fowler, James City Co.
Long, Richd., 1653, by Robt. Parfitt and Wm. Hatcher, Lancaster Co.
Long, Wm., 1653, by John Merryman and Morgan Haynes, Lancaster
    Co.
Long, Wm., 1637, by Daniell Gookins, New Norfolk Co.
Long, Ralph, 1638, by John George, Charles City Co.
Long, Richard, 1642, by Richard Gregson, Elizabeth City Co.
Long, Lewis, 1639, by Richard Preston, Upper New Norfolk Co.
Long, Tho., 1638, by Wm. Cloys, Charles River Co.
Long, Wm., 1654, by Wm. Beach, Westmoreland Co.
Long, Wm., 1654, by Arthur Nash, New Kent Co.
Long, Tho., 1654, by Abraham Moon, Gloucester Co.
Long, Jammiay, 1655, by Henry Huberd, ——— Co.
Long, Robert, 1655, by Henry Huberd, ——— Co.
Long, John, 1655, by Lt. Col. Tho. Swan, Surry Co.
Long, Michael, 1656, by John Wood, ——— Co.
Long, Wm., 1651, by Hugh Fauch and James Magregory, Northum-
    berland Co.
Long, Wm., 1643, by Samuell Abbott, James City Co.
Long, Jon., 1637, by Capt. Francis Eppes, Charles City Co.
Long, Robert, his wife, and Robert and John, his sons, 1643, by John
    Sherlocke, Isle of Wight Co.
Long, Robt., 1643, by Capt. John Upton, Isle of Wight Co.
Long, Jon., 1637, by Capt. Thomas Panlett, Charles City Co.
Long, James, 1642, by Robert Lawrance, Isle of Wight Co.
Long, Ann, 1635, by Capt. Adam Thoroughgood, ——— Co.
Long, Wm., 1650, by Nathaniell Jones, Northampton Co.
Long, Edward, 1649, by Frances Land, Norfolk Co.
Long, Tho., 1649, by John Dennis, ——— Co.
Long, Wm., 1648, by Randall Crew, Nansemond Co.
Long, Law., 1651, by Ashwell Battrie, Yorke Co.
Longdale, Abigole, 1651, by John Thomas, Gloucester Co.
Longe, Jon., 1653, by Wm. Hunt, ——— Co.
Longe, Tho., 1653, by Corbet Piddles, Northumberland Co.
Longe, Wm., 1652, by Tobias Horton, Lancaster Co.
Longe, Wm., 1652, by Andrew Munrow, Northumberland Co.
Longe, James, 1652, by Andrew Munrow, Northumberland Co.
Longe, Lawrence, 1654, by John Wyre, John Gillet, Andrew Gilson
    and John Phillipps, ——— Co.
Longe, Teague, 1650, by Nicholas Waddilow, Northampton Co.
Longingham, Mary, 1655, by Martin Hammond, ——— Co.

Longland, Wm., 1650, by Richard Tye and Charles Sparrowe, Charles City Co.
Longrane, Winifrid, 1636, by Georg Travellor, Accomack Co.
Longworth, James, 1652, by Mr. Edwin Connaway, ——— Co.
Longworthy, John, 1637, by Oliver Sprye, New Norfolk Co.
Loody, Henry, 1649, by Wm. Nesum, Tho. Sax, Miles Barthasby and John Pyne, Northampton Co.
Looker, Cheespeon, 1656, by Margaret Miles, Westmoreland Co.
Lopeat, Wm., 1653, by John Earle, Northumberland Co.
Lopphom, John, 1648, by Lewis Burwell, Cent., ——— Co.
Lorain, Lymon, 1635, by George Minifye, James City Co.
Lordy, John, 1648, by Lewis Burwell, Gent, ——— Co.
Lorymore, Thomas, 1646, by Lancaster Loevit, ——— Co.
Lorne, Tho., 1650, by George Pate, Charles City Co.
Lorum, Symon, 1636, by Mr. George Menifye, James City Co.
Losway, John, 1649, by Richard Kemp, Esq., (Sec. of State), ——— Co.
Louch, Roger, 1635, by Vectoris Christmas, Elizabeth City Co.
Loude, Richard, ———, by Lt. Coll. John Cheeseman, ——— Co.
Loudell, George, 1648, by Lewis Burwell, Gent., ——— Co.
Louder, Rich., 1637, by Capt. John Howe, Accomac Co.
Louder, Wm., 1649, by Mr. Wm. Presly, Northumberland Co.
Louder, James, 1648, by Geo. Hardy, Tho. Wombwell, and Peter Hall, Isle of Wight Co.
Loue, Eliza., 1652, by Mr. Tho. Curtis, ——— Co.
Loughton, Leonard, 1637, by Elizabeth Parker, Henrico Co.
Lownd, Alex., 1637, by Thomas Barnard, Warwick River Co.
Lovas, George, 1654, by John Newman, Lancaster Co.
Love, Richard, 1642, by John Robins, ——— Co.
Love, Rose, 1654, by R. Lawson, ——— Co.
Loveday, Fra., 1653, by Francis Grey, Charles City Co.
Loveing, Tho., 1638, by Georg Mynifie (merchant), ——— Co.
Lovell, Mary, 1653, by Tho. Davis, ——— Co.
Lovell, Grace, 1651, by Richard Grigson, ——— Co.
Lovell, Ann., 1651, by Richard Whitehurst, Lower Norfolk Co.
Loverton, Tho., 1650, by Francis Hobbs, ——— Co.
Lovett, Ann, 1652, by Tho. Boswell, ——— Co.
Lovett, Mary, 1650, by Francis Hobbs, ——— Co.
Low, Robt., 1638, by Thomas Dewe, Upper New Norfolk Co.
Low, Peter, 1637, by Capt. Thomas Panlett, Charles City Co.
Lowden, John, 1638, by Mr. John Gookins, Upper New Norfolk Co.
Lowder, Wm., 1638, by Richard Wilcox, James City Co.
Lowder, Henry, 1638, by John Batts and John Davis, Charles River Co.
Lowe, Ralph, 1652, by Richard Nelmes, Northumberland Co.
Lowe, Tho., 1639, by Richard Corke, Gent., Henrico Co.
Lowe, Richard, 1656, by Humphry Tabb, Gent., Elizabeth City Co.
Lowe, Robt., 1637, by Tho. Powell, New Norfolk Co.
Lowe, Mary, 1648, by Tho. Broughton, ——— Co.
Lowell, Mary, 1653, by Tho. Bourne, Lamcaster Co.
Lowell, Tho., 1653, by Tho. Griffin, Lancaster Co.
Lowell, Hugh, 1656, by Richard Barnhouse, Gent., James City Co.
Lowell, Robert, 1637, by Francis Fowler, James River Co.

Lowell, Thomas, 1637, by Leonard Yeo, Elizabeth City Co.
Lowen, Richard, 1652, by Mrs. Jane Harmer, Northumberland Co.
Lowne, Tho., 1653, by Henry Lowne, Henrico Co.
Lownes, Mary, and wife, 1652, by Richard Starnell, ———— Co.
Lownes, Edward, 1637, by Capt. Henry Browne, James City Co.
Lownee, Henry, 1645, by Michael Masters, Henrico Co.
Lowrey, Elinor, 1649, by Wm. Batt, James City Co.
Lowrey, Ema., 1649, by Wm. Batt, James City Co.
Loyd, Hugh, 1654, by Edward Revell, Northampton Co.
Loyd, Edw., 1654, by Edward Revell, Northampton Co.
Loyd, Jon., 1653, by Robert Brasseur, Nansemond Co.
Loyd, Marg., 1653, by Richard Thomas, Henrico Co.
Loyd, John, 1652, by John Pounsey, ———— Co.
Loyd, Mary, 1639, by John Burland, Charles River Co.
Loyd, Josepe, 1639, by Justinian Cooper, Isle of Wight Co.
Loyd, David, 1638, by John Robins, James City Co.
Loyd, Hugh, 1639, by William Wigg, ———— Co.
Loyd, Morris, 1642, by Capt. Samuell Mathews, Esq., ———— Co.
Loyd, Ann, 1653, by Richard Burton, ———— Co.
Loyd, Amy, 1650, by Jervace Dodson, Gent, Northumberland Co.
Loyd, John, 1642, by Thomas Guyer, ———— Co.
Loyd, Theod., 1635, by Capt. Thos. Willowbye, ———— Co.
Loyd, John, 1643, by Capt. Samuell Mathews, Esq., ———— Co.
Loyd, Wm., 1642, by Hugh Gwyn, Gent., ———— Co.
Loyd, James, 1650, by Mr. James Williamson, ———— Co.
Loyer, Brasenburn, 1638, by Thomas Dew, Upper New Norfolk Co.
Loyne, John, 1648, by Wm. Ewen, James City Co.
Loyse, John, 1638, by Capt. Christopher Wormley, Charles River Co.
Lucas, Wm., 1652, by Mr. Edwin Connaway, ———— Co.
Lucas, Clothyer, 1652, by John Fleet, Yorke Co.
Lucas, Wm., 1652, by Mr. David Fox, Lancaster Co.
Lucas, Tho., Jr., 1652, by Tho. Lucas, Gent. (his father), Lancaster Co.
Lucas, Edward, 1652, by John Catlett and Ralph Rouzee, ———— Co.
Lucas, ————, 1652, by Tho. Lucas, Gent. (her husband),Lancaster Co.
Lucas, Martha, 1652, by John Catlett and Ralph Rouzee, ———— Co.
Lucas, Wm., 1653, by Capt. Robt. Abrahal, York Co.
Lucas, Rogers, 1651, by Coll. Guy Molsworth, ———— Co.
Lucas, Jane, 1651, by Coll. Guy Molsworth, ———— Co.
Lucas, Wm., 1650, by John Mangor, ———— Co.
Lucas, Robert, 1636, by Christopher Calthropp, Charles River Co.
Lucas, Tho., 1648, by Lewis Burwell and Tho. Haws, York River Co.
Lucas, Robert, 1636, by Wm. Coleman, Charles Rievr Co.
Lucas, Roger, 1636, by Samuel Edwards, James City Co.
Lucas, Samuel, 1635, by Charles Harwer, ———— Co.
Lucas, Jane, 1637, by Francis Poythers, Charles City Co.
Lucas, Rich., 1637, by Charles Barcroft, Isle of Wight Co.
Lucas, Samuell, 1638, by Robt. Holt and Richard Bell, James City Co.
Lucas, Richard, 1650, by Jervace Dodson, Gent., Northumberland Co.
Lucas, Sam., 1655, by Southy Littleberry, Northampton Co.
Lucas, Eliz., 1654, by Capt. David Mansell, Westmoreland Co.
Lucas, Ed., 1654, by Tho. and Henry Preston, ———— Co.

Lucas, Richard, 1639, by John Jackson, Charles River Co.
Lucas, Wm., 1640, by Thomas Cansey ——— Co.
Lucas, Samuell, 1640, by Robert Holt, James City Co.
Luco, Anth., 1640, by Robert Holt, James City Co.
Lucas, Robert, 1639, by Walter Cooper, James City Co.
Lucham, Eliz., 1654, by Nich. Merywether, Westmoreland Co.
Lucking, George, 1635, by Daniel Cugley, Accomac Co.
Luckins, Eliza., 1639, by John Pawley, James City Co.
Luckston, Edward, 1638, by Randall Crew, Upper New Norfolk Co.
Luco, Antho., 1637, by Robt. Holt and Richard Bell, James City Co.
Lucy, Jaone, 1653, by Abraham Moone, Lancaster Co.
Lucye, Hester, 1654, by John Drayton, Westmoreland Co.
Ludd, Thomas, 1651, by Richard Grigson, ——— Co.
Ludicus, La., 1652, by Mr. James Warradine, ——— Co.
Ludicus, Eliz., 1653, by Mr. James Warradine, ——— Co.
Luddington, Allen, 1642, by Hugh Gwyn, Gent., ——— Co.
Luddington, Samuell, 1650, by Thomas Mulford, Nansemond Co.
Ludlow, Gabriell, 1652, by Col. Geo. Ludlow, Esq., Gloucester Co.
Lodlow, Tho., 1652, by Col. Geo. Ludlow, Esq., Gloucester Co.
Ludlow, Wm., 1654, by John Sherrett, ——— Co.
Ludson, John, 1654, by John Drayton, Westmoreland Co.
Ludwell, James, 1656, by Capt. Henry Fleete, ——— Co.
Ludwell, Tho., 1646, by Col. Henry Bishopp, James City Co.
Lue, Tho., 1653, by Richard Braine, Charles Co.
Luellin, Jenkin, 1653, by Charles Scarburg, Northampton Co.
Luellin, Rc., 1651, by Mr. Rowland Burnham, ——— Co.
Lufurrier, Anthony, 1637, by Peter Roy and William Jacob, Isle of
    Wight Co.
Luggett, Georg, 1642, by John Smith, James City Co.
Luke, Wm., 1654, by Coll. Jno. Matron, Westmoreland Co.
Lumbert, Wm., 1652, by John Godfrey, Lower Norfolk Co.
Lumbrey, Dominick, 1643, by Capt. Wm. Peirce, Esq., ——— Co.
Lumley, Dom, 1650, by Capt. Moore Fautleroy, ——— Co.
Lunn, John, 1653, by Richard Burton, ——— Co.
Luntsford, The Ladey, 1650, by Sr. Tho. Luntsford, Kt., and Baronett,
    ——— Co.
Luntsford, Mrs. Elizabeth, 1650, by Sr. Tho. Luntsford, Kt., and Barro-
    nett, ——— Co.
Luntsford, Mrs. Mary, 1650, by Sr. Tho. Luntsford, Kt, and Barronett,
    ——— Co.
Luntsford, Wm., Esq., 1650, by Sr. Tho. Luntsford, Kt., and Barronett,
    ——— Co.
Luntsford, Mrs. Phillipa, 1650, by Sr. Tho. Luntsford, Kt., and Bar-
    ronett, ——— Co.
Lupton, John, 1638, by Byron Smith, Henrico Co.
Lupo, Wm., 1643, by Sir Francis Wyatt, Kt., ——— Co.
Lupton, John, 1652, by John Greenbough, Henrico Co.
Lurks, Nicho., 1651, by Mr. Rowland Burnham, ——— Co.
Lurner, Sam., 1635, by George Minifie, James City Co.
Lushby, Robert, 1652, by Tho. Cartwright, Lower Norfolk Co.
Lusse, Mary, 1639, by Richard Corke, Gent., Henrico Co.

Lustcomb, Thomas, 1647, by Thomas Wright, Lower Norfolk Co.
Lutton, Elizabeth, 1652, by Tho. Steevens, Lancaster Co.
Luter, Thomas, 1637, by Rich. Bennett, New Norfolk Co.
Luter, Thomas, 1635, by Richard Bennett, ——— Co.
Luther, John, 1642, by Tho. Curtis, ——— Co.
Lutton, Robt., 1636, by Francis Maulden, ——— Co.
Lux, Thomason, 1635, by Wm. Garry, Accomacke Co.
Lewindall, Tho., 1654, by John Watson and John Bognall, Westmore-
     land Co.
Lyall, Dennis, 1649, by Mr. Henry Woodhouse, Lower Norfolk Co.
Lyddal, Geo., 1654, by Capt. John West, Esq., Gloucester Co.
Lyddeatt, Rich., 1655, by Mr. Tho. Peck, Gloucester Co.
Lyel, Eliz., 1647, by James Warradine, ——— Co.
Lyell, Dennis, 1652, by Mr. Edwin Connaway, ——— Co.
Lyke, Ann, 1642, by John Smith, James City Co.
Lylley, ———, 1642, by John Lylley (her husband), ——— Co.
Lylls, Martha, 1646, by John Ashcomb, Upper Norfolk Co.
Lyme, John, 1648, by Richard Lee, Gent., ——— Co.
Lymon, Amy, 1655, by Richard Price, New Kent Co.
Lymon, Jon., 1635, by Charles Harwer, ——— Co.
Lyna, Arthur, 1655, by John Westlock, Northampton Co.
Lyna, Rose, 1655, by John Westlock, Northampton Co.
Lyna, Mary, 1655, by John Westlock, Northampton Co.
Lynar, John, 1653, by Edward Kemp, Geo. Cortlough, and John
     Meredith, Lancaster Co.
Lynce, Nehemiah, 1655, by Wm. Wright, Gent., Nansemond Co.
Lynch, Jeremiah, 1638, by Capt. Christopher Wormley, Charles River
     Co.
Lyne, Fra., 1651, by Toby Norton, Northampton Co.
Lynge, Michl., 1655, by Wm. Wright, Gent., Nansemond Co.
Lyner, Silvester, 1654, by John Wyre, John Gillet, Andrew Gilson, and
     John Phillipps, ——— Co.
Lynn, Fra., 1651, by Abraham Moone and (Thomas Griffin), Lancaster
     Co.
Lynn, James, 1655, by John Nicholls, Northampton Co.
Lynsey, Robt., 1652, by Mr. Tho. Purifye and Mrs. Temperence
     Reppett, ——— Co.
Lyon, John, 1656, by Wm. Crump and Mr. Humphry Vaulx, James
     City Co.
Lyonel, Step., 1654, by Thomas Binus, Surry Co.
Lysemy, Sus., 1654, by John Wyre, John Gillet, Andrew Gilson and
     John Phillipps, ——— Co.
Lyster Morris, 1654, by Richard Jacob, Northampton Co.

M

Mabb, Tho., 1643, by Sir Francis Wyatt, ——— Co.
Mabor, Gile, 1651, by Mr. Rowland Burnham, ——— Co.
Macalster, 1654, by Valentine Patten, Westmoreland Co.
Macalster, John, 1654, by Valentine Patten, Westmoreland Co.
Macalster, Gowry, 1654, by Valentine Patten, Westmoreland Co.

Macalster, Hector, 1654, by Robert Hubard, Westmoreland Co.
Macargoe, John, 1652, by Major Lewis Burwell and Lucy, his wife, ——— Co.
Macay, John, 1651, by John Hull, Northumberland Co.
Mackall, Danll., 1653, by Edward Dobson, ——— Co.
Maccome, Jon., 1653, by Henry Lee, Yorke Co.
Machin, Eliza., 1635, by Edmund Scarbourgh, Accomack Co.
Macdnell, John, 1650, by John Mangor, ——— Co.
Mace, Gilbert, 1650, by Ralph Green, ——— Co.
Mace, Jon., 1637, by Henry Perry, Charles River Co.
Machoone, Dorrenum, 1656, by John Billiott, Northampton Co.
Mackgahaye, Wm., 1653, by Mr. Wm. Hoccaday, Yorke Co.
Mack-Person, Laugham, 1653, by Tho. Kidd, Lancaster Co.
Mack-Manor, Pat., 1653, by Jno. Edwards, Lancaster Co.
Mack Maroe, John, 1655, by David Boucher, Isle of Wight Co.
Mackan, John, 1652, by Nicho. George, Tho. Taberer, and Humphry Clarke, ——— Co.
Mackarle, Alexander, 1652, by Joseph Gregory, ——— Co.
Mackdall, Gilbert, 1652, by Major Lewis Burwell and Lucy, his wife, ——— Co.
Mackdoneal, Oneath, 1655, by John Browne, Gent., Northampton Co.
Mackdonell, Tho., 1653, by Tho. Speoke, ——— Co.
Mackdonell, Dan, 1653, by Tho. Speoke, ——— Co.
Mackee, Neale, 1652, by Nicholas George, ——— Co.
Mackelane, Wently, 1655, by John Wise, Northampton Co.
Mackelanna, Taberor, 1653, by Tho. Speoke, ——— Co.
Mackell, Sanders, 1653, by Richard Carey, ——— Co.
Mackeney, James, 1656, by John Wood, ——— Co.
Mackenly, Wm., 1653, by John Ware, ——— Co.
Macker, Owen, 1637, by Geo. Hull, Charles River Co.
Macker, Joane, 1654, by John Whithers and Stephen Garey, Westmoreland Co.
Mackerell, Elizabeth, 1655, by Peter Ford, Gloucester Co.
Mackernall, Dennis, 1654, by Edw. Welch, ——— Co.
Mackert, John, 1655, by Christopher Calvert, Northampton Co.
Macknilliam, John, 1655, by Mary Lewis, Northampton Co.
Mackery, Wm., 1653, by Richard Carey, ——— Co.
Mackery, Ja., 1650, by George Pate, Charles City Co.
Mackerye, Mich., 1653, by Wm. Hunt, ——— Co.
Mackfassum, John, 1650, by Wm. Clapham, ——— Co.
Mackinellan, ———, 1656, by Tabitha and Matilda Scarburgh, Northampton Co.
Mackland, Dan., 1653, by Mr. Edmund Bowman, ——— Co.
Macklatt, John, 1653, by Edward Kemp, Geo. Cortlough, and John Meredith, Lancaster Co.
Macklett, Allen, 1650, by John Cox, —— —Co.
Mackmun, James, 1653, by James Bonner, Lancaster Co.
Mackniel, James, 1652, by John Bayles, Lancaster Co.
Mackreall, Jno., 1648, by Lewis Burwell and Tho. Haws, York River Co.
Mackwell, James, 1653, by Abraham Moon, Lancaster Co.
Mackroe, Patrick, 1653, by Tho. Davis, ——— Co.

Macurt, Owen, 1655, by Tho. Leatherberry, Northampton Co.
Madby, John, 1650, by Sr. Tho. Luntsford, Kt., and Barronett, ———
    Co.
Maddin, Hen., 1643, by Henry Neale, James City Co.
Maddison, John, 1642, by Capt. Daniell Gookin, ———Co.
Maddison, Richard, 1638, by Thomas Swan, James Citie Co.
Maddison, Rich., 1635, by Wm. Swan, James Co.
Maddox, Alice, 1656, by George Abbott, Nansemond Co.
Maddox, Mary, 1653, by Tho. Todd, ——— Co.
Maddox, Edward, 1652, by Lawrence Dameron, Northumberland Co.
Made, Narmad, 1652, by Capt. John West, Esq., ——— Co.
Mader, Ambrose, 1636, by Peter Johnson, Warrisquinoake Co.
Mader, Jno., 1653, by Jno. Edwards, Lancaster Co.
Madero, Thomasen, 1653, by Mr. Wm. Hoccaday, Yorke Co.
Madison, Edwd., 1650, by Wingfield Webb, and Richard Pate, ———
    Co.
Madix, Katherine, 1652, by Nicho. Morris, Northumberland Co.
Madox, John, 1654, by Major Miles Carey, Westmoreland Co.
Madlock, Robert, 1638, by Thomas Clipwell, James City Co.
Madrin, Owin, 1640, by Thomas Harvey, James City Co.
Madwell, Wm., 1637, by Tho. Symmons, Charles River Co.
Madwell, William, 1639, by John Kempe, James City Co.
Madwell, Wm., 1639, by Tho. Symons, James City Co.
Madworth, Wm., 1637, by Daniell Gookins, New Norfolk Co.
Maealster, Gawry, 1654, by Robert Hubard, Westmoreland Co.
Maealster, John, 1654, by Robert Hubard, Westmoreland Co.
Maeshall, Jno., 1650, by Richard Tye and Charles Sparrowe, Charles
    City Co.
Mafield, Wm., 1653, by Charles Grymes, Lancaster Co.
Mage, Richard, 1642, by Adam Cooke, Charles County.
Magee, Jon., 1635, by Capt. Adam Thoroughgood, ——— Co.
Magler, Jno., 1653, by John Edwards, Lancaster Co.
Magson, Jon., 1643, by Capt. Wm. Perice, Esq., ——— Co.
Maguiry, Charles, 1653, by Major Abra. Wood, Charles City Co.
Mahonney, Dennis, 1635, by Tho. Butler Clark and Pastor of Denbie,
    Warrasquinoake Co.
Mahoone, David, 1656, by Wm. and Hancock Lee, Gloucester Co.
Maistone, Tho., 1650, by Sr. Tho. Lunstford, Kt., and Barronett,
    ——— Co.
Maidstone, Isabell, 1650, by Sr. Tho. Luntsford, Kt., and Barronett,
    ——— Co.
Maior, Wm., 1643, by John Freeme, Charles Co.
Maior, Geo., 1643, by Lt. Wm. Worleidge, ——— Co.
Maior, John, 1640, by John Maior, Accomack Co.
Maior, Jane, 1640, by John Maior, Accomack Co.
Maior, Eliz., 1642, by Stephen Gill, ——— Co.
Maior, Robert, 1642, by Adam Cooke, Charles County.
Maine, Grigory, 1650, by Lewis Burwell, Gent., Northumberland Co.
Mainson, John, 1643, by Richard Richards, Charles River Co.
Major, Herman, 1649, by Richard Vaughan, Northampton Co.
Major, Tho., 1653, by Charles Scarburgh, Northampton Co.

Major, Phi., 1637, by Capt. Thomas Panlett, Charles City Co.
Major, Rich., 1655, by Major Wm. Hoccaday, New Kent Co.
Major, Tho., 1645, by Francis Martin, Northampton Co.
Major, Eliza., 1645, by Francis Martin, Northampton Co.
Major, John, 1645, by Francis Martin, Northampton Co.
Major, Edward, 1645, by Francis Martin, Northampton Co.
Major, John, 1654, by Mrs. Mgt. Brent, Westmoreland Co.
Major, Fran., 1645, by Francis Martin, Northampton Co.
Major, Tho., 1652, by Mr. John Brown, Northampton Co.
Makefoshion, Jno., 1655, by Richard Jones, ——— Co.
Maker, Owen, 1651, by Edward Deggs, Esq., Yorke Co.
Makester, Rich., 1637, by Capt. Henry Browne, James River Co.
Makey, Danl., 1652, by George Kemp, Lower Norfolk Co.
Makin, Tho., 1653, by Robt. Wild and Phillip Chesley, York Co.
Makins, Dunkin, 1654, by Major Abraham Wood, Henrico Co.
Makinlton, And., 1653, by Charles Grimes, Lancaster Co.
Malam, Eliza., 1647, by Richard Stearnell, Lower Norfolk Co.
Maland, Fra., 1652, by John Johnson, Northampton Co.
Maldin, John, 1652, by Edward Cannon and Tho. Allen, Lower Norfolk
    Co.
Male, Martin, 1653, by Colo. Wm. Clayborne (Sec. of State), ——— Co.
Males, Robt., 1653, by Geo. Taylor, Lancaster Co.
Maley, Daniell, 1647, by John Sidney, Lower Norfolk Co.
Malfe, Wm., 1650, by Richard Axom and Tho. Godwin, ——— Co.
Malfe, Tho., 1650, by Richard Axom and Tho. Godwin, ——— Co.
Malferd, Tho., 1653, by by Margarett Upton, Lancaster Co.
Malladine, John, 1655, by Edmund Scarbourgh, Jr., and Littleton
    Scarbourgh, Northampton Co.
Mallard, Fra., 1654, by Mrs. Fra. Harrison, widow, Westmoreland Co.
Mallard, Tho., 1646, by Sir William Berkley, ——— Co.
Mallerd, Tho., 1653, by Tho. Mallard, Northumberland Co.
Mallery, Richd., 1649, by Wm. Nesum, Tho. Sax, Miles Bathasby
    and John Pyne, Northumberland Co.
Mallery, Roser, 1655, by John Woodward, Gloucester Co.
Mallry, Cormack, 1655, by Jon Smilley, ——— Co.
Mallett, Wm., 1635, by Thos. Crompe, James Co.
Malliose, Edward, 1652, by Richard Coleman, ——— Co.
Malton, Ja., 1653, by Capt. Robt. Abrahal, Gloucester Co.
Man, Thomas, 1638, by Hugh Allen, Charles River Co.
Man, Robt., 1637, by James Berry, Accomack Co.
Man, Robert, 1636, by James Berry, Accomack Co.
Man, Nich., 1636, by Justinian Cooper, Warrasquinoake Co.
Man, ———, 1653, by Robert Bouth, Yorke Co.
Manchest, Jno., 1645, by Michael Masters, Henrico Co.
Manckes, Gilbert, 1637, by Henry Perry, Charles River Co.
Mander, Welts, 1651, by John King, Gloucester Co.
Mandor, Randall, 1647, by John Brooch, York River Co.
Manet, Wal., 1637, by Daniell Gookins, New Norfolk Co.
Manfelld, Robt., 1652, by Richard Longe, ——— Co.
Mangor, John, 1650, by Wm. Clapham, ——— Co.
Maning, Joan, 1652, by Robert Lendall, ——— Co.

Manker, Robt., 1650, by Capt. Moore Fautleroy, ——— Co.
Manly, Jon., 1637, by Joseph Cobb, Isle of Wight Co.
Manly, John, 1636, by John Neale, Accomack Co.
Manly, Jon, 1637, by Joseph Cobb, Isle of Wight Co.
Maning, Jane, 1652, by John Gresham, Northumberland Co.
Manough, Patrick, 1653, by Geo. Thompson, ——— Co.
Mann, Tho., 1650, by Capt. Moore Fautleroy, ——— Co.
Mann, Christian, 1648, by Nicholas Dixson, Nansemond Co.
Mann, Nicholas, 1642, by Justinian Cooper, Isle of Wight Co.
Mann, Tho., 1650, by John Garwood, Nansemond Co.
Mann, Benja., 1652, by Capt. John West, Esq., ——— Co.
Mannce, Wm., 1637, by Thomas Cansey, Charles City Co.
Manner, Tho., 1653, by Nicholas Meriwether, Lancaster Co.
Manner, Marg., 1654, by John Watson and John Bognall, Westmoreland
　　Co.
Manners, Jos., 1635, by Wm. Swan, James Co.
Manning, Lazarus, 1635, by Charles Harwer, ——— Co.
Manse, Alex., 1651, by James Thelaball, Lower Norfolk Co.
Mansel, Jno., 1653, by Wm. Sidner, Lancaster Co.
Mansell, John, 1650, by George Taylor, ——— Co.
Manser, Tho., 1653, by Tho. Davis, Gent., Nansemond Co.
Mansfield, Tho., 1649, by John King, Yorke Co.
Mansfield, Jane, 1654, by Capt. David Mansell, Westmoreland Co.
Mansfeild, Eliza., 1654, by Capt. David Mansell, Westmoreland Co.
Mansfeild, Vincent, 1653, by Colo. Wm. Clayborne (Sec. of State),
　　——— Co.
Mansfeild, Wm., 1654, by Walter Dickenson, Lancaster Co.
Mansliepp, Richard, 1638, by Randall Crew, Upper New Norfolk Co.
Mantone, Will, 1653, by Major Abra. Wood, Charles City Co.
Mapp, John, 1654, by Richard Allen, Northampton Co.
Mapps, Robert, 1652, by Mr. John Brown, Northampton Co.
Maple, John, 1652, by Nicho. Sebrell, Northumberland Co.
Mapleton, Jacob, 1651, by Tho. Wilsford, Gent., ——— Co.
Mappind, John, 1649, by Francis Brown, Northumberland Co.
Marale, Geo., 1652, by Toby Smith, Gent., Lancaster Co.
Marbury, Richard, 1643, by Wm. Storey, Upper Norfolk Co.
Marcall, Rice, 1635, by Thos. Harris, Henrico Co.
Marchall, Wm., 1648, by Wm. Ewen, James City Co.
Marchall, Henry, 1635, by McWilliam Stone, ——— Co.
Marchlam, Tho., 1648, by Tho. Lambert, Lower Norfolk Co.
Mardure, Wm., 1653, by Peter Knight and Baker Cutt, ——— Co.
Mare, John, 1651, by Robt. Newman, Northumberland Co.
Marea, Anna, 1654, by Mrs. Fra. Harrison, widow, Westmoreland Co.
Marecroft, Sam., 1653, by Tho. Hampton, ——— Co.
Marenhana, Edmd., 1652, by Tho. Todd, ——— Co.
Mareland, Darmett, 1652, by Nicholas Waddilow, Northampton Co.
Marely, Robt., 1655, by Geo. Coltclough, Northumberland Co.
Marfee, James, 1637, by William Parry, New Norfolk Co.
Margaret, James, 1655, by Richard Codsford, Westmoreland Co.
Margarett, Small, 1637, by John Moone, Isle of Wight Co.
Margaretts, John, 1653, by Abraham Moon, Lancaster Co.

Margeson, Rob., 1655, by Jer. Dodson, Gent., Lancaster Co.
Margetts, Jno., 1654, by Rich. Bunduch, Northampton Co.
Margorane, Herbert, 1656, by Roger Wolmsly and Richard Ingram, James City Co.
Margrave, Tho., 1649, by Edmund Scarburgh, Jr., Northampton Co.
Margrave, Ad., 1648, by Wm. Ewen, James City Co.
Margret, James, 1654, by Nath. Pope, Westmoreland Co.
Margritts, Wm., 1650, by John Baytes, Northumberland Co.
Marin, Eliza, 1655, by Philip Charles, ——— Co.
Maris, Mary, 1650, by Wm. Yarrett and Fra. Wittington, ——— Co.
Mark, And., 1654, by Edw. Welch, ——— Co.
Markason, Robt., 1653, by Richard Vardy, James City Co.
Markedon, John, 1638, by Robert Freeman, James City Co.
Marke, Eliza., 1652, by Peter Knight, Gloucester Co.
Marke, Alexander, 1652, by Mr. Tho. Curtis, ——— Co.
Marke, Sara, 1650, by George Pate, Charles City Co.
Markes, Jon., 1643, by John Freeme, Charles Co.
Markes, John, 1643, by Tho. Wheeler, Charles City Co.
Markes, Peter, 1643, by Thomas Wheeles, Charles City Co.
Markes, Rich., 1645, by Lawrence Ward and John King, Isle of Wight Co.
Marken, Patience, 1648, by John Landman, Nansemond Co.
Marken, Patience, 1649, by Tho. Dale, ——— Co.
Markham, John, 1639, by Tho. Stamp, James City Co.
Markham, John, 1638, by Thomas Stampe, James City Co.
Markham, Susan, 1636, by Thos. Markham, Henrico Co.
Markham, Tho., 1637, by Thomas Markham, Henrico Co.
Markham, Susan, 1637, by Thomas Markham, Henrico Co.
Marks, John, 1655, by Symon Symons, Charles City Co.
Marks, Brice, 1638, by Stephen Charlton, Accomack Co.
Marleaw, Eliza., 1651, by Capt. Geo. Read, Lancaster Co.
Marleaw, Capt. Nico., 1651, by Capt. Geo. Read, Lancaster Co.
Marlett, Davy, 1654, by Robert Hubard, Westmoreland Co.
Marlin, Geo., 1656, by Tho. Rolfe, Gent., James City Co.
Marlin, Jon., 1636, by Richard Cocke, ——— Co.
Marlin, Edwd., 1651, by Richard Smith, Northampton Co.
Marloe, Wm., 1654, by Wm. Thorne, Northampton Co.
Marloe, Mary, 1653, by Rawleigh Travers, ——— Co.
Marmaduke, Richard, 1638, by Capt. Christopher Wormley, Charles River Co.
Marmore, Elizabeth, 1638, by Stephen Hamblyn, Charles City Co.
Marner, Adrian, 1638, by Wm. Clays, Charles River Co.
Marogan, John, 1651, by Hugh Fauch and James Magregory, Northumberland Co.
Maron, Ann, 1651, by Wm. Rennales, Northumberland Co.
Marrell, John, 1649, by Edmund Scarburgh, Jr., Northampton Co.
Marres, Robt., 1656, by Wm. Pulliam, New Kent Co.
Marriot, Henry, 1646, by Thomas Bahe, Upper Norfolk Co.
Marrow, Geo., 1647, by Richard Bland, ——— Co.
Marrowe, Alen, 1650, by John Hallawes, Gent., Northumberland Co.
Marsam, Edward, 1642, by Tho. Curtis, ——— Co.

Marsh, Lewis, 1643, by Mr. Moore Fautleory, Upper Norfolk Co.
Marsh, Hugh, 1650, by Tho. Vaus, Gent., Northumberland Co.
Marsh, James, 1650, by John Armesbee, Northumberland Co.
Marsh, Francis, 1643, by Mr. Moore Fautleroy, Upper Norfolk Co.
Marsh, John, 1643, by Mr. Moore Fautleroy, Upper Norfolk Co.
Marsh, Joseph, 1638, by John Fludd, James City Co.
Marsh, Thomas, 1637, by Thomas Holt, New Norfolk Co.
March, Tho., 1652, by Richard Coleman, ——— Co.
Marshall, Wm., 1643, by William Ewins, James City Co.
Marshall, Mrs. Tho., 1650, by Sr. Tho. Luntsford, Kt., and Barronett, ——— Co.
Marshall, John, 1642, by John Sweete, ——— Co.
Marshall, John, and two children, 1650, by Mr. James Williamson, ——— Co.
Marshall, Henry, 1649, by Richard Kemp, Esq. (Sec. of State), ——— Co.
Marshall, John, 1646, by John Hill, Norfolk Co.
Marshall, Edw., 1648, by Thomas Woodhouse, James City Co.
Marshall, Edward, 1638, by John Batts and John Davis, Charles River Co.
Marshall, Jno., 1644, by James Taylor and Lawrence Baher, James City Co.
Marshall, Henry, 1638, by George Higgin, Charles River Co.
Marshall, John, 1636, by Joane Bennett, Charles River Co.
Marshall, Thos., 1635, by Capt. Adam Thoroughgood, ——— Co.
Marshall, Anne, 1653, by John Jaliffe, Isle of Wight Co.
Marshall, Wm., 1653, by Major John Westhrope, Charles City Co.
Marshall, John, 1656, by Lewis Perry, ——— Co.
Marshall, Hen., 1638, by Capt. Christopher Wormley, Charles River Co.
Marshall, Walter, 1639, by John Well, Charles City Co.
Marshall, Anne, 1642, by Christopher Boyce, ——— Co.
Marshell, Jno., 1653, by Frances Emperor, Hugh Gale, and Edward Morgan, Lower Norfolk Co.
Marsly, Jon., 1637, by Jonathan Longworth, New Norfolk Co.
Marsly, Jon., 1637, by Jonathan Langworth, New Norfolk Co.
Marston, Sil., 1651, by Mr. Wm. Armestead, ——— Co.
Marsse, Bryan, 1654, by Mrs. Mgt. Brent, Westmoreland Co.
Marstien, Wm., 1637, by Mathew Edloe, ——— Co.
Martaye, Edward, 1653, by Tho. Speake, ——— Co.
Martiall, Jno., 1648, by Job. Chanter, Lower Norfolk Co.
Martian, Eliz., 1639, by Capt. Nicholas Martian, her father, Charles River Co.
Martian, Jane, 1639, by Capt. Nicholas Martian, her husband, Charles River Co.
Martian, Nicho., 1639, by Capt. Nicholas Martian, his father, Charles River Co.
Marthdon, Mathew, 1635, by Capt. Wm. Pierse, ——— Co.
Martin, John, 1651, by John Hull, Northumberland Co.
Martin, Robert, 1650, by Richard Dunning, ——— Co.
Martin, John, 1654, by Mr. Tho. Fowke, Westmoreland Co.

Martin, Phillip, 1648, by John Seward, Isle of Wight Co.
Martin, Wm., 1646, by Col. Henry Bishopp, James City Co.
Martin, Joseph, 1650, by John Hany, Northumberland Co.
Martin, Mary, 1650, by Robert Blake and Samuell Elridge, Isle of Wight Co.
Martins, Maryall, 1648, by Richard Lee, Gent., ——— Co.
Martin, Capt. Nich., 1648, by Geo. Read, Gent., ——— Co.
Martin, Eliza., 1648, by George Read, Gent., ——— Co.
Martin, Mrs. Lane, 1648, by George Read, Gent., ——— Co.
Martin, John, 1653, by Charles Scarburg, Northampton Co.
Martin, Robert, 1643, by Sir Francis Wyatt, Kt., ——— Co.
Martin, Nich., 1638, by Randall Crew, Upper New Norfolk Co.
Martin, Robert, 1638, by John Cookeney, Henrico Co.
Martin, Nathaniel, 1637, by Leonard Yeo, Elizabeth City Co.
Martin, Arthur, 1637, by Rich. Bennett, New Norfolk Co.
Martin, Tho., 1637, by Mathew Edloe, ——— Co.
Martin, Thom., 1636, by James Vanerit, Elizabeth City Co.
Martin, Robert (servant), 1635, by William Stafford, ——— Co.
Martin, Arthur, 1635, by Richard Bennett, ——— Co.
Martin, Nich., 1635, by Rich. Peirce, James City Co.
Martin, John, 1653, by Tho. Todd, ——— Co.
Martin, John, 1653, by Tho. Hawkins, Northumberland Co.
Martin, Henry, 1639, by Georg Minifye, Esq., Charles River Co.
Martin, John, 1639, by Richard Corke, Gent., Henrico Co.
Martin, Wm., 1638, by John Moye, Lower New Norfolk Co.
Martin, Nicholas, 1638, by Rich. Hill and Roger Arnwood, James City Co.
Martin, Agnis, 1639, by William Canhcoe, Charles River Co.
Martin, Nicho., 1642, by Capt. Samuell Mathews, Esq., ——— Co.
Martin, Richard, 1642, by Lieut. Francis Mason, ——— Co.
Martin, Edward, 1650, by Richard Smith, Northampton Co.
Martin, John, 1655, by Mrs. Margaret Brent, Lancaster Co.
Martin, Danl., 1654, by Benjamin Mathews, Northampton Co.
Martin, Mary, 1654, by Major Miles Carey, Westmoreland Co.
Martin, Dudgell, 1652, by Capt. Tho. Hackett, Lancaster Co.
Martin, Dudyill, 1652, by Nathaniel Bacon, Isle of Wight Co.
Martin, Wm., 1652, by Mrs. Mry Brent, Northumberland Co.
Martin, John, 1652, by Mr. John Browne, Northampton Co.
Martin, Joan, 1653, by Robt. Blake, Isle of Wight Co.
Martine, John, 1654, by Mr. Wm. Westerhouse, Northampton Co.
Marton, Ralph, 1651, by Mr. Wm. Armestead, ——— Co.
Marton, Geo., 1653, by Robt. Saven, ——— Co.
Marton, Geo., 1653, by Wm. Debram, ——— Co.
Marton, Jos., 1694, by Mr. Edmund Scarburg, Northampton Co.
Marton, Mathew, 1639, by Thomas Mathews, Henrico Co.
Martyn, Elizabeth, wife of Robt. Martin, 1638, by Robert Martin, Lower New Norfolk Co.
Martyn, Robt., 1638, by Robt. Martin, Lower New Norfolk Co.
Martyn, Patience, 1641, by Garrett Stephens, Warwick River Co.
Martyn, Eliza., 1653, by John Edwards, Lancaster Co.
Marve, Hanna, 1638, by Richard Milton, Charles City Co.

Marvell, John, 1653, by Charles Scarburg, Northampton Co.
Marvell, John, 1652, by Mr. John Browne, Northampton Co.
Mary, John, 1651, by Abraham Moone and (Thomas Griffin), Lancaster Co.
Moryow, Henry, 1647, by Tho. Gibson, York Co.
Mason, Mary, wife Francis Mason, 1742, by Lieut. Francis Mason, ——— Co.
Mason, Francis, 1642, by Lieut. Francis Mason, ——— Co.
Mascall, Richard, 1638, by Capt. Thom. Harris, Henrico Co.
Mascall, Wm., 1642, by Georg Busse, ——— Co.
Mascull, Susan, 1654, by Humphry Haggett, Lancaster Co.
Mase, Thomas, 1648, by Lewis Burwell, Gent., ——— Co.
Masey, John, 1638, by Mr. Walter Ashton, Charles City Co.
Masgarke, Jaques, 1642, by Peter Johnson, New Norfolk Co.
Masgrove, Wm., 1638, by Christopher Wormley, Charles River Co.
Mash, Thomas, 1638, by Thomas Clipwell, James City Co.
Mash, Tho., 1653, by John Merryman and Morgan Haynes, Lancaster Co.
Mash, Wm., 1652, by Richard Dudley, ——— Co.
Mashfeild, Edmd., 1654, by Capt. John West, Esq., Gloucester Co.
Masie, Ann, 1650, by Mr. Anthony Ellyot, ——— Co.
Mason, Ann, 1654, by John Wyre, John Gillet, Andrew Gilson and John Phillipps, ——— Co.
Mason, Wm., 1646, by Col. Henry Bishopp, James City Co.
Mason, Henry, 1646, by Wm. Hockaday, York Co.
Mason, Tho., 1650, by Mr. Stephen Hamelin, Charles City Co.
Mason, Jon., 1643, by Rowland Burnham, Yorke Co.
Mason, Tho., 1650, by Mr. Epaphroditus Lawson, ——— Co.
Mason, Edward, 1648, by Georg Read, Gent., ——— Co.
Mason, Tho., 1646, by Sir William Berkeley, ——— Co.
Mason, Charles, 1637, by Henry Perry, Charles River Co.
Mason, John, 1641, by John Gookin, Lower Norfolk Co.
Mason, Jon., 1637, by Cheney Boyes, Charles City Co.
Mason, Jon., 1636, by Cheney Boyse, Charles City Co.
Mason, Robt., 1635, by Thom. Phillipps, James City Co.
Mason, Peter, 1656, by Sir Henry Chichley, ——— Co.
Mason, Tho., 1656, by Sir Henry Chichley, —— —Co.
Mason, John, (and Sarah his wife), 1650, by Tho. Parker, Isle of Wight Co.
Mason, Wm., 1652, by Tho. Greenwood, Isle of Wight Co.
Mason, Robert, 1639, by Georg Minifye, Esq., Charles River Co.
Mason, James, 1638, by Thomas Croutch, James City Co.
Mason, John, 1642, by John Beale, ——— Co.
Mason, Charles, 1637, by Henry Perry, Charles River Co.
Mason, Ann, 1642, by Lieut. Francis Mason, ——— Co.
Mason, Robt., 1642, by Capt. Daniell Gookin, ——— Co.
Mason, Robert, 1655, by Martin Hamond, ——— Co.
Mason, Mary, 1653, by John Bishop and James Mason, Surry Co.
Masse, Alex., 1637, by James Thelaball, Lower Norfolk Co.
Massell, John, 1655, by John Lawson, Lancaster Co.
Masser, Thomas, 1650, by Nicholas Jernen, Gent., ——— Co.

Massey, Roger, 1654, by John Wyre, John Gillet, Andrew Gilson and John Phillipps, ——— Co.
Massey, Robt., 1653, by Toby Horton, Lancaster Co.
Masters, Thomas, 1639, by Edward Prince, Charles City Co.
Masters, Robt., 1638, by Robt. Martin, Lower New Norfolk Co.
Masterson, Elizabeth, 1655, by Mr. Tho. Ballard, Gloucester Co.
Matham, John, 1638, by Christopher Branch, Henrico Co.
Matham, Wm., 1652, by Tho. Steevens, Warwick Co.
Mather, Tho., 1653, by Coll. Fran. Epps, Esq., Charles City Co.
Mathereel, Wm., 1637, by Tho. Wheeler, Charles City Co.
Mathering, N., 1655, by John Lawson, Lancaster Co.
Mathew, Robt., 1651, by James Baldridge and Capt. Tho. Baldrige, Northumberland Co.
Mathew, John, 1651, by Hugh Fauch and James Magregory, Northumberland Co.
Mathew, Jon., 1639, by John Pawley, James City Co.
Mathew, John, 1656, by Wm. and Hancock Lee, Gloucester Co.
Mathew, John, 1651, by John Smithey, ——— Co.
Mathews, Antho., 1638, by John Seaward, Isle of Wight Co.
Mathews, Robt., 1654, by Capt. Giles Brent, Westmoreland Co.
Mathews, Benj., 1653, by Richard Burton, ——— Co.
Mathews, Edwd., 1651, by Roger Johns, Northampton Co.
Mathews, Ellinor, 1651, by Robt. Bradshaw, Charles River Co.
Mathews, Wm., 1651, by Coll. Richard Lee, Esq., Gloucester Co.
Mathews, Ann, 1650, by George Taylor, ——— Co.
Mathews, John, 1650, by Hump Lyster, ——— Co.
Mathews, Jno., 1648, by Wm. Edwards and Rice Edwards, James City Co.
Mathews, Phill, 1653, by Sampson Robins, Northampton Co.
Mathews, Morrice, 1653, by Edward Harrington, Northampton Co.
Mathews, Naurice, 1653, by Charles Scarburg, Northampton Co.
Mathews, Richard, 1643, by Epaphroditus Lawson, Upper Norfolk Co.
Mathews, Robert, 1643, by Sir Francis Wyatt, Kt., ——— Co.
Mathews, John, 1637, by Capt. Thomas Flint, Warwick River Co.
Mathews, John, 1637, by William Spencer, ——— Co.
Mathews, Rich., 1637, by Charles Barcroft, Isle of Wight Co.
Mathews, John, 1635, by William Spencer, ——— Co.
Matthews, Mary, 1653, by Wm. Hunt, ——— Co.
Matthews, Winifred, 1654, by Tho. Morecock, James City Co.
Mathews, Ellynor, 1654, by Nich. Merywether, Westmoreland Co.
Mathews, Barbara, 1656, by James Price, Northampton Co.
Mathews, Wm., 1638, by Cobb Howell, Lower New Norfolk Co.
Mathews, Roger, 1639, by Thomas Mathews, Henrico Co.
Mathews, Winifred, 1655, by Nich. Bush, James City Co.
Mathews, Jacob, 1647, by Leonard Pettock, Accomac Co.
Mathews, Tho., 1652, by Robt. Bauldry, York Co.
Mathewson, James, 1655, by Saml. Eldridge, ——— Co.
Mathaw, John, 1635, by Christopher Branch, Henrico Co.
Mathias, Mathew, 1651, by Richard Whitehurst, Lower Norfolk Co.
Mathis, Ann, 1635, by William Carter, Henrico Co.
Mathis, Ann, 1638, by William Carter, James City Co.

Mathy, Elizabeth, 1654, by Tho. Deynes,
Matthewes, Richard, 1650, by Jervace Dodson, Gent., Northumberland Co.
Matthews, Morris, 1651, by Jonos Jackson, Northampton Co.
Mattocks, Ann, 1656, by Mr. Henry Soanes, New Kent Co.
Matter, Wm., 1652, by Edward Revell, Northampton Co.
Maties, Alex., 1638, by Roger Davis, Charles City Co.
Matley, John, 1652, by John Pead, ——— Co.
Matlin, John, 1650, by Silvester Thatcher and Tho. Whitlocke, ——— Co.
Maton, Nicholas, 1638, by Edward Hill, Charles City Co.
Matricks, Alex, 1652., by Littleton Scarburgh, ——— Co.
Mattro, John, 1655, by Sam. Sollace and Robert Trolliver, Gloucester Co.
Matrun, William, 1635, by Mc William Stone, ——— Co.
Maurice, Williams, 1637, by Humphry Loyd, Charles River Co.
Maurice, Geo., 1656, by Major Wm. Lewis, ——— Co.
Maulden, Katherin, 1636, by Francis Maulden, ——— Co.
Maulden, William, 1635, by Robert Sheppard, ——— Co.
Mavellis, Claus, 1653, by John Dipdal, Charles City Co.
Maw, Tho., 1651, by Humphry Tabb, Northumberland Co.
Maway, Tho., 1655, by Edmund Scarbourgh, Jr., and Littleton Scarbourgh, Northampton Co.
Mawgery, James, 1650, by James Arrorke, ——— Co.
Mawsler, Loves, and Jane, his daughter, and Jane, his wife, 1650, by Lewis Burwell, Gent., ——— Co.
Max, Rob., 1655, by Southy Littleberry, Northampton Co.
Maxe, Robt., 1636, by James Knott, Elizabeth City Co.
Maxe, Robt., 1637, by James Knott, New Norfolk Co.
Maxfield, John, 1638, by Augustine Warner, Charles River Co.
Maxney, Cha., 1638, by William Clarke, Henrico Co.
Maxney, Charles, 1636, by Wm. Clarke, Henrico Co.
Maxrell, Alex., 1650, by George Pate, Charles City Co.
May, Margaret, 1655, by Major Miles Carey, Warwick Co.
May, William, 1648, by Mr. Thomas Davies, Isle of Wight Co.
May, Robt., 1638, by William Parker, Upper Norfolk Co.
May, Edwd., 1643, by Rich. Hoe, Gent., ——— Co.
May, Edward, 1637, by Robert Bennett, New Norfolk Co.
May, Nick., 1641, by Wm. Storey, Upper Norfolk Co.
May, Hannah, 1637, by Francis Osborne, ——— Co.
May, Jon., 1642, by Stephen Gill, Yorke River Co.
May, John, 1642, by Thomas Ray, ——— Co.
Maydley, Peter, 1645, by Michail Master, Henrico Co.
Mayden, Jon., 1653, by Wm. Johnson, Henrico Co.
Maye, Alice, 1648, by John Ellis, James Joones and John Taylor, Northampton Co.
Mayes, Henry, 1650, by Richard Budd, Northumberland Co.
Nayle, Wm., 1650, by Richard Tye and Charles Sparrowe, Charles City Co.
Mayler, Jone, 1639, by Walter Cooper, James City Co.
Maylor, Wm., 1639, by Lieut. Richard Popeley, ——— Co.

Mayne, Samll., 1648, by Lewis Burwell and Tho. Haws, York River Co.
Mayne, Susan, 1650, by Nathaniell Jones, Northumberland Co.
Mayne, John, 1655, by Mrs. Margaret Brent, Lancaster Co.
Mays, Edward, 1635, by Robert Bennett, ———— Co.
Mayses, John, 1656, by John Wood, ———— Co.
Maze, Robt., 1643, by Francis Rice, ———— Co.
McCloyden, Rose, 1654, by Richard Kellam, Northampton Co.
Mead, Jon., 1636, by Capt. Thomas Willoughby, ———— Co.
Mead, Jon., 1643, by Richard Kemp, Esq., James City Co.
Meadcrofts, Christopher, 1656, by Maj. Wm. Lewis, ———— Co.
Meades, Tho., 1638, by John Gater, Lower New Norfolk Co.
Meades, Thomas, 1636, by John Gater, Elizabeth City Co.
Meader, Nich., 1638, by Abraham Wood, Charles City Co.
Meader, Jon., 1638, by William Clarke, Henrico Co.
Meadwell, Wm., 1643, by Tho. Symonds, ———— Co.
Meadwell, Mary, 1655, by Jenken Price, Northampton Co.
Meal, Robert, 1654, by Tho. Deynes, ———— Co.
Mealy, Kath., 1654, by John Wyre, John Gillet, Andrew Gilson and John Phillipps, ———— Co.
Meares, John, 1654, by Col. Hump. Higgenson, Esq., and Abraham Moone, Westmoreland Co.
Meares, Tho., 1650, by Wm. Yarrett and Fra. Whittington, ———— Co.
Meares, Anne, 1654, by Francis Gray, ———— Co.
Meares, Humphry, 1654, by Francis Gray, ———— Co.
Meares, Henry, 1638, by Joseph Harmon, James City Co.
Meares, Henry, 1635, by William Beard, James City Co.
Meares, Bartholomew, 1655, by Wm. Taylor, Northampton Co.
Meares, Walter, 1653, by Francis Emepror, Lower Norfolk Co.
Meares, Hump., and Anne his wife, 1653, by Samuell Parry, Lancaster Co.
Mccane, Kath., 1655, by George Parker, Northampton Co.
Mecannick, Dan., 1653, by Capt. Robt. Abrall, ———— Co.
Mecunny, Mecum, 1652, by Nicholas Waddilow, Northampton Co.
Medcalfe, C—, 1650, by Mr. James Willaims, ———— Co.
Medcalfe, Pete, 1648, by Geo. Hardey, Tho. Wombwell, and Peter Hall, Isle of Wight Co.
Medcalfe, Jeffery, 1645, by John Rode, Warwick Co.
Medcalfe, Henry, 1637, by John Wilkins, New Norfolk Co.
Medcalfe, Henry, 1636, by John Wilkins, Accomack Co.
Medcalfe, Wm., 1639, by Lieut. Richard Popeley, ———— Co.
Medcalfe, Christopher, 1635, by Richard Tisdale, ———— Co.
Medcalfe, Jno., 1654, by John Wyre, John Gillett, Andrew Gilson and John Phillipps, ———— Co.
Medlam, Agnis, 1635, by John Wilkins, Accomack Co.
Medlam, Agnes, 1637, by John Wilkins, New Norfolk Co.
Medland, Geo., 1642, by Wm. Pudivatt, Isle of Wight Co.
Medle, Robt., 1637, by Hen. Thompson, James River Co.
Medley, Robert, 1650, by Robert Bird, ———— Co.
Medley, Robert, 1641, by Ambrose Bennett, Isle of Wight Co.
Medley, Wm., 1650, by John Sevier, ———— Co.

Medralfe, George, 1652, by Ralph Horsley, Northumberland Co.
Medralfe, Charles, 1652, by Ralph Horsley, Northumberland Co.
Medralfe, Wm., 1652, by Ralph Horsley, Northumberland Co.
Mee, Geo., 1635, by Capt. A. Throughgood, ———— Co.
Meekes, John, 1654, by Toby Smith, Lancaster Co.
Meekes, John, 1652, by Lawrence Dameron, Northumberland Co.
Mekins, Anne, 1653, by John Medstard, and John Edwards, Northumberland Co.
Meekins, Jno. 1654, by John Wyre, John Gillet, Andrew Gilson and John Phillipps, ———— Co.
Meeleger, John, 1651, by James Thelaball, Lower Norfolk Co.
Meerfin, Griffin, 1637, by Daniell Gookins, New Norfolk Co.
Meggs, George, 1652, by John Wareham, Northumberland Co.
Melder, John, 1636, by Wm. Clarke, Henrico Co.
Melham, James, 1643, by John Freeme, Charles Co.
Melelr, John, 1649, by Mr. Ralph Barlowe, Northampton Co.
Melling, Anne, 1653, by Wm. Mellin, Northampton Co.
Melling, Wm., 1653, by Wm. Mellin, Northampton Co.
Mellock, Jno., 1650, by Capt. Moore Faulteroy, ———— Co.
Mellon, Nich., 1653, by Capt. Robt. Abrahal, Gloucester Co.
Melner, Tho., 1650, by David Peebles, Charles City Co.
Milton, Hannah, 1638, by Tho. Melton (her husband), Lower New Norfolk Co.
Melton, Thomas, 1635, by Capt. Adam Thoroughgood, ———— Co.
Melvice, Agnes, 1654, by Nich. Merywether, Westmoreland Co.
Mendrose, Sanders, 1653, by Tho. Todd, ———— Co.
Menslye, Georg., 1638, by Christopher Thomas, Accomac Co.
Menter, David, 1636, by Bridges Freeman, ———— Co.
Mentin, Jon., 1635, by William Barber (a mariner), Charles City Co.
Mentoe, Nicholas, 1650, by Sr. Tho. Luntsford, Kt., and Barronett, ———— Co.
Mercer, Richard, 1643, by Mr. Moore Fautleroy, Upper Norfolk Co.
Mercer, Robert, 1637, by Henry Perry, Charles River Co.
Mercer, Robt., 1637, by Henry Perry, Charles River Co.
Mercer, John, 1642, by Capt. Samuell Mathews, ———— Co.
Mercey, Jno., 1650, by Jervace Dodson, Northumberland Co.
Merchant, Jeffy, 1637, by Wm. Prior, Gent., Charles River Co.
Meredith, Tho., 1650, by John Mattrum, Northumberland Co.
Meredith, David, 1650, by Francis Hobbs, ———— Co.
Meredith, John, 1637, by Capt. Henry Browne, James River Co.
Merifield, Abra., 1646, by Tho. Savedge, Northampton Co.
Merler, John, 1636, by Christopher Calthropp, Charles River Co.
Mermaduke, Richd., 1649, by Capt. Ralph Wormeley, ———— Co.
Merte, John, 1651, by Joseph Croshawe, Yorke Co.
Merr, John, 1652, by John Bryan, ———— Co.
Merredith, Tho., 1638, by John Gater, Lower New Norfolk Co.
Merrett, William, 1637, by Thomas Barnard, Warwick River Co.
Merrick, Thomas, 1643, by Robert Lawrance, Isle of Wight Co.
Merrick, Wm., 1654, by John Wyre, John Gillet, Andrew Gilson and John Phillipps, ———— Co.
Merrick, Howel, 1654, by Col. Argoll Yardley, Northampton Co.

Merrick, Hen., 1635, by Mr. Geo. Keth, Charles River Co.
Merriday, John, 1638, by John Yates, Lower New Norfolk Co.
Merrideth, Fr., 1638, by John Gater, Upper New Norfolk Co.
Merrideth, Thomas, 1636, by John Gater, Elizabeth City Co.
Merrideth, Francis, 1636, by John Gater, Elizabeth City Co.
Merrie, Savage, 1637, by Lt. John Upton, Isle of Wight Co.
Merrifell, Kath., 1655, by Mary Lewis, Northampton Co.
Merrill, Peirce, 1655, by Wm. Botham, Westmoreland Co.
Merriman, Sarah, 1635, by James Merriman, Charles City Co.
Merrit, Wm., 1653, by Margarett Upton, Lancaster Co.
Merror, Nicho., 1648, by Richard Lee, Gent., ———— Co.
Merrott, James, 1650, by George Taylor, ———— Co.
Merry, Jon., 1643, by Richard Kemp, Esq., James City Co.
Merry, Isam, 1636, by John Roberts, Elizabeth City Co.
Merryman, Audry, 1649, by John Merriman, ———— Co.
Merryman, Ann, 1643, by James Merryman, Charles City Co.
Mesele, Jos., 1643, by Joseph Croshawe, ———— Co.
Meshen, Henry, 1637, by John Dennett, Charles River Co.
Mess, Wm., 1655, by John Westlock, Northampton Co.
Messard, Deborah, 1635, by Anthony Jones, ———— Co.
Messenger, Hercules, 1638, by Wm. Carter, James City Co.
Messer, James, 1653, by Charles Grymes, Lancaster Co.
Methrole, Tho., 1643, by Capt. Samuell Mathews, Esq., ———— Co.
Metton, George, 1654, by John Williams, Northumberland Co.
Meviry, Daniell, 1636, by Cheney Boyse, Charles City Co.
Michaell, Richard, 1645, by James Bruss, Northampton Co.
Michaell, Edwd., 1648, by Tho. Braughton, ———— Co.
Michaell, Wm., 1652, by Tho. Teakle, Northampton Co.
Michaell, Palentine, 1653, by Colo. Wm. Clayborne (Sec. of State),
    ———— Co.
Michalla, Hugh, 1650, by Mr. Robt. Holt, James City Co.
Michallen, Jno., 1654, by Tho. Willoughby, Lower Norfolk Co.
Michell, Jno., 1650, by Richard Axom, and Tho. Godwin, ———— Co.
Michell, Thos., 1636, by John Neale, Accomack Co.
Michell, John, 1636, by Georg Travellor, Accomack Co.
Michell, Joanna, 1637, by Theodore Moyser, James City Co.
Michell, Henry, 1653, by John Gillett, Lancaster Co.
Michell, Walter, 1652, by Mr. Tho. Curtis, ———— Co.
Michem, John, 1652, by Nicho. Morris, Northumberland Co.
Nichols, Jon., 1636, by Robert Hollom, Henrico Co.
Michwell, Tho., 1650, by John Landman, ———— Co.
Micklesworth, Wm., 1637, by Capt. Thomas Osborne, Henrico Co.
Mickly, Jno., 1654, by Tho. Willoughby, Lower Norfolk Co.
Middleton, Joane, 1652, by Wm. Up Thomas, ———— Co.
Middleton, Owen, 1647, by Elizabeth Barcroft, Isle of Wight Co.
Middleton, Owen, 1650, by Anthony Fulgam, ———— Co.
Middleton, Mary, 1644, by James Taylor and Lawrence Baker, James
    City Co.
Middleton, Catherine, 1647, by Thomas Johnson, Gent., Northampton
    Co.

Middleton, James, 1638, by Percivall, Champion, Upper New Norfolk Co.
Middleton, Wm., 1638, by Thomas Plomer and Samuell Edmonds, James City Co.
Midleton, James, 1637, by Percival Champion, New Norfolk Co.
Middleton, Tho., 1655, by Dr. Giles Mode, New Kent Co.
Middleton, John, 1656, by Mr. Martin Baker, New Kent Co.
Middleton, Mary, ——, by Mr. John Page, —— Co.
Middleton, John, 1652, by Capt. Tho. Hackett, Lancaster Co.
Middleton, Robert, 1653, by Collo. Wm. Taylor, Esq., Gloucester Co.
Middlemore, Geo., 1654, by Martin Coale, Northumberland Co.
Midleton, Nich., 1638, by Joseph Harmon, James City Co.
Middip, John, 1636, by Wm. Parker, Warrasquinoake Co.
Midelewood, Wm., 1650, by James Hurd, —— Co.
Middleton, Wm., 1649, by Capt. Ralph Wormeley, —— Co.
Midleton, With., 1635, by William Beard, James City Co.
Midleton, John, 1639, by Wm. Denham, Isle of Wight Co.
Midleton, John, 1642, by Lieut. Francis Mason, —— Co.
Midlemane, Geo., ——, by Capt. Daniel Luellin, —— Co.
Midlux, Henry, 1654, by Lt. Colo. John Cheeseman and (John Addeston), —— Co.
Miffoner, Mary, 1656, by Francis Hutchins, Nansemond Co.
Mike, Ann, 1642, by Thomas Loving, James City Co.
Milborne, Rich., 1635, by Henry Harte, James City Co.
Milday, Edw., 1650, by John Sevier, —— Co.
Miles, Tho., 1650, by John Hany, Northumberland Co.
Miles, John, 1647, by Thomas Johnson, Gent., Northampton Co.
Miles, Hen., 1653, by Wm. Hunt, —— Co.
Miles, Adam, 1656, by Mr. Martin Baker, New Kent Co.
Miles, Wm., 1642, by John Smith, James City Co.
Miles, Robt., Jr., 1642, by Wm. Ireland and Robt. Wallis, Yorke Co.
Miles, Barbara, 1642, by Wm. Ireland and Robert Wallis, York, Co.
Miles, John, 1652, by Tho. Steevens, Lancaster Co.
Miles, John, 1652, by Mr. Wm. Waters, Northampton Co.
Miles, Hump., 1652, by Mr. Richard Cocke, Henrico Co.
Milford, Sarah, 1653, by Geo. Watts, Northumberland Co.
Mill, John, 1654, by John Watson and John Bognall, Westmoreland Co.
Mill, James, 1655, by Edward Pettaway, Surry Co.
Millard, Jones, Child Richard Millard, 1650, by Sr. Tho. Luntsford, Kt., and Barronett, —— Co.
Millard, Richard, 1650, by Sr. Tho. Luntsford, Kt., and Barronett, —— Co.
Millard, Richard, 1638, by John Watkins, James Cittie Co.
Millen, Heebert, 1651, by Capt. John West, Esq., Yorke Co.
Millen, Barthol, 1642, by Adam Cooke, Charles Co.
Miller, Tho., 1651, by Wm. Taylor, Northumberland Co.
Miller, Kath., 1651, by George Eaton, —— Co.
Miller, Joseph, 1651, by Richard Whitehurst, Lower Norfolk Co.
Miller, Edw., 1643, by Henry Neale, James City Co.
Miller, Xtop., 1650, by Capt. Moore Faulteroy, —— Co.

Miller, Joan, 1649, by Bertram Obert, ——— Co.
Miller, Fr., 1637, by Capt. Thomas Flint, Warwick River Co.
Miller, John, 1653, by Joseph Croshaw, York Co.
Miller, Wm., 1653, by Charles Grymes, Clerk, Lancaster Co.
Miller, Richard, 1653, by Charles Grymes, Lancaster Co.
Miller, Richard, 1643, by John Neale, Gent., Northampton Co.
Miller, Dorothy, 1656, by Mr. Henry Soanes, New Kent Co.
Miller, James, 1651, by Joseph Hayes, Gent., Yorke Co.
Miller, Andrew, 1653, by Mr. Wm. Fry, James City Co.
Miller, Dorothy, 1653, by Mr. Wm. Fry, James City Co.
Miller, Margarett, 1638, by Richard Mairon, Charles River Co.
Miller, Richard, 1638, by Richard Mairon, Charles River Co.
Miller, Georg, 1638, by John George, Charles City Co.
Miller, Pat., 1650, by John Garwood, Nansemond Co.
Miller, Jno., 1643, by Fra. Mason, Henrico Co.
Miller, John, 1655, by Richard Price, New Kent Co.
Miller, Sarah, 1656, by John Williams, Lower Norfolk Co.
Miller, James, 1655, by Mrs. Margaret Brent, Lancaster Co.
Miller, Jane, 1653, by Mr. Edmund Bowman and Richard Starnell, ——— Co.
Miller, John, 1654, by Mr. Francis Hamond, York Co.
Miller Dorothy, 1652, by Mr. Henry Soane, ——— Co.
Miller, Tho., 1652, by Mr. Peter Knight, Gloucester Co.
Miller, James, 1653, by Francis Emperor, Hugh Gale, and Edward Morgan, Lower Norfolk Co.
Millett, Fra., 1651, by Edward Degg, Esq., Yorke Co.
Millett, Francis, 1651, by Capt. John West, Esq., Yorke Co.
Millett, Henry, 1651, by Capt. John West, Esq., Yorke Co.
Millett, Ralph, 1653, by Peter Knight, Northumberland Co.
Millicent, James, 1653, by Joseph Hogkinson, Lower Norfolk Co.
Millington, Joan, 1650, by Geo. Ludlow, Esq., Northumberland Co.
Millocha, Ja., 1649, by John Sibsey, Lower Norfolk Co.
Mills, Joan, 1654, by Wm. Thorne, Northampton Co.
Mills, John, 1642, by Hugh Gwyn, Gent., ——— Co.
Mills, Luke, 1638, by Thomas Gray, James City Co.
Mills, Alice, 1637, by Capt. Henry Browne, James City Co.
Mills, John, 1637, by John Baker, Henrico Co.
Mills, And., 1656, by Silvester Thatcher, ———Co.
Mills, Abigall, 1656, by Major Wm. Lewis, ——— Co.
Mills, Miles, 1650, by James Hurd, ——— Co.
Mills, Susan, 1637, by Capt. Francis Eppes, Charles City Co.
Mills, Jon., 1642, by Stephen Gill, ——— Co.
Mills, Lewis, 1642, by John Resbury, ——— Co.
Mills, John, 1652, by Mr. Henry Soane, ——— Co.
Mills, Cornelius, 1653, by Capt. Francis Patt, Northampton Co.
Milshire, John, 1653, by Capt. Francis Patt, Northampton Co.
Milton, Wm., 1654, by Lieut. Coll. Giles Brent, Westmoreland Co.
Milton, Wm., 1651, by John Rookwood, Gent., Northumberland Co.
Milton, Wm., 1651, by Lieut. Coll. Giles Brent, Northumberland Co.
Milton, Wm., 1638, by Edward Hill, Charles City Co.
Minefrid, Anne, 1652, by Capt. John West, Esq., ——— Co.

Minen, George, 1650, by Anthony Fuljam, ———— Co.
Minner, Geo., 1647, by Elizabeth Barcroft, Isle of Wight Co.
Mines, Ralph, 1650, by Mr. Anthony Ellyot, ———— Co.
Minifie, Chas., 1643, by Wm. Warcler, ———— Co.
Minifie, Wm., 1639, by Georg Minifye, Esq., Charles River Co.
Minnees, Tho., 1653, by Capt. Robt. Abrall, ———— Co.
Minnes, Tho., 1651, by Robert Abrall, Yorke Co.
Minnocks, Wm., 1638, by William Croutch, Lower Norfolk Co.
Minor, Katherine, 1643, by Edward Dobson, ———— Co.
Minshem, Eliz., 1654, by Alexander, Portus and Tho. Williams, Lancaster Co.
Minstrill, Tho., 1651, by Humphry Tabb, Northumberland Co.
Mint, John, 1650, by John Mattrum, Northumberland Co.
Minter, Jon., 1638, by Wm. Baker and Associates, Charles City Co.
Minter, Grace, 1638, by Edward Minter (her husband), James City Co.
Minter, Jon., 1635, by Edward Minter, James Co.
Minter, Ruth, 1635, by Edw. Minter, James Co.
Minter, Annie, 1635, by Edw. Minter, James Co.
Minton, David, 1637, by Bridges Freeman, James City Co.
Misle, Luke, 1635, by Thomas Gray, James Co.
Mission, John, 1646, by Geo. Ludlow, Esq., York Co.
Mitcalfe, John, 1652, by Mrs. Jane Harmer, Horthumberland Co.
Mitchener, Sanders, 1654, by Wm. Thorne, Northampton Co.
Mithell, Math., 1650, by Silvester Thatcher and Tho. Whitlocke, ————
    Co.
Mitchell, Edw., 1643, by Elizabeth Hull, ———— Co.
Mitchell, Tho., 1638, by John Cockeney, Henrico Co.
Mitchell, Thos., 1637, by Capt. Adam Thoroughgood, New Norfolk Co.
Mitchell, Wm., 1636, by Elizabeth Hawkins, Charles River Co.
Mitchell, Thomas, 1637, by John Redman and John Neale, Accomac
    Co.
Mitchell, Hen., 1653, by Richard Thomas, Henrico Co.
Mitchell, Wm., 1655, by Tho. Leatherberry, Northampton Co.
Mitchell, James, 1638, by John Robins, James City Co.
Michell, Aline, 1656, by Wm. Justice, Charles City Co.
Mitchell, Henry, 1656, by Wm. Millinge, Northampton Co.
Mitchell, Jo., 1653, by Ferdinando Austin, Charles City Co.
Moby, John, 1651, by Thomas Keeling, Lower Norfolk Co.
Moales, Eliz., 1654, by Capt. David Mansell, Westmoreland Co.
Mose, David, 1653, by Geo. Watts, Northumberland Co.
Mocellett, John, 1655, by George Parker, Northampton Co.
Mocconey, Maccum, 1655, by Nich. Waddilow, Northampton Co.
Mochin, Tho., 1651, by John Hull, Northumberland Co.
Mock, David, 1638, by William Morgan, ———— Co.
Mockero, Mary, 1655, by Christopher Calvert, Northampton Co.
Mockland, Morgan, 1654, by Lule Billington, Accomac Co.
Mockland, Doc., 1655, by Nich. Waddilow, Northampton Co.
Mockay, James, 1653, by Tho. Todd, ———— Co.
Mockay, Jno., 1654, by Capt. Augustine Warner and Mr. John Robins,
    ———— Co.
Mocklayne, John, 1650, by George Taylor, ———— Co.

Mocklesly, Daniel, 1650, by George Pate, Charles City Co.
Macartee, Elisca, 1653, by Tho. Speoke, ———— Co.
Mockworth, Arthur, 1643, by Capt. Samuell Mathews, Esq., ————
    Co.
Modnell, Edmund, 1652, by Richard King, Lower Norfolk Co.
Mogeredge, Richard, 1654, by John Drayton, Westmoreland Co..
Mohunharaya, Hugh, 1653, by John Dipdall, Charles City Co.
Molford, Rebecca, 1656, by Wm. Crump and Mr. Humphry Vaulx,
    James City Co.
Molline, Willm., 1653, by Mr. Wm. Hoccaday, Yorke Co.
Molocklan, Dennis, 1656, by John Billiott, Northampton Co.
Molton, Jasper, 1637, by Henry Wilsom, Accomack Co.
Momfort, Richard, 1641, by Wm. Storey, Upper Norfolk Co.
Momus, Joseph, 1638, by Thomas Swan, James Citie Co.
Monahan, Wm., 1654, by James Yates, ———— Co.
Monday, Thomas, 1637, by Theodore Moyser, James City Co.
Monder, James, 1655, by Ralph Green, New Kent Co.
Mondy, John, 1642, by Wm. Eyres, Upper New Norfolk Co.
Mondye, Symon, 1636, by Robert West, Elizabeth City Co.
Monford, Jeffry, 1654, by John Drayton, Westmoreland Co.
Monger, Elizabeth, 1651, by James Allen, Northumberland Co.
Montgomery, Neale, 1650, by George Pate, Charles City Co.
Monkes, Frank, 1652, by Tho. Steevens, Lancaster Co.
Moon, William, 1637, by Georg White, New Norfolk Co.
Moone, Tho., 1652, by Littleton, Scarburgh, ———— Co.
Moone, Henry, 1637, by Humphry Higginson, Gent, ———— Co.
Moone, John, 1649, by Joseph Croshawe, Yorke Co.
Moone, Susan, 1635, by John Moone, Warrasquinoake Co.
Moone, Abraham, 1638, by Epaphroditus Lawson, Upper Norfolk Co.
Moone, Abraham, 1639, by Lieut. Richard Popeley, ———— Co.
Moone, Arthur, 1652, by Mr. Wm. Waters, Northampton Co.
Moody, Mary, 1641, by William Yarrett, New Norfolk Co.
Moold, Francis, 1643, by Richard Richards, Charles River Co.
Moor, Jno., 1645, by John Rode, Warwick Co.
Moor, Tho., 1654, by Robert Holt, James City Co.
Moor, Susan, 1653, by Toby Horton, Lancaster Co.
Moor, Edward, 1652, by Richard Coleman, ———— Co.
Moor, Hen., 1653, by Wm. Morgan, ———— Co.
Mooringe, John, 1652, by Tho. Greenwood, Isle of Wight Co.
Mooreland, 1637, by Capt. Robt. Helgate, Charles River Co.
Moorecroft, Henry, 1640, by Christopher Kirke, Accomack Co.
Moore, Rebecca, 1651, by Richard Smith, Northampton Co.
Moore, Kath., 1651, by Richard Smith, Northampton Co.
Moore, Ann, 1651, by Robert Abrall, Yorke Co.
Moore, Richard, 1646, by Richard Moore and William Welton, Upper
    Norfolk Co.
Moore, Jon., 1643, by Capt. Samuell Mathews, Esq., ———— Co.
Moore, John, 1646, by John Ashcomb, Upper Norfolk Co.
Moore, Dan., 1650, by John Hallawes, Gent., Northumberland Co.
Moore, Henry, 1643, by Wm. Gapinge, James City Co.
Moore, Eliz., 1650, by John Mattrum, Northumberland Co.

Moore, Joane, 1650, by Capt. Moore Faulteroy, ——— Co.
Moore, Wm., 1650, by Wm. Hodgson, Yorke Co.
Moore, George, 1650, by John Mangor, ——— Co.
Moore, Tho., 1649, by Edmund Scarburgh, Jr., Northampton Co.
Moore, Wm., 1648, by Tho. Lambert, Lower Norfolk Co.
Moore, Nat., 1650, by Edward Walker, Northumberland Co.
Moore, Edward, 1653, by Sampson Robins, Northampton Co.
Moore, Tho., 1653, by Edward Harrington, Northampton Co.
Moore, Thomas, 1653, by Charles Scarburg, Northampton Co.
Moore, Aldalo, 1645, by William Daynes, Lower Norfolk Co.
Moore, John, 1643, by Thomas Cassen, ——— Co.
Moore, Nath., 1638, by Capt. Tho. Harris, Henrico Co.
Moore, John, 1638, by Robert Freeman, James City Co.
Moore, Nich., 1637, by Capt. Thomas Flint, Warwick River Co.
Moore, Eliz., 1637, by Henry Perry, Charles River Co.
Moore, Daniell, 1651, by Thomas Thornbrough, Northumberland Co.
Mooreton, Ralph, 1651, by Thomas Thornbrough, Northumberland Co.
Moore, Thomas, 1637, by John Neale, Accomack Co.
Moore, Jane, 1637, by John Hucks, James Citie Co.
Moore, Robt., 1637, by Richard Bennett, New Norfolk Co.
Moore, Nath., 1635, by Thos. Harris, Henrico Co.
Moore, Wm., 1635, by Mr. Geo. White, minister of the Word of God,
——— Co.
Moore, Edward, 1651, by Mr. Arthur Price, Yorke Co.
Moore, Jeffery, 1654, by Nich. Merywether, Westmoreland Co.
Moore, Tho., 1655, by Wm. Wright, Gent., Nansemond Co.
Moore, Calleat, 1656, by Tabitha and Matilda Scarburgh, Northampton
Co.
Moore, Richard, 1566, by Edward Moore, Northampton Co.
Moore, Mary, 1656, by Edward Moore, Northampton Co.
Moore, Edw., Jr., 1656, by Edward Moore, Sr., Northampton Co.
Moore, John, 1652, by Mr. James Warradine, ———, Co.
Moore, Richard, 1652, by Mrs. Elinor Brocas, Lancaster Co.
Moore, Ann, 1653, by Capt. Robt. Abrall, ——— Co.
Moore, Thomas, 1649, by Thomas Curtis. ——— Co.
Moore, Thomas, 1546, by Rich. Moore and William Welton, Upper
Norfolk Co.
Moore, Eliz., 1637, by Henry Perry, Charles River Co.
Moore, Joseph, 1642, by Thomas Symmons, ——— Co.
Moore, Tho., 1638, by Robert Freeman, James City Co.
Moore, Richard, 1639, by John White, James Citie Co.
Moore, Richard, 1639, by Thomas Stoute, James City Co.
Moore, Jane, 1639, by John Knipe, James City Co.
Moore, Thomas, 1651, by John Martin and (Lancaster Lovett), Lower
Norfolk Co.
Moore, Dorcas, 1651, by Abraham Moon (Thomas Griffin), Lancaster
Co.
Moore, Rebecca, 1650, by Richard Smith, Northampton Co.
Moore, Henry, 1650, by Wm. Morgan, ——— C.
Moore, Miles, 1652, by Daniell Welch, Lancaster Co.
Moore, Augustine, 1652, by Augustine Moore (his father), ——— Co.

Moore, Anne, 1652, by Augustine Moore (her husband), ———— Co.
Moore, Jeffery, 1653, by Nicho. Meriwether, Northumberland Co.
Moore, Richard, 1653, by Mr. Wm. Hoccaday, Yorke Co.
Moore, Richd., 1653, by John Earle, Northumberland Co.
Moore, Robert, 1635, by Richard Bennett, ———— Co.
Moores, Rich., 1649, by Wm. Hoccaday, ———— Co.
Moorey, Tho., 1643, by John Hoddin, ———— Co.
Moosh, Joseph, 1650, by Capt. John Flood, Gent., and Jno. Flood, an
    ancient planter, ———— Co.
Morane, Dermot, 1655, by Matilda Scarbourgh, Northampton Co.
More, Natha., 1648, by Francis Ceely, ———— Co.
More, William, 1647, by John Brooch, York River Co.
More, Doro., 1647, by John Brooch, York River Co.
More, Cicely, 1656, by Tho. Busby, Surry Co.
More, Jon., 1643, by Richard Kemp, Esq., James City Co.
More, Morocco, 1653, by Robt. Blake, Isle of Wight Co.
Morecock, Tho., 1651, by Tho. Hales and Tho. Sheppard, Northumber-
    land Co.
Morecocke, Geo., 1652, by Richard Coleman, ———— Co.
Morehead, John, 1656, by John Symons, Nansemond Co.
Morethrope, Thos., 1635, by Robert Hollow, Henrico Co.
Morey, George, 1652, by Mr. Tho. Purifye and Mrs. Temperence Rep-
    pett, ———— Co.
Morfey, Mary, 1650, by William Gooch, Gent., ———— Co.
Morg, Wm., 1656, by Tabitha and Matilda Scarburgh, Northampton
    Co.
Morgan, Tho., 1655, by Capt. Tho. Davis, Warwick Co.
Morgan, Edward, 1651, by Mr. Wm. Armestead, ———— Co.
Morgan, Dorothy, 1651, by Edward Greenwood, James City Co.
Morgan, Wm., 1651, by Lieut. Coll. Anthony Elliott, ———— Co.
Morgan, Fra., 1648, by John Seward, Isle of Wight Co.
Morgan, Richard, 1642, by Richard Morgan, Charles Co.
Morgan, Griffin, 1650, by Wm. Clapham, ———— Co.
Morgan, Abraham, 1649, by Mr. Ralph Barlowe, Northampton Co.
Morgan, Henry, 1652, by Tobias Horton, Lancaster Co.
Morgan, Wm., 1645, by Zachary Cripps, Warwick Co.
Morgan, Alice, 1643, by Tho. Taylor, Warwick Co.
Morgan, Wm., 1638, by Thomas Stout, ———— Co.
Morgan, Tho., 1638, by Capt. Tho. Harris, Henrico Co.
Morgan, Edward, 1638, by Thomas Watts, Lower New Norfolk Co.
Morgan, Margarett, 1638, by Wm. Morgan, her husband, James City
    Co.
Morgan, John, 1638, by Wm. Hatfield, Upper New Norfolk Co.
Morgan, Evan, 1637, by Capt. Thomas Panlett, Charles City Co.
Morgan, John, 1653, by Colo. Wm. Clayborne (Sec. of State), ———— Co.
Morgan, Edw., 1637, by Daniell Gookins, New Norfolk Co.
Morgan, Fra., 1654, by Wm. Robinson and Cornelius Johnson, West-
    moreland Co.
Morgan, John, 1635, by John Armie, Warrasquionaoke, Co.
Mogan, Meredith, 1641, by Ambrose Bennett, Isle of Wight Co.
Morgan, Edward, 1638, by Mr. John Gookins, Upper New Norfolk Co.

Morgan, Mathew, 1638, by Wm. Banister, —— Co.
Morgan, Tho., 1637, by Zacheriah Cripps, Warwick River Co.
Morgan, John, 1638, by William Clarke, Charles River Co.
Morgan, Margaret, 1636, by William Morgan, James City Co.
Morgan, Edward, 1637, by John Burnette, New Norfolk Co.
Morgan, Evans, 1635, by John Upton, Warrasquinoake Co.
Morgan, Robt., 1635, by Jno. Upton, Warrasquinoake Co.
Morgan, Edo., 1636, by John Goodin, Gent., —— Co.
Morgan, Jon., 1636, by James Place, Henrico Co.
Morgan, Tho., 1635, by Thos. Harris, Henrico Co.
Morgan, John, 1635, by John Parrott, —— Co.
Morgan, Thom., 1635, by Arthur Washington, Warwick Co.
Morgan, Wm., 1653, by Henry Soanes, Gent., Gloucester Co.
Morgan, Henry, 1654, by Mr. Giles Brent, Westmoreland Co.
Morgan, Wm., 1656, by Mr. Henry Soanes, New Kent Co.
Morgan, Walton, 1656, by Margaret Miles, Westmoreland Co.
Morgan, Francis, Gent., 1653, by John Hillier, Northumberland Co.
Morgan, James, 1653, by Abraham Moon, Lancaster Co.
Morgan, John, 1639, by Richard Parsons, Lower New Norfolk Co.
Morgan, William, 1639, by Mathew, Gough, Henrico Co.
Morgan, Tho., 1638, by Christopher Branch, Henrico Co.
Morgan, Tho., 1642, by Daniell Lewellyn, —— Co.
Morgan, Henry, 1648, by George White, Lower Norfolk Co.
Morgan, Mary, 1652, by Anthony Doney and Enoch Hawkes, Lan-
    casterCo.
Morgan, Isaac, 1652, by Edward Cannon and Tho. Allen, Lower Nor-
    folk Co.
Morgan, Fra., 1652, by Elias Edmonds, Lancaster Co.
Morgan, Fra., 1652, by Mr. Nicholas Jernew, Gloucester Co.
Morgan, Howell, 1653, by Colo. Wm. Clayborne (Sec. of State), ——
    Co.
Morgan, Tho., 1653, by Xpher Rivers, —— Co.
Morgate, Peter, 1638, by Thomas Dew, Upper New Norfolk Co.
Morgin, Tho., 1645, by Zachary Cripps, Warwick Co.
Morgrave, Adam, 1643, by William Ewins, James City Co.
Morganson, Richard, 1652, by Nathaniel Bacon, Isle of Wight Co.
Morggon, Allen, 1642, by Capt. Samuell Mathews, Esq., —— Co.
Morgrave, Merca, 1648, by Richard Wyatt, —— Co.
Morland, Tho., 1650, by John Hany, Northumberland Co.
Morley, Robt., 1654, by Francis Gray, —— Co.
Morley, Sym., 1636, by Richard Cocke, —— Co.
Morley, Wm., 1656, by Tho. Rolfe, Gent., James City Co.
Morley, Tho., 1652, by Capt. Francis Morgan and Ralph Green,
    Gloucester Co.
Morley, Symon, 1639, by Richard Corke, Gent., Henrico Co.
Morley, Eliza., 1654, by Robert Younge, Lancaster Co.
Morley, Robt., 1653, by Samuell Parry, Lancaster Co.
Moroise, Nicho., 1653, by Robt. Brasseur, Nansemond Co.
Morraine, John, 1655, by Edward Lucas, —— Co.
Morraine, Kennet, 1655, by Edward Lucas, —— Co.
Morrice, James, 1645, by Michall Masters, Henrico Co.

Morrall, Anne, 1653, by John Barrow, Surry Co.
Morrell, David, 1656, by Capt. Henry Fleete, ——— Co.
Morrell, Tho., 1638, by John Robins, James City Co.
Morian, Mary, 1655, by Edward Pettaway, Surry Co.
Morrice, James, 1654, by Francis Smith and Mr. John Smith, Westmoreland Co.
Morrice, James, 1651, by Hugh Fauch and James Magregory, Northumberland Co.
Morrice, Eliza., 1653, by Peter Knight and Baker Cult, ——— Co.
Morrice, Rice, 1653, by Peter Knight and Baker Cult, ——— Co.
Morrice, Nicholas, 1641, by John Seaward, Isle of Wight Co.
Morrice, Richard, 1641, by Ambrose Bennett, Isle of Wight Co.
Morrice, Wm., 1639, by Rich. Hoe, James City Co.
Moriell, Da., 1653, by Oliver Segar, Lancaster Co.
Morrin, Dan., 1653, by Jno Hansford, Gloucester Co.
Morris, Tho., 1654, by Major Wm. Andrews, Northampton Co.
Morris, Xper, 1653, by Thomas Kidd, Lancaster Co.
Morris, Edwd., 1648, by John Ellis, James Joones and John Taylor, Northampton Co.
Morris, Joseph, 1650, by George Goldsmith, ——— Co.
Morris, Edward, 1649, by Nicholas Waddilow, Northampton Co.
Morris, Evan., 1648, by Tho. Braughton, ——— Co.
Morris, John, 1652, by Tobias Horton, Lancaster Co.
Morris, Evan., 1643, by Elizabeth Hull, ——— Co.
Morris, John, 1643, by Thomas Cassen, Lower Norfolk Co.
Morris, Sarah, 1643, by Phillipp Taylor, Northampton Co.
Morris, Eliza., 1638, by Stephen Webb, James Citie Co.
Morris, Wm., 1643, by Tho. Williams, ——— Co.
Morris, Wm., 1643, by Rich. Hoe, Gent., ——— Co.
Morris, Richard, 1643, by Sir Francis Wyatt, Kt., ——— Co.
Morris, William, 1638, by Ambrose Bennett, Isle of Wight Co.
Morris, James, 1637, by Edward Tunstall, Henrico Co.
Morris, Rich., 1637, by Capt. John Howe, Accomac Co.
Morris, Robt., 1635, by Hugh Cox, Charles City Co.
Morris, John, 1642, by Wm. Barnard, Esq., Isle of Wight Co.
Morris, John, 1636, by John Laydon, Warwick River Co.
Morris, John, 1636, by Joane Bennett, Charles River Co.
Morris, James, 1636, by Edward Tunstall, ——— Co.
Morris, Thom., 1637, by Mathew Edloe, ——— Co.
Morris, Rich., 1637, by Rich. Bennett, New Norfolk Co.
Morris, Richard, 1635, by Richard Bennett, ——— Co.
Morris, Simon, 1653, by Richard Well, Northumberland Co.
Morris, John, 1655, by Wm. Wright, Gent., Nansemond Co.
Morris, Eliza., 1652, by Mr. Edwin Connaway, ——— Co.
Morris, Richard, 1638, by Thomas Ellis, Henrico Co.
Morris, Jacob, 1639, by Abraham Wood, Henrico Co.
Morris, Richard, 1642, by Lieut. Francis Mason, ——— Co.
Morris, Jenkin, 1655, by Walter Dickenson, Lancaster Co.
Morris, Frederick, 1653, by James Turner, ——— Co.
Morris, Jno., 1654, by John Wyre, John Gillet, Andrew Gilson and John Phillipps, ——— Co.

Morris, Mary, 1653, by Peter Knight, Northumberland Co.
Morris, Wm., 1650, by Wm. Yarrett and Fra. Wittington, ———— Co.
Morris, Edward, 1653, by Peter Knight, Northumberland Co.
Morris, Fra., 1652, by Mr. Wm. Waters, Northampton Co.
Morris, Tho., ————, by Lt. Coll. John Cheesman, ———— Co.
Morris, Wm., 1653, by Xpher Rivers, ———— Co.
Morris, Mary, 1653, by John Earle, Northumberland Co.
Morrison, Major Richard, 1651, by Winifred Morrison, ———— Co.
Morrison, Winifred, 1648, by Major Richard Morrison, Elizabeth City Co.
Morrison, Henry, 1648, by Major Richard Morrison, Elizabeth City Co.
Morrison, Richard, 1648, by Major Richard Morrison, Elizabeth City Co.
Morrison, Major Francis, 1650, by Mrs. Winifred Morrison, ———— Co.
Morrison, Mary, 1652, by Wm. Owen and Wm. Morgan, ———— Co.
Morry, Morley, 1656, by Tabitha and Matilda Scarburgh, Northampton Co.
Morry, Eliz., 1641, by Thomas Morrey, Isle of Wight Co.
Mors, Wm., 1649, by Arthur Allen, James City Co.
Morse, Rebecca, 1652, by Richard Starnell, ———— Co.
Morse, Wm., 1656, by Geo. Abbott, Nansemond Co.
Morsh, Richard, 1653, by Tho. Speoke, ———— Co.
Morslay, Mary, 1653, by John King, Surry Co.
Morksly, Wm., 1652, by Richard Dudley, ———— Co.
Mort, Richard, 1653, by George Collins, ———— Co.
Morte, Jesper, 1642, by Edmund Scarburgh, Accomack Co.
Morphew, Michaell, 1639, by Richard Preston, Upper New Norfolk Co.
Morter, Tho., 1639, by Georg Minifye, Esq., Charles River Co.
Morth, James, 1654, by Abraham Moone, ———— Co.
Mortlye, Jon., 1635, by Francis Fowler, James City Co.
Mortimer, Rowland, 1639, by John Lewis, Isle of Wight Co.
Morton, Wm., 1636, by William Melling, Accomack Co.
Morton, Margarett, 1650, by John Smith, ———— Co.
Morton, Thomas, 1649, by Joseph Croshawe, Yorke Co.
Morton, Wm., 1655, by Dr. Giles Mode, New Kent Co.
Morton, Jos., 1650, by John Sevier, ———— Co.
Moskall, Susan, 1650, by John Landman, ———— Co.
Moss, Jane, 1653, by Richard Major, Gloucester Co.
Moss, Wm., 1656, by John Bromfeild, James City Co.
Moss, Edward, 1655, by Ralph Green, New Kent Co.
Mosse, Ribert, 1650, by Richard Axom and Tho. Godwin, ———— Co.
Mosse, Richard, 1651, by Mr. Arthur Price, Yorke Co.
Mosse, Eliz., 1639, by John Well, Charles City Co.
Mosley, Robt., 1654, by Mr. Tho. Fowke, Westmoreland Co.
Moseley, Eliz., 1650, by Lewis Burwell, Gent., Northumberland Co.
Moseley, Samuell, 1650, by Lewis Burwell, Gent., Northumberland Co.
Moseley, Fra., 1650, by Capt. Moore Fautleroy, ———— Co.
Moseley, Jos., 1650, by Wm. Hodgson, Yorke Co.
Moseley, Wm., 1650, by Wm. Underwood, Gent., ———— Co.
Moseley, Jos., 1637, by Daniell Gookins, New Norfolk Co.

Moseley, Richard, 1653, by Edward Dobson, ——— Co.
Moseley, Ann, 1652, by Robert Lendall, ——— Co.
Moseley, Wm. and Arthur, 1653, by Wm. Moseley (their father), Lower Norfolk Co.
Moseley, Susanna, 1653, by Wm. Moseley, Lower Norfolk Co.
Moseley, Robert, 1640, by Mr. Bridges Freeman, James City Co.
Moseley, Wm., 1642, by Adam Cooke, Charles Co.
Moseley, Fra., 1647, by John Brooch, York River Co.
Mostly, Robert, 1655, by John Cool, James City Co.
Mothell, Edward, 1653, by Tho. Read, Northumberland Co.
Motly, John, 1637, by Francis Fowler, James River Co.
Mott, Fra., 1653, by Peter Knight and Baker Cult, ——— Co.
Motts, Willi, 1638, by Thomas Swan, James Citie Co.
Motts, Wm., 1635, by Wm. Swan, James Co.
Moubert, Elizabeth, 1652, by John Robinson, Jr., Northampton Co.
Mould, John, 1651, by Joseph Croshaw, Yorke Co.
Mould, John, 1653, by Tho. Griffin, Lancaster Co.
Moulder, Jon., 1643, by Richard Kemp, Esq., James City Co.
Moult, Wm., 1638, by Stephen Charlton, Accomack Co.
Mouncer, James, 1638, by Christopher Lawson, ——— Co.
Mounford, Margaret, 1653, by George Wadding, Lancaster Co.
Mountford, Geo., 1652, by Nicho. George, Tho. Taberer and Humphry Clarke, ——— Co.
Mouse, Arnall, 1650, by Capt. Richard Bond, Charles City Co.
Mouse, Robt., 1639, by Robt. Newman, Warwick River Co.
Mouser, John, 1648, by Geo. Hardey, Tho. Wombwell, and Peter Hall Isle of Wight Co.
Mouson, John, 1651, by Joseph Croshaw, Yorke Co.
Moye, Dorothy, 1638, by John Moye (her husband), Lower New Norfolk Co.
Moyes, John, 1637, by Leonard Yeo, Elizabeth City Co.
Moyle, Edward, 1654, by Mrs. Fra. Harrison, widow, Westmoreland Co.
Moyle, Roger, 1652, by Henry Fleete, Lancaster Co.
Moyles, Wm., 1637, by Nathaniel Floyd, Isle of Wight Co.
Moyses, Theodor, 1643, by Georg Levitt, ——— Co.
Moyses, Chri., 1638, by Stephen Charlton, Accomack Co.
Moyon, Tirish, 1656, by Tabitha and Matilda Scarburgh, Northampton Co.
Mowser, James, 1635, by Richard Tisdale, ——— Co.
Mucer, Eliz., 1654, by Capt. Nich. Marteaw, Westmoreland Co.
Muckeford, John, 1648, by Wm. Ewen, James City Co.
Mud, Jane, wife of Peter Mudd, 1640, by Thomas Harvey, James City Co.
Mudd, Peter, 1640, by Thomas Harvey, James City Co.
Mugg, Samuell, 1651, by Abraham Moone and (Thomas Griffin), Lancaster Co.
Muher, And., 1654, by Nich. Merywether, Westmoreland Co.
Mukee, John, 1655, by Lt. Col. Anthony Ellyott, ——— Co.
Mulbkin, Arche, 1654, by Thomas Binus, Surry Co.
Mule, Wm., 1654, by Col. Argoll Yardley, Northampton Co.

Mullett, Tho., 1653, by Charles Grymes, Lancaster Co.
Mullins, John, 1652, by Capt. Augustine Warner, ——— Co.
Munck, John, 1648, by Wm. Ewen, James City Co.
Munday, Mary, 1650, by John Mangor, ——— Co.
Munday, John, 1652, by John Robbins, Northampton Co.
Munday, John, 1655, by Southy Littleberry, Northampton Co.
Munday, Wm., 1639, by Georg Minifye, Esq., Charles River Co.
Munday, Robert, 1638, by John Walton, Accomac Co.
Munger, Georg, 1638, by Nicholas Georg and John Grynisditch, Isle
  of Wight Co.
Muns, Tho., 1653, by Richard Lee, Lancaster Co.
Muns, Wm., 1653, by Richard Lee, Lancaster Co.
Munroe, And., 1654, by Tho. Hobkins, Lancaster Co.
Munteth, Wm., 1656, by Wm. Bird, ——— Co.
Murbee, James, 1652, by Jno. Robinson, Lancaster Co.
Murcocke, Georg., 1642, by Henry Ballard, Warwick Co.
Murden, John, 1655, by Tho. Willess, Lancaster Co.
Murferry, Edwd., 1649, by Capt. Ralph Wormeley, ——— Co.
Murfield, Wm., 1638, by Capt. Christopher Wormley, Charles River
  Co.
Murkead, James, 1655, by John Dorman, Northampton Co.
Murr, Daniell, 1637, by Cheney Boyes, Charles City Co.
Murrall, Wm., 1653, by John Barrow, Surry Co.
Murrey, Jno., 1650, by Capt. More Fautleroy, ——— Co.
Murrey, Sanders, 1643, by John Hoddin, ——— Co.
Murry Daniel, 1656, by Francis Hutchins, Nansemond Co.
Murritt, Henry, 1651, by Rowland Morgan, Lower Norfolk Co.
Murrowes, David, 1651, by Richard Whitehurst, Lower Norfolk Co.
Murry, Robt., 1656, by Geo. Abbott, Nansemond Co.
Murry, Alexander, 1652, by Christopher Lewis, Isle of Wight Co.
Murns, Wm., 1639, by Richard Johnson, Henrico Co.
Musgrey, Jno., 1648, by Wm. Ewen, James City Co.
Musgrove, Tho., 1651, by Richard Vaughan, Northampton Co.
Musgrove, Grace, 1651, by John Thomas, Gloucester Co.
Musgrove, Tho., 1643, by Henry Neale, James City Co.
Musgrove, Thos. 1652, by Littleton, Scarburgh, ——— Co.
Musgrove, John, 1638, by Henry Catelyn, Upper Norfolk Co.
Musgrove, Jno., 1637, by Henry Catalyn, New Norfolk Co.
Muskatina, Ja., 1654, by Edward Simpson, Gloucester Co.
Muskatina, Ja., 1652, by Henry Tyler, Charles River Co.
Mussett, Francis, 1637, by John Orchard, James Citie Co.
Mutford, George, 1655, by Henry Huberd, ——— Co.
Mutton, Mary, 1648, by Randall Crew, Nansemond Co.
Mutton, Kath., 1653, by Robt. Sorrel, ——— Co.
Mutton, Kath., 1655, by Martin Hamond, ——— Co.
Muxford, Robt., 1638, by Jeremiah Dickinson, James City Co.
Muxford, John, 1643, by William Ewins, James City Co.
Myller, Ann, 1650, by Elias Edmonds, ——— Co.
Myles, Robert, Sr., 1650, by Wingfield Webb and Richard Pate, ———
  Co.

Myles, Robert, Jr., 1650, by Wingfield Webb and Richard Pate, ———
 Co.
Myles, John, 1638, by Richard Bennett, Isle of Wight Co.
Myles, Kath., 1650, by Wingfield Webb and Richard Pate, ——— Co.
Mynor, Ann, 1637, by Christopher Woodward, Charles City Co.

N

Nablett, Mary, 1636, by James Berry, Accomack Co.
Nahan, Rebecca, 1652, by John Fleet, Yorke Co.
Nailes, James, 1653, by John Gillett, Lancaster Co.
Naipes, Henry, 1652, by Capt. Augustine Warner, ——— Co.
Nakes, Andrew, 1650, by Capt. Moore Fautleroy, ——— Co.
Nance, Alice, 1639, by Rich. Nance, her husband now, Henrico Co.
Napier, Patrick, 1655, by Peter Ford, Gloucester Co.
Nargatt, Henry, 1649, by John Trussells, ——— Co.
Narton, Wm., 1653, by Elianor Brocas, Lancaster Co.
Nash, Margarett, 1654, by Francis Smith and Mr. John Smith, West-
 moreland Co.
Nash, Tho., 1655, by Henry Huberd, ——— Co.
Nash, John, 1652, by Wm. Up Thomas, ——— Co.
Nash, Edward, 1652, by Henry Nicholls, Lancaster Co.
Nash, Danll., 1653, by Geo. Thompson, Gloucester Co.
Nash, Robt., 1635, by Francis Fowler, James City Co.
Nash, Robert, 1637, by Francis Fowler, James River Co.
Naylor, James, 1653, by Geo. Taylor, Lancaster Co.
Naylor, Tho., 1653, by John Phillips, ——— Co.
Naylor, John, 1655, by Walter Dickenson, Lancaster Co.
Naylor, John, 1655, by Robert Castle, James City Co.
Neah, Wm., 1636, by Cheney Boyse, Charles City Co.
Neal, James, 1654, by John Wyre, John Gillet, Andrew Gilson and
 John Phillipps, ——— Co.
Neale, Thomas, 1636, by Mary Boxe, Henrico Co.
Neale, Wm., 1637, by Cheney Boyes, Charles City Co.
Neale, Jon., 1635, by John Moone, Warrasquinoake Co.
Neale, Thos., 1637, by Mary Box, Henrico Co.
Neale, Pearce, 1635, by John Neale, Accomack Co.
Neale, Jno., 1643, by Henry Neale, James City Co.
Neale, Xtop., 1650, by Richard Axom and Tho. Godwin, ——— Co.
Neal, Peter, 1650, by John Catlett and Ralph Rowsey, ——— Co.
Neale, John, 1650, by John Bone, ——— Co.
Neale, Joane, 1649, by Wm. Nesum, Tho. Sax, Miles Bathasby and
 John Pyne, Northampton Co.
Neale, Peirce, 1651, by James Davis, Northampton Co.
Neale, Ann, 1651, by James Thelaball, Lower Norfolk Co.
Neale, John, 1653, by Tho. Todd, ——— Co.
Neale, Ruth, 1653, by Jervais Dodson, Northumberland Co.
Neale, Anthony, 1652, by Mr. Wm. Waters, Northampton Co.
Neale, Peter, 1652, by Tho. Lucas, Gent., Lancaster Co.
Neale, James, 1652, by Anthony Doney and Enoch Hawker, Lancaster
 Co.

Neale, Richard, 1652, by Tho. Preston, ——— Co.
Neale, Eliz., 1654, by John Watson and John Bognall, Westmoreland Co.
Nealy, Teague, 1655, by Edmund Scarbourgh, Jr., and Littleton Scarbourgh, Northampton Co.
Neare, Tho., 1637, by Nathaniel Floyd, Isle of Wight Co.
Neave, John, 1650, by Mr. Robt. Holt, James City Co.
Neavor, Richard, 1654, by John Newman, Lancaster Co.
Needam, ———, 1652, by Elias Edmonds, Lancaster Co.
Needham, Thos., 1638, by Mr. Robert Bennett, Upper Norfolk Co.
Needham Thomas, 1639, by Capt. Rich. Townsend, Charles River Co.
Needum, Eliz., 1653, by Samuell Bonam, Northumberland Co.
Neegh, Tho., 1651, by Mr. Rowland Lawson, ——— Co.
Neele, George, 1635, by John Parrott, ——— Co.
Nelmes, Robt., 1653, by Capt. Francis Patt, Northampton Co.
Nelson, Prevost, 1652, by Tho. Stevens, Lancaster Co.
Nelson, Mathew, 1639, by Edward Panderson, ——— Co.
Nelson, Francis, 1656, by Wm. Justice, Charles City Co.
Nelson, Mary, 1637, by James Berry, Accomack Co.
Nelson, John, 1636, by John Chew, Gent., Charles River Co.
Nelson, George, 1649, by Edmund Scarburgh, Jr., Northampton Co.
Nelson, Prowess, 1653, by Charles Grymes, Clerk, Lancaster Co.
Nelson, Tho., 1653, by Charles Grymes, Lancaster Co.
Nelsonn, Mary, 1636, by James Berry, Accomack Co.
Nelsonn, Henry, 1641, by Ambrose Bennett, Isle of Wight Co.
Nelve, Carmack, 1655, by Maltilda Scarbourgh, Northampton Co.
Nemo, John, 1642, by Christopher Boyce, ——— Co.
Nerey, Alex., 1638, by Benjamin Carrill, James City Co.
Nero, Rich., 1637, by Edward Travis, James City Co.
Neroy, Alex., 1636, by Nathan Martin, Henrico Co.
Nerton, William, 1637, by William Prior, Charles River Co.
Nerve, John, 1646, by Geo. Ludlow, Esq., York Co.
Nesse, Wm., 1637, by Justinian Cooper, Isle of Wight Co.
Nesse, Wm., 1636, by Justinian Cooper, Warrasquinoak Co.
Nessum, Edwd., 1649, by Stephen Gill, York Co.
Nestry, Dorothy, 1655, by Wm. Wright, Gent., Nansemond Co.
Neswid, John, 1653, by Colo. Wm. Clayborne (Sec. of State), ——— Co.
Netheritt, Nicho., 1652, by Tho. Steevens, ——— Co.
Nethfeild, Georg, 1642, by Georg Harding, ——— Co.
Nett, Nich., 1639, by Mathew Gough, Henrico Co.
Neucombe, Hen., 1653, by Major Abra. Wood, Charles City Co.
Nevera, Jane, 1655, by George Parker, Northampton Co.
Nevil, Rich., 1650, by Mr. Anthony Ellyot, ——— Co.
New, Rich., 1638, by Edward Travis and John Johnson, James City Co.
New House, John, 1638, by Robt. Holt and Richard Bell, James City Co.
Newark, Wm., 1654, by Abrahma Moone, ——— Co.
Newkerke, Robert, 1635, by William Wilkinson (minister), ——— Co.
Newkerke, Robt., 1637, by Wm. Wilkinson, New Norfolk Co.
Newarke, Jon., 1635, by Capt. Adam Thoroughgood, ——— Co.
Newball, Francis, 1651, by Joseph Croshaw, Yorke Co.

Newberry, Ro., and his wife, 1653, by Symon Thorogood, Elizabeth City Co.
Newby, Henry, 1651, by Joseph Hayes, Gent., Yorke Co.
Newby, John, 1643, by Epaphroditus Lawson, Upper Norfolk Co.
Newby, Henry, 1655, by Mrs. Margaret Brent, Lancaster Co.
Newby, Robt., 1656, by Vincent Stanford, ———— Co.
Newcomb, Arthur, 1653, by Tho. Bourn, Lancaster Co.
Newcombe, Ann, 1654, by John Wyre, John Gillett, Andrew Gilson and John Phillipps, ———— Co.
Newell, Dan., 1654, by Thomas Binns, Surry Co.
Newell, Jon., 1637, by Capt. Francis Turner, Charles River Co.
Newell, Peter, 1653, by Capt. Wm. Whittington, Northampton Co.
Newell, Wm., 1654, by Mr. Tho. Fowke, Westmoreland Co.
Newer, Jon., 1637, by Arthur Smith, Isle of Wight Co.
Newes, Joan, 1656, by John Billiott, Northampton Co.
Newett, Winifrid, 1636, by John Dunston, James City Co.
Newett, Winifred, 1639, by John Dunston, James City Co.
Newill, Richard, 1651, by Richard Bayly, ———— Co.
Newgent, Clerist, 1635, by Capt. Adam Thoroughgood, ———— Co.
Newgent, Wm., 1654, by John Wyre, John Gillett, Andrew Gilson and John Phillipps, ———— Co.
Newham, John, 1653, by Mr. Robt. Bourne and Mr. Daniel Parke, York Co.
Newhouse, John, 1640, by Robt. Holt, James City Co.
Newland, Mary, 1646, by Thomas Holmes, Yorke River Co
Newland, Richd., 1653, by Capt. Natha. Hurd, Warrick Co.
Newland, Rebecca, 1639, by John Pawley, James City Co.
Newley, Robert, 1656, by Vincent Stanford, ———— Co.
Newman, Alice, 1638, by John Moone, ———— Co.
Newman, Robt., 1637, by Robt. Newman, New Norfolk Co.
Newman, Robert, 1636, by John Laydon, Warwick River Co.
Newman, John, 1635, by Capt. Adam Thoroughgood, Henrico Co.
Newman, Jon., 1636 by James Vaneirt, Elizabeth City Co.
Newman, John, 1635, by Capt. Wm. Pierse, ———— Co.
Newman, Eliz., 1650, by John Hany, Northumberland Co.
Newman, Alice, 1650, by Tho. Wilkinson, ———— Co.
Newman, Susan, 1650, by Richard Axom and Tho. Godwin, ———— Co.
Newman, John, 1643, by Robert Haies, Lower Norfolk Co.
Newman, Susana, wife of Tho. Newman, 1650, by Capt. Moore Fautleroy, ———— Co.
Newman, Tho., 1659, by Capt. Moore Fautleroy, ———— Co.
Newman, Eliza., 1650, by John Olian, James City Co.
Newman, Ellis, 1650, by John Cox, ———— Co.
Newman, Susan, 1651, by Henry Singleton ———— Co.
Newman, Ann., 1651, by Henry Singleton, ———— Co.
Newman, Tho. (and Susanna his wife), 1651, by Henry Singlton, ———— Co.
Newman, Susan, 1653, by Tho. Griffin, Lancaster Co.
Newman, Wm., 1652, by Mr. Geo. Foster, Northumberland Co.
Newman, Richard, 1639, by Henry Perry, Charles City Co.
Newman, Alice, 1641, by Ambrose Bennett, Isle of Wight Co.

Newman, Tho., 1638, by Georg Mynifie (merchant), —— Co.
Newman, Sam., 1654, by John Wyre, John Gillet, Andrew Gilson and John Phillips, —— Co.
Newman, Tho., 1654, by Capt. David Mansell, Westmoreland Co.
Newman, Susan, 1654, by John Newman, Lancaster Co.
Newman, Robt., 1654, by Francis Smith and Mr. John Smith, Westmoreland Co.
Newman, Robt., 1656, by Richard Gible, Northumberland Co.
Newman, John, 1648, by George White, Lower Norfolk Co.
Newman, Jon., 1642, by Adam Cooke, Charles Co.
Newnom, John, 1648, by James Mason, James City Co.
Newsom, Eliz., 1653, by John Cox, Lancaster Co.
Newsom, James, 1642, by Wm. Ireland and Robt. Wallis, Yorke Co.
Newton, Robt., 1638, by Jeremiah Dickenson, James City Co.
Newton, John, 1643, by Capt. John Upton, Isle of Wight Co.
Newton, Richard, 1635, by Charles Harwer, —— Co.
Newton, Francis, 1635, by Capt. Adam Thoroughgood, —— Co.
Newton, John, 1650, by Epa. Lawson, —— Co.
Newton, John, 1648, by Tho. Ludwell, Gent., James City Co.
Newton, Fra., 1648, by Richard Lee, Gent., —— Co.
Newton, Ph., 1648, by John Smith, Lower Norfolk Co.
Newton, James, 1651, by Joseph Croshaw, Yorke Co.
Newton, Wm., 1653, by Abraham Moon, Lancaster Co.
Newton, John, 1653, by Abraham Moon, Lancaster Co.
Newton, John, 1653, by Wm. Thomas, Northumberland Co.
Newton, Wm., 1652, by John Bayles, Lancaster Co.
Newton, Joane, 1652, by Augustine Moore, —— Co.
Newton, Tho., 1654, by John Wyre, John Gillet, Andrew Gilson and John Phillips, —— Co.
Newton, Tho., 1655, by Southy Littleberry, Northampton Co.
Neworth, Wm., 1653, by Wm. Hardidge, Northumberland Co.
Nicholas, Wm., 1643, by Peter Knight, Isle of Wight Co.
Nicholas, Jon., 1653, by Wm. Sidner, Lancaster Co.
Nicholas, Richard, 1639, by Samuell Jackson, Isle of Wight Co.
Nichols, Roger, 1635, by Stephen Webb, —— Co.
Nichols, Walter, 1637, by Capt. Thomas Panlett, Charles City Co.
Nichols, Samll., 1650, by Silvester Thatcher and Tho. Whitlocke, —— Co.
Nichols, Andrew, William and Elizabeth, children of Andrew Nichols, 1648, by Richard Whitehurst, Norfolk Co.
Nichols, Elizabeth, wife of Andrew Nichols, 1648, by Richard Whitehurst, Norfolk Co.
Nichols, Andrew, 1648, by Richard Whitehurst, Norfolk Co.
Nichols, Wm., 1653, by Frances Symons, Northumberland Co.
Nichols, Eliz., 1653, by John Bebey, Lancaster Co.
Nichols, ——, 1653, by Henry Lowne, Henrico Co.
Nichols, Elinor, 1653, by Sampson Robins, Northampton Co.
Nichols, Fr., 1641, by Ambrose Bennett, Isle of Wight Co.
Nichols, Wm., 1642, by William Eyres, Upper New Norfolk Co.
Nicholls, Samuell, 1647, by Thomas Johnson, Gent., Northampton Co.
Nicholls, Sands, 1645, by Mr. Bartholomew Hoskins, —— Co.

Nicholls, Mary, 1652, by Gawen Lancaster, Charles River Co.
Nicholls, James, ——, by Lt. Coll. John Cheesman, —— Co.
Nicholls, John, 1652, by John Smith, —— Co.
Nicholls, Wm., 1652, by Nicho. Morris, Northumberland Co.
Nicholls, Elinor, 1653, by Sampson Robins, Northampton Co.
Nicholls, Nicho., 1653, by Sampson Robins, Northampton Co.
Nicholls, John, 1653, by Sampson Robins, Northampton Co.
Nicholls, John, 1655, by Peter Ford, Gloucester Co.
Nicholls, Wm., 1654, by Nicholas Morris, Northumberland Co.
Nicholls, Mary, 1656, by Lewis Perry, —— Co.
Nicbolson, Eliz., 1635, by William Spencer, —— Co
Nicholson, George, 1635, by Stephen Webb, —— Co.
Nicalson, Richard, 1650, by Silvester Thatcher and Tho. Whitlocke, —— Co.
Nicholson, Jane, 1652, by Nicholas Waddilow, Northampton Co.
Nicholson, Eliz., 1637, by William Spencer, —— Co.
Nicholson, Alex., 1650, by George Pate, Charles City Co.
Nicholson, Ralph, 1650, by Hump. Lyster, —— Co.
Nicholson, Phillip, 1651, by Robert Cade, —— Co.
Nicholson, Ja., 1653, by Mr. Wm. Hoccaday, Yorke Co.
Nicholson, Wm., 1652, by Tho. Cartwright, Lower Norfolk Co.
Nicholson, Jáne, 1655, by Nich. Waddilow, Northampton Co.
Nicholson, Jane, 1655, by Nich. Waddilow, Northampton Co.
Nicholson, Wm., 1655, by John Lawson, Lancaster Co.
Nicheson, Edward, 1651, by Thomas Keeling, Lower Norfolk Co.
Nigent, Robert, 1646, by Edward Hall, Lower Norfolk Co.
Night, Robt., 1648, by Wm. Edwards and Rice Edwards, James City Co.
Nightingale, Tho., 1648, by Georg Read, Gent., —— Co.
Nimcahoe, Knora, 1656, by John Billiott, Nansemond Co.
Nimfe, Charles, 1642, by Thomas Bagwell, Charles City Co.
Nitingale, Kath., 1649, by Christop. Kemp, James City Co.
Niren, Godfrid, 1652, by Peter Knight, Gloucester Co.
Noble, Michaell, 1643, by Thomas Frye, James City Co.
Noble, Wm., 1637, by Henry Bradley, New Norfolk Co.
Noble, Robert, 1650, by Mrs. Winefrid Morrison, —— Co.
Noble, Grace, 1654, by Nich. Merywether, Westmoreland Co.
Noble, Miles, 1653, by Mr. Wm. Fry, James City Co.
Noble, George, 1655, by Robt. Nicholson, Charles City Co.
Nobli, William, 1640, by Henry Bradley, New Norfolk Co.
Nockey, Tho., 1655, by Wm. Steevens, Northampton Co.
Nokes, Wm., 1654, by Humphry Haggett, Lancaster Co.
Noles, Eliz., 1655, by Symon Symons, Charles City Co.
Nolton, John, 1637, by Theodore Moyser, James City Co.
Novell, Mary, 1653, by John Medstard and John Edwards, Northumberland Co.
Nookes, Henry, 1653, by Wm. Debram, —— Co.
Noole, William, 1642, by Henry Bradley, Upper Norfolk Co.
Norcott, Wm., 1637, by Capt. Thomas Flint, Warwick River Co.
Norden, Walter, 1637, by John Moone, Isle of Wight Co.
Norman, Peter, 1638, by Mr. John Gookins, Upper New Norfolk Co.
Norman, Mary, 1638, by Mr. John Gookins, Upper New Norfolk Co.

Norman, Austice, 1637, by Daniell Gookins, New Norfolk Co.
Norman, Mary, 1636, by John Gookin, Gent., ——— Co.
Norman, Peter, 1637, by Daniell Gookins, New Norfolk Co.
Norman, Henry, 1642, by Thomas Say, ——— Co.
Norman, Henry, 1637, by Daniell Gookins, New Norfolk Co.
Norman, Peter, 1636, by John Gookin, Gent., ——— Co.
Norman, Peter, 1637, by John Gookins, New Norfolk Co.
Norman, Mary, 1637, by John Gookin, New Norfolk Co.
Norman, Edward, 1651, by Joseph Croshaw, Yorke Co.
Norman, Stephen, 1652, by Nicholas George, ——— Co.
Norman, Dickery, 1638, by Capt. Christopher Wormley, Charles River
    Co.
Norman, Tho., 1654, by Major Wm. Andrews, Northampton Co.
Norman, Jno., 1654, by Coll. Jno. Matron, Westmoreland Co.
Norman, Elizabeth, 1655, by Francis Clay, Gent., Northumberland Co
Norman, Henry, 1654, by Mr. Mordecay Cooke, ——— Co.
Normenswell, Edwd., 1653, by Capt. Francis Patt, Northampton Co.
Norrell, Walter, 1650, by George Pate, Charles City Co.
Norrice, Tho., 1643, by John Carter, ——— Co.
Norrie, Savage, 1635, by Jno. Upton, Warrasquinoake Co.
Norris, Rich., 1643, by Richard Kemp, Esq., James City Co.
Norris, Thomas, 1647, by Lawrence Peeters, "Nansimum" Co.
Norris, Eliz., 1639, by Stephen Webb, James City Co.
Norts, Ma., 1647, by John Brooch, York River Co.
Norts, James, 1652, by Mr. David Fox, Lancaster Co.
North, John, 1642, by John Towlson, Accomack Co.
North, Wm., 1651, by Coll. Guy Molsworth, ——— Co.
North, Wm., 1651, by Robt. Vans, Gent., Yorke Co.
North, James, 1651, by Abraham Moone and (Thomas Griffin), Lan-
    caster Co.
North, John, 1653, by Major Abra Wood, Charles City Co.
North, Fra., 1654, by John Watson and John Bognall, Westmoreland
    Co.
North, Ann, 1654, by John Watson and John Bognall, Westmoreland
    Co.
North, Anth., 1654, by Alexander Portus and Tho. Williams, Lancaster
    Co.
North, James, 1654, by Toby Smith, Lancaster Co.
Northam, Toby, 1647, by Stephen Horsey and Nicho. Waddilow,
    Northampton Co.
Northerne, John, 1636, by Richard Cocke, ——— Co.
Norton, Jon., 1637, by Joseph Cobb, Isle of Wight Co.
Norton, William, 1635, by Wm. Prior, ——— Co.
Norton, Margaret, 1647, by Stephen Horsey and Nicho. Waddilow,
    Northampton Co.
Norton, Ann, 1643, by John Norton (her husband), James City Co.
Norton, Walter, 1649, by Mr. Ralph Barlowe, Northampton Co.
Norton, Richard, 1651, by Humphry Tabb, Northumberland Co.
Norton, John, 1652, by Mrs. Mary Brent, Northumberland Co.
Norton, John, 1637, by Joseph Cobb, Isle of Wight Co.
Norton, Xtope, 1648, by George White, Lower Norfolk Co.

Nors, Tho., 1646, by Joseph Croshawe, Charles River Co.
Norway, John, 1638, by Georg Mynifie (merchant), ——— Co.
Nowell, Wm., 1639, by Robert Newman, Warwick River Co.
Norwood, Richard, 1643, by Sir Francis Wyatt, Kt., ——— Co.
Nosencroft, Mandelin, 1640, by William Hampton, Elizabeth City Co.
Nosworthy, Ann, 1639, by Tristram Nosworthy, Upper Norfolk Co.
Northrock, Marke, 1651, by Henry Singleton, ——— Co.
Nousier, John, 1650, by Mr. James Williamson, ——— Co.
Novis, Richd., 1654, by Mr. Francis Hamond, York Co.
Nowell, Mary, 1653, by Abraham Moone, Lancaster Co.
Nowell, Tho., 1654, by John Battel, ——— Co.
Nowell, Peeter, 1647, by Wm. Whitington, Northampton Co.
Nowell, Rich., 1637, by James Knott, New Norfolk Co.
Nugent, Christopher, 1638, by Cobb Howell, Lower New Norfolk Co.
Nullall, Robt., 1650, by Capt. Moore Fautleroy, ——— Co.
Nurden, Tho., 1649, by Tho. Bourne, ——— Co.
Nurdon, Tho., 1651, by Ashwell Battin, Yorke Co.
Nursirie, Daniel, 1635, by Stephen Webb, ——— Co.
Nurton, Henry, 1654, by Francis Smith and Mr. John Smith, West-
    moreland Co.
Nurton, John, 1652, by Mrs. Jane Harmer, Northumberland Co.
Nurton, Wm., 1649, by Wm. Hoccaday, ——— Co.
Nurton, John, 1643, by John Norton, James City Co.
Nurton, Jon., 1638, by John Jackson and Eliza Kingswill, James City
    Co.
Nussor, Robt., 1650, by Capt. Moore Fautleroy, ——— Co.
Nusum, Wm., 1650, by Capt. Moore Fautleroy, ——— Co.
Nute, Winifred, 1637, by Capt. John Howe, Accomac Co.
Nute, Thom., 1637, by Capt. John Howe, Accomac Co.
Nutt, James, 1655, by Patrick Miller, Lancaster Co.
Nutt, Wm., 1636, by Bridges Freeman, ——— Co.
Nutt, Wm., 1637, by Bridges Freeman, James City Co.
Nuttall, Robt., 1637, by Thomas Hampton New Norfolk Co.
Nutter, James, 1652, by Capt. Tho. Hackett, Lancaster Co.

O

Oatelys, Phillipp, 1636, by Hannibal Fletcher, James City Co.
Oates, Greg., 1637, by Jonathan Langworth, New Norfolk Co.
Obed, John, 1650, by Mrs. Frances Townshend, Northumberland Co.
Obert, Bertrum, 1654, by Wm. Lea, Charles City Co.
Obbins, Faulkerd, 1652, by John Robinson, Jr., Northampton Co.
Ockmond, John, 1656, by Tabitha and Matilda Scarburgh, North-
    ampton Co.
Octies, Tho., 1649, by John Dennis, ——— Co.
Odait, Elin, 1649, by Mr. Ralph Barlowe, Northampton Co.
Odaley, Daniel, 1656, by Major Wm. Lewis, ——— Co.
Odell, Henry, 1654, by Robert Hubard, Westmoreland Co.
Odell, Henry, 1654, by Valentine Patten, Westmoreland Co.
Offdale, Use., 1654, by John Phillips and John Batts, Lancaster Co.
Offeild, Henry, 1650, by Capt. Richard Bond, Charles City Co.

Ogar, James, 1655, by George Truett, Northampton Co.
Ogee, Dun, 1655, by Sampson Robins, Northampton Co.
Oger, Morris, 1650, by John Cooke, Northumberland Co.
Ogestor, Elenor, 1656, by Tho. Harris, Lancaster Co.
OKell, Rich., 1654, by Mr. Francis Hamond, York Co.
Oldum, Percy and Eliza., his wife, 1643, by Phillip Taylor, Northampton Co.
Oldum, James, 1643, by Phillipp Taylor, Northampton Co.
Oldis, John, 1637, by Leonard Yeo, Elizabeth City Co.
Oldis, James, 1652, by Mr. David Fox, Lancaster Co.
Oleves, Walter, 1651, by Joseph Hayes, Gent., Yorke Co.
Oliver, Nich., 1636, by Wm. Clarke, Henrico Co.
Oliner, Nich., 1636, by Richard Cocke, ——— Co.
Olliner, George, 1636, by Wm. Ravenett, Warwick River Co.
Ollaver, Wm., 1645, by John Rode, Warwick Co.
Olivee, John, 1648, by Geo. Hardey, Tho. Wombwell and Peter Hall, Isle of Wight Co.
Oliver, Edward, 1638, by Randall Crew, Upper New Norfolk Co.
Oliver, Eliz., 1643, by Casar Puggett, Lower Norfolk Co.
Oliver, Nich., 1638, by William Clarke, Henrico Co.
Oliver, Richard, 1642, by Stephen Hamblyn, York Co.
Oliver, Walter, 1655, by Mrs. Margaret Brent, Lancaster Co.
Oliver, Geo., 1654, by John Drayton, Westmoreland Co.
Oliver, Mary, 1651, by George Eaton, ——— Co.
Oliver, John, 1642, by Christopher Boyce, ——— Co.
Omallin, Patt., 1651, by John Adleston, ——— Co.
Omelle, Dollo., 1656, by Tabitha and Matilda Scraburgh, Northampton Co.
Onesley, Wm., 1651, by Wm. Parry, Northumberland Co.
Onwell, Luke, 1652, by John Greenbough, Henrico Co.
Open, Richard, 1646, by Geo. Ludlow, Esq., York Co.
Oran, Robert, 1642, by Tymothy Fenn, Isle of Wight Co.
Orchard, Anne, 1636, by John Orchard, James City Co.
Orchard, Mary, 1637, by John Orchard (her husband), James Citie Co.
Orchard, Ann, 1637, by John Orchard (her husband), James Citie Co.
Ord, Wm., 1653, by John Poye, ——— Co.
Orde, Margaret, 1648, by Robert Pitt, Isle of Wight Co.
Ordean, John, 1655, by John Browne, Gent., Northampton Co.
Organ, Lawrence, 1654, by John Whithers and Stephen Garey, Westmoreland Co.
Orley, Tho., 1653, by Tho. Keene, Northumberland Co.
Orly, Tho., 1653, by Colo. Wm. Clayborne (Sec. of State), ——— Co.
Ororke, Tho., 1652, by Tho. Glossock, Lancaster Co.
Orphiw, Edmund, 1655, by Lieut. Coll. John Walker, ——— Co.
Orpewood, Richard, 1654, by Edward Parker, Westmoreland Co.
Orrawane, John, 1655, by George Truett, Northampton Co.
Orrey, Robt., 1654, by Col. Hump. Higgenson, Esq., and Abraham Moone, Westmoreland Co.
Orton, John, 1654, by Col. Hump. Higgenson, Esq., and Abraham Moone, Westmoreland Co.
Osberton, Alexander, 1636, by Samuel Edwards, James City Co.

Osborne, Richd., 1653, by Capt. Francis Patt, Northampton Co.
Osborne, Tho., 1637, by Thomas Osborne, Jun., Henrico Co.
Osborne, Rich., 1637, by Jonathan Langworth, New Norfolk Co.
Osborne, Mary, 1637, by Jno. Broche, Charles River Co.
Osbourne, John, 1653, by Alexander Addison, ——— Co.
Osheelivan, Margt., 1654, by Luke Billington, Accomac Co.
Osman, Adam, 1653, by Gregory Rawlins, Surry Co.
Osmotherly, Wm., 1637, by Eleanor Day and Thos. Emmerson, War-
    wick River Co.
Others, Thom., 1636, by John Seaward, Isle of Wight Co.
Ottamon, Teague, 1655, by John Woodward, Gloucester Co.
Otter, Thomas, 1638, by Edmund Scarborough, Accomac Co.
Otteway, Richard, 1652, by Richard Hill, Northampton Co.
Ourton, Tymothy, 1643, by Capt. Samuell Mathews, Esq., ——— Co.
Outsis, Mary, 1652, by Mrs. Mary Brent, Northumberland Co.
Overton, Mary, 1655, by John Dorman, Northampton Co.
Overy, Mathew, 1649, by Edmund Scarburgh, Jr., Northampton Co.
Owberry, John, 1636, by Wm. Ravenett, Warwick River Co.
Owen, John, 1653, by Abraham Moone, Northumberland Co.
Owen, Thomas, 1632, by Hannibal Fletcher, ——— Co. In the ship
    Susan of London.
Owen, Morring, 1651, by John Rookwood, Gent., Northumberland Co.
Owen, Edw., 1636, by Wm. Julian, Elizabeth City Co.
Owen, Rowland, 1636, by Wm. Armistead, Elizabeth City Co.
Owen, Tho., 1637, by John Broche, Charles River Co.
Owen, Marie, 1655, by Wm. Wright, ——— Co.
Owen, Mark, Wm., 1655, by George Truett, Northampton Co.
Owen, Teague, 1655, by Wm. Steevens, Northampton Co.
Owen, Morrice, 1654, by Lieut. Coll. Giles Brent, Westmoreland Co.
Owen, Edward, 1635, by Robert Sheppard, ——— Co.
Owen, John, 1652, by Wm. Moore, ——— Co.
Owen, John, 1652, by Christopher Lewis, Isle of Wight Co.
Owen, John, 1652, by John Johnson, Northampton Co.
Owen, John, 1653, by Geo. Cable, ——— Co.
Owen, Jon., 1653, by James Johnson, Nansemond Co.
Owen, John, 1651, by Phillip Hunley, ——— Co.
Owen, David, 1651, by Edward Degg, Esq., Yorke Co.
Owen, William, 1650, by Nicholas Perkins, Henrico Co.
Owens, John, 1655, by Christopher Calvert, Northampton Co.
Owens, Mary, 1655, by Christopher Calvert, Northampton Co.
Owens, Tho., 1655, by Christopher Calvert, Northampton Co.
Owens, Richard and wife, 1652, by Tho. Green, ——— Co.
Owens, Walter, 1650, by Mr. James Williamson, ——— Co.
Owens, Richd., 1649, by Mr. Nesum and others, Northumberland Co.
Owin, Tho., 1654, by Col. Hump. Higgenson, Esq., and Abraham Moone
    Westmoreland Co.
Owin, Movies, 1651, by Lieut. Coll. Giles Brent, Northumberland Co.
Owly, Robt., 1648, by George Read, Gent., ——— Co.
Ownce, Jno., 1651, by Ashwell Batlin, Yorke Co.
Owtey, Edward, 1648, by Lewis Burwell, Gent., ——— Co.
Oxford, Wm., 1636, by John Orchard, James City Co.

Oxford, Christopher, 1635, by William Ravenett, Denbeigh Co.
Oxford, Xpher, 1654, by John Drayton, Westmoreland Co.
Oxford, John, 1652, by Mrs. Jane Harmer, Northumberland Co.
Oxford, Joseph, 1650, by John Bone, ——— Co.
Oxford, Wm., 1637, by John Orchard, James Citie Co.
Oyles, Nicho., 1649, by Nicholas Waddilowe, Northampton Co.
O'Carby, Dan., 1655, by Lt. Col. Anthony Ellyott, ——— Co.
O'Crahan, Patrick, 1656, by Wm. and Hancock Lee, Gloucester Co.
O'Drenne, John, 1655, by Lt. Coll. Anthony Ellyott, ——— Co.
O'Derrick, Tho., 1655, by John Woodward, Gloucester Co.
O'Derrick, Tho., 1655, by Lt. Col. Anthony Ellyott, ——— Co.
O'Fahee, 1655, by Hugh Yeo, Northampton Co.
O'Fallo, Teague, 1655, by Capt. Henry Fleet, ——— Co.
O'Farne, Dormot, 1656, by Wm. and Hancock Lee, Gloucester Co.
O'Gley, Frorell, 1656, by Tabitha and Matilda Scarburgh, Northampton Co.
O'Graham, Donell, 1655, by Hugh Yeo, Northampton Co.
O'Grangenes, John, 1655, by John Smithey, ——— Co.
O'Harratt, Richard, 1655, by Richard Lee, Coll. Gloucester Co.
O'Harrough, Rich., 1655, by Lt. Col. Anthony Ellyott, ——— Co.
O'Lanny, Nella, 1656, by Tabitha and Matilda Scarburgh, Northampton Co.
O'Leaby, Owin, 1655, by Lt. Coll. Anthony Elyott, ——— Co.
O'Leally, John, 1656, by Wm. and Hancock Lee, Gloucester Co.
O'Lire, Jane, 1656, by Tabitha and Matilda Scraburgh, Northampton Co.
O'Loffe, Gwalle, 1656, by Tabitha and Matilda Scarburgh, Northampton Co.
O'Lyn, Tho., 1655, by Lieut. Col. John Walker, ——— Co.
O'Mally, Commack, 1655, by Coll. Richard Lee, Gloucester Co.
O'Morpher, Connor, 1655, by John Woodward, Gloucester Co.
O'Maulins, Teague, 1655, by John Hampton, ——— Co.
O'Naught, Wm., 1655, by Hugh Yeo, Northampton Co.
O'William, John, 1656, by Tabitha and Matilda Scarburgh, Northampton Co.

P

Pace, Henry, 1638, by William Cotten, Accomack Co.
Pack, Christ., 1642, by Thomas Osborne, Henrico Co.
Packer, Joan, 1654, by Col. Argoll Yardley, Northampton Co.
Packford, Wm., 1637, by Thomas Sawyer, New Norfolk Co.
Packhurst, Anthony, 1642, by John Brooch, Charles River Co.
Packman, Geo., 1642, by Peter Rigby, ——— Co.
Pacton, John, 1650, by Stephen Charlton, Northampton Co.
Pacye, Henry, 1640, by John Holloway, Accomack Co.
Padgett, Ann, 1653, by Tho. Cowlinge, ——— Co.
Paddison, Tho., 1642, by Wm. Warren, ——— Co.
Paddison, Robert, 1656, by John Bromfeild, James City Co.
Page, Edward, 1635, by Anthony Jones, ——— Co.
Page, Eliza., ———, by Mr. John Page, ——— Co.

Page, Alice, ——, by Mr. John Page, ——— Co.
Page, Mary, ——, by Mr. John Page, ——— Co.
Page, Tho., 1652, by Tho. Lucas, Gent., Lancaster Co.
Page, Robt., 1653, by Margarett Upton, Lancaster Co.
Page, John, 1650, by John Mangor, ——— Co.
Page, Richard, 1646, by Joseph Croshawe, Charles River Co.
Page, Joans, 1656, by John Phips, James City Co.
Page, Joans, 1654, by Mrs. Fra. Harrison (widow), Westmoreland Co.
Page, Rob., 1654, by Coll. Jno. Matrom, Westmoreland Co.
Page, Annis, 1640, by William Crannage, Isle of Wight Co.
Page, Nath., 1638, by John Robins, James City Co.
Pagg, Joseph, 1650, by John Essix, Northumberland Co.
Pagett, Thomas, 1639, by William Burdett, Accomack Co.
Paggett, Richard, 1649, by Mr. Nesum and others, Northumberland
    Co.
Pain, Sam., 1654, by Robert Holt, James City Co.
Paine, Florentine, 1642, by Richard Lee, ——— Co.
Paine, Georg., 1638, by Randolph Crew, Upper New Norfolk Co.
Paine, Majery, 1652, by Daniell Welsh, Lancaster Co.
Paine, Richard, 1635, by John Armie, Warrasquinoake Co.
Paine, Florentine, 1651, by Richard Grigson, ——— Co.
Paine, Henry, 1652, by Christopher Lewis, Isle of Wight Co.
Paine, Robt., 1653, by Roger Walker, Northumberland Co.
Paine, John, 1642, by Richard Morgan, Charles Co.
Paine, Wm., 1642, by Thomas Guyer, ——— Co.
Paine, Wm., 1642, by Capt. Daniell Gookin, ——— Co.
Paine, Elizabeth, 1656, by Tho. Busby, Surry Co.
Paine, Margaret, 1656, by Mr. Jno. Paine, ——— Co.
Paine, Mary, 1654, by Nath. Pope, Westmoreland Co.
Paine, John, 1653, by Mathew Williams, James City Co.
Paine, Mary, 1654, by Mr. Francis Hamond, York Co.
Painter, Richard, 1654, by Walter Dickenson, Lancaster Co.
Painter, John, 1639, by Capt. Rich. Townsend, Charles River Co.
Palam, John, 1653, by Abraham Moon, Lancaster Co.
Pale, Wm., 1636, by John Harlowe, Accomack Co.
Pall, Wm., 1656, by Capt. Henry Fleete, ——— Co.
Pallard, Digon, 1649, by Henry White, James City Co.
Pallington, Rebecca, 1639, by Robt. Newman, Warwick River Co.
Palmer, Jon., 1638, by Epaphroditus Lawson, Upper Norfolk Co.
Palmer, Edward, 1635, by Capt. Adam Thoroughgood, ——— Co.
Palmer, Sarah, 1637, by Lt. Richard Popeley, New Norfolk Co.
Palmer, Edward, 1638, by John Caudgen, Charles River Co.
Palmer, Howell, 1638, by Warradin, Charles City Co.
Palmer, Sarah, 1653, by Wm. Wyatt, Gloucester Co.
Palmer, Henry, 1650, by Stephen Charlton, Northampton Co.
Palmer, Sarah, 1636, by Henry Southell, ——— Co.
Palmer, Wm., 1635, by Capt. Thos. Willowbye, ——— Co.
Palmer, Mary, by Joseph Croshaw, York Co.
Palmer, Martin, and Mary his wife, 1653, by Joseph Croshaw, York
    Co.
Palmer, Elinor, 1652, by Richard Coleman, ——— Co.

Palmer, Edward, 1652, by John Greenbough, Henrico Co.
Palmer, Ann, 1651, by Wm. Rennoles, Northumberland Co.
Palmer, Hen., 1650, by Wm. Yarrett and Fra. Wittington, ——— Co.
Palmer, Edward, 1642, by Francis England, Isle of Wight Co.
Palmer, John, 1649, by Christop. Lewis, James City Co.
Palmer, Richard, 1655, by Mr. Robert Bowne, and Mr. Daniel Parke, York Co.
Palmer, Rebecca, 1642, by Thomas Loving, James City Co.
Palmer, Eliza., 1650, by John Garwood, Nansemond Co.
Palmer, Mary, 1654, by John Watson and John Bognall, Westmoreland Co.
Palmer, Eliz., 1654, by Edw. Welch, ——— Co.
Palmer, James, 1654, by Col. Argoll Yardley, Northampton Co.
Palmer, William, 1639, by Peter Ridley, James City Co.
Palmer, Henry, 1638, by Richard Milton, Charles City Co.
Palmer, Jane, 1637, by John Baker, Charles City Co.
Palmer, Priscilla, 1637, by John Baker, Charles City Co.
Palmer, Mary, 1654, by R. Lawson, ——— Co.
Palmeton, Sarah, 1653, by Francis Hale, ——— Co.
Pancell, Edwd., 1648, by Francis Fludd, York Co.
Panckherst, Tho., 1654, by Francis Smith and Mr. John Smith, Westmoreland Co.
Pancroft, Eliza., 1652, by Henry Barlow, ——— Co.
Pancroft, Abra., 1652, by Henry Barlow, ——— Co.
Panell, Marga., 1653, by Charles Scarburg, Northampton Co.
Panier, John, 1638, by Roger, Davis, Charles City Co.
Panthurst, Abra., 1636, by John Neale, Accomack Co.
Pantry, Wm., 1653, by Henry Deadman, Lancaster Co.
Paptass, Jno., 1651, by Mr. Wm. Armestead, ——— Co.
Parce, Tho., 1653, by Samuell Parry, Lacaster Co.
Parchmore, Peter, 1648, by Richard Lee, Gent., ——— Co.
Parcroft, Tho., 1639, by Richard Corke, Gent., Henrico Co.
Pardy, Eliz., 1654, by John Watson and John Bognall, Westmoreland Co.
Pargiter, John, 1638, by Thomas Stout, ——— Co.
Park, Sarah, 1655, by Mathew Hubard, Gent., York Co.
Parke, Edwd., 1649, by Wm. Nesum, Tho. Sax, Miles Bathasby and John Pyne, Northampton Co.
Parke, Robt., 1654, by Wm. Johnson, Northampton Co.
Parke, Wm., Sr., 1655, by Mathew Huberd, Gent., York Co.
Parke, Wm., Jr., 1655, by Mathew Huberd, Gent., York Co.
Parke, ———, 1655, by Mr. Robt. Bourne and Mr. Daniel Parke (her husband), York Co.
Parke, John, 1652, by Robert Elam, Henrico Co.
Parkes, Wm., 1656, by Tho. Meredith, New Kent Co.
Parkes, John, 1644, by Stephen Taylor, ——— Co.
Parkes, Robert, 1639, by Robert Eley, Isle of Wight Co.
Parkin, Robert, 1640, by William Crannage, Isle of Wight Co.
Parks, Tho., 1647, by Wm. Whitington, Northampton Co.
Parks, Thomas, 1635, by Thomas Harwood, ——— Co.
Parkenson, Tim., 1653, by Edward Hamond, Northampton Co.

Parkenson, Ro., 1654, by Mr. Francis Hamond, York Co.
Parker, Elizabeth (widdowe), 1635, by Capt. Adam Thoroughgood, Henrico Co.
Parker, Jon., 1637, by John Upton, Isle of Wight Co.
Parker, Jno., 1635, by Jno Upton, Warrasquinoake Co.
Parker, Tho., 1643, by John Sweete, Isle of Wight Co.
Parker, Andrew, 1638, by Richard Milton, Charles City Co.
Parker, James, 1637, by Lt. John Upton, Isle of Wight Co.
Parker, Richard, 1653, by Capt. Francis Morgan, Gloucester Co.
Parker, Jno., 1653, by Capt. Francis Morgan, Gloucester Co.
Parker, John, 1653, by Wm. Havett, ——— Co.
Parker, James, 1650, by Stephen Charlton, Northampton Co.
Parker, Richard, 1645, by Thomas Davis, Warwick Co.
Parker, John, 1645, by Justinian Cooper, Gent., Isle of Wight Co.
Parker, Richard, 1653, by John Hillier, Northumberland Co.
Parker, Ellin, 1653, by Major Abra. Wood, Charles City Co.
Parker, Fra., 1652, by John Meredith, Lancaster Co.
Parker, Elizabeth, 1652, by Isaac Richeson, Lancaster Co.
Parker, Susan, 1652, by Collo. Hugh Gwin, ——— Co.
Parker, Tho., 1652, by Gregory Parrett, Lower Norfolk Co.
Parker, Joane, Elizabeth, Thomas, Francis, 1650, by Thomas Parker (their father), Isle of Wight Co.
Parker, Martha, 1651, by Edmond Welch, ——— Co.
Parker, Richard, 1651, by Capt. Tho. Davis, Northumberland Co.
Parker, Tho., 1653, by Richard Major, Gloucester Co.
Parker, Tho., 1653, by Robert Brasseur, Nansemond Co.
Parker, James, 1650, by Sr. Tho. Luntsford, Kt., and Barronett, ——— Co.
Parker, George, 1649, by Mr. Ralph Barlowe, Northampton Co.
Parker, Ann, 1649, by Mr. Ralph Barlowe, Northampton Co.
Parker, Richard, 1649, by John Dennis, ——— Co.
Parker, Ann, 1655, by Wm. Wright, Gent., Nansemond Co.
Parker, Phillip, 1655, by Capt. Tho. Davis, Warwick Co.
Parker, Wm., 1642, by Hugh Gwyn, Gent., ——— Co.
Parker, Tho., 1646, by Thomas Brown, Lower Norfolk Co.
Parker, Tho., 1642, by Richard Maior, Charles River Co.
Parker, Richard, 1647, by Lawrence Peterse, "Nansimum" Co.
Parker, Rich., 1646, by William Hockaday, York Co.
Parker, Charles, 1650, by John Hull, Northumberland Co.
Parker, Ann, 1656, by Wm. Pulliam, New Kent Co.
Parker, Richard, 1654, by John Wyre, John Gillet, Andrew Gilson and John Phillipps, ——— Co.
Parker, Joan, 1654, by Wm. Johnson, Northampton Co.
Parker, John, 1655, by George Parker, Northampton Co.
Parker, Joane, 1655, by Richard Price, New Kent Co.
Parker, John, 1642, by William Lawson, Isle of Wight Co.
Parker, John, 1638, by Lieut. John Upton, Isle of Wight Co.
Parker, Jon., 1638, by Elizabeth Grayne, Charles City Co.
Parkhurst, Antho., 1647, by John Brooch, York River Co.
Parksly, Wm., 1636, by Christopher Cathropp, Charles River Co.
Parish, Edward, 1635, by Capt. Adam Thoroughgood, ——— Co.

Parmeton, John, 1653, by Francis Hale, ——— Co.
Parmeton, Nathaniel, 1653, by Francis Hale, ——— Co.
Parnell, Wm., 1651, by Capt. John West, Esq., Yorke Co.
Parook, Giles, 1654, by Mr. Francis Hamond, York Co.
Parr, Margt., 1637, by Cheney Boyes, Charles City Co.
Parr, Margery, 1636, by Cheney Boyse, Charles City Co.
Parr, Robert, 1637, by John Chew, Charles River Co.
Parr, Thomas, 1651, by Mr. Arhtur Price, Yorke Co.
Parr, Edward, 1649, by Stephen Gill, York Co.
Parr, Mary, 1653, by Tobey Horton, Lancaster Co.
Parramore, Edwd., 1643, by Wm. Butler, James City Co.
Parramore, Rob., 1654, by Col. Argoll Yardley, Northampton Co.
Parrett, Edw., 1652, by Henry Woodhouse, Lower Norfolk Co.
Parrett, Symon, 1654, by Christopher Regault, Gloucester Co.
Parrey, Robert, 1643, by Capt. Samuell Mathews, Esq., ——— Co.
Parricoat, Phill, 1653, by Charles Scarburg, Northampton Co.
Parrinter, Richard, 1654, by Abraham Moone, ——— Co.
Parris, Arundell, 1642, by Hugh Gwyn, Gent., ——— Co.
Parris, John, 1654, by Roger Walters, Northumberland Co.
Parris, Arrundill, 1653, by Mr. Henry Soanes, Gloucester Co.
Parris, John, 1653, by Roger Walter, Northumberland Co.
Parrit, James, 1648, by John Seward, Isle of Wight Co.
Parrott, Prunella, 1635, by John Parrott (her husband), ——— Co.
Parrot, Joan, 1652, by Wm. Colborne, Northampton Co.
Parrs, Anthony, 1653, by Wm. Wyatt, Gloucester Co.
Parry, Tho., 1652, by Richard Coleman, ——— Co.
Parry, Wm., 1652, by Nathaniel Bacon, Isle of Wight Co.
Parry, Roger, 1653, by Wm. Haynes, ——— Co.
Parry, Edmd., 1654, by Richard Jones, James City Co.
Parry, Elizab., 1653, by John Hillier, Northumberland Co.
Parry, Ann, 1652, by Mr. Tho. Curtis, ——— Co.
Parry, Tho., 1653, by Wm. Debram, ——— Co.
Parry, Robt., 1652, by Rice Jones, Lancaster Co.
Parry, Eliza., 1652, by Mrs. Anna Barnett, Gloucester Co.
Parry, Eliza., 1653, by Capt. Francis Morgan, Gloucester Co.
Parry, Wm., 1636, by Francis Maulden, ——— Co.
Parry, Ann, 1637, by William Parry, New Norfolk Co.
Parry, Wm., 1636, by John Neale, Accomack Co.
Parry, Wm., 1642, by Capt. Samuell Mathews, Esq., —— —Co.
Parry, Ra., ——, by Tho. Lucas, ——— Co.
Parry, Samll., 1650, by Mr. Stephen Hamlin, Charles City Co.
Parry, Samuel, 1656, by Sir Henry Chichley, ——— Co.
Parry, Eliz., 1654, by Wm. Robinson and Cornelius Johnson, West-
    moreland Co.
Parson, John, 1638, by Lt. Robt. Sheppard, James City Co.
Parsons, James, 1637, by John Upton, Isle of Wight Co.
Parsons, James, 1635, by Jno. Upton, Warrasquinoake Co.
Parsons, John, 1637, by Lt. John Upton, Isle of Wight Co.
Parsons, Sara, 1652, by Tho. Glascock, Lancaster Co.
Parsons, Eliza., ——, by Mr. John Page, ——— Co.
Parsons, John, 1653, by Geo. Hack, Northampton Co.

Parsons, Katherine, 1645, by James Bruss, Northampton Co.
Parsons, Wm., 1653, by Charles Grymes, Lancaster Co.
Parsons, Grace, 1651, by Mr. Arthur Price, Yorke Co.
Parsons, Henry, 1643, by William Ewins, James City Co.
Parsons, Edward, 1639, by John Wright, Upper New Norfolk Co.
Parsons, Edward, 1639, by Justinian Cooper, Isle of Wight Co.
Parsons, James, 1638, by Lieut. John Upton, Isle of Wight Co.
Parsons, Wm., 1638, by John George, Charles City Co.
Parsons, Thomas, 1639, by John White, James Citie Co.
Parsons, Thomas, 1639, by John White, James Citie Co.
Parteele, Tho., 1651, by Humphry Tabb, Northumberland Co.
Partin, Ralph, 1653, by Capt. Francis Patt, Northampton Co.
Partin, Robert, 1648, by John Seward, Isle of Wight Co.
Partin, Acces, Rebecca and Deborah, daughters of Robert Partin, 1648,
    by John Seward, Isle of Wight Co.
Partin, Margaret, wife of Robert Partin, 1648, by John Seward, Isle
    of Wight Co.
Partin, Robt., Jr., 1648, by John Seward, Isle of Wight Co.
Partir, Math., 1652, by Nicholas Wadilow, Northampton Co.
Partridge, Nester, 1636, by Wm. Clarke, Henrico Co.
Partirdge, Hester, 1638, by William Clark, Henrico Co.
Partridge, Wm., 1652, by Robert Elam, Henrico Co.
Parvin, John, 1648, by George Read, Gent., ——— Co.
Parvoll, Tho., 1650, by Mordecay Cooke, ——— Co.
Paskall, Phill., 1652, by Mrs. Mary Brent, Northumberland Co.
Paskins, Edw., 1636, by John Neale, Accomack Co.
Peasley, Joseph, 1656, by Major Wm. Lewis, ——— Co.
Pasmore, John, 1638, by Roger Davis, Charles City Co.
Passmore, Mary (wife John Passmore), 1638, by Roger Davis, Charles
    City Co.
Passe, Tho., 1653, by Wm. Debram, ——— Co.
Passe, John, 1652, by Col. Geo. Ludlow, Esq., Gloucester Co.
Pate, Richard, 1636, by Walter Hacker, James River Co.
Pate, Wm., 1637, by Francis Fowler, James River Co.
Pate, John, 1653, by Joseph Hogkinson, Lower Norfolk Co.
Pate, John, 1651, by Edmond Welch, ——— Co.
Pate, Henry, 1656, by Mr. Henry Soanes, New Kent Co.
Pate, Katherine, 1656, by Mr. Henry Soanes, New Kent Co.
Pate, Elizabeth, 1656, by Mr. Henry Soanes, New Kent Co.
Pateman, Eliz., 1653, by Robert Brasseur, Nansemond Co.
Paternoster, Abra., 1651, by Humphry Tabb, Northumberland Co.
Patient, Arthur, 1637, by Theodore Moyser, James City Co.
Patlyon, John, 1654, by Francis Gray, ——— Co.
Patt, Jno., Jr., 1653, by Capt. Francis Patt, Northampton Co.
Patt, Bridgett, 1653, by Capt. Francis Patt, Northampton Co.
Patt, Hatill, 1653, by Capt. Francis Patt, Northampton Co.
Patt, Fra., 1653, by Capt. Francis Patt, Northampton Co.
Patt, John, 1652, by Mr. Tho. Brice, Lancaster Co.
Patrick, Wm., 1637, by Henry Hart, James Citie Co.
Patrick Henry, 1636, by Edward Minter, ——— Co.
Patrick, Hen., 1638, by Edward Minter, James City Co.

Patrick, John, 1638, by William Banister, ——— Co.
Patrick, Isabell, 1653, by Capt. Robt. Abrall, ——— Co.
Patrick, Leo., 1646, by Sir William Berkeley, ——— Co.
Patrick, John, 1651, by Humphry Tabb, Northumberland Co.
Patrick, Seath., 1646, by Joseph Croshawe, Charles River Co.
Patricke, Tho., 1643, by Robert Pitt, Isle of Wight Co.
Patridge, Wm., 1650, by George Pate, Charles City Co.
Patt, John, 1646, by Tho. Savedge, Northampton Co.
Pattblade, Tho., 1654, by Col. Hump. Higgenson, Esq., and Abraham
    Moone, Westmoreland Co.
Pattent, Eliz., 1653, by Wm. Johnson, Henrico Co.
Patter, Jon., 1635, by Thos. Butler Clark and Pastor of Denbie, War-
    rasquinoake Co.
Patter, Cuthbert, 1654, by Sr. Henry Chickly, Kt., Lancaster Co.
Pattison, James, 1636, by John Neale, Accomack Co.
Pattison, Henry, 1635, by Hugh Cox, Charles City Co.
Paul, Pat., 1648, by Wm. Barret, ——— Co.
Paul, John, 1650, by Richard Hull, ——— Co.
Paule, Francis, 1637, by Thomas Paule, James City Co.
Paule, Mathew, 1637, by Thomas Paule, James City Co.
Paule, Thos., 1637, by Thomas Paule, James City Co.
Paule, Stephen, 1643, by Robert Pitt, Isle of Wight Co.
Paulett, Chidock, 1637, by Capt. Thomas Paulett, Charles City Co.
Paulwin, Hester, 1652, by Christopher Robinson, and John Sturdwant,
    Henrico Co.
Paulsans, John, 1652, by Capt. Augustine Warner, ——— Co.
Pauncy, John, 1651, by Edward Deggs, Esq., Yorke Co.
Paverell, Georg., 1639, by Mark Johnson, Elizabeth City Co.
Pavy, Wm., 1648, by Tho. Lambert, Lower Norfolk Co.
Pawan, Mary, 1653, by Jno. Hansford, Gloucester Co.
Pawly, John, 1635, by Capt. Wm. Pierse, ——— Co.
Pawre, John, 1652, by Richard Hatton and Lambett Lambettson,
    Lancaster Co.
Pawre, Peter, 1652, by Richard Hatton, and Lambett Lambettson,
    Lancaster Co.
Pawre, Reynold, Jr., 1652, by Richard Hatton and Lambett Lambett-
    son, Lancaster Co.
Pawre, Gawt., 1652, by Richard Hatton and Lambett Lambettson,
    Lancaster Co.
Pawre, Reynold, 1652, by Richard Hatton and Lambett Lambettson,
    Lancaster Co.
Payne, Robert, 1653, by Roger Walter, Northumberland Co.
Payne, Tho., 1652, by Elias Edmonds, Lancaster Co.
Payne, Sarah, 1652, by Mr. Henry Pitt, ——— Co.
Payne, Edw., 1650, by Mr. Epaphroditus Lawson, ——— Co.
Payne, Tho., 1650, by John Garwood, Nansemond Co.
Payne, Tho., 1645, by Michael Masters, Henrico Co.
Payne, Jno. Jr., 1656, by Mr. Jno. Paine, ——— Co.
Payne, Richard, 1654, by Mr. Francis Hamond, York Co.
Paynes, Tho., 1850, by David Peebles, Charles City Co.
Paynter, Tho., 1643, by John Hoddin, ——— Co.

Paynter, Robt., 1654, by Valentine Patten, Westmoreland Co.
Paynter, Wm., 1655, by Nich. Bush, James City Co.
Payse, Tho., 1648, by Richard Pettibon, ——— Co.
Payton, Mary, 1653, by Edward Kemp, Geo. Cortlough, and John
    Meredith, Lancaster Co.
Payton, Peter, 1636, by William Julian, Elizabeth City Co.
Payton, Mary, 1650, by Wm. Yarrett and Fra. Wittington, ——— Co.
Peach, Dasabell, 1651, by Edward Deggs, Esq., Yorke Co.
Peach, Tho., 1653, by Denis Coniers, Lancaster Co.
Peach, Wm., 1653, by Denis Coniers, Lancaster Co.
Peach, Wm., 1643, by Rowland Burnham, Yorke Co.
Peacock, Tho., 1635, by William Barber (a mariner), Charles City Co.
Peacock, Mathew, 1651, by Coll. Richard Lee, Esq., Gloucester Co.
Peacock, Robert, 1653, by Mr. Edmund Bowman, ——— Co.
Peacock, Micahell, 1642, by Daniell Lewellyn, ——— Co.
Peacock, Tho., 1646, by David Jones, Charles City Co.
Peacock, Rideord, 1656, by Mr. Jno. Paine, ——— Co.
Peacock, Richard, 1642, by Capt. Samuell Mathews, Esq., ——— Co.
Pead, Mary, 1652, by John Pead, ——— Co.
Pead, Robert, 1651, by Joseph Croshaw, Yorke Co.
Peadle, Cosbett, 1643, by Richard Kemp, Esq., James City Co.
Peadle, Henry, 1639, by Justinian Cooper, Isle of Wight Co.
Peagler, Joane, 1648, by Richard Lee, Gent., ——— Co.
Peake, Matthew, 1636, by John Harlowe, Accomack Co.
Peake, Thomas, 1635, by Daniel Cugley, Accomac Co.
Peake, John, 1652, by Lt. Coll. John Cheesman, ——— Co.
Peake, Thos., 1642, by Adam Cooke, Charles Co.
Peake, William, 1643, by Capt. Samuell Mathews, Esq., ——— Co.
Peal, Jon., 1637, by Wm. Farrar, Henrico Co.
Peale, Wm., 1651, by John Thomas, Gloucester Co.
Peale, Fra., 1635, by Thomas Crompe, James Co.
Pearce, Edward, 1635, by William Wilkinson (minister), ——— Co.
Pearce, Wm., 1636, by John Neale, Accomack Co.
Pearce, Edw., 1637, by William Wilkinson, New Norfolk Co.
Pearce, John, 1653, by Colo. Wm. Clayborne (Sec. of State), ——— Co.
Peace, Anthony, 1650, by John Mangor, ——— Co.
Pearce, Robert, 1636, by John Neale, Accomack Co.
Peare, John, 1653, by Edward Harrington, Northampton Co.
Peare, Henry, 1653, by Edward Harrington, Northampton Co.
Peare, Tho., 1650, by Mr. Anthony Ellyott, ——— Co.
Peare, Edward, 1653, by Edward Harrington, Northampton Co.
Peare, Elizabeth, 1653, by Edward Harrington, Northampton Co.
Peareene, Thomas, 1639, by John Bell, Charles River Co.
Pearepoint, Wm., 1643, by John Freeme, Charles Co.
Pearle, Franc, 1635, by William Spencer, ——— Co.
Pearle, Francis, 1637, by William Spencer, ——— Co.
Pearle, Andrew, 1653, by Hopkins Howell, Nansemond Co.
Peasant, William, 1638, by Mr. John Gookins, Upper New Norfolk Co
Pearse, Robert, 1637, by Thomas Davis, New Norfolk Co.
Peasley, Susan, 1650, by Henry Peaseley, ——— Co.
Pearson, Tho., 1636, by Richard Cocke, ——— Co.

Pearson, Mary, 1646, by Sir William Berkley, —— Co.
Peasint, William, 1637, by John Burnette, New Norfolk Co.
Peasly, Magd., 1653, by John Ware, —— Co.
Peasly, Henry, 1650, by Henry Peaseley, —— Co.
Peasly, Michael, 1650, by Henry Peaseley, —— Co.
Peasley, Wm., 1654, by Mr. Francis Hamond, York Co.
Peat, John, 1649, by John Libsey, Lower Norfolk Co.
Peay, Mary, 1654, by Mr. Giles Brent, Westmoreland Co.
Peck, John, 1651, by Wm. Parry, Northumberland Co.
Peck, John, 1654, by Francis Smith and Mr. John Smith, Westmore-
    land Co.
Peck, Elizabeth, 1655, by Mr. Tho. Peck, Gloucester Co.
Pickering, Jon., 1653, by Gregory Rawlins, Surry Co.
Peckering, Joan, 1653, by Samuell Bonam, Northumberland Co.
Peckers, Mary, 1650, by Geo. Ludlow, Esq., Northumberland Co.
Peckstone, Tho., 1655, by Mr. Tho. Peck, Gloucester Co.
Pedegrew, Andrew, 1652, by Nicholas Waddilow, Northampton Co.
Pedigrew, And., 1655, by Nich. Waddilow, Northampton Co.
Pedlers, Roger, 1655, by Dr. Giles Mode, New Kent Co.
Pedocke, Eliza., 1650. by Stephen Charlton, Northampton Co.
Pedocke, Eliza., 1649, by Henry Bishopp, Northampton Co.
Pee, John, 1651, by James Foster, Nansemond Co.
Peele, John, 1652, by John Howett, Northumberland Co.
Peele, Luke, 1654, by Mr. Francis Hamond, York Co.
Peerce, Eliz., 1650, by Epa. Lawson, —— Co.
Peerce, Hen., 1650, by John Landman, —— Co.
Peeroy, Ann, 1648, by Geo. Hardy, —— Co.
Peeter, Alice, 1653, by Fra. Gower, Lancaster Co.
Peeters, Tho., 1643, by Richard Richards, Charles River Co.
Peeters, Lawrence, 1646, by Thomas Bahe, Upper Norfolk Co.
Peeterson, Neele, 1653, by John Gillett, Lancaster Co.
Peggatt, Walter, 1650, by Richard Tye and Charles Sparrowe, Charles
    City Co.
Peggin, Dan., 1652, by Lawerence Dameron, Northumberland Co.
Peggis, Garrett, 1654, by Henry Walker, James City Co.
Peiden, Rose, 1643, by Richard Kemp, Esq., James City Co.
Peio, John, 1650, by John Hallawes, Gent., Northumberland Co.
Peirce, Wm., 1635, by Jno. Sparks, —— Co.
Peirce, Wm., 1637, by Wm. Prior, Charles River Co.
Peirce, William, 1637, by William Prior, Charles River Co.
Peirce, David, 1637, by Humphry Loyd, Charles River Co.
Peirce, Wm., 1642, by John Boyles, —— Co.
Peirce, John, 1643, by Casar Puggett, Lower Norfolk Co.
Peirce, Wm., 1643, by Capt. John Upton, Isle of Wight Co.
Peirce, Eliza., 1643, by Capt. John Upton, Isle of Wight Co.
Peirce, Wm., 1652, by Tho. Harwood, —— Co.
Peirce, Wm., 1648, by Mr. Phillip Bennet, Nansemond Co.
Peirce, John, 1648, by John Saynes, James City Co.
Peirce, Robt., 1651, by Robt. Bradshaw, Charles River Co.
Peirce, Ed., 1653, by Tho. Willis, York Co.

Peirce, Mrs., 1650, by Sr. Tho. Luntsford, Kt., and Baronnett, ——— Co.
Peirce, Jane, 1650, by Richard Tye and Charles Sparrowe, Charles City Co.
Peirce, Geo., 1650, by Capt. Ishiell Linch, ——— Co.
Peirce, Kath., 1650, by Mr. James Williamson, ——— Co.
Peirce, John, 1649, by Joseph Croshawe, Yorke Co.
Peirce, John, 1648, by Georg Read, Gent, ——— Co.
Peirce, Wm., 1648, by Thomas Hart, James City Co.
Peirce, Chr., 1645, by Francis Martin, Northampton Co.
Peirce, Robt., 1643, by Fra. Mason, Lower Norfolk Co.
Peirce, Mary, 1647, by John Sidney, Lower Norfolk Co.
Peirce, Hen., 1654, by Col. Argoll Yardley, Northampton Co.
Peirce, George, 1652, by Robert Younge, Lancaster Co.
Peirce, Giles, 1655, by Coll. Richard Lee, Gloucester Co.
Peirce, John, 1639, by William Davis, James City Co.
Peirce, Thomas, 1639, by Lieut. Richard Popeley, ——— Co.
Peirce, Richard, 1638, by Christopher Branch, Henrico Co.
Perice, Mary, 1638, by Epaphroditus Lawson, Upper New Norfolk Co.
Peircifull, Robt., 1642, by John Meakes, ——— Co.
Percival, Richard, 1653, by Tho. Kibby, Northumberland Co.
Peircey, Fra., 1653, by John Debar, ——— Co.
Peircy, Abraham, 1653, by John Debar, Lower Norfolk Co.
Peircy, Mary, 1653, by Tho. Youl, Northumberland Co.
Peirse, Wm., 1643, by Wm. Berryman, Northampton Co.
Pelard, James, 1648, by John Seward, Isle of Wight Co.
Pelcock, Barthoe, 1640, by Thomas Harvey, James City Co.
Pellet, Ann, 1653, by Corbet Piddle, Northumberland Co.
Pelhive, Abraham, 1636, by Izabell Thresher, ——— Co.
Pelliboner, Kath., 1652, by Capt. Augustine Warner, ——— Co.
Pelloone, John, 1655, by Lt. Col. Tho. Swan, Surry Co.
Pellton, Wm., N., 1656, by Mr. Henry Soanes, New Kent Co.
Pelover, James, 1655, by Lt. Col. Tho. Swan, Surry Co.
Pembridge, Tho., 1643, by Wm. Butler, James City Co.
Pender, Thomas, 1638, by Alice Edloe, Henrico Co.
Pendergast, Phillipp, 1643, by Mr. John Bishopp, James City Co.
Pendergast, Phillip, 1647, by James Warradine, ——— Co.
Pendergast, Phil., 1655, by Richard Hamlet, James City Co.
Peneale, Mary, 1654, by Mr. Tho. Fowke, Westmoreland Co.
Penenton, Jno., 1654, by Wm. Beach, Westmoreland Co.
Penhorne, Christopher, 1637, by Wm. Farrar, Henrico Co.
Penifell, Sym., 1654, by Capt. Nich. Marteaw, Westmoreland Co.
Penill, Rich., 1637, by Capt. Henry Browne, James City Co.
Pensint, Wm., 1636, by John Gookin, Gent., ——— Co.
Penington, Wm., 1652, by James Forster and Audry Bonny, ——— Co.
Penington, Jno., 1654, by Capt. Nich. Marteaw, Westmoreland Co.
Penkney, James, 1635, by William Pilkington, ——— Co.
Penn, Wm., 1652, by Tho. Hoane, ——— Co.
Penn, Tho., 1652, by Tho. Hoane, ——— Co.
Penn, Rog., 1652, by Mr. George Clapham, ——— Co.
Penn, Elizabeth, 1650, by Wm. Underwood, Gent., ——— Co.

Penne, Rich., 1648, by Wm. Ewen, James City Co.
Pennell, George, 1656, by Mr. Tho. Purifoy, ——— Co.
Penny, Wm., 1643, by Robert Lawrance, Isle of Wight Co.
Pensint, Wm., 1637, by Daniell Gookins, New Norfolk Co.
Penton, Tho., 1640, by Thomas Stegg, Charles City Co.
Peogler, John, 1646, by John Flyne, Yorke Co.
Pep, Joyce, 1652, by Mrs. Mary Brent, Northumberland Co.
Pepper, Wm., 1652, by John Pounsey, ——— Co.
Pepper, John, 1653, by Robert Chewninge, Lancaster Co.
Pepper, Henry, 1643, by Richard Jackson, Isle of Wight Co.
Peppett, Fra., 1653, by Mr. Wm. Hoccoday, Yorke Co.
Peppin, Wm., ———, by Mr. Wm. Presly, Northumberland Co.
Pepping, Mathew, 1655, by Southy Littleberry, Northampton Co.
Perce, Katherine, 1635, by William Spencer, ——— Co.
Percevale, Robert, 1649, by Mr. Robert Parker, Northampton Co.
Perchin, Jno., 1650, by Mrs. Frances Townshend (widdow), Northum-
    berland Co.
Percival, Eliz., 1654, by Richard Kellam, Northampton Co.
Percivall, John, 1650, by John Mattum, Northumberland Co.
Percie, Jno., 1635, by Capt. Adam Thoroughgood, ——— Co.
Peremeter, John, 1648, by Richard Lee, Gent., ——— Co.
Perfect, Robert, and wife, 1650, by Wm. Yarrett and Fra. Wittington,
    ——— Co.
Perine, Ursula, 1651, by Edward Symson, Gloucester Co.
Perkes, Edward, 1635, by John Leonard, Warrasquinoake Co.
Perkins, Ellin, 1635, by Jno. Sparks, ——— Co.
Perkins, Roger, 1652, by Col. Geo. Ludlow, Esq., Gloucester Co.
Perkins, Geo., 1652, by John Pounsey, ——— Co.
Perkins, Davy, 1651, by Capt. Stephen Gill, Northumberland Co.
Perkins, Dinah, 1651, by Mr. Rowland Burnham, ——— Co.
Perkins, Tho., 1643, by John Neale, Gent, Northampton Co.
Perkins, George, 1653, by Colo. Wm. Clayborne (Sec. of State), ———
    Co.
Perkins, Mary, 1650, by Nicolas Perkins, Henrico Co.
Perkins, Wm., 1650, by Wm. Clapham, ——— Co.
Perkins, Samll, 1650, by George Taylor, ——— Co.
Perkins, Tho., 1642, by Capt. Daniell Gookins, ——— Co.
Perkins, James, 1642, by Capt. Daniell Gookins, ——— Co.
Perkins, Robt., 1642, by Wm. Durant, ——— Co.
Perkins, Tho., 1650, by Wingfield Webb and Richard Pate, ——— Co.
Perkins, Jane, 1650, by Wingfield Webb and Richard Pate, ——— Co.
Perkins, Obedience, 1656, by Wm. Pope, Nansemond Co.
Perkins, Tho., 1656, by Mr. Henry Soanes, New Kent Co.
Perkins, Andrew, 1638, by Lieut. John Upton, Isle of Wight Co.
Perkins, Nicholas, 1641, by Brayant Smith, Henrico Co.
Perren, Richard, 1654, by Nich. Meriwether, Westmoreland Co.
Perren, Andrew, 1655, by George Kibble, Lancaster Co.
Perrie, Francis, 1637, by Jon. Brodie, Charles River Co.
Perrie, Peter, 1647, by Tho. Gibson, York Co.
Perrie, Wm., 1650, by David Peibles, Charles City Co.
Perrigoe, Wm., 1654, by Capt. Nich. Marteaw, Westmoreland Co.

Perrin, Arthur, 1638, by Georg Mynifie (merchant), ——— Co.
Perrin, Richard, 1653, by Nicho. Meriwether, Northumberland Co.
Perrin, Richard, 1637, by Thomas Weston, Charles River Co.
Perrin, Richard, 1637, by Thomas Osborne, Jr., Henrico Co.
Perrin, John, 1642, by William Prior, Gent., ——— Co.
Perrocks, Tho., 1638, by Wm. Barker and Associates, Charles City Co.
Perry, Rich., 1635, by Wm. Swan, James Co.
Perry, Robert, 1639, by Richard Nance, Henrico Co.
Perry, Robert, 1637, by Patrick Kennedye, New Norfolk Co.
Perry, Edward, 1637, by Henry Perry, Charles River Co.
Perry, Ann, 1643, by Mr. Moore Fautleroy, Upper Norfolk Co.
Perry, Rich., 1638, by Thomas Swan, James Citie Co.
Perry, Elizabeth, 1652, by Elias Edmonds, Lancaster Co.
Perry, Eliza., 1651, by Mrs. Anna Bernard, Northumberland Co.
Perry, Ann, 1651, by Phillip Hunley, ——— Co.
Perry, Sa., 1653, by Corbet Piddle, Northumberland Co.
Perry, Joan, 1654, by Hugh Lee, Northumberland Co.
Perry, Edw., 1654, by Hugh Lee, Northumberland Co.
Perry, Edmond, 1653, by Colo. Wm. Clayborne (Sec. of State), ———
    Co.
Perry, Ezekiell, 1643, by Wm. Butler, James City Co.
Perry, Ann, 1655, by Richard Coole and David Anderson, Westmore-
    land Co.
Perry, Tho., 1656, by Geo. Abbott, Nansemond Co.
Perry, Eliz., 1654, by John Wyre, John Gillet, Andrew Gilson and
    John Phillipps, ——— Co.
Perry, Edward, 1637, by Henry Perry, Charles River Co.
Perry, Richard, 1656, by Robt. Bayly, Northampton Co.
Person, Thomas, 1639, by Thomas Stoute, James City Co.
Person, John, 1648, by Nicholas Dixson, Nansemond Co.
Person, Tho., 1639, by Richard Corke, Gent., Henrico Co.
Person, Ralph, 1637, by Capt. John Howe, Accomac Co.
Person, Kath., 1636, by John Seaward, Isle of Wight Co.
Persons, Joane, 1650, by Wm. Clapham, ——— Co.
Persons, Henry, 1648, by Wm. Ewen, James City Co.
Pertirson, Sanders, 1652, by Tho. Teakle, Northampton Co.
Peter, John, 1649, by Mr. Ralph Barlowe, Northampton Co.
Peter, Elizabeth, 1650, by Andrew Gilson, ——— Co.
Peters, Edmd., 1653, by Wm. Walker, Northumberland Co.
Peters, Anne, 1652, by Wm. Morton, Lower Norfolk Co.
Peters, Henry, 1652, by Richard Hill, Northampton Co.
Peters, William, 1635, by Thomas Harwood, ——— Co.
Peters, Jon., 1637, by Richard Bennett, New Norfolk Co.
Peters, Wm., 1653, by James Turner, ——— Co.
Peters, Edmond, 1654, by John Whithers and Stephen Garey, West-
    moreland Co.
Peters, He., 1655, by John Ayres, ——— Co.
Peterson, Cor., 1653, by Edward Dobson, ——— Co.
Peterson, Neale, 1653, by Wm. Sidner, Lancaster Co.
Peterson, Barnett, 1650, by Capt. Chas. Leech, Yorke Co.
Peterson, Evor., 1653, by Eppy Bonison, Lancaster Co.

Peterson, Ann, 1638, by Benjamin Carrill, James City Co.
Peterson, Wm., 1638, by John Bough, Henrico Co.
Peterson, Eyver, 1654, by John Wyre, John Gillet, Andrew Gilson and John Phillipps, ——— Co.
Peterson, Pe., 1655, by Mr. Tho. Peck, Gloucester Co.
Petick, Eliz., 1641, by Stephen Charleton, Accomack Co.
Petick, Leonard, 1641, by Stephen Charleton, Accomack Co.
Pett, William, 1637, by Thomas Davis, New Norfolk Co.
Pett, Francis, 1652, by Mrs. Elinor Brocas, Lancaster Co.
Pett, Mathew, 1651, by Toby Norton, Northampton Co.
Pett, Fra., 1649, by Wm. Hoccaday, ——— Co.
Pettibone, Richard, 1639, by Richard Preston, Upper New Norfolk Co.
Pettin, James, 1649, by Richard Parrett, ——— Co.
Pettis, Step., 1637, by Mathew Edloe, ——— Co.
Pettits, Ann, 1656, by Richard Gible, Northumberland Co.
Pettit, Rich., 1636, by Samuel Curby, James City Co.
Pettriman, Robt., 1642, by Henry Coleman, Elizabeth City Co.
Pettus, Jr., Thomas, 1643, by Capt. Thomas Pettus, ——— Co.
Petway, Rich., 1635, by John Moone, Warrasquinoake Co.
Petwell, Robt., 1636, by Samuel Curby, James City Co.
Pevvis, Richard, 1654, by Mr. Mordecay Cooke, ——— Co.
Pew, Richard, 1637, by William Reynolds, Charles River Co.
Pew, George, 1652, by Henry Smith, Jr., ——— Co.
Pewer, Grigs, 1651, by Abraham Moone and (Thomas Griffin), Lancaster Co.
Peyston, Robt., 1654, by John Sharpe, Lancaster Co.
Peyter, Wm., 1646, by Thomas Bahe, Upper Norfolk Co.
Pharin, Phillipp, 1637, by Robert Bennett, New Norfolk Co.
Pharrin, Phill., 1635, by Robert Bennett, ——— Co.
Phelps, Robert, 1639, by Samuell Almond, Henrico Co.
Phelps, Robt., Thos. Cosby's servant, 1637, by Arthur Bayly and Thos. Crosby, Henrico Co.
Philcock, Richd., 1643, by Samuell Abbott, James City Co.
Phillips, Ann, 1651, by Thomas Bridge, Lower Norfolk Co.
Phillipps, Eliz., 1635, by Tho. Phillipps, her father, James City Co.
Phillips, Wm., 1656, by Wm. Justice, Charles City Co.
Phillips, Tho., 1650, by Jervace Dodson, Gent., Northumberland Co.
Phillips, Edward, 1655, by Dr. Giles Mode, New Kent Co.
Phillips, Lucy, 1654, by Col. Hump. Higgenson, Esq., and Abraham Moone, Westmoreland Co.
Phillips, David, 1654, by John Cox, Lancaster Co.
Phillips, John, 1654, by Abraham Moone, ——— Co.
Phillips, Elizabeth, 1654, by Major Abraham Wood, Henrico Co.
Phillips, Wm., 1654, by Arthur Nash, New Kent Co.
Phillips, Sarah, 1654, by John Wyre, John Gillet, Andrew Gilson and John Phillipps, ——— Co.
Phillips, Eliza., 1654, by John Wyre, John Gillet, Andrew Gilson and John Phillipps, ——— Co.
Phillips, Richard, 1654, by Col. Argoll Yardley, Northampton Co.
Phillips, Ann, 1656, by Wm. Crump and Mr. Humphry Vaulx, James City Co.

Phillips, Elizabeth, 1653, by Nicholas Meriwether, Lancaster Co.
Phillips, David, 1650, by Samuell Smith, Northumberland Co.
Phillips, Martha, 1655, by Wm. Wright, Gent., Nansemond Co.
Phillips, Wm., 1650, by Edward James, ———— Co.
Phillips, Mr. David, 1650, by Sr. Tho. Luntsford, Kt. and Barronnett,
———— Co.
Phillips, Eliza., 1650, by John Major, Northampton Co.
Phillips, Wm., 1653, by Augustine Gillet, Upper Norfolk Co.
Phillips, Robert, 1651, by Wm. Parry, Northumberland Co.
Phillips, Tho., 1651, by Richard Turney, Northumberland Co.
Phillips, Wm., 1648, by Wm. Ewen, James City Co.
Phillips, Dav., 1648, by Wm. Barret, ———— Co.
Phillips, Robert, 1648, by Tho. Braughton, ———— Co.
Phillips, Elizabeth, 1652, by Elias Edmonds, Lancaster Co.
Phillips, John, 1652, by John Chambers, Northumberland Co.
Phillips, Mathew, 1651, by Thomas Bridge, Lower Norfolk Co.
Philliph, Jeffery, 1652, by Robert West, Charles City Co.
Phillipp, Elig., 1635, by Tho. Phillipps, James City Co.
Phillipps, Georg., 1638, by Alice Edloe, Henrico Co.
Phillipps, John, 1638, by John Stratton, Lower New Norfolk Co.
Phillipps, Lewis, 1638, by Lieut. John Upton, Isle of Wight Co.
Phillipps, Eliz., 1639, by Justinian Cooper, Isle of Wight Co.
Phillipps, Robert, 1640, by Thomas Harvey, James City Co.
Phillipps, John, 1643, by Capt. Samuell Mathews, Esq., ———— Co.
Phillipps, Eliz., 1650, by Robert Blake and Samuell Elridge, Isle of
Wight Co.
Phillipps, Wm., 1643, by Rich. Hoe, Gent., ———— Co.
Phillipps, Eliz., 1637, by Cheney Boyes, Charles City Co.
Phillipps, Morgan, 1637, by Daniell Gookins, New Norfolk Co.
Phillipps, Lewis, 1637, by John Upton, Isle of Wight Co.
Phillipps, Robt., 1643, by Elizabeth Hull, ———— Co.
Phillipps, Richard, 1635, by Alexander Stonar, ———— Co.
Phillipps, Eliz., 1635, by Wm. Barber (a mariner), Charles City Co.
Phillips, John, 1653, by Sampson Robins, Northampton Co.
Phillips, Michael, 1653, by John Knott, ———— Co.
Phillipps, Lewis, 1637, by Lt. John Upton, Isle of Wight Co.
Phillipps, Jon, 1637, by Capt. Adam Thoroughgood, New Norfolk Co.
Phillipps, Edw., 1638, by Nicholas Sabrell, James City Co.
Phillipps, Eliz., 1638, by Wm. Barker and Associates, Charles City Co.
Phillipps, John, 1636, by Christopher Burroughs, Elizabeth City Co.
Phillipps, Lewis, 1635, by Jno. Upton, Warrasquinoake Co.
Phillipps, Jon., 1635, by Capt. Adam Thoroughgood, ———— Co.
Phillipps, Eliz., 1636, by Cheney Boyse, Charles City Co.
Phillipps, Robt., 1637, by John Graves, Elizabeth City Co.
Phillipps, Tho., 1637, by John Graves, Elizabeth City Co.
Phillipps, Rich., 1637, by Tho. Wheeler, Charles City Co.
Phillipson, Robt., 1640, by Robert Holt, James City Co.
Phillipson, Robt., 1638, by Robt. Holt and Richard Bell, James City
Co.
Philpot, Rich., 1648, by Randall Crew, Nansemond Co.
Philpot, Jon., 1653, by Wm. Johnson, Henrico Co.

Phipps, John, 1654, by Robert Holt, James City Co.
Phipps, Edw., 1654, by Capt. David Mansell, Westmoreland Co.
Pickeringe, Geo., 1655, by Mr. Wm. Nutt, Northumberland Co.
Pickering, Joane, 1642, by Richard Lee, ——— Co.
Pickery, Edm., 1650, by Richard Tye and Charles Sparrowe, Charles City Co.
Pickfizzell, Giles, 1655, by John Dorman, Northampton Co.
Pidd, William, 1648, by Lewis Burwell, Gent., ——— Co.
Piddington, Christopher, 1638, by Oliver Sprye, Upper New Norfolk Co.
Pidiston, Sam., 1650, by Daniell Luellin, Charles City Co.
Pierce, Richard, 1635, by Christopher Branch, Henrico Co.
Piggett, Wm., 1654, by Sarah Hancock, Lower Norfolk Co.
Piggott, ———, 1655, by John Biggs, Lower Norfolk Co.
Pigson, Jon., 1636, by Izabell Thresher, ——— Co.
Pike, Wm., 1650, by James Metgrigar and Hugh Foutch, Northumberland Co.
Piland, James, 1642, by Francis England, Isle of Wight Co.
Piland, Alexandra, wife of James Piland, 1642, by Francis England, Isle of Wight Co.
Piland, Alexandria, 1642, by John Sweete, ——— Co.
Piland, Joane, 1641, by John Sweete, ——— Co.
Pilcher, Tho., 1652, by Wm. Colborne, Northampton Co.
Pilkington, Margaret, 1635, by William Pilkington, ——— Co.
Pillard, Benj., 1642, by Stephen Hamblyn, York Co.
Pillars, Jasper, 1648, by Randall Crew, Nansemond Co.
Pilsberry, Henry, 1649, by John Walthams, Northampton Co.
Pincher, Barah, 1651, by James Thelaball, Lower Norfolk Co.
Pincher, Wm., 1637, by Lt. John Upton, Isle of Wight Co.
Pincher, Wm., 1635, by Jno. Upton, Warrasquinoake Co.
Pincher, Wm., 1637, by John Upton, Isle of Wight Co.
Pinches, Jon., 1635, by Capt. Thos. Willowbye, Elizabeth City Co.
Pinkhorne, John, 1652, by Nicholas George, ——— Co.
Pinkard, Tho., 1655, by Wm. Wright, Gent., Nansemond Co.
Pinke, Fra., 1650, by John Mattrum, Northumberland Co.
Pinion, Wm., 1643, by John Wall, ——— Co.
Pinn, Robt., 1649, by Stephen Gill, York Co.
Pinn, Dorothy, 1637, by Humphry Higginson, Gent., ——— Co.
Pinner, James, 1643, by John Freeme, Charles Co.
Pinox, Jane, 1653, by Coll. Wm. Taylor, Esq., Gloucester Co.
Pinser, Geo., 1635, by Osbourne Jeakin, Chas. City Co.
Piper, John, 1654, by John Skerrett, ——— Co.
Piper, John, 1650, by Walter Boradhurst, ——— Co.
Piper, Jon., 1636, by James Knott, Elizabeth City Co.
Piper. John, 1637, by James Knott, New Norfolk Co.
Pippin, Wm., 1638, by Richard Wilcox, James City Co.
Pitcher, John, 1653, by Charles Scarburg, Northampton Co.
Pitcher, Mary, 1650, by Robert Bird, ——— Co.
Pitchfork, Walter, 1648, by Georg Read, Gent., ——— Co.
Pistole, Eliz., 1636, by John Neale, Accomack Co.
Pistole, Robt., 1636, by John Neale, Accomack Co.

Pitt, Richard, 1653, by Samuell Parry, Lancaster Co.
Pitt, Math., 1642, by John Harlow, Accomack Co.
Pitts, Richard, 1651, by Robt. Newman, Northumberland Co.
Pitts, Richard, 1654, by Francis Gray, ———— Co.
Pitts, Edward, 1635, by Capt. Adam Thoroughgood, ———— Co.
Pitts, Saml., 1652, by Capt. Augustine Warner, ———— Co.
Pitts, John, 1649, by John Trussells, ———— Co. ·
Pitts, Tho., 1654, by Henry Walker, James City Co.
Pittsway, Edward (son), 1638, by Robert Pittsway (his father), Charles River Co.
Pittsway, Mary (wife), 1638, by Robert Pittsway (her husband), Charles River Co.
Pittsway, Mary (daughter), 1638, by Robert Pittsway (her father), Charles River Co.
Pittway, Robt., 1637, by Edward Travis, James City Co.
Pittway, Evan, 1639, by Edward Travis, James City Co.
Pixley, Benjamin, 1639, by Georg Minifye, Esq., Charles River Co.
Place, Mary, 1636, by John Place (her husband), Elizabeth City Co.
Place, James, 1636, by Robert Hollom, Henrico Co.
Placenett, Tho., 1653, by Wm. Walker, Northumberland Co.
Plaine, Hen., 1654, by Capt. Nich. Marteaw, Westmoreland Co.
Plaine, Robt., 1638, by Thomas Burbage, Accomack Co.
Planer, Elizabeth, 1652, by Tho. Lucas, Gent., Lancaster Co.
Plant, Rich., 1638, by John Bough, Henrico Co.
Plart, Tho., 1638, by Sarah Cloyden, Isle of Wight Co.
Platford, Tho., 1654, by Capt. John West, Esq., Gloucester Co.
Platt, Gilbert, 1635, by Capt. Adam Thoroughgood, Henrico Co.
Platt, Law., 1652, by Mr. John Cheesman, ——— —Co.
Platt, Tho., 1642, by Christopher Boyce, ———— Co.
Player, Richd., 1653, by Margarett Upton, Lancaster Co.
Playstone, Ann, 1652, by Col. Geo. Ludlow, Esq., Gloucester Co.
Playstone, Ann, Sr., 1652, by Col. Geo. Ludlow, Esq., Gloucester Co.
Playstow, Ann, Jr., 1642, by Wm. Durant, ———— Co.
Playstow, Ann, Sr., 1642, by Wm. Durant, ———— Co.
Plesberry, Wm., 1638, by John Gater, Lower New Norfolk Co.
Pledge, Nich., 1636, by Wm. Clarke, Henrico Co.
Pleg, Nich., 1638, by William Clarke, Henrico Co.
Pletsoe, George, 1652, by Collo. Hugh Gwin, ———— Co.
Pliny, John, 1637, by Percival Champion, New Norfolk Co.
Plowman, Edwd., 1638, by John Jackson and Eliza Kingswill, James City Co.
Pluckett, Tho., 1651, by Richard Turney, Northumberland Co.
Plunckett, James, 1638, by Bennett Freeman, James City Co.
Plucknett, Tho., 1654, by John Whithers and Stephen Garey, Westmoreland Co.
Plunket, James, 1655, by Capt. George Floyd, New Kent Co.
Plumblye, Phillipp, 1638, by John Seaward Isle of Wight Co.
Plumby, Eliza, 1650, by Rice Jones, ———— Co.
Plumer, Fra., 1654, by R. Lawson, ———— Co.
Plumer, Peter, 1656, by Wm. Justice, Charles City Co.
Plumer, John, 1650, by John Garwood, Nansemond Co.

Plummer, Jo., 1653, by Wm. and George Worseman, Henrico Co.
Plummer, John, 1642, by John Harlowe, Northampton Co.
Plummor, Morris, 1656, by Capt. Richard Lee, Gloucester Co.
Plumpton, Henry, ——, by Mr. Wm. Presly, Northumberland Co.
Plunknett, Edw., 1642, by Stephen Gill, Yorke River Co.
Pocen, Mathew, 1639, by Wm. Barker, Charles City Co.
Pockett, Wm., 1637, by Capt. Henry Browne, James City Co.
Pockett, Jo., 1637, by John Graves, Elizabeth City Co.
Poggett, Ann, 1650, by Richard Axom and Tho. Godwin, —— Co.
Pograve, Gregory, 1637, by Thomas Addison, New Norfolk Co.
Pointean, James, 1637, by Peter Roy and William Jacob, Isle of Wight Co.
Pointer, Robt., 1654, by Robert Hubard, Westmoreland Co.
Polden, Richard, 1646, by Sir William Berlkey, —— Co.
Pollard, John, 1642, by Peter Rigby, —— Co.
Polly, Wm., 1653, by Charles Grymes, Lancaster Co.
Polwort, John, 1655, by Capt. Henry Fleet, —— Co.
Pomery, Henry, 1636, by Georg Sapheir, Elizabeth City Co.
Pond, John, 1643, by Robert Lawrance, Isle of Wight Co.
Pone, Tho., 1656, by John Wood, —— Co.
Ponier, Tho., 1656, by Sir Henry Chichley, —— Co.
Pontian, Ja., 1648, by Richard Pettibon, —— Co.
Ponton, John, 1635, by Capt. Adam Thoroughgood, —— Co.
Pool, George, 1650, by James Hurd, —— Co.
Pool, David and Mary, his wife, 1655, by Geo. Coltclough, Northumberland Co.
Poobat, Jon, 1635, by Pierce Lemon, Charles City Co.
Pooey, John, 1643, by Edward Murfey and John Vaughan, —— Co.
Poole, Richard, G., 1635, by Capt. Adam Thoroughgood, —— Co.
Poole, Thomas, 1635, by George Minifie, James City Co.
Poole, Thomas, 1636, by Mr. Georg Minifye, James City Co.
Poole, David, Mary, his wife, Martin, his son, Jane, his daughter, 1653, by Samuell Parry, Lancaster Co.
Poole, Danll., 1653, by Tho. Salisbury, Northumberland Co.
Poole, Adrion, 1653, by Gregory Rawlins, Surry Co.
Poole, Robert, 1649, by Mr. Nesum and others, Northumberland Co.
Poole, Tho., 1655, by Wm. Wright, Gent., Nansemond Co.
Poole, Robt., 1642, by Thomas Loving, James City Co.
Poole, John, 1654, by Col. Argoll Yardley, Northampton Co.
Poole, John, 1654, by Tho. Harmanson, Northampton Co.
Poole, Martin, 1655, by Wm. Little, Northumberland Co.
Poole, Jane, 1655, by Wm. Little, Northumberland Co.
Poole, John, 1655, by Major Wm. Lewis, New Kent Co.
Poole, John, 1638, by Capt. Christopher Wormley, Charles River Co.
Poole, Mary, 1655, by John Hinman, Northampton Co.
Pooly, Jon., 1643, by Capt. Samuell Mathews, Esq., —— Co.
Pooly, Elian, 1643, by Capt. Wm. Peirce, Esq., —— Co.
Poope, Michael, 1653, by Peter Knight and Baber Cutt, —— Co.
Pope, John, 1650, by Capt. Moore Fautleroy, —— Co.
Pope, Fra., 1652, by Edward Revell, Northampton Co.
Pope, Fra., 1654, by Edward Revell, Northampton Co.

Popewell, John, 1637, by James Knott, New Norfolk Co.
Popeplewell, Jon., 1636, by James Knott, Elizabeth City Co.
Popler, Elizabeth, 1655, by Jer. Dodson, Gent., Lancaster Co.
Poranton, Edw., 1637, by Theodore Moyser, James City Co.
Porichard, Richd., 1653, by Capt. Francis Patt, Northampton Co.
Port, Perey, 1653, by John Dipdall, Charles City Co.
Porter, Nicholas, 1637, by Joseph Jolly, Charles River Co.
Porter, Nicholas, 1636, by Joseph Jolly, Charles River Co.
Porter, Wm., 1653, by Capt. Francis Morgan, Gloucester Co.
Porter, James, 1643, by Wm. Warder, ——— Co.
Porter, Wm., 1652, by Tho. Leechman, and John Bennett, Gloucester Co.
Porter, Wm., 1653, by Colo. Wm. Clayborne (Sec. of State), ——— Co.
Porter, Mathew, 1655, by Nich. Waddilow, Northampton Co.
Porter, Edmond, Sr., 1639, by Edmond Porter, Isle of Wight Co.
Porter, Edmond, Jr., 1639, by Edmond Porter, Isle of Wight Co.
Porter, Edmond, 1642, by Christopher Boyce, ——— Co.
Porter, Robt., 1647, by Richard Morgan, Lower Norfolk Co.
Porter, Jon., Sr., 1642, by Christopher Boyce, ——— Co.
Porter, Jon., Jr., 1642, by Christopher Boyce, ——— Co.
Porter, Manasa, 1642, by Christopher Boyce, ——— Co.
Porter, Nicholas, 1656, by Mr. Martin Baker, New Kent Co.
Porter, Elizabeth, 1656, by Mr. Martin Baker, New Kent Co.
Porter, Nicholas, 1656, by Mr. Martin Baker, New Kent Co.
Porter, Wm., 1654, by John Wyre, John Gillet, Andrew Gilson and John Phillipps, ——— Co.
Porter, Rich., 1654, by Richard Codsford, Westmoreland Co.
Porter, Wm., 1654, by Richard Codsford, Westmoreland Co.
Porter, Joan, 1654, by Tho. Deynes, ——— Co.
Porten, Mary, 1650, by Capt. Moore Fautleroy, ——— Co.
Portus, Alex., 1650, by Edward James, ——— Co.
Posey, Fr., 1637, by Wm. Farrar, Henrico Co.
Post, Jacob, 1651, by Capt. Tho. Davis, Northumberland Co.
Possell, Wm., 1635, by Christopher Branch, Henrico Co.
Possell, Wm., 1638, by Christopher Branch, Henrico Co.
Possin, Ruth, 1635, by Samuel Weaver, ——— Co.
Poteete, Ann, 1639, by John Poteete, Charles River Co.
Potteete, Georg, 1638, by Thomas Stegg, Charles City Co.
Potery, Ann, 1642, by Walter Chiles, Charles Co.
Pothres, Francis, 1642, by Robert Eyres, Lower New Norfolk Co.
Pott, Lucretia, 1653, by Charles Scarburg, Northampton Co.
Potter, Eliza., 1644, by Edwyn Conaway, Northampton Co.
Potter, John, 1638, by Hugh Allen, Charles River Co.
Potter, Elizabeth, 1648, by Francis Fludd, York Co.
Potter, John, 1651, by Thomas Keeling, Lower Norfolk Co.
Potter, Eliza., 1650., by George Taylor, ——— Co
Potter, Tho., 1654, by Tho. Deynes, ——— Co.
Pottman, Tho., 1640, by Thomas Stegg, Charles City Co.
Potts, Tho., 1653, by Abraham Moon, Lancaster Co.
Potts, Lucretea, 1652, by Mr. Tho. Teagle, Northampton Co.
Potts, Lucrecia, 1649, by Edmund Scarburgh, Jr., Northampton Co.

Potuxon, Thomas, 1637, by Hen. Woodhouse, New Norfolk Co.
Poudle, Henry, 1639, by Richard Corke, Gent., Henrico Co.
Poulter, Tho., 1650, by Capt. Moore Fautleroy, ——— Co.
Poultner, Tho., 1650, by Capt. Moore Fautleroy, ——— Co.
Poulton, John, 1650, by Geo. Goldsmith, ——— Co.
Poutlon, Wm., 1643, by Richard Kemp, Esq., James City Co.
Pountney, Wm., 1649, by Rich. Croshaw, Yorke Co.
Pouson, Jos., 1647, by John Brooch, York River Co.
Porry, Wm., 1638, by William Berryman, Accomack Co.
Powel, Robt., 1653, by Robt. Sorrel, ——— Co.
Powell, Richard, 1642, by Wm. Warren, ——— Co.
Powell, Ellen, 1642, by Tho. Curtis, ——— Co.
Powell, Robert, 1651, by Geo. Trabett, and Henry Edwards, North-
    ampton Co.
Powell, Richard, 1642, by John Waltham, Jr., Accomac Co.
Powell, Ann, 1642, by John Bayles, ——— Co.
Powell, Ra., 1645, by Justinian Cooper, Gent., Isle of Wight Co.
Powell, Richard, 1635, by Samuel Weaver, ——— Co.
Powell, Ann, 1635, by Wm. Prior, ——— Co.
Powell, Rich., 1635, by Samuel Weaver, ——— Co.
Powell, Thomas, 1636, by Christopher Calthropp, Charles River Co.
Powell, Jon., 1637, by Thomas Addison, New Norfolk Co.
Powell, Thomas, 1636, by Walter Hacker, James River Co.
Powell, John, 1636, by Walter Hacker, James River Co.
Powell, Ann, 1637, by William Prior, Charles River Co.
Powell, Margarett, 1636, by Richard Cocke, ——— Co.
Powell, Henry, 1637, by Christopher Stokes, Warwick River Co.
Powell, Robt., 1638, by Abraham Wood, Charles City Co.
Powell, Henry, 1637, by Christopher Stoakes, Charles River Co.
Powell, Phillipp, 1637, by David Mansell, James City Co.
Powell, Thomas, 1637, by William Spencer, ——— Co.
Powell, Jon., 1636, by Peter Johnson, Warrasquinoake Co.
Powell, Rich., 1637, by Thomas Nestor, Charles River Co.
Powell, Leigh, 1635, by Hugh Cox, Charles City Co.
Powell, Wm., 1652, by Anthony Doney and Enoch Hawker, Lancaster
    Co.
Powell, Winifred, 1653, by Tho. Hawkins, Northumberland Co.
Powell, Wm., 1653, by Tho. Hawkins, Northumberland Co.
Powell, Anne, 1653, by Abraham Moone, Northumberland Co.
Powell, Tho., 1653, by John Gillett, Lancaster Co.
Powell, Serah, 1651, by Thomas Manning, Warwick Co.
Powell, Plie, 1635, by David Mansell, James Co.
Powell, Thomas, 1635, by William Spencer, ——— Co.
Powell, Richard, 1635, by McWilliam Stone, ——— Co.
Powell, Ann, 1645, by John Rode, Warwick Co.
Powell, John, 1644, by Edwyn Conaway, Northampton Co.
Powell, John, 1653, by Edward Dobson, ——— Co.
Powell, Tho., 1653, by George Wadding, Lancaster Co.
Powell, Elizabeth, 1652, by Capt. John West, Esq., ——— Co.
Powell, Tho., 1652, by Peter Knight, Gloucester Co.
Powell, Wm., 1652, by Capt. Augustine Warner, ——— Co.

Powell, Sarah, 1652, by Tho. Steevens, Lancaster Co.
Powell, Anne, 1652, by Tobias Horton, Lancaster Co.
Powell, John, 1652, by John Howett, Northumberland Co.
Powell, Tho., 1653, by Wm. Sidner, Lancaster Co.
Powell, Isab., 1653, by Tho. Mallard, Northumberland Co.
Powell, Richard, 1653, by Colo. Wm. Clayborne (Sec. of State), ———
    Co.
Powell, Margaret, 1653, by Tho. Bourne, Lancaster Co.
Powell, Tho., 1650, by Stephen Hamlin, Charles City Co.
Powell, Wm., 1643, by Robert Pitt, Isle of Wight Co.
Powell, Richard, 1650, by Capt. Moore Fautleroy, ——— Co.
Powell, John, 1648, by Francis Fludd, York Co.
Powell, Gabriell, 1655, by Southy Littleberry, Northampton Co.
Powell, Howell, 1642, by Hugh Gwyn, Gent., ——— Co.
Powell, Walter, 1643, by Capt. Samuell Mathews, Esq., ——— Co.
Powell, Madelew, 1646, by John Ashcomb, Upper Norfolk Co.
Powell, Tho., 1656, by Margaret Miles, Westmoreland Co.
Powell, Richard, 1654, by Sinkler Pagett, Nansemond Co.
Powell, Harbert, 1654, by Clement Thurush, Lancaster Co.
Powell, Hen., 1654, by Christopher Boon, Westmoreland Co.
Powell, John, 1654, by Edward Simpson, Gloucester Co.
Powell, James, 1655, by John Motley, Northumberland Co.
Powell, Wm., 1654, by Wm. Mells, Lancaster Co.
Powell, David, 1640, by William Crannage, Isle of Wight Co.
Powell, Robert, 1639, by William Parry, Elizabeth City Co.
Powell, William, 1639, by Henry Bagwell, Accomack Co.
Powell, Robert, 1642, by Richard Gregson, Elizabeth City Co.
Powell, Wm., 1639, by Georg Minifye, Esq., Charles River Co.
Powell, Henry, 1641, by Samuell Firment, Upper New Norfolk Co.
Powell, Margarett, 1639, by Richard Corke, Gent., Henrico Co.
Powell, Hen., 1635, by Christopher Stoakes, Elizabeth Co.
Powell, Samuell, 1637, by Capt. John Howe, Accomac Co.
Powell, Edward, 1654, by John Thomas, Nansemond Co.
Powett, Mary, 1650, by Mr. James Williamson, ——— Co.
Powlerheele, Wm., 1643, by Casar Puggett, Lower Norfolk Co.
Powlter, Andrew, 1642, by Humphry Tabb, Elizabeth City Co.
Powndle, Henry, 1636, by Richard Cocke, ——— Co.
Powis, Robert, 1649, by Robert Mosely, Gent., ——— Co.
Poyner, Ambrose, 1639, by Edward Travis, James City Co.
Praise, Wm., 1644, by Stephen Taylor, ——— Co.
Praise, Biggony, 1654, by Tho. Harmonson, Northampton Co.
Pratt, Jon., 1637, by Wm. Farrar, Henrico Co.
Pratt, Andrew, 1637, by Elizabeth Parker, Henrico Co.
Pratt, John, 1651, by Wm. Taylor, Northumberland Co.
Pratt, Mary, 1653, by Wm. Dittye, Charles City Co.
Pratt, Tho., 1655, by Mr. Tho. Ballard, Gloucester Co.
Prawer, George, 1635, by William Spencer, ——— Co.
Prebedy, Georg, 1639, by Richard Nance, Henrico Co.
Preddery, Dan., 1651, by Thomas Thornbrough, Northumberland Co.
Preese, Tho., 1639, by John Pawley, James City Co.
Pren, John, 1640, by Thomas Causey, ——— Co.

Prene, ———, 1652, by Elias Edmonds, Lancaster Co.
Prentice, Val., 1654, by Major Miles Carey, Westmoreland Co.
Prenthall, Brd., 1654, by Capt. Nich. Marteaw, Westmoreland Co.
Prenton, James, 1654, by James Yates, ——— Co.
Presall, Alex., 1650, by John Garwood, Nansemond Co.
Prescon, Tho., 1656, by Wm. Crump and Mr. Humphry Vaulx, James City Co.
Prescot, John, 1653, by James Johnson, Nansemond Co.
Prese, Richard, 1642, by Thomas Ransha, Warwick Co.
Presly, Peter, ———, by Mr. Wm. Presly, Northumberland Co.
Presly, Jane, ———, by Mr. Wm. Presly (her husband), Northumberland Co.
Presly, Payle, ———, by Mr. Wm. Presly, Northumberland Co.
Press, Hugh, 1637, by John Moone, Isle of Wight Co.
Press, Nicholas, 1655, by Peter Starchey, ——— Co.
Prestee, Richard, 1638, by Thomas Croutch, James City Co.
Preston, Thomas, 1637, by William Wilkinson, New Norfolk Co.
Preston, John, 1650, by John Sevier, ——— Co.
Preston, Tho., 1650, by George Pate, Charles City Co.
Preston, John, 1652, by Tho. Mairy, ——— Co.
Preston, Wm., 1653, by John Edwards, Lancaster Co.
Powell, John, 1642, by Francis England, Isle of Wight Co.
Powell, Hugh, 1650, by Robert Bird, ——— Co.
Preston, Tho., 1653, by Symon Thorogood, Elizabeth City Co.
Preston, Edward, 1649, by Mr. Robert Parker, Northampton Co.
Preston, John, 1648, by Randall Crew, Nansemond Co.
Preston, Hen., 1642, by Samuell Abbott, ——— Co.
Preston, Joseph, 1654, by Edw. Welch, ——— Co.
Preston, Sam., 1642, by Capt. Samuell Mathews, Esq., ——— Co.
Prett, John, 1643, by Joseph Croshawe, ——— Co.
Prettyman, Mr. Tho., 1656, by Wm. Johnson, ——— Co.
Prewitt, Thomas, 1636, by Joane Bennett, Charles River Co.
Price, Laydran, 1635, by George Minifie, James City Co.
Price, Jon., 1637, by Wm. Farrar, Henrico Co.
Price, Margary, 1637, by John Orchard, James Citie Co.
Price, Thomas, 1636, by Capt. Thos. Willoughby ——— Co.
Price, Letition, 1636, by Mr. Georg Minifye, James City Co.
Price, John, 1637, by Percival Champion, New Norfolk Co.
Price, Robt., 1647, by Lawrence Peters, "Nansimum" Co.
Price, Henry, 1637, by Daniell Gookins, New Norfolk Co.
Price, Tho., 1653, by Coll. Fran. Epps, Esq., Charles City Co.
Price, Fran., 1653, by Coll. Fran. Epps, Esq., Charles City Co.
Price, Tho., 1653, by Tho. Hackett, ——— Co.
Price, Alice, 1653, by Charles Scarburg, Northampton Co.
Price, Barbara, 1650, by Stephen Charlton, Northampton Co.
Price, Tho., 1643, by Casar Puggett, Lower Norfolk Co.
Price, Jane, 1645, by Michael Masters, Henrico Co.
Price, Wm., 1653, by Capt. Francis Patt, Northampton Co.
Price, Tho., 1653, by Capt. Francis Patt, Northampton Co.
Price, John, 1653, by Abraham Moon, Lancaster Co.
Price, James, 1653, by Wm. Leech, Lancaster Co.

Price, William, 1652, by John Johnson, Northampton Co.
Price, Wm., 1652, by Mr. Tho. Purifye and Mrs. Temperence Reppitt, ——— Co.
Price, Alice, 1652, by Dr. George Hack, Northampton Co.
Price, Tho., 1652, by Rice Hughes, ——— Co.
Price, Walter, 1648, by Wm. Barret, ——— Co.
Price, Henry, 1648, by Wm. Edwards and Rice Edwards, James City Co.
Price, Elizabeth, 1651, by Mr. Wm. Armestead, ——— Co.
Price, George, and Mary, his wife, 1651, by Edward Greenwood, James City Co.
Price, Kath., 1653, by Wm. Johnson, Henrico Co.
Price, John, 1653, by Tho. Kibby, Northumberland Co.
Price, John, 1653, by Corbet Piddle, Northumberland Co.
Price, Ann, 1650, by Andrew Gilson, ——— Co.
Price, Lewis, 1650, by Hump. Lyster, ——— Co.
Price, John, 1650, by Capt. Moore Faulteroy, ——— Co.
Price, James, 1650, by John Mangor, ——— Co.
Price, John, 1649, by Capt. Ralph Wormeley, ——— Co.
Price, Jno., 1646, by Henry Sedenden, Northampton Co.
Price, Geo., 1647, by Richard Bland, ——— Co.
Price, Maurice, 1643, by William Ewins, James City Co.
Price, Henry, 1643, by Randall Holt, ——— Co.
Price, Tho., 1646, by Col. Henry Bishopp, James City Co.
Price, Hanna, 1654, by John Watson and John Bognall, Westmoreland Co.
Price, Ann, 1654, by Andrew Gibson, ——— Co.
Price, Joan, 1654, by Arthur Nash, New Kent Co.
Price, David, 1654, by Coll. Jno. Matrom, Westmoreland Co.
Price, Ann, 1655, by George Wall, Westmoreland Co.
Price, Mary, 1653, by Mr. Edmund Bowman, and Richard Starnell ——— Co.
Price, Humphry, 1639, by Edward Panderson, ——— Co.
Price, Hercules, 1639, by Lieut. Richard Popeley, ——— Co.
Price, Jone, 1639, by John Howell, Henrico Co.
Price, John, 1639, by John Pawley, James City Co.
Price, Hugh, 1638, by Thomas Burbage, Accomack Co.
Price, Wm., 1641, by Thomas Pitt, Charles City Co.
Price, John, 1642, by John Smith, James City Co.
Price, Wm., 1642, by Ellis Richerdson, Yorke Co.
Price, Ben., 1654, by Mr. Tho. Fowke, Westmoreland Co.
Price, Wm., 1654, by Coll. Hump. Higgenson, Esq., and Abraham Moone, Westmoreland Co.
Price, Tho., 1655, by Wm. Williams, Northumberland Co.
Price, Wm., 1656, by Wm. Justice, Charles City Co.
Price, Rich., 1637, by John Davis, James City Co.
Prichard, Tho., 1643, by Sir Francis Wyatt, Kt., ——— Co.
Prichard, Tho., 1642, by Christopher Boyce, ——— Co.
Prichard, Alice, 1647, by Elizabeth Barcroft, Isle of Wight Co.
Pritchard, ———, 1654, by John Watson and John Bognall, Westmoreland Co.

Prichard, Tho., 1655, by Mr. Tho. Ballard, Gloucester Co.
Prichard, Richard, 1639, by William Davis, James City Co.
Prichard, Rowland, 1638, by Thomas Clipwell, James City Co.
Pricklove, Geo., 1637, by Mathew Edloe, ——— Co.
Priddy, Robt., 1654, by Capt. John West, Esq., Gloucester Co.
Pridutt, Joane, 1650, by Geo. Goldsmith, ——— Co.
Prince, Edw., 1635, by Wm. Berriman, Accomack Co.
Prince, Edmund, 1643, by Wm. Berryman, Northampton Co.
Prince, Edward, 1646, by John Ashcomb, Upper Norfolk Co.
Prince, Thomas, 1639, by Georg Minifye, Esq., Charles River Co.
Prince, James, 1638, by Georg Mynifie (merchant), ——— Co.
Prior, ———, 1642, by William Prior, Gent. (her husband), ——— Co
Prior, Mrs. Margaret, 1637, by Wm. Prior, Gent. (her husband), ———
    Co.
Prise, Jon., 1635, by John Moone, Warrasquinoake Co.
Pritchard, Robt., 1637, by Thomas Barnard, James City Co.
Pritchard, Pallardary, 1653, by Mr. Wm. Debram, ——— Co.
Pritchett, Tho., 1653, by John Coale, James City Co.
Pritchett, Tho., 1650, by Richard Tye and Charles Sparrowe, Charles
    City Co.
Pritchett, Ralph, 1654, by James Yates, ——— Co.
Prite, Silvant, ———, by Lt. Coll. John Cheesman, ——— Co.
Primock, Rich., 1637, by Theodore Moyser, James City Co.
Proby, Geo., 1647, by Richard Bland, ——— Co.
Proby, Richard, 1655, by Mr. Tho. Ballard, Gloucester Co.
Procier, Morris, 1649, by Richard Kemp, Esq. (Sec. of State), ———
    Co.
Procter, Anth., 1638, by Randall Crew, Upper New Norfolk Co.
Procter, Ambrose, 1637, by Nathaniel Floyd, Isle of Wight Co.
Proctor, John, 1649, by Joseph Croshawe, Yorke Co.
Prosser, John, 1653, by Tho. Scoggin, Northumberland Co.
Prosser, Morris, 1638, by Capt. Christopher Wormley, Charles River
    Co.
Prosser, Ann, 1636, by John Neale, Accomack Co.
Prosser, Jane, 1635, by Capt. Adam Thoroughgood, ——— Co.
Prosser, Georg, 1637, by William Spencer, ——— Co.
Prounce, James, 1654, by Fra. Spright, Nansemond Co.
Prouse, Emblence, 1639, by John Wright, Upper New Norfolk Co.
Prout, Wm., 1653, by Tho. Hawkins, Northumberland Co.
Provo, Marke, 1654, by Francis Gray, ——— Co.
Provose, Marke, 1642, by Lieut. Francis Mason, ——— Co.
Prowse, John, S., 1639, by Richard Maior, Charles River Co.
Prowse, John, 1639, by Samuell Jackson, Isle of Wight Co.
Pryce, Wm., 1654, by Richard Walker, ——— Co.
Pryce, John, 1655, by Wm. Wright, Gent., Nansemond Co.
Pryde, Wm., ———, by Tho. Binns, Surry Co.
Pryer, John, 1655, by Southy Littleberry, Northampton Co.
Pryse, Jane, 1653, by Major Abra. Wood, Charles City Co.
Puckerell, Mary, 1655, by Mr. Anthony Langston, New Kent Co.
Puckerell, Tho., 1655, by Tho. Willoughby, Lower Norfolk Co.
Puckering, Richard, 1655, by Southy Littleberry, Northampton Co.

Puckrell, Mary, 1655, by Robt. Priddy, New Kent Co.
Pudivatt, Jane, 1642, by Wm. Pudivatt (her husband), Isle of Wight Co.
Pue, Wm., 1654, by John Drayton, Westmoreland Co.
Puflord, John, 1649, by Capt. Ralph Wormeley, ——— Co.
Pugly, Wm., 1648, by Wm. Ewen, James City Co.
Puiser, Geo., 1637, by Francis Osborne, ——— Co.
Pullapin, Jno., 1635, by Wm. Gary, Accomack Co.
Puller, John, 1652, by John Sharpe, Lancaster Co.
Pulmon, Richard, 1652, by John Pounsey, ——— Co.
Pullock, David, 1640, by Richard Williams, Charles City Co.
Pullum, Edward, 1636, by Wm. Clarke, Henrico Co.
Pullum, Edmund, 1638, by William Clark, Henrico Co.
Pulson, Daniel, 1652, by Tho. Holliwell, ——— Co.
Pumfrey, John, 1635, by William Heires, Warrasquinoake Co.
Pumocke, Tho., 1652, by Wm. Owen and Wm. Morgan, ——— Co.
Pumwell, John, 1653, by Colo. Wm. Clayborne (Sec. of State), ——— Co.
Pungly, Susan, 1653, by Peter Knight and Baker Cutt, ——— Co.
Pupill, Jane, 1649, by John Walthams, Northampton Co.
Purdie, Richard, 1646, by Sir William Berkley, ——— Co.
Purce, Tho., 1642, by Tho. Curtis, ——— Co.
Purchase, Henry, 1652, by Tho. Steevens, Lancaster Co.
Purchass, Henry, 1652, by Ralph Paine, ——— Co.
Purches, Robt., 1635, by Francis Fowler, James City Co.
Purcy, Katherine, 1635, by John Leonard, Warrasquinoake Co.
Purfitt, Kola, 1635, by Robert Hollom, Henrico Co.
Purkeys, Robert, 1637, by Francis Fowler, James River Co.
Purnell, Wm., 1638, by Capt. Tho. Harris, Henrico Co.
Purnell, Wm., 1635, by Thos. Harris, Henrico Co.
Purnell, John, 1652, by Mr. David Fox, Lancaster Co.
Purnell, Marg., 1652, by Dr. George Hack, Northampton Co.
Purnell, Math., 1652, by Richard Nelmes, Northumberland Co.
Purnell, 1654, by John Drayton, Westmoreland Co.
Purner, Tho., Jr., 1650, by John Smith, ——— Co.
Purner, Dorothy, wife of Tho. Purner, 1650, by John Smith, ——— Co.
Purner, Tho., Sr., 1650, by John Smith, ——— Co.
Purney, John, 1639, by John Pawley, James City Co.
Purr, Robt., 1636, by John Chew, Gent., Charles River Co.
Pursell, Tho., 1653, by Robt. Brasseur, Nansemond Co.
Purt, James, 1653, by John Bell, Lancaster Co.
Purton, Tymo., 1649, by Wm. Hoccaday, ——— Co.
Pusie, Elizabeth, 1656, by Mr. Jno. Paine, ——— Co.
Puters, John, 1635, by Richard Bennett, ——— Co.
Pye, Elizabeth, 1656, by Francis Hutchins, Nansemond Co.
Pye, John, 1654, by Obed. Williams, York Co.
Pye, John, 1649, by Wm. Hoccaday, ——— Co.
Pye, Eliza., 1651, by Edward Deggs, Esq., Yorke Co.
Pye, John, 1652, by Mrs. Elinor Brocas, Lancaster Co.
Pye, Joseph, 1652, by Mr. Tho. Curtis, ——— Co.
Pylar, Wm., 1650, by Mr. Stephen Hamelin, Charles City Co.

Pyman, Lawrance, 1638, by William Wigg, James City Co.
Pymm, Eliza., 1650, by George Goldsmith, ———Co.
Pynel, John, 1650, by Mr. Epaphroditus Lawson, ——— Co.

Q

Quainer, Tho., 1653, by Charles Grymes, Lancaster Co.
Qually, Joane, 1653, by Colo. Wm. Clayborne (Sec. of State), ———
    Co.
Qearle, Richard, 1640, by John George, Charles City Co.
Quarrell, Elen, 1638, by Epaphroditus Lawson, Upper New Norfolk
    Co.
Quash, Francis, 1642, by Thomas Osborne, Henrico Co.
Quayle, Jno., 1650, by John Landman, ——— Co.
Quayles, Richard, 1639, by Samuell Watkeyes, Charles River Co.
Quelche, William, 1639, by Thomas Sheppey, Henrico Co.
Quesenbury, John, 1651, by Richard Turner, Northumberland Co.
Quick, Richard, 1651, by Henry Hackery, ——— Co.
Quick, John, 1656, by George Abbott, Nansemond Co.
Quilt, Samuel, 1652, by Richard Starnell, ——— Co.
Quimbee, Ann, 1651, by Mr. Rowland Burnham, ——— Co.
Quinbrough, And., 1650, by John Hallawes, Gent., Northumberland
    Co.
Quinee, Tho., 1652, by Tho. Steevens, Lancaster Co.

R

Rabb, John, 1654, by Phillip Chesly and Dan. Wilde, York Co.
Rabbish, James, 1642, by Lieut. Francis Mason, ——— Co.
Raby, Robert, 1637, by Robert Bennett, New Norfolk Co.
Rabye, Robt., 1637, by Justinian Cooper, Isle of Wight Co.
Rabye, Robert, 1635, by Robert Bennett, ——— Co.
Racher, Manns, 1635, by Richard Tisdale, ——— Co.
Rack, Isaac, 1655, by Ralph Green, New Kent Co.
Raddish, David, 1642, by John Robins, ——— Co.
Radford, Tho., 1647, by Richard Morgan, Lower Norfolk Co.
Radford, John, 1652, by Tho. Todd, ——— Co.
Radford, William, 1636, by Wm. Hatcher, Henrico Co.
Radford, Rich., 1637, by Wm. Hatcher, ——— Co.
Radish, Jon., 1637, by Henry Perry, Charles River Co.
Radley, Richard, 1649, by Edmund Scarburgh, Jr., Northampton Co.
Radway, Wm., 1638, by Wm. Barker and Associates, Charles City Co.
Radway, Issin, 1638, by Wm. Baker and Associates, Charles City Co.
Radway, Jane, 1635, by William Barber (a mariner), Charles City Co.
Radway, Wm., 1635, by Wm. Barber (a mariner), Charles City Co.
Raed, Tho., 1656, by Sir Henry Chichley, ——— Co.
Rafe, Mary, 1653, by Richard Carey, ——— Co.
Raffle, Wm., 1652, by Tho. Holliwell, ——— Co.
Ragg, Ann, 1650, by Thomas Mulford, Nansemond Co.
Ragg, Benj., 1635, by Wm. Barber (a mariner), Charles City Co.
Raggerd, Rich., 1638, by Jonathan Longworth, Lower New Norfolk Co.

Raiman, Richard, 1653, by Colo. Wm. Clayborne (Sec. of State), ——— Co.
Rainalls, John, 1654, by Mrs. Mgt. Brent, Westmoreland Co.
Raine, Rowland, 1636, by John Wilkins, Accomack Co.
Rainhard, Nicholas, 1646, by Elizabeth and Ratchell Robins, Northampton Co.
Raison, Francis, 1639, by Edward Travis, James City Co.
Ralfe, Margarett, 1643, by Thomas Cassen, Lower Norfolk Co.
Ralluram, George, 1635, by Robert Bennett, ——— Co.
Ralph, Sam., 1653, by Tho. Salisbury, Northumberland Co.
Ram, Fra., 1654, by John Drayton, Westmoreland Co.
Rammell, Rice, 1654, by Col. Argoll Yardley, Northampton Co.
Rampsie, Wm., 1652, by Richard Starnell, ——— Co.
Ramsden, John, 1652, by Col. Geo. Ludlow, Esq., Gloucester Co.
Ramsden, John, 1642, by Wm. Durant, ——— Co.
Ramsen, Penelope, 1635, by Wm. Neesam, James City Co.
Ramsey, Eliza., 1642, by John Beale, ——— Co.
Ramsey, James, 1654, by Mrs. Mgt. Brent, Westmoreland Co.
Ramsey, Sam., 1635, by Osbourne Jenkin, Charles City Co.
Ramsey, Bar., 1653, by Henry Lee, Yorke Co.
Ramzee, Elinor, 1653, by Peter Knight and Baker Cult, ——— Co.
Randall, John, 1655, by Mrs. Magraret Brent, Lancaster Co.
Randall, James, 1650, by Sr. Tho. Luntsford, Kt., and Baronnett, ——— Co.
Randall, John, 1639, by Edward Prince, Charles City Co.
Randall, Blanch, 1654, by John Wyre, John Gillet, Andrew Gilson and John Phillipps, ——— Co.
Randall, Mary, 1654, by Rich. Bunduch, Northampton Co.
Randall, Thomas, 1636, by Anthony Jones, Warwick Co.
Randoll, Tho., 1655, by Major Wm. Lewis, New Kent Co.
Ranes, Robert, 1655, by Capt. Tho. Davis, Warwick Co.
Range, John, 1653, by Tho. Hancks, Gloucester Co.
Rankin, Lawlin, 1650, by Capt. Moore Fautleroy, ——— Co.
Ransby, Samuel, 1637, by Francis Osborne, ——— Co.
Ranshaw, Katharine, 1635, by William Ranshaw, Elizabeth City Co.
Ranson, Robert, 1635, by Richard Bennett, ——— Co.
Rapwell, John, 1651, by Capt. Tho. Davis, Northumberland Co.
Raror, Eliz., 1654, by John Williams, Northampton Co.
Rach, Richard, 1650, by Henry Peaseley, ——— Co.
Rash, Walter, 1648, by Mr. Bartholomew Haskins, Lower Norfolk Co.
Rash, Tho., 1653, by Tho. Hawkins, Northumberland Co.
Rashe, John, 1635, by William Heires, Warrasquinoake Co.
Rassell, Mary, 1650, by John Cox, ——— Co.
Rassell, Elizabeth, 1652, by Ambrose Dixon and Stephen Horsely, Jr., Northampton Co.
Rastill, Tho., 1649, by Arthur Allen, James City Co.
Rasto, John, 1636, by Joane Bennett, Charles River Co.
Ratchliff, Charles, 1650, by Stephen Charlton, Northampton Co.
Ratford, Eleanor, 1653, by Charles Grymes, Lancaster Co.
Rathbourne, Wm., 1654, by Wm. Beach, Westmoreland Co.
Rathropp, Jon., 1643, by Capt. Samuell Mathews, Esq., ——— Co.

Ratiffe, Edward, 1639, by Richard Preston, Upper New Norfolk Co.
Ratsham, John, 1637, by Capt. Henry Browne, James River Co.
Rattams, Tho., 1647, by John Brooch, York River Co.
Ravely, Jason, 1648, by Wm. Edwards and Rice Edwards, James City Co.
Raven, Peter, 1648, by George White, Lower Norfolk Co.
Raven, John, 1651, by Lieut. Coll. Giles, Brent Northumberland Co.
Raven, John, 1651, by John Rookwood, Gent., Northumberland Co.
Raven, Peter, 1653, by Margarett Upton, Lancaster Co.
Raven, John, 1654, by Lieut. Coll. Giles Brent, Westmoreland Co.
Raw, Margarett, 1638, by Capt. Christopher Wormley, Charles River Co.
Rawboard, Mannering, 1642, by John Ewens, Jr., Charles City Co.
Rawden, Robert, 1636, by Edward Tonstall, ——— Co.
Rawdon, Mathew, 1650, by Samuell, Smith Northumberland Co.
Rawell, Eliz., 1635, by Thos. Butler Clark and Pastor of Denbie, Warrasquinoake Co.
Rawford, Thomas, 1635, by William Ranshaw, Elizabeth City Co.
Rawles, Mary, 1653, by James Bonner, Lancaster Co.
Rowles, Fra., 1655, by Southy Littleberry, Northampton Co.
Rawley, Tho., 1650, by Mr. Epaphroditus Lawson, ——— Co.
Rawlins, Charles, 1653, by Tho. Hampton, ——— Co.
Rawlins, John, 1652, by Wm. UpThomas, ——— Co.
Rawlins, Charles, 1653, by Dennis Conniers, Lancaster Co.
Rawlins, Rogr., 1654, by John Sharpe, Lancaster Co.
Rawlins, Rich., 1654, by Nath. Pope, Westmoreland Co.
Rawlins, Walter, 1654, by Capt. Giles Brent, Westmoreland Co.
Rawlins, Jeremy, 1655, by Dr. Giles Mode, New Kent Co.
Rawlins, Walter, 1654, by Abraham Moon, Gloucester Co.
Rawlins, William, 1635, by Samuel Weaver, ——— Co.
Rawlins, Richard, 1650, by George Pate, Charles City Co.
Rawlinson, Robt., 1650, by Mr. Robt. Holt, James City Co.
Rawlinson, John, 1652, by Tho. Todd, ——— Co.
Rawlings, Christopher, 1639, by Edward Prince, Charles City Co.
Rawlings, John, 1642, by Richard Gregson, Elizabeth City Co.
Rawlings, Richard, 1654, by Abraham Moon, Gloucester Co.
Rawlings, William, 1637, by Thomas Weston, Charles River Co.
Rawlings, Wm., 1637, by John Hucks, James Citie Co.
Rawlington, Edw., 1639, by Richard Nance, Henrico Co.
Rawlson, Jas., 1654, by Richard Walker, ——— Co.
Ray, John, 1650, by Mr. Stephen Hamelin, Charles City Co.
Ray, Elizabeth, 1653, by Maj. John Westhrope, Charles City Co.
Ray, Abe, 1652, by Capt. Augustine Warner, ——— Co.
Ray, John, 1652, by Richard Coleman, ——— Co.
Ray, ———, wife of Thos. Ray, 1642, by Thomas Ray, ——— Co.
Ray, Darby, 1642, by Thomas Ray, ——— Co.
Ray, ———, 1641, by Richard Jackson, Isle of Wight Co.
Ray, John, 1642, by William Eyres, Upper New Norfolk Co.
Ray, John, 1656, by Sir. Henry Chichley, ——— Co.
Ray, Benj., 1638, by Wm. Baker and Associates, Charles City Co.
Raye, Henry, 1643, by Richard Richards, Charles River Co.

Raymon, Nicholas, 1638, by Capt. Christopher Wormley, Charles River Co.
Raymond, Arthur, 1639, by William Burdett, Accomack Co.
Raynard, Robt., 1643, by Sir Francis Wyatt, Kt., ——— Co.
Rayne, Andrew, 1656, by John Rosier Clarke, Westmoreland Co.
Raynes, Robt., 1652, by Anthony Doney and Enoch Hawker, Lancaster Co.
Rayne, Rowland, 1637, by John Wilkins, New Norfolk Co.
Rayson, Mathew, 1637, by James Harrison, James City Co.
Read, Elliam, 1643, by John Wall, ——— Co.
Read, Rich., 1650, by Wm. Yarrett and Fra. Wittington, ——— Co.
Read, John, 1649, by Tho. Dale, ——— Co.
Read, John, 1649, by Francis Brown, Northumberland Co.
Read, Mr. George, 1648, by Georg Read, Gent., ——— Co.
Read, Wm., 1652, by Wm. Owen and Wm. Morgan, ——— Co.
Read, Stephen, 1651, by Mr. Antho. Steevens, Northampton Co.
Read, Archibald, 1653, by Tho. Keene, Northumberland Co.
Read, Walter, 1652, by Mrs. Elnor Brocas, Lancaster Co.
Read Walter, 1652, by Edward Cole, Northumberland Co.
Read, John, 1651, by Thomas Keeling, Lower Norfolk Co.
Read, Geo., 1641, by Samuell Firmer, Upper New Norfolk Co.
Read, Thos., 1639, by Randall Holt, James City Co.
Read, John, 1654, by John Drayton, Westmoreland Co.
Read, Walter, 1654, by Andrew Gibson, ——— Co.
Read, Peter, 1654, by Walter Brookes, Charles City Co.
Read, Owen, 1655, by George Frizell and Tho. Moore, Northampton Co.
Read, John, 1648, by John Landman, Nansimond Co.
Read, Thomas, 1635, by Thomas Harwood, ——— Co.
Read, Robert, 1637, by Zachariah Cripps, Warwick River Co.
Read, John, 1636, by Wm. Ravenett, Warwick River Co.
Read, Thomas, 1636, by Randall Holt, James City Co.
Read, Wm., 1637, by Thomas Hampton, New Norfolk Co.
Read, John, 1636, by Robert Hollam, Henrico Co.
Reade, Fra., 1652, by Capt. Francis Morgane and Ralph Green, Gloucester Co.
Reades, Eliza., 1642, by Justinian Cooper, Isle of Wight Co.
Reading, John, 1653, by Colo. Wm. Clayborne (Sec. of State), ——— Co.
Readwood, John, 1643, by Edward Murfey and John Vaughan, ——— Co.
Reale, Tyanell, 1650, by Mrs. Frances Townshend (widow), Northumberland Co.
Reames, Thomas, 1638, by Mathew Ireland, Charles River Co.
Reasley, Michael, 1650, by Henry Peaslye, ——— Co.
Reason, John, 1649, by Robert Mosely, Gent., ——— Co.
Reason, Henry, 1635, by William Dawson, ——— Co.
Reaves, John, 1650, by Lawrence Peters, Nansemond Co.
Rebell, Wm., 1638, by Robert Freeman, James City Co.
Reboone, Anth., 1638, by John Robins, James City Co.
Rece, Nicho., 1654, by Edward Revell, Northampton Co.

Rechordson, Ja., 1649, by Mr. Nesum and others, Northumberland Co.
Recnolds, Geo., 1652, by Anthony Doney and Enoch Hawkes, Lancaster Co.
Red, David, 1637, by William Spencer, ——— Co.
Redd, John, 1654, by Toby Smith, Lancaster Co.
Redchester, John, 1653, by Jervais Dodson, Northumberland Co.
Redder, Sarah, 1654, by John Watson and John Bognall, Westmoreland Co.
Redding, Richard, 1656, by Wm. Johnson, ——— Co.
Reddinge, Robt., 1643, by Randall Holt, ——— Co.
Reddock, John, 1650, by Francis Hobbs, ——— Co.
Reddock, Alex., 1653, by Tho. Hampton, ——— Co.
Rede, Robt., 1645, by Zachary Cripps, Warwick Co.
Redicke, John, 1643, by Thomas Taylor, Warwick Co.
Redman, Mary, 1652, by Christopher Lewis, Isle of Wight Co.
Redman, Richard, 1639, by Samuell Watkeyes, Charles River Co.
Redman, Jno., 1655, by Robt. Priddy, New Kent Co.
Redman, Wm., 1642, by Justinian Cooper, Isle of Wight Co.
Redman, Wm., 1637, by Justinian Cooper, Isle of Wight Co.
Redman, Wm., 1636, by Justinian Cooper, Warrasquinoake, Co.
Redman, Richard, 1649, by Joseph Croshawe, Yorke Co.
Redock, Rich., 1637, by Nathaniel Floyd, Isle of Wight Co.
Redwood, James, 1648, by Francis Fludd, York Co.
Reed, Geo., 1643, by Capt. Samuell Mathews, Esq., ——— Co.
Reed, Julian, 1639, by Georg Minifye, Esq., Charles River Co.
Reekes, Richard, 1653, by John Gillett, Lancaster Co.
Reeme, Jno., 1637, by John Dennett, Charles River Co.
Rees, Elizabeth, 1648, by Richard Lee, Gent., ——— Co.
Reese, Thomas, 1648, by John King and Lawrence Ward, Isle of Wight Co.
Reeses, Edward, 1650, by Richard Smith, Northampton Co.
Reense, Mary, 1653, by Mr. Wm. Hoccaday, Yorke Co.
Reeve, Thos., 1637, by Lt. John Upton, Usle of Wight Co.
Reeve, Fr., 1635, by William Stafford, ——— Co.
Reeve, Deenis, 1635, by Capt. Thos. Willowbye, ——— Co.
Reeves, Jon, 1642, by Thomas Loving, James City Co.
Reeves, Charles, 1652, by Capt. Augustine Warner, ——— Co.
Reeves, Edw., 1651, by Richard Smith, Northampton Co.
Reeves, John, 1652, by Robert West, Charles City Co.
Reeves, Wm., 1652, by Littleton, Scarburg, ——— Co.
Reeves, Lawrence, 1638, by Capt. Christopher Wormley, Charles River Co.
Reeves, John, 1642, by Capt. Samuell Mathews, Esq., ——— Co.
Reeves, Jove, 1643, by Edward Murfy and John Vaughan, ——— Co.
Reeves, John, 1642, by John Ewens, Jr., Charles City Co.
Reeves, John, 1636, by Robert West, Elizabeth City Co.
Reeves, Robt., 1635, by Thos. Shippen, ——— Co.
Reid, David, 1651, by Richard Vaughan, Northampton Co.
Reigner, Barton, 1651, by Thomas Thornbrough, Northumberland Co.
Rekey, Mary, 1651, by Mr. Wm. Armestead, ——— Co.

Relas, Thomas, 1635, by Jno. Upton, Warrasquinoake Co.
Reley, Tho., 1654, by Col. Hump. Higgenson, Esq., and Abraham Moone, Westmoreland Co.
Relue, David, 1655, by Matilda Scarbourgh, Northampton Co.
Reman, Nich., 1654, by Francis Gray, ——— Co.
Remerts, John, 1653, by Wm. Leech, Lancaster Co.
Remington, 1643, by Richard Kemp, Esq., James City Co.
Remington, Silvester, 1654, by John Drayton, Westmoreland Co.
Remmons, Wm., 1654, by Wm. Beach, Westmoreland Co.
Rends, Wm., 1655, by John Biggs, Lower Norfolk Co.
Renall, Randall, 1639, by William Burdett, Accomack Co.
Renell, Austin, 1637, by Capt. John Howe, Accomac Co.
Renells, Fra., 1655, by Wm. Hall, New Kent Co.
Renolls, Eliz., 1654, by John Watson and John Bognall, Westmoreland Co.
Renolls, Robt., 1654, by Major Wm. Andrews, Northampton Co.
Renolls, Y. ———, 1654, by Major Wm. Andrews, Northampton Co.
Renolls, Ann, 1655, by Capt. George Floyd, New Kent Co.
Renols, Mary, 1653, by Tho. Griffin, Lancaster Co.
Rena, Harry, 1654, by Tho. Hobkins, Lancaster Co.
Rennells, Wm., 1654, by John Hallawes, Westmoreland Co.
Rennoles, Ann., 1650, by Capt. Richard Bond, Charles City Co.
Rennoles, Ann, 1651, by Wm. Rennoles, Northumberland Co.
Renney, John, 1652, by Mr. Tho. Teagle, Northampton Co.
Renny, John, 1653, by Charles Scarburg, Northampton Co.
Report, John, 1653, by Wm. Leech, Lancaster Co.
Reppon, Ellis, 1640, by Randall Crew, Upper Norfolk Co.
Repserry, John, 1646, by John Hill, Norfolk Co.
Resbury, Jno., 1653, by Frances Emperor, Hugh Gale and Edward Morgan, Lower Norfolk Co.
Reslye, Chil., 1654, by Robert Holt, James City Co.
Resir, Richard, 1651, by Robert Abrall, Yorke Co.
Rest, Walter, 1639, by Stephen Webb, James City Co.
Reston, Jon., 1637, by Henry Perry, Charles River Co.
Rethstreete, Rich., 1653, by Ralph Green, Gloucester Co.
Reve, Robert, 1653, by Mr. James Tooke, Isle of Wight Co.
Revell, John, 1652, by Robert Elam, Henrico Co.
Revelle, Eliz., 1637, by Hugh Wynn, Isle of Wight Co.
Revelle, Tho., 1653, by George Collins, ——— Co.
Reves, Thomas, 1648, by Lewis Burwell, Gent., ——— Co.
Rewed, Jarvis, 1637, by John Brodwell, James City Co.
Rey, Everard, 1653, by Corbet Piddle, Northumberland Co.
Rey, George, 1649, by Robert Mosely, Gent., ——— Co.
Rey, Eliz., 1650, by Capt. Moore Fautleroy, ——— Co.
Reycock, Bryan, 1637, by Francis Poythers, Charles City Co.
Reylue, Tho., 1655, by Matilda Scarbourgh, Northampton Co.
Reymon, Tho., 1651, by Abraham Moone and (Thomas Griffen), Lancaster Co.
Reyneond, Tho., 1642, by John Pratt, Henrico Co.
Reyner, Jone, wife of Wassett Reyner, 1648, by Georg Read, Gent., ——— Co.

Reyner, Wassett, 1648, by Georg Read, Gent., ——— Co.
Reynold Alex., 1648, by Lewis Burwell and Tho. Haws, York River Co.
Reynold, Peter, 1654, by Richard Jones, James City Co.
Reynolds, Wm., 1648, by John Seward, Isle of Wight Co.
Reynolds, John, 1653, by John Dipdall, Charles City Co.
Reynolds, Rich., 1652, by Henry Palin and John Singleton, ——— Co.
Reynolds, Geo., 1653, by Robert Tomlin, ——— Co.
Reynolds, Tho., 1637, by Henry Perry, Charles River Co.
Reynolds, Mary, 1637, by John Judson, Charles River Co.
Reynolds, Gilbert, 1642, by Thomas Symmons, ——— Co.
Reynolds, Wm., 1638, by Christopher Lawson, James City Co.
Reynolds, Richard, 1638, by John George, Charles City Co.
Reynolds, Nich., 1642, by Hugh Gwyn, Gent., ——— Co.
Reynolds, Wm., and others, 1642, by Augustine Warner, ——— Co.
Reynolls, Mary, 1654, by John Newman, Lancaster Co.
Reynolds, Edw., 1638, by John Poteet, Charles River Co.
Reynolds, Eliz., 1638, by John Poteet, Charles River Co.
Reynolds, Gilbert, 1638, by Joseph Moore, Elizabeth City Co.
Reynolds, Richard, 1637, by James Knott, New Norfolk Co.
Reynolds, Thos., 1637, by Henry Perry, Charles River Co.
Reynolds, Edward, 1635, by Capt. Adam Thoroughgood, ——— Co.
Reynolds, William, 1637, by Rich. Bellane and Christopher Lawson,
    James City Co.
Reynolls, Wm., 1652, by John Meredith, Lancaster Co.
Reynolls, Richard, 1652, by Mr. Henry Soane, ——— Co.
Reynolls, Wm., 1653, by Tho. Hawkins, Northumberland Co.
Rhoades, Robt., 1638, by Stephen Charlton, Accomack Co.
Rhodes, Africa, 1650, by John Garwood, Nansemond Co.
Rible, Richard, 1639, by Justinian Cooper, Isle of Wight Co.
Ribone, Antho., 1642, by Lieut. Francis Mason, ——— Co.
Rice, Eulherd, 1636, by John Dansey, James City Co.
Rice, Peter, 1635, by Robert Bennett, ——— Co.
Rice, Wm., 1638, by John Gater, Lower New Norfolk Co.
Rice, Hoary, 1656, by Sir Henry Chichley, ——— Co.
Rice, John, 1639, by Rich. Hoe., James City Co.
Rice, David, 1642, by John Benton, ——— Co.
Rice, James, 1653, by Wm. Leech, Lancaster, Co.
Rice, Kath., 1653, by Robert Tomlin, ——— Co.
Rice, Jane, 1651, by Audery Bennett, Nansemond Co.
Rice, Peter, 1651, by Audery Bennett, Nansemond Co.
Rice, Peter, 1637, by Robert Bennett, New Norfolk Co.
Rice, Henry, 1652, by Capt. Henry Fleet, Lancaster Co.
Rice, Jno., 1653, by Robt. Parfitt and Wm. Hatcher, Lancaster Co.
Rice, Ri., 1650, by Capt. Moore Faultleroy, ——— Co.
Rice, David, 1650, by Francis Hobbs, ——— Co.
Rice, Henry, 1650, by Mr. Stephen Hamelin, Charles City Co.
Rich, Jones, 1638, by John Moone, ——— Co.
Ritch, David, 1656, by Mr. Martin Baker, New Kent Co.
Rich, Abraham, 1653, by James Turner, ——— Co.
Rich., Eliz., 1654, by John Phillips and John Batts, Lancaster Co.
Rich, Miles, 1654, by Robert Tomlin, ——— Co.

Rich, Elizabeth, 1653, by Capt. Robt. Abrall, ——— Co.
Richard, Tho., 1648, by John Landman, Nansimond Co.
Richard, Tho. Up., 1650, by Mr. Stephen Hamelin, Charles City Co.
Richard, William, 1648, by Georg Read, Gent., ——— Co.
Richard, Lawrence, 1653, by Wm. Langly, Lower Norfolk Co.
Richard, Mande, 1642, by Stephen Gill, Yorke River Co.
Richardes, Ann, 1650, by Edward James, ——— Co.
Richard, Tho., 1654, by Toby Smith, Lancaster Co.
Richards, Eliza., 1647, by Leonard Pettock, Accomac Co.
Richards, John, 1648, by John Seward, Isle of Wight Co.
Richards, Jos., 1648, by John Seward, Isle of Wight Co.
Richards, Ann, 1646, by John Broach, York Co.
Richards, Eliza., 1643, by Richard Richards, Charles River Co.
Richards, Mr. Richard, 1643, by Richard Richards, Charles River Co.
Richards, James, 1650, by Mr. Epaphroditus Lawson, ——— Co.
Richards, Robt. 1650, by Hump. Lyster, ——— Co.
Richards, Wm., 1650, by Capt. Moore Fautleroy, ——— Co.
Ritchards, Walter, 1650, by Capt. Moore Fautleroy, ——— Co.
Richards, Tho., 1649, by Tho. Dale, ——— Co.
Richards, Wm., 1649, by Mr. Wm. Hoccaday, ——— Co.
Richards, Richard, 1651, by Richard Bayly, ——— Co.
Richards, Jno., 1653, by Geo. Thompson, Gloucester Co.
Richards, Jno., 1653, by John Coale, James City Co.
Richards, John, 1652, by Col. Geo. Ludlow, Esq., Gloucester Co.
Richards, Tho., 1650, by Capt. Richard Bond, Charles City Co.
Richards, Eliza., 1651, by Mr. Robert Abrall, Yorke Co.
Richards, James, 1652, by John Taylor, Lancaster Co.
Richards, Elizab., 1652, by Mrs. Jane Harmer, Northumberland Co.
Richards, James, 1652, by Henry Woodhouse, Lower Norfolk Co.
Richards, Griff., 1653, by George Collins, ——— Co.
Richards, Jon., 1651, by John Thomas, Gloucester Co.
Richards, Wm., 1642, by Thomas Symmons, ——— Co.
Richards, John, 1639, by Georg Minifye, Esq., Charles River Co.
Richards, John, 1638, by Thomas Clipwell, James City Co.
Richards, Jane, 1656, by Mr. Tho. Purifoy, ——— Co.
Richards, Wm., 1654, by Col. Argoll Yardley, Northampton Co.
Richards, Jon., 1642, by Wm. Durant, ——— Co.
Richards, Wm., 1656, by Wm. Pulliam, New Kent Co.
Richards, Wm., 1637, by Daniell Gookins, New Norfolk Co.
Richards, Florence, 1637, by John Upton, Isle of Wight Co.
Richards, Wm., 1642, by Wm. Warren, ——— Co.
Richards, Arch., 1636, by Wm. Bibby, Accomack Co.
Richards, Joseph, 1635, by Mr. Robert Cane, ——— Co.
Richards, Wm., 1635, by Anthony Jones, ——— Co.
Richards, Florence, 1635, by Jno. Upton, Warrasquinoake Co.
Richards, Wm., 1636, by Joseph Moore, Elizabeth Citie Co.
Richards, John, merchant, 1652, by John Spiltimber and John Brady,
    ——— Co.
Richards, Jon., 1643, by Mr. Phillipp Bennett, Upper Norfolk Co.
Richards, Tho., 1643, by Tho. Cassen, Lower Norfolk Co.
Richards, William, 1638, by Joseph Moore, Elizabeth City Co.

Richards, John, 1645, by Zachary Cripps, Warwick Co.
Richards, David, 1654, by Walter Dickenson, Lancaster Co.
Richardson, Symon, 1636, by Wm. Clarke, Henrico Co.
Richardson, Wm., 1637, by Wm. Farrar, Henrico Co.
Richardson, Luke, 1636, by John Chandler, Elizabeth Citie Co.
Richardson, Learward, 1637, by Henry Catalyn, New Norfolk Co.
Richardson, Leonard, 1638, by Henry Catelyn, Upper Norfolk Co.
Richardson, Tho., 1643, by Wm. Warder, ——— Co.
Richardson, Robt., 1655, by Mr. Tho. Peck, Gloucester Co.
Richardson, Isaac, 1650, by Wingfield Webb and Richard Paile, ———
    Co.
Richardson, Tho., 1642, by Daniell Lewellyn, ——— Co.
Richardson, Tho., 1642, by Thomas Bagwell, Isle of Wight Co.
Richardson, Isabell, 1642, by Hugh Gwyn, Gent., ——— Co.
Richardson, Dorothy, 1655, by Richard Price, New Kent Co.
Richardson, Nich., 1655, by Jer. Dodson, Gent., Lancaster Co.
Richardson, Peter, 1638, by Capt. Christopher Wormley, ——— Co.
Richardson, Tho., 1638, by Christopher Branch, Henrico Co.
Richardson, Robt., 1639, by Thomas Faulkner, ——— Co.
Richeson, Barnaby, 1639, by Samuell Almond, Henrico Co.
Richeson, Eliz., 1654, by Walter Brookes, Charles City Co.
Richardson, Peter, 1651, by Capt. Stephen Gill, Northumberland Co.
Richardson, Barbary, 1653, by Major Abra. Wood, Charles City Co.
Richinson, John, 1648, by Mr. Phillip Bennet, Nansemond Co.
Richardson, Mary, 1645, by Mr. Bartholomew Hoskins, ——— Co.
Richardson, Evan., 1648, by Tho. Ludwell, Gent., James City Co.
Richardson, John, 1650, by Mr. James Williams, ——— Co.
Richardson, Mary, 1649, by Rowland Burneham, Gent., ——— Co.
Richardson, Bridgett, 1649, by Mr. Ralph Barlowe, Northampton Co.
Richardson, Tho., 1650, by Capt. Moore Fautlcroy, ——— Co.
Richett, Christo., 1639, by John Burland, Charles River Co.
Richey, Susan, 1635, by John Dennett, James Co.
Rickett, Francis, 1643, by John Freeme, Charles Co.
Rickett, Fra., 1654, by Coll. Jno. Matrom, Westmoreland Co.
Ricketts, Edw., 1642, by Wm. Barnard, Esq., Isle of Wight Co.
Ricketts, Wm., 1650, by Capt. Richard Bond, Charles City Co.
Ricroft, Silvanus, 1648, by Richard Wyatt, ——— Co.
Ricroft, Richard, 1640, by Thomas Stegg, Charles City Co.
Richford, Mary, 1653, by Benjamin Brasseur, ——— Co.
Richford, John, 1638, by Richard Wilcox, James City Co.
Riddle, James, 1651, by George Eaton, ——— Co.
Riddly, Will, 1653, by Henry Lowne, Henrico Co.
Riddly, James, 1636, by Robt. Hollom, Henrico Co.
Riddling, Tho., 1650, by George Pate, Charles City Co.
Rider, Wm., 1639, by Samuell Almond, Henrico Co.
Rider, Wm., 1647, by Thomas Johnson, Gent., Northampton Co.
Rider, Willis, servant of Thos. Crosby, 1637, by Arthur Bayly and Tho.
    Crosby, Henrico Co.
Rider, Sarah, 1636, by Wm. Neesam, James City Co.
Ridges, Richard, 1648, by Richard Thompson, Northumberland Co.
Ridges, Richard, 1639, by William Parry, Elizabeth City Co.

Ridges, Richard, 1653, by Mrs. Mary Brent, ——— Co.
Ridgett, Tho., 1642, by Stephen Gill, Yorke River Co.
Ridle, John, 1652, by Mrs. Elnor Brocas, Lancaster Co.
Ridley, Tho., 1647, by Richard Bland, ——— Co.
Riddly, Tho., 1651, by John Addleston, ——— Co.
Ridley, Wm., 1639, by Samuell Almond, Henrico Co.
Ridley, Ann, 1638, by Capt. Thomas Harris, Henrico Co.
Ridly, John, 1654, by Tho. Hobkins, Lancaster Co.
Ridly, Wm., 1637, by Arthur Bayly and Tho. Crosby, Henrico Co.
Ridly, Ann, 1635, by Thos. Harris, Henrico Co.
Ridmore, Sarah, 1653, by Coll. Wm. Taylor, Esq., Gloucester Co.
Ridford, John, ———, by Mr. Wm. Presly, Northumberland Co.
Rigby, Robert, 1642, by Georg Busse, ——— Co.
Rigby, Roger, 1638, by John Robins, ——— Co.
Rigby, Robert, 1638, by Wm. Rookins, James City Co.
Rigby, Dorothy, 1639, by Peter Rigby (her husband), Charles River
    Co.
Riggons, John, 1656, by George Kibble, Lancaster Co.
Rigie, Abraham, 1653, by John Maddison, Gloucester Co.
Riggs, Rich., 1637, by Arthur Smith, Isle of Wight Co.
Rightsome, Ann, 1638, by John Fludd, James City Co.
Right, Wm., 1652, by Peter Knight, Gloucester Co.
Right, John, 1654, by Humphry Haggett, Lancaster Co.
Right, Giles, 1642, by John Pratt, Henrico Co.
Right, John, 1638, by John Fludd, James City Co.
Right, Jason, 1637, by Lt. Richard Popeley, New Norfolk Co.
Right, Jathen, 1636, by Henry Southell, ——— Co.
Rigsby, James, 1637, by Wm. Farrar, Henrico Co.
Ridue, John, 1655, by Lt. Col. Anthony Ellyott, ——— Co.
Ridyer, Rich., 1637, by William Parry, New Norfolk Co.
Rilby, Wm., 1652, by Mr. Henry Soane, ——— Co.
Riley, Richd., 1649, by Wm. Nesum, Tho. Sax, Miles Bathasby and
    John Pyne, Northampton Co.
Rilly, Richard, 1651, by John Adleston, ——— Co.
Rily, Dorothy, 1652, by John Johnson, Northampton Co.
Ring, John, 1649, by Edmund Scarburgh, Jr., Northampton Co.
Ringall, Tho., 1642, by Capt. Daniell Gookin, ——— Co.
Rineley, Jason, 1636, by Wm. Neesam, James City Co.
Ripley, John, 1636, by Edward Drew, Accomack Co.
Riplye, Tho., 1653, by Coll. Fran. Epps, Esq., Charles City Co.
Rippin, Alice, 1650, by Mr. Epaphroditus Lawson, ——— Co.
Rippin, Christ., 1637, by Cheney Boyes, Charles City Co.
Rippin, Christ., 1636, by Cheney Boyse, Charles City Co.
Rippon, Ann, 1640, by Randall Crew, Upper Norfolk, Co.
Rishixt, Wm., and wife, 1654, by Christopher Regault, Gloucester Co.
Risby, Robert, 1636, by William Rookins, James City Co.
Risden, Phillip, 1653, by Anto. Hoskins, Northampton Co.
Risdon, Landma, 1655, by Arthur Upshott, Northampton Co.
Risdon, James, 1655, by Arthur Upshott, Northampton Co.
Risdon, Mary, 1655, by Arthur Upshott, Northampton Co.
Riss, William, 1635, by McWilliam Stone, ——— Co.

Risson, Blandma, 1655, by Hugh Yeo, Northampton Co.
Rith, Row., 1652, by John Johnson, Northampton Co.
Rivers, Joan, 1653, by Mr. Wm. Hoccaday, Yorke Co.
Roads, Roger, 1655, by Wm. Steevens, Northampton Co.
Roads, Jon., 1636, by John Chandler, Elizabeth Citie Co.
Roades, Richard, 1638, by Percivall Champion, Charles River Co.
Roath, Wm., 1652, by John Johnson, Northampton Co.
Roades, Christopher, 1638, by Rich. Ewen, Upper New Norfolk Co.
Robb, Tho., 1655, by Jer. Dodson, Gent., Lancaster Co.
Robbins, Edward, 1646, by Elizabeth and Ratchell Robins, North-
    ampton Co.
Robert, Williams, 1651, by Wm. Rennoles, Northumberland Co.
Roberts, John, 1638, by Mr. Walter Ashton, Charles City Co.
Roberts, Morgan, 1637, by Lt. John Upton, Isle of Wight Co.
Roberts, Fra., 1650, by Richard Jacob, Northampton Co.
Roberts, Ewen, 1643, by Robert Pitt, Isle of Wight Co.
Roberts, Francis, 1650, by Sr. Tho. Luntsford, Kt., and Barronett,
    ——— Co.
Roberts, Edmond, 1650, by Sr. Tho. Luntsford, Kt., and Barronett,
    ——— Co.
Roberts, Gab., 1650, by Mr. Epaphroditus Lawson, ——— Co.
Roberts, Edw., 1650, by Wm. Holder, ——— Co.
Roberts, John, 1650, by Capt. Ishiell Linch, ——— Co.
Roberts, Wm., 1649, by Stephen Gill, York Co.
Roberts, Ed., 1653, by Capt. Nathaniel Hurd, Warrick Co.
Roberts, Lewis, 1652, by Mr. John Cheesman, ——— Co.
Roberts, Eliza., 1652, by John Robinson, Jr., Northampton Co.
Roberts, Ben., 1651, by Edward Deggs, Esq., Yorke Co.
Roberts, Wm., 1651, by Capt. Stephen Gill, Northumberland Co.
Roberts, John, 1653, by Abraham Moon, Lancaster Co.
Roberts, James, 1652, by Wm. Morton, Lower Norfolk Co.
Roberts, Samuel, 1652, by Wm. Morton, Lower Norfolk Co.
Roberts, Wm., 1652, by Mr. Edwin Connaway, ——— Co.
Roberts, John, Jr., 1652, by Mr. Edwin Connaway, ——— Co.
Roberts, John, Sr., 1652, by Mr. Edwin Connaway, ——— Co.
Roberts, Anne, 1652, by Mr. Edwin Connaway, ——— Co.
Roberts, Geo., 1652, by Arthur Upshott, Northampton Co.
Roberts, Jno., 1652, by Arthur Upshott, Northampton Co.
Roberts, Richd., 1653, by Gregory Rawlins, Surry Co.
Roberts, Jon., 1654, by Alex. Madocks and James Jones, Northampton
    Co.
Roberts, Peter, 1642, by John Robins, ——— Co.
Roberts, Henry, 1639, by Justinian Cooper, Isle of Wight Co.
Roberts, Edward, 1639, by Justinian Cooper, Isle of Wight Co.
Roberts, John, 1639, by Thomas Curtis, ——— Co.
Roberts, John, 1638, by John Walton, Accomac Co.
Roberts, Ralph, 1638, by David Mansell, James City Co.
Roberts, Edward, 1641, by Samuell Firment, Upper New Norfolk Co.
Roberts, Tho., 1641, by Garrett Stephens, Warwick River Co.
Roberts, Thomas, 1638, by Oliver Sprye, Upper New Norfolk Co.
Roberts, Morgan, 1638, by Lieut. John Upton, Isle of Wight Co.

Roberts, Wm., 1654, by John Wyre, John Gillett, Andrew Gilson and John Phillipps, ———Co.
Roberts, Ann., 1654, by Edwin Conaway, Lancaster Co.
Roberts, Mary, 1655, by Peter Ford, Gloucester Co.
Roberts, Sarah, 1655, by Mr. Wm. Nutt, Northumberland Co.
Roberts, Wm., 1655, by Wm. Wright, Gent., Nansemond Co.
Roberts, David, 1656, by Roger Wolmsly and Richard Ingram, James City Co.
Roberts, Rob., 1654, by Col. Argoll Yardley, Northampton Co.
Roberts, John, 1653, by Ralph Green, Gloucester Co.
Roberts, Peter, 1642, by Stephen Gill, Yorke River Co.
Roberts, Edw., 1650, by John Garwood, Nansemond Co.
Roberts, John, 1650, by John Garwood, Nansemond Co.
Roberts, John, 1650, by Bertram Obert, ——— Co.
Roberts, Edward, 1643, by Epaphroditus Lawson, Upper Norfolk Co.
Roberts, Evan., 1643, by Rich. Hoe, Gent., ——— Co.
Roberts, Jon., 1637, by Capt. Thomas Flint, Warwick River Co.
Roberts, Edw., 1637, by Humphry Loyd, Charles River Co.
Roberts, John, 1642, by Tho. Curtis, ——— Co.
Roberts, Morgan, 1637, by John Upton, Isle of Wight Co.
Roberts, Jon., 1636, by Thomas Curtis, Charles River Co.
Roberts, James, 1637, by Wm. Farrar, Henrico Co.
Roberts, Gris., 1637, by Mathew Edloe, ——— Co.
Roberts, Fr., 1637, by Mathew Edloe, ——— Co.
Robers, Thom., 1637, by Mathew Edloe, ——— Co.
Robertton, John, 1655, by Wm. Steevens, Northampton Co.
Robin, Sampson, 1635, by McWilliam Stone, ——— Co.
Robins, John, 1643, by Capt. Samuell Mathews, Esq., ——— Co.
Robins, Judith, 1650, by Francis Hobbs, ——— Co.
Robins, Joseph, 1650, by Wm. Underwood, Gent., ——— Co.
Robins, Sam., 1653, by Sampson Robins, Northampton Co.
Robins, Alice, 1653, by Sampson Robins, Northampton Co.
Robins, Mrs. Grace, 1643, by Obedience Robins, Gent., Northampton Co.
Robins, Dorothy, 1638, by John Robins, ——— Co.
Robins, Alice (second wife), 1638, by John Robins, James City Co.
Robins, Dorothy, (first wife) 1638, by John Robins (her husband), James City Co.
Robins, John, 1655, by Lt. Col. Anthony Ellyott, ——— Co.
Robins, Hen., 1654, by Phillip Chesly and Dan. Wilde, York Co.
Robins, Lawrance, 1637, by Arthur Smith, Isle of Wight Co.
Robins, Robt., 1637, by Tho. Symmons, Charles River Co.
Robins, Henry, 1637, by Arthur Bayly, Henrico Co.
Robenson, Jno., 1654, by Mr. Francis Hamond, York Co.
Robinson, Tho., 1643, by William Ewins, James City Co.
Robinson, Gab., 1650, by Mr. Stephen Hamelin, Charles City Co.
Robinson, John, 1650, by Mr. Epaphroditus Lawson, ——— Co.
Robinson, Nich., 1643, by Robert Haies, Lower Norfolk Co.
Robinson, Ellin, 1649, by Bertram Obert, ——— Co.
Robinson, Frances, 1648, by John Manning, Lower Norfolk Co.
Robinson, Symon, 1645, by Mr. Robt. Eyres, ——— Co.

Robinson, Wm., 1649, by Capt. Ralph Wormeley, ——— Co.
Robinson, Step., 1648, by Tho. Lambert, Lower Norfolk Co.
Robinson, Wm., 1653, by John Merryman and Morgan Haynes, Lancaster Co.
Robinson, James, 1652, by Lt. Coll. John Cheesman, ——— Co.
Robinson, John, 1652, by Capt. Augustine Warner, ——— Co.
Robinson, Marga., 1652, by Wm. Ratton and Richard Flint, Lancaster Co.
Robinson, Elinor, 1651, by Audery Bennett, Nansemond Co.
Robinson, Lucy, 1653, by Wm. Hardidge, Northumberland Co.
Robinson, John, 1652, by Mr. David Fox, Lancaster Co.
Robinson, Fra., 1652, by Mr. Tho. Brice, Lancaster Co.
Robinson, Susanna (alis Corker), 1653, by Wm. Moseley, Lower Norfolk Co.
Robinson, Margaret, 1654, by Francis Gray, ——— Co.
Robinson, Hen., 1654, by Francis Gray, ——— Co.
Robinson, Lucy, 1653, by Abraham Moone, Lancaster Co.
Robinson, John, 1653, by Peter Knight and Baker Cult, ——— Co.
Robinson, Sarah, 1652, by George Hemp, Lower Norfolk Co.
Robinson, Wm., Sr., 1652, by George Hemp, Lower Norfolk Co.
Robinson, Wm., Jr., 1652, by George Hemp, Lower Norfolk Co.
Robinson, Nicholas, 1639, by Walter Pakes, ——— Co.
Robinson, Thomas, 1640, by Thomas Stegg, Charles City Co.
Robinson, Richard, 1642, by Wm. Ireland and Robt. Wallis, Yorke Co.
Robinson, Nich., 1639, by Walter Pakes, James City Co.
Robinson, Andrew, 1638, by Wm. Carter, James City Co.
Robinson, Margarett, 1642, by John Beale, ——— Co.
Robinson, Thomas, 1639, by William Barker, James City Co.
Robinson, Robt., 1654, by John Drayton, Westmoreland Co.
Robinson, Simon, 1654, by Humphry Belt, Lower Norfolk Co.
Robinson, Richard, 1656, by Vincent Stanford, ——— Co.
Robinson, Mary, 1656, by Richard Gible, Northumberland Co.
Robinson, Christo., 1642, by John Ewens, Jr., Charles City Co.
Robinson, Phillipp, 1643, by Phillipp Taylor, Northampton Co.
Robinson, Jon., 1643, by Mr. Phillipp Bennett, Upper Norfolk Co.
Robinson, Wm., 1643, by John Sweete, Isle of Wight Co.
Robinson, Edwd., 1643, by Rich. Hoe, Gent., ——— Co.
Robinson, Mathew, 1638, by Wm. Baker and Associates, Charles City Co.
Robinson, Georg, 1638, by Cornelius Loyd, Charles River Co.
Robinson, Jon., 1638, by Stephen Charlton, Accomack Co.
Robinson, John, 1637, by Richard Bennett, New Norfolk Co.
Robinson, James, 1637, by William Spencer, ——— Co.
Robinson, Mary, 1637, by Humphry Higginson, Gent., ——— Co.
Robinson, James, 1637, by Hugh Wynn, Isle of Wight Co.
Robinson, John, 1636, by Richard Bennett, ——— Co.
Robinson, Ann, 1637, by Thomas Barnard, Warwick River Co.
Robinson, Henry, 1636, by John Neale, Accomack Co.
Robinson, Andrew, 1635, by William Carter, Henrico Co.
Robinson, Patrick, 1637, by Wm. Farrar, Henrico Co.
Robinson, Tho., 1636, by James Place, Henrico Co.

Robinson, Tho., 1635, by Wm. Barber (a mariner), Charles City Co.
Robinson, William, 1635, by Joseph Johnson, —— Co.
Robrisius, John, 1653, by Charles Grymes, Clerk, Lancaster Co.
Robinson, Giles, 1656, by Vincent Stanford, —— Co.
Roch, Symon, 1654, by Mrs. Fra. Harrison, widow, Westmoreland Co.
Roch, John, 1643, by Capt. Samuell Mathews, Esq., —— Co.
Roche, James, 1637, by Arthur Smith, Isle of Wight Co.
Rocke, Fr., 1646, by David Jones, Charles City Co.
Rochester, John, 1638, by Thomas Watts, Lower New Norfolk Co.
Rock, Anthony, 1648, by Lewis Burwell, Gent., —— Co.
Rocks, Antho., 1643, by Richard Kemp, Esq., James City Co.
Rockly, Rich., 1639, by John Pawley, James City Co.
Rockwell, Tho., 1639, by Robert Rockwell, Upper New Norfolk Co.
Rockwell, Mary, 1637, by Robt. Rockwell, New Norfolk Co.
Rockwell, Thomasin, 1637, by Robt. Rockwell, New Norfolk Co.
Rockwell, Sarah, 1637, by Robert Rockwell (her husband), New Norfolk Co.
Rockwood, Anth., 1638, by Joseph Harmon, James City Co.
Rockwood, Anthony, 1635, by William Beard, James City Co.
Rodgeson, James, 1637, by Bridges Freeman, James City Co.
Rodish, Wm., 1637, by Henry Perry, Charles River Co.
Rods, James, 1653, by Abraham Moon, Lancaster Co.
Rodye, Robt., 1636, by Justinian Cooper, Warrasquinoak Co.
Roe, Jon., 1637, by Daniel Gookins, New Norfolk Co.
Roe, Jon., 1637, by Arthur Smith, Isle of Wight Co.
Roe, James, 1654, by John Hallawes, Westmoreland Co.
Roe, Mary, 1639, by Robert Rockwell, Upper New Norfolk Co.
Roe, James, 1653, by John Debar, —— Co.
Roe, Charles, 1653, by Peter Knight, Northumberland Co.
Roe, John, 1653, by Peter Knight, Northumberland Co.
Roe, Ann, 1653, by Tho. Davis, —— Co.
Roe, Ri., 1650, by Wm. Clapham, —— Co.
Roger, Tho., 1643, by Richard Kemp, Esq., James City Co.
Roger, Jon., 1643, by John Freeme, Charles Co.
Roger, Hugh, 1650, by David Peibles, Charles City Co.
Roger, Mr. John, 1642, by John Garrett, Upper New Norfolk Co.
Roger, Might, 1635, by Edmund Scarborough, Accomack Co.
Rogers, Wm., 1650, by Lawrence Peters, Nansemond Co.
Roger, Nicholas, 1646, by Thomas Holmes, Yorke River Co.
Rogers, Henry, 1650, by Geo. Ludlow, Esq., Northumberland Co.
Rogers, James, 1650, by Mr. James Williams, —— Co.
Rogers, Phill., 1648, by Wm. Ewen, James City Co.
Rogers, John, 1653, by John Dipdall, Charles City Co.
Roggers, Mary, 1651, by Rowland Morgan, Lower Norfolk Co.
Rogers, Thomas, 1639, by Nicholas Comings, Charles River Co.
Rogers, Elian, 1639, by Robert Eley, Isle of Wight Co.
Rogers, John, 1638, by Georg Mynifie (merchant), —— Co.
Rogers, Wm., 1639, by Richard Corke, Gent., Henrico Co.
Rogers, Francis, 1638, by Thomas Clipwell, James City Co.
Rogers, Tho., 1654, by John Phillips and John Batts, Lancaster Co.
Rogers, Wm., 1653, by Ferdinando Austin, Charles City Co.

Rogers, Nicholas, 1645, by Mark Johnson, Elizabeth City Co.
Rogers, Ellin, 1638, by Joseph Harmon, James City Co.
Rogers, Thos., 1637, by Humphry Higginson, Gent., ——— Co.
Rogers, Charles, 1637, by Francis Fowler, James River Co.
Rogers, Chas., 1635, by Francis Fowler, James City Co.
Rogers, Wm., 1636, by Richard Cocke, ——— Co.
Roggers, John, 1650, by Lewis Burwell, Gent., Northumberland Co.
Roggett, Wm., 1649, by Robert Mosely, Gent., ——— Co.
Roles, Robt., 1637, by Theodore Moyser, James City Co.
Rolfe, Thomas, 1635, by Capt. Wm. Pierse, ——— Co.
Rolles, Wm., 1644, by John Hill, Gent., Upper Norfolk Co.
Rolland, John, 1653, by Charles Grymes, Clerk, Lancaster Co.
Roland, Francis, 1656, by Margaret Miles, Westmoreland Co.
Ronch, Richard, 1643, by Richard Kemp, Esq., James City Co.
Rondall, Joseph, 1651, by Lieut. Collo. Giles Brent, Northumberland
     Co.
Rood, Wm., 1642, by Capt. Samuell Mathews, Esq., ——— Co.
Rooch, Wm., 1652, by Dr. George Hack, Northampton Co.
Rooke, Danl., 1652, by Mr. Henry Pitt, ——— Co.
Rooks, Richard, 1638, by Benjamin Carrill, James City Co.
Roose, John, 1653, by Patrick Margraffe, ——— Co.
Roote, Richard, 1652, by Tho. Todd, ——— Co.
Roote, ———, 1641, by Richard Jackson, Isle of Wight Co.
Rope, Tho., 1652, by Tho. Green, ——— Co.
Roper, Phillipp, 1643, by Randall Holt, ——— Co.
Rosburye, Jon., 1637, by James Harrison, James City Co.
Rose, Alex., 1654, by Thomas Binus, Surry Co.
Rose, Wm, and wife, 1653, by Wm. Knott, Surry Co.
Rose, Henry, 1639, by John Kempe, James City Co.
Rose, Mabell, 1639, by John Pawley, James City Co.
Rose, Morrice, 1639, by Richard Corke, Gent., Henrico Co.
Rose, Wm., 1654, by Nich. Merywether, Westmoreland Co.
Rose, Richard, 1654, by Mark Foster, ——— Co.
Rose, Rob., 1655, by John Hinman, Northampton Co.
Rose, Wm., 1367, by Capt. Thomas Panlett, Charles City Co.
Rose, Charles, 1636, by William Julian, Elizabeth City Co.
Rose, Morrice, 1636, by Richard Cocke, ——— Co.
Rosh, John, 1651, by Joseph Croshaw, Yorke Co.
Rosler, John, 1652, by Henry Fleete, Lancaster Co.
Rosier, Eliza., 1650, by John Rosier, Northumberland Co.
Rosier, Morgan, 1637, by Cheney Boyes, Charles City Co.
Rosier, Morgan, 1636, by Cheney Boyse, Charles City Co.
Roseires, John, 1649, by Wm. Batt, James City Co.
Ross, John, 1652, by Col. Geo. Ludlow, Esq., Gloucester Co.
Ross, Wm., 1653, by Nicho. Meriwether, Northumberland Co.
Ross, John, 1654, by John Grey, Northampton Co.
Rosse, Thomas, 1642, by Thomas Loving, James City Co.
Rosse, Alex., 1650, by Mr. James Williamson, ——— Co.
Rosse, John, 1652, by Mr. George Clapham, ——— Co.
Rosse, James, 1642, by Capt. Samuell Mathews, ——— Co.
Rosser, Eliz., 1654, by Tho. Salsbury, Lancaster Co.

Roston, Thomas, 1639, by John Pawley, James City Co.
Rotherum, Georg, 1637, by Robert Bennett, New Norfolk Co.
Ronfe, Symon, 1638, by Jeremiah Dickenson, James City Co.
Rouncifull, Henry, 1636, by Justinian Cooper, Warrasquinoak Co.
Rouncifull, Henry, 1637, by Justinian Cooper, Isle of Wight Co.
Round, Togue, 1655, by Tho. Leatherberry, Northampton Co.
Rouse, James, 1653, by Wm. Debram, ——— Co.
Rouse, Wm., 1653, by Geo. Wadding, Lancaster Co.
Rouse, Wm., 1653, by Edward Kemp, Geo. Cortlough and John Meredith, Lancaster Co.
Rouse, Walter, 1652, by Tho. Steevens, ——— Co.
Rouse, Walter, 1654, by John Wyre, John Gillett, Andrew Gilson and John Phillipps, ——— Co.
Rouse, Dan., 1654, by Col. Hump. Higgenson, Esq., and Abraham Moone, Westmoreland Co.
Rouse, Tho., 1638, by John Gater, Lower New Norfolk Co.
Rouse, Thos., 1635, by John Gater, Elizabeth City Co.
Rouston, John, 1642, by Thomas Guyer, ——— Co.
Rout, Hugh, 1642, by William Eyres, Upper New Norfolk Co.
Routh, John, 1652, by John Pouncey, ——— Co.
Rouzee, Martha, 1652, by John Catlett and Ralph Rouzee, ——— Co.
Rouzee, Sarah, 1652, by John Catlett, and Ralph Rouzee ———Co.
Rouzee, Kath., 1652, by Tho. Lucas, Gent., Lancaster Co.
Rouzee, Sarah, 1652, by Tho. Lucas, Gent., Lancaster Co.
Roverton, Daniel, 1655, by Mr. Anthony Lansgton, New Kent Co.
Row, Teague, 1655, by George Frizzell and Tho. Moore, Northampton Co.
Rowdell, Tho., 1635, by Anthony Jones, ——— Co.
Rowden, Robert, 1637, by Edward Tunstall, Henrico Co.
Rowry, Rowryae, 1653, by Edward Kemp, Geo. Cortlough and John Meredith, Lancaster Co.
Rowland, Fra., 1649, by Wm. Hoccaday, ——— Co
Rowland, Lewis, 1652, by July Gardner, Northampton Co.
Rowland, James, 1651, by Phillip Hunley, ——— Co.
Rowland, Lewis, 1653, by Charles Scarburg, Northampton Co.
Rowland, Tho., 1655, by Lt. Col. Anthony Ellyott, ——— Co.
Rowland, John, 1655, by John Motley, Northumberland Co.
Rowland, John, 1635, by John Dennett, James Co.
Rowles, Jno., 1653, by Francis Emperor, Hugh Gale, and Edward Morgan, Lower Norfolk Co.
Rowles, Georg, 1637, by Robert Bennett, New Norfolk Co.
Rowlett, Jon., 1635, by John Moone, Warrasquinoake Co.
Rowly, Wm., 1638, by Elizabeth Grayne, Charles City Co.
Rowne, Robert, 1652, by Ralph Paine, ——— Co.
Rownfifall, Hen., 1642, by Justinian Cooper, Isle of Wight Co.
Rowsen, Wm., 1654, by Toby Smith, Lancaster Co.
Rowson, Robt., 1637, by Rich. Bennett, New Norfolk Co.
Roy, Hugh, 1654, by Capt. Nich. Marteaw, Westmoreland Co.
Roy, Hen., 1637, by Peter Roy and William Jacob, Isle of Wight Co.
Roy, Margaret, 1637, by Peter Roy and William Jacob, Isle of Wight Co.

Royall, Henry, 1637, by Joseph Royall, Henrico Co.
Royall, Thomasin, 1637, by Joseph Royall (her husband), Henrico Co.
Royall, Ann, 1637, by Jospeh Royall (she being his now wife), Henrico Co.
Roye, John, 1652, by Tho. Holliwell, ——— Co.
Royly, Joane, 1651, by Capt. John West, Esq., Yorke Co.
Royly, John, 1651, by Capt. John West, Esq., Yorke Co.
Rumball, John, 1652, by Clement Thrush, Lancaster Co.
Rube, Dorothy, 1639, by Thomas Stoute, James City Co.
Rubie, Jon., 1638, by John Fludd, James City Co.
Ruck, Wm., 1652, by Capt. John West, Esq., ——— Co.
Rucoate, Anne, 1654, by Humphry Haggett, Lancaster Co.
Rude, A., 1653, by Geo. Taylor, Lancaster Co.
Rudderford, Jane, 1649, by Frances Land, Norfolk Co.
Rudrick, Edw., 1644, by Stephen Taylor, ——— Co.
Rufe, Mary, 1635, by Capt. William Pierse, ——— Co.
Ruffe, Edward, 1655, by Wm. Wright, Gent, Nansemond Co.
Ruffle, Reese, 1652, by Mr. George Clapham, ——— Co.
Rugg, Benj., 1643, by Wm. Warder, ——— Co.
Rule, Dorothy, 1640, by Henry Porter and Raphaell Joyner, James City Co.
Rule, Dorothy, 1639, by John White, James Citie Co.
Rulford, Tho., 1651, by Tho. Wilsford, Gent., ——— Co.
Rundsay, Robert, 1651, by George Ludlow, Esq., ——— Co.
Ruse, Dan., 1655, by Gilbert Deacon, Henrico Co.
Rush, Jon., 1642, by Thomas Osborne, Henrico Co.
Rush, George, 1654, by Francis Gray, ——— Co.
Rush, Geo., 1651, by Robt. Newman, Northumberland Co.
Rush, Wm., 1650, by Sr. Tho. Luntsford, Kt., and Barronett, ——— Co.
Rusham, Anne, 1653, by Robt. Parfitt, and Wm. Hatcher, Lancaster Co.
Russe, Wm., 1642, by Adam Cooke, Charles Co.
Russell, John, 1653, by Colo. Wm. Clayborne (Sec. of State), ——— Co.
Russell, Alice, 1653, by John King, Surry Co.
Russell, Wm., 1648, by Thomas Woodhouse, James City Co.
Russell, Richard, 1648, by Richard Thompson, Northumberland Co.
Russell, Ann, 1649, by Mr. Henry Lee, Yorke Co.
Russell, Robert, 1649, by Henry Brakes, Lower Norfolk Co.
Russell, John, 1650, by Mr. Tho. Spake, ——— Co.
Russell, Tho., 1650, by George Taylor, ——— Co.
Russell, Rich., 1636, by James Knott, Elizabeth City Co.
Russell, Dennis, 1635, by Capt. Adam Thoroughgood, ——— Co.
Russell, Jon., 1635, by John Moone, Warrasquinoake Co.
Russell, Charles, 1637, by Capt. Thomas Osborne, Henrico Co.
Russell, Rich., 1637, by James Knott, New Norfolk Co.
Russell, Joane, 1645, by William Daynes, Lower Norfolk Co.
Russell, Wm., 1643, by Pierce Lemon, Charles City Co.
Russell, Katherine, 1656, by Margaret Miles, Westmoreland Co.
Russell, Susan, 1654, by Col. Hump Higgenson, Esq., and Abraham Moone, Westmoreland Co.
Russell, Tho., 1654, by Walter Pritchard, ——— Co.

Russell, Wm., 1654, by John Watson and John Bognall, Westmoreland Co.
Russer, Morgan, 1639, by Thomas Mathews, Henrico Co.
Russey, Elizabeth, 1637, by Robert Bennett, New Norfolk Co.
Rute, Dorothy, 1639, by Samuell Trigg and Raphael Joyner, James City Co.
Rutkin, Henry, 1635, by Richard Bennett, ——— Co.
Rutkin, Henry, 1637, by Rich. Bennett, New Norfolk Co.
Rutkin, Henry, 1635, by Richard Bennett, Warrasquinoak Co.
Rutland Rich., 1641, by Thomas Morsey, Isle of Wight Co.
Rutt, Jeremiah, 1640, by Toby Smith, Warwick River Co.
Rutter, John, 1642, by William Prior, Gent., —— —Co.
Ryall, Jsoeph, 1636, by Hannah Boysc, Henrico Co.
Ryall, Joseph, 1637, by Hannah Boyes, Henrico Co.
Ryall, Edwd., 1651, by James Baldridge and Capt. Tho. Baldridge, Northumberland Co.
Ryalls, Ann, 1655, by George Mosely, Gloucester Co.
Ryalls, Sarah, 1655, by George Moseley, Gloucester Co.
Ryland, Tho., 1650, by Thomas Powell, ——— Co.
Ryley, Ann, 1653, by Tho. Kibby, Northumberland Co.
Ryman, Nicholas, 1639, by John Poteete, Charles River Co.
Rythe, Chr., 1645, by John Rode, Warwick Co.
Rytherland, Rich., 1648, by John Twy, James City Co.

S

Sabin, Susan, 1653, by Robt. Savin, ——— Co.
Sabin, Thomas, 1642, by Georg Harding, ——— Co.
Sabin, Tho., 1648, by Richard Pettibon, ——— Co.
Sable, Geo., 1652, by Mrs. Elnor Brocas, Lancaster Co.
Sabrell, Richard, 1650, by Walter Broodhurst, ——— Co.
Sacker, Edward, 1652, by John Robinson, Jr., Northamton Co.
Sackes, Tho., 1649, by Capt. Ralph Wormeley, ——— Co.
Sactor, Richard, 1649, by Richard Croshaw, Yorke Co.
Sadd, Richard, 1638, by Joseph Farge, Charles City Co.
Sadlington, Jonas, 1637, by Lt. John Upton, Isle of Wight Co.
Saddington, Jonas, 1637, by John Upton, Isle of Wight Co.
Sadlington, Jonas, 1635, by Jno. Upton, Warrasquinoake Co.
Sadler, Eliz., Sr., 1640, by William Crannage, Isle of Wight Co.
Sadler, Edmund, Sr., 1640, by William Crannage, Isle of Wight Co.
Sadler, Eliz., Jr., 1640, by William Crannage, Isle of Wight Co.
Sadler, Mary, 1640, by William Crannage, Isle of Wight Co.
Sadler, Edmund, Jr., 1640, by William Crannage, Isle of Wight Co.
Sadler, Mary, 1640, by William Crannage, Isle of Wight Co.
Sadler, Martha, 1654, by Francis Smith and Mr. John Smith, Westmoreland Co.
Sadler, Eliz., 1653, by James Turner, ——— Co.
Sadler, Edward, 1637, by Wm. Cranage, New Norfolk Co.
Sadler, Tho., 1636, by John Neale, Accomack Co.
Sadler, Thomas, 1637, by John Redman and John Neale, Accomac Co.
Sadler, John, 1652, by Daniel Welch, Lancaster Co.

Sadler, Roger, 1652, by Daniel Welch, Lancaster Co.
Sadler, Dorothy, 1652, by Daniel Welch, Lancaster Co.
Sadler, John, 1652, by Daniel Welch, Lancaster Co.
Sadler, Alice, 1651, by Thomas Thornbrough, Northumberland Co.
Sadler, Eliz., 1653, by Francis Hale, ——— Co.
Sadler, Geo., 1652, by John Meredith, Lancaster Co.
Sadleway, Xtop., 1650, by Lewis Burwell, Gent., Northumberland
     Co.
Sadome, Allen, 1639, by Thomas Grey, James City Co.
Sage, Gregory, 1643, by Obedience Robins, Gent., Northmapton Co.
Sagent, Fra., 1653, by John Gillett, Lancaster Co.
Saiferne, James, 1647, by John Brooch, York River Co.
Saines, Wm., 1653, by Peter Knight, Northumberland Co.
Saintpere, Nath., 1653, by Robert Saven, ——— Co.
Saker, Tho., 1653, by Wm. Bebram, ——— Co.
Sale, Eliz., 1639, by Georg Mallen, James City Co.
Sale, ———, 1653, by Henry Lowne, Henrico Co.
Salisberry, Robert, 1650, by John Brown, Northampton Co.
Salisbury, Roger, 1638, by William Parker, Upper Norfolk Co.
Salisbury, Robert, 1646, by John Brown, Northampton Co.
Salisbury, Robt., 1650, by John Brown, Northampton Co.
Salsbury, Robt., 1637, by Alice Edloe, Henrico Co.
Salle, Elion, 1642, by Thomas Gwyn, ——— Co.
Sallett, Gyles, 1642, by Humphry Tabb, Elizabeth City Co.
Sallett, Charles, 1643, by John Hoddin, ——— Co.
Sallett, Giles, 1651, by Humphrey Tabb, Northumberland Co.
Salmon, Jane, 1655, by Dr. Giles Mode, New Kent Co.
Salmon, Jane, 1653, by Capt. Francis Patt, Northampton Co.
Salmon, Edward, 1651, by Richard Vaughan, Northampton Co.
Salsberry, Tho., 1646, by John Ashcomb, Upper Norfolk Co.
Salsbury, Edward, 1638, by Georg Mynifie (merchant), ——— Co.
Salsbury, Wm., 1642, by Capt. Samuell Mathews, Esq., ——— Co.
Salsbury, Robert, 1642, by John Browne, Accomac Co.
Salter, Robt., 1639, by Richard Maior, Charles River Co.
Salter, Edward, 1638, by Christopher Branch, Henrico Co.
Salter, Edward, 1639, by Thomas Mathews, Henrico Co.
Sadler, Thomas, 1642, by Roger Symomns, ——— Co.
Salter, Rich., 1654, by Mr. Francis Hamond, York Co.
Salter, Fra., 1655, by John Coole, James City Co.
Salter, John, 1650, by Wm. Clapham, ——— Co.
Salter, Robert, 1649, by Joseph Croshawe, Yorke Co.
Salter Edward, 1651, by Coll. Guy Molsworth, ——— Co.
Saltrea, John, 1639, by Henry Perry, Charles City Co.
Salvadge, Jno., 1651, by Edmond Welch, ——— Co.
Sames, Eliz., 1639, by John Dunston, James City Co.
Sames, Eliz., 1636, by John Dunston, James City Co.
Sampson, James, 1638, by John Walton, Elizabeth City Co.
Sampson, Alex., 1654, by Arthur Nash, New Kent Co.
Sampson, Edwd., 1653, by Francis Clay, Northumberland Co.
Samuell, Edward, 1643, by Edward Murfey and John Vaughan, ———
     Co.

Sandall, Edw., 1637, by Eleanor Day and Thom. Emmerson, Warwick River Co.

Sandall, Edw., 1636, by Elilnor Dey and Thos. Emmerson, Warwick River Co.

Sanderby, Tho., 1642, by Wm. Barnard, Esq., Isle of Wight Co.

Sanders, Tho., 1653, by Charles Grymes, Clerk, Lancaster Co.

Sanders, Richard, 1639, by Samuell Trigg and Raphael Joyner, James City Co.

Sanders, William, 1638, by Thomas Burbage, Accomack Co.

Sanders, Isabell, 1638, by Wm. Morgan, ———— Co.

Sanders, Michaell, 1642, by William Prior, Gent., ———— Co.

Sanders, Wm., 1639, by Wm. Barker, Charles City Co.

Sanders, Robert, 1638, by Thomas Symons, Upper Norfolk Co.

Sanders, Margarett, 1638, by Mr. Thomas Wallis, James City Co.

Sanders, Jon., 1637, by Johanthon Longworth, New Norfolk Co.

Sanders, Eliz., 1643, by Phillipp Taylor, Northampton Co.

Sanders, Richard, 1637, by Bridges Freeman, ———— Co.

Sanders, Jon., 1636, by James Vanerit, Elizabeth City Co.

Sanders, Kath., 1635, by Henry Daniell, James City Co.

Sanders, Herny, 1643, by Capt. Samuell Mathews, Esq., ———— Co.

Sanders, Thomas, 1646, by Joseph Croshawe, Charles River Co.

Sanders, Eustace, 1649, by Bestram Obert, ———— Co.

Sanders, Ann, 1650, by Capt. Richard Bond, Charles City Co.

Sanders, Tho., 1652, by Tho. Steevens, Lancaster Co.

Sanders, Elizabeth, 1651, by Robt. Bradshaw, Charles River Co.

Sanders, Tho., and Grace, his wife, 1653, by Denis Coniers, Lancaster Co.

Sanders, Cor., 1653, by Capt. Robt. Abrahal, Gloucester Co.

Sanderson, Jane, daughter of Henry Sanderson, 1650, by Lewis Burwell, Gent., Northumberland Co.

Sanderson, Henry, 1650, by Lewis Burewll, Gent., Northumberland Co.

Sanderson, Tho., 1651, by Richard Whitehurst, Lower Norfolk Co.

Sandish, Stephen, 1642, by Wm. Warren, ———— Co.

Sands, Mary, 1648, by Major Richard Morrison, Elizabeth City Co.

Sands, David, 1653, by Major John Westhrope, Charles City Co.

Sanford, Wm., 1655, by Lt. Col. Tho. Swan, Surry Co.

Sanham, John, 1637, by John Moon, Isle of Wight Co.

Sanner, Sarah, 1642, by Wm. Eyres, Upper New Norfolk Co.

Sanson, Wm., 1656, by Mr. Martin Baker, New Kent Co.

Sany James, 1643, by Edward Murfey and John Vaughan, ———— Co.

Sapcoate, Robert, 1655, by Wm. Wright, Gent., Nansemond Co.

Sar, Wm., 1654, by Robert Hubard, Westmoreland Co.

Sarah, Grace, 1651, by Abraham Moone and (Thomas Griffen), Lancaster Co.

Sareland, Oliver, 1654, by Tho. Salsbury, Lancaster Co.

Sareland, Oliver, 1652, by Ambrose Dixon and Stephen Horsely, Northampton Co.

Sargent, Arthur, 1643, by Tho. Faylor, Warwick Co.

Sarrigg, John, 1654, by Tho. Willoughby, Lower Norfolk Co.

Sarrow, Benja., 1652, by Collo. Hugh Gwin, ———— Co.

Sarslett, Xtop., 1650, by John Hany, Northumberland Co.

Sarson, Rich., 1654, by Col. Hump. Higgenson, Esq., and Abraham Moone, Westmoreland Co.
Sarsonn, Wm., 1638, by John Fludd, James City Co.
Sassell, Richard, 1655, by Wm. Wright, Gent., Nansemond Co.
Sassell, John, 1639, by John Graves, Elizabeth City Co.
Satchell, Eliza., 1650, by Epa. Lawson,,—— Co.
Saughier, Eliz., Senior, 1637, by Geo. Saughier, Eliz. City Co.
Saughier, Robt., 1637, by Geo. Saughier, Eliz. City Co.
Saughier, Eliz., Junior, by George Saughier, Eliz. City Co.
Saunder, Ann, 1654, by John Drayton, Westmoreland Co.
Saunders, Jon., 1637, by Jonathan Longworth, New Norfolk Co.
Saunders, Mary, 1654, by Tho. Bell, Northampton Co.
Saunders, Elizabeth, 1654, by Robt. Bowers, —— Co.
Saunders, Wm., 1654, by Robt. Bowers, —— Co.
Saunders, Edw., Gent., 1654, by Nich. Merywether, Westmoreland Co.
Saunders, Richard, 1636, by Bridges Freeman, —— Co.
Saunders, Edwd., 1654, by John Watson and John Bognall, Westmoreland Co.
Saunderson, Mountecue and brother, 1654, by Nich. Merywether, Westmoreland Co.
Savage, Rich., 1640, by John Holloway, Accomack Co.
Savage, James, 1654, by Coll. Jno. Matrom, Westmoreland Co.
Savage, Richard, 1638, by William Parker, Upper Norfolk Co.
Savage, Fr., 1637, by Lt. John Upton, Isle of Wight Co.
Savage, Thos. (a servant), 1635, by Wm. Garry, Accomack Co.
Savage, Fr., 1637, by John Upton, Isle of Wight Co.
Savage, Frank, 1635, by Jno. Upton, Warrasquinoake Co.
Savage, Mart., 1649, by Capt. Ralph Wormeley, —— Co.
Savage, Willm., 1648, by Thomas Woodhouse, James City Co.
Savage, Wm., 1653, by James Mason, James City Co.
Savary, Wm., 1637, by Jno. Broche, Charles River Co.
Savell, Tho., 1637, by Bennett Freeman, James City Co.
Saven, Robt., Sr., 1653, by Robt. Saven, —— Co.
Saverne, Bridgett, wife of Jno. Saverne, Sr., 1646, by Tho. Savidge, Northampton Co.
Saverne, Jno., Jr., 1646, by Tho. Savedge, Northampton Co.
Savidge, Tho., 1650, by Henry Peaseley, —— Co.
Savidge, Robert, 1653, by Charles Grymes, Lancaster Co.
Savidge, Robert, 1652, by Tho. Steevens, Lancaster Co.
Savill, Eliza., 1652, by Mr. Edwin Connaway, —— Co.
Savin, Robt., 1643, by John Sweete, Isle of Wight Co.
Savoy, Tho., 1652, by Richard Coleman, —— Co.
Sawyer, Lidia, 1655, by Mr. John Mottrow, Northumberland Co.
Sawyer, Wm., 1650, by Mordecay Cocke, —— Co.
Sawyer, Tho., 1653, by Charles Grymes, Lacaster Co.
Sawyer, Frances, 1637, by Thomas Sawyer, New Norfolk Co.
Sawyer, Fra., 1635, by David Mansell, James Co.
Sawyer, Wm., 1642, by John Resbury, —— Co.
Sawyer, Tho., 1650, by Tho. Tilsey, James City Co.
Sawyer, Mary, 1649, by Tho. Harwood, —— Co.
Sawyer, Francis, 1652, by Mr. Tho. Sawyer, Lower Norfolk Co.

Sawyer, Nich., 1652, by Mrs. Jane Harmer, Northumberland Co.
Sax, Bassett, 1646, by Geo. Ludlow, Esq., York Co.
Sax, Thomas, 1638, by Capt. Christopher Wormley, Charles River Co.
Say, John, 1639, by Lieut. Richard Popeley, ——— Co.
Say, Jane, 1650, by John Lacker, ——— Co.
Say, Hugh, 1650, by Tho. Vans, Gent., Northumberland Co.
Saye, John, 1637, by Percival Champion, New Norfolk Co.
Saye, John, 1648, by John Ellis, Janus Joones, and John Taylor, North-
    ampton Co.
Sayer, Mary, 1643, by Obedience Robins, Gent., Northampton Co.
Sayle, Hump., 1651, by Edward Deggs, Esq., Yorke Co.
Sayler, Anne, 1653, by Tho. Sawyer, ——— Co.
Sayler, Ralph, 1649, by Tho. Spake, Gent., Northumberland Co.
Sayne, Hump., 1654, by Col. Argoll Yardley, Northampton Co.
Saynes, Geo., 1654, by Wm. Beach, Westmoreland Co.
Saysell, John, 1653, by Mrs. Mary Brent, ——— Co.
Saysill, John, 1645, by William Cock, Elizabeth City Co.
Scag, Tho., 1654, by Mr. Mordecay Cooke, ——— Co.
Scale, Wm., 1656, by John Wood, ——— Co.
Scales, Geo., 1636, by John Seaward, Isle of Wight Co.
Scales, John, 1651, by Edward Deggs, Esq., Yorke Co.
Scales, John, 1652, by Capt. Augustine Warner, ——— Co.
Scarbourgh, Tho., 1639, by Edward Travis, James City Co.
Scarborough, Hannah, 1635, by Capt. Edmund Scarborough, Accomack
    Co.
Scarbourgh Mathew, 1635, by McWilliam Stone, ——— Co.
Scarburg, John, 1652, by John Gresham, Northumberland Co.
Scarburg, Tho., 1653, by Richard Carey, ——— Co.
Scarburgh, Mary, 1640, by Edmund Scarburgh (her husband), Acco-
    mack Co.
Scarburgh, Kath., 1652, by Mr. Tho. Curtis, ——— Co.
Scarbrow, Richard, 1656, by Sir Henry Chichley, ——— Co.
Scarfe, Moses, 1653, by Richard Carey, ——— Co.
Scary, Robert, 1635, by David Jones, Charles City Co.
Scatchwench, Mary, 1650, by Stephen Charlton, Northampton Co.
Scatchwench, Eliza., 1650, by Stephen Charlton, Northampton Co.
Scat, Jon., 1635, by Capt. Thos. Willowbye, ——— Co.
Scearle, John, 1647, by Leonard Pettock, Accomac Co.
Schin, Winfred, 1654, by Mr. Wm. Westerhouse, Northampton Co.
Schin, Mary, 1654, by Mr. Wm. Westerhouse, Northampton Co.
Schin, Law., 1654, by Mr. Wm. Westerhouse, Northampton Co.
Scibbs, John, 1652, by Francis Fleetwood, Lower Norfolk Co.
Scifeild, Samuell, 1653, by Colo. Wm. Clayborne (Sec. of State), ———
    Co.
Scocher, John, 1643, by Henry Neale, James City Co.
Scoggin, Geo., 1653, by Wm. Sidner, Lancaster Co.
Scope, Tho., 1651, by Abraham Moone and (Thomas Griffen), Lancaster
    Co.
Scott, James, 1637, by Thos. Hampton Clarke, New Norfolk Co.
Scott, Richard, 1655, by George Frizell, and Tho. Moore, Northampton
    Co.

Scott, Daniell, 1638, by Christopher Burrough, Lower Norfolk Co.
Scott, Dan., 1637, by Henry Perry, Charles River Co.
Scott, Jon., 1637, by Daniell Gookins, New Norfolk Co.
Scott, Tho., 1650, by George Pate, Charles City Co.
Scott, Wm., 1637, by Lt. John Upton, Isle of Wight Co.
Scot, Wm., 1637, by John Upton, Isle of Wight Co.
Scott, Henry, 1637, by Bridges Freeman, James City Co.
Scott, Wm., 1635, by Jno. Upton, Warrasquinoake Co.
Scott, Hen., 1636, by Bridges Freeman, ——— Co.
Scott, Robt., 1650, by Richard Tye and Charles Sparrowe, Charles City
    Co.
Scott, Tho., 1650, by Capt. Moore Fautleroy, ——— Co.
Scott, Barbery, 1653, by John Levistone, Gloucester Co.
Scott, Joane, 1653, by Abraham Moone, Lancaster Co.
Scott, Wm., 1653, by Tho. Hampton ——— Co.
Scott, Tho., 1649, by Edmund Scarburgh, Jr., Northampton Co.
Scott, Wm., 1651, by John Adleston, ——— Co.
Scott, Wm., 1652, by John Bryan, ——— Co.
Scott, Wm., 1653, by John Barbur, ——— Co.
Scott, James, 1653, by Richard Budd, Northumberland Co.
Scott, Wm., 1653, by Wm. Hunt, ——— Co.
Scott, Kath., 1653, by Wm. Hunt, ——— Co.
Scott, Hen., 1653, by Richard Smith, Lancaster Co.
Scott, James, 1655, by Edward Moore, Northampton Co.
Scoe, John, 1655, by Moses Lynton, Lower Norfolk Co.
Scott, Arthur, 1635, by John Leonard, Warrasquinoake Co.
Scott, Charles, 1654, by Francis Smith and Mr. John Smith, Westmore-
    land Co.
Scott, Wm., 1654, by John Drayton, Westmoreland Co.
Scott, Wm., 1642, by Thomas Ray, ——— Co.
Scott, Dan., 1637, by Henry Perry, Charles River Co.
Scott, Nicholas, 1640, by Georg Traveller, Accomack Co.
Scott, Robt., 1652, by Tho. Greenwood, Isle of Wight Co.
Scratton, Sisley, 1649, by Edmund Scarburgh, Jr., Northampton Co.
Scrivener, Mathew, 1653, by Charles Grymes, Lancaster Co.
Scruggs, Rich., 1655, by John Lynge, James City Co.
Scruggs, Rich., 1655, by Henry Barlow, ——— Co.
Scull, John, 1645, by William Storey, Upper Norfolk Co.
Seabottom, Jon., 1653, by Samuell Bonam, Northumberland Co.
Seaburne, John, 1636, by John Yates, Elizabeth City Co.
Seaburne, Nicholas, 1636, by John Yates, Elizabeth City Co.
Seaden, John, 1653, by Dennis Conniers, Lancaster Co.
Seadgall, Hump., 1650, by Epa. Lawson, ——— Co.
Seager, Jon., 1643, by Capt. Samuell Mathews, Esq., ——— Co.
Seagrosse, Amy, 1652, by Christopher Lewis, Isle of Wight Co.
Seale, Henry, 1637, by Capt. Thomas Osborne, Henrico Co.
Seale, Mary, 1652, by Anthony Hoskins, Northampton Co.
Seales, Wm., 1652, by John Puncey, ——— Co.
Sealing, Mary, 1653, by Peter Knight, Northumberland Co.
Sealling, Nich., 1635, by Wm. Swan, James Co.
Seame, John, 1638, by Capt. Tho. Harris, Henrico Co.

Seamer, Owen, 1639, by Justinian Cooper, Isle of Wight Co.
Seamer, Francis, 1637, by John Neale, Accomack Co.
Seaper, John, 1646, by Coll Henry Bishopp, James City Co.
Seaper, John, 1655, by Matilda Scarbourgh, Northampton Co.
Search, Eliza., 1653, by Jno. Hansford, Gloucester Co.
Searell, Nich., 1637, by Capt. John Howe, Accomac Co.
Seargent, John, 1652, by Capt. John West, Esq., ———— Co.
Searle, John, 1639, by John Kempe, James City Co.
Searle, Gabriell, 1640, by John Holloway, Accomack Co.
Searle, Jon., 1635, by Tho. Harris, Henrico Co.
Searle, John, 1652, by John Halton, ———— Co.
Seaton, John, 1637, by Mathew Edloe, ———— Co.
Seave, Ralph, 1648, by Francis Ceely, ———— Co.
Seavell, David, 1652, by Henry Fleete, Lancaster Co.
Seaver, Hugh, 1639, by Henry Perry, Charles City Co.
Seavoble, John, 1648, by John Seward, Isle of Wight Co.
Seawell, Tho., 1638, by Wm. Clays, Charles River Co.
Seawell, Jarvis, 1637, by Bennett Freeman, James City Co.
Seawell, Tho., 1649, by Mr. Wm. Hoccaday, ———— Co.
Seawell, Mercy, 1637, by Bridges Freeman, James City Co.
Seawell, Tho., 1647, by Symon Symons, Nansemond Co.
Sebeard, John, 1639, by Thomas Sheppey, Henrico Co.
Seberry, John, 1638, by John Robins, James City Co.
Sebocke, Wm., 1652, by Mrs. Mary Brent, Northumberland Co.
Secker, Geo., 1643, by Epaphroditus Lawson, Upper Norfolk Co.
Secroft, John, 1650, by George Gill, Yorke Co.
Sedberry, Peter, 1638, by Cornelius Loyd, ———— Co.
Sedgwick, Joseph, 1635, by by Capt. Adam Thoroughgood, ———— Co.
Seeleyn, Mary, 1653, by Jno. Edwards, Lancaster Co.
Seely, John, 1654, by Francis Smith and Mr. John Smith, Westmoreland Co.
Seemer, John, 1650, by Mr. Epaphroditus Lawson, ———— Co.
Seene, John, 1636, by Samuel Edwards, James City Co.
Seere, Fra., 1651, by Thomas Keeling, Lower Norfolk Co.
Segar, Francis, 1637, by David Mansell, James City Co.
Segrave, Joane, 1654, by John Wyre, John Gillet, Andrew Gilson and John Phillipps, ———— Co.
Selby, Robt., 1637, by James Knott, New Norfolk Co.
Selby, Robt., 1636, by James Knott, Elizabeth City Co.
Selbee, Robert, 1638, by Robert Freeman, James City Co.
Seldome, Wm., 1638, by Robert Pitts, Isle of Wight Co.
Selickley, Timo., 1650, by Lewis Burewll, Gent., ———— Co.
Selker, Robert, 1636, by Christopher Calthropp, Charles River Co.
Sellick, Saml., 1654, by Col. Argoll Yardley, Northampton Co.
Selly, John, 1638, by Edmund Scarborough, Accomac Co.
Selly, John, 1651, by James Allen, Northumberland Co.
Semaster, Hen., 1642, by Capt. Samuell Mathews Esq., ———— Co.
Sen, Stephen, 1642, by John Boyles, ———— Co.
Senter, Wm., 1652, by Tho. Preston, ———— Co.
Septon, John, 1650, by Richard Tye and Charles Sparrowe, Charles City Co.

Serby, Robt., 1652, by Richard Starnell, —— Co.
Seretfeeld, Tho., 1653, by Charles Grymes, Clerk, Lancaster Co.
Seriver, Jos., 1650, by John Mangor, —— Co.
Sergeant, Wm., 1638, by Roger Davis, Charles City Co.
Sergeant, Fra., 1653, by Wm. Sidner, Lancaster Co.
Serjant, Jno., 1654, by Toby Smith, Lancaster Co.
Sermoner, Edwd., 1652, by Wm. Colborne, Northampton Co.
Serrell, Robert, 1637, by James Harrison, James City Co.
Serridon, Tho., 1642, by Francis Mandlin, Upper New Norfolk Co.
Session, Judith, 1645, by Zachary Cripps, Warwick Co.
Sethel, Eliza., 1655, by John Lawson, Lancaster Co.
Settler, Judith, 1643, by Walter Aston, Gent., Charles City Co.
Sevens, Tho., 1653, by Robert Bouth, Yorke Co.
Seward, James, 1655, by Lt. Col. Tho. Swan, Surry Co.
Sewell, Lane, 1652, by Mrs. Jane Harmer, Northumberland Co.
Sewell, John, 1639, by Edward Travis, James City Co.
Sewell, Tho., 1637, by Jno. Brache, Charles River Co.
Sewell, Richard, 1651, by Capt. Stephen Gill, Northumberland Co.
Sewell, Martha, 1652, by Henry Weeker, —— Co.
Sexton, Richard, 1653, by Charles Grimes, Lancaster Co.
Sexton, Nich., 1654, by Sr. Henry Chickley, Kt., Lancaster Co.
Sey, Wm., 1642, by Richard Maior, Charles River Co.
Seymor, Tho., 1641, by Samuell Firment, Upper New Norfolk Co.
Seyton, Dorcas, 1652, by Wm. Capps, Lower Norfolk Co.
Shade, Henry, 1652, by Edward Cannon and Tho. Allen, Lower Norfolk
    Co.
Shaddock, John, 1637, by Elizabeth Parker, Henrico Co.
Shakley, John, 1650, by John Mattrum, Northumberland Co.
Shadwell, Overner, 1650, by Anthony Ellyot, Gent., —— Co.
Shagbrough, Joane, 1651, by George Ludlow, Esq., —— Co.
Shallamine, John, 1655, by Edward Lucas, —— Co.
Shallock, John, 1638, by Lieut. John Upton, Isle of Wight Co.
Shandall, Antho., 1646, by John Broach, York Co.
Shanks, John, 1650, by Tho. Gerrord, Gent., Northumberland Co.
Shapwell, William, 1638, by Henry Catelyn, Upper Norfolk Co.
Share, Hellen, 1650, by Elias Edmonds, —— Co.
Share, Jacob, 1652, by Capt. John West, Esq., —— Co.
Sharp, Rich., 1639, by John Dunston, James City Co.
Sharp, Robt., 1636, by Georg Holmes, James City Co.
Sharg, Richard, 1636, by John Dunston, James City Co.
Sharp, Ann, wife of Barker, 1636, by Peter Johnson, Warrasquinoake
    Co.
Sharpe, Robt., 1637, by Georg Holmes, James City Co.
Sharpe, Tho., 1650, by Hump. Lyster, —— Co.
Sharpe, Robt., 1652, by Ralph Horsely, Northumberland Co.
Sharpe, Richard, 1649, by Joseph Croshawe, Yorke Co.
Sharpe, Jon., 1638, by Wm. Hatfield, Upper New Norfolk Co.
Sharpe, Olver, 1651, by Giles Lawrence and John Turner, Nansemond
    Co.
Sharpe, Sarah, 1654, by Mr. Giles Brent, Westmoreland Co.
Sharpe, Rebecca, 1637, by Capt. John Howe, Accomac Co.

Sharpe, Wm., 1654, by John Sharpe, Lancaster Co.
Sharpe, Henry, 1654, by James Yates, ——— Co.
Sharpe, Tho., 1652, by Mrs. Jane Harmer, Northumberland Co.
Sharpe, Andrew, 1653, by Mr. Wm. Hoccoday, Yorke Co.
Sharpe, Robert, 1638, by David Mansell, James City Co.
Sharpe, Wm., 1641, by Garrett Stephens, Warwick River Co.
Sharpe, Richard, 1651, by Robt. Bradshaw, Charles River Co.
Sharp, Fra., 1653, by Leonard Chamberlaine, Gloucester Co.
Sharper, Jones, 1650, by Capt. Moore Fautleroy, ——— Co.
Sharpless, Eliz., 1651, by Capt. Geo. Read, Lancaster Co.
Sharples, Tho., 1639, by Georg Minifye, Esq., Charles River Co.
Sharples, Eliz., 1639, by Capt. Nicholas Martian, Charles River Co.
Shatbones, Rich., 1635, by Christo. Stoakes, Elizabeth City Co.
Shaw, Wm., 1642, by Lieut. Francis Mason, ——— Co.
Shaw, James, 1655, by Jer Dodson, Gent., Lancaster Co.
Shaw, Ann, 1655, by George Parker, Northampton Co.
Shaw, Susan, 1655, by John Palmer, Northumberland Co.
Shaw, John, 1642, by George Busse, ——— Co.
Shaw, Francis, 1643, by John Sweete, Isle of Wight Co.
Shaw, Richard, 1639, by William Davis, James City Co.
Shaw, Walter, 1638, by Walter Chiles, Charles City Co.
Shaw, Nich., 1637, by Cheney Boyes, Charles City Co.
Shaw, Wm., 1636, by John Neale, Accomack Co.
Shaw, Ann, 1635, by James Knott, Elizabeth City Co.
Shaw, William, 1643, by Geo. Gilbert, James City Co.
Shaw, John, 1650, by Capt. Moore Fautleroy, ——— Co.
Shaw, Anne, 1652, by Mr. Tho. Purifye and Mrs. Temperence Peppitt,
    ——— Co.
Shaw, Ann, 1653, by Peter Knight, Northumberland Co.
Sheaphard, Nath., 1654, by Roger Walters, Northumberland Co.
Sheappard, Elin., 1654, by Capt. Nich. Marteau, Westmoreland Co.
Sheppard, Jon., 1638, by Wm. Hatfield, Upper New Norfolk Co.
Sheppard, Richard, 1644, by James Taylor and Lawrence Baker, James
    City Co.
Sheppard, John, 1642, by John Brooch, Charles River Co.
Sheppard, Priscilla, 1635, by Robert Sheppard (her husband), ———
    Co.
Sheppard, Priscilla, Dorothy and Mary, 1650, by Capt. Robert Sheppard
    ——— Co.
Sheppard, Edward, 1650, by Daniell Suellin, Charles City Co.
Sheppard, Mr. John and Anne, his wife, 1642, by Stephen Gill, Yorke
    River Co.
Shearmon, Abraham, 1648, by John Seward, Isle of Wight Co.
Sheave, Georg, 1637, by Thomas Hampton, New Norfolk Co.
Sheeles, Jon., 1653, by Roger Walker, Northumberland Co.
Sheeles, John, 1653, by Roger Walter, Northumberland Co.
Sheen, Ellen, 1650, by Mr. James Williamson, ——— Co.
Sheep, Allen, 1649, by Richard Parret, ——— Co.
Sheeres, Susan, 1651, by Capt. Tho. Davis, Northumberland Co.
Sheeves, Geo., 1656, by Richard Wheeler, Lower Norfolk Co.
Sheild, Thomas, 1638, by Mr. Walter Ashton, Charles City Co.

Sheild, Walter, 1650, by Richard Tye and Charles Sparrowe, Charles City Co.
Sheir, Geo., 1653, by Margarett Upton, Lancaster Co.
Shekells, Barbery, 1656, by George Kibble, Lancaster Co.
Sheld, Tho., 1651, by Mrs. Anna Bernard, Northumberland Co.
Shell, John, 1643, by Thomas Hughes, Charles River Co.
Shelley, Thos., 1642, by Capt. Samuell Mathews, Esq., ——— Co.
Shelton, Fr., 1638, by John Fludd, James City Co.
Shelton, Fra., 1654, by Robert Hubard, Westmoreland Co.
Shelton, Rich., 1638, by Hugh Allen, Charles River Co.
Shelton, Fra., 1654, by Valentine Patten, Westmoreland Co.
Shelly, Roger, 1637, by William Spencer, ——— Co.
Sheely, Roger, 1656, by Wm. and Hancock Lee, Gloucester Co.
Shelly, Edw., 1650, by Tho. Gerrord, Gent., Northumberland Co.
Shelly, John, 1653, by Wm. Cox, ——— Co.
Shepard, Susan, 1643, by Casar Puggett, Lower Norfolk Co.
Sheppe, Edward, 1653, by John Shepperd, Northumberland Co.
Shepheard, Tho., 1649, by John Walthams, Northampton Co.
Shepherd, Nath., 1653, by Roger Walker, Northumberland Co.
Shepperd, John, 1638, by Georg Mynifie (merchant), ——— Co.
Shepperd, Wm., 1642, by Capt. Daniell Gookin, ——— Co.
Shepperd, Jon., 1643, by Richard Kemp, Esq., James City Co.
Shepperd, Tho., Jr., 1653, by John Shepperd, Northumberland Co.
Shepperd, Mr. Tho., Sr., 1653, by John Shepperd, Northumberland Co
Shepping, Jno., 1651, by Joseph Croshaw, Yorke Co.
Sherborne, James, 1642, by Roger Symmons, ——— Co.
Sherborne, James, 1639, by Georg Minifye, Esq., Charles River Co.
Sheres, Susan, 1653, by John Debar, Lower Norfolk Co.
Sheriffs, Tho., 1649, by John Sibsey, Lower Norfolk Co.
Sherland, Wm., 1653, by Capt. Wm. Whittington, Northampton Co.
Sherlocke, John, 1643, by Capt. John Upton, Isle of Wight Co.
Sherly, Henry, 1654, by Henry Walker, James City Co.
Sherman, James, 1643, by Francis Rice, ——— Co.
Sheerman, Edm., 1650, by Mr. Epaphroditus Lawson, ——— Co.
Sherman, Wm., 1652, by John Godfrey, Lower Norfolk Co.
Shermoner, Edward, 1653, by Charles Scarburg, Northampton Co.
Sheers, James, 1639, by Georg Minifye, Esq., Charles River Co.
Sheers, Wm., 1643, by Capt. William Peirce, Esq., ——— Co.
Sheeres, John, 1652, by Nicho. George, Tho. Taberer, and Humphry Clarke, ——— Co.
Sherwood, John, 1639, by Edward Panderson, ——— Co.
Sherwood, Mary, 1656, by Wm. Justice, Charles City Co.
Sherwood, Jane, 1653, by Robt. Warren, Northampton Co.
Sherwood, Hump., 1648, by Wm. Edwards and Rice Edwards, James City Co.
Sherry, Susan, 1650, by Edward Grimes, ——— Co.
Shevarne, Henry, 1652, by Augustine Moore, ——— Co.
Shewell, Sam., 1653, by Capt. Wm. Whittington, Northampton Co.
Shewell, Mary, 1652, by Edward Cannon and Tho. Allen, Lower Norfolk Co.
Shipcott, Thomas, 1648, by Mr. Thomas Davies, Isle of Wight Co.

Shinger, Edw., 1656, by Richard Barnhouse, Gent., James City Co.
Shipp, Richard, 1650, by John Cox, ——— Co.
Shippard, Adrell, 1654, by John Drayton, Westmoreland Co.
Shippard, Ann, 1654, by Henry Walker, James City Co.
Shippard, Eliz., 1654, by Robert Yoe, Westmoreland Co.
Shippe, Daniell, 1653, by John Shepperd, Northumberland Co.
Shippey, Edw., 1637, by Capt. Thos. Panlett, Charles City Co.
Shippey, Eliza, 1637, by Thomas Shippey, Henrico Co.
Shirle, Tho., 1643, by Wm. Warder, ——— Co.
Shirt, John, 1648, by Georg Read, Gent., ——— Co.
Shoare, Robert, 1656, by Richard Barnhouse, Gent., James City Co.
Shoemaker, Wm., 1652, by Mr. Richard Cocke, Henrico Co.
Shoke, John, 1636, by Richard Cocke, ——— Co.
Shone, Teage, 1655, by Christopher Calvert, Northampton Co.
Shore, Kath., 1636, by Richard Cocke, ——— Co.
Shore, Jonas, 1639, by Richard Cocke, Gent., Henrico Co.
Shore, John, 1639, by Richard Cocke, Gent., Henrico Co.
Shore, Katherine, 1639, by Richard Cocke, Henrico Co.
Shore, James, 1636, by Richard Cocke, ——— Co.
Short, William, 1635, by Capt. Wm. Peirse, ——— Co.
Short, Wm., 1649, by Robert Mosely, Gent., ——— Co.
Short, John, 1652, by Daniell Welch, Lancaster Co.
Shorn, Nicho., 1636, by Cheney Boyes, Charles City Co.
Short, William, 1639, by Thomas Grey, James City Co.
Shorpe, Henry, 1649, by Richard Parrett, ——— Co.
Short, Wm., 1654, by Edward Simpson, Gloucester Co.
Short, John, 1656, by Wm. Crump and Mr. Humphry Vaulx, James City
    Co.
Short, Robt., 1643, by John Sweete, Isle of Wight Co.
Shorte, Wm., 1639, by John Kempe, James City Co.
Short, David, 1653, by Mr. Tho. Breman, Gloucester Co.
Shorton, Mary, 1636, by Joseph Moore, Elizabeth City Co.
Shorter, John, 1638, by Thomas Clipwell, James City Co.
Shorter, Mary, 1638, by Joseph Moore, Elizabeth City Co.
Shott, Walch, Richd., 1650, by Bertram Obert, ——— Co.
Shotworth, Dan., 1652, by Mr. John Brown, Northampton Co.
Should, Jonathan, 1652, by Dr. Geo. Hack, Northampton Co.
Shoute, Henry, 1650, by Henry Peaseley, ——— Co.
Shovelock, Hen., 1642, by by Stephen Gill, ——— Co.
Showell, Jonath., 1653, by Charles Scarburg, Northampton Co.
Shrallop, Tinsley, 1647, by Jonathan Gills, Northampton Co.
Shrefter, John, 1651, by John Hull, Northumberland Co.
Shrews, Tho., 1653, by Joseph Hogkinson, Lower Norfolk Co.
Shuett, Richard, 1641, by Wm. Storey, Upper Norfolk Co.
Shull, John, 1643, by William Storey, Upper Norfolk Co.
Shullivan, Daniel V., 1656, by Nicholas Waddilow, Northampton Co.
Shullivan, Dorman, V., 1656, by Nicholas Waddilow, Northampton Co.
Shurley, Wm., 1652, by Major Lewis Burwell, and Lucy his wife, ———
    Co.
Shurly, Eliz., 1636, by John Neale, Accomack Co.
Shutle, John, 1642, by Stephen Gill, ——— Co.

Shute, Martin, 1642, by Richard Maior, Charles River Co.
Sicah, Robt., 1656, by Nathaniel Pope, Gent., Westmoreland Co.
Sickard, Symon, 1654, by John Skerrett, ——— Co.
Sidney, Robert, 1650, by John Mangor, ——— Co.
Sdney, Eliza., 1655, by Richard Hamlet, James City Co.
Sidney, Eliza., 1643, by Mr. John Bishopp, James City Co.
Signett, Balden, 1639, by Robt. Newman, Warwick River Co.
Siler, Robert, 1639, by Capt. Robt. Felgate, Charles River Co.
Silke, Anne, 1653, by John Levistone, Gloucester Co.
Silley, Edward, 1638, by Henry Catelyn, Upper Norfolk Co.
Sillingat, Dorothy, 1648, by Lewis Burwell and Thomas Hawes, York
    River Co.
Sillis, Marke, 1650, by Tho. Blogg, Northumberland Co.
Sillito, Roger, 1643, by Wm. Warder, ——— Co.
Sillward, Jon., 1635, by John Moone, Warrasquinoake Co.
Siliston, Kath., 1651, by Humphry Tabb, Northumberland Co.
Silver, Mary, 1643, by John Freeme, Charles Co.
Silvester, Phillipp, 1643, by Wm. Warder, ——— Co.
Silvester, Phillipp, 1642, by Thomas Bagwell, Charles City Co.
Simco, Ann, 1653, by Colo. Wm. Clayborne (Sec. of State), ——— Co.
Simmers, John, 1656, by Herbert Smith, Gent., Westmoreland Co.
Simmons, Oliver, 1638, by Roger Davis, Charles City Co.
Simons, Ed., 1655, by Mr. Anthony Langston, New Kent Co.
Simons, Milicent, 1653, by Richard Pinner, ——— Co.
Simpkin, Edward, 1637, by Theodore Moyser, James City Co.
Simpkins, Ralph, 1636, by Henry Southell, ——— Co.
Simpkins, Ralph, 1637, by Lt. Richard Popeley, New Norfolk Co.
Simpson, Wm., 1637, by Rich. Bennett, New Norfolk Co.
Simpson, John, 1639, by Edward Panderson, ——— Co.
Simpson, Patrick, 1639, by Edward Panderson, ——— Co.
Simpson, Dan., 1654, by James Yates, ——— Co.
Simpson, Tho., 1654, by John Whithers and Stephen Garey, West-
    moreland Co.
Simpson, Ann, 1655, by Mr. Tho. Ballard, Gloucester Co.
Simpson, Edward, 1655, by Francis Clay, Gent., Northumberland Co.
Simpson, Robt., 1637, by Edward Travis, James City Co.
Simpson, Robt., 1638, by Edw. Travis and John Johnson, James City
    Co.
Simpson, William, 1635, by Richard Bennett, ——— Co.
Simpson, James, 1636, by Richard Cocke, ——— Co.
Simpson, John, 1643, by Wm. Morgan, ——— Co.
Simpson, Thomas, 1642, by Christopher Boyce, ——— Co.
Simson, Richard, 1643, by John Batts, James City Co.
Simpson, John, 1652, by Mr. Peter Knight, Gloucester Co.
Simpson, Kath., 1653, by Edward Hall, Lower Norfolk Co.
Simpson, Tho., 1653, by Francis Emperor, Hugh Gale, and Edward
    Morgan, Lower Norfolk Co.
Simpson, Ed., 1653, by Capt. Nathaniel Hurd, Warrick Co.
Simpson, Grace, 1653, by Geo. Taylor, Lancaster Co.
Sims, Andrew, 1635, by Wm. Andrews, Accomac Co.
Sinchard, Jon., 1635, by Mr. Geo. Keth, Charles River Co.

Sinckler, John, 1655, by Lt. Col. Tho. Swan, Surry Co.
Sinckler, Margarett, 1638, by James Warradin, Charles City Co.
Sinckler, Morrice, 1653, by Francis Gray, Charles City Co.
Sinclear, Jean, 1655, by Lt. Col. Tho. Swan, Surry Co.
Sincler, Abrahm, 1656, by John Bromfield, James City Co.
Singleer, Edmund, 1656, by Nathaniel Pope, Gent., Westmoreland Co.
Singleton, Hen., 1637, by John Graves, Elizabeth City Co.
Singleton, Henry, 1651, by Wm. Parry, Northumberland Co.
Singleton, Grace, 1653, by Francis Grey, Charles City Co.
Singleton, John, 1651, by Richard Ripley, —— Co.
Sinill, Thomas, 1642, by John Robins, —— Co.
Sinpiocks, Alex., ——, by Mr. Robt. Fontaine, Lower Norfolk Co.
Sipley, Tho., 1643, by Capt. Thomas Pettus, —— Co.
Sipsone, John, 1653, by Peter Knight and Baker Cutt, —— Co.
Siropp, Alice, 1653, by Richard Braine, Charles Co.
Siscock, Jon., 1637, by Cheney Boyes, Charles City Co.
Sissell, Wm., 1654, by Francis Land, Lower Norfolk Co.
Sivelian, Elinor, 1653, by Wm. Menux and Demetre Murreen, ——
    Co.
Skarfe, Bryan, 1650, by Mr. Anthony Ellyot, —— Co.
Skepp, Math., 1646, by Herbert Smith, Gent., Westmoreland Co.
Skeed, Wm., 1654, by John Thomas, Nansemond Co.
Skepner, Edward, 1650, by Capt. Moore Fautleroy, —— Co.
Skidmore, Augustine, 1638, by Lieut. John Upton, Isle of Wight Co.
Skinham, Wm., 1652, by Capt. Augustine, Warner, —— Co.
Skiddiner, John, 1653, by Peter Knight, Northumberland Co.
Skinner, Robert, 1651, by Wm. Taylor, Northumberland Co.
Skinner, Wm., 1653, by Charles Scarburg, Northampton Co.
Skiffin, Wm., 1650, by Mr. John Hallawes, Northumberland Co.
Skinner, Joane, 1649, by Ronert Moseley, Gent., —— Co.
Skinner, Edw., 1650, by Anthony Ellyot, Gent., —— Co.
Skidd, John, 1650, by Capt. Moore Fautleroy, —— Co.
Skirrick, Thom., 1638, by Capt. Christopher Wormley, Charles River
    Co.
Skinner, Richard, 1655, by Southy Littleberry, Northampton Co.
Skillome, Dorothy, 1638, by John Batts and John Davis, Charles River
    Co.
Skinner, Ruth, 1635, by George Minifie, James City Co.
Skinner, Antho., 1636, by Mr. Georg Menifye, James City Co.
Skinner, Martin, 1643, by John Hoddin, —— Co.
Sknens, William, 1635, by Jeremiah Clement, —— Co.
Slade, Geo., 1654, by Capt. John West, Esq., Gloucester Co.
Shadock, Peter, 1654, by John Sharpe, Lancaster Co.
Slae, Jane, 1653, by Peter Knight, Northumberland Co.
Slaughter, Anne, 1653, by Wm. Thomas, Northumberland Co.
Slanton, Mary, 1653, by Augustine Gillet, Upper Norfolk Co.
Slarkey, Peter, 1649, by Stephen Gill, York Co.
Slate, John, 1653, by Coll. Wm. Taylor, Esq., Gloucester Co.
Slater, Arthur, 1655, by Robt. Nicholson, Charles City Co.
Slater, Leonard, 1639, by Tho. Boulding, Elizabeth City Co.
Slaughter, Dorothy, 1655, by Southy Littleberry, Northampton Co.

Slaughter, Mary, 1656, by Mr. Tho. Purifoy, ——— Co.
Slaughter, Sarah, 1654, by Daniel Boucher, Isle of Wight Co.
Slaughter, Rebecca, 1635, by Charles Harwer,——— Co.
Sled, Henry, 1648, by Richard Lee, Gent., ——— Co.
Sledwell, Tho., 1655, by John Nicholls, Northampton Co.
Sleepway, John, 1649, by Richard Vaughan, Northampton Co.
Sleeve, Ellin, 1648, by Geo. Hardy, ——— Co.
Sleighter, Anne, 1653, by Abraham Moon, Lancaster Co.
Sleerman, Anne, 1652, by Henry Tyler, Charles River Co.
Sley, Undell, 1656, by Tabitha and Matilda Scarburgh, Northampton
     Co.
Slight, George, 1652, by Rice Jones, Lancaster Co.
Slinger, Peter, 1642, by Stephen Gill, Yorke River Co.
Slinton, Wm., 1654, by Peter Knight, Northumberland Co.
Slurly, Agnes, 1637, by Thomas Osborne (Jun.), Henrico Co.
Slye, Jeremiah, 1638, by Robert Freeman, James City Co.
Small, Eliz., 1639, by Justinian Cooper, Isle of Wight Co.
Small, Margarett, 1637, by John Moone, Isle of Wight Co.
Small, Wm., 1651, by Joseph Croshaw, Yorke Co.
Small, Henry, 1636, by Richard Young, Warwick Co.
Smallwood, Jno., 1637, by David Mansell, James City Co.
Smalecomb, Tho., 1647, by John Brooch, York River Co.
Smalernell, Fra., 1656, by Tabitha and Matilda Scarburgh, North-
     ampton Co.
Smalledge, Jon., 1635, by David Mansell, James Co.
Smallodge, Jo., 1635, by Capt. Wm. Pierse, ——— Co.
Smallwood, Mathew, 1652, by John Fleet, Lancaster Co.
Smally, Margarate, 1635, by Capt. William Pierse, ——— Co.
Smarby, Wm., 1650, by Mr. James Williamson, ——— Co.
Smarlort, Wm., 1643, by Wm. Barnard, Esq., Isle of Wight Co.
Smarte, Wm., 1643, by William Batts, ——— Co.
Smart, Wm., 1647, by Jonathan Gills, Northampton Co.
Smart, John, 1653, by Major John Westhrope, Charles City Co.
Smarth, Wm., 1656, by Wm. Millinge, Northampton Co.
Smarts, Tho., 1648, by Major Richard Morrison, Elizabeth City Co.
Smith, Wm., 1637, by Daniell Gookins, New Norfolk Co.
Smith, Jane, 1650, by Lewis Burwell, Gent., ——— Co.
Smith, Robt., 1637, by Daniell Gookins, New Norfolk Co.
Smith, John, 1638, by John Woodliffe, Charles City Co.
Smith, Symon, 1646, by John Brown, Northampton Co.
Smith, John, 1645, by Zachary Cripps, Warwick Co.
Smith, Hester, 1645, by Zachary Cripps, Warwick Co.
Smith, Massey, 1650, by Richard Dunning, ——— Co.
Smith, George, 1646, by Lancaster Levilt, ——— Co.
Smith, Gabriell, 1643, by Tho. Faylor, Warwick Co.
Smith, John, 1637, by Zacheriah Cripps, Warwick River Co.
Smith, John, 1637, by Francis Fowler, James River Co.
Smith, Edward, 1637, by Francis Fowler, James River Co.
Smith, Mary, 1635, by Richard Durrant, James Co.
Smith, Jon., 1635, by Francis Fowler, James City Co.
Smith, Henry, 1642, by Joseph Royall, ——— Co.

Smith, Katherine (wife), 1642, by Joseph Royall, ——— Co.
Smith, Saunders, 1641, by Wm. Storey, Upper Norfolk Co.
Smith, Thomas, 1635, by William Spencer, ——— Co.
Smith, Richard, 1635, by Robert Bennett, ——— Co.
Smith, Ann, 1636, by Thos. Smith, Accomack Co.
Smith, Sarah, 1636, by Thomas Smith, Accomack Co.
Smith, Joseph, 1637, by Henry Poole, New Norfolk Co.
Smith, Rich., 1637, by Henry Perry, Charles River Co.
Smith, Thomas, 1637, by Robert Taylor, New Norfolk Co.
Smith, Grace, 1637, by Thomas Weston, Charles River Co.
Smith, Thos., 1637, by William Spencer, ——— Co.
Smith, James, 1637, by Justinian Cooper, Isle of Wight Co.
Smith, Richard, 1637, by Justinian Cooper, Isle of Wight Co.
Smith, Rich., 1637, by Robert Bennett, New Norfolk Co.
Smith, Martha, 1638, by Georg White, clerk, Upper New Norfolk Co.
Smith, Rebecca, 1637, by Robt. Martin, Lower New Norfolk Co.
Smith, Richard, 1643, by Mr. John Bishopp, James City Co.
Smith, John, 1639, by Edward Oliver, James City Co.
Smith, Rich., 1638, by Joseph Harmon, James City Co.
Smith, Alice, 1637, by Arthur Smith, Isle of Wight Co.
Smith, Tho., 1643, by Phillipp Taylor, Northampton Co.
Smith, Thos., 1638, by William Croutch, Lower Norfolk Co.
Smith, Alice, 1642, by John King, Charles River Co.
Smith, Tho., 1655, by Lt. Col. Thomas Swan, Surry Co.
Smith, John, 1653, by Fredinando Austin, Charles City Co.
Smith, Sarah, 1653, by Mr. Edmund Bowman, ——— Co.
Smith, Robt., 1655, by Dr. Giles Mode, New Kent Co.
Smith, John, 1655, by Capt. Henry Fleet, ——— Co.
Smith, Mary, 1655, by Mr. Anthony Langston, New Kent Co.
Smith, John, 1655, by Jenkin Price, Northampton Co.
Smith, Jno., 1655, by Mr. Wm. Nutt, Northumberland Co.
Smith, Wm., 1655, by Mr. Tho. Ballard, Gloucester Co.
Smith, James, 1655, by Mr. Tho. Ballard, Gloucester Co.
Smith, Robt., 1654, by John William, Northumberland Co.
Smith, Sarah, 1656, by Margaret Miles, Westmoreland Co.
Smith, Jno., 1656, by Mr. Martin Baker, New Kent Co.
Smith, Ann, 1656, by James Price, Northampton Co.
Smith, Ann, 1656, by John Billiott, Northampton Co.
Smith, John, Jr., 1656, by Maj. Wm. Lewis, ——— Co.
Smith, John, Sr., 1656, by Major Wm. Lewis, ——— Co.
Smith, Robert, 1655, by George Kibble, ——— Co.
Smith, John, 1655, by Wm. Wright, Gent., Nansemond Co.
Smith, Daniel, 1654, by Francis Smith and Mr. John Smith, Westmoreland Co.
Smith, Mary, 1654, by Capt. Augustine Warner and Mr. John Robins, ——— Co.
Smith, Mary, 1654, by Humphry Dennis, Gloucester Co.
Smith, Mary, 1656, by Mr. Jno. Paine, ——— Co.
Smith, Robt., 1656, by Daniel Jaines and Jno. Jenings, ——— Co.
Smith, Tho., 1656, by John Wood, ——— Co.
Smith, Richard, 1655, by Southy Littleberry, Northampton Co.

Smith, Geo., 1655, by Southy Littleberry, Northampton Co.
Smith, Richard, 1655, by Southy Littleberry, Northampton Co.
Smith, Sarah, 1656, by Nicholas Smith (her husband), Isle of Wight Co.
Smith, John, 1654, by Alexander Portus and Tho. Williams, Lancaster Co.
Smith, Jeffery, 1654, by Arthur Nash, New Kent Co.
Smith, Sarah, 1654, by Edward Simpson, New Kent Co.
Smith, Eliz., 1654, by Richard Codsford, Westmoreland Co.
Smith, Ann, 1654, by Capt. Nich. Marteaw, Westmoreland Co.
Smith, John, 1654, by Wm. Beach, Westmoreland Co.
Smith, Geo., 1654, by Robert Yoe, Westmoreland Co.
Smith, John, Sr., 1654, by Rich. Bunduch, Northampton Co.
Smith, Phillis, 1654, by Rich. Bunduch, Northampton Co.
Smith, John, Jr., 1654, by Rich. Bunduch, Northampton Co.
Smith, George, 1654, by Rich. Bunduch, Northampton Co.
Smith, Ann, 1654, by Rich. Bunduch, Northampton Co.
Smith, Tho., 1654, by Tho. Salsbury, Lancaster Co.
Smith, Eliz., 1654, by John Wyre, John Gillet, Andrew Gilson and John Phillipps, ——— Co.
Smith, Rich., 1637, by Henry Perry, Charles River Co.
Smith, Symon, 1642, by John Browne, Accomac Co.
Smith, Thomas, 1638, by Rich. Hill and Roger Armwood, James City Co.
Smith, John, 1638, by Edward Oliver, ——— Co.
Smith, John, 1639, by Richard Corke, Gent., Henrico Co.
Smith, John, and three wives, Alice, Eliz., and Sarah, 1642, by John Smith, James City Co.
Smith, Mary, 1642, by William Lawson, Isle of Wight Co.
Smith, Tho., 1638, by Georg Mynifie (merchant), ——— Co.
Smith, Edw., 1639, by William Wigg, ——— Co.
Smith, William, 1641, by Ambrose Bennett, Isle of Wight Co.
Smith, Henry, 1639, by Samuell Jackson, Isle of Wight Co.
Smith, James, 1639, by Henry Perry, Charles City Co.
Smith, Georg, 1639, by Tho. Symons, James City Co.
Smith, John, 1639, by John Smith and Christo. Bea, Elizabeth City Co.
Smith, Sarah, 1639, by Thomas Smith (her husband), Accomac Co.
Smith, Ann, 1639, by Tho. Smith (her father), Accomac Co.
Smith, Richard, 1639, by Henry Bogwell, Accomack Co.
Smith, Henry, 1639, by Lieut. Richard Popeley, ——— Co.
Smith, John, 1639, by Edward Oliver, James City Co.
Smith, 1639, by Capt. Nichloas Martian, Charles River Co.
Smith, Tho., 1652, by Tho. Todd, ——— Co.
Smith, Eliza., 1653, by Capt. Francis Morgan, Gloucester Co.
Smith, John, 1652, by Mrs. Jane Harmer, Northumberland Co.
Smith, Will, 1653, by Coll. Wm. Taylor, Esq., Gloucester Co.
Smith, James, 1652, by Gregory Parrett, Lower Norfolk Co.
Smith, Thos., 1640, by William Hampton, Isle of Wight Co.
Smith, Tho., 1652, by Teague Floyne, Lancaster Co.
Smith, Alexand., 1653, by John Holding, York Co.
Smith, Tho., 1652, by Wm. Gautlett, ——— Co.

Smith, Saml., ——, by Mr. John Page, —— Co.
Smith, Nicho., 1652, by Joseph Gregory, —— Co.
Smith, Wm., 1653, by John Earle, Northumberland Co.
Smith, Mary, 1654, by Richard Budd, —— Co.
Smith, Eliz., 1653, by Wm. Walker, Northumberland Co.
Smith, John, 1651, by Coll. Richard Lee, Esq., Gloucester Co.
Smith, Richard, 1651, by Robert Abrall, Yorke Co.
Smith, Wm., 1653, by Nathaniel Hickmon, Northumberland Co.
Smith, Jon., 1653, by Capt. Natha. Hurd, Warrick Co.
Smith, Tho., 1653, by James Bonner, Lancaster Co.
Smith, Geo., 1653, by Joseph Croshaw, York Co.
Smith, Geo., 1653, by Frances Emperor, Hugh Gale and Edward Morgan, Lower Norfolk Co.
Smith, John, 1653, by John Shepperd, Northumberland Co.
Smith, Kath., 1653, by Charles Scraburg, Northampton Co.
Smith, George, 1652, by John Robbins, Northampton Co.
Smith, John, 1652, by Henry Hoodhouse, Lower Norfolk Co.
Smith, George, 1653, by Elias Hartru, Northampton Co.
Smith, Joyce, 1652, by Edward Revell, Northampton Co.
Smith, Tho., 1651, by Joseph Croshaw, Yorke Co.
Smith, Alex., 1651, by Capt. Stephen Gill, Northumberland Co.
Smith, Peter, 1651, by Thomas Thornbrough, Northumberland Co.
Smith, Thomas, 1651, by Wm. Hampton, —— Co.
Smith, Jane, 1651, by Wm. Rennales, Northumberland Co.
Smith, John, 1651, by Richard Coleman, Yorke Co.
Smith, John, 1651, by Mrs. Anna Bernard, Northumberland Co.
Smith, Mary, 1651, by Phillip Charles, James City Co.
Smith, Tho., 1650, by James Hurd, —— Co.
Smith, Mary, 1651, by Plamer Hinton, —— Co.
Smith, Alexander, 1651, by Wm. Vincent, Northumberland Co.
Smith, James, 1651, by Wm. Vincent, Northumberland Co.
Smith, Ann, 1651, by Richard Smith, Northampton Co.
Smith, Richard, 1650, by Mr. Robt. Holt, James City Co.
Smith, Richard, 1651, by John Adleston, —— Co.
Smith, Wm., 1651, by Robert Holt, James City Co.
Smith, James, 1648, by John Smith, Lower Norfolk Co.
Smith, Nicho., 1647, by Symon Symons, Nansemond Co.
Smith, Eliza., 1648, by Tho. Lambert, Lower Norfolk Co.
Smith, Phil., 1648, by Richard Pettibon, —— Co.
Smith, Sarah, 1649, by Stephen Gill, York Co.
Smith, Fra., 1649, by Stephen Gill, York Co.
Smith, Nicho., 1649, by Mr. Wm. Hoccaday, —— Co.
Smith, Rich., 1649, by Stephen Gill, York Co.
Smith, Geo., 1648, by George Read, Gent., —— Co.
Smith, Richard, 1649, by Capt. Ralph Wormeley, —— Co.
Smith, Margary, 1648, by Bartholomew Hoskins, —— Co.
Smite, John, 1649, by Nicholas Waddilowe, Northampton Co.
Smith, Wm., 1649, by Francis Brown, Northumberland Co.
Smith, John, 1648, by Lewis Burwell, Gent., —— Co.
Smith, Henry, 1650, by Nicho. Jernew, Yorke Co.
Smith, Richard, 1652, by Mr. Edwin Connaway, —— Co.

Smith, Wm., 1652, by Edward Cole, Northumberland Co.
Smith, John, 1653, by Tho. Hawkins, Northumberland Co.
Smith, Alex., 1653, by Jno. Robinson, Lancaster Co.
Smith, John, 1652, by Mrs. Anna Barnett, Gloucester Co.
Smith, Wm., 1652, by Anthony Doney and Enoch Hawker, Lancaster Co.
Smith, Richard, 1652, by Anthony Doney and Enoch Hawker, Lancaster Co.
Smith, Daniel, 1652, by Tho. Hoane, ——— Co.
Smith, Wm., 1646, by Joseph Croshawe, Charles River Co.
Smith, Richard, 1650, by Capt. Moore Fautleroy, ——— Co.
Smith, Symon, 1650, by John Brown, Northampton Co.
Smith, Geo., 1650, by Edward Walker, Northumberland Co.
Smith, Cassairainjews, 1650, by Sr. Tho. Luntsford, Kt., and Barron-nett, ——— Co.
Smith, Wm., 1650, by David Peibles, Charles City Co.
Smith, Wm., 1650, by Richard Tye and Charles Sparrowe, Charles City Co.
Smith, Edward, 1643, by Tho. Evans, ——— Co.
Smith, Tho., 1643, by Thomas Wheeler, Charles City Co.
Smith, Henry, 1650, by Nicholas Jernew, Gent., ——— Co.
Smith, Symon, 1650, by John Browne, Northampton Co.
Smith, John, 1650, by Silvester Thatcher and Tho. Whitlocke, ——— Co.
Smith, Susanah, 1650 ,by John Major, Northampton Co.
Smith, Hannah, 1650, by Samuell Smith (her husband), Northumber-land Co.
Smith, Richard, 1647, by James Warradine, ——— Co.
Smith, Jon., 1643, by Capt. Samuell Mathews, Esq., ——— Co.
Smith, Silvester, 1643, by Capt. Samuell Mathews, Esq., ——— Co.
Smith, Jo., 1647, by Richard Bland, ——— Co.
Smith, Richard, 1646, by Samuell Abbott, Nansemond Co.
Smith Richard, 1648, by Lewis Burwell and Tho. Haws, York River Co.
Smith, Uryas, 1648, by Lewis Burwell and Tho. Haws, York River Co.
Smith, John, 1654, by Sr. Henry Chickly, Kt., Lancaster Co.
Smith, John, 1653, by Richard Burton, ——— Co.
Smith, Wm., 1654, by Edw. Welch, ——— Co.
Smith, Nich., 1654, by John Watson and John Bognall, Westmoreland Co.
Smith, Ann, 1654, by John Watson and John Bognall, Westmoreland Co.
Smith, Geo., 1643, by Tho. Symonds, ——— Co.
Smith, James, 1642, by Justinian Cooper, Isle of Wight Co.
Smith, Wm., 1643, by Banjemin Harryson, Gent., James City Co.
Smith, Tho., 1643, by Benjamin Harryson, Gent., James City Co.
Smith, Robert, 1650, by Capt. Charles Leech, Yorke Co.
Smith, Ann, 1650, by Richard Smith, Northampton Co.
Smith, Wm., 1650, by Mrs. Frances Townshend (widow), Northumber-land Co.
Smith, Tho., 1642, by Richard Maior, Charles River Co.

Smith, Henry, 1642, by Adam Cooke, Charles County.
Smith, Samuell, 1642, by Adam Cooke Charles County.
Smith, Richard, 1645, by Justinian Cooper, Gent., Isle of Wight Co.
Smith, Lew., 1636, by Bridges Freeman, ——— Co.
Smith, Grace, 1635, by Samuel Weaver, ——— Co.
Smith, Rich., 1635, by Justinian Cooper, Warrasquinoake Co.
Smith, James, 1636, by Justinian Cooper, Warrasquinoak Co.
Smith, Jon., 1636, by Epaphroditus Lawson, Warwick Co.
Smith, Eliz., 1635, by Henry Coleman, Elizabeth Co.
Smith, Robert, 1635, by Thomas Harwood, ——— Co.
Smith, Thomas, 1635, by Thomas Harwood, ——— Co.
Smith, Thomas, 1635, by McWilliam Stone, ——— Co.
Smith, William, 1635, by Josepe Johnson, ——— Co.
Smith, James, 1635, by John Armie, Warrasquinoake Co.
Smith, James, 1635, by Richard Bennett, ——— Co.
Smith, Hen., 1635, by Francis Fowler, James City Co.
Smith, John, 1636, by Richard Cocke, ——— Co.
Smith, Thos., 1636, by Robt Hollom, Henrico Co.
Smith, Anne, 1635, by McWilliam Stone, ——— Co.
Smith, Jon., 1637, by Wm. Farrar, Henrico Co.
Smith, James, 1637, by Rich. Bennett, New Norfolk Co.
Smith, Ursula, 1637, by William Frye, James City Co.
Smith, Jarvis, 1637, by Thomas Hampton, New Norfolk Co.
Smith, Toby, 1637, by Thomas Holt, New Norfolk Co.
Smith, Williams, 1637, by Thomas Holt, New Norfolk Co.
Smith, Rich., 1636, by John Neale, Accomack Co.
Smith, Katharine, 1636, by John Neale, Accomack Co.
Smith, Wm., 1637, by Theodore Moyser, James City Co.
Smith, Thomas, 1635, by Capt. Adam Thoroughgood, ——— Co.
Smith, Tho., 1637, by Bridges Freeman, James City Co.
Smith, Jon., 1637, by Wm. Farrar, Henrico Co.
Smith, Eliz., 1653, by Richard Carey, ——— Co.
Smith, William, 1651, by Henry Hackery, ——— Co.
Smith, Fra., 1651, by Richard Grigson, ——— Co.
Smith, Robert, 1651, by Mr. Rowland Lawson, ——— Co.
Smith, Wm., 1651, by Mr. Wm. Armestead, ——— Co.
Smith, Edw., 1651, by Toby Norton, Northampton Co.
Smith, Tho., 1653, by Major John Westhrope, Charles City Co.
Smith, Mary, 1653, by Tho. Cowlinge, ——— Co.
Smith, Rich., 1653, by John Phillips, ——— Co.
Smith, John and Mary, his wife, 1653, by Tho. Scoggin, Northumber-
    land Co.
Smith, John and Joan, his wife, 1653, by Edward Dobson, ——— Co.
Smithson, Wm., 1652, by Nicholas Waddilow, Northampton Co.
Smith, Law., 1652, by Capt. Augustine Warner, ——— Co.
Smith, Aphroh., 1652, by John Robinson, Jr., Northampton Co.
Smith, Wm. Tho., 1652, by John Robinson, Jr., Northampton Co.
Smith, Kath., 1652, by Mr. Tho. Teagle, Northampton Co.
Smith, Ursela, 1652, by Peter Knight, Gloucester Co.
Smith, John, 1652, by Peter Knight, Gloucester Co.
Smith, Tho., 1652, by Henry Fleete, Lancaster Co.

Smith, Tho., 1652, by Ambrose Dixon and Stephen Horsely, Jr., North-
ampton Co.
Smith, Richard, 1652, by Tho. Hoane, ——— Co.
Smister, Hugh, 1649, by Mr. Wm. Hoccaday, ——— Co.
Smithark, Henry, 1636, by John Oberry, ——— Co.
Smithcock, Henry, 1639, by Rose Oberye, ——— Co.
Smither, Geo., 1653, by Richard Starnell, ——— Co.
Smither, Geo., 1652, by Robert Elam, Henrico Co.
Smithfield, Hen., 1642, by Stephen Gill, ——— Co.
Smithell, Wm., 1642, by Stephen Gill, ——— Co.
Smithson, Tho., 1654, by John Cox., Lancaster Co
Smithson, Wm., 1656, by Nicholas Waddilow, Notrhampton Co.
Smithwick, Hugh, 1642, by Wm. Eyres, Upper New Norfolk Co.
Smithwood, Rob., 1652, by Mr. Tho. Gutheridge, Lower Norfolk Co.
Smithvest, Edw., 1643, by Richard Kemp, Esq., James City Co.
Smyth, John, 1643, by John Batts, James City Co.
Smyth, Richd., 1649, by Wm. Nesum, Tho. Sox, Miles Bathasby and
John Pyne, Northampton Co.
Smythwood, Robt., 1647, by Thomas Wright, Lower Norfolk Co.
Smycott, Jno., 1650, by Thomas Powell, ——— Co.
Smylewood, Symon, 1652, by Anthony Doney and Enoch Hawker,
Lancaster Co.
Snackson, Monte, 1638, by Sarah Cloyden, Isle of Wight Co.
Snapes, Wm., 1653, by Richard Lee, Lancaster Co,
Snea, Richard, 1636, by Wm. Rainshaw, Elizabeth City Co.
Sneade, Robt., 1654, by John Wyre, John Gillett, Andrew Gilson and
John Phillipps, ——— Co.
Sneade, John, 1652, by Mrs. Elnor Brocas, Lancaster Co.
Sneade, Alice, 1635, by Samuel Sneade, James Co.
Sneade, Wm., 1635, by Samuel Sneadc, James Co.
Sneale, Dorothy, 1636, by Richard Young, Warwick Co.
Sneale, Eliz., 1636, by Richard Young, Warwick Co.
Sneale, Alice, 1636, by Richard Young, Warwick Co.
Sneale, Elizabeth, 1636, by Richard Young, Warwick Co.
Sneale, John, 1636, by Richard Young, Warwick Co.
Sneldon, Dyana, 1649, by Robert Mosely, Gent., ——— Co.
Snelgreene, Susan, 1639, by John Osborne, James Cittie Co.
Snell, Jno., 1656, by John Curtis, Gloucester Co.
Snelling, Richd., 1653, by Jno. Edwards, Lancaster Co.
Snellinge, Jno., 1653, by Edward Dobson, ——— Co.
Snellocke, Jon., 1643, by Capt. Wm. Peirce, Esq., ——— Co.
Sneyre, Jane, 1648, by Randall Crew, Nansemond Co.
Snoddy, Dan., 1654, by Tho. Willoughby, Lower Norfolk Co.
Snodell, Wm., 1654, by Phillip Chesly and Dan. Wilde, York Co.
Snow, George, 1649, by John Walthams, Northampton Co.
Snead, Peter, 1654, by Francis Gray, ——— Co.
Snow, Martha, 1637, by John Upton, Isle of Wight Co.
Snow, Hen., 1638, by William Carter, James City Co.
Snow, Martha, 1637, by Lt. John Upton, Isle of Wight Co.
Snow, Henry, 1635, by William Carter, Henrico Co.
Snow, Tho., 1654, by Sinkler, Pagett, Nansemond Co.

Snowe, Mary, 1650, by Lewis, Burwell Gent., ——— Co.
Snowe, Fran., 1650, by Lewis Burwell, Gent., ——— Co.
Snowe, Tho., 1651, by James Foster, Nansemond Co.
Snowson, John, 1641, by William Yarrett, New Norfolk Co.
Soane, Judith, Jr., 1651, by Henry Soane, James City Co.
Soane, Jiudth, Sr., 1651, by Henry Soane, James City Co.
Soane, John, 1651, by Henry Soane, James City Co.
Soane, Eliza., 1651, by Henry Soane, James City Co.
Sockbone, James, 1654, by Tho. Harmanosn, Northampton Co.
Soleacut, Dennis, 1655, by Tho. Leatherberry, Northampton Co.
Solbey, Tho., 1652, by Mr. John Brown, Northampton Co.
Soll, Augues, 1650, by Mr. Epaphroditus Lawson, ——— Co.
Sollis, Roger, 1652, by Nichols Sebrell, York Co.
Somerfale, Thos., 1638, by William Clarke, Henrico Co.
Somersate, Thomas, 1636, by Wm. Clarke, Henrico Co.
Somers, Alexander, 1655, by Gilbert Deacon, Henrico Co.
Somerton, Jon., 1654, by Robert Holt, James City Co.
Soper, Greg., 1637, by Arhutr Smith, Isle of Wight Co.
Soopson, Tho., 1648, by Geo. Hardy, Tho. Wombwell and Peter Hall, Isle of Wight Co.
Sooter, John, 1649, by Wm. Peerce and Frances Symons, Northumberland Co.
Sorrell, John, 1652, by Francis Fleetwood, Lower Norfolk Co.
Sorrell, Robt., 1652, by Francis Fleetwood, Lower Norfolk Co.
Sorrell, John, 1647, by Thomas Wright, Lower Norfolk Co.
Sorrel, Robt., 1653, by Richard Carey, ——— Co.
Sorrell, Robt., 1651, by Thomas Keeling, Lower Norfolk Co.
Sorrell, Robt., 1647, by Thomas Wright, Lower Norfolk Co.
Sorwell, Wm., and Eliz., his wife, 1643, by Edward Murfey and John Vaughan, ——— Co.
Souchack, Philip, 1655, by Arthur Upshott, Northampton Co.
Soule, Wm., 1652, by Mr. Wm. Warters, Northampton Co.
Southurn, Tho., 1653, by Francis Grey, Charles City Co.
Southerne, Sarah, 1655, by Tho. Welsford, Gent., Westmoreland Co.
Southerland, Ajex., 1654, by Mr. Francis Hamond, York Co.
South, Jno., 1656, by Daniel Jaines and Jno. Jenings, ——— Co.
South, Wm., 1655, by Wm. Steevens, Northampton Co.
South, John, 1655, by George Kibble, ——— Co.
Southern, Thos. 1656, by Nihcolas Waddilow, Northampton Co.
Southerland, Gil., 1655, by John Synge, James City Co.
Southerland, Gilbert, 1655, by Henry Barlow, ——— Co.
Southerwood, Isaac, 1642, by Samuell Abbott, ——— Co.
Southerne, Thomas, 1635, by William Clark, Warrasquinoake Co.
South, John, 1650, by Capt. Charles Leech, Yorke Co.
Southerne, Edward, 1647, by Stephen Harsey, and Nich. Waddilow Northampton Co.
Southerby, Dan., 1653, by Joseph Hogkinson, Lower Norfolk Co.
Southerne, Edwd., 1649, by Nicholas Waddilowe, Northampton Co.
Southerwood, Is., 1652, by Mr. Edmond Overman, York Co.
Spaine, Tho., 1641, by Richard Jackson, Isle of Wight Co.
Spalding, Tho., ———, by Mr. Wm. Presly, Northumberland Co.

Spach, Edward, 1642, by Luce Webster, York Co.
Spackman, Nath., 1637, by Capt. Thomas Osborne, Henrico Co.
Spackman, Rich., 1637, by John Upton, Isle of Wight Co.
Spackman, Rich., 1635, by Jno. Upton, Warrasquinoake Co.
Spackman, Dorothy, 1635, by John Spackman (her husband), Warrasquinoake Co.
Spackman, Joyce, 1635, by John Spackman (her father), Warrasquinoake Co.
Spackman, Rosamond, 1635, by John Spackman, Warrasquinoake Co.
Spackford, Wm., 1638, by Thomas Sawyer, New Norfolk Co.
Spare, Alice, 1635, by Josepe Johnson, ——— Co.
Sparlocke, Mary, 1652, by Joane Yates, Lower Norfolk Co.
Sparke, Sarah, 1654, by Robert Yoe, Westmoreland Co.
Sparke, Anne, 1635, by Capt. Adam Thoroughgood, ——— Co.
Spacke, Mr. Tho., 1649, by Tho. Spoke, Gent., Northumberland Co.
Sparks, Thomas, 1638, by Edmund Scarborough, Accomac Co.
Sparks, Frances, 1638, by John Robins, James City Co.
Sparkes, Jon. (a servant), 1635, by Wm. Gary, Accomac Co.
Sparkes, Grace, 1635, by Jno. Sparkes, ——— Co.
Sparks, John, 1635, by Capt. Wm. Pierse, ——— Co.
Sparkes, Mary, 1635, by Jno. Sparkes, ——— Co.
Sparkes, Culbert, 1650, by Wm. Clapham, ——— Co.
Sparks, John, 1653, by Wm. Wyatt, Gloucester Co.
Sparkes, Elizabeth, 1650, by Henry Lee and Wm. Clapham, ——— Co.
Sparkes, Wm., 1651, by Joseph Croshaw, Yorke Co.
Sparkman, Nicho., 1650, by Capt. Moore Fautleroy, ——— Co.
Sparrow, Thomas, 1637, by James Knott, New Norfolk Co.
Sparrow, Thos., 1636, by James Knott, Elizabeth City Co.
Sparrow Alice, 1654, by Phillip Chesly and Dan. Wilde, York Co.
Sparrow, John, 1653, by Nicholas Perry, Charles City Co.
Sparshott, Edw., Sen., 1638, by Edw. Sparshott, Charles City Co.
Sparshott, Edw., Jr., 1638, by Edward Sparshott, Charles City Co.
Sparshott, Edw., Sen., 1638, by Edward Sparshott, Charles City Co.
Spatch, Edward, 1646, by Lucy Webster, Judith and Jame Webster, James City Co.
Spayford, Jno., 1649, by Robert Mosely, Gent., ——— Co.
Speare, Robert, 1653, by Wm. Blackey, ——— Co.
Spearman, Jam., 1650, by William Gooch, Gent., ——— Co.
Speckman, Tho., 1653, by John Ware, ——— Co.
Speechly, Eliz., 1650, by Wm. Clapham, ——— Co.
Speed, Jeffry, 1655, by John Cool, James City Co.
Speed, Robert, 1649, by Mr. Robert Parker, Northampton Co.
Speevy, Geo., 1643, by Thomas Dew, Upper Norfolk Co.
Speich, Wm., 1635, by Capt. Adam Thoroughgood, ——— Co.
Speight, Francis, 1642, by Wm. Eyres, Upper New Norfolk Co.
Spell, George, 1656, by John Rosier, Clarke, Westmoreland Co.
Spences, John, 1649, by Mr. Robert Parker, Northampton Co.
Spence, Robt., 1654, by Edward Simpson, New Kent Co.
Spence, Richard, 1651, by Joseph Croshaw, Yorke Co.
Spence, Wm., 1653, by John Bennett, of Normany, Northumberland Co.

Spencer, William, 1638, by Oliver Sprye, Upper New Norfolk Co.
Spencer, Mary, 1655, by Wm. Wright, Gent., Nansemond Co.
Spencer, John, 1656, by Richard Barnhouse, Gent., James City Co.
Spencer, Kath., 1643, by Sir Francis Wyatt, Kt., ——— Co.
Spencer, Jane, 1652, by Mr. George Clapham, ——— Co.
Spencer, Edwd., 1649, by Tho. Dale, ——— Co.
Spencer, Jon., 1638, by Mr. Thomas Wallis, James City Co.
Spencer, Ralph, 1649, by Jospeh Croshawe, Yorke Co.
Spencer, Nicholas, 1637, by William Spencer, ——— Co.
Spencer, Robt., 1651, by George Eaton, ——— Co.
Spencer, Alice, 1652, by Clement Thrush, ——— Co.
Spencer, Edw., 1648, by John Landman, Nansimond Co.
Spencer, Nicholas, 1635, by William Spencer, ——— Co.
Spencer, Wm., 1642, by Thomas Loving, James City Co.
Spencer, Susan, 1653, by John Earle, Northumberland Co.
Spencer, Francis, 1643, by John Foster, Northampton Co.
Spencer, Fran., 1652, by Tho. Hallinard, ——— Co.
Spendlowe, Ralph, 1653, by Mr. Wm. Fry, James City Co.
Spenke, Robt., 1637, by Arthur Boyly and Tho. Crosby, Henrico Co.
Spenne, Richard, 1649, by Wm. Hoccaday, ——— Co.
Spering, Joseph, 1638, by Lieut. Robt. Sheppard, James City Co.
Spice, Georg., 1638, by John Robins, James City Co.
Spicer, Peter, 1656, by Tho. Busby, Surry Co.
Spicer, Edward, 1643, by William Batts, ——— Co.
Spicer, Edward, 1645, by Mr. Bartholomew Hoskins, ——— Co.
Spicer, Sam., 1653, by Charles Gyrmes, Clerk, Lancaster Co.
Spiltimber, John, 1635, by Thomas Harwood, ——— Co.
Spilman, Ann, 1655, by Hugh Yeo., Northampton Co.
Spin., Roger, 1654, by Rich Bunduch, Northampton Co.
Spincke, Tho., 1646, by Col. Henry Bishopp, James City Co.
Spittlewood, Sarah, 1646, by Geo. Ludlow, Esq., York Co.
Spockman, Rich., 1637, by Lt. John Upton, Isle of Wight Co.
Spooner, Wm., 1650, by Andrew Gilson, ——— Co.
Sporling, Richard, 1650, by James Metgrigar and Hugh Foutch, North-
  umberland Co.
Spratt, Charles, 1651, by Mr. Wm. Armestead, ——— Co.
Spragon, Ja., 1653, by Capt. Natha. Hurd, Warrick Co.
Spraklin, Robert, 1649, by Nicholas Waddilowe, Northampton Co.
Sprand, Margarett, Sr., 1651, by Thomas Watts, Jr., Northumberland
  Co.
Sprand, Margarett, Jr., 1651, by Thomas Watts, Jr., Northumberland
  Co.
Sprason, Wm., 1636, by Georg Travellor, Accomack Co.
Spreatt, John, 1653, by Peter Knight and Baker Cutt, ——— Co.
Spring ,Rose, ———, Mr. Robt. Fontaine, Lower Norfolk Co.
Spring, Rose, 1651, by John Mantin and (Lancaster Lovett), Lower
  Norfolk Co.
Spring, Joseph, 1635, by William Clard, Warrasquinoake Co.
Spring, Robt., 1635, by Capt. Adam Thoroughgood, ——— Co.
Spring, Paul, 1653, by James Magregory and Hugh Hauch, Northumber-
  land Co.

Spring, Joan, 1653, by James Magregory and Hugh Fauch, Northumberland Co.
Spring, Ro., 1652, by Toby Smith, Gent., Lancaster Co.
Springwell, Alice, 1653, by Symon Peeters, Lower Norfolk Co.
Sprogge, Edw., 1650, by Geo. Ludlow, Gent., Northumberland Co.
Sprons, John, 1649, by Joseph Croshawe, Yorke Co.
Sprouce, Alice, 1642, by Tho. Guyer, ——— Co.
Spry, Wm., 1648, by Lewis Burwell and Tho. Haws, York River Co.
Sprye, Oliver, 1639, by Richard Parsons, Lower New Norfolk Co.
Sprye, Oliver, 1636, by Oliver Sprye, Warrisquinoak Co.
Spuer, Margarett, 1643, by Sir Francis Wyatt, Kt., ——— Co.
Spure, Bridgett, 1650, by Richard Tye and Charles Sparrowe, Charles City Co.
Spurnell, Richard, 1653, by Peter Knight and Baker Cutt, ——— Co.
Spurjoye, Georg. 1639, by Edward Prince, Charles City Co.
Spurrier, Michael, 1635, by Richard Peirce, Jamse City Co.
Spurway, John, 1637, by Leonard Yeo, Elizabeth City Co.
Square, John, 1654, by Tho. Harmanson, Northampton Co.
Squire, John, 1654, by Major Miles Carey, Westmoreland Co.
Squire, Robt., 1637, by John Baker, Charles City Co.
Squires, Nich., 1654 by, Major Wm. Andrews, Northamptin Co.
Squire, Wm., 1656, by Richard Barnhouse, Gent., James City Co.
Stacie, Geo., 1642, by Justinian Cooper, Isle of Wight Co.
Stacie, Eliz., 1643, by John Wall, ——— Co.
Stacy, Tho., 1656, by Mr. Martin Baker, New Kent Co.
Stacy, Geo., 1637, by Justinian Cooper, Isle of Wight Co.
Stacy, Geo., 1636, by Justinian Cooper, Warrasquinoake Co.
Stafford, Peter, 1653, by Mr. Henry Soanes, Gloucester Co.
Stafford, Christs, 1635, by William Stafford, ——— Co.
Stafford, Rebecca, 1635, by William Stafford, ——— Co.
Staimes, Geo., 1653, by Denis Coniers, Lancaster Co.
Stakes, Jane, 1653, by John King, Surry Co.
Stalling, Nich., 1638, by Thomas Swan, James Citie Co.
Stallings, Nich. and wife, 1655, by Wm. Wright, Gent., Nansemond Co.
Stalmy, Wm., 1650, by John Mangor, ——— Co.
Stamey, Robt., 1636, by Wm. Eyres, Warrasquinoake Co.
Stanbye, John, 1639, by William Burdett, Accomack Co.
Standy, Hugh, 1642, by Edmund Scarburgh, Accomack Co.
Staininbrow, John, 1654, by Alexander Portus and Tho. Williams, Lancaster Co.
Stamner, Ann, 1650, by Jervace Dodson, Gent., Northumberland Co.
Standly, Alice, 1654, by Francis Smith and Mr. John Smith, Westmoreland Co.
Stanforb, Hugh, 1653, by Joseph Croshaw, York Co.
Stanford, Nell, 1652, by Capt. Tho. Hackett, Lancaster Co.
Stanford, Ann, 1637, by Henry Perry, Charles River Co.
Standford, Abraham, 1654, by Fra. Spright, Nansemond Co.
Stanford, Vincent, 1656, by Richard Gible, Northumberland Co.
Stanford, Ann, 1655, by Mr. Anthony Langston, New Kent Co.
Stanford, Ann, 1637, by Henry Perry, Charles River Co.
Stanfast, Mary, 1652, by John Robinson, Jr., Northampton Co.

Stanfast, James, 1652, by John Robinson, Jr., Northampton Co.
Stang, Robert, 1642, by Wm. Eyres, Upper New Norfolk Co.
Stankey, Francis, 1650, by John Cox, ——— Co.
Stanks, James, 1642, by Abraham English, ——— Co.
Standish, Geo., 1643, by Rich. Hoe, Gent., ——— Co.
Standish, Dorothy, 1638, by Wm. Barker and Associates, Charles City Co.
Standish, Stephen, 1637, by Francis Fowler, James River Co.
Stanfield, Symon, 1635, by Capt. Adam Thoroughgood, ——— Co.
Standish, Dorothy, 1635, by William Barber (a mariner), Charles City Co.
Standish, Ja., 1646, by Henry Sedenden, Northampton Co.
Stanley, Christopher, 1652, by Ambrose Dixon and Stephen Horsely, Jr., Northampton Co.
Stanley, Wm., 1648, by John Baldwin, Northampton Co.
Stanley, Wm., 1649, by Nicholas Waddilow, Northampton Co.
Stanley, Alice, 1652, by Tho. Hoane, ——— Co.
Stanley, Geo., 1656, by Vincent Stanford, ——— Co.
Stanley, John, 1639, by William Burdett, Accomack Co.
Stanly, Adam, 1653, by Jon. Slaughter, ——— Co.
Stanly, Hugh, 1649, by Mr. Edmund Scraburg, Northampton Co.
Stanly, Judith, 1655, by Major Wm. Hoccaday, New Kent Co.
Stanly, Wm., 1654, by Tho. Willoughby, Lower Norfolk Co.
Stanfield, Lawrence, 1646, by Elizabeth & Ratchell Robins, Northampton Co.
Stannerd, Wm., 1652, by John Pounsey, ——— Co.
Stanny, Joan, 1643, by Mr. More Fautleroy, Upper Norfolk Co.
Stanton, Henry, 1653, by Tho. Speoke, ——— Co.
Stanton, Tho., 1643, by Wm. Berryman, Northampton Co.
Stanton, Christopher, 1638, by Richard Milton, Charles City Co.
Stanton, Robt., 1642, by Thomas Osborne, Henrico Co.
Stanton, Mary, 1655, by Lt. Col. Anthony Ellyott, ——— Co.
Stanton, Mary, 1656, by George Kibble, Lancaster Co.
Stanton, Richard, 1655, by Matilda Scrabourgh, Northampton Co.
Stanton, Mary, 1653, by Robert Woody, Lower Norfolk Co.
Staple, James, 1655, by Wm. Hall, New Kent Co.
Staples, Eliz., 1651, by George Eaton, ——— Co.
Staples, Richard, 1655, by Symon Symons, ——— Co.
Staples, Richd., 1650, by Francis Hobbs, ——— Co.
Starch, Wm., 1639, by Justinian Cooper, Isle of Wight Co.
Starcky, Adam, 1635, by John Slaughter, ——— Co.
Stardy, Edwd., 1654, by Mr. Fra. Harrison, widow, Westmoreland Co.
Starford, Margarett, 1639, by Thomas Marsh, Upper Norfolk Co.
Stare, John, 1653, by Colo. Wm. Clayborne (Sec. of State), ——— Co.
Starkey, Peter, 1652, by Capt. Francis Morgan and Raplh Green, Gloucester Co.
Starkey, Phill., 1652, by Richard Coleman, ——— Co.
Starky, Wm., 1652, by Henry Barlow, ——— Co.
Starling, Wm., 1647, by Jonathan Gills, Northampton Co.
Staffleson, Staffle, 1650, by Richard Axom and Tho. Godwin, ——— Co.

Starnell, Richd., 1652, by Francis Fleetwood, Lower Norfolk Co.
Starnell, Rich., 1646, by Thomas Brown, Lower Norfolk Co.
Starnell, Rich., 1652, by Arhtur Upshall, Northampton Co.
Starr, Eliz., 1642, by Peter Ribgy, ——— Co.
Stathard, Pit., 1650, by Richard Tye and Charles Sparrowe, Charles City Co.
Statherd, Fra., 1654, by Arthur Nash, New Kent Co.
Staunton, Wm., 1655, by John Nicholls, Northampton Co.
Staunton, Robt., 1655, by John Nicholls, Northampton Co.
Stawe, John, ———, by Tho. Meares, Lower Norfolk Co.
St. Clare, Neal, 1654, by John Drayton, Westmoreland Co.
Stead, Tho., 1649, by Wm. Nesum, Tho. Sax, Miles Bathasby and John Pyne, Northampton Co.
Steare, Joan, 1654, by Wm. Johnson, Northampton Co.
Steed, Jno., 1650, by Mr. Anthony Ellyot, ——— Co.
Steeler, Elizabeth, 1649, by Richard Parrett, ——— Co.
Steele, Jeffery, 1637, by Henry Perry, Charles River Co.
Steele, Tho., 1638, by William Carter, James City Co.
Steele, Henry, 1648, by Francis Ceely, ——— Co.
Steel, Clement, 1651, by Lieut. Collo. Giles Brent, Northumberland Co.
Steephens, Wm., 1653, by Abraham Moone, Lancaster Co.
Steers, Robt., 1637, by Charles Barcroft, Isle of Wight Co.
Steeres, Robt., 1650, by Jervace Dodson, Gent, Northumberland Co.
Steerman, Tho., 1653, by Colo. Wm. Clayborne, (Sec. of State) ——— Co.
Steere, John, 1653, by Francis Hale, ——— Co.
Steevens, Edward, 1654, by George Kibble, Lancaster Co.
Steevens, John, 1656, by Wm. Crump and Mr. Humphry Vaulx, James City Co.
Steevens, Ann, 1655, by Lt. Col. Anthony Ellyott, ——— Co.
Steevens, John, 1650, by Stephen Charlton, Northampton Co.
Steevens, Tho., 1650, by Wingfield Webb and Richard Pate, ——— Co.
Steevens, Richd., 1650, by Robert Bird, ——— Co.
Steevens, John, 1653, by Capt. Robt. Abrall, ——— Co.
Steevens, Richd., ———, by Mr. Wm. Presly, Northumberland Co.
Steevens, Ann, 1651, by Mr. Robert Abrall, Yorke Co.
Steeven, Richard, 1651, by Robt. Bradshaw, Charles River Co.
Steevens, Wm., 1653, by Richard Budd, Northumberland Co.
Steevenson, And., 1650, by Hump. Lyster, ——— Co.
Stevenson, Phill., 1652, by Augustine Moor, ——— Co.
Stefferton, Francis, 1635, by William Heires, Warrasquinoake Co.
Stella, Johanna, 1654, by Tho. Pencherman, York Co.
Stensby, Anthony, 1636, by John Neale, Accomack Co.
Stensbye, Anthony, 1637, by John Redman and John Neale, Accomac Co.
Stensbye, Anth., 1637, by John Wilkins, New Norfolk Co.
Stensbye, Robert, 1637, by John Wilkins, New Norfolk Co.
Stephen, Wm., 1653, by James Turner, ——— Co.
Stephens, Rich., 1638, by Richard Wilcox, James City Co.
Stephens, Peter, 1639, by John Jackson, Charles River Co.
Stephens, Edward, 1654, by Richard Allen, Northampton Co.

Stephens, Ann, 1655, by Wm. Steevens (her husband), Northampton Co.
Stephens, Edward, 1656, by Herbert Smith, Gent., Westmoreland Co.
Stephens, Wm., 1656, by Mr. Henry Soanes, New Kent Co.
Steevens, Edward, 1654, by Robert Younge, Lancaster Co.
Stephens, Mary, 1655, by John Wyere, Lancaster Co.
Stephens, Margt., 1655, by John Wyere, Lancaster Co
Stephens, Tho., 1638, by Geo. Lobb, Tho. Perce, Tho. Warne, James City Co.
Stephens, Jon., 1637, by Capt. Thomas Flint, Warwick River Co.
Stephens, Archelans, 1638, by Stephen Charlton, Accomack Co.
Stephens, Archelaus, 1637, by Percival Champion, New Norfolk Co.
Stephenson, Christ., 1637, by Elizabeth Parker, Henrico Co.
Stephens, Peter, 1637, by John Jackson, Charles River Co.
Stephens, Henry, 1638, by John Woodliffe, Charles City Co.
Stephens, Rich., 1637, by Leonard Yeo., Elizabeth City Co.
Stephens, Phillipp, 1636, by Capt. Thomas Willowby, ——— Co.
Stephans, Tho., 1635, by Wm. Pilkington, ——— Co.
Stephenes, Wm., 1646, by Tho. Savedge, Northampton Co.
Stephens, Richard, 1653, by John Ashby and Jh. Hamper, ——— Co.
Stephens, Wm., 1653, by John Asbhy and Jh. Hamper, ——— Co.
Stephens, Jon., 1653, by Robert Brasseur, Nansemond Co.
Stephens, Tho., 1654, by Robert Holt, James City Co.
Stephens, Wm., 1653, by Peter Knight, Northumberland Co.
Stephens, Samuel, 1653, by Wm. Debram, ——— Co.
Stephens, Rich., 1643, by Capt. Samuell Mathews, Esq., ——— Co.
Stephens, Tobias, 1646, by Thomas Bahe, Upper Norfolk Co.
Stephen, Ro., 1650, by Richard Axom and Tho. Godwin, ——— Co.
Stephens, John, 1635, by William Ranshaw, Elizabeth City Co.
Stephenson, Ann, 1636, by Wm. Julian, Elizabeth City Co.
Stepping, Daniell, 1650, by Hump. Lyster, ——— Co.
Sterkey, Pet., 1649, by Capt. Ralph Wormeley, ——— Co.
Steren, Wm., 1636, by Wm. Bibby, Accomack Co.
Sterling, Wm., 1656, by Wm. Willinge, Northampton Co.
Sterling, Tho., 1655, by Symon Symons, ——— Co.
Sternall, Richard, 1638, by Wm. Rainshaw, Lower New Norfolk Co.
Sternes, Dorothy, 1651, by Phillip Charles James City Co.
Stersmone, Ann, 1653, by Robt. Sorrel, ——— Co.
Stevens, Wm., 1637, by Capt. Adam Thoroughgood, Elizabeth City Co.
Stevens, Hen., 1637, by Christopher Woodward, Charles City Co.
Stevens, Henry, 1637, by Cheney Boyes, Charles City Co.
Stevens, Tho. Mount, 1652, by Tho. Steevens, Lancaster Co.
Steevens, Jno., 1650, by Capt. Richard Bond, Charles City Co.
Stevens, John, 1651, by Mr. Robert Abrall, Yorke Co.
Stevens, Wm., 1650, by William Gooch, Bent., ——— Co.
Steward, Jno., 1651, by Edmond Welch, ——— Co.
Steward, John, 1639, by Tristram Nosworthy, Upper Norfolk Co.
Steward, Andrew, 1656, by Tho. Stephens, Surry Co.
Steward, Roger, 1655, by Wm. Wright, Gent., Nansemond Co.
Steward, Elin, 1656, by Mr. Tho. Purifoy, ——— Co.
Steward, Neal, 1655, by Lt. Col. Anthony Ellyott, ——— Co.

Steward, Patrick, 1655, by Jer. Dodson, Gent., Lancaster Co.
Steward, Charles, 1635, by Edward Osborne, Henrico Co.
Steward, David, 1652, by Anthony Hoskins, Northampton Co.
Steward, Jno., 1652, by Tho. and Wm. Leithermore, ——— Co.
Stewart, Charles, 1638, by Christopher Branch, Henrico Co.
Stewardson, Alice, 1647, by Stephen Harsey and Nicho. Waddilow, Northampton Co.
Stewardson, Alex., 1649, by Nicholas Waddilow, Northampton Co.
Stibbs, John, 1646, by Thomas, Brown, Lower Norfolk Co.
Stickden, Edw., 1635, by Wm. Garry, Accomack Co.
Stidwell, Tho., 1648, by John Ellis, Janus Joones and John Taylor, Northampton Co.
Stidwell, Thomas, 1636, by Edward Drew, Accomack Co.
Stile, Eliza., 1656, by Lewis Perry, ——— Co.
Stiles, Nathaniell, 1639, by Edward Panderson, ——— Co.
Stiles, Robert, 1643, by Thomas Frye, James City Co.
Stiler, Hugh, 1647, by James Warradine, ——— Co.
Stilit, Tho., 1650, by Capt. Moore Faulteroy, ——— Co.
Stillard, Wm., 1655, by John Biggs, Lower Norfolk Co.
Stillger, Antho., 1650, by John Hayny, Northumberland Co.
Stilt, Bar., 1655, by John Coole, James City Co.
Stingsby, Robert, 1636, by Wm. Fookes, ——— Co.
Stinter, Richard, 1638, by Georg Mynifie (merchant), ——— Co.
Stinsby, Antho., 1636, by John Wilkins, Accomack Co.
Stipthorp, Hen., 1648, by Francis Ceely, ——— Co.
Stoakes, Lan., 1653, by Charles Grymes, Clerk, Lancaster Co.
Stockdell, John, 1635, by Thomas Harwood, ——— Co.
Stockden, Tymothy, 1638, by Thomas Isles, Charles River Co.
Stockley, Francis, 1651, by Jonas Jackson, Northampton Co.
Stockell, Jane, 1646, by Sir William Berkley, ——— Co.
Stockhouse, Robert, 1637, by John Redman and John Neale, Accomac Co.
Stockhouse, Robt., 1636, by John Wilkins, Accomack Co.
Stockhouse, Robert, 1636, by John Neale, Accomack Co.
Stockwell, Tho., 1654, by John Phillips and John Batts, Lancaster Co.
Stockwell, Rose, 1650, by Hugh Lee, Northumberland Co.
Stockwell, Marg., 1653, by Robert Brasseur, Nansemond Co.
Stocks, Daniell, 1639, by William Burdett, Accomack Co.
Stoddon, William, 1635, by George Minifie, James City Co.
Stodon, Wm., 1636, by Mr. Geo. Menifye, James City Co.
Stogdell, John, 1650, by James Hurd, ——— Co.
Stokes, Thomas, 1638, by Wm. Clays, Charles River Co.
Stokes, Eliza., Jr., 1637, by Christopher Stokes, Charles River Co.
Stokes, Christopher, Jr., 1637, by Christopher Stokes, Charles River Co.
Stokes, Hen., 1637, by Christopher Stokes, Charles River Co.
Stokes, Eliza., 1637, by Christopher Stokes, Charles River Co.
Stokes, Willi, 1637, by Christopher Stokes, Charles River Co.
Stokes, Lancellott, 1637, by Christopher Stokes, Warwick River Co.
Stokes, Robert, 1637, by William Spencer, ——— Co.
Stokes, Robert, 1635, by William Spencer, ——— Co.

Stoner, Alex., 1638, by John Jackson and Eliza Kingswill, James City Co.
Stonar, Jane, 1635, by Alexander Sontar (her husband), ——— Co.
Stommer, Daniell, 1653, by Charles Grymes, Lancaster Co.
Stonard, Joseph, 1654, by John Watson and John Bognall, Westmoreland Co.
Stone, Edward, 1642, by Thomas Todd, Lower New Norfolk Co.
Stone, Robt., 1654, by Richard Harrison, Westmoreland Co.
Stone, Edward, 1655, by Mr. Tho. Peck, Gloucester Co.
Stone, Robert, 1654, by Nich. Merywether, Westmoreland Co.
Stone, Moyses, 1637, by Arthur Smith, Isle of Wight Co.
Stone, Francis, 1637, by Elizabeth Parker, Henrico Co.
Stone, Jerimy, 1637, by Bridges Freeman, James City Co.
Stone, Andrew, 1635, by McWilliam Stone, ——— Co.
Stone, Jeremiah, 1636, by Bridges Freeman, ——— Co.
Stone, Joyce, 1642, by Christopher Boyce, ——— Co.
Stone, Hannah, 1653, by Jno. Hansford, Gloucester Co.
Stone, Wm., 1652, by John Howett, Northumberland Co.
Stone, Nicholas, 1650, by Mr. James Williamson, ——— Co.
Stone, Mathew, 1651, by Wm. Taylor, Northumberland Co.
Stone, Wm., 1652, by Richard Coleman, ——— Co.
Stone, George, 1653, by Tho. Griffin, Lancaster Co.
Stone, Edward, 1650, by Mr. Epaphroditus Lawson, ——— Co.
Stone, Richard, 1653, by Charles Grymes, Clerk, Lancaster Co.
Stonner, John, 1644, by Elizabeth Harmer, Northampton Co.
Stonner, Alexander, 1652, by Mr. Geo. Foster, Northumberland Co.
Stoole, Thomas, 1642, by John Lylley, ——— Co.
Stoont, Anne, 1653, by Francis Emperor, Lower Norfolk Co.
Stoper, Samll., 1650, by Andrew Gilson, ——— Co.
Stoppee, Sa., 1651, by Mr. Rowland Burnham, ——— Co.
Storrey, Jo., 1650, by Robert Blake and Samuell Elridge, Isle of Wight Co.
Story, James, 1655, by Ralph Green, New Kent Co.
Storey, William, 1645, by William Storey, Upper Norfolk Co.
Story, Francis, 1648, by Wm. Barret, ——— Co.
Stoton, Anthony, 1637, by William Spencer, ——— Co.
Stott, Hen., 1654, by John Watson and John Bognall, Westmoreland Co.
Stow, John, 1654, by Arthur Nash, New Kent Co.
Stout, Mary, 1654, by Sarah Hancock, Lower Norfolk Co.
Stout, Thomas, 1638, by Joseph Harmon, James City Co.
Stoute, Jane, 1655, by Tho. Jones, James City Co.
Stoute, John, 1635, by William Beard, James City Co.
Stowell, Ralph, 1641, by Stephen Charlton, Accomack Co.
Stowhill, Anne, 1652, by John Bryan, ——— Co.
Stowly, Michaell, 1642, by Thomas Ransha, Warwick Co.
Stowther, Phill., 1652, by Anthony Doney and Enoch Hawkes, Lancaster Co.
Strader, Richard, 1647, by Richard Bland, ——— Co.
Straing, Wm., 1638, by Wm. Barker and Associates, Charles City Co.
Strand, Tho., 1650, by George Pate, Charles City Co.

Strange, Nicho., 1638, by John Robins, James City Co.
Strange, Wm., 1641, by Thomas Pitt, Charles City Co.
Strange, Wm., 1635, by William Barber (a mariner), Charles City Co.
Strange, Benjamin, 1652, by Tho. Holme, Yorke Co.
Strange, Benj., 1653, by Tho. Holmes, York Co.
Strathridge, Tho., 1654, by Wm. Thorne, Northampton Co.
Stratter, Mathew, 1652, by Mrs. Mary Brent, Northumberland Co.
Stratton, Sisley, 1647, by Edmond Scarborough, Northampton Co.
Stratton, Alice, 1654, by Tho. Stratton, Northampton Co.
Stratton, Henry, 1641, by Thomas Morrey, Isle of Wight Co.
Stratton, Saran, 1649, by Thomas Coniers, Eliz. City Co.
Stratton, Richard, 1651, by Joseph Croshaw, Yorke Co.
Stratton, Walter, 1655, by Mr. Tho. Peck, Gloucester Co.
Stratchy, Edmond, 1651, by George Ludlow, Esq., ———— Co.
Straw, John, 1638, by Walter Chiles, Charles Citie Co.
Strawbrocke, John, 1635, by Robert Shepperd, ———— Co.
Streate, Antho., 1635, by William Spencer, ———— Co.
Streatly, Mary, 1654, by Lt. Colo. John Cheeseman and (John Adleston,) ———— Co.
Streces, Wm., 1652, by Capt. Augustine Warner, ———— Co.
Stretcher, Andrew, 1636, by Wm. Armestead, Elizabeth City Co.
Stretcher, James, 1650, by Thomas Mulford, Nansemond Co.
Street, Hump., 1653, by James Turner, ———— Co.
Streete, Anth., 1637, by William Spencer, ———— Co.
Streets, Ann, 1638, by John Bough, Henrico Co.
Streete, Fra., 1652, by John Greenbough, Henrico Co.
Street, Eliza., 1652, by Mr. George Clapham, ———— Co.
Street, Eliza., 1652, by Nicho. Sebrell, Northumberland Co.
Street, Richd., 1653, by Richard Foster, Lower Norfolk Co.
Street, Tho., 1653, by Colo. Wm. Clayborne (Sec. of State), ———— Co.
Street, Robt., 1650, by John Hallawes, Gent., Northumberland Co.
Street, Robt., 1650, by John Hallawes, Gent., Northumberland Co.
Street, Hump., 1650, by William Gooch, Gent., ———— Co.
Stretchey, Rose, 1636, by John Oberry, ———— Co.
Stretchleigh, James, 1650, by Thomas Mulford, Nansemond Co.
Stretton, Eliza., 1650, by Elias Edmondes, ———— Co.
Strey, Oliv., 1638, by John Stratton, Lower New Norfolk Co.
Strichly, Edmond, 1646, by William Hockaday, York Co.
Stringer, James, 1647, by Tho. Godby, Lower Norfolk Co.
Stringer, John, 1651, by Wm. Taylor, Northumberland Co.
Stringer, Lettice, 1653, by Tho. Kibby, Northumberland Co.
Strong, Leonard, 1655, by Wm. Wright, Gent., Nansemond Co.
Stronge, Edw., 1637, by Capt. Adam Thoroughgood, New Norfolk Co.
Stronge, Alex., 1650, by John Lacker, ———— Co.
Stong, James, 1642, by George Harding, ———— Co.
Strong, Edw., 1635, by Capt. Adam Thoroughgood, ———— Co.
Strong, James, 1653, by John Bell, Lancaster Co.
Stronge, Abraham, 1653, by Peter Knight, Northumberland Co.
Strong, Mary, 1650, by Tho. Gerrord, Gent., Northumberland Co.
Stroud, Tho., 1652, by George Pace, Charles City Co.
Strowd, Thomas, 1642, by John Ewes, Jr., Charles City Co.

Strutton, Wm., 1637, by Capt. Thomas Flint, Warwick River Co.
Stuper, Sam., 1654, by Andrew Gibson, —— Co.
Stuard, James, 1651, by John Martin and (Lancaster Lovett), Lower Norfolk Co.
Stuart, Robt., 1652, by Col. Geo. Ludlow, Esq., Gloucester Co.
Stuart, Walter, 1653, by Jervais Dodson, Northumberland Co.
Stuart, Henry, 1653, by Geo. Watts, Northumberland Co.
Stuart, Oneale, 1652, by Nathaniel Bacon, Isle of Wight Co.
Stubbs, Isabell, 1638, by William Clarke, Henrico Co.
Stubbs, Daniell, 1645, by Zachary Cripps, Warwick Co.
Stubbs, Daniell, 1637, by Zachariah Cripps, Warwick River Co.
Stubbs, Hontford, 1637, by Capt. Henry Browne, James City Co.
Stubs, Izabell, 1636, by Wm. Clarke, Henrico Co.
Stubberd, Jno., 1653, by Wm. Walker, Northumberland Co.
Stubberts, John, 1654, by John Whithers and Stephen Garey, Westmoreland Co.
Stuble, Richard, 1653, by Jervais Dodson, Northumberland Co.
Stud, Thomas, 1651, by Wm. Rennales, Northumberland Co.
Studdell, Tho., 1654, by Christopher Regault, Gloucester Co.
Studdell, Tho., his wife and child, 1654, by Christopher Regault, Gloucester Co.
Stukely, James, 1639, by Lieut. Richard Popeley, —— Co.
Stulton, Rich., 1638, by Nicholas Georg and John Gryrisditch, Isle of Wight Co.
Stunnerson, Sarah, 1643, by Sir Francis Wyatt, Kt., —— Co.
Stupp, Natha., 1653, by Roger Walter, Northumberland Co.
Sturdey, James, 1652, by Christopher Robinson and John Sturdevant, Henrico Co.
Sturdge, Ri., 1650, by Wm. Clapham, —— Co.
Sturrupp, Jno., 1646, by William Hockaday, York Co.
Styam, John, 1649, by Capt. Ralph Wormeley, —— Co.
Styles, Jane, 1649, by Edmund Scarburgh, Jr., Northampton Co.
Substance, Ann, 1653, by Richard Burton, —— Co.
Subtill, Henry, 1652, by Tho. Preston, Jr., —— Co.
Subtell, Henry, 1654, by John Williams, Northumberland Co.
Succor, Henry, 1650, by Wm. Underwood, Gent., —— Co.
Such, George, 1656, by Edward Robinson and Tho. Hall, Lower Norfolk Co.
Sudbery, Robert, 1638, by Lt. John Upton, Isle of Wight Co.
Sudwell, Hen., 1653, by Richard Carey, —— Co.
Sullivan, Onory, 1656, by Capt. Wm. Confell, —— Co.
Sullivant, Elizabeth, 1655, by Wm. Walker, Northumberland Co.
Sumer, Benjamin, 1655, by Wm. Johnson and Stephen Horsey, Northampton Co.
Sumere, Miles, 1637, by Georg Burcher, James City Co.
Sumers, Robt., 1638, by Richard Kemp, Esq., —— Co.
Sumervile, Garrett, 1639, by Walter Cooper, James City Co.
Summer, Richard, 1638, by Lieut. John Upton, Isle of Wight Co.
Summers, Alex., 1638, by Joseph Boarne, Charles City Co.
Sumner, Mary, 1653, by Capt. Francis Patt, Northampton Co.
Sumptner, Eliza., 1651, by Audery Bennett, Nansemond Co.

Sures, Samll., 1648, by Richard Wyatt, ——— Co.
Surtue, Wm., 1651, by John Hull, Northumberland Co.
Sunkler, Neale, 1653, by Tho. Hampton ——— Co.
Sutch, Geo., 1653, by John Custis, Northampton Co.
Sutton, Richard, 1638, by Thomas Stampe, James City Co.
Sutton, Eliza., 1653, by Charles Grymes, Lancaster Co.
Sutton, Jon., 1653, by Robert Brasseur, Nansemond Co.
Sutton, Robt., 1653, by Johnn Sheerlock, Lancaster Co.
Sutton, John, 1652, by Mr. Edwin Connaway, ——— Co.
Sutton, Tho., 1643, by Richard Kemp, Esq., James City Co.
Sutton, Wm., 1636, by Mr. Georg Minifye, James City Co.
Sutton, William, 1635, by George Minifie, James City Co.
Sutton, John, 1642, by Wm. Barnard Esq., Isle of Wight Co.
Sutton, Richard, 1637, by Edward Travis, James City Co.
Sutton, Tho., 1655, by Peter Starchey, ——— Co.
Sutton, Richard, 1639, by Walter Cooper, James City Co.
Sutton, Wm., 1642, by Capt. Samuell Mathews, Esq., ——— Co.
Sutton, Geo., 1642, by Thomas Ransha, Warwick Co.
Sutton, Richard, 1639, by Edward Travis, James City Co.
Sutton, Richard, 1639, by Thomas Slamp, James City Co.
Sutton, Annis, 1639, by William Burdett, Accomack Co.
Swaddin, Kath., 1649, by Richard Parrett, ——— Co.
Swan, Edward, 1638, by Thomas Swan, James Citie Co.
Swan, John, 1638, by Thomas Swan, James Citie Co.
Swan, Jon., 1635, by Wm. Swan, James Co.
Swan, Edw., 1635, by Wm. Swan, James Co.
Swan, Fra., 1652, by John Wareham, Northumberland Co.
Swan, Geo., 1652, by Robert Elan, Henrico Co.
Swane, Samll., 1637, by Capt. Henry Browne, James City Co.
Swann, Ann, 1649, by Edmund Scarburgh, Jr., Northampton Co.
Swann, Richard, 1646, by Sir William Berkley, ——— Co.
Swann, Martha, 1635, by Jno. Upton, Warrasquinoake Co.
Swanson, Robert, 1649, by John Dennis, ——— Co.
Swain, Ann (wife Thom. Swain), 1638, by Thomas Plomer and Samuell
    Edmonds, James City Co.
Swaine, Thos., wife, 1653, by Martin, Cole, Northumberland Co.
Swaine, Stephen, 1635, by Capt. Adam Thoroughgood, ——— Co.
Swaine, Tho., 1638, by Thom Plomer and Samuell Edmonds, James
    City Co.
Swart, Jon., 1643, by Richard Kemp, Esq., James City Co.
Swayne, Sith., 1645, by Richard Jacob, Northampton Co.
Sweet, George, 1653, by Capt. Francis Pate, Northampton Co.
Sweetaple, Geo., 1651, by Edward Deggs, Esq., Yorke Co.
Sweet, Wm., 1654, by Col. Argoll Yardley, Northampton Co.
Sweetman, Margaret, 1656, by Wm. Bird, ——— Co.
Sweny, Edmund, son of An. Bowles, Jr., 1656, by Mr. Tho. Purifoy,
    ——— Co.
Sweney, Elizabeth, 1656, by Mr. Tho. Purifoy, ——— Co.
Sweney, Mary, 1656, by Mr. Tho. Purifoy, ——— Co.
Swest, Thomas, 1642, by Joseph Royall, ——— Co.
Swett, Robt., 1638, by Lt. Robt. Sheppard, James City Co.

Swifte, John, 1636, by Cheney Boyse, Charles City Co.
Swift, Jon., 1637, by Cheney Boyes, Charles City Co.
Swift, Thos., 1638, by Joseph Royall, Charles Citie Co.
Swillivon, Cornelius, 1637, by Wm. Prior, Charles River Co.
Swinburne, Wm., 1655, by Marhew Huberd, Gent., York Co.
Swilliams, Corn., 1642, by John Bayles, ———— Co.
Sybley, Charles, 1650, by Mr. Epaphroditus Lawson, ———— Co.
Syer, Tho., 1650, by Robert Blake and Samuell Elridge, Isle of Wight
     Co.
Sykamore, Jon., 1637, by Henry Perry, Charles River Co.
Syker, John, 1637, by Thomas Sawyer, New Norfolk Co.
Sykes, Jon., 1642, by Francis England, Isle of Wight Co.
Sygmar, Rowland, 1639, by Robert Newman, Warwick River Co.
Symber, Wm., 1637, by John Graves, Elizabeth City Co.
Symber, Tho., 1647, by Symon Symons, Nansemond Co.
Symcocks, Alis, 1651, by John Martin and (Lancaster Lovett), Lower
     Norfolk Co.
Symes, Tho., 1653, by Colo. Wm. Clayborne (Sec. of State), ———— Co.
Symkins, Tho., 1652, by Mr. Geo. Foster, Northumberland Co.
Symmons, Tho., 1644, by Elizabeth Harmer, Northampton, Co.
Symmons, Symon, 1637, by Henry Perry, Charles River Co.
Symonds, Wm., 1650, by Richard Tye and Charles Sparrowe, Charles
     City Co.
Symonds, Symon, 1643, by Mr. John Bishopp, James City Co.
Symond, Roger, 1646, by Sir William Berkley, ———— Co.
Symon, Elizabeth, 1650, by Capt. Moore Fautleroy, ———— Co.
Symon, Sarah, 1642, by John Brooch, Charles River Co.
Symons, Wm., 1653, by David Phillips, Northumberland Co.
Symons, Richard, 1650, by James Hurd, ———— Co.
Symons, Gama., 1648, by Richard Pettibon, ———— Co.
Symons, Richard, 1649, by Bartholomew, Hoskins, ———— Co.
Symons, Richard, 1652, by Rice Hughes, ———— Co.
Symons, Jon., 1637, by Hen. Woodhouse, New Norfolk Co.
Symons, Thos., 1637, by Hen. Woodhouse, New Norfolk Co.
Symons, Fr., 1643, by Thomas Cassen, Lower Norfolk Co.
Symons, John, 1643, by Mr. Phillipp Bennett, Upper Norfolk Co.
Symons, Francis, 1650, by Mrs. Frances Townshend, Northumberland
     Co.
Symons, Henry, 1638, by Wm. Hatcher, ———— Co.
Symons, Hen., 1638, by Robert Pitts, Isle of Wight Co.
Symons, Richard, 1637, by Christopher Stokes, Warwick River Co.
Symons, Thos., 1638, by Stephen Charlton, Accomack Co.
Symons, Tho., 1654, by Toby Smith, Lancaster Co.
Symons, John, 1655, by Souhty Littleberry, Northampton Co.
Symons, Francis, 1638, by Lieut. John Upton, Isle of Wight Co.
Symons, Gilbert, 1642, by Capt. Samuell Mathews, Esq., ———— Co.
Sympson, Seth., 1651, by Audery Bennett, Nansemond Co.
Sympson, Dan,. 1649, by Tho. Dale, ———— Co.
Symson, Tho., 1651, by Capt. Stephen Gill, Northumberland Co.
Symson, Tho., 1649, by John Waltham, Northampton Co.
Symson, Thomas, 1645, by John Rode, Warwick River Co.

Syneson, John, 1650, by John Hallawes, Gent., Northumberland Co.
Synsbury, Ro., 1654, by Major Miles Carey, Westmoreland Co.

T

Tabb, Tho., 1643, by Georg Levitt, ———— Co.
Taberer, Joshua, 1652, by Nicho. George, Tho. Taberer and Humphry Clarke, ———— Co.
Taberer, Tho., 1552, by Mr. Peter Knight, Gloucester Co.
Taberer, Anne, 1652, by Daniell Welch, Lancaster Co.
Taball, Dermon, 1653, by Richard Carey, ———— Co.
Tabrer, Anne, 1652, by Tho. Boswell, ———— Co.
Tabor, John, 1639, by Georg Minifye, Esq., Charles River Co.
Tacker, Danll., 1651, by Richard Ripley, ———— Co.
Taesly, Rich., 1655, by John Watson, Lancaster Co.
Taffe, Joane, 1654, by Richard Allen, Northampton Co.
Tagle, Wm., 1655, by Wm. Walker, Northumberland Co.
Takes, Margarett, 1651, by Edward Symson, Gloucester Co.
Talbott, Peter, 1642, by Georg Smith, Accomack Co.
Talbott, Geo., 1637, by Thomas Davis, New Norfolk Co.
Talbott, Hercules, 1654, by Arthur Nash, New Kent Co.
Talbott, Sarah, 1655, by Mr. Tho. Ballard, Gloucester Co.
Talbott, Jon., 1642, by John Davis, Henrico Co.
Talbott, John, 1642, by Daniell Lewellyn, ———— Co.
Talbott, Peter, 1643, by Capt. Thomas Pettus, ———— Co.
Talbott, John, 1652, by Henry Fleete, Lancaster Co
Talbott, Wm., 1652, by Henry Fleete, Lancaster Co.
Talbott, Wm., 1652, by Edward Coles, Northumberland Co.
Talgate, Humitiation, 1649, by Christop. Lewis, James City Co.
Talker, Geo., 1651, by William Ginsey, Yorke Co.
Tall, Wm., 1653, by Oliver Segar, Lancaster Co.
Tallenson, Wm., 1650, by Mrs. Francis Townshend, Northumberland Co.
Talley, Eliza, 1638, by Benjamin Carrill, James City Co.
Talley, Elias, 1637, by Capt. Thomas Paulett, Charles City Co.
Tally, Eliza., 1636, by Nathan Martin, Henrico Co.
Tallin, Pat., 1652, by Mrs. Jane Harmer, Northumberland Co.
Talling, Patrick, 1638, by John Jackson and Eliza. Kingswill, James City Co.
Tallisfnevre, John, 1652, by Richard Coleman, ———— Co.
Tallock, James, 1638, by Lieut. John Upton, Isle of Wight Co.
Tallot, John, 1650, by John Mangor, ———— Co.
Talridge, Richd., 1653, by Richard Slaughter, Nansemond Co.
Talson, Jno., 1648, by Lewis Burwell and Tho. Haws, York River Co.
Tam, Martin, 1638, by Augustine Warner, Charles River Co.
Tame, Henry, 1642, by Thomas Bagwell, Charles City Co.
Tamon, Jon., 1653, by Capt. Nathaniel Hurd, Warrick Co.
Tandey, Wm., 1650, by Wm. Clapham, ———— Co.
Tandy, Wm., 1643, by Thomas Taylor, Warwick Co.
Tanner Barbay, 1635, by Capt. Wm. Pierse, ———— Co.
Tanner, Abram., 1655, by Robt. Nicholson, Charles City Co.

Tanner, Benj., 1644, by Stephen Taylor, ——— Co.
TapLady, John, 1649, by Capt. Ralph Wormeley, ——— Co.
Tapp, Thos., 1643, by Thomas Hughes, Charles River Co.
Tappin, Hen., 1642, by Stephen Gill, Yorke River Co.
Tarbooke, Robert, 1642, by Stephen Hamblyn, York Co.
Tarington, Mary, 1650, by Hump. Lyster, ——— Co.
Tarling, Richard, 1639, by Stephen Webb, James City Co.
Tarlrupe, Richard, 1652, by Mrs. Mary Brent, Northumberland Co.
Tarrington, Robt., 1652, by Capt. Augustine Warner, ——— Co.
Tarry, Tho., 1638, by Georg Mynifie (merchant), ——— Co.
Tarry, Elizabeth, 1656, by Nicholas Waddilow, Northampton Co.
Tascure, Isabell, 1653, by Samuell Parry, Lancaster Co.
Tassell, Robt., 1637, by John Jackson, Charles River Co.
Tatham, John, 1652, by Mr. George Clapham, ——— Co.
Tatnam, Silvester, 1635, by Thomas Harwood, ——— Co.
Tatum, Mary, 1638, by Nathaniell Tatum (her father), Charles City Co.
Tatum, Ann, 1638, by Nathaniell Tatum (her husband), Charles City
    Co.
Tatum, Robt., 1646, by Tho. Savedge, Northampton Co.
Tatum, Ralph, 1642, by John Benton, ——— Co.
Tavern, Giles, 1639, by Capt. Nicholas Martian, Charles River Co.
Taverne, Francis, 1642, by Wm. Durant, ——— Co.
Taverne, Fra., 1652, by Col. Geo. Ludlow, Esq., Gloucester Co.
Taverner, Dan., 1654, by Edw. Welch, ——— Co.
Taverner, Giles, 1654, by Francis Gray, ——— Co.
Tarling, Rich., 1636, by Stephen Webb, James City Co.
Tawney, Ann, 1656, by Mr. Tho. Purifoy, ——— Co.
Tawson, Elizabeth, 1655, by Robt. Priddy, New Kent Co.
Tayler, Anthony, 1637, by Francis Fowler, James River Co.
Tayler, Robert, 1642, by Thomas Guyer, ——— Co.
Taylor, Wm., 1649, by Francis Brown, Northumberland Co.
Taylor, Joseph, 1653, by Jno. Hansford, Gloucester Co.
Taylor, Jane, 1643, by Phillipp Taylor, Northampton Co.
Taylor, Phillipp, Sr., 1643, by Phillipp Taylor, Northampton Co.
Taylor, Zachariah, 1638, by Georg White, Clerk, Upper New Norfolk
    Co.
Taylor, William, 1638, by Lieut. Robt. Sheppard, James City Co.
Taylor, Giles, 1638, by Wm. Hatcher, ——— Co.
Taylor, Zachariah, 1637, by Georg White, New Norfolk Co.
Taylor, Thomas, 1637, by James Knott, New Norfolk Co.
Taylor, Wm., 1637, by Henry Snaile, Isle of Wight Co.
Taylor, John, 1635, by Francis Fowler, James City Co.
Taylor, Robert, 1643, by Mr. John Bishopp, James City Co.
Taylor, ———, 1637, by Phillipp Taylor (her husband), Accomack Co.
Taylor, Florence, 1637, by Thomas Barnard, James City Co.
Taylor, Georg, 1636, by John Seaward, Isle of Wight Co.
Taylor, Henry, 1635, by Jno. Sparkes, ——— Co.
Taylor, Thomas, 1635, by George Minifie, James City Co.
Taylor, Thomas, 1637, by Rich. Bellane and Christopher Lawson,
    James City Co.
Taylor, Wm., 1636, by John Dunston, James City Co.

Taylor, Georg, 1637, by Thomas Holt, New Norfolk Co.
Taylor, Samuel, 1637, by Thomas Holt, New Norfolk Co.
Taylor, John, 1635, by Jeremiah Clement, ——— Co.
Taylor, Jon., 1636, by Wililam Coleman, Charles River Co.
Taylor, Arthur, 1637, by Patrick Kennedye, New Norfolk Co.
Taylor, Thomas, 1636, by Mr. Georg Menefee, James City Co.
Taylor, Thos., 1636, by James Knott, Elizabeth City Co.
Taylor, Wm., 1650, by Mrs. Frances Townshend, Northumberland Co.
Taylor, Anna, 1640, by Elias Taylor, Accomack Co.
Taylor, Geo., 1639, by Robt. Newman, Warwick River Co.
Taylor, Robt., 1639, by Abraham Wood, Henrico Co.
Taylor, Thomas, 1639, by Walter Cooper, James City Co.
Taylor, William, 1639, by John Dunston, James City Co.
Taylor, John, 1637, by Thom. Harwood, Charles River Co.
Taylor, James, 1638, by William Morgan, ——— Co.
Taylor, Wm., 1638, by John Powell, Elizabeth City Co.
Taylor, William, 1638, by Lieut. John Upton, Isle of Wight Co.
Taylor, Wm., 1640, by Randall Crew, Upper Norfolk Co.
Taylor, Thomas, 1640, by Randall Crew, Upper Norfolk Co.
Taylor, Thomas, 1639, by Richard Bell, James City Co.
Taylor, Abr., 1654, by John Watson and John Bognall, Westmoreland Co.
Taylor, Ann, 1654, by John Wyre, John Gillet, Andrew Gilson and John Phillipps, ——— Co.
Taylor, Mary, 1654, by Major Miles Carey, Westmoreland Co.
Taylor, Ann, 1654, by Major Miles Carey, Westmoreland Co.
Taylor, John, 1654, by John Drayton, Westmoreland Co.
Taylor, Fra., 1655, by Mathew Huberd, Gent., York Co.
Taylor, Ellin, 1655, by Major Wm. Lewis, New Kent Co.
Taylor, Stephen, 1654, by Nicholas Morris, Northumberland Co.
Taylor, Jno., 1655, by John Ayres, ——— Co.
Taylor, Richard, 1654, by Francis Smith and Mr. John Smith, Westmoreland Co.
Taylor, John, 1654, by Francis Smith and Mr. John Smith, Westmoreland Co.
Taylor, John, 1656, by Wm. Crump and Mr. Humphry Vaulx, James City Co.
Taylor, James, 1650, by John Rosier, Northumberland Co.
Taylor, Robt.,1656, by Sir Henry Chichley, ——— Co.
Taylor, Margarett, 1644, by Stephen Taylor (her husband), ——— Co.
Taylor, Thomas, 1642, by Daniell Lewellyn, ——— Co.
Taylor, Arthur, 1642, by Thomas Loving, James City Co.
Taylor, Eliz., 1643, by Edward Murfey and John Vaughn, ———Co.
Taylor, Wm., 1648, by Lewis Burwell and Tho. Haws, York River Co.
Taylor, Robt., 1650, by Mr. Stephen Hamelin, Charles City Co.
Taylor, Tho., 1642, by Hugh Gwyn, Gent., ——— Co.
Taylor, Richard, 1650, by Edward Walker, Northumberland Co.
Taylor, Tho., 1650, by Richard Tye and Charles Sparrowe, Charles City Co.
Taylor, John, 1650, by Tho. Gerrord, Gent., Northumberland Co.
Taylor, Kath., 1650, by Wm. Yarrett and Fra. Wittington, ——— Co.

Taylor, Symon, 1650, by Capt. Moore Fautleroy, ——— Co.
Taylor, Nicho., 1650, by Elyas Edmonds, ——— Co.
Taylor, Robt., 1648, by John King and Lawrence Ward, Isle of Wight Co.
Taylor, Mary, 1650, by John Sever, ———Co.
Taylor, Eidith, 1648, by Lewis Burwell, Gent., ——— Co.
Taylor, Elias and wife, 1648, by Lewis Burwell and Tho. Haws, York River Col
Taylor, Wm., 1648, by Geo. Hardy, Tho. Wombwell and Peter Hall, Isle of Wight Co.
Taylor, John, 1648, by Geo. Hardy,Tho. Wombwell, and Peter Hall, Isle of Wight Co.
Taylor, Rich., 1653, by Capt. Francis Patt, Northampton Co.
Taylor, Ann, 1653, by Fra. Gower, Lancaster Co.
Taylor, Phillip, 1652, by Capt. Henry Fleet, Lancaster Co.
Taylor, John, 1652, by Tho. Cartwright, Lower Norfolk Co.
Taylor, Tho., 1653, by Robert Bouth, Yorke Co.
Taylor, Alice, 1653, by Jno. Hansford, Gloucester Co.
Taylor, John, 1651, by John Senior, ——— Co.
Taylor, John, 1651, by James Foster, Nansemond Co.
Taylor, Wm., 1651, by Mr. Wm. Armestead, ——— Co.
Taylor, Tho., 1651, by Mr. Antho. Steevens, Northampton Co.
Taylor, Walker, 1656, by Capt. Wm. Canfill, Surry Co.
Taylor, Richard, 1651, by Capt. John West, Esq., Yorke Co.
Taylor, Mathew, 1652, by Augustine Moore, ——— Co.
Tayton, Xtop., 1645, by Zachary Cripps, Warwick Co.
Taytor, John, 1654, by Capt. Nich. Marteau, Westmoreland Co.
Teagg, John, 1652, by Edward Revell, Northampton Co.
Teagg, John, 1652, by Andrew Munrow, Northumberland Co.
Teagee, Brian, 1655, by Sampson Robins, Northampton Co.
Teague, Dennis, 1655, by Richard Price, New Kent Co.
Tealter, Walter, 1649, by Rich. Croshaw, Yorke Co.
Tecknor, Tho., 1652, by Richard Coleman, ——— Co.
Teeling, Francis, 1655, by John Green, ——— Co.
Tegume, David, 1652, by Henry Tyler, Charles River Co.
Temnan, Phill., 1651, by Abraham Moone and (Thomas Griffin), Lancaster Co.
Tempest, Edward, 1653, by Tho. Speoke, ——— Co.
Tempest, Robt., 1635, by Mr. Geo. Keth, Charles River Co.
Temperance, John, 1642, by Abraham English, ——— Co.
Tenches, Edward, 1637, by Theodore Moyser, James City Co.
Tengood, Richard, 1649, by Mr. Edmund Scarburg, Northampton Co.
Tenman, Robert, 1636, by Hannibal Fletcher, James City Co.
Tennant, Christopher, 1635, by John Sparkes, ——— Co.
Teogue, John and Nichols (Irishmen), 1654, by John Drayton, Westmoreland Co.
Teppett, Robert, 1635, by Thomas Harwood, ——— Co.
Tero, John, 1650, by John Hallawes, Gent., Northumberland Co.
Terrey, Glannell, 1656, by Tabitha and Matilda Scarburgh, Northampton Co.
Terrill, Jane, 1652, by Robert West, Charles City Co.

Terry, Wm., 1653, by Mr. James Tooke, Isle of Wight Co.
Terry, Sarah, 1653, by Richard Pinner, ———— Co.
Terry, Gabrielle, 1650, by Mr. Robt. Holt, James City Co.
Tervant, Tho., 1654, by Francis Smith and Mr. John Smith, Westmoreland Co.
Tetzell, Danll., 1654, by Richard Budd, Northampton Co.
Tetzell, Danll., Sr., 1654, by Richard Budd, ———— Co.
Teuricke, James, 1653, by Colo. Wm. Clayborne (Sec. of State), ———— Co.
Teye, Katherine, 1651, by Mr. Wm. Armestead, ———— Co.
Thack, Virgil, 1651, by Thomas Clifton, Northampton Co.
Tharpp, Wm., 1655, by Richard Codsford, Westmoreland Co.
Theboult, Clemt., 1643, by Tho. Cassen, Lower Norfolk Co.
Therg, Mr. James, 1655, by Major Wm. Lewis, New Kent Co.
Thickman, Wm., 1650, by Mr. John Hallawes, Northumberland Co.
Thickpenny, John, 1654, by Edw. Welch, ———— Co.
Thiggeson, Joane, 1636, by Edward Tonstall, ———— Co.
Thimbleby, Richard, 1638, by Thomas Swan, James Citie Co.
Thimbley, Rich., 1635, by Wm. Swan, James Co.
Thocker, Silvester, 1650, by Mr. James Williamson, ———— Co.
Thocker, Hen., 1642, by Hugh Gwyn, Gent., ———— Co.
Thocker, Henry, 1652, by Capt. Augustine Warner, ———— Co.
Thomas, Hoell, 1655, by Mr. Anthony Langston, New Kent Co.
Thomas, Grace, 1654, by Nich. Merywether, Westmoreland Co.
Thomas, Roger, 1656, by Silvester Thatcher, ———— Co.
Thomas, John, 1655, by Major Miles Cary, Warwick Co.
Thomas, Fra., 1655, by Richard Coole and David Anderson, Westmoreland Co.
Thomas, Wm., 1655, by John Earle, Northumberland Co.
Thomas, Arundl., 1656, by Tebitha and Matilda Scarburgh, Northampton Co.
Thomas, Tho., 1656, by Sir Henry Chichley, ———— Co.
Thomas, Grace, 1654, by Abra. Moone, Lancaster Co.
Thomas, Richard, 1654, by John Phillips and John Batts, Lancaster Co.
Thomas, Robt., 1654, by Randall Chamblett, ———— Co.
Thomas, Wm., 1654, by Capt. Augustine Warner and Mr. John Robins, ———— Co.
Thomas, Wm., 1654, by Walter Dickenson, Lancaster Co.
Thomas, Wm., 1655, by Richard Codsford, Westmoreland Co.
Thomas, Wm., 1642, by Cornelius de Hull, ———— Co.
Thomas, John, 1647, by Richard Bland, ———— Co.
Thomas, John, Jr., 1643, by Capt. Samuell Mathews, Esq., ———— Co.
Thomas, Wm., 1643, by Capt. Samuell Mathews, Esq., ———— Co.
Thomas, Edward, 1650, by Tho. Blogg, Northumberland Co.
Thomas, Aebie, 1650, by Tho. Wilkinson, ———— Co.
Thomas, Wm., 1650, by Epa. Lawson, ———— Co.
Thomas, Tho., 1650, by Mr. Epaphroditus Lawson, ———— Co.
Thomas, Morgan, 1650, by Richard Axom, and Tho. Godwin ———— Co
Thomas, Daniell, 1650, by Hump. Lyster, ———— Co.
Thomas, Jura, 1650, by Hump. Lyster, ———— Co.

Thomas, Robt., 1650, by Capt. Moore Fautleroy, ——— Co.
Thomas, Elcino, 1650, by Nicho. Jernew, Yorke Co.
Thomas, John, 1649, by Mr. Robert Parker, Northampton Co.
Thomas, Roger, 1650, by Tho. Hawkins, Charles River Co.
Thomas, Dorothy, 1649, by John Thomas (her husband), York Co.
Thomas, Edward, 1649, by Wm. Nesum, Tho. Sax, Miles Bathasby
    and John Pyne, Northampton Co.
Thomas, Richard, 1650, by Mr. James Williamson, ——— Co.
Thomas, John, 1649, by Richard Kemp, Esq. (Sec. of State), ——— Co.
Thomas, Abra., 1648, by Bartholomew Hoskins, ——— Co.
Thomas, Wm., 1649, by Stephen Gill, York Co.
Thomas, John, 1649, by Mr. Wm. Hoccaday, ——— Co.
Thomas, Wm., 1648, by Mr. Phillip Bennet, Nansemond Co.
Thomas, John, 1648, by Richard Lee, Gent., ——— Co.
Thomas, Gabrell, 1648, by Wm. Barret, ——— Co.
Thomas, Sym., 1648, by Wm. Barret, ——— Co.
Thomas, Eliz., 1654, by Edward Revell, Northampton Co.
Thomas, Evan, 1653, by David Phillips, Northumberland Co.
Thomas, Sarah, 1653, by Wm. Hunt, ——— Co.
Thomas, Ev., 1653, by Wm. Hunt, ——— Co.
Thomas, Phild., 1653, by Wm. Hunt, ——— Co.
Thomas, ———, 1653, by Wm. Thomas (her husband), Lancaster Co.
Thomas, Joane, 1653, by John Hillier, Northumberland Co.
Thomas, Wm., 1653, by John Hillier, Northumberland Co.
Thomas, Geo., 1653, by John Holding, York Co.
Thomas, Eliz., 1652, by Mr. Nicholas Jernew, Gloucester Co.
Thomas, Phill., 1652, by Christopher Lewis, Isle of Wight Co.
Thomas, Wm., 1652, by John Taylor, Lancaster Co.
Thomas, George, 1652, by Mr. Edward Travis, James City Co.
Thomas, Wm., 1652, by Nicho. George, Tho. Taberer and Humphry
    Clarke, ——— Co.
Thomas, Francis, 1652, by Mr. Henry Soane, ——— Co.
Thomas, Wm., 1653, by Tho. Read, Northumberland Co.
Thomas, John, 1652, by Tho. Hackett, ——— Co.
Thomas, Wm., 1653, by Gregory Penot, Isle of Wight Co.
Thomas, John, 1653, by Richard Smith, Northampton Co.
Thomas, James, 1651, by John Thomas, Gloucester Co.
Thomas, Kath., 1651, by John Thomas, Gloucester Co.
Thompson, Sara., 1651, by Lancaster Lovett, Lower Norfolk Co.
Thomas, Wm., 1651, by Edward Deggs, Esq., Yorke Co.
Thomas, Edw., 1651 by John Adleston, ——— Co.
Thomas, Richard, 1651, by Mr. Arthur Price, Yorke Co.
Thomas, Henry, 1643, by John Hoddin, ——— Co.
Thomas, Wm., 1638, by John Batts and John Davis, Charles River Co.
Thomas, Richard, 1638, by John Batts and John Davis, Charles River
    Co.
Thomas, John, 1638, by George Higgins, Charles River Co.
Thomas, Wm., 1643, by Capt. John Upton, Isle of Wight Co.
Thomas, Mary, 1643, by John Hoddin, ——— Co.
Thomas, Lowry, 1638, by Randall Crew, Upper New Norfolk Co.
Thomas, John, 1637, by Elizabeth Parker, Henrico Co.

Thomas, Jon., 1637, by Daniell Gookins, New Norfolk Co.
Thomas, Lazarus, 1638, by Wm. Morgan, ——— Co.
Thomas, Wm., 1635, by Christopher Wooddard, ——— Co.
Thomas, Eliz., 1637, by Phillipp Taylor, Accomack Co.
Thomas, Henry, 1637, by Capt. Robt. Helgate, Charles River Co.
Thomas, Phillipp, 1637, by Christopher Woodward, Charles City Co.
Thomas, John, 1636, by Elizabeth Packer, Henrico Co.
Thomas, Wm., 1637, by Wm. Farrar, Henrico Co.
Thomas, Margaret, 1637, by Richard Greete (her husband), ——— Co
Thomas, Eliza., 1637, by Thomas Hampton Co. New Norfolk Co.
Thomas, Thomas, 1637, by Thomas Hampton, New Norfolk Co.
Thomas, Robert, 1635, by George Minifie, James City Co.
Thomas, Robert, 1636, by Mr. Georg Menifye, James City Co.
Thomas, Privett, 1636, by Thomas Privett, Charles River Co.
Thomas, Richard, 1635, by John Davis, James City Co.
Thomas, Wm., 1651, by Richard Coleman, Yorke Co
Thomas, John, 1639, by Rich. Hoe, James City Co.
Thomas, Christopher, Sr., 1638, by Christopher Thomas, Accomac Co.
Thomas, Christopher, Jr., 1638, by Christopher Thomas, Accomac Co.
Thomas, Jon., 1642, by Capt. Samuell Mathews, Esq., ——— Co.
Thomas, John, 1638, by Capt. Christopher Wormley, Charles River Co.
Thomas, Christ., 1637, by Nathaniel Floyd, Isle of Wight Co.
Thomas, Robt., 1642, by John Benton, ——— Co.
Thomas, Robert, 1639, by William Barker, James City Co.
Thomas, John, 1639, by Henry Perry, Charles City Co.
Thomas, Thorand, 1654, by Col. Argoll Yardley, Northampton Co.
Thomasin, his wife (Raynes), 1637, by John Wilkins, New Norfolk Co.
Thomason, a maid, 1649, by Richard Kemp, Esq., Sec. of State, ———
    Co.
Thomblin, Sara, 1650, by Richard Axom and Tho. Godwin, ——— Co.
Thomlin, Sara, 1650, by Richard Axom and Tho. Godwin, ——— Co.
Thornbury, Richard, 1650, by Capt. John Flood, Gent., and Jno. Flood,
    an ancient planter, James City Co.
Thomlinson, Tho., 1653, by John Madison, Gloucester Co.
Thompkin, Rich., 1648, by John Seward, Isle of Wight Co.
Thompson, Eliz., 1655, by Mr. Anthony Langston, New Kent Co.
Thompson, Robert, 1656, by George Kibble, Lancaster Co.
Thompson, Ann, 1656, by George Kibble, Lancaster Co.
Thompson, John, 1653, by Samuell Parry, Lancaster Co.
Thompson, John, 1654, by Wm. Thorne, Northampton Co.
Tompson, Robert, 1655, by George Kibble, ——— Co.
Thompson, Joseph, 1655, by Dr. Giles Mode, New Kent Co.
Thompson, Wm., 1655, by George Frizell and Tho. Moore, North-
    ampton Co.
Thompson, David, 1656, by Edward Robinson and Tho. Hall, Lower
    Norfolk Co.
Thompson, Sara, ———, by Robt. Fontaine, Lower Norfolk Co.
Thompson, Thos., 1656, by Humphry Tabb, Gent., Elizabeth City Co.
Thompson, Robert, 1656, by Daniel Jines and Jno. Jenings, ——— Co.
Thompson, Law., 1656, by Mr. John Paine, ——— Co.
Thompson, Ann, 1650, by John Garwood, Nansemond Co.

Thompson, Milliscent, 1650, by Tho. Tilsley, James City Co.
Thompson, Robert, 1650, by Capt. Charles Leech, Yorke Co.
Thompson, Eldred, 1643, by Samuell Abbott, James City Co.
Thompson, Tho., 1646, by Samuell Abbott, Nansemond Co.
Thompson, Margaret, 1646, by Col. Henry Bishopp, James City Co.
Thompson, Ja., 1646, by David Jones, Charles City Co.
Thompson, Jane, 1650, by David Peible, Charles City Co.
Thompson, Sara, 1650, by John Mattrum, Northumberland Co.
Thompson, Tho., 1650, by Mr. Epaphroditus Lawson, ——— Co.
Thompson, John, 1649, by Edmund Scarburgh, Jr., Northampton Co.
Thompson, Henry, 1649, by John King, Yorke Co.
Thompson, John, 1649, by Nicholas Waddilow, Northampton Co.
Thompson, Wm., 1653, by Robert Tomplin, ——— Co.
Thompson, Francis, 1653, by Wm. Johnson, Lower Norfolk Co.
Thompson, Edward, 1653, by Colo. Wm. Clayborne (Sec. of State),
     ——— Co.
Thompson, John, 1653, by Colo. Wm. Clayborne (Sec. of State), ———
     Co.
Thompson, Makum, 1653, by Geo. Watts, Northumberland Co.
Thompson, Clare, 1653, by John Shepperd, Northumberland Co.
Thompson, Geo., 1653, by John Shepperd, Northumberland Co.
Thompson, Elizabeth, 1652, by Mr. Tho. Purifye and Mrs. Temperence
     Reppitt, ——— Co.
Thompson, John, 1652, by Ralph Horsely, Northumberland Co.
Thompson, Richd., 1652, by Tho. Holliwell, ——— Co.
Thompson, Robt., 1652, by Richard Nelmes, Northumberland Co.
Thompson, John, 1652, by Littleton Scarburg, ——— Co.
Thompson, Rice, 1653, by Peter Knight and Baker Cutt, ——— Co.
Thompson, John, 1652, by Littleton Scarburg, ——— Co.
Thompson, John, 1651, by Richard Kellum, Northampton Co.
Thompson, Thomas, 1646, by Lancaster Levit, ——— Co.
Thompson, Willi, 1643, by George Levitt, ——— Co.
Thompson, Tho., 1643, by John Hoddin, ——— Co.
Thompson, John, 1643, by John Hoddin, ——— Co.
Thomspon, Ann, 1637, by Arthur Smith, Isle of Wight Co.
Thompson, Judith, 1638, by Randall Crew, Upper New Norfolk Co.
Thompson, Hen., 1637, by Edward Morth, James City Co.
Thompson, William, 1635, by John Leonard, Warrasquinoake Co.
Thompson, Thos., 1637, by Francis Poythers, Charles City Co.
Thompson, William, 1635, by Capt. Wm. Pierse, ——— Co.
Thompson, Ann, 1653, by Tho. Philpot, Northumberland Co.
Thompson, Rich., 1637, by Tho. Symmons, Charles River Co.
Thompson, Jam., 1650, by George Pate, Charles City Co.
Thompson, James, 1639, by Richard Corke, Gent., Henrico Co.
Thompson, Danll., 1650, by George Pate, Charles City Co.
Thomson, Wm., 1642, by Victoris Christmas and Francis Finch, ———
     Co.
Thompsond, Edwd., 1642, by Wm. Eyres, Upper New Norfolk Co.
Thomson, Jane, 1650, by John Hallawes, Gent., Northumberland Co.
Thomson, Wm., 1650, by Epa. Lawson, ——— Co.
Thomnes, Ralph, 1644, by John Hill, Gent., Upper Norfolk Co.

Thooneford, Samuell, 1637, by Thomas Osborne (Jun.), Henrico Co.
Thoonecroft, Edward, 1640, by Elias Taylor, Accomack Co.
Thorncombe, Wm., 1637, by Cheney Boyes, Charles City Co.
Thorncomb, Wm., 1636, by Cheney Boyse, Charles City Co.
Thorne, Thomas, 1650, by Thomas Mulford, Nansemond Co.
Thorne, Anna, 1651, by James Foster, Nansemond Co.
Thorne, Thom., 1638, by John Moye, Lower New Norfolk Co.
Thronberry, Rich., 1638, by John Fludd, James City Co.
Thorneton, Wm., 1642, by William Prior, Gent., ——— Co.
Thorneton, Rich., 1637, by Theodore Moyser, James City Co.
Thornton, Adam, 1651, by Capt. Staphen Gill, Northumberland Co.
Thorowgood, Tho., 1655, by John Hinman, Northampton Co.
Thorowgood, John, 1650, by Silvester Thatcher, and Tho. Whitlocke,
    ——— Co.
Thoroughgood, Elin., 1651, by Coll. Guy Molsworth, ———Co.
Thoroughgood, Mary, 1638, by Phillipp Clarke, James City Co.
Thoroughgood, Dann., 1635, by Capt. Adam Thoroughood, ——— Co.
Thoroughgood, Thomas, 1635, by Capt. Adam Thoroughgood, ———
    Co.
Thoroughgood, Sarah, 1635, by Capt. Adam Thoroughgood (her hus-
    band), ——— Co.
Thoroughgood, Thomas, 1639, by William Davis, James City Co.
Thorp, Ann, 1653, by Toby Horton, Lancaster Co.
Thorp, Mayses, 1655, by John Palmer, Northumberland Co.
Throp, Clerist, 1637, by Margaret Rogers, New Norfolk Co.
Thorpe, Tho., 1654, by John Cox, Lancaster Co.
Thorpe, John, 1650, by Bertram Obert, ——— Co.
Thorpe, John, 1650, by Nathaniel Jones, Northumberland Co.
Thorpe, Wm., 1650, by Mrs. Winefrid, Morrison, ——— Co.
Thorpe, Wm., 1643, by Thomas Hughes, Charles River Co.
Thorpe, John, 1653, by Dennis Conniers, Lancaster Co.
Thorpe, Walter, 1653, by John Earle, Northumberland Co.
Thorpe, Tho., 1653, by John Earle, Northumberland Co.
Thorpe, Daniell, 1643, by Georg Levitt, ——— Co.
Thorpe, Christ, 1636, by Edward Rogers, Warrasquinoake Co.
Thourleson, John, 1650, by John Hallawes, Gent., Northumberland Co
Thrope, Mary, 1652, by Capt. Augustine Warner, ——— Co.
Thraile, Tho., 1654, by Humphry Dennis, Gloucester Co.
Thrasher, Ann, 1650, by Richard Smith, Northampton Co.
Thresher, Ann, 1651, by Richard Smith, Northampton Co.
Thresher, Wm., 1649, by Richard Vaughan, Northampton Co.
Thresher, Robert, (Jr.), 1636, by Izabell Thresher, ——— Co.
Thresher, Izabell, 1636, by Izabell Thresher, ——— Co.
Thresher, Robt., 1636, by Izabell Thresher, ——— Co.
Thrickmorton, Robt., 1645, by Wm. Jacob, Upper Norfolk Co.
Thrift, James, 1639, by Justinian Cooper, Isle of Wight Co.
Thrift, James, 1639, by John Wright, Upper New Norfolk Co.
Thrope, Richard, 1653, by Wm. Cox, ——— Co.
Thorndon, Robert, 1648, by Lewis Burwell, Gent., ——— Co.
Throughtgood, Rich., 1650, by Elias Edmondes, ——— Co.
Thrush, Wm., 1655, by Wm. Botham, Westmoreland Co.

Thrush, Fra., 1653, by Wm. Sidner, Lancaster Co.
Thucker, John, 1650, by Lieut. Wm. Worleich, ——— Co.
Thunder, Peter, 1642, by Wm. Durant, ——— Co.
Thunder, Peter, 1652, by Col. Geo. Ludlow, Esq., Gloucester Co.
Thurman, Jane, 1637, by John Wilkins, New Norfolk Co.
Thurpless, Eliza, 1648, by George Read, Gent., ——— Co.
Thurlley, Hen., 1650, by Richard Tye and Charles Sparrowe, Charles
    City Co.
Thurten, Thomas, 1636, by Edward Tonstall, ——— Co.
Thurston, Edw., 1650, by Mr. Stephen Hamelin, Charles City Co.
Townson, Hen., 1643, by Capt. Samuell Mathews, Esq., ——— Co.
Tiballs, Edward, 1652, by Mrs. Elinor Brocas, Lancaster Co.
Tibball, Peter, 1656, by Tho. Harris, Lancaster Co.
Tibbs, Michaell, 1637, by John Baker, Charles River Co.
Tidderson, Richard, 1653, by Richard Major, Gloucester Co.
Tidney, Richard, 1653, by Mathew Tomlin, Northumberland Co.
Tielet, John, 1648, by Robert Pitt, Isle of Wight Co.
Tiffeney, John, 1638, by Henry Catalyn, Upper Norfolk Co.
Tiffiney, John, 1637, by Henry Catalyne, New Norfolk Co.
Trigg, Paul, 1654, by Tho. Willoughby, Lower Norfolk Co.
Tildamus, Ann, 1654, by Major Miles Carey, Westmoreland Co.
Tilkin, Robert, 1650, by Capt. Charles Leech, Yorke Co.
Till, Daniell, 1655, by George Parker, Northampton Co.
Till, John, 1650, by Capt. Moore Fautleroy, ——— Co.
Tilman, Christopher, 1638, by Georg Mynifie (merchant), ——— Co.
Tillney, Symon, 1639, by Robert Newman, Warwick River Co.
Tillet, Marg., 1653, by Wm. Colborne, Northampton Co.
Tillett, Margarett, 1653, by Charles Scarburg, Northampton Co.
Tilly, Anthony, 1654, by Robert Younge, Lancaster Co.
Tilly, ———, 1653, by Charles Scarburg, Northampton Co.
Tilsley, Thomas, 1638, by John Robins, James City Co.
Tilson, Richard, 1650, by Henry Peaseley, ——— Co.
Timball, Lydia, 1653, by Mr. James Tooke, Isle of Wight Co.
Tinason, Richard, 1654, by Francis Smith and Mr. John Smith, West-
    moreland Co.
Tingle, John, 1650, by Mr. James Williamson, ——— Co.
Tinkins, Robt., 1651, by John Hull, Northumberland Co.
Tinley, Richard, 1651, by Richard Whitehurst, Lower Norfolk Co.
Tinwell, John, 1637, by Francis Osborne, ——— Co.
Tiplady, John, 1639, by Christopher Boyse, Charles River Co.
Tipladge, Jno., 1645, by John Rode, Warwick Co.
Tipler, Mary, 1651, by Christopher Burroughs, Lower Norfolk Co.
Tisley, Rich., 1638, by John Gater, Lower New Norfolk Co.
Tirloe, Jos., 1636, by Francis Maulden, ——— Co.
Titon, Wm., 1638, by John Moye, Lower New Norfolk Co.
Titus, Tho., 1654, by John Drayton, Westmoreland Co.
Tirrall, Morrice, 1653, by Toby Harton, Lancaster Co.
Tirrell, Edward, 1653, by Joseph Croshaw, York Co.
Tockewood, Eliz., 1643, by Tho. Dew, Upper Norfolk Co.
Todd, Wm., 1651, by Mr. Antho. Steevens, Northampton Co.
Todd, Geo., 1650, by Wm. Yarrett and Fra. Wittington, ——— Co.

Todd, Wm., 1654, by Christopher Regault, Gloucester Co.
Todd, Mathew, 1646, by John Broach, York Co.
Todd, Thomas, 1642, by Roger Symmons, ——— Co.
Todd, Elizabeth, 1637, by Thomas Todd (her husband), New Norfolk Co.
Todd, Robert, 1647, by Thomas Johnson, Gent., Northampton Co.
Todd, Mary, 1652, by John Howett, Northumberland Co.
Todd, Tho., 1652, by Tobias Horton, Lancaster Co.
Todman, Richd., 1653, by Robt. Sorrel, ——— Co.
Todwell, Hen., 1652, by Capt. Francis Morgan, and Ralph Green Gloucester Co.
Thombs, Richard, 1636, by James Place, Henrico Co.
Tomkeson, John, 1637, by Francis Fowler, James River Co.
Tomkin, Henry, 1652, by Mr. Nicholas Jernew, Gloucester Co.
Tomkins, Hump., 1652, by Capt. Francis Morgan and Ralph Green, Gloucester Co.
Tomkins, Robt., 1653, by Wm. Wyatt, Gloucester Co.
Tomlin, Henry, 1638, by Edmund Scarborough, Accomac Co.
Tomlin, Jon., 1642, by William Lawson, Isle of Wight Co.
Tomlin, Mathew, 1637, by Nathaniel Floyd, Isle of Wight Co.
Tonlim, Henry, 1640, by Edmund Scarburgh, Accomack Co.
Tomlin, Wm., 1652, by Dr. George Hack, Northampton Co.
Tomlin, Wm., 1653, by Charles Scarburg, Northampton Co.
Tomlins, Patience, 1651, by John Stratton, Lower Norfolk Co.
Tomlinson, Jon., 1636, by Cheney Boyse, Charles City Co.
Tomlinson, Joane, 1636, by Cheney Boyse, Charles City Co.
Tomlinson, Edward, 1637, by Jonathan Longworth, New Norfolk Co.
Tomlinson, John, 1637, by Arthur Smith, Isle of Wight Co.
Tomlinson, Joane, 1637, by Cheney Boyes, Charles City Co.
Tomlinson, John, 1637, by Cheney Boyes, Charles City Co.
Tomlinson, Edward, 1637, by Jonathan Longworth, New Norfolk Co.
Tompkins, Tho., 1636, by John Chew, Gent., Charles River Co.
Tompkins, Thom., 1637, by John Chew, Charles River Co.
Tompson, Edwd., 1637, by Mathew Edloe, ——— Co.
Tompkinson, John, 1635, by Francis Fowler, James City Co.
Tompson, Henry, 1635, by Jeremiah Clement, ——— Co.
Tompkins, John, 1638, by John Bishop, James City Co.
Tompson, Humphry, 1639, by Randall Holt, James City Co.
Tompson, Hen., 1643, by Richard Richards, Charles River Co.
Thompson, Grace, 1653, by Evan Davis and Henry Nicholls, Lancaster Co.
Tomroy, Marg., 1653, by Richard Carey, ——— Co.
Tomson, Edw., 1650, by John Hallawes, Gent., Northumberland Co.
Tonell, Tho., 1654, by John Newman, Lancaster Co.
Tonery, Fra., 1654, by John Watson and John Bognall, Westmoreland Co.
Tonerson, Georg, 1636, by Stephen Webb, James City Co.
Tonlson, Edward, 1639, by Stephen Webb, James City Co.
Tonne, Rich., 1649, by Tho. Spoke, Gent., Northumberland Co.
Tonstall, Martha, 1636, by Edward Tonstall, (her husband) ——— Co.
Toogood, Joseph, 1654, by Tho. Willoughby, Lower Norfolk Co.

Toogood, Edward, 1656, by Richard Gible, Northumberland Co.
Tooke, James, 1637, by William Spencer, ——— Co.
Toole, John, 1655, by John Dorman, Northampton Co.
Tooales, John, 1656, by John Billiott, Northampton Co.
Toolye, Thomas, 1638, by John Fludd, James City Co.
Tooly, Tho., 1654, by Robert Hubard, Westmoreland Co.
Toomes, Alice, 1650, by Mr. Anthony Ellyot, ——— Co.
Toomes, Ann, 1655, by Lt. Col. Anthony Ellyott, ——— Co.
Toppin, John, 1652, by Robert West, Charles City Co.
Toprell, Mary, 1653, by Wm. Cox, ——— Co.
Tordall, George, 1655, by John Lawson, Lancaster Co.
Torme, John, 1653, by Tho. Todd, ——— Co.
Torner, Sa., 1652, by George Pace, Charles City Co.
Torringe, Geo., 1653, by Charles Grymes, Lancaster Co.
Torrowgood, Tho., 1656, by Mr. Henry Soanes, New Kent Co.
Toshan, John, 1656, by Margaret Miles, Westmoreland Co.
Tovey, John, 1653, by Tho. Speoke, ——— Co.
Towell, Jon., 1637, by Capt. Thomas Panlett, Charles City Co.
Tower, Robt., 1654, by Col. Argoll Yardley, Northampton Co.
Towerman, Ann, 1653, by Robt. Blake, Isle of Wight Co.
Towers, Wm., 1637, by Wm. Farrar, Henrico Co.
Towers, Elizabeth, 1654, by Tho. Deynes, ——— Co.
Towers, James, 1654, by Benjamin Mathews, Northampton Co.
Towke, Richd., 1653, by Henry Lee, Yorke Co.
Towmes, John, 1652, by Mrs. Jane Harmer, Northumberland Co.
Town, James, 1651, by John King, Gloucester Co.
Townd, Edmond, 1650, by John Cooke, Northumberland Co.
Towney, Isaac, 1654, by John Drayton, Westmoreland Co.
Towning, Thos., 1637, by Mathew Atkinson, New Norfolk Co.
Townsend, Robt., 1643, by Casar, Puggett Lower Norfolk Co.
Tows, Robt., 1644, by John Hill, Gent., Upper Norfolk Co.
Townsend, Francis, 1639, by Capt. Rich. Townsend, Charles River Co.
Townshend, John, 1655, by Moses Lynton, Lower Norfolk Co.
Towne, John, 1649, by Mr. Tho. Spake, Northumberland Co.
Townsehend, Jno., 1653, by Capt. Robt. Abrahal, York Co.
Townshend, Richd., 1653, by Capt. Francis Patt, Northampton Co.
Townsend, Wm., 1653, by Edward Dobson, ——— Co.
Townsend, Job., 1652, by Wm. Ratton and Richard Flint, Lancaster Co.
Townsend, John, 1651, by Christopher Burroughs, Lower Norfolk Co.
Townsend, Wm., 1635, by Thos. Smith, James Co.
Towton, Anto., 1654, by Col. Argoll Yardley, Northampton Co.
Trace, John, 1652, by Mr. Tho. Curtis, ——— Co.
Tracye, Robt., 1653, by Roger Walter, Northumberland Co.
Tracy, Mary, 1654, by John Wyre, John Gillet, Andrew Gilson and John Phillipps, ——— Co.
Tracy, Robert, 1653, by Roger Walker, Northumberland Co.
Trade, Thomas, 1643, by Thomas Glascocke, Warwick River Co.
Traneere, James, 1635, by John Parrott, ——— Co.
Traniell, John, 1646, by Lancaster Levilt, ——— Co.
Trassy, Teague, 1655, by Matilda Scarbourgh, Northampton Co.

Trasey, Robert, 1654, by Roger Walters, Northumberland Co.
Travellor, Alice, 1636, by Georg Travellor, Accomack Co.
Travis, Walter, 1637, by Edward Travis, James City Co.
Travis, Walter, 1638, by Edward Travis and Jon. Johnson, James City Co.
Travers, James, 1653, by Peter Knight, Northumberland Co.
Trayton, Kath., 1653, by Wm. Sidner, Lancster Co.
Trayillis, Richd., 1651, by Ashwell Battin, Yorke Co.
Treamer, Jacob, 1654, by John Wyre, John Gillet, Andrew Gilson and John Phillipps, —— Co.
Treble, Wm., Sr., 1640, by Thomas Harvey, James City Co.
Treble, Wm., Jr., 1640, by Thomas Harvey, James City Co.
Tredescant, John, 1642, by Bertram Hobert, —— Co.
Tredisken, John, 1654, by Wm. Lea, Charles City Co.
Tree, Humphry, 1643, by John Batts, James City Co.
Treedle, Eliz., 1650, by John Sevier, —— Co.
Treffe, Joyce, 1654, by John Wyre, John Gillet, Andrew Gilson, and John Phillipps, —— Co.
Trelbeck, Miles, 1650, by Lawrence Peters, Nansemond Co.
Trelawney, Robt., 1643, by John Sweete, Isle of Wight Co.
Trencher, Symon, 1637, by Francis Osborne, —— Co.
Trendale, Paul, 1637, by John Wilkins, New Norfolk Co.
Trendall, Paul, 1636, by John Wilkins, Accomack Co.
Trenis, Jacob, 1656, by Robt. Bayly, Northampton Co.
Trenor, Jno., 1651, by Geo. Colclough, Gent., Northumberland Co.
Trent, Jno., 1653, by Frances Emperor, Hugh Gale and Edward Morgan, Lower Norfolk Co.
Trent, Humphry, 1638, by Percivall Champion, Upper New Norfolk Co.
Trent, John, 1647, by Thomas Wells, Lower Norfolk Co.
Treplana, Tho., 1653, by Colo. Wm. Clayborne (Sec. of State), —— Co.
Tresilian, Kather., 1643, by Capt. Samuell Mathews, Esq., —— Co.
Trevannion, Tho., 1645, by Thomas Davis, Warwick Co.
Trevalin, Alice, 1652, by Tho. Steevens, Lancaster Co.
Trevell, Eliza., 1642, by Wm. Durant, —— Co.
Trevis, Wm., 1656, by Robt. Bayly, Northampton Co.
Trevill, Eliza, 1652, by Col. Geo. Ludlow, Esq., Gloucester Co.
Trevett, Georg, 1640, by Christopher Kirke, Accomack Co.
Trewet, John, 1694, by Mr. Edmund Scarburgh, Northampton Co.
Triggs, Wm., 1640, by Henry Porter and Raphaell Joyner, James City Co.
Trigg, Samuel, 1640, by Henry Porter and Raphaell Joyner, James City Co.
Trigg, Elian, wife of Saml. Trigg, 1640, by Henry Porter and Raphaell Joyner, James City Co.
Trigg, William, 1639, by Samuell Trigg and Raphael Joyner, James City Co.
Trigg, Samuell, 1635, by Thomas Harwood, —— Co.
Trigg, Ellian, wife of Saml. Trigg, 1639, by Saml. Trigg and Raphael Joyner, James City Co.
Tingy, Jon., 1636, by James Vanerit, Elizabeth City Co.

Triggs, Lan., 1651, by Capt. John West, Esq., Yorke Co.
Tripp, Edw., 1649, by Richard Bayly, Northampton Co.
Trolman, ———, 1640, by John George, Charles City Co.
Trollock, Jon., 1642, by Stephen Gill, ——— Co.
Tross, Thos., 1640, by John Radford, Lower Norfolk Co.
Troton, Nicholas, 1638, by Thomas Beerboge, Upper New Norfolk Co.
Trotter, John, 1653, by Tho. Holmes, York Co.
Trotter, Tho., 1638, by William Banister, ——— Co.
Trotter, Joane, 1653, by Jno. Hansford, Gloucester Co.
Trovell, Sarah, 1648, by Wm. Edwards and Rice Edwards, James City Co.
Trowers, Baughley, 1656, by Mr. Jno. Paine, ——— Co.
Truce, Abig., 1654, by Mr. Francis Hamond, York Co.
True, Walter, 1652, by Tho. Preston, ——— Co.
True, Anne, 1654, by Humphry Haggett, Lancaster Co.
Truman, Jno., 1654, by John Watson and John Bognall, Westmoreland Co.
Trueman, Robt., 1656, by Mr. Henry Soanes, New Kent Co.
Truitt, John, 1642, by Edmund Scarburgh, Accomack Co.
Trulton, Geo., 1653, by Christopher Boyce, Northumberland Co.
Trustall, Robert, 1639, by Thomas Mathews, Henrico Co.
Truth, Fra., 1653, by John Gillett, Lancaster Co.
Tuata, Tho., 1649, by John Merriman, ——— Co.
Tuck, Ann, 1656, by William Bird, ——— Co.
Tuck, Woodham, 1642, by Lieut. Francis Mason, ——— Co.
Tucker, Leonnider and wife, 1650, by Thomas Powell, ——— Co.
Tucker, John, 1643, by Lt. Wm. Worleidge, ——— Co.
Tucker, Allen, 1638, by Abraham Wood, Charles City Co.
Tucker, Alex., 1635, by William Clark, Warrasquinoake Co.
Tucker, Allen, 1636, by Wm. Clarke, Henrico Co.
Tucker, Barthol., 1639, by Tristram Nosworthy, Upper Norfolk Co.
Tucker, Tho., 1654, by John Watson and John Bognall, Westmoreland Co.
Tucker, John, 1642, by Samuell Abbott, ——— Co.
Tucker, Wm., 1650, by Daniell Luellin, Charles City Co.
Tucker, Wm., 1650, by Richard Tye and Charles Sparrowe, Charles City Co.
Tucker, Ailee, 1649, by Arthur Allen, James City Co.
Tucker, John, 1652, by Mr. Edward Overman, York Co.
Tue, John, 1654, by Tho. Hobkins, Lancaster Co.
Tuffes, Tho., 1656, by Wm. Pulliam, New Kent Co.
Tuffnell, John, 1650, by Richard Cheeseman, ——— Co.
Tuggell, Tho., 1654, by Obed. Williams, York Co.
Tull, Tho., 1654, by John Watson and John Bognall, Westmoreland Co.
Tulley, John, 1640, by John Holloway, Accomack Co.
Tungleburg, Wm., 1653, by Charles Grymes, Lancaster Co.
Tunstall, Martha, 1637, by Edward Tunstall (her husband), Henrico Co.
Tupp, Edwd., 1654, by Wm. Bacon, Northumberland Co.
Tute, James, 1652, by Mrs. Jane Harmon, Northumberland Co.
Tutton, Hen., 1638, by Walter Chiles, Charles Citie Co.

Tutty, Tho., 1653, by Capt. Francis Patt, Northampton Co.
Turbuck, Willi, 1641, by Thomas Morrey, Isle of Wight Co.
Tureton, Robert, 1653, by Colo. Wm. Clayborne (Sec. of State), ——— Co.
Turfry, Richard, 1642, bh Capt. Humphry Higgenson, ———Co.
Turk, Antho., 1636, by Mr. Georg Minifye, James City Co.
Turke, Wm., 1647, by Richard Bland, ——— Co.
Turkey, Peter John, 1637, by Edward Travis, James City Co.
Turner, Thomas, 1645, by William Jones, Northampton Co.
Turner, John, 1639, by Edward Oliver, James City Co.
Turner, Geo., 1644, by John Hill, Gent., Upper Norfolk Co.
Turner, Sarah, 1655, by John Lawson, Lancaster Co.
Turner, John, 1637, by Humphry Higginson, ——— Co.
Turner, Robt., 1637, by Robert Throckmorton, Charles River Co.
Turner, James, 1635, by Pierce Lemon, Charles City Co.
Turner, Tobias, 1642, by Geo. Adkins and Wm. Foster, ——— Co.
Turner, Robert, 1637, by Wm. Farrar, Henrico Co.
Turner, Richard, 1637, by Francis Poytheis, Charles City Co.
Turner, Fr., 1637, by Theodore Moyser, James City Co.
Turner, Samuel, 1636, by Mr. Georg Minifye, James City Co.
Turner, Horman, 1637, by Patrick Kennedye, New Norfolk Co.
Turner, Thomas, 1636, by Richard Cocke, ——— Co.
Turner, Iatharios, 1635, by Wm. Andrews, Accomac Co.
Turner, Wm., 1643, by Mr. Phillipp Bennett, Upper Norfolk Co.
Turner, John, 1638, by Georg Mynifie (merchant), ——— Co.
Turner, Robert, 1637, by Robert Throckmorton, Charles River Co.
Turner, Richard; 1639, by Georg Minifye, Esq., Charles River Co.
Turner, John, 1638, by Edward Oliver, ——— Co.
Turner, Abraham, 1642, by Abraham Turner, ——— Co.
Turner, John, 1639, by Edward Oliver, James City Co.
Turner, Wm., 1639, by Capt. Nicholas Martian, Charles River Co.
Turner, Ann, 1637, by Capt. Francis Eppes, Charles City Co.
Turner, John, 1654, by John Watson and John Bognall, Westmoreland Co.
Turner, Richard, 1653, by Anto. Hoskins, Northampton Co.
Turner, Bryan, 1654, by John Newman, Lancaster Co.
Turner, Em., 1654, by John Newman, Lancaster Co.
Turner, Tho., 1655, by Lt. Col. Anthony Ellyott, ——— Co.
Turner, Abigall, 1655, by John Green, ——— Co.
Turner, Mary, 1653, by James Turner, ——— Co.
Turner, Margaret, 1656, by Mr. Martin Baker, New Kent Co.
Turner, Jam., 1650, by John Rosier, Northumberland Co.
Turner, Geo., 1642, by Stephen Gill, Yorke River Co.
Turner, Nicho., 1650, by Mrs. Frances Townshend (widow), Northumberland Co.
Turner, John, 1650, by John Landman, ——— Co.
Turner, John, 1643, by Capt. Samuell Mathews, Esq., ——— Co.
Turner, George, 1650, by Ralph Green, ——— Co.
Turner, Mary, 1650, by Ralph Green, ——— Co.
Turner, Mary, 1642, by Thomas Plummer, ——— Co.

Turner, John, 1650, by Richard Tye and Charles Sparrowe, Charles City Co.
Turner, Henry, 1650. by Richard Tye and Charles Sparrowe, Charles City Co.
Turner, Jane, 1650, by Wm. Clapham, ――― Co.
Turner, Eliz., 1650, by Capt. Moore Fautleroy, ――― Co.
Turner, Jno., 1653, by Capt. Francis Patt, Northampton Co.
Turner, E―――, 1653, by Tho. Griffin, Lancaster Co.
Turner, Bryan, 1653, by Tho. Griffin, Lancaster Co.
Turner, Elizabeth, 1653, by Charles Kiggen, York Co.
Turner, Simon, 1652, by Capt. John West, Esq., ――― Co.
Turner, Tho., 1652, by Mr. Tho. Gutheridge, Lower Norfolk Co.
Turner, George, 1653, by Robert Bouth, Yorke Co.
Turner, Mary, 1653, by Robert Bouth, Yorke Co.
Turner, John, 1653, by Francis Hale, ――― Co.
Turner, John, 1651, by Richard Wooton, Northumberland Co.
Turner, Ann, 1651, by Capt. Tho. Daivs, Northumberland Co.
Turney, James, 1652, by Capt. Francis Morgan, and Ralph Green, Gloucester Co.
Turpey, Jno., 1653, by Joseph Croshaw, York: Co.
Turtley, Anis, 1638, by Wm. Carter, James City Co.
Turtley, Avis, 1635, by Wm. Carter, James City Co.
Turth, Robt., 1653, by Colo. Wm. Clayborne (Sec. of State), ――― Co.
Turton, Timo., 1653, by Richard Jackson, ――― Co.
Turton, Miller, 1652, by Mr. Tho. Curtis, ――― Co.
Turton, Tymonthy, 1652, by Mrs. Elinor Brocas, Lancaster Co.
Turvy, John, 1638, by Edw. Travis, and John Johnson, James City Co.
Tuscome, Tho., 1652, by Mr. Tho. Gutheridge, Lower Norfolk Co.
Tustall, Robt., 1650, by Geo. Ludlow, Esq., Northumberland Co.
Tustion, Charles, 1648, by Georg Read, Gent., ――― Co.
Twinn, Ann., 1655, by Nich. Wadilow, Northampton Co.
Twinn, Tho., ―――, by Mr. John Page, ――― Co.
Twilly, Hum., 1651, by John Martin and (Lancaster Lovett), Lower Norfolk Co.
Twillye, Hum., ―――, by Mr. Robt. Fontaine, Lower Norfolk Co.
Tyball, Edward, 1649, by Capt. Ralph Wormeley, ――― Co.
Tybatts, Edward, 1649, by Wm. Hoccaday, ――― Co.
Tydder, Hugh, 1637, by Mathew Edloe, ――― Co.
Tye, Richard, 1642, by Adam Cooke, Charles Co.
Tyler, Tho., 1635, by Osbourne Jenkin, Charles City Co.
Tyler, Mary, 1652, by Henry Tyler, Charles River Co.
Tyler, Robert, 1654, by Mr. Giles Brent, Westmoreland Co.
Tyler, James, 1655, by Henry Barlow, ――― Co.
Tyler, James, 1655, by John Lynge, James City Co.
Tyler, Wm., 1654, by Capt. Nich. Marteaw, Westmoreland Co.
Tyler, Eliz., 1654, by Capt. Nich. Marteaw, Westmoreland Co.
Tyler, Anth., 1635, by John Upton, Warrasquinoake, Co.
Tyler, Thomas, 1637, by Francis Osborne, ――― Co.
Tyler, Antho., 1637, by John Upton, Isle of Wight Co.
Tyler, Robert, 1637, by Capt. Robert Helgate, Charles River Co.
Tyler, Anth., 1637, by Lt. John Upton, Isle of Wight Co.

Tymon, Sarah, 1642, by William Tymon (her husband), Charles River Co.

Tyngle, Antho., 1648, by Geo. Hardy, Tho. Wombwell and Peter Hall, Isle of Wight Co.

Tyres, Daniell, 1653, by Major Abra. Wood, Charles City Co.

Tyrrill, James, 1648, by Lewis Burwell, Gent., ——— Co.

Tysley, Richard, 1636, by John Gates, Elizabeth City Co.

Tyson, Georg, 1642, by John Moone, Isle of Wight Co.

U

Udday, Sanders, 1651, by Lieut. Collo. Giles Brent, Northumberland Co.

Uggins, Tho., 1653, by Tho. Todd, ——— Co.

Uggins, Edward, 1653, by George Collins, ——— Co.

Underfield, Wm., 1656, by Mr. Tho. Purifoy, ——— Co.

Underhill, Henry, 1653, by Richard Vardy, James City Co.

Underhill, Mr. Jno., 1651, by Lieut. Collo. Giles Brent, Northumberland Co.

Underhill, Mr. John, 1655, by Mrs. Margaret Brent, Lancaster Co.

Underwood, John, 1646, by Edward Hall, Lower Norfolk Co.

Underwood, Mary, wife Mr. Geo. Underwood, 1650, by Capt. Moore Fautleroy, ——— Co.

Underwood, Mr. Geo., 1650, by Capt. Moore Fautleroy, ——— Co.

Underwood, Ann, 1650, by Capt. Moore Fautleroy, ——— Co.

Underwood, Tho., 1650, by Capt. Moore Fautleroy, ——— Co.

Underwood, Wm., 1650, by Wm. Underwood, Gent. (his father), ——— Co.

Underwood, Mary, 1650, by Wm. Underwood, Gent. (her husband), ——— Co.

Underwood, Wm., 1642, by Justinian Cooper, Isle of Wight Co.

Union, Mary, 1654, by Richard Allen, Northampton Co.

Upchurch, Mich., 1654, by Valentine Patten, Westmoreland Co.

Upchurch, Mich., 1654, by Robert Hubard, Westmoreland Co.

Upoman, Edward, 1652, by Littleton Scarburg, ——— Co.

Uprence, Ri., 1650, by Hump. Lyster, ——— Co.

Upton, Dorothy, 1654, by Tho. Felton, Charles City Co.

Usher, 1653, by Anto. Hoskins, Northampton Co.

Usklye, Wm., 1653, by Roger Walker, Northumberland Co.

Uteley, James, 1643, by Rowland Burnham, Yorke Co.

Uxer, Mary, 1642, by Wm. Whitington, Northampton Co.

Uxor, Mary, 1653, by Capt. Wm. Whitington, Northampton Co.

Upwilliams, Tho., 1653, by Charles Scarburg, Northampton Co.

V

Vacseen, James, 1637, by John Clarkson, Charles River Co.

Vaeker, Dan., 1653, by Ferdinando Austin, Charles City Co.

Vaine, John, 1643, by Capt. Thomas Pettus, ——— Co.

Valeveo, Wm., 1653, by Peter Knight and Baker Cutt, ——— Co.

Valler, Wm., 1650, by Capt. Moore Fautleroy, ——— Co.

Vallett, John, 1639, by Capt. Nicholas Martian, Charles River Co.
Vallin, Joane, ——, by Mr. John Page, —— Co.
Valrey, Geo., 1650, by Thomas Powell, —— Co.
Van De Powke, ——, 1656, by Mr. Tho. Purifoy, —— Co.
Vand, Hump., 1648, by Lewis Burwell, Gent., —— Co.
Vand, Thomas, 1648, by Lewis Burwell, Gent., —— Co.
Vans, Robert, 1654, by Mr. Francis Hamond, York Co.
Vans, Susan, 1654, by Mr. Francis Hamond, York Co.
Vans, Eliz., 1654, by Mr. Francis Hamond, York Co.
Vans, Hump., 1654, by Mr. Francis Hamond, York Co.
Vans, John, 1638, by John George, Charles City Co.
Vanse, David, 1656, by George Kibble, Lancsater Co.
Varbread, Wm. 1653, by Capt. Wm. Whittington, Northampton Co.
Vardale, Rich., 1638, by Thomas Stout, —— Co.
Vardall, Richard, 1639, by William Davis, James City Co.
Vardy, Elizabeth, 1653, by Richard Vardy, James City Co.
Vargan, James, 1650, by Francis Hobbs, —— Co.
Varlow, Peter, 1635, by Daniel Cugley, Accomac Co.
Varly, Symon, 1650, by Lewis Burwell, Gent., Northumberland Co.
Varnham, John, 1656, by Herbert Smith, Gent., Westmoreland Co.
Vase, Rich., 1636, by Elizabeth Packer, Henrico Co.
Vase, Richard, 1637, by Elizabeth Parker, Henrico Co.
Vase, Henry, 1653, by Anto. Hoskins, Northampton Co.
Vassal, John, 1650, by Robert Blake and Samuell Elridge, Isle of Wight
    Co.
Vaster, Eliza., 1635, by John Vaster, Warrasquinoake Co.
Vauche, Kath., 1651, by Richard Wooton, Northumberland Co.
Vauche, Oliver, 1651, by Richard Wooton, Northumberland Co.
Vaughan, Rowd., 1636, by James Vanerit, Elizabeth City Co.
Vaughan, Patrick, 1635, by Nathaniel Hooke, —— Co.
Vaughan, John, 1637, by John Chew, Charles River Co.
Vaughan, David, 1637, by James Harrison, James City Co.
Vaughan, Lewis, 1636, by James Knott, Elizabeth City Co.
Vaughan, John, 1636, by John Chew, Gent., Charles River Co.
Vaughan, Thom., 1638, by Tristrum Nosworthy, —— Co.
Vaughan, Lewis, 1637, by James Knott, New Norfolk Co.
Vanhan, John, 1637, by John Moone, Isle of Wight Co.
Vaughan, Francis, 1644, by John Hill, Gent., Upper Norfolk Co
Vaughan, Eliza., 1643, by Walter Aston, Gent., Charles City Co.
Vaughan, Edwd., 1644, by John Hill, Gent., Upper Norfolk Co.
Vaughan, Jon., 1642, by Capt. Daniell Gookin, —— Co.
Vaughan, Christ., 1642, by Capt. Daniell Gookin, —— Co.
Vaughan, Xph., 1655, by Geo. Coltclough, Northumberland Co.
Vaughan, Elizabeth, 1654, by Daniel Boucher, Isle of Wight Co.
Vaughan, Mary, 1639, by Henry Bogwell, Accomack Co.
Vaughan, Patrick, 1638, by Lieut. John Upton, Isle of Wight Co.
Vaughan, Tho., 1653, by Wm. Hardidge, Northumberland Co.
Vaughan, Symon, 1651, by Wm. Hampton, —— Co.
Vaughan, Xtopher, 1653, by Samuell Parry, Lancaster Co.
Vaughan, Tho., 1653, by Abraham Moone, Lancaster Co.
Vaughan, John, 1652, by Mrs. Jane Harmer, Northumberland Co.

Vaughan, Xtopher, 1652, by John Hatton, ——— Co.
Vaughan, Geo., 1648, by Richard Pettibon, ——— Co.
Vaugran, Jon., 1638, by John Jackson and Eliza Kingswill, James City Co.
Vaukes, Peter, 1651, by Richard Wooton, Northumberland Co.
Vauson, Richard, 1643, by Capt. Samuell Mathews, Esq., ——— Co.
Vauston, Richard, 1637, by Thom. Harwood, Charles River Co.
Vausum, John, 1652, by Richard Hatton and Lambett Lambettson, Lancaster Co.
Vaultres, John, 1656, by Mr. Martin Baker, New Kent Co.
Veach, James, 1654, by Nicholas Morris, Northumberland Co.
Veale, Jane, 1636, by Wm. Parker, Warrasquinoake Co.
Veare, Mary, 1642, by Justinian Cooper, Isle of Wight Co.
Vecery, Ann, 1650, by Capt. Moore Fautleory, ——— Co.
Vehen, Daniel, 1652, by Augustine Moore, ——— Co.
Velayne, Jerimiah, 1642, by Wm. Eyres, Upper New Norfolk Co.
Velley, Wm., 1650, by Sr. Tho. Luntsford, Kt., and Barronnett, ——— Co.
Venable, Richard, 1635, by Alexander Stonar, ——— Co.
Venner, Wm., 1654, by Humphry Haggett, Lancaster Co.
Venice, Wm., 1639, by Christopher Boyse, Charles River Co.
Venice, Wm., 1642, by Christopher Boyce, ——— Co.
Venicoyih, Anne, 1650, by Anthony Fuljam, ——— Co.
Venison, Ben., 1654, by Capt. David Mansell, Westmoreland Co.
Vensey, Weymouth, 1635, by Capt. Tho. Willowbye, Elizabeth City Co.
Vert, Wm., 1652, by Peter Knight, Gloucester Co.
Vessell, Joyce, 1645, by Zachary Cripps, Warwick Co.
Vessell, Josias, 1653, by Charles Grymes, Lancaster Co.
Vicaris, Peter, 1651, by Audery Bennett, Nansemond Co.
Vicard, Wm., 1648, by Tho. Ludwell, Gent., James City Co.
Viccars, Biyan, 1639, by Edward Travis, James City Co.
Viccars, Francis, 1639, by Lieut. Richard Popeley, ——— Co.
Viccars, Mary, 1639, by Richard Nance, Henrico Co.
Vigeo, Gesper, 1655, by John Watson, Lancaster Co.
Villnott, Walter, 1650, by Tho. Tilsley, James City Co.
Vincent, Thomas, 1637, by John Wilkins, New Noriolk Co.
Vincent, Thos., 1636, by John Wilkins, Accomack Co.
Vincent, Hen., 1635, by Samuel Sneade, James Co.
Vincent, Eliza., 1656, by John Evans, Northampton Co.
Vincent, Eliz., 1654, by John Watson and John Bognall, Westmoreland Co.
Vincent, James, 1653, by Mathew, Tomlin, Northumberland Co.
Vincent, Elyas, 1651, by Capt. Stephen Gill, Northumberland Co.
Vincles, Michaell, 1637, by Rich. Preston, ——— Co.
Vining, Jno. 1635, by Thom. Smith, James Co.
Vinson, Wm., 1637, by John Moon, Isle of Wight Co.
Vinson, Phillip, 1652, by Richard Coleman, ——— Co.
Vinquit, Walter, 1643, by Obedience Robins, Gent., Northampton Co.
Vipon, Thos., 1639, by Thomas Faulner, ——— Co.
Virer, James, 1652, by John Robbins, Northampton Co.
Virgin, Robert, 1637, by John Moone, Isle of Wight Co.

Viriam, Richard, 1650, by Mordecay Cooke, ——— Co.
Virose, Ann, 1648, by Mr. Bartholomew Haskins, Lower Norfolk Co.
Vissett, Francis, 1636, by Robert Hollom, Henrico Co.
Vivin, Mary, 1652, by Robert West, Charles City Co.
Vokes, Wm., 1652, by Mr. Henry Pitt, ——— Co.
Vonably, 1653, by John Hopkin Howell, Nansemond Co.
Voyce, Jonathan, 1643, by Obedience Robins, Gent., Northampton Co.
Voyle, John, 1652, by John Meredith, Lancaster Co.
Vuwin, Katharine, 1637, by Georg Vuwin, New Norfolk Co.
Vuwin, Elizabeth, 1637, by Georg Vuwin, New Norfolk Co.
Vye, Eliza., 1650, by Lawrence Peters, Nansemond Co.
Vynall, Alice, 1646, by Sir William Berkley, ———— Co.

W

Wacmatt, James, 1652, by Christopher Lewis, Isle of Wight Co.
Waddington, Ra., 1652, by Tho. Steevens, Lancaster Co.
Waddington, Jno., 1654, by Peter Knight, Northumberland Co.
Waddington, Ralph, 1653, by Charles Grymes, Clerk, Lancaster Co.
Waddington, Hannah, 1636, by Henry Southell, ——— Co.
Wade, Rich., 1642, by Stephen Gill, ——— Co.
Wade, Antho., 1654, by Robert Holt, James City Co.
Wade, Mary, 1653, by John Bishop and James Mason, Surry Co.
Wade, Thomas, 1637, by Alice Edloe, Henrico Co.
Wade, Eliz., 1654, by John Watson and John Bognall, Westmoreland
    Co.
Wade, Tho., 1653, by John Maddison, Gloucester Co.
Wade, Wm., 1656, by Richard Gible, Northumberland Co.
Wade, Phillipp, 1642, by John King, Charlse River Co.
Wade, Edward, 1638, by Robt. Martin, Lower New Norfolk Co.
Wade, John, 1642, by Bartholomew Knipe, ——— Co.
Wader, Wm., 1635, by Thos. Bagwell, ——— Co.
Wadingham, Phill., 1654, by Toby Smith, Lancaster Co.
Wadlowe, Tho., ———, by Mr. John Page, ——— Co.
Waedce, Tho., 1649, by Tho. Harwood, ——— Co.
Waffeild, Morcop, 1656, by Tabitha and Matilda Scarburgh, North-
    ampton Co.
Wagett, Tho., 1653, by Samuell Parry, Lancaster Co.
Waggott, Thom., 1639, by Georg Minifye, Esq., Charles River Co.
Wagstaff, Mary, 1655, by Mrs. Margaret Brent, Lancaster Co.
Waight, Edward, 1655, by Dr. Giles Mode, New Kent Co.
Waines, Geo., 1653, by Charles Grymes, Lancaster Co.
Waiters, Margt., 1643, by Obedience Robins, Gent., Northampton Co.
Wakefeild, Jno., 1635, by Capt. Adam Thoroughgood, ——— Co.
Wakes, Jonathan, 1636, by John Laydon, Warwick River Co.
Wakefeild, John, 1650, by Elias, Edmonds, ——— Co.
Wakefeild, Geo., 1654, by Nicholas Morris, Northumberland Co.
Wakefield, Thos., 1637, by Theodore Moyser, James City Co.
Wakeland, Anne, 1641, by Tho. Mathews, ——— Co.
Wakin, Thomas, 1650, by Lewis Burwell, Gent., Northumberland Co.
Waking, Rich., 1648, by John Seward, Isle of Wight Co.

Wakins, Edward, 1638, by John Robins, James City Co.
Waklin, Anth., 1636, by Richard Cocke, ——— Co.
Wahab, Geo., 1655, by Richard Jones, ——— Co.
Wahoope, Archibald, ——, by Mr. Robt. Fontaine, Lower Norfolk Co.
Walbeck, Kath., 1653, by Jervais Dodson, Northumberland Co.
Walers, John, 1636, by John Dansey, James City Co.
Walby, Henry, 1653, by Wm. Debram, ——— Co.
Walch, Edmund, 1655, by John Hampton, ——— Co.
Walcoke, Robt., 1643, by Capt. Samuell Mathews, Esq., ——— Co.
Walden, Wm., 1654, by Mr. Tho. Fowke, Westmoreland Co.
Walden, Edward, 1651, by Capt. Stephen Gill, Northumberland Co.
Waldgrave, Edward, 1653, by Edward Kemp, Geo. Cortlough and John
    Meredith, Lancaster Co.
Waldgrave, Charles, 1653, by Edward Kemp, Geo. Cortlough and John
    Meredith, Lancaster Co.
Waldrom, Tho., 1642, by Thomas Osborne, Henrico Co.
Waldon, Phillip, 1655, by Major Wm. Hoccaday, New Kent Co.
Waldren, Henry, 1653, by Dennis Conniers, Lancaster Co.
Waldron, Joice, 1653, by Richard Budd, Northumberland Co.
Wale, John, 1655, by John Woodward, Gloucester Co.
Walemon, John, 1654, by John Grey, Northampton Co.
Walfe, Robert, 1654, by John Battell, ——— Co.
Walford, John, 1638, by William Croutch, Lower Norfolk Co.
Walgrane, Geo., 1650, by Capt. Moore Fautelroy, ——— Co.
Walgrow, Tho., 1656, by Vincent Stanford, ——— Co.
Walker, Richd., 1650, by Tho. Gerrord, Gent., Northumberland Co.
Walker, John, 1655, by Wm. Wright, Gent., Nansemond Co.
Walker, Henry, 1651, by Mr. Robert Abrall, Yorke Co.
Walker, Alice, 1651, by Wm. Hampton, ——— Co.
Walker, Phillipp, 1637, by Henry Perry, Charles River Co.
Walker, John, 1653, by Colo. Wm. Clayborne (Sec. of State), ——— Co.
Walker, Henry, 1653, by John Dipdall, Charles City Co.
Walker, Mary, 1653, by Wm. Johnson, Lancaster Co.
Walker, Mr. John, 1651, by Richard Ripley, ——— Co.
Walker, Henry, 1653, by Nicho. Meriwether, Northumberland Co.
Walker, John, 1651, by Joseph Croshaw, Yorke Co.
Walker, Andrew, 1562, by George Pace, Charles City Co.
Walker, Mary, 1652, by Nathaniel Bacon, Isle of Wight Co.
Walker, Tho., 1652, by Nicho. George, Tho. Taberer and Humphry
    Clarke, ——— Co.
Walker, Mary, 1652, by Capt. Tho. Hackett, Lancaster Co.
Walker, John, 1652, by Mr. Edwin Connaway, ——— Co.
Walker, Jane, 1653, by Mr. Wm. Fry, James City Co.
Walker, James, 1638, by John Stratton, Lower New Norfolk Co.
Walker, Morris, 1649, by Capt. Ralph Wormeley, ——— Co.
Walker, Phillipp, 1637, by Henry Perry, Charles River Co.
Walker, Morris, 1638, by Capt. Christopher Wormley, Charles River
    Co.
Walker, Elizabeth, 1655, by Peter Ford, Gloucester Co.
Walker, Henry, 1654, by Nich. Merywether, Westmoreland Co.
Walker, John, 1655, by Samuel Smith, James City Co.

Walker, Hen., 1636, by James Vanerit, Elizabeth City Co.
Walker, Jon., 1636, by Cheney Boyse, Charles City Co.
Walker, Andrew, 1650, by George Pate, Charles City Co.
Walker, John, 1654, by Robt. Bowers, —— Co.
Walker, Wm., 1654, by Tho. Felton, Charles City Co.
Walker, Jno., 1646, by Joseph Croshawe, Charles River Co.
Walker, John, 1650, by Edward Walker, Northumberland Co.
Walker, Sarah, 1650, by Edward Walker (her husband), Northumberland Co.
Walker, Isabel, 1650, by Wm. Clapham, —— Co.
Walker, Sarah, 1649, by Henry Brakes, Lower Norfolk Co.
Walker, Tho., 1649, by Capt. Ralph Wormeley, —— Co.
Walker, Samll., 1639, by Georg Minifye, Esq., Charles River Co.
Walker, Edw., 1643, by William Mills, Isle of Wight Co.
Walker, Robt., 1656, by John Wood, —— Co.
Walker, Wm., 1656, by Wm. Pulliam, New Kent Co.
Walker, Wm., 1656, by Mr. Jno. Paine, —— Co.
Walker, Phillipp, 1637, by Henry Perry, Charles River Co.
Walker, Oliver, 1637, by John Dennett, Charles River Co.
Walker, Roger, 1637, by Daniell Gookins, New Norfolk Co.
Walker, John, 1636, by John Seaward, Isle of Wight Co.
Walker, Lawer, 1637, by Cheney Boyes, Charles City Co.
Walker, Jon., 1637, by Cheney Boyes, Charles City Co.
Walker, Jane, 1637, by Henry Hart, James Citie Co.
Walker, Edward, 1636, by John Laydon, Warwick River Co.
Wall, Richard, 1649, by Ralph Harsly, Northumberland Co.
Wall, Richard, 1637, by Thomas Markham, Henrico Co.
Wall, Wm., 1635, by Wm. Barber, Charles City Co.
Wall, Jon., 1638, by William Clarke, Henrico Co.
Wall, Richard, 1636, by Thomas Markham, Henrico Co.
Wall, John, 1636, by Wm. Clarke, Henrico Co.
Wallbrooke, Joane, 1651, by George Ludlow, Esq., —— Co.
Waller, Wm., 1637, by Francis Osborne, —— Co.
Waller, John, 1655, by Dr. Giles Mode, New Kent Co.
Waller, John, 1654, by Wm. Johnson, Northampton Co.
Walters, Tho., 1642, by Lieut. Francis Mason, —— Co.
Wallett, James, 1636, by Richard Bennett, —— Co.
Walley, Eliz., 1650, by Lewis Burwell, Gent., Northumberland Co.
Wallice, Matt, 1648, by John Landman, Nansimond Co.
Wallis, Christop., 1652, by John Smith, —— Co.
Wallis, James, 1651, by James Ward, Charles City Co.
Wallis, John, 1639, by Richard Johnson, Henrico Co.
Wallis, Rebecca, wife of Robt. Wallis, 1642, by Wm. Ireland, and Robt. Wallis, Yorke Co.
Wallis, Edmond, 1652, by Capt. Augustine Warner, —— Co.
Wallis, Peter, 1650, by Wm. Hodgson, Yorke Co.
Wallis, Mathew, 1649, by Tho. Dale, —— Co.
Wallis, John, 1639, by William Burdett, Accomack Co.
Wallis, Thomas, 1645, by Michall Masters, Henrico Co.
Wallis, Thomas, 1638, by Mr. Thomas Wallis, James City Co.

Wallis, Eliz., 1635, by Thos. Butler Clark and Pastor of Denbie, Warrasquinoake Co.
Wallis, Edmond, 1635, by Capt. Adam Thoroughgood, ——— Co.
Walsgrane, Chr., 1649, by John Dennis, ——— Co.
Walser, Mary, 1635, by Thom. Bailie, Chas. City Co.
Walsh, Tho., 1643, by Capt. John Upton, Isle of Wight Co.
Walshway, Charles, 1652, by Tho. Steevens, ——— Co.
Walson, Adam, 1650, by Epa. Lawson, ——— Co.
Walstone, Samuel, 1653, by Mr. Wm. Baldwen, York Co.
Walter, Peter, 1641, by Ambrose Bennett, Isle of Wight Co.
Walter, Wm., 1638, by Robert Pitt, Isle of Wight Co.
Walter, Wm., 1648, by John Seward, Isle of Wight Co.
Walter, Eliz., 1643, by Edward Murfey and John Vaughan, ——— Co.
Walter, Sibbill, 1638, by Percivall Champion, Upper New Norfolk Co.
Walter, Richard, 1638, by Wm. Hatfield, Upper New Norfolk Co.
Walter, John, 1635, by William Dawson, ——— Co.
Walters, John, 1637, by Patrick Kennedye, New Norfolk Co.
Walters, Edmund, 1648, by Mr. Thomas Davies, Isle of Wight Co.
Walters, Wm., 1642, by Stephen Gill, Yorke River Co.
Walters, Eliza., 1653, by Capt. Robt. Abrall, ——— Co.
Walters, Wm., 1652, by Mrs. Elnor Brocas, Lancaster Co.
Walters, Natha., 1652, by Collo. Hugh Gwin, ——— Co.
Walters, Elizabeth, 1651, by Mr. Robert Abrall, Yorke Co.
Walters, Joane, 1637, by Francis Osborne, ——— Co..
Waltham, Hen., 1637, by Christopher Stokes, Charles River Co.
Waltham, Wm., 1638, by Thomas Burbage, Accomack Co.
Waltham, Samuell, 1637, by Christopher Stoakes, Charles River Co.
Waltham, John, Sr., 1642, by John Waltham, Jr., Accomac Co.
Walton, John, 1653, by Henry Soanes, Gent., Gloucester Co.
Walton, Samll., 1651, by Robert Cade, ——— Co.
Walton, John, 1654, by John Drayton, Westmoreland Co.
Walton, Richard, 1650, by Robert Blake and Samuell Elridge, Isle of Wight Co.
Walton, George, 1635, by Alexander Stonar, ——— Co.
Walton, Marg., 1635, by William Beard, James City Co.
Walton, Jeffry, 1636, by Mr. Georg Menifye, James City Co.
Walton, John, 1650, by Henry Lee and Wm. Clapham, ——— Co.
Walton, John, 1649, by Tho. Dale, ——— Co.
Walton, John, 1656, by Tabitha and Matilda Scarburgh, Northampton Co.
Walton, Jno., 1648, by John Landman, Nansimond Co.
Walton, Margarett, 1638, by Joseph Harmon, James City Co.
Walton, Daniell, 1638, by Lieut. Robt. Sheppard, James City Co.
Walton, Samuell, 1637, by Christopher Stokes, Warwick River Co.
Walton, Jno., 1637, by Jno. Broche, Charles River Co.
Walton, Robert, 1636, by John Laydon, Warwick River Co.
Wambly, James, 1637, by Georg Holmes, James City Co.
Wand, John, 1652, by Nathaniel Bacon, Isle of Wight Co.
Wand, John, 1651, by Richard Vaughan, Northampton Co.
Wand, Jane, 1643, by Robert Haies, Lower Norfolk Co.

Waneman, Ann, 1653, by Colo. Wm. Clayborne (Sec. of State), ———
Co.
Wanes, Richard, 1636, by Edward Drew, Accomack Co.
Wanklin, Anthony, 1639, by Richard Corke, Gent., Henrico Co.
Wanton, James, 1637, by Capt. Thomas Osborne, Henrico Co.
Waplett, Thomas, 1639, by Thomas Mathews, Henrico Co.
Wapp, John, 1654, by John Curtis, Accomac Co.
Wapshatt, Jane, 1652, by Anthony Hoskins, Northampton Co.
Waraner, Math., 1637, by Wm. Farrar, Henrico Co.
Warbleton, Tho., 1653, by Wm. Debram, ——— Co.
Warburton, Ann, 1656, by Geo. Abbott, Nansemond Co.
Ward, Ann, 1651, by James Ward, Charles City Co.
Ward, Barth., 1651, by Richard Whitehurst, Lower Norfolk Co.
Ward, John, 1652, by Capt. Tho. Hackett, Lancaster Co.
Ward, Wm., 1653, by Charles Grimes, Lancaster Co.
Ward, Katherine, 1652, by Col. Geo. Ludlow Esq., Gloucster Co.
Ward, Jon., 1640, by John Holloway, Accomack Co.
Ward, Silvester, 1640, by Thomas Stegg, Charles City Co.
Ward, Peter, 1654, by Tho. Hobkins, Lancaster Co.
Ward, Robert, 1654, by Edward Simpson, Gloucester Co.
Ward, Robt., 1650, by James Williamson, ——— Co.
Ward, James, 1648, by Richard Lee, Gent., ——— Co.
Ward, Mathew, 1639, by Georg Minifye, Esq., Charles River Co.
Ward, William, 1638, by Mr. Walter Askton, Charles City Co.
Ward, Robt., 1640, by John Geary, Upper Norfolk Co.
Ward, Robt., 1639, by Lieut. Richard Popeley, ——— Co.
Ward, Robert, 1642, by Daniell Lewellyn, ——— Co.
Ware, Fra., 1653, by John Ware, ——— Co.
Ware, Kath., 1653, by John Ware, ——— Co.
Ward, Tho., 1643, by Fra. Mason, Lower Norfolk Co.
Ward, Sam., 1645, by Richard Jacob, Northampton Co.
Ward, John, 1637, by Elizabeth Parker, Henrico Co.
Ward, Thomas, 1637, by Jonathan Langworth, New Norfolk Co.
Ward, Susan, 1637, by Francis Fowler, James River Co.
Ward, Susan, 1635, by Francis Fowler, James City Co.
Ward, Robert, 1637, by Jno. Broche, Charles River Co.
Ward, Rich., 1636, by Capt. John Chelsman, Charles River Co.
Ward, Roger, 1635, by Capt. Adam Thoroughgood, ——— Co.
Ward, Jon., 1636, by Elizabeth Packer, Henrico Co.
Ward, Rich., 1635, by John Cheeseman, Charles River Co.
Ward, John, 1637, by John Ward, James Citie Co.
Ward, Henry, 1637, by Francis Osborne, ——— Co.
Ward, William, 1637, by Thomas Hampton, New Norfolk Co.
Ward, Thomas, 1635, by McWilliam Stone, ——— Co.
Ward, Robert, 1648, by Geo. Hardey, Tho. Wombwell and Peter Hall,
Isle of Wight Co.
Ward, Thoms, 1637, by Jonathan Longworth, New Norfolk Co.
Ward, Cleri., 1636, by James Vanerit, Elizabeth City Co.
Ward, Jon., 1636, by James Place, Henrico Co.
Ward, Grace, 1636, by James Place, Henrico Co.
Ward, Eliz., 1636, by James Place, Henrico Co.

Ward, Jeremiah, 1637, by Patrick Kennedye, New Norfolk Co.
Wards, Tho., 1649, by Henry Brakes, Lower Norfolk Co.
Wardell, Tohe, 1654, by Francis Smith and Mr. John Smith, Westmoreland Co.
Wardell, Mathew, 1655, by Southy Littleberry, Northampton Co.
Warden, Jon., 1637, by Capt. Francis Eppes, Charles City Co.
Warder, Geo., 1635, by John Moone, Warrasquinoake Co.
Wardley, Tho., 1654, by Henry Walker, James City Co.
Wardy, Roger, 1654, by Wm. Mells, Lancaster Co.
Ware, Jon., Sr., and Margarett, his wife, 1653, by John Ware, —— Co.
Ware, Jon., Jr., 1653, by John Ware, —— Co.
Ware, John, 1653, by William Johnson, Lancaster Co.
Ware, Tho., 1652, by Ambrose Dixon and Stephen Horsely, Northampton Co.
Ware William, 1641, by Thomas Bernard, Warwick River Co.
Ware, Nich., 1648, by George White, Lower Norfolk Co.
Ware, John, 1655, by Peter Ford, Gloucester Co.
Wariner, Susan, 1652, by Tobias Horton, Lancaster Co.
Warington, Eliz., 1653, by Margarett Upton, Lancaster Co.
Warmer, Henry, 1655, by Robt. Nicholson, Charles City Co.
Warne, Thos., 1636, by Richard Peirce, James City Co.
Warnell, Robt., 1637, by Joseph Royall, Henrico Co.
Warner, Henry, 1636, by John Neale, Accomack Co.
Warner, Mary, 1652, by Capt. Augustine Warner, —— Co.
Warner, John, 1652, by Nicho. Morris, Northumberland Co.
Warner, Mary, 1638, by Augustine Warner, Charles River Co.
Warner, Tho., 1643, by Tho. Symmonds, —— Co.
Warner, John, 1654, by Nicholas Morris, Northumberland Co.
Warner, Tho., 1643, by Mr. John Bishopp, James City Co.
Warner, Henry, 1637, by John Redman and John Neale, Accomac Co.
Warner, Augustine, 1635, by Capt. Adam Thoroughgood, —— Co.
Warninger, William, 1638, by Mr. Thomas Wallis, James City Co.
Warrall, Joseph, 1652, by Capt. John West, Esq., —— Co.
Warrell, Wm., 1654, by Walter Dickenson, Lancaster Co.
Warren, Mr., 1650, by Sr. Thomas Luntsford, Kt. and Baronnett, —— Co.
Warren, John, 1655, by Wm. Wright, Gent., Nansemond Co.
Warren, Anthony, 1655, by Wm. Wright, Gent., Nansemond Co.
Warren, Henry, 1637, by Robert Throckmorton, Charles River Co.
Warren, Wm., 1652, by Mr. Wm. Waters, Northampton Co.
Warren, Tho., 1647, by James Warradine, —— Co.
Warren, Jon., 1638, by Richard Wilcox, James City Co.
Warren, Abra., 1654, by Arthur Nash, New Kent Co.
Warren, Eliza., 150, by Capt. Moore Fautleroy, —— Co.
Wariner, Tho., 1650, by Capt. Moore Fautleroy, —— Co.
Warren, Thomas, 1642, by Capt. Daniell Gookin, —— Co.
Warren, John, ——, by Mr. Wm. Presly, Northumberland Co.
Warren, William, 1639, by Robert Eley, Isle of Wight Co.
Warren Richard, 1655, by Wm. Johnson and Stephen Horsey, Northampton Co.
Warren, Wm., 1647, by Thomas Johnson, Gent., Northampton Co.

Warren, Henry, 1637, by Robert Throckmorton, Charles River Co.
Warren, Amos, 1642, by Wm. Warren, ——— Co.
Warren, David, 1637, by Capt. Henry Browne, James City Co.
Warrenford, Peter, 1637, by John Redman and John Neale, Accomac Co.
Warrenford, Peter, 1636, by John Neale, Accomack Co.
Warster, Richard, 1635, by McWilliam Stone, ——— Co.
Was, Wm., 1635, by Capt. A. Thoroughgood, ——— Co.
Washborne, Daniell, 1641, by Thomas Morrey, Isle of Wight Co.
Washington Richard, 1639, by Peter Rigby, Charles River Co.
Waslon, Elizabeth, 1651, by Richard Turney, Northumberland Co.
Wassall, Wm., 1652, by Capt. John West, Esq., ——— Co.
Wate, Mathew, 1653, by John Ashby and Jh. Hamper, ——— Co.
Waterhouse, Wm., 1654, by Obed. Williams, York Co.
Waterhouse, Samuell, 1642, by Cornelius de Hull, ——— Co.
Waterman, Richd., 1652, by Mrs. Mary Brent, Northumberland Co.
Waterman, Georg, 1639, by Edward Drew, Accomack Co.
Waterman, Ann, 1638, by Geo. Lobb, Tho. Perce, Tho. Warne, James River Co.
Waterman, Ann, 1636, by John Chew, Gent., Charles River Co.
Waterman, Ann, 1637, by John Chew, Charles River Co.
Waters, Lt. Edw., 1652, by Mr. Wm. Waters, Northampton Co.
Waters, John, 1652, by Capt. Tho. Hackett, Lancaster Co.
Waters, Wm., 1648, by George White, Lower Norfolk Co.
Waters, Eliz., 1647, by Elizabeth Barcroft, Isle of Wight Co.
Waters, Geo., 1642, by Capt. Humphry Higgenson, ——— Co.
Waters, Georg, 1639, by Wm. Barker, Charles City Co.
Waters, Eliz., 1650, by Anthony Fuljam, ——— Co.
Waters, Wm., 1648, by Francis Ceely, ——— Co.
Waters, John, 1639, by Wm. Denham, Isle of Wight Co.
Waters, Edw., 1647, by Thomas Johnson, Gent., Northampton Co.
Waters, Roger, 1637, by Arthur Smith, Isle of Wight Co.
Waters, Jon., 1635, by Capt. Adam Thoroughgood, ——— Co.
Waters, Mary, 1636, by Wm. Parker, Warrasquinoake Co.
Watkin, Phillip, 1656, by Wm. Millinge, Northampton Co.
Watkins, Jno., 1651, by Wm. Hampton ——— Co.
Watkins, John, 1653, by Charles Grymes, Lancaster Co.
Watkins, Alice, 1654, by Walter Pritchard, ——— Co.
Watkins, Edward, 1654, by John Wyre, John Gillet, Andrew Gilson and John Phillipps,——— Co.
Watkins, Geo., 1654, by Robert Hubard, Westmoreland Co.
Wattkins, Phillipp, 1647, by Jonathan Gills, Northampton Co.
Watkins, Thomas, 1647, by John Sidney, Lower Norfolk Co.
Watkins, Mary, 1654, by John Thomas, Nansemond Co.
Watkins, Eliz., 1654, by Major Wm. Andrews, Northampton Co.
Watkins, Wm., 1643, by Richard Richards, Charles River Co.
Watkins, Eliz., 1640, by Edmund Scarburgh, Accomack Co.
Watkins, Rich., 1643, by John Foster, Northampton Co.
Watkins, Geo., 1638, by John Fludd, James City Co.
Watkins, Thos., 1637, by Thomas Weston, Charles River Co.
Watkins, Alice, 1638, by William Carter, James City Co.

Watkins, Nich., 1639, by William Wigg, ——— Co.
Watkins, Morgan, 1637, by John Baker, Henrico Co.
Watkins, Alice, 1635, by William Carter, Henrico Co.
Watkins, Thomas, 1635, by Samuel Weaver, ——— Co.
Wattkins, Phillip, 1649, by Edmund Scarburgh, Jr., Northampton Co.
Watt, The Plowman, 1650, by Andrew Gilson, ——— Co.
Watts, Eliz., 1651, by Thomas Watts, Jr., Northumberland Co.
Watts, Susan, 1651, by Thomas Watts, Jr., Northumberland Co.
Watts, Edmond, ———, by Lt. Coll. John Cheesman, ——— Co.
Watts, Peter, 1654, by Alex. Madocks and James Jones, Northampton Co.
Watts, Tho., 1652, by Wm. Owen and Wm. Morgan, ——— Co.
Watts, Robt., 1652, by Henry Weeker, ——— Co.
Watts, Stephen, 1653, by Abraham Moone, Northumberland Co.
Watts, Wm., 1652, by Thomas Bell, Gloucester Co.
Watts, Edward, 1640, by William Wigg, James City Co.
Watts, Wm., 1656, by Thomas Bell, Gloucester Co.
Watts, Geo., and wife, 1656, by Margaret Miles, Westmoreland Co.
Watts, Wm., 1650, by Capt. Moore Fautleroy, ——— Co.
Watts, Sara., 1649, by Robert Mosely, Gent., ——— Co.
Watts, Martha, 1650, by John Watts, Gent. (her husband), ——— Co.
Watts, John, 1649, by Edmund Scarburgh, Jr., Northampton Co.
Watts, Wm., 1649, by Richard Kemp, Esq. (Sec. of State), ——— Co.
Watts, Charity, wife Wm. Watts, 1649, by Richard Kemp, Esq. (Sec. of State), ——— Co.
Watts, Susan, wife Tho. Watts, 1649, by Mr. Henry Woodhouse, Lower Norfolk Co.
Watts, Tho., 1649, by Mr. Henry Woodhouse, Lower Norfolk Co.
Watts, Wm., 1638, by John Wayne, Charles River Co.
Watts, Jeremiah, 1638, by Edw. Sparshott, Charles City Co.
Watts, Richard, 1642, by John Ewers, Jr., Charles City Co.
Watts, Tho., 1642, by Stephen Gill, Yorke River Co.
Watts, Ger., 1638, by Edward Sparshott, Charles City Co.
Watts, Henry, 1643, by John Sherlocke, Isle of Wight Co.
Watts, Henry, 1643, by Capt. John Upton, Isle of Wight Co.
Watts, Christopher (Junior), 1636, by Capt. Christopher Calthropp, Charles River Co.
Watts, Christopher (Senior), 1636, by Capt. Christopher Calthropp, Charles River Co.
Watts, Thomas, 1636, by John Laydon, Warwick River Co.
Watten, Jenkin, 1654, by Major Miles Carey, Westmoreland Co.
Wattin, John, 1636, by Richard Cocke, ——— Co.
Watton, Thos., 1639, by John Pawley, James City Co.
Watton, John, 1656, by Mr. Henry Soanes, New Kent Co.
Watson, Marg., 1653, by Corbet Piddle, Northumberland Co.
Watson, Art., 1653, by Robert Woodey, Lower Norfolk Co.
Watson, Nicho., 1653, by Capt. Robt. Abrahal, York Co.
Watson, Ann, 1653, by Francis Hale, ——— Co.
Watson, Alexander, 1653, by Mr. Wm. Hoccoday, York Co.
Watson, Joane, 1651, by Robert Holt, James City Co.
Watson, Tho., 1653, by Tho. Keene, Northumberland Co.

Watson, John, 1652, by Littleton Scarburg, ——— Co.
Watson, Andrew, 1653, by Joseph Hogkinson, Lower Norfolk Co.
Watson, James, 1653, by Wm. Knott, Surry Co.
Watson, Geo., 1653, by John King, Surry Co.
Watson, Mary, 1653, by James Watson (her husband), Isle of Wight Co.
Watson, Richard, 1652, by John Wareham, Northumberland Co.
Watson, Alice, 1654, by John Watson and John Bognall, Westmoreland
    Co.
Watson, Eliz., 1654, by Robert Hubard, Westmoreland Co.
Watson, Samuel, 1635, by Christopher Stoakes, Elizabeth Co.
Watson, Isaac, 1656, by Tho. Merredith, New Kent Co.
Watson, Richard, 1649, by Edmund Scarburgh, Jr., Northampton Co.
Watson, Jeffery, 1649, by Tho. Dale, ——— Co.
Watson, John, 1648, by James Mason, James City Co.
Watson, Arthur, 1649, by John Sibsey, Lower Norfolk Co.
Watson, Henry, 1645, by Mr. Robt. Eyers, ——— Co.
Watson, Richard, 1649, by Capt. Ralph Wormeley, ——— Co.
Watson, Alin, 1655, by George Truett, Northampton Co.
Watson, Abraham, 1650, by Tho. Tilsley, James City Co.
Watson, Eliz., 1635, by Jon. Watson (her husband), ——— Co.
Wattson, Wm., 1654, by Col. Hump. Higgenson, Esq., and Abraham
    Moone, Westmoreland Co.
Wattson, Nicholas, 1640, by Thomas Causey, ——— Co.
Watty, Wm., 1635, by Christopher Stoakes, Elizabeth Co.
Watty, Wm., 1637, by Christopher Stoakes, Charles River Co.
Waxell, Tobias, 1636, by Wm. Neesam, James City Co.
Way, Henry, 1652, by John Pouncey, ——— Co.
Way, George, 1648, by Richard Lee, Gent., ——— Co.
Way, John, 1636, by John Dansey, James City Co.
Wayder, Wm., 1638, by Thomas Bogwell, Charles City Co.
Waydon, Hugh, 1650, by John Olian, James City Co.
Waye, John, 1654, by Tho. Harmanson, Northampton Co.
Wayles, Oliver, 1653, by Charles Grymes, Lancaster Co.
Wayne, Mary, 1653, by Robert Bouth, Yorke Co.
Wayne, John, 1653, by Robert Bouth, Yorke Co.
Wayne, John, 1648, by Tho. Browne, York Co.
Wayne, Amy, 1638, by John Wayne (her husband), Charles River Co.
Weaborne, Robt., 1653, by Abraham Moon, Lancaster Co.
Weaker, Lawrance, 1636, by Cheney Boyse, Charles City Co.
Weaner, John, 1638, by Thomas Bogwell, Charles City Co.
Weather, Nich., 1647, by Richard Bland, ——— Co.
Weathurs, Wm., 1650, by John Hallawes, Gent., Northumberland Co.
Weaver, Richard, 1652, by Christopher Lewis, Isle of Wight Co.
Weaver, John, 1639, by Henry Perry, Charles City Co.
Weaver, Jno., 1635, by Thos. Baywell, ——— Co.
Weaver, John, 1651, by Wm. Vincent, Northumberland Co.
Weavor, Richàrd, 1653, by Tho. Griffin, Lancaster Co.
Web, Tho., 1655, by Gilbert Deacon, Henrico Co.
Webb, Fayth, 1651, by Ashwell Battin, Yorke Co.
Webb, Tho., 1654, by Abra. Moone, Lancaster Co.
Webb, Giles, 1653, by Robert Tomlin, ——— Co.

Webb, Step., 1651, by Mr. Rowland Burnham, ——— Co.
Webb, Giles, 1653, by John Gillett, Lancaster Co.
Webb, Giles, 1652, by Tho. Todd, ——— Co.
Webb, Wm., 1653, by Patrick Margraffe, ——— Co.
Webb, Alice, 1639, by Walter Pakes, James City Co.
Webb, Robert, 1639, by Stephen Webb, James City Co.
Webb, Stephen, 1639, by Stephen Webb, James City Co.
Webb, Clare, 1639, by Stephen Webb, James City Co.
Webb, Rich., 1646, by Samuell Abbott, Nansemond Co.
Webb, Giles, 1646, by Thomas Bahe, Upper Norfolk Co.
Webb, Edwd., 1547, by Richard Stearnell, Lower Norfolk Co.
Webb, Francis, 1656, by Tho. Merredith, New Kent Co.
Webb, Tho., 1654, by Nich. Merywether, Westmoreland Co.
Webb, Eliza., 1642, by Francis England, Isle of Wight Co.
Webb, Wm., 1642, by Capt. Daniell Gookin, ——— Co.
Webb, William, 1642, by Walter Chiles, Charles Co.
Webb, William, 1648, by Lewis Burwell, Gent., ——— Co.
Webb, Alice, 1639, by Justinian Cooper, Isle of Wight Co.
Webb, Mary, 1639, by John Well, Charles City Co.
Webb, Nicholas, 1645, by William Daynes, Lower Norfolk Co.
Webb, Richard, 1643, by Epaphroditus Lawson, Upper Norfolk Co.
Webb, Robert, 1638, by Stephen Webb, James Citie Co.
Webb, Clare, 1638, by Stephen Webb, James Citie Co.
Webb, Thomas, 1635, by John Armie, Warrasquinoake Co.
Webb, Wm., 1654, by Mr. Francis Hamond, York Co.
Webb, Wm., 1643, by Tristram Nosworthy, Isle of Wight Co.
Webber, Jno., 1630, by Jno. Russell, ——— Co.
Webher, John, 1654, by Col. Argoll Yardley, Northampton Co.
Weblin, Henry and wife, 1650, by John Bone, ——— Co.
Weblin, Henry, 1635, by John Leonard, Warrasquinoake Co.
Webster, Francis, 1639, by Edward Oliver, James City Co.
Webster, Nicho., 1653, by John Maddison, Gloucester Co.
Webster, Richard, 1642, by John George, Charles City Co.
Webster, Francis, 1639, by Edward Oliver, James City Co.
Webster, Susan, 1646, by Lucy Webster, Judith and Jane Webster, James City Co.
Webster, Lucien, 1642, by Luce Webster, Yorke Co.
Webster, Tho., 1642, by Luce Webster, York Co.
Webster, Nath., 1642, by Hugh Gwyn, Gent., ——— Co.
Webster, Francis, 1638, by Edward Oliver, ——— Co.
Webster, Wm., 1653, by Henry Lowne, Henrico Co.
Webster, Tho., 1653, by Nicholas Meriwether, Lancaster Co.
Weddington, Hannah, 1637, by Lt. Rich. Popeley, New Norfolk Co.
Wedge, Margt., 1653, by Tho. Holmes, York Co.
Wedlow, Nicholas, 1647, by Stephen Harsey and Nicho. Waddilow, Northampton Co.
Weed, Hen., 1654, by Wm. Bacon, Northumberland Co.
Weed, Henry, 1649, by Richard Bayly, Northampton Co.
Weekes, Ralph, 1654, by Francis Smith and Mr. John Smith, Westmoreland Co.
Weekes, Tho., 1651, by Mr. Robert Abrall, Yorke Co.

Weekes, Robert, 1654, by Edward Simpson, Gloucester Co.
Weekes, Wm., 1635, by Capt. Adam Thoroughgood, ——— Co.
Weekes, William, 1645, by Capt. Wm. Pierse, ——— Co.
Weekes, Robt., 1636, by James Knott, Elizabeth City Co.
Weeks, Richard, 1635, by Capt. Wm. Pierse, ——— Co.
Weeks, Jon., 1643, by George Levitt, ——— Co.
Wegan, Jon., 1637, by Thomas Osborne, Jr., ——— Co.
Weghtman, Antho., 1653, by Wm. Knott, Surry Co.
Weinne, Tho., 1653, by John Ware, ——— Co.
Welbeloved, Math., 1653, by John Hillier, Northumberland Co.
Welbeloved, Math., 1652, by Mr. Edwin Connaway, ——— Co.
Wilborough, Richard, 1653, by Abraham Moone, Northumberland Co.
Welbourne, Robt., 1652, by John Bayles, Lancaster Co.
Welbourne, Mathew, 1653, by Charles Grimes, Lancaster Co.
Welby, Alice, 1654, by John Wyre, John Gillet, Andrew Gilson and
    John Phillipps, ——— Co.
Welbourn, Sam, 1654, by Major Miles Carey, Westmoreland Co.
Welch, John, 1653, by Tho. Griffin, Lancaster Co.
Welch, Jno., 1651, by Mr. Rowland Burnham, ——— Co.
Welch, Joan, 1651, by Mr. Rowland Burnham, ——— Co.
Welch, James, 1652, by Mr. David Fox, Lancaster Co.
Welch, James, 1653, by Abraham Moone, Lancaster Co.
Welch, Tho., 1652, by Anthony Hoskins, Northampton Co.
Welch, Rich., 1654, by Valentine Patten, Westmoreland Co.
Welch, Gilbert, 1654, by Col. Argoll Yardley, Northampton Co.
Welch, David, 1654, by Arthur Nash, New Kent Co.
Welch, Rich., 1654, by Robert Hubard, Westmoreland Co.
Welch, Tho., 1650, by Epa Lawson, ——— Co.
Welch, Rice, 1650, by Mr. Epaphroditus Lawson, ——— Co.
Welch, Jane, 1650, by Capt. Moore Fautleroy, ——— Co.
Welch, Morgan, 1650, by Capt. John Flood, Gent., and Jno. Flood, an
    ancient planter, James City Co.
Welch, Joone, 1649, by John Cabbedge, Lower Norfolk Co.
Welch, Robt., 1638, by Thomas Grey, James City Co.
Welch, Daniell, 1638, by John Moone, ——— Co.
Welch, Morgan, 1638, by John Fludd, James City Co.
Welch, Nich., 1635, by Thos. Butler Clark and Pastor of Danbie, War-
    rasquinoake Co.
Welch, Mary, 1637, by Francis Osborne, ——— Co.
Welchman, Jno., 1650, by Capt. Moore Fautleroy, ——— Co.
Welchurch, Hen., 1645, by Wm. Jacob, Upper Norfolk Co.
Welcoxe, Grace, 1652, by Col. Geo. Ludlow, Esq., Gloucester Co.
Weldy, Wm., 1642, by Capt. Daniell Gookin, ——— Co.
Welden, Peter, 1645, by Mr. Robt. Eyres, ——— Co.
Welding, Samuel, 1651, by Richard Turney, Northumberland Co.
Wellford, John, 1637, by Francis Fowler, James River Co.
Wellington, Martha, 1653, by John Edwards, Lancaster Co.
Wellingworth, Jon., 1642, by John Pratt, Henrico Co.
Wellman, Richard, 1636, by John Dunston, James City Co.
Wellman. Richard, 1639, by John Dunston, James City Co.
Wellon, William, 1636, by John Laydon, Warwick River Co.

Wells, Rich., 1654, by Abra. Moone, Lancaster Co.
Wells, Wm., 1651, by Phillip Hunley, ——— Co.
Wells, Eliza., 1652, by Gilbert Blunt, ——— Co.
Wells, Elizabeth, 1652, by Isaac Richeson, Lancaster Co.
Wells, Tho., 1653, by Charles Grimes, Lancaster Co.
Wells, James, 1654, by John Watson and John Bognall, Westmoreland
    Co.
Wells, Mary, 1654, by Robert Hubard, Westmoreland Co.
Wells, John, 1638, by Wm. Rainshaw, Lower New Norfolk Co.
Wells, Edward, 1643, by Peter Knight, Isle of Wight Co.
Wells, John, 1656, by George Kibble, Lancaster Co.
Wells, Richard, 1654, by Nich. Merywether, Westmoreland Co.
Wells, Mary, 1654, by Fra. Spright, Nansemond Co.
Wells, Pru., 1654, by Robert Younge, Lancaster Co.
Wells, Richard, 1654, by Mr. Giles Brent, Westmoreland Co.
Wells, Edmond, 1642, by Adam Cooke, Charles Co.
Wells, Richard, 1650, by Mrs. Frances Townshend (widow), Northum-
    berland Co.
Wells, Tho., 1650, by Bertram Obert, ——— Co.
Wells, Geo., 1645, by Michael Masters, Henrico Co.
Wells, Wm., 1645, by James Bruss, Northampton Co.
Wells, Walter, 1643, by Casar Puggett, Lower Norfolk Co.
Wells, John, 1638, by Joseph Royall, Charles Citie Co.
Wells, Robert, 1637, by James Knott, New Norfolk Co.
Wells, Mary, 1636, by John Wilkins, Accomack Co.
Wells, Greg, 1635, by Capt. Wm. Pierse, ——— Co.
Wells, Jon., 1637, by Joseph Royall, Henrico Co.
Wells, Richard, 1637, by Francis Poythers, Charles City Co.
Wells, Mary, 1637, by John Wilkins, New Norfolk Co.
Wells, Tho., 1650, by George Pate, Charles City Co.
Wellshaw, Jon., 1642, by John Beale, ——— Co.
Wellson, Wm., 1656, by Nicholas Waddilow, Northampton Co.
Welsh, Thomas, 1638, by Lieut. John Upton, Isle of Wight Co.
Welshe, Robt., 1635, by Thoma Gray, James Co.
Welton, Wm., 1651, by Wm. Taylor, Northumberland Co.
Wenet, John, 1655, by Wm. Wright, Gent., Nansemond Co.
Wenner, Thos., 1635, by John Moone, Warrasquinoake Co.
Werden, Geo., 1650, by Mrs. Frances Townshend, Northumberland Co.
Werrott, Jane, 1651, by Audery Bennett, Nansemond Co.
Wenterton, Wm., 1656, by Richard Gible, Northumberland Co.
Wentworth, Ken., 1652, by Robert West, Charles City Co.
Weorington, Tho., 1656, by Sir Henry Chichley, ——— Co.
Wesby, John, 1642, by Wm. Barnard, Esq., Isle of Wight Co.
Wescorne, Wm., 1636, by Wm. Neesam, James City Co.
Wesfeild, Hen., 1650, by Elias Edmonds, ——— Co.
Westerfield, Jane, 1635, by Capt. Adam Thoroughgood, ——— Co.
Wesgate, Ellen, ———, by Henry Wesgate, Lower Norfolk Co.
Wesh, Mrs. Ann, 1651, by Capt. John West, Esq., Yorke Co.
Wesh, John, Jr., 1651, by Capt. John West, Esq., Yorke Co.
Wesh, James, 1653, by Wm. Hardidge, Northumberland Co.
Weslall, Richard, 1650, by George Taylor, ——— Co.

Weslike, Ann, 1641, by Wm. Storey, Upper Norfolk Co.
Wesson, Ri., 1650, by Wm. Clapham, ——— Co.
Wesson, Eliza., 1649, by John Waltham, Northampton Co.
West, Phillip, 1653, by Colo. Wm., Clayborne (Sec. of State), ———
    Co.
West, James, 1653, by John Merryman, and Morgan Haynes, Lancaster
    Co.
West, George, 1653, by Tho. Scoggin, Northumberland Co.
West, Thos., 1652, by Charles Scarburg, Northampton Co.
West, Susanna, 1652, by Robert West, Charles City Co.
West, John, 1652, by Robert West, Charles City Co.
West, Mary, 1652, by Tho. Stevens, Lancaster Co.
West, Mary, 1652, by Nicholas George, ——— Co.
West, Tho., 1653, by Charles Scarburgh, Northampton Co.
West, Toby, 1653, by John Barrow, Surry Co.
West, Tho., 1652, by Tho. Glascock, Lancaster Co.
West, Elizabeth, 1653, by Wm. Moseley, Lower Norfolk Co.
West, Mary, 1656, by Mr. Martin Baker, New Kent Co.
West, Wm., 1656, by Mr. Martin Baker, New Kent Co.
West, Henry, 1656, by Mr. Martin Baker, New Kent Co.
West, Robt., 1656, by Mr. Martin Baker, New Kent Co.
West, Robt., 1650, by Richard Tye and Charles Sparrowe, Charles
    City Co.
West, Tho., 1650, by John Mattrum, Northumberland Co.
West, Henry, 1650, by John Mattrum, Northumberland Co.
West, Henry, 1649, by Mr. Tho. Spake, Northumberland Co.
West, Geo., 1650, by Capt. Moore Fautleroy, ——— Co.
West, Richd., 1650, by Mr. Tho. Spake, Northumberland Co.
West, Anthony, 1649, by Capt. Randall Harle, Northampton Co.
West, Kath., 1649, by Capt. Randall Harle, Northampton Co.
West, Ann, wife Anthony West, 1649, by Capt. Randall Harle, North-
    ampton Co.
West, John, 1649, by Capt. Randall Harle, Northampton Co.
West, Robert, 1639, by John Lewis, Isle of Wight Co.
West, Humphry, 1642, by John Styles, Isle of Wight Co.
West, Wm., 1642, by Justinian Cooper, Isle of Wight Co.
West, Richard, 1637, by Francis Fowler, James River Co.
West, Humphry, 1638, by Ambrose Bennett, Isle of Wight Co.
West, Rich., 1635, by Francis Fowler, James City Co.
West, Grace, 1636, by John Yates, Elizabeth City Co.
West, John, 1636, by Richard Cocke, ——— Co.
Westbrooke, James, 1653, by Peter Knight and Baker Cutt, ——— Co.
Westerhouse, Barbary, 1654, by Mr. Wm. Westerhouse, Northampton
    Co.
Westerhouse, Peter, 1654, by Mr. Wm. Westerhouse, Northampton Co.
Westerhouse, Wm., Jr., 1654, by Mr. Wm. Westerhouse, Sr., North-
    ampton Co.
Westerhouse, Adrian, 1654, by Mr. Wm. Westerhouse, Northampton
    Co.
Westerhouse, Sedia, 1654, by Mr. Wm. Westerhouse, Northampton Co.
Westake, Jon., 1642, by Capt. Samuell Mathews, Esq., ——— Co.

Westerlincke, Martin, and wife and child, 1653, by Richard Jackson, —— Co.
Westhead, Peter, 1645, by Tho. Steevens, Elizabeth City Co.
Westhery, Rich., 1646, by Sir William Berkley, —— Co.
Westlock, Ann, 1640, by Randall Crew, Upper Norfolk Co.
Westly, Ann, 1636, by Wm. Fookes, —— Co.
Weston, Phill., 1652, by Gregory Parrett, Lower Norfolk Co.
Weston, Richard, 1652, by Mr. Peter Knight, Gloucester, Co.
Weston, Phillip, 1646, by Tho. Miles, Elizabeth City Co.
Weston, Chris., 1648, by Wm. Edwards and Rice Edwards, James City Co.
Weston, Jam., 1650, by Capt. Moore Fautleroy, —— Co.
Weston, Rich., 1638, by Mr. Thomas Wallis, James City Co.
Weston, Rich., 1637, by Theodore Moyser, James City Co.
Weston, John, 1637, by John Chew, Charles River Co.
Weston, Jno., 1635, by Anthony Jones, —— Co.
Westone, John, 1652, by Mr. George Clapham, —— Co.
Westrill, James, 1653, by Tho. Mallard, Northumberland Co.
Westwell, Robert, 1635, by Capt. Adam Thoroughgood, —— Co.
Westwood, Robt., 1653, by Tho. Cowlinge, —— Co.
Westwood, Tho., 1650, by Capt. Ishiell Linch, —— Co.
Westwood, Robt., 1643, by Sir Francis Wyatt, Kt., —— Co.
Westwood, Wm., 1638, by Thomas Stout, —— Co.
Westwood, Wm., 1637, by Capt. Henry Browne, James City Co.
Wetcomb, Geo., 1649, by Wm. Peerce and Frances Symons, Northumberland Co.
Wethell, Tho., 1652, by Wm. Moore, —— Co.
Wetherby, David, 1636, by John Neale, Accomack Co.
Wetherbye, Tho., 1637, by Thomas Weston, Charles River Co.
Wethersby, Barth., 1652, by Lawerence Dameron, Northumberland Co.
Wetts, Tho., 1648, by Tho. Lambert, Lower Norfolk Co.
Weworth, Wm., 1653, by Abraham Moone, Lancaster Co.
Weyncke, Margaret, 1646, by David Jones, Charles City Co.
Wgnn, Christopher, 1638, by John Moye, Lower New Norfolk Co.
Whadsey, Peter, 1636, by Elizabeth Packer, Henrico Co.
Whalps, Tw., 1653, by Major John Westhrope, Charles City Co.
Wharton, Geo., 1643, by Georg Levitt, —— Co.
Wheafeby, James, 1650, by Sr. Tho. Luntsford, Kt., and Barronnett, —— Co.
Wheatly, Danl., 1654, by Gregory Wills and Richard Williams, James City Co.
Wheatly, Wm., 1638, by Wm. Cloys, Charles River Co.
Wheatly, Ann, 1650, by Silvester Thatcher and Tho. Whitlocke, —— Co.
Wheatly, Ellis, 1655, by Wm. Graves, York Co.
Wheatley, David, 1645, by James Bruss, Northampton Co.
Wheatley, Wm., 1646, by Col. Henry Bishopp, James City Co.
Wheatley, David, 1651, by Toby Norton, Northampton Co.
Wheatley, Eliza., 1649, by Richard Bayly, Northampton Co.
Wheatley, Lydia, 1649, by Richard Bayly, Northampton Co.
Wheeler, Wm., 1654, by Edw. Cole, Northampton Co.

Wheeler, Francis, 1651, by John Hull, Northumberland Co.
Wheeler, Elin., 1651, by John Hull, Northumberland Co.
Wheeler, John, 1654, by Tho. Harmason, Northampton Co.
Wheeler, Fra., 1652, by John Fleet, Lancaster Co.
Wheeler, Francis, 1642, by John Beale, ——— Co.
Wheeler, Wm., 1654, by Tho. Hobkins, Lancaster Co.
Wheeler, Edward, 1642, by Lieut. Francis Mason, ——— Co.
Wheeler, Rich., 1637, by James Knott, New Norfolk Co.
Wheeler, Thomas, 1637, by Cheney Boyes, Charles City Co.
Wheeler, Wm., 1636, by John Yates, Elizabeth City Co.
Wheeler, Rich., 1636, by James Knott, Elizabeth City Co.
Wheeler, Dorothy, 1635, by Capt. Adam Thoroughgood, ——— Co.
Wheeley, Tho., 1652, by Tho. Bell, Gloucester Co.
Wherry, Robt., 1653, by Richard Major, Gloucester Co.
Wherry, Robt., 1642, by Richard Maior, Charles River Co.
Wherwood, Nich., 1636, by Mr. Georg Menifye, James City Co.
Whetle, Robt., 1635, by Capt. Adam Thoroughgood, ——— Co.
Wheydon, Clement, 1636, by Wm. Ravenett, Warwick River Co.
Whielie, Tho., 1636, by Cheney Boyse, Charles City Co.
Whidon, Clemt., 1654, by John Drayton, Westmoreland Co.
Whidow, Clement, 1650, by Mr. Stephen Hamelin, Charles City Co.
Whissellwhite, Will., 1651, by Richard Wooton, Northumberland Co.
Whiltey, Rich., 1654, by Capt. Nich. Marteaw, Westmoreland Co.
Whitacre, Ann, 1636, by Wm. Fookes, ——— Co.
Whitaker, John, 1639, by Peter Ridley, James City Co.
Whitby, Tho., 1654, by Francis Smith, and Mr. John Smith, West-
    moreland Co.
Whitby, Mrs. Kath., 1654, by Francis Smith and Mr. John Smith,
    Westmoreland Co.
Whitby, Danl., 1653, by Hen. Soanes, Gent., Gloucester Co.
Whitby, Mr. Wm., 1652, by Tho. Steevens, Lancaster Co.
Whilby, Edward, 1654, by John Watson and John Bognall, Westmore-
    land Co.
Whitby, Daniel, 1656, by Mr. Henry Soanes, New Kent Co.
Whitby, Wm., 1654, by Capt. Nich. Marteaw, Westmoreland Co.
White, John, 1637, by Thomas Hampton, New Norfolk Co.
White, Eliza., 1637, by Thomas Hampton, New Norfolk Co.
White, Edward, 1637, by Thomas Hampton, New Norfolk Co.
White, Tho., 1654, by Francis Smith and Mr. John Smith, Westmore-
    land Co.
White, Wm., 1652, by John Cheesman, ——— Co.
White, Fra., 1654, by Edw. Cole, Northampton Co.
White, Francis, 1651, by Wm. Parry, Northumberland Co.
White, John, 1651, by Richard Walker, Northumberland Co.
White, Mary, 1651, by Richard Walker, Northumberland Co.
White, Joseph, 1651, by Richard Walker, Northumberland Co.
White, Richard, 1651, by Richard Walker, Northumberland Co.
White, Murael, 1653, by Wm. Morgan, ——— Co.
White, Hen., 1653, by Wm. and George Worsman, Henrico Co.
White, Tho., 1653, by Colo. Wm. Clayborne (Sec. of State), ——— Co.
White, Richard, 1651, by James Davis, Northampton Co.

White, Ann, 1651, by Thomas Keeling, Lower Norfolk Co.
White, Ann, 1651, by Winifrid Morrison, ——— Co.
White, Patrick, 1653, by Richard Lake, Lancaster Co.
White, Wm., 1653, by Wm. Sidner, Lancaster Co.
White, Catherine, 1653, by Wm. Cox, ——— Co.
White, Wm., 1651, by Edward Deggs, Esq., Yorke Co.
White, Robt., 1653, by Abraham Moon, Lancaster Co.
White, John, ———, by Capt. Daniel Luellin, ——— Co.
White, Peter, 1653, by Nicho. Meriwether, Northumberland Co.
White, John, 1654, by Richard Kellam, Northampton Co.
White, Robert, 1652, by John Bayles, Lancaster Co.
White, Geo., 1652, by Capt. Augustine Warner, ——— Co.
White, Cicely, 1653, by Jervais Dodson, Northumberland Co.
White, Peter, 1652, by Henry Woodhouse, Lower Norfolk Co.
White, John, 1653, by Edward Hall, Lower Norfolk Co.
White, Wm., 1653, by Edward Hall, Lower Norfolk Co.
White, Anne, 1652, by Augustine Moore, ——— Co.
White, Edward, 1652, by Capt. Tho. Hackett, Lancaster Co.
White, Mary, 1652, by Christopher Lewis, Isle of Wight Co.
White, Neale, 1652, by Mr. Richard Cocke, Henrico Co.
White, Robt., 1654, by Edw. Welch, ——— Co.
White, John, 1654, by Martin Coale, Northumberland Co.
White, Simon, ———, by Lt. Coll. John Cheesman, ——— Co.
White, Anne, 1653, by Capt. Giles Brent, Northumberland Co.
White, Anne, 1654, by John Black, ——— Co.
White, Nath., 1741, by Ambrose Bennett, Isle of Wight Co.
White, John, 1642, by Thomas Wombwell, James City Co.
White, Margaret, 1648, by George White (her husband), Lower Norfolk
    Co.
White, John, 1650, by John Hany, Northumberland Co.
White, Nicho., 1648, by Wm. Ewen, James City Co.
White, Tho., 1648, by Wm. Edwards and Rice Edwards, James City Co.
White, Richard, 1640, by Elias Taylor, Accomack Co.
White, Wm., 1655, by John Motley, Northumberland Co.
White, Morris, 1655, by John Smithey, ——— Co.
White, Peter, 1654, by Nich. Merywether, Westmoreland Co.
White, James, 1654, by Major Miles Carey, Westmoreland Co.
White, William, 1650, by Lieut. Wm. Worleich, ——— Co.
White, Anne, 1650, by Robert Bird, ——— Co.
White, Grace, 1650, by Wm. Hodgson, Yorke Co.
White, William, 1642, by John Sweete, ——— Co.
White, John, 1650, by John Bone, ——— Co.
White, Richard, 1649, by Edmund Scarburgh, Jr., Northampton Co.
White, Fra., 1649, by Richard Bayly, Northampton Co.
White, Fra., 1648, by Bartholomew Hoskins, ——— Co.
White, Richard, 1647, by John Brooch, York River Co.
White, Phillipp, 1642, by Capt. Sameull Mathews, Esq., ——— Co.
White, Katherine, 1640, by Phillip Clarke, James City Co.
White, Wm., 1639, by Richard Corke, Gent., Henrico Co.
White, Edward, 1639, by Wm. Denham, Isle of Wight Co.
White, Charles, 1639, by Samuell Almond, Henrico Co.

White, Richard, 1639, by John Loraine, Isle of Wight Co.
White, John, 1642, by Richard Gregson, Elizabeth City Co.
White, Michael, 1655, by Lt. Col. Tho. Swan, Surry Co.
White, John, 1642, by John Styles, Isle of Wight Co.
White, John, 1656, by Sir Henry Chichley, ——— Co.
White, Michaell, 1650, by Wm. Morgan, ——— Co.
White, James, 1643, by Samuell Abbott, James City Co.
White, John, 1643, by William Jacob, Lower Norfolk Co.
White, Lawrance, 1643, by Phillipp Taylor, Northampton Co.
White, Thos., 1638, by Joseph Boarne, Charles City Co.
White, John, 1638, by William Croutch, Lower Norfolk Co.
White, Peter, 1638, by Georg White Clerk, Upper New Norfolk Co.
White, Blanka, 1638, by Georg White, Clerk (her husband), Upper New
    Norfolk Co.
White, Nich., 1638, by Stephen Charlton, Accomack Co.
White, Tho., 1638, by Thomas Sawyer, New Norfolk Co.
White, Peter, 1637, by Georg White, New Norfolk Co.
White, Blanch, 1637, by Georg White (her husband), New Norfolk Co.
White, Jon., 1637, by Capt. Thomas Osborne, Henrico Co.
White, Geo., 1637, by Daniell Gookins, New Norfolk Co.
White, Charles, 1637, by Arthur Bayly and Tho. Crosby, Henrico Co.
White, Oliver, 1643, by William Storey, Upper Norfolk Co.
White, Jon., 1635, by John Moone, Warrasquinoake Co.
White, Peter, 1635, by Richard Bennett, ——— Co.
White, Nicholas, 1637, by Margaret Rogers, New Norfolk Co.
White, Franc., 1637, by John Graves, Elizabeth City Co.
White, Nich., 1636, by Edward Rogers, Warrasquinoake Co.
White, Peter, 1637, by Richard Bennett, New Norfolk Co.
White, Wm., 1636, by Richard Cocke, ——— Co.
White, Niccodemus, 1635, by Capt. Wm. Pierse, ——— Co.
White, Joan, 1654, by Richard Jacob, Northampton Co.
Whitaker, Geo., 1638, by Robert Freeman, James City Co.
Whitecroft, Robt., 1640, by Thomas Causey, ——— Co.
Whitecroft, Robt., 1653, by Capt. Robt. Abrahal, Gloucester Co.
Whitefare, Robt., 1655, by Robert Castle, James City Co.
Whitehart, William, 1639, by Henry Bogwell, Accomack Co.
Whitehead, Arth., 1643, by Mr. Obedience Robins, Northampton Co.
Whitehead, Wm., 1655, by Jenkin Price, Northampton Co.
Whitehead, James, 1638, by Benjamin Carrill, James City Co.
Whitehead, George, 1635, by Capt. Adam Thoroughgood, ——— Co.
Whitehurst, Wm., 1636, by James Vanerit, ——— Co.
Whitehurst, Wm., 1636, by James Vanerit, Elizabeth City Co.
Whiteredge, Wm., 1637, by Thomas Todd, New Norfolk Co.
Whitehorne, Ann, 1635, by Capt. Adam Thoroughgood, ——— Co.
Whitewell, Eliz., 1653, by Robert Tomlin, ——— Co.
Whiteworth, Alice, 1652, by Clement Thrush, Lancaster Co.
Whiteworth, Robt., 1656, by George Abbott, Nansemond Co.
Whitfield, Gilbert, 1637, by Daniell Gookins, New Norfolk Co.
Whitfield, Wm., 1636, by John Chandler, Elizabeth Citie Co.
Whitefield, Richard, 1635, by Thomas Warren, Charles City Co.
Whithorne, Arunges, 1653, by Charles Grimes, Lancaster Co.

Whitill, Geo., 1654, by Andrew Gibson, ——— Co.
Whiting, Robert, 1653, by Charles Grymes, Lancaster Co.
Whiting, Edward, 1653, by Nicho. Meriwether, Northumberland Co.
Whiting, Owen, 1643, by Richard Jackson, Isle of Wight Co.
Whiting, Edward, 1654, by Nich. Merywether, Westmoreland Co.
Whiting, Ann, 1643, by James Whiting (her husband), ——— Co.
Whiting, James, 1638, by Mr. Thomas Wallis, James City Co.
Whiting, Chri., 1636, by Wm. Fookes, ——— Co.
Whiting, Richard, 1637, by Francis Poythers, Charles City Co.
Whiting, Jones, 1635, by Mr. Geo. Keth, Charles River Co.
Whiting, Rebecca, 1635, by Mr. Geo. Keth, Charles River Co.
Whitting, Richard, 1650, by John Rosier, Northumberland Co.
Whitinge, Tho., 1654, by Edward Revell, Northampton Co.
Whitington, Lucan, 1647, by Wm. Whitington (her husband), North-
    ampton Co.
Whittington, Tho., 1652, by Tho. Greenwood, Isle of Wight Co.
Whittington, Mary, 1653, by Capt. Wm. Whittington (her husband),
    Northampton Co.
Whitler, Tho., 1656, by Wm. Justice Charles City Co.
Whitley, Richard, 1646, by Joseph Croshawe, Charles River Co.
Whittey, Randall, 1638, by Lieut. Robt. Sheppard, James City Co.
Whitliffe, Alice, 1650, by Henry Brooke, Northumberland Co.
Whitlift, Robt., 1650, by Henry Brooke, Northumberland Co.
Whitlift, David, 1650, by Henry Brooke, Northumberland Co.
Whitlock, Tho., 1638, by Richard Bennett, Isle of Wight Co.
Whitlock, Tho., 1650, by Mr. James Williamson, ——— Co.
Whitlock, Ann, 1651, by Mrs. Anna Bernard, Northumberland Co.
Whitlockee, Anne, 1652, by Mrs. Anna Barnett, Gloucester Co.
Whitly, David, 1654, by Gregory Wells and Richard Williams, James
    City Co.
Whitmore, Robt., and his wife, 1653, by Samuell Parry, Lancaster Co.
Whitmore, Mary, 1637, by Thomas Todd, New Norfolk Co.
Whitney, Thos., 1635, by Thos. Butler Clark and Pastor of Denbie,
    Warrasquinoake Co.
Whitson, Ann, 1654, by Major Miles Carey, Westmoreland Co.
Whitsorrell, Morrice, 1656, by John Billiott, Northampton Co.
Whittecure, George, 1650, by John Cooke, Northumberland Co.
Whittle, Geo., 1650, by Andrew Gibson, ——— Co.
Whitle, Robert, 1637, by Capt. Adam Thoroughgood, New Norfolk Co.
Whitway, Edwd., 1650, by John Hany, Northumberland Co.
Whitty, John, 1656, by Mr. Henry Soanes, New Kent Co.
Whoop, John, 1652, by Mr. Edwin Connaway, ——— Co.
Whoorewood, Nicholas, 1635, by George Minifie, James City Co.
Whorsen, Matt., 1650, by Capt. Moore Fautleroy, ——— Co.
Wleming, John, 1653, by Joseph Croshaw, York Co.
Wichard, James, 1654, by Tho. Willoughby, Lower Norfolk Co.
Wicke, Romor, 1656, by Tabitha and Matilda Scarburgh, Northampton
    Co.
Wickes, Henry, 1651, by Thomas Axby, Northumberland Co.
Wictor, Mich., 1652, by Richard Coleman, ——— Co.
Widdowes, Henry, 1638, by Lieut. Robt. Shepperd, Jamas City Co.

Widnell, Mich., 1653, by Joseph Croshaw, York Co.
Wigg, Ann, 1650, by Silvester Thatcher and Tho. Whitlocke, ——— Co.
Wigg, Robert, 1638, by William Wigg, James City Co.
Wiggs, Eliza., 1652, by Daniell Welch, Lancaster Co.
Wiggan, Fra., 1652, by Tho. Boswell, ——— Co.
Wiggen, Martha, 1654, by John Wyre, John Gillet, Andrew Gilson and
    John Phillipps, ——— Co.
Wigmore, Elias, 1637, by Henry Perry, Charles River Co.
Wignull, Thos., 1656, by Wm. Millinge, Northampton Co.
Wignall, Alex., 1656, by Wm. Millinge, Charles City Co.
Wignall, Thomas, 1647, by Jonathan Gills, Northampton Co.
Wignall, Wm., 1650, by Andrew Gilson, ——— Co.
Wignall, Will., 1654, by Andrew Gibson, ——— Co.
Wignall, Alex., 1647, by Jonathan Gills, Northampton Co.
Wignoll, Margarett, 1638, by Wm. Morgan, ——— Co.
Wiggs, Eliza., 1652, by Tho. Boswell, ——— Co.
Wike, Alex., 1642, by William Prior, Gent., ——— Co.
Wilbains, Edward, 1635, by George Minifie, James City Co.
Wilchin, Rochell, 1654, by Richard Wilchin (her husband), Gloucester
    Co.
Wilcon, Peter, 1650, by Capt. Moore Fautleroy, ——— Co.
Wilcockes, John, 1652, by James Forster and Audry Best, ——— Co.
Wilcocks, Tho., 1654, by Elizabeth Hutton, Surry Co.
Wilcocks, John, 1654, by Elizabeth Hutton, Surry Co.
Wilcocks, Math., 1655, by Mr. Wm. Nutt, Northumberland Co.
Wilcocks, Tymothy, 1650, by Mrs. Frances Townshend, Northumber-
    land Co.
Wilcocks, John, 1636, by James Vanerit, Elizabeth City Co.
Wilcock, Georg., 1637, by Oliver Sprye, New Norfolk Co.
Wilcox, Henry, 1655, by Dr. Giles Mode, New Kent Co.
Wilcox, Henry, 1655, by John Motley, Northumberland Co.
Wilcox, Joan, 1654, by Henry Walker, James City Co.
Wilcox, Michaell, 1642, by Wm. Durant, ——— Co.
Wilcox, Margt., 1653, by James Turner, ——— Co.
Wilcox, Roger, 1642, by Capt. Daniell Gookin, ——— Co.
Wilcox, Grace, 1642, by Wm. Durant, ——— Co.
Wilcox, Wm., 1652, by Col. Geo. Ludlow, Esq., Gloucester Co.
Wilcox, Michael, 1652, by Col. Geo. Ludlow, Esq., Gloucester Co.
Wilcox, Mary, 1653, by John Edwards, Lancaster Co.
Wild, Robert, 1649, by John Trussells, ——— Co.
Wilham, Morris, 1653, by John Edwards, Lancaster Co.
Wilken, Frances, daughter of Elias Taylor, 1648, by Lewis Burwell and
    Tho. Haws, York River Co.
Wilkey, Mary, 1653, by Peter Knight, Northumberland Co.
Wilks, Jno., 1648, by George Read, Gent., ——— Co.
Wilks, John, 1655, by Wm. Steevens, Northampton Co.
Wilkes, Tho., 1653, by Ferdinando Austin, Charles City Co.
Wilkeson, Jno., 1643, by Seth Ward, Henrico Co.
Wilkins, Katharine, 1639, by Edward Travis, James City Co.
Wilkins, Katharine, 1637, by Edward Travis, James City Co.
Wilkins, Tho., 1644, by Toby Smith, Gent., Upper Norfolk Co.

Wilkins, Humphry, 1643, by Tho. Evans, ——— Co.
Willkins, Rich., 1654, by Richard Codsford, Westmoreland Co.
Wilkins, Richard, 1654, by John Wyre, John Gillet, Andrew Gilson and
    John Phillipps, ——— Co.
Wilkins, Richard, 1653, by Capt. Francis Morgan, Gloucester Co.
Wilkins, Rich., 1652, by Tho. Leechman and John Bennett, Gloucester
    Co.
Wilkins, David, 1653, by Tho. Hawkins, Northumberland Co.
Wilkins, Edward, 1653, by Tho. Hackett, ——— Co.
Wilkinson, Robt., 1638, by Georg Mynifie (merchant), ——— Co.
Wilkinson, Naiomy, 1635, by William Wilkinson (minister), ——— Co.
Wilkinson, Antho., 1651, by James Thelaball, Lower Norfolk Co.
Wilkinson, Wm., 1639, by John Pawley, James City Co.
Wilkinson, Antho., 1653, by Tho. Davis, ——— Co.
Wilkinson, Matt., 1653, by Augustine Gillet, Upper Norfolk Co.
Wilkinson, ———, 1654, by Randal Chamly, Lancaster Co.
Wilkinson, John, 1652, by Capt. Augustine Warner, ——— Co.
Wilkinson, John, 1656, by Richard Gible, Northumberland Co.
Wilkinson, Ann, 1656, by Richard Gible, Northumberland Co.
Wilkinson, Robt., 1635, by William Stafford, ——— Co.
Wilkinson, (Mrs. Moony), 1637, by Wm. Wilkinson, New Norfolk Co.
Wilkinson, John, 1637, by Wm. Prior, Charles River Co.
Wilkinson, Mr. Willi., 1637, by William Wilkinson, New Norfolk Co.
Wilkinson, Willi., 1635, by William Wilkinson (minister), ——— Co.
Wilkins, Thomas, 1637, by Arthur Smith, Isle of Wight Co.
Wilkinson, Tho., 1655, by Major Miles Cary, Warwick Co.
Wilkinson, John, 1639, by Georg Minifye, Esq., Charles River Co.
Wilkinson, Joane, 1639, by Georg Minifye, Esq., Charles River Co.
Wilkinson, Mary, 1648, by Richard Wyatt, ——— Co.
Wilkinson, Robert, 1649, by Tho. Harwood, ——— Co.
Wilkinson, Henry, 1650, by Lawrence Peters, Nansemond Co.
Wilkenson, Mary, 1654, by John Sharpe, Lancaster Co.
Wilkinson, James, 1650, by Tho. Blogg, Northumberland Co.
Wilkenson, Mar., 1654, by John Watson and John Bognall, Westmore-
    land Co.
Wilkenson, James, 1654, by Mrs. Fra. Harrison (widow), Westmoreland
    Co.
Wilkenson, Tho., 1655, by George Wall, Westmoreland Co.
Wilkenson, Mann, 1655, by George Parker, Northampton Co.
Willard, Richard, 1654, by Francis Smith and Mr. John Smith, West-
    moreland Co.
Willboone, William, 1637, by John Wilkins, New Norfolk Co.
Willbourne, Wm., 1636, by John Wilkins, Accomack Co.
Wille, Ann, 1648, by James Miller, ——— Co.
Wille, Eman, Elizabeth, his wife, and six children, 1653, by Peter
    Knight and Baker Cutt, ——— Co.
Willeford, William, 1638, by Robt. Holt and Richard Bell, James City
    Co.
Willford, Edward, 1635, by Capt. Wm. Pierse, ——— Co.
Willford, John, 1653, by Alexander Addison, ——— Co.
Willes, Eliz., 1654, by Nich. Merywether, Westmoreland Co.

Willie, Tho., 1655, by Tho. Hale, Northumberland Co.
Willett, John, 1653, by John Merryman and Morgan Haynes, Lancaster Co.
Willett, Robert, 1653, by Geo. Wadding, Lancaster Co.
Willet, Richard, 1653, by Edward Kemp, Geo. Cortlough, and John Meredith, Lancaster Co.
Willett, James, 1652, by John Taylor, Lancaster Co.
Willetts, John, 1655, by Richard Codsford, Westmoreland Co.
Willett, Edw., 1654, by Walter Dickenson, Lancaster Co.
Willett, Geo., 1652, by Robert West, Charles City Co.
Willett, Peter, 1638, by Richard Wilcox, James City Co.
Willett, James, 1637, by Richard Bennett, New Norfolk Co.
Willet, Peter, ——, by Mr. Wm. Presly, Northumberland Co.
Willett, David, 1654, by Christopher Boon, Westmoreland Co.
Willett, Sarah, 1654, by Toby Smith, Lancaster Co.
Willett, Hen., 1640, by Thomas Harvey, James City Co.
Willett, John, 1652, by Tho. Hackett, —— Co.
William, John, 1648, by George White, Lower Norfolk Co.
William, Masser, 1650, by Nicho. Jernew, Yorke Co.
Williams, Thos., 1639, by Rich. Hoe, James City Co.
Williams, Joane, 1655, by John Hinman, Northampton Co.
Williams, Jane, 1655, by John Hinman, Northampton Co.
Williams, Eliz., 1650, by Thomas Powell, —— Co.
Williams, Lewis, 1650, by Capt. Richard Bond, Charles City Co.
Williams, James, 1651, by Mr. Robert Abrall, Yorke Co.
Williams, Thomas, 1651, by Wm. Rennales, Northumberland Co.
Williams, Henry, 1654, by Robert Holt, James City Co.
Williams, Tho., 1654, by Robert Holt, James City Co.
Williams, Ellinor, 1653, by Mathew Tomlin, Northumberland Co.
Williams, Jon., 1653, by Leonard Chamberlaine, Gloucester Co.
Williams, Hum., 1653, by Richard Jackson, —— Co.
Williams, Owen, 1652, by Wm. Colborne, Northampton Co.
Williams, Jon., 1642, by John Smith, James City Co.
Williams, Henry, 1653, by Richard Foster, Lower Norfolk Co.
Williams, Tho., 1651, by Ashewell Battin, Yorke Co.
Williams, Mor., 1651, by Ashwell Battin, Yorke Co.
Williams, Owen, 1651, by Richard Smith, Northampton Co.
Williams, David, 1651, by Richard Smith, Northampton Co.
Williams, John, 1651, by Mr. Arthur Price, Yorke Co.
Williams, Wm., 1651, by John Rookwood, Gent., Northumberland Co.
Williams, Francis, 1651, by John King, Gloucester Co.
Williams, Wm., 1651, by Lieut. Coll. Giles Brent, Northumberland Co.
Williams, Gilbert, 1653, by Richard Carey, —— Co.
Williams, Jno., 1651, by Capt. Stephen Gill, Northumberland Co.
Williams, Edmond, 1653, by Nicho. Meriwether, Northumberland Co.
Williams, Jno., 1653, by Geo. Wadding, Lancaster Co.
Williams, James, 1653, by Abrahma Moon, Lancaster Co.
Williams, Jeffery, 1653, by Evan Davis and Henry Nicholls, Lancaster Co.
Williams, John, 1653, by Edward Kemp, Geo. Cortlough and John Meredith, Lancaster Co.

Williams, Henry, 1654, by Rich. Jones, James City Co.
Williams, Mary, 1653, by Mr. Henry Soanes, ——— Co.
Williams, Phillip, 1653, by Jno. Rosyer, Northumberland Co.
Williams, Elizabeth, 1653, by Tho. Morgan, ——— Co.
Williams, Jon., 1654, by Edw. Cole, Northampton Co.
Williams, Richd., 1654, by Richard Budd, ——— Co.
Williams, David, 1652, by John Taylor, Lancaster Co.
Williams, Morgan, 1639, by William Davis, James City Co.
Williams, Richard, 1654, by Wm. Wells, Lancaster Co.
Williams, Jane, 1656, by John Evans, Northampton Co.
Williams, Morgan, 1656, by John Bromfeild, James City Co.
Williams, Thom., 1654, by Obed. Williams, York Co.
Williams, Tho., 1655, by George Kibble, Lancaster Co.
Williams, Wm., 1654, by Lieut. Coll. Giles Brent, Westmoreland Co.
Williams, Edwd., 1655, by John Marshall, Isle of Wight Co.
Williams, Wm., 1655, by Lt. Col. Anthony Ellyott, ——— Co.
Williams, Edward, 1654, by Nich. Merywether, Westmoreland Co.
Williams, Ann, 1654, by Tho. Hobkins, Lancaster Co.
Williams, John, 1654, by Capt. Augustine Warner and Mr. John Robins, ——— Co.
Williams, Richard, 1654, by Capt. Augustine Warner and Mr. John Robins, ——— Co.
Williams, David, 1654, by Abraham Moone, ——— Co.
Williams, John, 1655, by Mr. Tho. Peck, Gloucester Co.
Williams, Phillip, 1654, by John Rosyer, Clerk, ——— Co.
Williams, Ja., 1654, by Walter Dickenson, Lancaster Co.
Williams, Rich., 1655, by John Wyere, Lancaster Co.
Williams, Rice, 1652, by Richard Coleman, ——— Co.
Williams, James, 1651, by Joseph Croshaw, Yorke Co.
Williams, Tho., 1652, by Mr. Nicholas Jernew, Gloucester Co.
Williams, Tho., 1652, by Anthony Doney and Enoch Hawker, Lancaster Co.
Williamson, Mathew, 1636, by Bridges Freeman, ——— Co.
Williams, Ellin, 1636, by James Knott, Elizabeth City Co.
Williams, Richard, 1636, by Epaphroditus Lawson, Warwick Co.
Williams, Thomas, 1635, by Richard Bennett, ——— Co.
Williams, Thomas, 1635, by John Armie, Warrasquinoake Co.
Williams, Jon., 1636, by Richard Cocke, ——— Co.
Williams, Evan, 1635, by William Spencer, ——— Co.
Williams, John, 1635, by Walter Hacker, James River Co.
Williams, Thos., 1637, by Richard Bennett, New Norfolk Co.
Williams, Edw., 1636, by Georg Mr. Menifye, James City Co.
Williams, Tho., 1637, by Wm. Farrar, Henrico Co.
Williams, Edw., 1635, by Capt. Adam Thoroughgood, ——— Co.
Williams, Richard, 1636, by Cheney Boyse, Charles City Co.
Williams, John, 1637, by Alice Edloe, Henrico Co.
Williamson, Mathew, 1637, by Bridges Freeman, James City Co.
Williams, Roger, 1635, by Thos. Butler Clark and Pastor of Denbie, Warrasquinoake Co.
Williams, Ann, 1635, by Thos. Butler Clark and Pastor of Denbie, Warrasquinoake Co.

Williams, Rich., 1637, by Cheney Boyes, Charles City Co.
Williams, Edw., 1637, by Thomas Osborne, Jr., Henrico Co.
Williams, Jenkins, 1638, by Capt. Christopher Wormley, Charles River Co.
Williams, Thos., 1635, by Christopher Wooddard, ——— Co.
Williams, Thos., 1635, by Wm. Swan, James Co.
Williams, Norman, 1635, by John Moone, Warrasquinoake Co.
Williams, Robt., 1637, by John Dennett, Charles River Co.
Williams, Edw., 1637, by Capt. Adam Thoroughgood, New Norfolk Co.
Williams, Evan, 1637, by William Spencer, ——— Co.
Williams, Ellin, 1637, by James Knott, New Norfolk Co.
Williams, Humphry, 1638, by Benjamin Carrill, James City Co.
Williams, Rowland, 1638, by Roger Davis, Charles City Co.
Williams, Wm., 1638, by Stephen Charlton, Accomack Co.
Williams, Margery, 1638, by Henry Williams, Accomack Co.
Williams, Tho., 1638, by Cornelius Loyd, ——— Co.
Williams, Tho., 1643, by Thomas Williams, ——— Co.
Williams, Tho., 1642, by Capt. Humphry Higgenson, ——— Co.
Williams, Tho., 1638, by Thomas Swan, James Citie Co.
Williams, Alice, 1638, by John Robins, ——— Co.
Williams, Walter, 1638, by William Parker, Upper Norfolk Co.
Williams, John, 1638, by John Seaward, Isle of Wight Co.
Williams, John, 1646, by Sir William Berkly, ——— Co.
Williams, Morgan, 1643, by John Carter, ——— Co.
Williams, John, 1647, by Tho. Gibson, York Co.
Williams, John, 1648, by Wm. Ewen, James City Co.
Williams, Geo., 1650, by John Essix, Northumberland Co.
Williams, Phillip, 1650, by John Hany, Northumberland Co.
Williams, James, 1650, by Nathaniell Jones, Northumberland Co.
Williams, Jno., 1650, by Mrs. Frances Townshend (widdow), Northumberland Co.
Williams, Robt., 1647, by James Warradine, ——— Co.
Williams, Rach., 1647, by James Warradine, ——— Co.
Williams, Morgan, 1647, by Lawrence Peeters, "Nansimum" Co.
Williams, John, 1643, by William Ewins, James City Co.
Williams, Jon., 1643, by Capt. Samuell Mathews, Esq., ——— Co.
Williams, Richard, 1643, by Capt. Samuell Mathews, Esq., ——— Co.
Williams, Tho., 1648, by John Seward, Isle of Wight Co.
Williams, Richard, 1646, by Samuell Abbott, Nansemond Co.
William, Edw., 1648, by John Landman, Nansimond Co.
Williams, Jane, 1645, by James Bruss, Northampton Co.
Williams, James, 1654, by Toby Smith, Lancaster Co.
Williams, Eliz., 1654, by John Williams, Northumberland Co.
Williams, David, 1650, by Richard Smith, Northampton Co.
Williams, Owin, 1650, by Richard Smith, Northampton Co.
Williams, Jon., 1642, by Christopher Boyce, ——— Co.
Williams, Jest., 1656, by Sir Henry Chichley, ——— Co.
Williams, John, 1650, by Mrs. Frances Townshend (widow), Northumberland Co.
Williams, James, 1656, by John Wood, ——— Co.
Williams, Richard, 1639, by Henry Perry, Charles City Co.

Williams, Nich., 1639, by Henry Bognell, Accomack Co.
Williams, Christi., 1638, by John George, Charles City Co
Williams, Jon., 1638, by Mr. Walter Ashton, Charles City Co.
Williams, Richard, 1638, by Mr. Walter Ashton, Charles City Co.
Williams, Roger, 1638, by Lieut. John Upton, Isle of Wight Co.
Willliams, Nicholas, 1638, by Christopher Lawson, James City Co.
Williams, ———, 1638, by William Morgan, ——— Co.
Williams, Tho., 1639, by Richard Corke, Gent., Henrico Co.
Williams, John, 1639, by Georg Minifye, Esq., Charles River Co.
Williams, Robert, 1639, by Georg Minifye, Charles River Co.
Williams, Robt., 1642, by Capt. Samuell Mathews, Esq., ——— Co.
Williams, Corn., 1642, by Capt. Samuell Mathews, Esq., ——— Co.
Williams, Rich., 1642, by Capt. Samuell Mathews, Esq., ——— Co.
Williams, Roger, 1642, by Capt. Samuell Mathews, Esq., ——— Co.
Williams, Ann, 1647, by John Brooch, York River Co.
Williams, Jno., 1649, by Mr. Wm. Hoccaday, ——— Co.
Williams, Tho., 1648, by James Mason, James City Co.
Williams, Jenkin, 1649, by Richard Kemp, Esq. (Sec. of State), ———
    Co.
Williams, Mary, 1649, by Joseph Croshawe, Yorke Co.
Williams, Mar., 1650, by Mr. James Williams, ——— Co.
Williams, Jno., 1649, by Wm. Nesum, Tho. Sax, Miles Bathasby and
    John Pyne, Northampton Co.
Williams, John, 1649, by John King, Yorke Co.
Williams, Edw., 1649, by Tho. Dale, ——— Co.
Williams, Robt., 1649, by Edmund Scarburgh, Jr., Northampton Co.
Williams, Perregrine, 1650, by Robert Bird, ——— Co.
Williams, Garrett, 1650, by John Mangor, ——— Co.
Williams, Morgan, 1650, by John Bone, ——— Co.
Williams, Jno., 1650, by Capt. Moore Fautleroy, ——— Co.
Williams, Jane, 1650, by Robert Bird, ——— Co.
Williamson, Francis, 1650, by Hump. Lyster, ——— Co.
Williams, John, 1650, by Richard Hull, ——— Co.
Williams, Charles, 1650, by Richard Hull, ——— Co.
Williams, John, 1650, by Sr. Tho. Luntsford, Kt., and Barronett, ———
    Co.
Williams, Joan, 1650, by Tho. Wilkenson, ——— Co.
Williams, John, 1643, by Robert Pitt, Isle of Wight Co.
Williams, Elinor, wife of Edm. Williams, 1650, by Nicholas Jernew,
    Gent., ——— Co.
Williams, Roger, 1653, by Mathew Williams, James City Co.
Williams, Mary, 1654, by Randall Chamblett, ——— Co.
Williams, Jno., 1654, by Tho. Bell, Northampton Co.
Williams, John, 1652, by Rice Hughes, ——— Co.
Williams, Hugh, 1650, by John Landman, ——— Co.
Williams, Henry, 1642, by William English, ——— Co.
Williams, John, 1638, by Thomas Todd, Lower New Norfolk Co.
Williams, Edward, 1642, by Richard Gregson, Elizabeth City Co.
Williams, Anne, 1653, by Mr. Wm. Fry, James City Co.
Williams, Jno., 1653, by Robert Bouth, Yorke Co.
Williams, Tho., ———, by Lt. Coll. John Cheesman, ——— Co.

Williams, James, 1652, by Capt. John West, Esq., ———— Co.
Williams, Roger, 1653, by Mr. Wm. Debram, ———— Co.
Williams, Martin, 1653, by Richard Braine, Charles Co.
Williams, Wm., 1652, by Mrs. Jane Harnett, Northumberland Co.
Williams, Edm., 1650, by Nicholas Jernew, Gent., ———— Co.
Williams, Ann, 1650, by Lewis Burwell, Gent., Northumberland Co.
Williams, Tho., 1650, by Ralph Green, ———— Co.
Williams, Tho., 1650, by John Essix, Northumberland Co.
Williams, Jane, 1654, by John Watson and John Bognall, Westmore-
  land Co.
Williams, John, 1652, by Mrs. Mary Brent, Northumberland Co.
  land Co.
Williams, Mary, 1652, by Dr. George Hack, Northampton Co.
Williams, John, 1652, by Tobias Horton, Lancaster Co.
Williams, Mary, 1653, by Abraham Moone, Northumberland Co.
Williams, Tho., 1652, by Wm. Ginsey, Gloucester Co.
Williams, Wm., 1652, by Mr. John Mottrom, Northumberland Co.
Williamson, Isaac, 1653, by Tho. Hampton, ———— Co.
Williams, Mary, 1653, by Charles Scarburg, Northampton Co.
Williams, Veven, 1653, by Charles Scarburg, Northampton Co.
Williams, Judeth, 1641, by Capt. John Cheesman, ———— Co.
Williams, Rich., 1642, by Christopher Boyce, ———— Co.
Williamson, David, 1638, by Thomas Burbage, Accomack Co.
Williamson, Ann, 1653, by Colo. Wm. Clayborne (Sec. of State), ————
  Co.
Williamson, Wm., 1653, by Colo. Wm. Clayborne (Sec. of State), ————
  Co.
Williamson, Richd., 1653, by Gregory Perrot, Isle of Wight, Co.
Williamson, Ja., 1654, by Col. Hump. Higgenson, Esq., and Abraham
  Moone, Westmoreland Co.
Wilkinson, Joyce, 1654, by Mrs. Fra. Harrison, widow, Westmoreland
  Co.
Williamson, Susanna, 1635, by Thos. Butler Clark and Pastor of Denbie,
  Warrasquinoake Co.
Williamson, Davis, 1637, by John Brodwell, James City Co.
Williamson, Max, 1638, by Stephen Charlton, Accomack Co.
Williamson, Alice, 1650, by Capt. Moore Fautleroy, ———— Co.
Wilkinson, John, 1643, by Wm. Morgan, ———— Co.
Williamson, Jon., 1643, by Capt. Samuell Mathews, Esq., ———— Co.
Willismson, Anthony, 1642, by Capt. Humphry Higgenson, ———— Co.
Williamson, Tho., 1649, by John Sybsey, Lower Norfolk Co.
WmSon, Andrew, 1653, by Richard Burton, ———— Co.
Williamson, John, 1640, by John Radford, Lower Norfolk Co.
Williamson, Richard, 1641, by Ambrose Bennett, Isle of Wight Co.
Wilkinson, Tho., 1654, by Phillip Chesly and Dan. Wilde, Yorke Co.
Willimot, Tho., 1652, by Henry Palin and John Singleton, ———— Co.
Willing, Robert, 1638, by Richard Bennett, Isle of Wight Co.
Willinger, Anthony, 1650, by Benedick Barbar, Gent., ———— Co.
Willington, Mary, 1653, by Abraham Moon, Lancaster Co.
Willmude, Mary, 1655, by John Jenkins, Northampton Co.
Willough, Peter, 1635, by Capt. Wm. Pierse, ———— Co.

Willoughby, John, 1653, by Charles Grymes, Clerk, Lancaster Co.
Willoughby, Fra., 1653, by Wm. Debram, ———— Co.
Willoughby, Thos., 1639, by Robt. Newman, Warwick River Co.
Willoughby, Alice, 1654, by Tho. Willoughby, Lower Norfolk Co.
Willoughby, Eliz., 1654, by Tho. Willoughby, Lower Norfolk Co.
Willis, Thomas, 1637, by Thomas Weston, Charles River Co.
Willis, Mary, 1653, by Thomas Willis, York Co.
Willis, ————, 1653, by Richard Stornell, ———— Co.
Willis, Ann, 1653, by James Watson, Isle of Wight Co.
Willis, Jane, 1652, by Tho. Steevens, Lancaster Co.
Willis, John, 1656, by Richard Gible, Northumberland Co.
Willis, Margery, 1654, by Capt. Nicho. Marteaw, Westmoreland Co.
Willis, Godfry, 1654, by Capt. Nich. Marteaw, Westmoreland Co.
Willis, Wm., 1653, by Anto. Hoskins, Northampton Co.
Willis, Thomas, 1635, by Samuel Weaver, ———— Co.
Willis, Eliza., 1637, by William Hatcher, ———— Co.
Willis, Eliz., 1636, by Wm. Clarke, Henrico Co.
Willis, Edward, 1635, by Thos. Butler Clark and Pastor of Denbie,
    Warrasquinoake Co.
Willis, Walter, 1637, by John Davis, James City Co.
Willis, Tho., 1637, by Phillipp Taylor, Accomack Co.
Willis, Walter, 1638, by Thomas Stampe, James City Co.
Willis, Eliz., 1638, by William Clarke, Henrico Co.
Willis, Tho., 1643, by Phillipp Taylor, Northampton Co.
Willis, Richard, 1650, by John Hallawes, Gent., Northumberland Co.
Willis, John, 1642, by Thomas Guyer, ———— Co.
Willis, Walter, 1639, by Thomas Stamp, James City Co.
Willis, Thomas, 1638, by Lieut. John Upton, Isle of Wight Co.
Willis, James, 1649, by George Burcher, Charles City Co.
Willis, John, 1650, by Thomas Mulford, Nansemond Co.
Willis, John, 1652, by Edward Willis, ———— Co.
Willis, Katherine, 1652, by Edward Willis, ———— Co.
Willis, Susana, 1652, by Edward Willis, ———— Co.
Willis, Rochell, 1652, by John Earle, Northumberland Co.
Willis, James, 1653, by Samuell Parry, Lancaster Co.
Willis, Henry, 1652, by Dr. George Hack, Northampton Co.
Willis, Anne, 1653, by John Gillett, Lancaster Co.
Willis, John, 1653, by John Gillett, Lancaster Co.
Willis, Jane, 1654, by Robert Tomlin, ———— Co.
Willow, Merra, 1642, by Lieut. Francis Mason, ———— Co.
Willowby, Kat., 1654, by Richard Hawkins, Westmoreland Co.
Wills, Jon., 1642, by John Benton, ———— Co.
Wills, Wm., 1650, by Nicho. Jernew, Yorke Co.
Wills, Elizabeth, 1638, by John Woodliffe, Charles City Co.
Wills, Wm., 1650, by Nicholas Jernew, Gent., ———— Co.
Wilmot, Tho., 1648, by Richard Wyatt, ———— Co.
Wilmott, Edward, 1635, by William Spencer, ———— Co.
Wilmott, Edward, 1637, by William Spencer, ———— Co.
Wilmott, Ann, 1650, by Richard Jacob, Northampton Co.
Wilmott, Anne, 1653, by Robert Bayly, Northampton Co.
Wiloge, Robert, 1650, by Mr. James Williamson, ———— Co.

Wilox, John, 1652, by John Robbins, Northampton Co.
Wiloxes, John, 1653, by Tho. Hampton, —— Co.
Wilsford, Tho., and Bridgett, his wife, 1653, by James Magregory and
    Hugh Fauch, Northumberland Co.
Wilshire, Wm., 1636, by Bridges Freeman, —— Co.
Wilshire, Wm., 1637, by Bridges Freeman, James City Co.
Wilsomis, Sarah, 1653, by John Hillier, Northumberland Co.
Wilson, Wm., 1652, by Nicholas Waddilow, Northampton Co.
Wilson, ——, 1654, by Randal Chamly, Lancaster Co.
Wilson, Jon., 1654, by Robert Holt, James City Co.
Wilson, Jon., 1653, by Jon. Slaughter, —— Co.
Wilson, Hen., 1653, by Tho. Youl, Northumberland Co.
Wilson, Gabriel, 1653, by Tho. Holmes, York Co.
Wilson, Jno., 1653, by Tho. Youl, Northumberland Co.
Wilson, Susan, 1653, by Capt. Francis Patt, Northampton Co.
Wilson, James, 1653, by Wm. Johnson, Lancaster Co.
Wilson, Wm., 1653, by John Shepperd, Northumberland Co.
Wilson, Ellen, 1653, by Richard Well, Northumberland Co.
Wilson, Thomas, 1653, by Charles Grymes, Lancaster Co.
Wilson, Robert, 1652, by John Meredith, Lancaster Co.
Wilson, Robt., 1652, by Col. Geo. Ludlow, Esq., Gloucester Co.
Wilson, Mathew, 1656, by Mr. Martin Baker, New Kent Co.
Wilson, Joan, 1655, by Richard Price, New Kent Co.
Wilson, Mar., 1654, by James Yates, —— Co.
Wilson, James, 1654, by Edward Simpson, Gloucester Co.
Wilson, Robt., 1652, by Collo. Hugh Gwin, —— Co.
Wilson, James, 1652, by Richard Coleman, —— Co.
Wilson, Richard, 1652, by Richard Coleman, —— Co.
Wilson, Wm., 1652, by Gregory Parrett, Lower Norfolk Co.
Wilson, James, 1652, by Nathaniel Bacon, Isle of Wight Co.
Wilson, Lane, 1637, by Hen. Woodhouse, New Norfolk Co.
Wilson, Mary, 1635, by Mr. Geo. Keth, Charles River Co.
Wilson, Scpian, 1648, by Geo. Hardey, Tho. Wombwell and Peter Hall,
    Isle of Wight Co.
Wilson, Wm., 1648, by John Smith, Lower Norfolk Co.
Wilson, Anth., 1648, by Lewis, Burwell, and Tho. Haws, York River Co.
Wilson, Wm., 1650, by Bertram Obert, —— Co.
Wilson, Sanders, 1655, by Southy Littleberry, Northampton Co.
Wilson, Tho., 1655, by Wm. Johnson and Stephen Horsey, Northamp-
    ton Co.
Wilson, Mary, 1647, by John Brooch, York River Co.
Wilson, Geo., 1649, by Capt. Ralph Wormeley, —— Co.
Wilson, James, 1649, by Stephen Gill, York Co.
Wilson, Lake, 1649, by John Walthams, Northampton Co.
Wilson, Mary, 1650, by John Cox, —— Co.
Wilson, Eliza., wife of Gabriell Wilson, 1650, by Capt. Moore Fautleroy,
    —— Co.
Willson, Gabriell, 1650, by Capt. Moore Fautleroy, —— Co.
Wilson, Tho., 1649, by Robert Mosely, Gent., —— Co.
Wilson, Wm., 1654, by John Sharpe, Lancaster Co.
Willson, Henry, 1654, by Richard Codsford, Westmoreland Co.

Wilson, Henry, 1654, by John Wyre, John Gillet, Andrew Gilson and John Phillipps, —— Co.
Wilson, John, 1654, by Col. Argoll Yardley, Northampton Co.
Wilson, Robt., 1653, by John Maddison, Gloucester Co.
Wilson, Henry, 1653, by Capt. Francis Morgan, Gloucester Co.
Wilson, Gabriell, 1652, by Tho. Holmes, Yorke Co.
Wilson, Mary, 1650, by John Major, Northampton Co.
Wilson, Eliza, 1650, by Richard Budd, Northumberland Co.
Wilson, Geo., 1652, by Ralph Paine, —— Co.
Wilson, John, 1652, by Augustine Moore, —— Co.
Wilson, Tho., 1654, by Francis Land, Lower Norfolk Co.
Willson, Jeffrey, 1654, by John Wyre, John Gillet, Andrew Gilson and John Phillipps, —— Co.
Willson, Robt., 1648, by Wm. Edwards and Rice Edwards, James City Co.
Willson, Jon., 1635, by John Spackman, Warrasquinoake Co.
Wilsonn, Elizabeth, 1636, by Wm. Neesam, James City Co.
Wilsonn, James, 1635, by Capt. Adam Thoroughgood, —— Co.
Wilsonn, Ruchard, 1636, by John Neale, Accomack Co.
Wilsonn, Gabriel, 1636, by Peter Johnson, Warrasquinoake Co.
Wilsonn, Nach., 1643, by Georg Levitt, —— Co.
Wilsonn, Eliza., 1642, by Adam Cooke, Charles Co.
Wilsonn, Edward, 1639, by Wm. Barker, Charles City Co.
Wilton, John, 1637, by Stephen Charlton, Accomack Co.
Willy, John, 1656, by Nicholas Waddilow, Northampton Co.
Winard, Tho., 1637, by John Chew, Charles River Co.
Winard, Thos., 1636, by John Chew, Gent., Charles River Co.
Wincen, Wm., 1652, by Mr. Henry Pitt, —— Co.
Wincock, Dorothy, 1652, by George Kemp, Lower Norfolk Co.
Winchell, Robt., 1653, by James Turner, —— Co.
Winchett, Ja., 1649, by Stephen Gill, York Co.
Winchester, Andrew, wife and Theoder, child, 1639, by Edward Panderson, —— Co.
Winchester, John, 1639, by Edward Panderson, —— Co.
Winchester, Jon., 1637, by Theodore Moyser, James City Co.
Winchester, John, 1636, by Wm. Hatcher, Henrico Co.
Winchester, John, 1637, by William Hatcher, —— Co.
Winchly, Mary, 1652, by Mrs. Jane Harmer, Northumberland Co.
Winders, James, 1642, by Peter Righby, —— Co.
Windeth, Fickler, 1645, by William Jones, Northampton Co.
Windell, Edward, 1650, by Thomas Mulford, Nansemond Co.
Windett, Ficler, 1652, by Mr. Tho. Gutheridge, —— Co.
Windett, Edward, 1638, by John Gater, Lower New Norfolk Co.
Windom, Edward, 1635, by Capt. Adam Thoroughgood, —— Co.
Wingatt, Roger, 1648, by Lewis Burwell and Thomas Haws, York River Co.
Winifrett, Wm., 1637, by John Chew, Charles River Co.
Winnifrett, Wm., 1636, by John Chew, Gent., Charles River Co.
Winifield, Wm., 1651, by Ashwell Battin, Yorke Co.
Winkeford, Jos., 1643, by Richard Richards, Charles River Co.
Winkle, Christopher, 1656, by John Lear, Westmoreland Co.

Wimbleton, Eliz., 1653, by James Johnson, Nansemond Co.
Wimpey, John, 1654, by Francis Smith and Mr. John Smith, Westmoreland Co.
Winley, Daire, 1635, by McWilliam Stone, ———— Co.
Winley, Robt., 1652, by Mr. John Browne, Northampton Co.
Wingfield, Thomas, 1636, by Walter Hacker, James River Co.
Winly, Nath., 1654, by Tho. Hobkins, Lancaster Co.
Winly, Nash, 1652, by Mrs. Elnor Brocas, Lancaster Co.
Winn, Jon., 1653, by Henry Lee, Yorke Co.
Winn, Anne, 1652, by Nicholas Waddilow, Northampton Co.
Winn, Elizabeth, 1656, by John Billiott, Northampton Co.
Winn, Eliza., 1652, by John Robbins, Northampton Co.
Winn, Anne, 1652, by John Robbins, Northampton Co.
Winn, Tho., 1654, by John Watson and John Bognall, Westmoreland Co.
Winn, Ann, 1650, by Mordecay Cook, ———— Co.
Winne, Katherine, 1652, by Anthony Doney and Enoch Hawker, Lancaster Co.
Winnall, John, 1635, by McWilliam Stone, ———— Co.
Winseill, Robert, 1646, by Sir William Berkley, ———— Co.
Winshaw, Roger, 1653, by Coll. Wm. Taylor, Esq., Gloucester Co.
Winthew, Constant, 1656, by Vincent Stanford, ———— Co.
Winter, Robt., 1651, by James Thelaball, Lower Norfolk Co.
Winter, Ann, 1649, by Edmund Scarburgh, Jr., Northampton Co.
Winter, Robert, 1649, by John Cabbedge, Lower Norfolk Co.
Winter, Richard, 1648, by Bartholomew Hoskins, ———— Co.
Winter, John, 1653, by Mr. Wm. Debram, ———— Co.
Winter, Rich., 1637, by Tho. Symmons, Charles River Co.
Winter, Ann, 1636, by Joane Bennett, Charles River Co.
Winter, William, 1635, by Jeremiah Clement, ———— Co.
Winterton, Mary, 1650, by John Mattrum, Northumberland Co.
Wirrall, Edw., 1654, by John Carr, ———— Co.
Wise, Hanna, 1655, by John Wise, Northampton Co.
Wisel, Nicholas, 1638, by Capt. Christopher Wormley, Charles River Co.
Wiseman, Robt., 1639, by Richard Johnson, Henrico Co.
Wiseman, John, 1652, by John Needles, ———— Co.
Wishart, Patrick, and five persons assigned from Mr. Edward Coye, 1638, by Thomas Beerboye, Upper New Norfolk Co.
Wishart, Patrick, 1656, by Tho. Harris, Lancaster Co.
Wishart, Patrick, 1638, by Thomas Beerboye, Upper New Norfolk Co.
Witcher, Henry, 1642, by Capt. Samuell Mathews, Esq., ———— Co.
Witen, Joyce, 1643, by Fra. Mason, Lower Norfolk Co.
Witch, Ann, 1646, by Joseph Croshawe, Charles River Co.
Withers, John, 1642, by Christopher Boyce, ———— Co.
Withers, Joe, 1635, by Capt. Adam Thoroughgood ,———— Co.
Withers, Stephen, 1635, by Capt. Adam Thoroughgood, ———— Co.
Withers, F., 1635, by William Beard, James City Co.
Withers, John, 1638, by Thomas Todd, Lower New Norfolk Co.
Withers, Fr., 1638, by Joseph Harmon, James City Co.
Witingale, Eliza., 1643, by William Mills, Isle of Wight Co.

Wittens, Richard, 1653, by Denis Coniers, Lancaster Co.
Wittington, Wm., 1642, by Wm. Barnard, Esq., Isle of Wight Co.
Wittington, Eliza., wife Fra. Wittington, 1650, by Wm. Yarrett and
    Fra. Wittington, ——— Co.
Wizard, Joane, 1653, by Colo. Wm. Clayborne (Sec. of State), ———
    Co.
Wiyfield, Philip, ——, by Tho. Binns, Surry Co.
Wohop, Arch., 1651, by John Martin and (Lancaster Lovett), Lower
    Norfolk Co.
Wolfe, Richard, 1646, by David Jones, Charles City Co.
Wombwell, Thom., 1638, by Christopher Lawson, James City Co.
Wombwell, Tho., 1648, by Wm. Edwards and Rice Edwards, James
    City Co.
Woomslye, Roger, 1647, by Leonard Pettock, Accomac Co.
Wood, Jon., 1653, by Wm. Johnson, Henrico Co.
Wood, John, 1642, by William Prior, Gent., ——— Co.
Wood, Leo., 1639, by Thomas Faulkner, ——— Co.
Wood, Peter, 1651, by George Eaton, ——— Co.
Wood, Wm., 1653, by Wm. Walker, Northumberland Co.
Wood, Eliz., 1653, by Richard Lake, Lancaster Co.
Wood, Wm., 1653, by Richard Carey, ——— Co.
Wood, Tho., 1652, by Mr. Nicholas Jernew, Gloucester Co.
Wood, Walter, 1652, by Mr. John Browne, Northampton Co.
Wood, Peter, 1652, by Mrs. Elnor Brocas, Lancaster Co.
Wood, Marg., 1654, by Francis Gray, ——— Co.
Wood, Walter, 1653, by Charles Scarburg, Northampton Co.
Wood, Tho., 1654, by Valentine Patten, Westmoreland Co.
Wood, Tho., 1654, by Robert Hubard, Westmoreland Co.
Wood, Jane, 1653, by Oliver Segar, Lancaster Co.
Wood, Wm., 1641, by Ambrose Bennett, Isle of Wight Co.
Wood, Edward, 1646, by John Ashcomb, Upper Norfolk Co.
Wood, Edward, 1647, by Symon Symons, Nansemond Co.
Wood, Peter, 1647, by John Brooch, York River Co.
Wood, Sclerams, 1656, by John Curtis, Gloucester Co.
Wood, Wm., 1654, by John Whithers and Stephen Garey, Westmore-
    land Co.
Wood, John, 1650, by William Gooch, Gent., ——— Co.
Wood, Walter, 1643, by Rowland Burnham, Yorke Co.
Wood, Wm., 1650, by Edward Walker, Northumberland Co.
Wood, Wm., 1650, by Robert Bird, ——— Co.
Wood, Wm., 1650, by Capt. John Flood, Gent., and Jno. Flood,
    ancient planter, James City Co.
Wood, Mary, 1648, by Lewis Burwell, Gent., ——— Co.
Wood, Edward, 1649, by Mr. Wm. Hoccaday, ——— Co.
Wood, Robt., 1642, by Capt. Samuell Mathews, Esq., ——— Co.
Wood, Thom., 1638, by Christopher Lawson, James City Co.
Wood, Wm., 1639, by Samuell Almond, Henrico Co.
Wood, Wm., 1639, by Edward Panderson, ——— Co.
Wood, Kath., 1650, by Richard Smith, Northampton Co.
Wood, Joane, 1656, by Capt. Henry Fleete, ——— Co.
Wood, Thomas, 1638, by John Fludd, James City Co.

Wood, Wm., 1638, by John Fludd, James City Co.
Wood, John, 1636, by Wm. Eyres, Warrasquinoake Co.
Wood, Arthur, 1636, by Richard Bennett, ——— Co.
Wood, John, 1636, by Wm. Fooks, Co.
Wood, Ralph, 1637, by Capt. Henry Browne, James River Co.
Wood, Arthur, 1637, by Rich. Bennett, New Norfolk Co.
Wood, Jon., 1635, by Capt. Tho. Willowbye, Elizabeth City Co.
Woods, Henry, 1635, by Capt. Adam Thoroughgood, ——— Co.
Woodall, Thomas, 1639, by John Dunston, James City Co.
Woodall, John, 1636, by Richard Peirce, James City Co.
Woodall, Tho., 1636, by John Dunston, James City Co.
Woodars, Wm., 1654, by Christopher Regault, Gloucester Co.
Woodbridge, Eliz., 1651, by Humphry Tabb, Northumberland Co.
Woodbridge, Eliza., 1642, by Humphry Tabb, Elizabeth City Co.
Woodcocke, John, 1639, by Walter Pakes, James City Co.
Woodcock, John, 1639, by Walter Pakes, ——— Co.
Woodcocke, John, 1637, by Argoll Yardely, New Norfolk Co.
Woodcock, George, 1636, by James Vanerit, Elizabeth City Co.
Woodcroft, Robt., 1654, by John Wyre, John Gillett, Andrew Gilson
    and John Phillipps, ——— Co.
Wooddard, ———, 1635, by Christopher Wooddard (her husband),
    ——— Co.
Woddy, Anthony, 1648, by Lewis Burwell and Tho. Haws, York River
    Co.
Wooderoft, Robt., 1649, by Tho. Dale, ——— Co.
Woodfield, Wm., 1652, by Mr. Tho. Teagle, Northampton Co.
Woodfield, Tho., 1653, by Charles Scarburg, Northampton Co.
Woodford, Richd., 1651, by Ashwell Battin, Yorke Co.
Woodford, Roger, 1652, by Nicholas Waddilow, Northampton Co.
Woodford, Roger, 1655, by Nich. Waddilow, Northampton Co.
Woodforde, Jon., 1638, by Stephen Charlton, Accomack Co.
Woodgate, Wm., 1635, by Wm. Barber (a mariner), Charles City Co.
Woodgate, Sarah, 1639, by Walter Cooper, James City Co.
Woodgate, Wm., 1638, by Wm. Barker and Associates, Charles City
    Co.
Woodhouse, Jon., 1654, by Lt. Colo. John Cheeseman (and John Adles-
    ton), ——— Co.
Woodhouse, Tho., 1653, by Colo. Wm. Clayborne (Sec. of State),
    ——— Co.
Woodhouse, Wm., 1642, by William Connhoe, ——— Co.
Woodhouse, Nich., 1654, by Arthur Nash, New Kent Co.
Woodhouse, Eliz., 1637, by Hen. Woodhouse, New Norfolk Co.
Woodhouse, Mary, 1637, by Hen. Woodhouse, New Norfolk Co.
Woolard, Sam., 1650, by Jervace Dodson, Gent., Northumberland Co.
Woolard, Ann. 1650, by Jervace Dodson, Gent., Northumberland Co.
Woolard, Geo., 1650, by Jervace Dodson, Gent., Northumberland Co.
Woodington, Jno., 1654, by Mr. Francis Hamond, York Co.
Woodmint, Mary, 1652, by Mr. Tho. Purifye and Mrs. Temperance
    Reppitt, ——— Co.
Woodnutt, Mary, 1652, by Col. Geo. Ludlow, Esq., Gloucester Co.

Woldridge, Timo., 1650, by Nicho. Jernew, Yorke Co.
Woldrige, John, 1646, by John Borach, York Co.
Woodrow, Joseph, 1651, by Robert Abrall, Yorke Co.
Woodrow, Jos., 1653, by Capt. Robt. Abrall, ——— Co.
Woodruffe, Robt., 1647, by Richard Bland ——— Co.
Woodruffe, Richard, 1643, by Capt. Samuell Mathews, Esq., ——— C.
Woodson, John, 1650, by Mr. Stephen Hamelin, Charles City Co.
Woodson, John, 1656, by Sir Henry Chichley, ——— Co.
Woodstock, Robert, 1653, by Wm. Debram, ——— Co.
Woodstock, Lew., 1635, by John Leonard Warrasquinoake Co.
Woodsworth, Richd., 1653, by Denis Conniers, Lancaster Co.
Woodwar, John, 1653, by James Turner, ——— Co.
Woodward, Samuell, 1650, by Samuell Smith, Northumberland Co.'
Woodward, Wm., 1642, by Justinian Cooper, Isle of Wight Co.
Woodward, Dorothy, 1637, by Christopher Woodward (she being his now wife), Charles City Co.
Woodward, Margaret, 1637, by Christopher Woodward (her husband), Charles City Co.
Woody, Symon, 1652, by Capt. Francis Morgan and Ralph Green, Gloucester Co.
Woody, Robt., 1656, by Mr. Martin Baker, New Kent Co.
Woodyard, Tho., 1654, by John Black, ——— Co.
Woodyard, Vincent, 1635, by William Ravenett, Denbeigh Co.
Woodyear, John, 1653, by Charles Grymes, Clerk, Lancaster Co.
Woofe, Dorothy, 1653, by Wm. Knott, Surry Co.
Woofed, Nich., 1640, by Thomas Stegg, Charles City Co.
Wookes, Mary, 1655, by Tho. Leatherberry, Northampton Co.
Woolaston, Geo., 1650, by Mr. Robt. Holt, James City Co.
Woolrich, Joane, 1635, by Thos. Shippey, ——— Co.
Woolridge, Tho., 1643, by Rowland Burnham, Yorke Co.
Woole, Samuel (a servant), 1635, by Wm. Gary, Accomack Co.
Wooleat, John, ———, by Tho. Meares, Lower Norfolk Co.
Wooleston, Ann, 1639, by William Wigg, ——— Co.
Wooles, John, 1654, by Col. Hump. Higgenson, Esq., and Abraham Moone, Westmoreland Co.
Woolest, Tho., 1652, by Mr. Henry Soanes, ——— Co.
Woolley, Wm., 1637, by Elizabeth Parker, Henrico Co.
Woolley, Wm., 1636, by Elizabeth Parker, Henrico Co.
Woolly, Wm., 1638, by Cornelius Loyd, ——— Co.
Woolfe, George, 1645, by John Baugh, Gent., Henrico Co.
Woolfe, Wm., 1636, by John Wilkins, Accomack Co.
Woolfe, William, 1637, by John Wilkins, New Norfolk Co.
Woolherne, Humphrey, 1637, by Wm. Spencer, ——— Co.
Woolman, Richard, 1653, by Francis Emperor, Lower Norfolk Co.
Woolmer, Tho., ———, by Henry Wesgate, Lower Norfolk Co.
Woolrich, Timo., 1650, by Nicholas Jernew, Gent., ——— Co.
Woolton, Wm., 1639, by Edward Panderson, ——— Co.
Woolly, Mr., 1653, by Francis Emperor, Hugh Gale and Edward Morgan, Lower Norfolk Co.
Wolly, Wm., 1647, by Richard Stearnell, Lower Norfolk Co.
Woorgen, Isaac, 1636, by Wm. Layton, ——— Co.

Woorke, William, 1637, by John Jackson, Charles River Co.
Wootton, Rich., 1642, by Christopher Boyce, ——— Co.
Wooton, Wm., 1653, by Robert Brasseur, Nansemond Co.
Wooton, Rich., 1638, by Thomas Todd, Lower New Norfolk Co.
Woover, Robt., 1638, by William Wigg, James City Co.
Wor, John, 1652, by Wm. Gautlett, ——— Co.
Wordroofe, Gran., 1653, by Mrs. Mary Brent, ——— Co.
Worke, William, 1639, by John Jackson, Charles River Co.
Worker, John, 1649, by Timothy Sodell, Yorke Co.
Workman, John, 1653, by Charles Grymes, Clerk, Lancaster Co.
Workman, Rich., 1648, by Tho. Braughton, ——— Co.
Workman, Wm., 1655, by Edward Pettaway, Surry Co.
Workman, Rich., 1654, by Major Miles Carey, Westmoreland Co.
Workman, Richard, 1643, by Elizabeth Hulle, ——— Co.
Workeman, Grace, 1643, by Tho. Williams, ——— Co.
Worleich, Jno., 1650, by Lieut. Wm. Worleich, ——— Co.
Worleich, Henry, 1649, by Lieut. Wm. Worleich, Elizabeth City Co.
Worleich, Mary, 1649, by Lieut. Wm. Worleich, Elizabeth City Co.
Worley, Elizabeth, 1652, by Tho. Lucas, Gent., Lancaster Co.
Wormeley, Mr. Ralph, 1649, by Richard Kemp, Esq. (Sec. of State),
——— Co.
Wormeley, Co., Xtopher, 1649, by Richard Kemp, Esq. (Sec. of State),
——— Co.
Wormeley, Mrs. Mary, 1649, by Richard Kemp, Esq., (Sec. of State),
——— Co.
Wormeley, Mrs. Agatha, 1649, by Richard Kemp, Esq. (Sec. of State),
——— Co.
Wormewell, Mary, 1635, by Capt. Tho. Willowbye, ——— Co.
Wormington, Jno., 1655, by John Marshall, Isle of Wight Co.
Worne, Tho., 1639, by Tho. Symons, James City Co.
Worrall, Robert, 1638, by Joseph Royall, Charles Cittie Co.
Worrell, James, 1650, by Henry Peaseley, ——— Co.
Worsby, Henry, 1651, by Richard Kellum, Northampton Co.
Woser, John, 1651, by Richard Wooton, Northumberland Co.
Woshbrow, Wm., 1654, by Robert Bowers, ——— Co.
Worship, Walter, 1643, by Wm. Berryman, ——— Co.
Worshipp, Walter, 1639, by Tho. Symons, James City Co.
Worshipp, Pru., 1653, by Jno. Hansford, Gloucester Co.
Wostarm, Andrew, 1645, by Zachary Cripps, Warwick Co.
Worth, John, 1636, by Nathan Martin, Henrico Co.
Worth, Roger, ———, by Lt. Coll. John Cheesman, ——— Co.
Worth, Mary, 1655, by Major Wm. Hoccaday, New Kent Co.
Worth, Peter, 1654, by Abraham Moone, ——— Co.
Worthing, Richard, 1652, by John Howett, Northumberland Co.
Wortman, Thos., 1643, by Robert Haies, Lower Norfolk Co.
Wortman, Ann, 1643, by Robert Haies, Lower Norfolk Co.
Wortman, Mary, 1643, by Robert Haies, Lower Norfolk Co.
Wortman, John, 1643, by Robert Haies, Lower Norfolk Co.
Wragg, Wm., 1654, by Edward Simpson, Gloucester Co.
Wrathersby, Thomas, 1635, by Samuel Weaver, ——— Co.
Wray, Thomas, 1636, by Thomas Wray, Charles River Co.

Wren, James, 1649, by Richard Bayly, Northampton Co.
Wren, James, 1654, by Wm. Bacon, Northumberland Co.
Wrenn, Fra., 1650, by George Goldsmith, ——— Co.
Wrenn, Nicho., 1653, by Mr. Wm. Baldwen, York Co.
Wrenn, Tho., 1638, by John Robins, James City Co.
Wrench, Ann, 1641, by John Gookin, Lower Norfolk Co.
Wridd, Jno., 1635, by Capt. Adam Thoroughgood, ——— Co.
Wrier, James, 1655, by John Coole, James City Co.
Wright, William, 1637, by Oliver Sprye, New Norfolk Co.
Wright, Jane, 1637, by Oliver Sprye, New Norfolk Co.
Wright, Ursula, 1642, by Justinian Cooper, Isle of Wight Co.
Wright, John, 1642, by Stephen Gill, Yorke River Co.
Wright, Simon, 1637, by Phillipp Taylor, Accomack Co.
Wright, Richard, 1636, by Walter Daniell, James City Co.
Wright, Elizabeth, 1637, by John Baker, Henrico Co.
Wright, Richard, 1636, by John Yates, Elizabeth City Co.
Wright, John, 1636, by Richard Peirce, James City Co.
Wright, Jon. (a servant), 1635, by Wm. Garry, Accomack Co.
Wright, Martha, 1655, by Wm. Hall, New Kent Co.
Wright, Jane, 1639, by Richard Parsons, Lower New Norfolk Co.
Wright, Wm., 1639, by Richard Parsons, Lower New Norfolk Co.
Wright, Richard, 1639, by Walter Daniell, James City Co.
Wright, John, 1638, by John Bishop, James City Co.
Wright, John, 1640, by Edmund Scarburgh, Accomack Co.
Wright, Samll., 1649, by Joseph Croshawe, Yorke Co.
Wright, Edward, 1649, by Mr. Nesum and others, Northumberland Co.
Wright, Marke, 1650, by Capt. Moore Fautleroy, ——— Co.
Wright, Phillis, 1649, by Robert Moseley, Gent., ——— Co.
Wright, John, 1650, by Capt. John Flood, Gent., and Jno. Flood, an ancient planter, James City Co.
Wright, John, 1650, by Capt. Moore Fautleroy, ——— Co.
Wright, Tho., wife and children, 1650, by Capt. Moore Fautleroy, ——— Co.
Wright, Richd., 1650, by Tho. Gerrord Gent., Northumberland Co.
Wright, John, 1650, by Richard Tye and Charles Sparrowe, Charles City Co.
Wright, Antho., 1650, by David Peibles, Charles City Co.
Wright, Jane, 1643, by Thomas Wheeler, Charles City Co.
Wright, Henry, 1650, by Lewis Burwell, Gent., Northumberland Co.
Wright, Tho., 1650, by Silvester Thatcher and Tho. Whitlocke, ——— Co.
Wright, Fra., 1654, by Edward Simpson, Gloucester Co.
Wright, John, 1654, by Robert Hubard, Westmoreland Co.
Wright, Joane, 1654, by Nich. Merywether, Westmoreland Co.
Wright, David, 1655, by Capt. Henry Fleet, ——— Co.
Wright, Robt., 1656, by John Evans, Northampton Co.
Wright, Giles, 1655, by Mrs. Margaret Brent, Lancaster Co.
Wright, Tho., 1647, by Tho. Godby, Lower Norfolk Co.
Wright, Wm., 1648, by George White, Lower Norfolk Co.
Wright, Wm., 1647, by Leonard Pettock, Accomac Co.

Wright, Jno., 1646, by Joseph Croshawe, Charles River Co.
Wright, John, 1653, by Robert Bouth, Yorke Co.
Wright, Gilbert, 1654, by Richard Walker, ——— Co.
Wright, Tea., 1654, by Rich. Bunduch, Northmapton Co.
Wright, Wm., 1654, by Mrs. Mgt. Brent, Westmoreland Co.
Wright, Wm., 1654, by Nath. Pope, Westmoreland Co.
Wright, Martha, 1654, by Robert Yoe, Westmoreland Co.
Wright, John, 1654, by Valentine Patten, Westmoreland Co.
Wright, Robt., 1654, by John Watson and John Bognall, Westmore-
land Co.
Wright, Wm., 1652, by Henry Nicholls, Lancaster Co.
Wright, Eliz., 1654, by John Watson and John Bognall, Westmoreland
Co.
Wright, Wm., 1652, by John Greenbough, Henrico Co.
Wright, Richard, 1652, by Mr. Nicholas Jernew, Gloucester Co.
Wright, Fra., 1654, by Edward Revell, Northampton Co.
Wright, Joane, 1653, by Nicho. Meriwether, Northumberland Co.
Wright, John, 1653, by Edward Kemp, Geo. Cortleigh and John Mere-
dith, Lancaster Co.
Wright, Jane, 1652, by Edward Wright (her husband), Yorke Co.
Wright, Richard, 1651, by Mr. Rowland Burnham, ——— Co.
Wright, Giles, 1651, by Lieut. Collo. Giles Brent, Northumberland Co.
Wright, Tho., 1653, by Gregory Rawlins, Surry Co.
Wright, Edward, 1643, by Capt. Thomas Pettus, ——— Co.
Wright, John, 1650, by Capt. Richard Bond, Charles City Co.
Wright, Ro., 1655, by John Hinman, Northampton Co.
Wright, Wm., 1637, by Francis Osborne, ——— Co.
Wrightwell, John, 1653, by Henry Corbell, Gloucester Co.
Wrisbone, Nath., 1653, by Richard Haines, ——— Co.
Wrist, Mutton, 1656, by Tabitha and Matilda Scarburgh, Northamp-
ton Co.
Writt, Edw., 1636, by John Wilkins, Accomack Co.
Wyaneford, Dorothy, 1649, by Henry Brakes, Lower Norfolk Co.
Wyatt, Tho., 1642, by John Waltham, Jr., Accomac Co.
Wyatt, Edwin, 1643, by Sir Francis Wyatt, Kt., ——— Co.
Wyatt, Tho., 1655, by Edward Moore, Northampton Co.
Wyatt, Andrew, 1654, by Major Miles Carey, Westmoreland Co.
Wyatt, Ann, 1653, by John Ashby and John Hamper, ——— Co.
Wyatt, Robt., 1639, by James Perron, Accomack Co.
Wye, George, 1650, by Mr. James Williamson, ——— Co.
Wye, Geo., 1643, by William Batts, ——— Co.
Wyer, Walker, 1650, by Edward James, ——— Co.
Wygood, Kath., 1643, by Tho. Evans, ——— Co.
Wygon, Anth., 1636, by Richard Cocke, ——— Co.
Wyld, Jon., 1653, by Geo. Taylor, Lancaster Co.
Wyne, John, 1637, by Henry Catalyn, New Norfolk Co.
Wynn, Mathew, 1636, by Wm. Julian, Elizabeth City Co.
Wynn, Hugh, 1637, by William Spencer, ——— Co.
Wynn, Garrett, 1647, by Elizabeth Barcroft, Isle of Wight Co.
Wynn, Anne, 1652, by Joane Yates, Lower Norfolk Co.
Wynn, Richard, 1652, by Wm. Owen and Wm. Morgan, ——— Co.

Wynton, Tho., 1654, by Walter Dickenson, Lancaster Co.
Wyth, Richard, 1635, by Charles Harwer, ——— Co.
Wyting, Tho., 1654, by Walter Dickenson, Lancaster Co.
Wyse, John, 1655, by Southy Littleberry, Northampton Co.
Wywell, Wm., 1647, by Thomas Johnson, Gent., Northampton Co.

X

Xnd, Alex., 1652, by Mr. Peter Knight, Gloucester Co.

Y

Yarblow, Christian, 1653, by Tho. Willis, York Co.
Yardley, Mrs. Anne, 1652, by John Robinson, Jr., Northampton Co.
Yarke, Edward, 1635, by Richard Bennett, ——— Co.
Yarnar, Anne, 1650, by Mr. James Williamson, ——— Co.
Yarner, Ann, 1648, by John Seward, Isle of Wight Co.
Yate, John, 1656, by Tho. Harris, Lancaster Co.
Yateman, Wm., 1651, by Wm. Hampton Co.
Yates, Richard, 1638, by John Yates, Lower New Norfolk Co.
Yates, Jone, 1638, by John Yates, Lower New Norfolk Co.
Yates, Robert, 1653, by Mr. Richard Barnhouse, Jr., Gloucester Co.
Yates, Stephen, 1653, by Richard Braine, Charles Co.
Yates, Samuel, 1653, by Richard Budd, Northumberland Co.
Yates, James, 1652, by John Howett, Northumberland Co.
Yates, John, 1649, by Thomas Curtis, ——— Co.
Yates, Margaret, 1649, by Tho. Curtis, ——— Co.
Yates, Henry, 1636, by James Knott, Elizabeth City Co.
Yates, Robt., 1635, by Wm. Barber (a mariner), Charles City Co.
Yates, Mary, 1636, by John Yates, Elizabeth City Co.
Yates, Jon., 1635, by Wm. Barber (a mariner), Charles City Co.
Yates, Richard, 1636, by John Yates, ——— Co.
Yates, Joane, 1636, by John Yates, ——— Co.
Yates, Robt., 1638, by Wm. Barker and Associates, Charles City Co.
Yates, Jon., 1638, by Wm. Barker and Associates, Charles City Co.
Yates, Henry, 1637, by James Knott, New Norfolk Co.
Yates, Mary, 1644, by James Taylor and Lawrence Baker, James City
     Co.
Yeardly, Frances, 1537, by Argoll Yeardly (her husband), New Norfolk
     Co.
Yellow, Eliza., 1652, by Mr. Tho. Sawyer, Lower Norfolk Co.
Yellow, Marg., 1653, by Tho. Sawyer, ——— Co.
Yenny, Robt., 1644, by John Hill, Gent., Upper Norfolk Co.
Yeo., Capt. Leonard, 1653, by John Shepperd, Northumberland Co.
Yeo, Mrs. Clare, 1653, by John Shepperd, Northumberland Co.
Yeo, Hugh, 1652, by Ambrose Dixon and Stephen Horsely, Jr., North-
     ampton Co.
Yeo, Wm., 1652, by Ambrose Dixon and Stephen Horsely, Jr., North-
     ampton Co.
Yeocke, Thomas, 1646, by Sir William Berkley, ——— Co.
Yeoman, Cesar, 1652, by Charles Scarburg, Northampton Co.

Yeomans, Geo., 1638, by Thomas Swan, James Citie Co.
Yeomans, Cester, 1653, by Charles Scarburg, Northampton Co.
Yeemans, Edw., 1652, by John Hatton, ——— Co.
Yepe, John, 1637, by William Spencer, ——— Co.
Yes, John, 1637, by Francis Osborne, ——— Co.
Yetman, Rosamar, 1637, by John Wilkins, New Norfolk Co.
Yetman, Rosamas, 1636, by John Wilkins, Accomack Co.
Yoanes, Timothy, 1635, by Wm. Garry, Accomack Co.
Yoe, Hugh, 1654, by Tho. Salsbury, Lancaster Co.
Yoe, Wm., 1654, by Tho. Salsbury, Lancaster Co.
Yoeman, James, 1656, by Lewis Perry, ——— Co.
Yoemann, Edward, 1652, by Christopher Lewis, Isle of Wight Co.
Yoemans, George, 1635, by Wm. Swan, James Co.
Yonall, Tho., 1653, by Colo. Wm. Clayborne (Sec. of State), ——— Co.
York, John, 1648, by Georg Read, Gent., ——— Co.
Yorke, Eliz., 1654, by John Watson and John Bognall, Westmoreland Co.
Yorke, Ann, 1639, by Wm. Barker, Charles City Co.
Yorke, Kath., 1637, by Cheney Boyes, Charles City Co.
Yorke Edward, 1637, by Rich. Bennett, New Norfolk Co.
Yorke, Catherine, 1636, by Cheney Boyse, Charles City Co.
Yorke, Edward, 1635, by Richard Bennett, Warrasquinoake Co.
Yorkshire, Kath., 1653, by Mr. Henry Soanes, ——— Co.
Youle, Tho., 1654, by Tho. Hobkins, Lancaster Co.
Young, Tho., 1655, by John Dorman, Northampton Co.
Young, Tho., 1656, by Major Wm. Lewis, ——— Co.
Young, Saml., 1654, by Richard Allen, Northampton Co.
Young, Edwin, 1641, by Thomas Pitt, Charles City Co.
Young, John, 1639, by Georg Higgins, Charles River Co.
Young, Peter, 1638, by Richard Kemp, Esq., ——— Co.
Young, Robt., 1638, by Thomas Burbage, Accomack Co.
Young, Richard, 1637, by David Winley, Accomac Co.
Young, Jane, 1637, by David Winley, Accomac Co.
Young, Christop., 1638, by Thomas Beerboge, Upper New Norfolk Co.
Young, Francis, 1639, by Georg Minifye, Esq., Charles River Co.
Young, Robert, 1639, by Richard Parsons, Lower New Norfolk Co.
Young, Martha, 1651, by Phillip Charles, James City Co.
Young, John, 1653, by Wm. Blackey, ——— Co.
Young, Robt., 1653, by Samuell Parry, Lancaster Co.
Young, Joan, 1653, by Colo. Wm. Clayborne (Sec. of State), ——— Co.
Young, Reynold, 1652, by Ralph Horsely, Northumberland Co.
Young, John, 1652, by Richard Hatton and Lambett Lambettson, Lancaster Co.
Young, Robt., 1652, by Peter Knight, Gloucester Co.
Young, Tho., 1694, by Mr. Edmund Scarburg, Northampton Co.
Young, Antho., 1648, by Wm., Ewen, James City Co.
Young, Ailee, 1649, by Frances Land, Norfolk Co.
Young, Ri., 1650, by Richard Tye and Charles Sparrowe, Charles City Co.
Young, Step., 1647, by Wm. Blackey, York Co.
Young, Christ, 1635, by Rich. Peirce, James City Co.

Young, Rich., 1635, by Jno. Upton, Warrasquinoake Co.
Young, Edward, 1636, by Edward Minter, ——— Co.
Young, Christo., 1635, by Richard Peirce, James City Co.
Young, Rich., 1637, by John Upton, Isle of Wight Co.
Young, Wm., 1641, by Wm. Burdett, Accomack Co.
Young, Ellis, 1642, by Geo. Adkins, and Wm. Foster, ——— Co.
Young, Richard, 1637, by Lt. John Upton, Isle of Wight Co.
Young, Florence, 1637, by Lt. John Upton, Isle of Wight Co.
Young, Jane, 1637, by Daniel Winley, Accomack Co.
Young, Richard, 1637, by Daniel Winley, Accomack Co.
Young, Edward, 1638, by Edward Minter, James City Co.
Young, Tho., 1643, by Sir Francis Wyatt, Kt., ——— Co.
Young, Cicely, 1643, by Wm. Morgan, ——— Co.
Young, Dilly, 1644, by James Taylor and Lawrence Baker, James City
    Co.
Younge, John, 1652, by Littleton Scarburg, ——— Co.
Younge, Thomas, 1654, by John Hallawes, Westmoreland Co.
Younge, Stephen, 1639, by Richard Maior, Charles River Co.
Yowell, Ann, Jr., 1654, by Tho. Hobkins, Lancaster Co.
Yowell, Ann, Sr., 1654, by Tho. Hobkins, Lancaster Co.
Yowell, Wm., 1654, by Tho. Hobkins, Lancaster Co.
Yowell, Tho., 1652, by John Johnson, Northampton Co.
Yowill, Wm., 1650, by Joh Hallawes, Gent., Northumberland Co.
Yowill, Ann, Jr., 1650, by John Hallawes, Gent., Northumberland Co.
Yowill, Ann, 1650, by John Hallawes, Gent., Northumberland Co.
Yowill, Tho. Jr., 1650, by John Hallawes, Gent., Northumberland Co.
Yowill, Tho., 1650, by John Hallawes, Gent., Northumberland Co.
Yutt, Wm., 1650, and wife, by Jervace Dodson, Gent., Northumber-
    land Co.

www.ingramcontent.com/pod-product-compliance
Lightning Source LLC
Chambersburg PA
CBHW021846020426
42334CB00013B/208